JUDITH SKUCE
Georgian College

Analyzing Data and Making Decisions

STATISTICS FOR BUSINESS

D1294729

PEARSON

Prentice Hall

Toronto

Library and Archives Canada Cataloguing in Publication

Skuce, Judith
    Analyzing data and making decisions: statistics for business / Judith Skuce.

Includes index.
ISBN-13: 978-0-13-197625-2
ISBN-10:   0-13-197625-7

1. Commercial statistics—Textbooks.   2. Decision making—Statistical methods—Textbooks.   I. Title.

HA29.S568 2007   650.01'5195   C2006-906398-2

ISBN-13: 978-0-13-197625-2
ISBN-10:   0-13-197625-7

Editor-in-Chief: Gary Bennett
Executive Editor: Samantha Scully
Executive Marketing Manager: Cas Shields
Developmental Editor: Eleanor MacKay
Production Editor: Cheryl Jackson
Copy Editor: Laurel Sparrow
Proofreader: Tom Gamblin
Production Coordinator: Christine Kwan
Composition: Integra
Photo Research: Sandy Cooke
Permissions Research: Beth McAuley
Art Director: Julia Hall
Cover and Interior Design: Anthony Leung
Cover Image: JupiterUnlimited

For permission to reproduce copyrighted material, the publisher gratefully acknowledges the copyright holders listed throughout the text and on this copyright page. Page 1: PAUL J. RICHARDS/AFP/GETTY; page 24: Jupiter Unlimited; page 88: © Helen King/CORBIS; page 137: Jupiter Unlimited; page 165: © Paul Broadbent/Alamy; page 204: Billy Lobo H./Shutterstock; page 237: © Chris Rout/Alamy; page 274: Shutterstock; page 298: © Alan Schein/zefa/Corbis; page 342: PhotoEdit; page 371: © Masterfile/www.masterfile.com; page 406: © George Robinson/Maxx Images.

Statistics Canada information is used with the permission of Statistics Canada. Users are forbidden to copy the data and redisseminate them, in an original or modified form, for commercial purposes, without permission from Statistics Canada. Information on the availability of the wide range of data from Statistics Canada can be obtained from Statistics Canada's Regional Offices, its World Wide Web site at http://www.statcan.ca, and its toll-free access number 1-800-263-1136.

1 2 3 4 5   11 10 09 08 07

Printed and bound in the United States.

Dedicated to the memory of Ruth Skuce (1928-2005), my mother and my first role model as an educator. Many people learned many things from my mother, and all of us miss her.

About the Author

Judith Skuce earned a Bachelor of Mathematics from the University of Waterloo and a Master of Arts in Political Economy from the University of Toronto. She spent many years as an economic policy advisor and manager for several Canadian government departments before joining Georgian College in 1990. Judith teaches Statistics and Economics in the Business and Management Studies department.

Brief Contents

PART I   INTRODUCTION   1

    CHAPTER 1   Using Data to Make Better Decisions   1

PART II   DESCRIPTIVE STATISTICS   24

    CHAPTER 2   Using Graphs and Tables to Describe Data   24

    CHAPTER 3   Using Numbers to Describe Data   88

PART III CONCEPTS OF INFERENTIAL STATISTICS   137

    CHAPTER 4   Calculating Probabilities   137

    CHAPTER 5   Probability Distributions   165

    CHAPTER 6   Using Sampling Distributions to Make Decisions   204

PART IV   MAKING DECISIONS   237

    CHAPTER 7   Making Decisions with a Single Sample   237

    CHAPTER 8   Estimating Population Values   274

    CHAPTER 9   Making Decisions with Matched-Pairs Samples,
                  Quantitative or Ranked Data   298

    CHAPTER 10   Making Decisions with Two Independent Samples,
                  Quantitative or Ranked Data   342

    CHAPTER 11   Making Decisions with Two or More Samples,
                  Qualitative Data   371

PART V   ANALYZING RELATIONSHIPS   406

    CHAPTER 12   Analyzing Relationships, Two Quantitative Variables 406

Contents

Preface   xvii

Excel Instructions and Templates   xxv

Table of Examples   xxix

Using Microsoft® Excel for Analyzing Data and Making
Decisions   xxxv

    Why Excel?   xxxv
    Excel Templates   xxxvi
    Excel Add-ins   xxxvi
    Excel Data Sets   xxxvi

PART I	INTRODUCTION	1
CHAPTER 1	Using Data to Make Better Decisions	1
	Introduction	1
1.1	Getting the Data	2
	Primary and Secondary Data	3
	Develop Your Skills 1.1	4
1.2	Sampling	5
	Why Sampling Is Necessary	5
	Nonstatistical Sampling	6
	Statistical Sampling	7
	Sampling and Nonsampling Error	11
	Develop Your Skills 1.2	11
1.3	Analyzing the Data	12
	Develop Your Skills 1.3	14
1.4	Making Decisions	15
	Develop Your Skills 1.4	17
1.5	Communication	17
	Develop Your Skills 1.5	19
1.6	A Framework for Data-Based Decision Making	19
	Chapter Summary	21
	Chapter Review Exercises	22

PART II DESCRIPTIVE STATISTICS   24

CHAPTER 2 Using Graphs and Tables to Describe Data   24

Introduction   24
2.1 Types of Data   25
    Quantitative and Qualitiative Data   26
    Quantitative Data: Discrete or Continuous   26
    Qualitative Data: Ranked or Unranked   27
    Cross-Sectional and Time-Series Data   28
    Develop Your Skills 2.1   28
2.2 Frequency Distributions and Histograms for
    Quantitative Data   28
    Stem-and-Leaf Displays   29
    Frequency Distributions   32
    Histograms   40
    Guide to Technique: Adjusting Excel's Histogram   42
    Symmetry and Skewness   45
    Comparing Histograms   47
    Guide to Technique: Comparing Histograms   42
    Develop Your Skills 2.2   49
2.3 Tables, Bar Graphs, and Pie Charts for
    Qualitative Data   52
    Bar Charts and Pie Charts for a Simple Table   52
    Bar Charts for Contingency Tables   57
    Develop Your Skills 2.3   58
2.4 Time-Series Graphs   60
    Develop Your Skills 2.4   63
2.5 Graphs of Paired Quantitative Data   64
    Develop Your Skills 2.5   67
2.6 Misleading and Uninteresting Graphs   69
    Misleading Graphs   69
    Uninteresting Graphs   76
    Develop Your Skills 2.6   77
    Chapter Summary   79
    Chapter Review Exercises   81

CHAPTER 3 Using Numbers to Describe Data   88

Introduction   88
3.1 Some Useful Notation   89
    Order of Operations   89
    Summation Notation   89
    Some Examples   90
    Develop Your Skills 3.1   93
3.2 Measures of Central Tendency   93
    The Mean   93
    The Median   97
    The Mode   99
    Guide to Decision Making: Choosing a Measure of
    Central Tendency   101
    Develop Your Skills 3.2   101

	3.3	Measures of Variability	101
		The Range	102
		The Standard Deviation	102
		The Interquartile Range	113
		Guide to Decision Making: Choosing a Measure of Variability	117
		Develop Your Skills 3.3	117
	3.4	Measures of Association	118
		The Pearson Correlation Coefficient for Quantitative Variables	118
		The Spearman Rank Correlation Coefficient for Ranked Variables	124
		Guide to Decision Making: Choosing a Measure of Association	128
		Develop Your Skills 3.4	128
		Chapter Summary	130
		Chapter Review Exercises	131

PART III CONCEPTS OF INFERENTIAL STATISTICS   **137**

CHAPTER 4		Calculating Probabilities	137
		Introduction	137
	4.1	Sample Spaces and Basic Probabilities	139
		Develop Your Skills 4.1	143
	4.2	Conditional Probabilities and the Test for Independence	143
		Conditional Probabilities	143
		The Test for Independence	145
		Develop Your Skills 4.2	147
	4.3	"And," "Or," and "Not" Probabilities	148
		"And" Probabilities	148
		"Or" Probabilities	152
		"Not" Probabilities	155
		Develop Your Skills 4.3	159
		Chapter Summary	160
		Chapter Review Exercises	161

CHAPTER 5		Probability Distributions	165
		Introduction	165
	5.1	Probability Distributions	166
		Building a Discrete Probability Distribution	166
		Mean and Standard Deviation of a Probability Distribution	168
		Develop Your Skills 5.1	170
	5.2	The Binomial Probability Distribution	171
		Conditions for a Binomial Experiment	171
		Mean and Standard Deviation of a Binomial Distribution	171
		Checking the Conditions for a Binomial Experiment	172
		Calculating Binomial Probabilities	173
		Calculating Binomial Probabilities with Excel	177
		Develop Your Skills 5.2	183

	5.3	The Normal Probability Distribution	183
		Develop Your Skills 5.3	198
		Chapter Summary	199
		Chapter Review Exercises	201

CHAPTER 6		Using Sampling Distributions to Make Decisions	204
		Introduction	204
	6.1	The Decision-Making Process for Statistical Inference	205
		Develop Your Skills 6.1	210
	6.2	The Sampling Distribution of the Sample Mean	211
		An Empirical Exploration of the Sampling Distributions of $\bar{x}$	215
		When Is the Sampling Distribution Normal? The Central Limit Theorem	218
		Guide to Decision Making: Using the Sampling Distribution of $\bar{x}$ When σ is Known	221
		Develop Your Skills 6.2	221
	6.3	The Sampling Distribution of the Sample Proportion	222
		Making Decisions About Population Proportions with the Binomial Distribution	222
		Guide to Decision Making: Using the Sampling Distribution of $\hat{p}$	230
		Develop Your Skills 6.3	231
	6.4	Hypothesis Testing	231
		Chapter Summary	232
		Chapter Review Exercises	234

PART IV MAKING DECISIONS

			237
CHAPTER 7		Making Decisions with a Single Sample	237
		Introduction	237
	7.1	Formal Hypothesis Testing	238
		The Null and Alternative Hypotheses	238
		One-Tailed and Two-Tailed Hypothesis Tests	239
		Making a Decision: Rejecting or Failing to Reject the Null Hypothesis	240
		Significance Level and Type I and Type II Errors	241
		Deciding on the Basis of p-Values	243
		Guide to Technique: Calculating p-Values	244
		Guide to Technique: Steps in a Formal Hypothesis Test	245
		Develop Your Skills 7.1	245
	7.2	Deciding About a Population Proportion	246
		Using the Excel Template for Making Decisions About a Population Proportion with a Single Sample	249
		Guide to Decision Making: Hypothesis Test About a Population Proportion	250
		Develop Your Skills 7.2	251
	7.3	Deciding About the Population Mean	251
		The t-Distribution	252
		Guide to Decision Making: Hypothesis Test About a Population Mean	266
		How Normal Is Normal Enough?	266

Develop Your Skills 7.3   267
Chapter Summary   268
Chapter Review Exercises   269

CHAPTER 8   Estimating Population Values   274

Introduction   274
8.1   Estimating the Population Proportion   276
Develop Your Skills 8.1   282
8.2   Estimating the Population Mean   283
Develop Your Skills 8.2   287
8.3   Selecting the Sample Size   287
    Sample Size to Estimate a Mean   287
    Sample Size to Estimate a Proportion   290
Develop Your Skills 8.3   291
8.4   Confidence Intervals and Hypothesis Tests   292
Develop Your Skills 8.4   293
Chapter Summary   294
Chapter Review Exercises   295

CHAPTER 9   Making Decisions with Matched-Pairs Samples, Quantitative or Ranked Data   298

Introduction   298
9.1   Matched Pairs, Quantitative Data, Normal Differences—The t-Test   300
    Guide to Decision Making: Matched Pairs, Quantitative Data, Normal Differences–The t-Test   307
    Confidence Interval Estimate of μ_D 308
Develop Your Skills 9.1   310
9.2   Matched Pairs, Quantitative Data, Non-Normal Differences—The Wilcoxon Signed Rank Sum Test   311
    Guide to Decision Making: Matched Pairs, Quantitative Data, Non-Normal Differences–The Wilcoxon Signed Rank Sum Test   324
    Quantitative Matched-Pairs Data: Which Test?   325
Develop Your Skills 9.2   325
9.3   Matched Pairs, Ranked Data—The Sign Test   327
    Guide to Decision Making: Matched Pairs, Ranked Data–The Sign Test   333
Develop Your Skills 9.3   333
Chapter Summary   335
Chapter Review Exercises   336

CHAPTER 10   Making Decisions with Two Independent Samples, Quantitative or Ranked Data   342

Introduction   342
10.1   Independent Samples, Normal Quantitative Data—The t-Test   343
    Equal or Unequal Variances?   349

Guide to Decision Making: Independent Samples, Normal
Quantitative Data–The *t*-Test   350
Confidence Interval for $\mu_1 - \mu_2$ 350
Develop Your Skills 10.1   353

10.2   Independent Samples, Non-Normal Quantitative Data
or Ranked Data—The Wilcoxon Rank Sum Test   354
Independent Samples, Non-Normal
Quantitative Data   355
Wilcoxon Rank Sum Test or *t*-Test   358
Independent Samples, Ranked Data   358
Guide to Decision Making: Independent Samples, Non-Normal
Quantitative Data or Ranked Data–The Wilcoxon Rank
Sum Test   360
Develop Your Skills 10.2   361

10.3   Comparing More than Two Populations   363
Chapter Summary   364
Chapter Review Exercises   366

CHAPTER 11   Making Decisions with Two or More Samples, Qualitative Data   371

Introduction   371
11.1   Comparing Two Proportions   372
Special Case: $H_0 : p_1 - p_2 = 0$ 373
General Case: $H_0 : p_1 - p_2 =$ Fixed Amount   376
Guide to Decision Making: Comparing Two Proportions   378
Confidence Interval Estimate of $p_1 - p_2$ 379
Develop Your Skills 11.1   380
11.2   Goodness-of-Fit Tests   381
Guide to Decision Making: Goodness-of-Fit Tests   389
Develop Your Skills 11.2   389
11.3   Comparing Many Population Proportions or Testing
Independence   391
Comparing Many Population Proportions   391
Testing for Independence   395
Guide to Decision Making: Contingency Table Tests   397
Develop Your Skills 11.3   399
Chapter Summary   401
Chapter Review Exercises   402

PART V ANALYZING RELATIONSHIPS   406

CHAPTER 12   Analyzing Relationships, Two Quantitative Variables   406

Introduction   406
12.1   Creating a Graph and Estimating the Relationship   407
Creating a Graph of the Relationship   408
Estimating the Relationship   410
Develop Your Skills 12.1   417
12.2   Assessing the Model   418
The Theoretical Model   418
Checking the Required Conditions   419

Guide to Decision Making: Checking Requirements for the
Linear Regression Model | 433
Develop Your Skills 12.2 | 434
12.3 Hypothesis Test About the Regression Relationship | 434
Guide to Decision Making: Testing the Slope of the
Regression Line | 439
Develop Your Skills 12.3 | 439
12.4 How Good Is the Regression? | 439
Develop Your Skills 12.4 | 442
12.5 Making Predictions | 442
Develop Your Skills 12.5 | 447
12.6 More Advanced Modelling | 447
Chapter Summary | 448
Chapter Review Exercises | 450

Appendix 1 Cumulative Binomial Tables | 454
Appendix 2 Standard Normal Table | 458
Appendix 3 Critical Values for the t-Distribution | 460
Appendix 4 Wilcoxon Signed Rank Sum Test Table, Critical
Values and p-values | 461
Appendix 5 Wilcoxon Rank Sum Test Tables, Critical Values | 462
Appendix 6 Critical Values for the χ^2-Distribution | 464
Glossary | 465
Index | 467

Preface

Employers consistently indicate that they want graduates of business programs to be able to think critically and use computers to organize and analyze data. A good statistics course should help students develop these skills. However, students consistently indicate that they fear their statistics course will be difficult, and their fears are often self-fulfilling.

This book is designed to help students overcome these fears. I have purposely used language that is simple and straightforward. Throughout the book, I have set my discussions about statistical techniques in the context of real or realistic business problems. Students are invited and encouraged to develop some intuition about what they are doing, to see that statistical techniques are, in fact, sensible, and not at all mysterious.

I place the focus *first* on the usefulness of a statistical technique, and then I fill in the details afterwards. For example, in Chapter 6, I discuss the usefulness of a sampling distribution for statistical inference at the beginning of the chapter, and then progress into detailed description of particular sampling distributions and the Central Limit Theorem.

Students who have understood *why* an analysis is done a particular way are better able to judge *what* to do in a new situation. Throughout the book, I have placed value on careful thinking, with assessments that are supported, but not replaced, by general guidelines. The approach I use is *not* mechanical. Instead, I have designed it to foster the ability of students to make good judgments.

I have focused the topic coverage in such a way as to make it less likely to overwhelm a student new to statistics. The text provides a thorough introduction to statistical analysis and enough detail that students will be able to use the techniques with confidence.

I cover statistics calculations for both manual and computer-based approaches. I believe it is important for students to understand how to work through the techniques on paper, to develop their intuition. Most courses also required the use of manual calculations in tests or exams. I also show students how to perform calculations using Excel, which is widely available. You will find more information about how I use Excel in this book in the introductory chapter, "Using Excel for Analyzing Data and Making Decisions."

ORGANIZATION

Part I provides a general overview of how data can be used to make better decisions. Part II covers the use of graphs, tables, and numbers to describe and summarize data. Part III introduces students to the underlying concepts of inferential statistics. Part IV applies these concepts to a series of hypothesis tests with associated confidence intervals. Part V discusses analyzing relationships and includes a thorough introduction to linear regression for two quantitative variables.

This book could be used as a foundation for a number of different statistics courses. I have designed Chapter 1 as a basic building block for any selection of topics covered in the book.

The entire book could be covered in two 14-week, 40–45 hour college courses. The first course would cover the first six, possibly seven, chapters; the second course would cover the remaining six, or five, starting with a review of Chapter 7.

A college limited to one 14-week, 40–45 hour course would typically cover the first seven (ideally eight) chapters. Some topics that could be omitted to ensure you would be able to cover up to the end of Chapter 8 are:

- the Empirical Rule in Chapter 3 (Section 3.3)
- the Spearman Rank Correlation Coefficient for Ranked Variables at the end of Chapter 3 (Section 3.4)
- Making Decisions about Population Proportions with the Binomial Distribution in Chapter 6 (Section 6.3)

I have included coverage of non-parametric methods for non-normal quantitative data, and ranked data in this textbook. Some introductory courses do not cover these topics; while this omission may be a necessary one, it is also one that may leave some students thinking that all quantitative data are normal! It is possible to use the text without covering these topics and without losing continuity. For example, such a course could cover Chapters 1–8 (omitting a discussion of the Spearman Rank Correlation Coefficient in Chapter 3), Section 9.1, Section 10.1, probably 10.3, and Chapters 11 and 12. The advantage of this book for such a course is that students would at least be made aware techniques exist to deal with non-normal or ranked data. Further, in the Guide to Technique, Guide to Decision Making, and Excel Templates, I have emphasized the necessity of checking for normality when analyzing quantitative data.

FEATURES

This book is designed first as a learning tool. I have presented a discussion of each new technique so that it flows naturally from the discussion that precedes it, which will allow students to make connections and build on previous knowledge.

I have included the following features to promote an ease of learning:

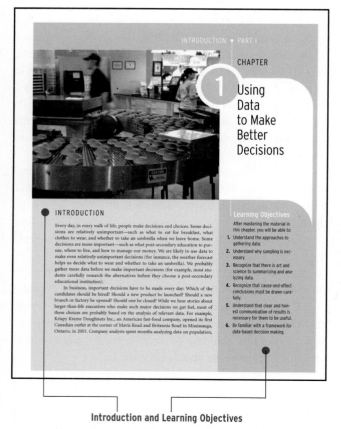

Introduction and Learning Objectives

Each chapter begins with a list of learning objectives, which provide an overview of the chapter content. The Introduction provides context for the chapter material by describing a business problem or problems relevant to the chapter's theme.

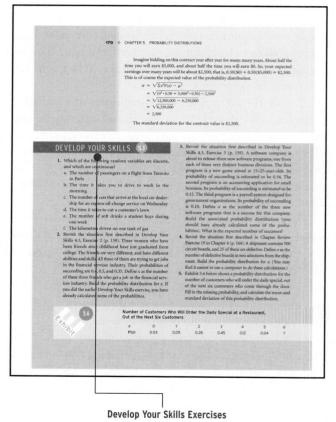

Develop Your Skills Exercises

At the end of every chapter section are questions designed to test and reinforce students' understanding of the material up to that point. I have developed the questions so that they are generally at the level of the examples I present in that section and provide immediate reinforcement of the material.

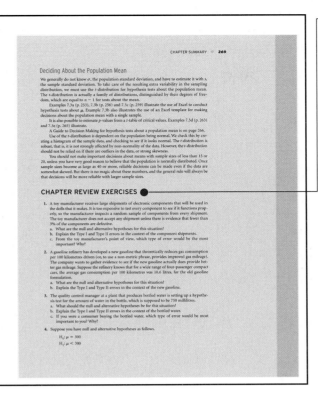

Deciding About the Population Mean

We generally do not know σ, the population standard deviation, and have to estimate it with s, the sample standard deviation. To take care of the resulting extra variability in the sampling distribution, we must use the t-distribution for hypothesis tests about the population mean. The t-distribution is actually a family of distributions, distinguished by their degrees of freedom, which are equal to n − 1 for tests about the mean.

Examples 7.3a (p. 253), 7.3b (p. 256) and 7.3c (p. 259) illustrate the use of Excel to conduct hypothesis tests about μ. Example 7.3b also illustrates the use of an Excel template for making decisions about the population mean with a single sample.

It is also possible to estimate p-values from a t-table of critical values. Examples 7.3d (p. 263) and 7.3e (p. 265) illustrate.

A Guide to Decision Making for hypothesis tests about a population mean is on page 266. Use of the t-distribution is dependent on the population being normal. We check this by creating a histogram of the sample data, and checking to see if it looks normal. The t-distribution is robust, that is, it is not strongly affected by non-normality of the data. However, the t-distribution should not be relied on if there are outliers in the data, or strong skewness.

You should not make important decisions about means with sample sizes of less than 15 or 20, unless you have very good reason to believe that the population is normally distributed. Once sample sizes become as large as 40 or more, reliable decisions can be made even if the data are somewhat skewed. But there is no magic about these numbers, and the general rule will always be that decisions will be more reliable with larger sample sizes.

CHAPTER REVIEW EXERCISES

1. A toy manufacturer receives large shipments of electronic components that will be used in the dolls that it makes. It is too expensive to test every component to see if it functions properly, so the manufacturer inspects a random sample of components from every shipment. The toy manufacturer does not accept any shipment unless there is evidence that fewer than 3% of the components are defective.
   a. What are the null and alternative hypotheses for this situation?
   b. Explain the Type I and Type II errors in the context of the component shipments.
   c. From the toy manufacturer's point of view, which type of error would be the most important? Why?

2. A gasoline refinery has developed a new gasoline that theoretically reduces gas consumption per 100 kilometres driven (or, to use a non-metric phrase, provides improved gas mileage). The company wants to gather evidence to see if the new gasoline actually does provide better gas mileage. Suppose the refinery knows that for a wide range of four-passenger compact cars, the average gas consumption per 100 kilometres was 10.6 litres, for the old gasoline formulation.
   a. What are the null and alternative hypotheses for this situation?
   b. Explain the Type I and Type II errors in the context of the new gasoline.

3. The quality control manager at a plant that produces bottled water is setting up a hypothesis test for the amount of water in the bottle, which is supposed to be 750 millilitres.
   a. What should the null and alternative hypotheses be for this situation?
   b. Explain the Type I and Type II errors in the context of the bottled water.
   c. If you were a consumer buying the bottled water, which type of error would be most important to you? Why?

4. Suppose you have null and alternative hypotheses as follows.
   $H_0: \mu = 300$
   $H_1: \mu < 300$

Chapter Review Exercises

Every chapter has a set of exercises designed to test and reinforce students' understanding of all of the chapter content. These questions require them to choose and apply the techniques in each chapter, but with no particular guidance about *which* technique to use. I have created these exercises so that in some instances they serve as building blocks for later discussions. All of the exercises are meaningful in the sense that they deal with realistic business problems or topics directly relevant to students' lives.

This book is also designed as a reference tool. Students will find the following features particularly helpful.

Guide to Technique and Guide to Decision Making

The Guide to Technique boxes and Guide to Decision Making boxes summarize the steps involved in certain important statistical tasks. For example, in Chapter 2, I have included a Guide to Technique box that covers the comparison of histograms (see page 42). All of the hypothesis tests covered in this text are summarized in a Guide to Decision Making box. These boxes summarize the type of data used and the type of decision involved in the test as well as all of the steps required to complete it. For an example of this type of box, see the Guide to Decision Making: *Matched Pairs, Quantitative Data, Normal Differences–The t-test* in Chapter 9 (see page 307). These guides are listed in the detailed table of contents for easy reference.

42 ● CHAPTER 2   USING GRAPHS AND TABLES TO DESCRIBE DATA

Of course, Excel's automatic histogram corresponds exactly to Excel's frequency distribution. The table and the graph produced by Excel look as shown below in Exhibit 2.30.

Exhibit 2.30

Raw Excel Frequency Distribution and Histogram

(a) Excel Frequency Distribution

Bin	Frequency
$ 199.99	5
$ 399.99	9
$ 599.99	19
$ 799.99	11
$ 999.99	6
$1,199.99	2
More	0

(b) Histogram

You can change elements in Excel's automatically produced histogram by clicking or right-clicking on those elements. There are a number of things to correct, as outlined in the Guide shown below.

Guide to Technique
Adjusting Excel's Histogram

1. The titles and axis labels must be informative. Click on each and type in titles and labels that allow the histogram to be interpreted without additional context.
2. The frequency legend is not required. Right-click on it and then click on **Clear**.
3. There should not be any spaces between the bars in a histogram (there are no spaces between the classes in the frequency distribution). Right-click on the bars, then click on **Format Data Series**, then click on the **Options** tab, then change the Gap width to 0, then click **OK**.
4. Convention has it that the x-axis of the histogram should show the *lower* limit of the class, but Excel's bin numbers are the *upper* included limit of each class. There is a trick to give the appearance of lower class limits: if you round the bin numbers on the worksheet, they will look like the lower limits of each class. Highlight the bin number cells on the worksheet, and then use the **Format** tool in Excel. Click on **Cells** . . . and then reduce **Decimal places**: to 0. Note that for this trick to work, you must always include decimal places in your bin numbers (e.g., a bin number of "199.99," not "199").[1]
5. The lower class limits should show at the left side of each associated bar, but Excel generally places the bin numbers on the chart under the middle of each bar. There is another trick to achieve approximately the right look: right-click on the x-axis labels, then click on **Format Axis** . . . , then click on the **Alignment** tab, and then set the orientation to −45 degrees.
6. Horizontal grid lines make it easier to interpret the heights of the bars on the histogram. Highlight the graph, then click on **Chart** on the toolbar. Click on **Chart Options** . . . , then tick the box beside **Major gridlines** under Value (Y) axis, then click **OK**.

[1] Probably because of the way Excel works, the traditional labelling convention (lower class limits on the x-axis of the histogram) is not always followed. You should communicate clearly that your histogram shows lower class limits (this will be obvious if your histogram is accompanied by a frequency distribution with clear class limits). You should also carefully examine any histogram you see, in case the standard convention is not followed.

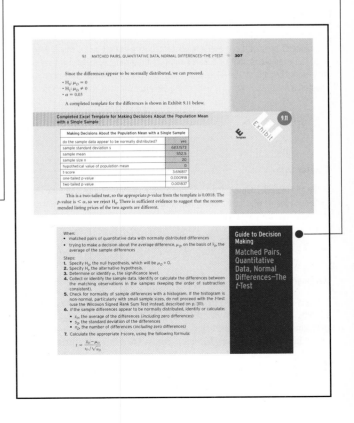

9.1   MATCHED PAIRS, QUANTITATIVE DATA, NORMAL DIFFERENCES–THE t-TEST   **307**

Since the differences appear to be normally distributed, we can proceed.

- $H_0: \mu_D = 0$
- $H_1: \mu_D \neq 0$
- $\alpha = 0.03$

A completed template for the differences is shown in Exhibit 9.11 below.

Exhibit 9.11

Completed Excel Template for Making Decisions About the Population Mean with a Single Sample

Making Decisions About the Population Mean with a Single Sample	
do the sample data appear to be normally distributed?	yes
sample standard deviation s	683.1573
sample mean	552.5
sample size n	20
hypothetical value of population mean	0
t-score	3.616817
one-tailed p-value	0.000918
two-tailed p-value	0.001837

This is a two-tailed test, so the appropriate p-value from the template is 0.0018. The p-value is < α, so we reject H_0. There is sufficient evidence to suggest that the recommended listing prices of the two agents are different.

Guide to Decision Making
Matched Pairs, Quantitative Data, Normal Differences–The t-Test

When:
- matched pairs of quantitative data with normally distributed differences
- trying to make a decision about the average difference, μ_D, on the basis of $\bar{x}_D$, the average of the sample differences

Steps:
1. Specify H_0, the null hypothesis, which will be $\mu_D = 0$.
2. Specify H_1, the alternative hypothesis.
3. Determine or identify α, the significance level.
4. Collect or identify the sample data. Identify or calculate the differences between the matching observations in the samples (keeping the order of subtraction consistent).
5. Check for normality of sample differences with a histogram. If the histogram is non-normal, particularly with small sample sizes, do not proceed with the t-test (use the Wilcoxon Signed Rank Sum Test instead, described on p. 311).
6. If the sample differences appear to be normally distributed, identify or calculate:
   - $\bar{x}_D$, the average of the differences (*including zero differences*)
   - s_D, the standard deviation of the differences
   - n_D, the number of differences (*including zero differences*)
7. Calculate the appropriate t-score, using the following formula:
   $$t = \frac{\bar{x}_D - \mu_D}{s_D / \sqrt{n_D}}$$

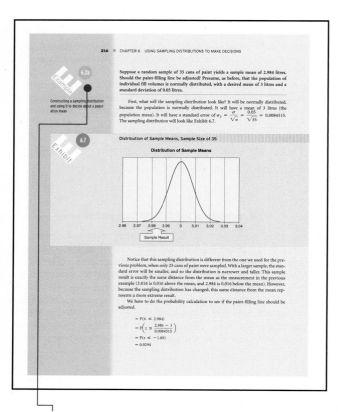

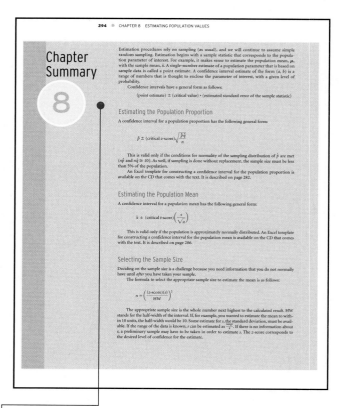

Annotated Examples

Every chapter has one or more examples that work through each of the statistical techniques I present. Each example also features a margin note, which describes what the example is about. Students will find the examples helpful references as they work through the Develop Your Skills and Chapter Review problems in each chapter. A list of the examples and their annotations follows this preface (p. xxvii).

Chapter Summaries

At the end of each chapter I have included a comprehensive summary of the chapter content. Students who have a firm grasp of what the chapter has covered will be able to use the summary for review and as a reference.

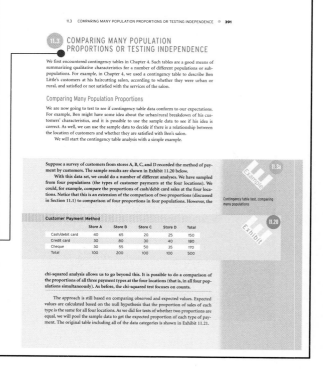

Meaningful Chapter and Section Headings

Students sometimes struggle to figure out which technique to apply to a particular problem; it is my hope with this book that this decision will actually prove to be quite simple to make. I have created descriptive chapter and section headings that convey the information students need to choose the correct statistical technique. For example, instead of a traditional title such as "Chi-Squared Tests", I use "Comparing Many Population Proportions" in Chapter 11. Students will find the listing of the first and second level of heading in the detailed table of contents in this text a useful reference.

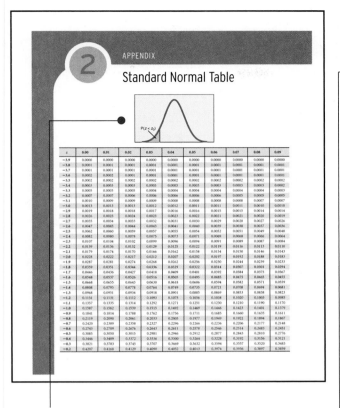

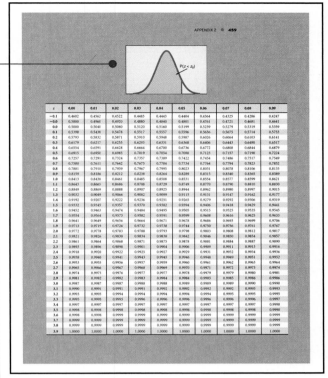

Carefully Designed Statistical Tables

Some of the tables in this text are presented using a non-standard approach so that they are easier for students to use and understand. For example, many books confine a normal table to one page and feature only the areas to the right of the mean. This design requires students to go through unnecessary mental hoops when doing normal probability calculations. In this book I have presented the table over two pages, which shows the areas to the left of the mean as well as to the right. Providing this additional information simplifies normal probability calculations for students and it means the presentation matches the way Excel calculates and displays normal probabilities.

Computers should make statistical analysis easier, not harder. Therefore, I have taken care to include several features that will ease students' introduction to using Excel for statistical analysis.

Excel Data Sets

I have created a number of data sets in Excel, which will allow students to work through the statistical techniques presented in the book. I have included data sets to accompany specific examples, Develop Your Skills questions, chapter-section discussions, and Chapter Review Exercises. All of the data sets appear on the Student CD-ROM that accompanies the text. Availability of a data set is highlighted with an Excel data set icon in the margin.

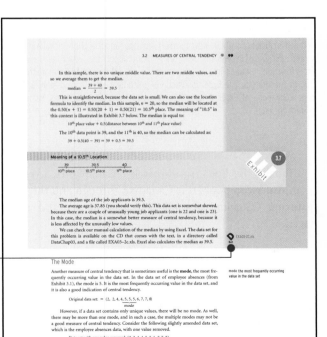

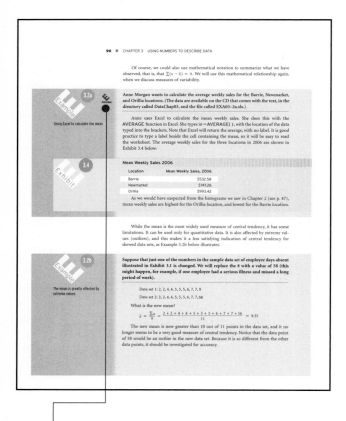

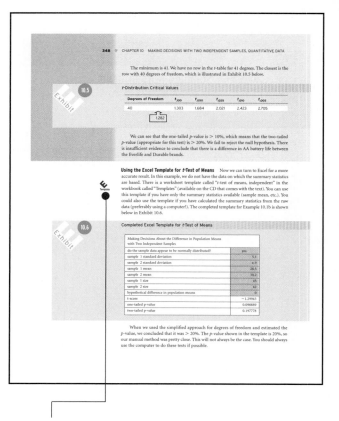

Excel Instructions

Detailed instructions about how to use Excel appear throughout. I have included screen captures of Excel dialogue boxes so that students can clearly see how to use Excel functions and add-ins. Each instance is highlighted with an Excel Instructions icon in the margin. The Excel instructions presume students have only a limited prior knowledge of Excel. A list of Excel instructions and templates follows this preface (p. xxiii).

Finally, this book is not merely a Canadianized version of an American book. It is Canadian through and through, featuring Canadian examples, measurements, and references.

SUPPLEMENTS

- **Instructor's Solutions Manual.** Full and detailed solutions are provided for all of the Develop Your Skills and Chapter Review exercises in the book. The solutions are "teaching" solutions that justify choice of technique and approach. Every effort has been made to ensure the solutions are correct and complete.

Excel Templates

I have included Excel templates that automate the calculations required for the hypothesis tests and confidence intervals I have included in this textbook. You will find the templates on the Student CD-ROM that accompanies the text. The templates are easy for students to use and feature cells that require input shaded in **"blue"**. The templates will remind students to check necessary conditions before proceeding with their calculations.

Excel Add-ins

Most of the Excel add-ins provided on the Student CD-ROM that accompanies the text are related to the ranking required for the non-parametric methods. Generally, the add-ins compute rank sums and provide them in the output. Students will then simply have to check conditions and do some further calculations. The add-ins are used to automate calculations that would be tedious for large data sets but they do not presume to automate the required decision making. Rather than trust the "magic" of computers, students will still have to think about their next steps and the decisions they will need to make.

The solutions are available in Word documents. I would recommend that these solutions be made available to students on a password-protected web site. Students develop confidence only when they can check their answers and make sure they are correct.

- **PowerPoint® Slides.** Properly designed with appropriate animations, PowerPoint slides can be very helpful to illustrate concepts. I recommend that you preview the slides that accompany this book before they are used in class. The animations can be very helpful, but not if they come as a surprise to the professor! The time spent in preparing them for your needs will yield real rewards in student learning.

- **Instructor's Resource Manual.** The Instructor's Resource Manual provides more detailed background for the discussion in the text. For example, occasionally a student will ask a professor to prove that

$$S = \sqrt{\frac{\sum(x - \bar{x})}{n - 1}} = \sqrt{\frac{\sum x^2 - \frac{(\sum x)^2}{n}}{n - 1}}$$

The IRM manual contains a suggested approach to proving this formula.

- **Pearson Education Canada Test Generator.** This powerful computerized testing package contains more than 600 multiple-choice, true/false, and short answer questions. Each question includes a correct answer, a skill and difficulty level rating, a chapter section reference, and a text page reference. This state-of-the-art software package in the Windows platform enables instructors to create tailor-made, error-free tests quickly and easily. The Custom Test allows instructors to create an exam, administer it traditionally or online, and evaluate and track students' results—all with the click of the mouse.

- **Companion Website (www.pearsoned.ca/skuce).** This website will be of interest to both instructors and students. Instructors can access the password-protected area of the website. It includes additional teaching tools, such as downloadable PowerPoint Slides, Instructor's Solutions Manual, Instructor's Resource Manual, and Pearson Education Canada Test Generator. Students will find additional true/false, multiple-choice, and fill-in-the-blank practice questions. Also available to students is a flashcard glossary of all the key terms from the text. Students can check out the Companion Website by going to www.pearsoned.ca/skuce and selecting the book cover for *Analyzing Data and Making Decisions: Statistics for Business* by Judith Skuce.

Where appropriate, I provide further explanation for the approaches I use in this text. For example, in Chapter 10, I recommend the unequal variances approach to the *t*-test of means as the default. I have provided an explanation for this approach in Chapter 10 of the Instructor's Resource Manual.

ACKNOWLEDGMENTS

This book began as a single chapter, which I wrote out of frustration with traditional material on sampling distributions. The journey from that first chapter to the book you hold in your hands has been a long and interesting one. I could not have travelled from there to here without the help of many people, and I would like to thank them.

Gary Bennett, Editor-In-Chief, Higher Education, displayed extraordinary persistence and patience as he gently persuaded me to take this project on. Gary's unwavering belief that this was a book worth writing has helped sustain me through many long hours and late nights. Samantha Scully in her capacity as Executive Editor for Accounting, Decision Sciences, and Finance, has provided effective leadership and support.

I have had the pleasure of working with two developmental editors. Angela Kurmey was very helpful in setting up the initial structure of the book. Eleanor MacKay has been extremely organized and thorough and has answered perhaps a million of my questions with unwavering good humour.

Cheryl Jackson's production editorial team and Christine Kwan's production team transformed a big box of pages of text into this book, and I consider that nothing short of a miracle. Anthony Leung provided a design that is not only beautiful, but highly functional. Laurel Sparrow edited the copy with remarkable attention to detail. Tom Gamblin, Catharine Haggert, and Torben Drewes provided crucial assistance to ensure that the text reads well and contains as few errors as possible. Beth McAuley took on the detailed task of obtaining the required permissions, which allowed the use of current and relevant examples in the text. Cas Shields, Executive Marketing Manager for Accounting, Management, General Business, Business Law and Decision Sciences, and her team have shown remarkable enthusiasm for this text.

I have been very positively impressed with the skill and dedication of everyone I have met at Pearson Canada, and I feel lucky to have their support.

My friend and colleague Dan Phillips created exactly the Excel add-ins that the book needed. I thank him for his skill and patience as we worked through the details.

I would also like to thank the following instructors who provided formal reviews of drafts of the manuscript:

- Margo Burtch, Seneca College
- Melanie Christian, St. Lawrence College

- Shari Corrigan, Camosun College
- David Gates, Vanier College
- John Henderson, Lambton College
- Marc Jerry, Mount Royal College
- Chris Kellman, British Columbia Institute of Technology
- Stephan Kogitz, Centennial College
- Karen A. Lawrence, Mohawk College
- Susan Vallery, Sir Sandford Fleming College

I want to thank Professor B. J. Marshman, who taught my class in advanced calculus at the University of Waterloo many years ago, and who remains a shining example of how to make complicated material more friendly and accessible to students.

Finally, I would like to thank all of the students who have attended my statistics classes over the years. I have learned a great deal from them.

Judith Skuce
2007

Excel Instructions and Excel Templates

The following is a list of Excel instructions and templates used in this text, for easy reference. Note: Excel's Data Analysis tools may need to be turned on. See Why Excel? on p. xxxv for more information. The Non-parametric Tools are Excel add-ins that come on the CD that accompanies this text, and must be installed. See Excel Add-ins on p. xxxvi for more information.

CHAPTER 2

Class Width Worksheet, Exhibit 2.11, p. 33

Data Analysis/Histogram for frequency distributions, p. 35

Data Analysis/Histogram for histograms, p. 41

Chart Wizard/Column chart for contingency tables, p. 58

Chart Wizard/Line chart for time-series data, p. 61

CHAPTER 3

AVERAGE function, p. 96

MEDIAN function, p. 97

MODE function, p. 100

STDEV function, p. 105

QUARTILE function, p. 115

PEARSON FUNCTION, p. 120

Non-parametric Tools/Spearman Rank Correlation Coefficient, p. 127

CHAPTER 5

BINOMDIST function, p. 177

NORMDIST function, p. 186

CHAPTER 7

Making Decisions About the Population Proportion with a Single Sample template, Exhibit 7.4, p. 249

TDIST function, p. 255

TDIST function with negative *t*-scores, p. 258

Making Decisions About the Population Mean with a Single Sample template,
   Exhibit 7.13, p. 259, Exhibit 7.15, p. 260

COUNT function, p. 259

CHAPTER 8

Confidence Interval Estimate for the Population Proportion template, Exhibit 8.9, p. 282

Confidence Interval Estimate for the Population Mean template, Exhibit 8.15, p. 286

CHAPTER 9

Making Decisions About the Population Mean with a Single Sample template
used with matched-pairs data, Exhibit 9.5, p. 303, Exhibit 9.11 p. 307

Data Analysis/*t*-Test: Paired Two Sample for Means, p. 304

Confidence Interval Estimate for the Population Mean template
used with matched-pairs data, Exhibit 9.13, p. 309

Non-parametric Tools/Wilcoxon Signed Rank Sum Test Calculations, p. 319

Making Decisions about Matched Pairs, Quantitative Data,
Non-normal Differences (WSRST) template, Exhibit 9.27, p. 320

Non-parametric Tools/Sign Test Calculations, p. 330

Making Decisions About Matched Pairs, Ranked Data (Sign Test)
template, Exhibit 9.40, p. 331

CHAPTER 10

Data Analysis/*t*-Test: Two-Sample Assuming Unequal Variances, p. 344, also p. 345

Making Decisions About the Difference in Population Means with
Two Independent Samples template, Exhibit 10.6, p. 348

Confidence Interval Estimate for the Difference in Population Means template, Exhibit 10.8, p. 352

Non-parametric Tools/Wilcoxon Rank Sum Test Calculations, p. 357

Making Decisions About Two Population Locations, Non-normal Quantitative Data or
Ranked Data (WRST) template, Exhibit 10.13, p. 358

CHAPTER 11

Data Analysis/Histogram to organize coded data, p. 375

Making Decisions About Two Population Proportions, Qualitative
Data template, Exhibit 11.1, p. 375, Exhibit 11.2, p. 377, Exhibit 11.30, p. 398

Confidence Interval Estimate for the Difference in Population Proportions template, Exhibit 11.3, p. 380

CHITEST function, p. 388

Non-parametric Tools/Chi-squared Expected Values Calculations, p. 394

CHAPTER 12

Data Analysis/Regression to get the least-squares line, p. 414

Data Analysis/Regression for analysis of residuals, p. 422

Data Analysis/Regression output for test of slope, p. 436

Data Analysis/Regression output for R2, p. 440

Prediction Interval Estimate for y, Given x template, p. 443

Confidence Interval Estimate for Average y, Given x template, Exhibit 12.45, p. 444

Table of Examples

CHAPTER 1

Example 1.1   Secondary data, p. 3
Example 1.2a   Nonstatistical sampling, p. 6
Example 1.2b   Nonstatistical sampling, p. 6
Example 1.2c   Random sampling with Excel, p. 8
Example 1.2d   Random sampling by polling companies, p. 10
Example 1.3   Analyzing the data, p. 12
Example 1.4a   Cause and effect cannot be concluded from observational studies, p. 16
Example 1.4b   Cause and effect may be concluded from experimental studies, p. 16
Example 1.5   State conclusions carefully, p. 18

CHAPTER 2

Example 2.2a   Setting up a frequency distribution with Excel, p. 38
Example 2.2b   Modifying Excel's automatic histogram, p. 43
Example 2.3   Using Excel to create a bar graph with coded data, p. 55
Example 2.4   Graphing time-series data, p. 62
Example 2.5   Graphing paired quantitative data, p. 66

CHAPTER 3

Example 3.1a   Evaluating Σx, p. 91
Example 3.1b   Evaluating Σx^2, p. 91
Example 3.1c   Evaluating $(\Sigma x)^2$, p. 91
Example 3.1d   Evaluating Σxy, p. 91
Example 3.1e   Evaluating $\Sigma(x - 6)$, p. 92
Example 3.1f   Evaluating $\Sigma(x - 6)^2$, p. 92
Example 3.1g   Evaluating $\Sigma\dfrac{(x - 6)^2}{n - 1}$, p. 92
Example 3.1h   Evaluating $\Sigma(x - 6)(y - 3)$, p. 93
Example 3.2a   Using Excel to calculate the mean, p. 96
Example 3.2b   The mean is greatly affected by extreme values, p. 96

Example 3.2c   Finding the median in a data set, p. 97
Example 3.3a   Calculating the standard deviation with Excel, p. 104
Example 3.3b   Calculating the standard deviation with the computational formula, p. 105
Example 3.3c   Applying the Empirical Rule, p. 112
Example 3.3d   Finding the 75th percentile, p. 114
Example 3.3e   Calculating the interquartile range, p. 115
Example 3.4a   Calculating the Pearson correlation coefficient, p. 124
Example 3.4b   Calculating the Spearman rank correlation coefficient, p. 125

CHAPTER 4

Example 4.1   Representing a sample space with a contingency table, a joint probability table,
                    and a tree diagram, p. 141
Example 4.2a   Calculating conditional probabilities, p. 145
Example 4.2b   Testing for independence, p. 146
Example 4.3a   The rule of multiplication: calculating "and" probability, p. 152
Example 4.3b   The rule of addition: calculating "or" probabilities, p. 154
Example 4.3c   Calculating probabilities with a tree diagram and probability rules, p. 157

CHAPTER 5

Example 5.1   Calculating the mean and standard deviation of a discrete probability distribution, p. 169
Example 5.2a   Calculating binomial probabilities with a formula, p. 176
Example 5.2b   Using Excel to calculate binomial probabilities, p. 178
Example 5.2c   Calculating binomial probabilities with tables, p. 182
Example 5.3a   Calculating normal probabilities with NORMDIST, p. 187
Example 5.3b   Using NORMINV to calculate x-values for normal probabilities, p. 190
Example 5.3c   Calculating normal probabilities with a table, p. 195

CHAPTER 6

Example 6.1   Using a sampling distribution to decide if a sample result is unusual, p. 210
Example 6.2a   Constructing a sampling distribution and using it to decide about a population mean, p. 214
Example 6.2b   Assessing population normality, constructing a sampling distribution, and using it to
                    decide about a population mean, p. 220
Example 6.3a   Using the binomial distribution to make a decision about a population proportion, p. 223
Example 6.3b   Using the sampling distribution of $\hat{p}$ to make a decision about a population proportion, p. 228
Example 6.3c   Using the sampling distribution of $\hat{p}$ to make a decision about a population proportion, p. 229

CHAPTER 7

Example 7.1a   Setting up correct null and alternative hypotheses, p. 238
Example 7.1b   Type I and Type II errors, p. 242

Example 7.1c   Calculating p-values, p. 244
Example 7.2a   Hypothesis test about a population proportion, summary data, p. 246
Example 7.2b   Hypothesis test about a population proportion with coded data, p. 248
Example 7.3a   Right-tailed hypothesis test about a population mean, raw data, p. 253
Example 7.3b   Left-tailed hypothesis test about a population mean, raw data, p. 256
Example 7.3c   Right-tailed hypothesis test about a population mean, raw data, p. 259
Example 7.3d   Estimating p-values from the table of critical values for the t-distribution, p. 263
Example 7.3e   Two-tailed hypothesis test about a population mean, summary data, p. 265

CHAPTER 8

Example 8.1   Constructing a confidence interval estimate for p, p. 281
Example 8.2   Constructing a confidence interval estimate for μ, p. 285
Example 8.3a   Deciding on sample size to estimate μ, p. 289
Example 8.3b   Deciding on sample size to estimate p, p. 291

CHAPTER 9

Example 9.1a   The t-test for matched pairs, raw data, p. 301
Example 9.1b   The t-test for matched pairs, raw data, p. 305
Example 9.1c   Confidence interval for μ_D, p. 308
Example 9.2a   Wilcoxon Signed Rank Sum Test, sample $\geq$ 25, p. 316
Example 9.2b   Wilcoxon Signed Rank Sum Test, small sample, raw data, p. 322
Example 9.3a   Sign Test, small sample, raw data, p. 327
Example 9.3b   Sign Test, large sample, summary data, using sampling distribution of $\hat{p}$, p. 331

CHAPTER 10

Example 10.1a t-test for independent samples, raw data, p. 345
Example 10.1b t-test for independent samples, summary data, p. 347
Example 10.1c   Confidence interval for difference in means, p. 351
Example 10.2a   Wilcoxon Rank Sum Test, sample size $\geq$ 10, p. 355
Example 10.2b   Wilcoxon Rank Sum Test, sample size $<$ 10, p. 359

CHAPTER 11

Example 11.1a   Comparing two proportions, special case, coded data, p. 375
Example 11.1b   Comparing two proportions, general case, summary data, p. 376
Example 11.1c   Confidence interval for difference in proportions, p. 379
Example 11.2a   Goodness-of-fit test, p. 382
Example 11.2b   Goodness-of-fit test, adjusting when $e_i < 5$, p. 386
Example 11.3a   Contingency table test, comparing many populations, p. 391
Example 11.3b   Contingency table for independence, p. 396

CHAPTER 12

Example 12.2a   Residuals with increasing variability, p. 423

Example 12.2b   Residuals not independent over time, p. 425

Example 12.2c   Residuals not independent over time, p. 426

Example 12.2d   Non-normal residuals, p. 427

Example 12.2e   Influential observations, p. 428

Example 12.3   Hypothesis Test of β_1 with Excel, p. 437

Example 12.4   Interpreting R^2, p. 442

Example 12.5   Calculating a confidence interval estimate for an average y,
                 given x, p. 446

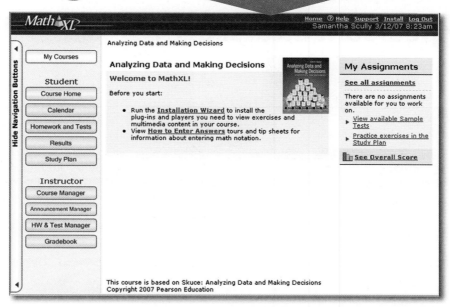

Access to MyStatLab is packaged at no extra cost with every new copy of *Analyzing Data and Making Decisions.* MyStatLab is a powerful new tool that:

- lets you identify your strengths and weaknesses using a diagnostic test and develops a personalized study plan for you that's keyed to your text

- provides you with exercises and problems, using an algorithmic engine that allows you to practise problems over and over again using different examples

- includes a brief animated video about the concepts explained in each chapter

- and more

You'll feel like you're back in class when you're doing your homework!

MyStatLab is powered by MathXL — go to **www.mathxl.com** to log in and get started!

A Great Way to Learn and Instruct Online

The Pearson Education Canada Companion Website is easy to navigate and is organized to correspond to the chapters in this textbook. Whether you are a student in the classroom or a distance learner you will discover helpful resources for in-depth study and research that empower you in your quest for greater knowledge and maximize your potential for success in the course.

[www.pearsoned.ca/skuce]

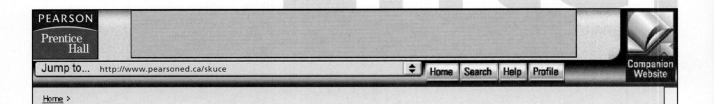

PEARSON
Prentice
Hall

Jump to...   http://www.pearsoned.ca/skuce   Home | Search | Help | Profile

Companion
Website

Home >

Companion Website

Analyzing Data and Making Decisions: Statistics for Business, by Judith Skuce

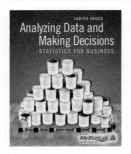

Student Resources

The modules in this section provide students with tools for learning course material. These modules include:
- Learning Objectives
- Chapter Summaries
- Self-Test
- Quizzes
- Glossary

In the quiz modules students can send answers to the grader and receive instant feedback on their progress through the Results Reporter. Coaching comments and references to the textbook may be available to ensure that students take advantage of all available resources to enhance their learning experience.

Instructor Resources

The modules in this section provide instructors with additional teaching tools. Downloadable PowerPoint Presentations, the Instructor's Solutions Manual and the Instructor's Resource Manual are just some of the materials that may be available in this section. Where appropriate, this section will be password protected. To get a password, simply contact your Pearson Education Canada Representative or call Faculty Sales and Services at 1-800-850-5813.

Using Microsoft® Excel for Analyzing Data and Making Decisions

Throughout this text, Microsoft Excel is the software that illustrates how the computer can be used to do statistical analysis. When you are learning new techniques, it is useful to do some of the analysis and calculations by hand (with a calculator), and you will probably have to do calculations with only a calculator in test and exam situations. However, no one actually does much statistical analysis without the use of a computer. Using a computer is an integral part of the techniques discussed in this text.

WHY EXCEL?

The Microsoft® Office software suite is widely used, in business and elsewhere. You probably already have some experience with Excel, and it is highly likely that this software is available to you at the educational institution where you are studying. It is also quite likely that Excel will be available to you in your workplace. For reasons of familiarity and availability, Excel was chosen to illustrate computer-based approaches to analyzing data and making decisions. Some basic facility with Excel is assumed (basic formulas, and use of Excel functions).

Excel has a built-in set of Data Analysis tools, which are used throughout the text. The standard installation of Excel does not usually include the Data Analysis tools, however, so you will have to follow these steps to activate them.

With a worksheet open in Excel:

1. Click on Tools
2. Click on Add-Ins . . . .
3. Put a tick mark beside Analysis Toolpak and Analysis Toolpak – VBA. See Exhibit 1.

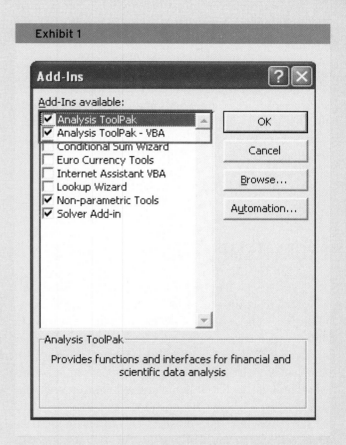

Exhibit 1

4. Click on OK.

When you attempt to do this, you may be asked for your installation disks for Excel.

After you complete these steps, when you click on Tools, Data Analysis . . . will be one of the available choices. Later in this text, you will be introduced to some of the Data Analysis tools.

While Excel is useful for an introductory course in statistics, it has some limitations. The CD that comes with this text contains some additional Excel tools, described in following sections. As well, you should be aware that Excel does not always handle missing data correctly. You should always examine your data sets carefully, and adjust for missing data. Some of Excel's routines produce unacceptable graphs (the histogram is one example). In any case where Excel's limitations could be a problem for the techniques covered here, advice is provided in the text. If you carry on in your study of statistics, you should consider learning how to use specialized statistical software.

Even if you choose to use another statistical analysis software package, the methods and concepts discussed in this book will still be helpful. Although your software output may look a little different from the Excel output described in the book, it will probably contain the same elements.

EXCEL TEMPLATES

The calculations required to analyze data or make decisions are repetitive. In some cases, Excel provides automatic functions to do some of the calculation required. In other cases, Excel formulas must be developed. A number of Excel templates with built-in formulas have been designed to assist you. The templates appear in one Excel workbook called Excel Templates. When you open this workbook you will see the individual templates organized by worksheet (see the worksheet tabs to locate the template you want). You will find instructions for selecting and using the Excel Templates workbook in Chapters 2, 7, 8, 9, 10, 11, and 12.

The templates contain some cells that require input from the user, and these cells are always shaded blue. Other cells contain formulas, and you should take care not to accidentally overwrite them. (The Excel worksheets are not protected, so that you can copy and paste the templates into the spreadsheets that contain the data you are analyzing, if you wish.) You can view the formulas, and if you have some experience with Excel, you should be able to see the direct correspondence between them and your manual calculations.

EXCEL ADD-INS

The CD that comes with the text also makes available some add-ins for procedures not covered in the standard Data Analysis tools. The add-ins do some calculations on sample data sets, simply automating what you would do by hand for small samples. The results of these calculations can then be input into the appropriate templates so that a final decision can be made. The use of the add-ins is described in the text, and there are also Help buttons to assist you.

The add-ins have to be installed. The instructions are as follows.

1. Locate the file called **Non_Parametric_Tools.xla** on your CD and then copy it to your computer, making a note about where you put the file. If you know where the other Excel add-ins are located in your file system, put this file in the same directory (but the file can be located anywhere).
2. Start Excel and, with a worksheet open, select Tools, then Add-Ins. The dialogue box will look approximately like Exhibit 1 shown on the previous page. However, you will not see Non-parametric Tools (if you do, tick the box beside it, click OK, and you are done!). You will have to select Browse and then click on **Non_Parametric_Tools.xla** when you locate it (according to your note in Step 1). Click OK.
3. You will now be returned to the Add-Ins dialogue box. The add-in Non-parametric Tools should now appear in the "Add-Ins available:" list. Tick the box and click OK.

Now that you are back to the usual view of Excel, select Tools. At the end of the menu you will see Non-parametric Tools. These tools are described in more detail in Chapters 9, 10, 11, and 12.

EXCEL DATA SETS

The data sets referenced in the text are available as Excel spreadsheets on the CD that accompanies the text. Data set files have been created for examples and exercises in Chapters 1, 2, 3, 6, 7, 8, 9, 10, 11, and 12. You will find the data set files organized by chapter. For example, the data files for Chapter 3 are in a directory called "DataChap03."

If a data set file is required to illustrate an example or for you to complete an exercise, you will find a data set icon in the margin. The file's name will either be with the icon or at the end of a question that uses the file. The file names have specific prefixes to help you identify them on the CD.

- The prefix "DYS" corresponds to the exercises in the Develop Your Skills sections (for example, "DYS02-2-1.xls").
- The prefix "CRE" corresponds to the Chapter Review Exercises (for example, CRE02-1.xls).

- The prefix "EXA" corresponds to examples in the text. For example, if a data set is available for Example 2.2a, the file is labelled EXA02-2a.xls.
- The prefix "SEC" is used when the data set is used in the general discussion in a particular section of the text. For example, a data set is introduced in Section 2.2, and it is labelled SEC02-2.xls.

Sometimes the same data file is used in a number of exercises. As a result, the same data set can have a number of different file names, one for each of the locations where the data set is used. This labelling system is designed to make it very easy for you to find the corresponding Excel files.

1 Using Data to Make Better Decisions

INTRODUCTION

Every day, in every walk of life, people make decisions and choices. Some decisions are relatively unimportant—such as what to eat for breakfast, what clothes to wear, and whether to take an umbrella when we leave home. Some decisions are more important—such as what post-secondary education to pursue, where to live, and how to manage our money. We are likely to use data to make even relatively unimportant decisions (for instance, the weather forecast helps us decide what to wear and whether to take an umbrella). We probably gather more data before we make important decisions (for example, most students carefully research the alternatives before they choose a post-secondary educational institution).

In business, important decisions have to be made every day: Which of the candidates should be hired? Should a new product be launched? Should a new branch or factory be opened? Should one be closed? While we hear stories about larger-than-life executives who make such major decisions on gut feel, most of these choices are probably based on the analysis of relevant data. For example, Krispy Kreme Doughnuts Inc., an American fast-food company, opened its first Canadian outlet at the corner of Mavis Road and Britannia Road in Mississauga, Ontario, in 2001. Company analysts spent months analyzing data on population,

Learning Objectives

After mastering the material in this chapter, you will be able to:

1. Understand the approaches to gathering data.

2. Understand why sampling is necessary.

3. Recognize that there is art and science to summarizing and analyzing data.

4. Recognize that cause-and-effect conclusions must be drawn carefully.

5. Understand that clear and honest communication of results is necessary for them to be useful.

6. Be familiar with a framework for data-based decision making.

traffic flow, and a host of other characteristics before choosing this location for the first Canadian Krispy Kreme outlet. Why?

> Using data to make decisions is better than guessing.

Collecting and analyzing data usually leads to a better understanding of the problem at hand, and a better decision about the solution, as you will see in the many examples in this text. For Krispy Kreme, all of the painstaking data evaluation paid off: its first Canadian location set a North American sales record for Krispy Kreme when it opened.[1]

It is likely that you are reading this book because you are enrolled in a course in "statistics." By convention and tradition, we use this term to refer to techniques for analyzing data and making decisions. However, the word "statistics" is not very illuminating to most people, and is fear-inspiring to many. What you should know is that there is nothing to be afraid of. If you can develop the habit of looking at the data carefully before you make decisions, and if you master at least some of the techniques described in this book, you will make better decisions. This approach is not only *not scary*, it can be a real plus for your life and your career.

The techniques involved in analyzing data and making decisions can also be fun. You might think of yourself as a data detective: you have to find the right data to help with the decision, and then you have to solve the mystery of what the data are telling you (or not telling you). It can be very satisfying to solve the mystery and arrive at the right decision.

This chapter provides you with a foundation for unravelling the mysteries of using data for decision making. Section 1.1 describes methods for getting the data you need. Section 1.2 describes the importance of sampling, and some of its challenges. Section 1.3 outlines the importance of analyzing the data that are collected, and Section 1.4 describes the kinds of conclusions that can (and cannot) be made from research studies. Section 1.5 stresses the importance of clearly communicating methods and conclusions. Section 1.6 provides a framework for a data-based decision-making approach, and describes how the material in this book relates to it.

 ## 1.1 GETTING THE DATA

Once you have understood the context of the problem at hand and identified the decision that is required, you will have to decide what data to collect. In some ways, this is the most important step in the process. Faulty data leads to faulty decisions.

There are two types of data that you might use to support decision making: data you collect yourself are *primary data*; and data already collected by someone else are *secondary data*. Suppose you wanted to know if the average mark on the last statistics test you wrote was more than 60%. One way to find out would be to ask every student what mark he or she received on the test, and then calculate the average. In this case, you

---

[1] As of the date of writing (summer 2006), Krispy Kreme is experiencing financial difficulties, which serves as a reminder that it takes more than one good decision to run a successful business. The store in Mississauga, however, is still operating.

would be collecting primary data. Alternatively, if you could get access to the teacher's marks database, you could use this secondary data to calculate the class average.

Primary and Secondary Data

Primary data are data that you collect yourself, for a specific purpose. The advantage of primary data collection is that you can collect exactly the data you need, and as a result you are in a much better position to make decisions. As well, you can design data collection methods so that it is possible to draw conclusions about cause-and-effect relationships. This is discussed in more detail in Section 1.4.

primary data data that you collect yourself, for a specific purpose

Many manufacturing enterprises have sophisticated systems to monitor quality continually. These companies collect a range of primary data so that they can adjust production processes when products do not meet specifications. For example, the "Six Sigma" approach to quality control was first introduced by Motorola Inc. in the mid-1980s. It began as a process to control the number of defects in a manufacturing setting, but has since developed into a system for controlling quality in a wide range of industries, including financial services and healthcare. The Six Sigma process relies on primary data collection.

The disadvantage of primary data is that collecting it tends to be costly or difficult, as it usually involves designing and implementing some kind of survey. For example, if you tried to collect the data about marks on the last statistics test from your classmates, you might find it very time-consuming. Just to start with, you might not even know who the students in your class are. If you could identify them accurately, some of them might refuse to tell you their test mark, and some might lie about it.

Secondary data is data that was previously collected by someone else. The advantage of secondary data is that it is usually cheaper to obtain than primary data. It may also be sufficient for your needs.

secondary data data that were previously collected by someone else

Suppose you wanted to know how the gross margin for your pharmacy in Cranbrook compared with other pharmacies in British Columbia. One of the easiest ways to get this data is through Statistics Canada.

Example 1.1

Secondary data

Exhibit 1.1 below shows the Statistics Canada data for pharmacies and personal care stores in British Columbia.

Exhibit 1.1

Statistics Canada Data for BC Pharmacies and Personal Care Stores			
	2003 Operating Statistics (Annual)		
	$ thousands		%
	Operating Revenues	Cost of Goods Sold	Expenses	Gross Margin
BC pharmacies and personal care stores	2,917,624	1,968,399	862,500	32.5

Source: Adapted from Statistics Canada website: http://www40.statcan.ca/101/cst01/trad38k.htm, accessed July 27, 2006.

There are many sources of secondary data about business activities in Canada. Most of these sources provide at least some of the available information on websites. Some useful sources are:

- Statistics Canada. This federal government agency collects all sorts of business information, and some of it is available for free. Libraries often house a selection of Statistics Canada publications. The website for Statistics Canada is **www.statcan.ca/start.html**, and the website for Statistics Canada business data is **http://commerce.statcan.ca/english/commerce**.
- Online databases, which can often be accessed through a library. Three are of particular interest:
  - Canadian Business & Current Affairs (CBCA) Business™. This online database collection provides access to a wide range of Canadian business periodicals.
  - ABI/INFORM. This online database is available in various forms. It provides access to over 3,800 business and management journals from around the world.
  - Business Source Premier (BSP). The Business Source Premier online service provides access to a collection of popular business magazines, scholarly journals and trade publications.
- Strategis Canada, a website produced by Industry Canada and available at **http://strategis.gc.ca**. The website provides access to 2 million electronic documents, with 50,000 links to related business sites.
- Provincial government websites, which provide a range of business information.
- Business publications, for example
  - *Canadian Business* magazine: **www.canadianbusiness.com/index.jsp**
  - *Maclean's* magazine: **www.macleans.ca/topstories/business/index.jsp**
  - *The Globe and Mail* Report on Business: **www.theglobeandmail.com/business**

This is just a short list of general business information sources. Industry-specific trade publications can also provide data to help you analyze your specific industry sector. Many of these sources provide at least some data on websites, however the ease of searching for information on the web should not prevent you from pursuing other sources of data (including those in print form). As well, you must recognize that many web-based sources of "data" are misleading, incomplete, biased, or just plain wrong.

It takes some skill to navigate the wide array of information available (especially on the Internet), and to identify which data sources are both useful and reliable. Librarians are trained in these activities, and when you are doing research a good librarian can be your best resource.

DEVELOP YOUR SKILLS

1. You are working in the bicycle manufacturing industry. You are interested in trends in household spending on bicycles and accessories. Find a secondary data source for this information.
2. If you were trying to control quality at your bicycle manufacturing plant, what primary and secondary data could you use?
3. Do you think data provided by government sources such as Statistics Canada are completely accurate and reliable? Do some research to see if your answer is correct.
4. Suppose you wanted to collect primary data about the music preferences of students at your school. How would you go about collecting it? What problems would you anticipate, and how would you solve them?
5. Choose a Canadian industry of interest to you. Try to come up with three sources of secondary data about the industry.

1.2   SAMPLING

The data you require to make a good decision are often not readily available. Even if you have the resources to do primary research, you will not likely be able to gather all the data you want.

Why Sampling Is Necessary

For example, as a business owner, you might be interested in characteristics of your current customers but not be able to survey all of them, either because you do not know how to contact them or because you cannot afford to. As a paint manufacturer, you might want to know that all of the cans coming off your production line contain the correct amount of paint, but you cannot (or cannot afford to) measure the paint level in all cans exactly. As a brewer, you might want to be sure that all of the beer you are producing is delicious, but obviously if you drank all of it to check, you would have none left to sell!

Fortunately, you do not need all of the data in order to make reliable decisions. Many of the techniques described in this text allow you to make decisions on the basis of sample data. For example, you might be interested in whether your customers react differently to your products according to their ages. The complete collection of data—the ages of all of your current and potential customers and their product preferences—is described as *population data*. **Population data** are the complete collection of *all* of the data of interest. Because of cost and difficulty in surveying *all* of the elements in the population, we survey only some of them. **Sample data** are a subset of population data.

Exhibit 1.2 below illustrates the difference between population data and sample data. Thousands of filled paint cans are coming off of a paint-production line. For quality control, a sample of these cans is examined.

population data the complete collection of *all* of the data of interest

sample data a subset of population data

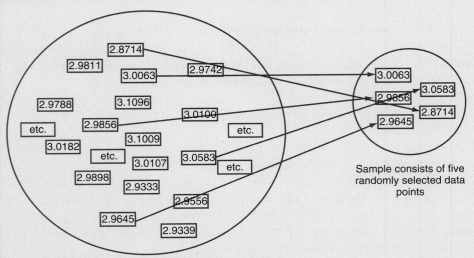

Population consists of thousands of data points, only some of which are illustrated

Sample consists of five randomly selected data points

The reliability of the conclusions that can be drawn about a population, on the basis of sample data, depends on the type of sampling used: statistical or nonstatistical sampling.

Nonstatistical Sampling

Nonstatistical sampling is sometimes referred to as *nonprobability sampling*. In **nonstatistical sampling**, the elements of the population are chosen for the sample by convenience, or according to the researcher's judgment. There is no way to estimate the probability (likelihood, or chance) that any particular element from the population will be chosen for the sample.

With nonstatistical sampling, there is no way to measure the reliability of the sample results, or whether the sample is representative of the population. Despite this, nonstatistical sampling can be useful. For example, although Statistics Canada uses statistical sampling for most of its data collection, it uses nonprobability sampling for testing questionnaires. Nonstatistical sampling can also legitimately be used to learn about emerging trends, or to test new product ideas. Focus groups are sometimes convened for these purposes. For example, if almost all of the people in a focus group hate a prototype product, this may mean that some adjustments are required.

nonstatistical sampling the elements of the population are chosen for the sample by convenience, or according to the researcher's judgment; there is no way to estimate the probability that any particular element from the population will be chosen for the sample

1.2a

Nonstatistical sampling

A retail store might take a convenience sample by surveying the first 50 customers who come into the store.

This could provide useful information, particularly if there is reason to believe that all customers of the store are essentially the same. But since customers 51 and up will not be chosen in such a sampling approach, its results should be used with caution. The customers who arrive at the store early may have very different characteristics and preferences from other customers.

1.2b

Nonstatistical sampling

The websites for some of Canada's newspapers conduct online polls and report results. For example, on June 9, 2006, *The Globe and Mail* posed this question: "Would you move if you could earn significantly more money at a job in another part of Canada?" (Source: "Poll Results," www.theglobeandmail.com, accessed June 9, 2006.)

Poll results were reported as follows: total votes were 17,979, with 61% voting "yes" and 39% voting "no."

The sampling approach here is nonstatistical, because responses were made by volunteers. Such a sample can be described as "self-selected," because the respondents themselves choose to provide sample data. The poll results should never be interpreted as representative of the views of all Canadians. At best, such a poll indicates the views of those who visited the newspaper's website and took the time to respond to the poll. But since one person could respond to the poll question many times, even this interpretation is risky. Such polls are best considered as entertainment.

Statistical Sampling

Statistical sampling is sometimes referred to as probability sampling. In **statistical sampling**, the elements of the population are chosen for the sample in a random fashion, with a known probability of inclusion. In this context, "random" does not mean "arbitrary" or "haphazard." It requires some thought and effort to select a random sample. The process will depend on the population being studied.

It is possible to make very reliable decisions about population data on the basis of data acquired through statistical sampling. The decision-making process is referred to as "inferential statistics." **Inferential statistics** is a set of techniques that allows reliable conclusions to be drawn about population data, on the basis of sample data. Usually, inferential statistics involves drawing some conclusion or estimating a population parameter on the basis of a sample statistic. For example, you might want to know the average amount of paint in *all* of the paint cans you produce. This average is a population parameter. A **parameter** is a summary measure of the population data. A **statistic** is a summary measure of the sample data. You might take a random sample of 30 paint cans, measure the amount of paint in each can exactly, and calculate a sample average. The average based on sample data is a sample statistic.

Reliable statistical inference is possible only if the sample data are a good reflection of population data. While even the best sampling techniques cannot *guarantee* this, with statistical sampling we can estimate and control the possibility of error. It is this control that makes statistical sampling such a powerful aid to decision making.

There are many possible methods of statistical sampling. The particular sampling plan will depend on the type of data being collected, the costs involved, and the goals of the analysis or decision. The simplest of the possible methods is simple random sampling, and the inferential techniques discussed in this text all assume simple random sampling. The methods required to analyze data from more complex sampling plans (e.g., systematic sampling, stratified sampling, cluster sampling) are extensions of the foundation techniques based on simple random sampling.

Simple random sampling is a sampling process that ensures that each element of the population is equally likely to be selected. Suppose that you wanted to collect test-mark data for a random sample of 10 of the students in your statistics class. One way to identify which students to survey is to ask the students to write their names on slips of paper. You could collect the slips of paper, and put them in a container of some kind, mix them up, and then ask someone to select 10 slips of paper from the container. You would then collect test mark data from the selected 10 students.

The population of interest is the test marks of all of the students in your statistics class. Will this procedure ensure that each element of the population is equally likely to be selected? Unfortunately, the answer is likely "no." Why? Unless your class is different from most other statistics classes, some students will be absent the day you conduct your survey. The absent students have no chance of being selected for the sample, and so you cannot say that your sampling procedure is random. Some elements of the population are less likely to be chosen.

In order to conduct a true random sample, you must start with a list of the elements in a population—this list is called a **frame**. Your teacher probably has a list of all of the students enrolled in your statistics class. How would this list be used to select a true random sample? You could write all of the names on slips of paper, mix them around in a hat, and

---

statistical sampling the elements of the population are chosen for the sample in a random fashion, with a known probability of inclusion

inferential statistics a set of techniques that allow reliable conclusions to be drawn about population data, on the basis of sample data

parameter a summary measure of the population data

statistic a summary measure of the sample data

simple random sampling a sampling process that ensures that each element of the population is equally likely to be selected

frame a list of the elements in a population

pull the names for the sample from the hat. Of course, this is a tedious process for large class sizes, and fortunately, more sophisticated methods are available. Computers allow us to use random number generation software to do the electronic equivalent of mixing up names in a hat and selecting some for the sample. Example 1.2c illustrates.

1.2c

Example

Random sampling with Excel

Instructions

Suppose your class has 60 students. You could number the student names from 1 to 60. Open a spreadsheet in Microsoft® Excel, and create a column of numbers from 1 to 60 (you can use Excel's autofill feature to create this list easily). Now you can use Excel to select a random sample from this frame. To do this, you will need to install the Data Analysis tools of Excel. Refer to the instructions for installing Data Analysis on page ii.

You can use Excel to generate a column of 60 random numbers beside the column of numbers from 1 to 60. Click on Tools, then select Data Analysis . . . , and select Random Number Generation. This will activate the window illustrated in Exhibit 1.3 below.

1.3

Exhibit

Random Number Generation in Excel

Random Number Generation   **[?] [X]**

Number of Variables: [1]   [OK]

Number of Random Numbers: [60]   [Cancel]

Distribution: [Uniform   ▼]   [Help]

┌─ Parameters ────────────────────────────────┐
│   │
│ Between [0]   and   [1]   │
│   │
│   │
└───┘

Random Seed: [   ]

┌─ Output options ────────────────────────────┐
│ (•) Output Range: [B1   ▦]   │
│ ( ) New Worksheet Ply: [   ] │
│ ( ) New Workbook   │
└───┘

You must enter

- Number of Variables, which in this case will be "1"
- Number of Random Numbers, which in this case will be "60"
- Distribution, which should always be Uniform (this ensures that each digit is equally likely to appear)
- Between defaults to "0" and "1," which is fine in this case
- Output Range, which is the top of the column next to the column containing the numbers 1–60.

The output you create will look something like the excerpt shown in Exhibit 1.4 below.

Excerpt of Excel Output for Random Number Generation
(only the first 12 rows are shown)

Exhibit 1.4

1	0.479446
2	0.490982
3	0.643391
4	0.308298
5	0.397809
6	0.024537
7	0.514634
8	0.26487
9	0.85815
10	0.530351
11	0.706015
12	0.457167

:
:

(columns continue)

The first column contains the numbers from 1 to 60, and the second column contains 60 random numbers between 0 and 1. Now you can use Excel to shuffle the first column according to the random numbers in the second column.

Place your cursor on one of the cells in the column of random numbers. Then select Data and Sort . . . , which will activate the window shown in Exhibit 1.5 below.

Sorting the Column of Numbers in Excel

Exhibit 1.5

You want to sort by the second column, which is the column of random numbers (check **Sort by**). Excel will usually automatically extend the sort to the adjacent column by default (read the dialogue box and change it if necessary). When you click **OK**, Excel will rearrange the numbers 1–60 in a random way, as shown in the excerpt in Exhibit 1.6.

Exhibit 1.6

Excerpt of Excel Output, with Frame Numbers Sorted by Random Numbers

6	0.024537
18	0.049593
21	0.052431
36	0.056063
26	0.068667
20	0.122562
56	0.122776
28	0.147954
23	0.153203
14	0.155858
60	0.170171
49	0.192694
22	0.213507

⋮

(columns continue)

The numbers in the first column—after you have electronically shuffled them around—represent the numbers you would pick out of the hat. If your sample size is 10, you would select the population elements corresponding to the first 10 numbers in column 1—that is, 6, 18, 21, 36, 26, 20, 56, 28, 23, and 14 (the shaded rows in Exhibit 1.6; these will not be shaded in Excel).

This discussion is designed to make you realize that taking a true random sample requires thought and effort. You may be able to create a true random sample if you are studying your own company. For example, you can probably take a random sample of employees or production output. You may also have sufficient data on hand to conduct a random sample of past customers. But you will never be able to conduct a true random sample of potential customers, because there is no way to know who they are.

Example 1.2d

Random sampling by polling companies

Polling companies who conduct opinion polls of the population at large are also challenged to identify a true random sample. Polling companies generally gather data by telephone interviews. Of course, this leaves out anyone who does not have a phone. In Canada, over 98% of households have at least one phone number, and this small difference between the sampled population and the target population is usually not considered to be a significant problem. The telephone survey approach makes it difficult to survey those who do not answer their phones or will not respond to telephone surveys. Polling companies go to considerable trouble to overcome these difficulties so that they can make reliable statements about survey results.

Sampling and Nonsampling Error

Sampling error is the difference between the true value of the population parameter and the value of the corresponding sample statistic; this difference arises because we are examining only a subset of the population. Sampling error is expected, because it would be unreasonable to expect the sample statistic to match the population parameter exactly. For example, if we managed to collect the test marks of a random sample of students, we would not expect the sample average mark to exactly match the true class average. Sampling error is something that we can estimate and control, as you will learn.

sampling error the difference between the true value of the population parameter and the value of the corresponding sample statistic; arises because we are examining only a subset of the population

Nonsampling errors are other kinds of errors that can arise in the process of sampling a population. Suppose you plan to survey past customers about their product preferences, and you decide to survey them by telephone. Here are some nonsampling errors that can occur.

nonsampling errors other kinds of errors that can arise in the process of sampling a population

1. Your survey frame may contain errors. Some customers may have been missed. Their phone numbers may have been incorrectly recorded or missing. Other information may not be correct. Such **coverage errors** arise because of inaccuracy or duplication in the survey frame.

   coverage errors errors that arise because of inaccuracy or duplication in the survey frame

2. Some of the customers you wish to speak to may never answer the phone. This causes **nonresponse error**, which arises when data cannot be collected for some elements of the sample.

   nonresponse error error that arises when data cannot be collected for some elements of the sample

3. There can be errors in acquiring the data. If the survey questions are biased or misleading, or difficult to understand, the customer being interviewed may not give truthful or accurate answers. If the interviewer is not well trained, he or she may influence the survey responses. These **response errors** arise because of problems with the survey collection instrument (e.g., the questionnaire), the interviewer (e.g., bias), the respondent (e.g., faulty memory), or the survey process (e.g., taking answers from someone other than the intended respondent).

   response errors errors that arise because of problems with the survey collection instrument (e.g., the questionnaire), the interviewer (e.g., bias), the respondent (e.g., faulty memory), or the survey process (e.g., not ensuring that the respondent fits into the target group)

4. There can be errors in recording the data, even when data are collected with the help of a computer, and this can lead to biased results. **Processing errors** occur when the data are being prepared for analysis.

   processing errors errors that occur when the data are being prepared for analysis

5. **Estimation errors** arise because of incorrect use of techniques, or calculation errors.

   estimation errors errors that arise because of incorrect use of techniques, or calculation errors

It is important that you recognize that nonsampling errors can invalidate the conclusions drawn from the sample. You should be watchful for nonsampling errors when you examine research done by others, and you should take great care to avoid these errors when you are sampling. With some effort, you can greatly minimize the possibility of nonsampling error.

DEVELOP YOUR SKILLS 1.2

1. Nowadays, many companies use customer relationship management (CRM) software to keep track of customer sales information, financing arrangements, and product preferences. Is this sample or population data?

See if you can find an article that describes how a particular company uses CRM data.

2. A restaurant owner decides to survey diners on Friday night, because he wants to collect a lot of data and Friday is always busy. Is this a statistical or a nonstatistical sample? Why? How much should the restaurant owner rely on the sample data?

3. "A new Ipsos-Reid survey conducted on behalf of Mosaik MasterCard finds that three-quarters (77%) of Canadian postsecondary students have at least one credit card. Of these students, 72% are currently carrying a balance, and 53% plan to pay it off entirely by their next statement due date." Are these population parameters or sample statistics? (Source: "School Credits of a Different Kind: The Mosaik MasterCard Back to School Student Survey on Credit Card Knowledge", **www.ipsos-na.com/news/pressrelease.cfm?id=2763**, accessed June 7, 2006.)

4. As part of an employee satisfaction survey, a research team wants to conduct in-depth interviews with a random sample of 10 employees. The company's employee list is available in an Excel spreadsheet that is on the CD that comes with this text, in the directory called DataChap01. Use Excel to create a random sample of 10 employees. See file called DYS01-2-4.xls.

5. Suppose Calgary Transit wants to do a survey to see if it can improve its services for people with disabilities. The organization decides to collect information through interviews of a random sample of riders. Outline some challenges Calgary Transit might face in gathering the data.

1.3   ANALYZING THE DATA

Once you collect the data you need, the information must be organized so that you can make sense of it. Raw (that is, unorganized) data usually do not tell us much.

Example 1.3

Analyzing the data

EXA01.3.xls

Suppose a Niagara region winery is interested in discovering if there is a difference between men's and women's average purchases from the winery. A random sample of 25 men and 28 women is selected, and their purchase amounts are collected. The data for purchases by men are as follows: $52.40, $20.67, $38.93, $51.32, $50.38, $46.80, $49.80, $43.19, $49.14, $22.96, $27.72, $15.71, $13.84, $24.27, $26.72, $10.58, $29.18, $31.15, $37.62, $31.61, $42.08, $31.56, $52.11, $34.98, $33.77. The data for purchases by women are: $46.32, $58.85, $47.82, $68.57, $13.80, $30.12, $37.30, $43.54, $24.73, $29.49, $67.55, $53.11, $13.17, $30.40, $49.42, $40.22, $53.99, $41.17, $28.36, $51.11, $34.76, $44.82, $58.00, $25.37, $67.25, $32.97, $31.09, $48.30.

Just looking at these lists of numbers does not tell us much. We cannot easily see if there is a difference in the purchases made by men and women. Probably one of your instincts is to calculate the men's and women's average purchases. The average is an example of a numerical summary measure, and is discussed along with other numerical summary measures in Chapter 3. It is often helpful to create a graph to summarize data, and such graphs are discussed in Chapter 2 of this text. The techniques in Chapters 2 and 3 are part of a branch of statistics called "descriptive statistics." Once you master these, you will be able to produce graphs and summary statistics that help you see the data more clearly. Exhibit 1.7 shows some graphs that organize and display the winery purchase data for men and women, as well as a table with some summary statistics.

Winery Purchase Data.

a)

b)

c)   **Summary Statistics for Winery Purchases**

Winery Purchases	average purchase	lowest purchase	highest purchase
by men	$34.74	$10.58	$52.40
by women	$41.84	$13.17	$68.57

These graphs and summary measures have probably helped you understand the two data sets better. You can see that the average purchase by women is higher than the average purchase by men. You can also see that there is greater variability in the purchases by women than the purchases by men. You will see summary measures in Chapters 2 and 3.

Descriptive statistics are a set of techniques to organize and summarize raw data. As you explore the possibilities for summarizing and describing data, you will discover that there is both art and science involved. While there are many guidelines to help you, you will usually have to make choices about presenting data. Your goal should always be to represent the data truthfully. You should also be aware that some will choose to confuse or misrepresent data, and you should always be alert to these possibilities. Even if you do not become a statistician, you should be an informed and suitably skeptical consumer of statistical analysis done by others. You will learn more as you explore Chapters 2 and 3.

descriptive statistics a set of techniques to organize and summarize raw data

DEVELOP YOUR SKILLS 1.3

1. An advertisement claims that prices for electronic organizers have decreased by 125%. What do you think of this claim?

2. Exhibit 1.8 shows two graphs depicting values of the Standard & Poor's/Toronto Stock Exchange Composite Index during the period from April 28 to June 8, 2006. Which graph is a better representation of the index during this time period?

(Source: S&P/TSX Composite Price History for Symbol TSX-1, April 28 to June 8, 2006. **http://investdb.theglobeandmail.com/ invest/invest-SQL/gx.price_history?pi_symbol=TSX-I** accessed June 8, 2006).

3. "[Student] Jack Gurley has shown astonishing progress in academic achievement over the last semester. Jack's average grade has increased by a substantial 20%." Based on this statement, what is your impression of Jack Gurley's academic success? (State your conclusion before you read any further.)

Now, here are the facts. Last semester, Jack's average grade was 32.8%. This semester, Jack's average grade is 20% higher, that is, 1.20(32.8%) =39.4%. While Jack's grades have improved, he is still a long way from academic success. How would you rewrite the initial statement in this question so that it was more honest?

4. You are the national manager for a company that provides express oil changes at a number of locations,

---

Exhibit 1.8

S&P/TSX Composite Index, April 28 to June 8, 2006

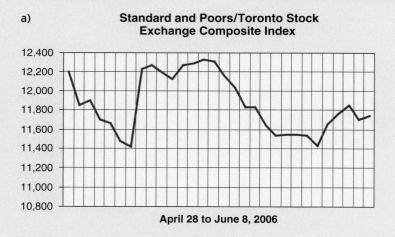

a) **Standard and Poors/Toronto Stock Exchange Composite Index**

April 28 to June 8, 2006

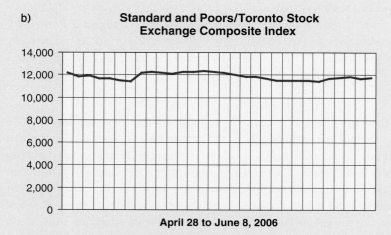

b) **Standard and Poors/Toronto Stock Exchange Composite Index**

April 28 to June 8, 2006

and you are concerned that the service level at one of these locations is not up to your standard. The location keeps records of its service completion times (from customer arrival to departure). You've asked to see these records, but the local manager says he's too busy to send them to you. He also claims that the maximum wait time during the recent quarter has decreased by 25%, compared with the previous quarter. Would you be satisfied, or would you insist on seeing the records?

5. Consider the graph shown in Exhibit 1.9 below. Do you think it is a fair representation of sales over the period?

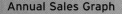
Annual Sales Graph

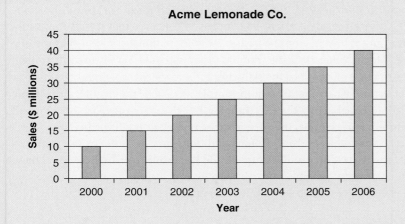

1.4   MAKING DECISIONS

After you have collected and analyzed the data, you will be in a position to make some decisions. The type of conclusion that you can draw depends on how the data were gathered.

Suppose a newspaper wants to know if its readers' average income has increased, compared with five years ago. This information could be very useful, because an attractive reader income profile helps to sell advertising. In this case, the decision to be made is a straightforward one: has readers' average income increased? By looking at the sample evidence, we can decide whether or not this appears to be the case, and you will learn reliable techniques to do this as you progress through this text. It is unlikely that the newspaper is particularly interested in *why* readers' average income has increased, if this turns out to be the case.

This is an example of an observational study. In an **observational study**, the researcher observes what is already taking place, and does not attempt to affect outcomes. Many marketing studies are observational in nature. Companies collect data about their customers in order to understand them better.

observational study the researcher observes what is already taking place, and does not attempt to affect outcomes

Sometimes research is aimed at understanding cause and effect, that is, pinpointing *why* an observed change or difference has occurred. Example 1.4a illustrates.

1.4a

Cause and effect cannot be concluded from observational studies

Suppose that the vice-president of operations is interested in how training methods affect the number of worker errors. One way to study this would be to record the number of errors for a random sample of workers at two different plants—one where training has taken place, and one where it has not.

The first decision that must be made is whether the sample data provide evidence to suggest that the error rates differ between the two plants. Once you have mastered the techniques in this text, you will be able to make this decision.

But there is also a further question. If the error rates differ, is it because of the training program? The vice-president might be tempted to conclude that it is. But this further conclusion cannot be made on the basis of an observational study such as the one described here. Factors other than the training program could have caused the difference in the error rates. For example, the skills and experience of the workers could affect the number of errors. Choosing a random sample at each plant may result in these factors being about equal across the two samples. But there are other factors that will not be randomized. For example, the supervisor at one plant might be better at motivating workers to make fewer errors. Traffic conditions may be better at one plant, so that the workers arrive less tired and frustrated, and less prone to error. Because of these other possibilities, it is not possible to make a strong conclusion about the cause of the differences in error rates on the basis of this observational study.

experimental study the researcher actively intervenes, designing the study so that conclusions about causation can be drawn

To make a stronger conclusion about the cause of any difference in error rates, the vice-president could conduct an experimental study. In an **experimental study**, the researcher actively intervenes, designing the study so that conclusions about causation can be drawn.

1.4b

Cause and effect may be concluded from experimental studies

Suppose an experimental study is designed as follows. A group of workers is randomly selected at a particular plant, and the numbers of errors made by the group are recorded over a period of time. The researcher then intervenes by putting the workers through a training program. The numbers of worker errors are recorded again after the training.

In this case, if the numbers of worker errors after the training are lower, it is easier to conclude that the training is the cause. However, even in this case, there could be other explanations. For example, the workers who took the training might have been motivated to pay particular attention and work carefully, simply because they were selected for the study. The results of the study might not generalize to the entire population of workers.

You can see from Example 1.4b that even experimental studies can have limitations, although generally they lead to stronger conclusions than observational studies. It is very important that you recognize what conclusions are justified—and what conclusions are *not* justified—from any particular research study. While statistical analysis can add to our understanding of the world, it cannot tell us everything.

This may surprise you. Many people expect that since statistical analysis involves data and mathematics (or at least arithmetic) and computers, the results should be very clear. This can sometimes be the case, but not always. The claim can be made that "using data to make decisions is better than guessing." This is true, but it does not imply that statistical techniques always lead to clear answers. Judgment is required to interpret the results of statistical analyses. In fact, judgment is required throughout the analysis, as you will see during your introduction to the techniques in this text. The ability to make good judgments develops with practice, experience, and reflection. This does not mean that anything goes, or that you can "prove" anything you want with statistics. Some conclusions and some choices are clearly unacceptable. In cases where judgment is required, you must be prepared to defend your choices objectively. And you should always critically evaluate the judgments made by others in their statistical analyses.

DEVELOP YOUR SKILLS 1.4

1. A study published in 2006 indicated that higher family incomes are associated with better physical, social/emotional, cognitive, and behavioural well-being among children (Source: "Study: Family Income and the Well-Being of Children," **www.statcan.ca/Daily/English/060511/d060511c.htm**, accessed June 8, 2006). Barbara Arneil, a political science professor at the University of British Columbia, was quoted in a related article in *The Globe and Mail* as saying that the findings suggest the following: "If the outcomes for our kids are better with higher incomes, the goal should be to get both parents into the work force." (Source: "Well-Off Children Do Better on Tests, Study Finds," **www.theglobeandmail.com**, accessed May 15, 2006). Should you agree with Professor Arneil's conclusion?

2. A study of 10,000 people born in the UK in 1958 revealed that a man 6 feet in height was more likely to have a partner and children than was a man of average height (5 feet, 10 inches). Does this mean that women prefer to marry tall men?

3. An insurance company with a number of branch offices across the country has designed a diary system for salespeople, which is designed to increase their productivity. The diary system is colour-coded: green is for time spent with clients making sales calls, blue is for time spent supporting existing clients, and red is down-time (lunch, travelling, etc.). The idea is that the visual cue of the coded diary will focus the salesperson's attention on sales. A number of poor performers were selected and introduced to the diary system. Average sales increased by 11%. Can we conclude that the diary system caused the increase?

4. If you wanted to test the effectiveness of the diary colour-coding system described in the previous exercise, how would you design your study?

5. An ice cream store hired a mascot to entice people into the store to buy ice cream. During the period when the mascot was working, sales increased by 15%. Can we conclude that the mascot caused the increase in sales?

1.5 COMMUNICATION

This text focuses on introductory techniques for analyzing data and making decisions about population data on the basis of sample data. Once you master these techniques, you will be on your way to becoming a successful data detective. However, your detective work will be useful only if you learn to communicate your methods and conclusions clearly.

When reporting on your statistical analysis, you should completely describe the problem at hand, and the goal of any decisions to be made. You should also provide information about how the data were collected, organized, and summarized, usually showing both graphs and numbers. Describe the statistical techniques you used, as well as any judgments about areas of uncertainty. Finally, make a clear statement of conclusions or decisions, with justification. You may provide the technical detail in the body of the report or in an appendix, but it must always be presented so that an informed reader can assess the methods used and whether the conclusions are justified. How much of the technical detail is included in the body of the report depends on its intended reader: a report written for colleagues who are familiar with statistics would be written differently than a report for a supervisor with little understanding of statistics.

It is also important that you state your conclusions carefully, as Example 1.5 illustrates.

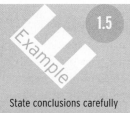

Example 1.5

State conclusions carefully

Consider a study of a newspaper's readers' incomes. Here are three different ways the conclusion of the study might be expressed:

1. With a p-value of 0.0123, H_0 is rejected.
2. The average income of this newspaper's readers has increased over the last five years.
3. Sample evidence suggests that the average income of this newspaper's readers has increased over the last five years.

While statement 1 might be technically correct, it cannot be understood without reference to the study. But this is a minor point. The more important problem is that most people would have no idea what this statement means, even after referring to the study! It is important that you learn to state the results of your statistical analysis in language that can be easily understood by almost anyone. While you need to understand the specialized language of statistics, you should also learn to translate it for an audience without statistical knowledge. Bosses and clients are not impressed by fancy jargon: they are frustrated by it.

Statement 2 is much more promising, because anybody could read it and understand it. However, this statement has a major problem: it does not even hint at the fact that this conclusion is made on the basis of sample results. Even if the sampling and the analysis were done properly, there is still a chance that a rare and unrepresentative sample was taken. The conclusion could be completely wrong. However, the statement does not even hint at this possibility, and so it is simply not correct, unless you have somehow managed to collect all the relevant population data.

Statement 3 is the best of the three, by far. First of all, it is understandable. It also indicates that a sample has been taken, and it is not nearly as definitive as statement 2. You might think that the differences between statement 2 and statement 3 are minor. The newspaper's employees are probably going to act and speak as if statement 2 were true, as they try to sell more newspaper ads, so why go to the bother of stating conclusions so carefully? The answer is quite simple: statement 2 is not truthful.

DEVELOP YOUR SKILLS 1.5

1. Identify the characteristics of the intended reader of your statistical analysis in the following situations, and describe how much technical detail you would plan to include in the body of the report.
   a. The national manager of quality control wants a report on quality control measures at the plant where you work.
   b. The human resources department has asked you to analyze the educational levels of middle managers in the organization.
   c. Your boss has asked you to prepare a report on a new product's characteristics, which will be used in a consumer magazine article about the product.

2. Comment on the following statement about a study based on a random sample of past customers of your firm: "Study results prove that our products are more attractive to younger buyers, so we should target the under-35 market."

3. One of the mistakes that beginning statisticians often make is to focus their reports on themselves, instead of on the data being analyzed. Instead of talking about what "I" did, you should be talking about what the data show. Rewrite the following statement with focus on the data, not the analyst.

   "I took a random sample of 30 paint cans off the line, and carefully measured the exact amount of paint in each can. The sample average was 3.012 litres, just a bit above the desired level of 3 litres. I plotted this on the control chart, and I noticed that this number was within control limits. So I concluded that there was no problem with the paint filling line."

4. Another mistake that beginning statisticians make is to use subjective language to describe results, thus influencing the reader's interpretation. The goal should be to let the data speak for themselves. Rewrite the following statement without the subjective flavour, and with the proper focus on the data. (Use your imagination to make the report more specific, if you wish.)

   "After extensive and painstaking analysis, I am delighted to conclude that our study shows that the new training program dramatically increased worker productivity. You should not hesitate to expand the training program across the nation, as the analysis is crystal-clear."

5. "The study concludes that being tall increases your chances of being a CEO." Do you think that this conclusion could be valid? How would you rewrite this to be more truthful?

1.6   A FRAMEWORK FOR DATA-BASED DECISION MAKING

A general approach to data-based decision making is outlined below. It summarizes the discussion in this chapter.

All of the steps in this process are important. Below are some comments about how these steps relate to the material in this text.

Steps in Data-Based Decision Making

1. Understand the problem and its context as thoroughly as possible. Be clear about the goal of a good decision.
2. Think about what kind of data would help you make a better decision. See if helpful data are already available somewhere. Decide how to collect data if necessary, keeping in mind the kind of conclusion you want to be able to make.

3. Collect the data, if the benefit of making a better decision justifies the cost of collecting and analyzing the data.
4. Examine and summarize the data.
5. Analyze the data in the context of the decision that is required. This may require using the sample data to:
   • estimate some unknown quantity
   • test if a claim (hypothesis) seems to be true
   • build a model.
6. Communicate the decision-making process. This requires:
   • a clear statement of the problem at hand, and the goal of the decision
   • a description of how the data were collected or located
   • a summary of the data
   • a description of the estimation, hypothesis test, or model-building process(es)
   • a statement of what decision should be made, with justification.

Step 1   In the pages of this book, you will find regular encouragement to *think* carefully about the problem at hand and how to approach it. Learning to do this successfully takes practice.

Steps 2 and 3   Generally, in this book, the data will be provided for you and simple random sampling will be assumed. If you continue your study of statistics beyond your introductory course, you will at some point have to gain knowledge and experience concerning primary research and design of experiments.

Step 4   Part II of the book (Chapters 2 and 3) provides an introduction to the methods of descriptive statistics.

Step 5   Most of this book is focused on inferential statistics. In Part III (Chapters 4–6), the concepts of inferential statistics are presented. Part IV (Chapters 7–11) introduces a range of techniques to use sample evidence to estimate unknown quantities or decide if a claim appears to be true. Part V (Chapter 12) introduces techniques to model the relationships between two quantitative variables.

Step 6   Throughout this text, there are Guides to Decision Making (see, for example, p. 101), which will help you with the technical side of the decision-making process. While this text does not focus on report writing, you may have an opportunity to develop your communication skills as you complete assignments associated with this course.

Chapter 1 has given you an overview of data-based decision making. The techniques you are about to learn are very powerful, but only if they are used correctly and wisely. You will be able to use this chapter as a reference when you are thinking about a business decision (or any other kind of decision) that you need to make.

Getting the Data

Primary data are data that you collect yourself, for a specific purpose. Secondary data are data that were previously collected by someone else. Some useful sources of secondary data about business activities in Canada are listed on page 4.

Sampling

Population data are the complete collection of *all* of the data of interest. Sample data are a subset of population data. The reliability of the conclusions that can be drawn about a population on the basis of sample data depends on the type of sampling used: statistical or nonstatistical sampling.

In nonstatistical sampling, the elements of the population are chosen for the sample by convenience, or according to the researcher's judgment. With nonstatistical sampling, there is no way to measure the reliability of the sample results, or whether the sample is representative of the population. Despite this, nonstatistical sampling can be useful for testing questionnaires, learning about emerging trends, or testing new product ideas.

Statistical sampling is sometimes referred to as probability sampling. In statistical sampling, the elements of the population are chosen for the sample in a random fashion, with a known probability of inclusion. It is possible to make very reliable decisions about population data on the basis of data acquired through statistical sampling, using a set of techniques called inferential statistics. Usually, inferential statistics involves drawing some conclusion or estimating a population parameter on the basis of a sample statistic. A parameter is a summary measure of the population data. A statistic is a summary measure of the sample data.

The simplest method of statistical sampling is simple random sampling. Simple random sampling is a sampling process that ensures that each element of the population is equally likely to be selected. In order to conduct a true random sample, you must start with a list of the elements in a population, which is called a frame. It is possible to use random number generation software to randomly select elements from the population, as Example 1.2c on pages 8–10 illustrates.

Sampling error is the difference between the true value of the population parameter and the value of the corresponding sample statistic, which arises because we are examining only a subset of the population. Sampling error is expected, and is something that we can estimate and control. Nonsampling errors are other kinds of errors that can arise in the process of sampling a population. Nonsampling errors can invalidate the conclusions drawn from the sample.

Analyzing the Data

Once you collect the data you need, the information must be organized so that you can make sense of it. Raw (that is, unorganized) data usually do not tell us much. Descriptive statistics are techniques to organize and summarize raw data.

Making Decisions

In an observational study, the researcher observes what is already taking place, and does not attempt to affect outcomes. Many marketing studies are observational in nature. Companies collect data about their customers in order to better understand them.

Sometimes research is aimed at understanding cause and effect, that is, *why* an observed change or difference has occurred. In an experimental study, the researcher actively intervenes, designing the study so that conclusions about causation can be drawn. Even experimental studies have their limitations in terms of establishing cause-and-effect relationships, particularly when human behaviour is being studied.

Judgment is required to interpret the results of statistical analyses. In cases where judgment is required, you must be prepared to defend your choices objectively. You should always critically evaluate the judgments made by others in their statistical analyses.

Chapter Summary

1

Communication

A report of any statistical analysis you do should completely describe the problem at hand, and the goal of any decisions to be made. It should also provide information about how the data were collected, organized, and summarized, usually showing both graphs and numbers. The statistical techniques used and any judgments about areas of uncertainty should also be described. Finally, a clear statement of conclusions or decisions should be made, with justification.

The technical detail may be provided in the body of the report or in an appendix, but it must always be presented so that an informed reader can assess the methods used and whether the conclusions are justified. How much of the technical detail is included in the body of the report depends on its intended reader.

A Framework for Data-Based Decision Making

A general approach to data-based decision making is outlined in the box on pages 19–20.

CHAPTER REVIEW EXERCISES

1. What are some of the difficulties in gathering data through personal interviews? As food for thought, watch some clips from a TV show segment called *Talking to Americans* (from *This Hour Has 22 Minutes*), in which Rick Mercer travelled to American cities and interviewed Americans about Canadian politics, geography, and weather. You will find some of these clips at **http://home.comcast.net/~wwwstephen/americans**.

2. A study conducted by a polling company for a major financial services provider indicates that 9 out of 10 Canadians consider the purchase of a home to be a good investment. Does this mean that buying a home is a good investment?

3. The Top 100 Employers list is compiled annually by Mediacorp Canada Inc. Mediacorp invites several thousand Canadian employers to complete an extensive application, and about a thousand apply. On the basis of the applications Mediacorp rates the employers, and publishes a book profiling the top 100. Do you think that this process is an effective way to identify Canada's "top 100" employers?

4. The government of Ontario began collecting data on "key performance indicators" (KPI) for colleges in 1998. Data on graduate employment rates, graduate satisfaction, and employer satisfaction are collected by external service providers through telephone surveys (some 40,000 graduates, 10,000 employers, and 90,000 current students are surveyed). The data are used as a basis for distributing some of the colleges' funding. Data on student satisfaction are collected by the colleges themselves using student surveys, and student graduation rates are calculated by the colleges. What are some of the difficulties that would be involved in collecting and interpreting these data?

5. Refer to Exercise 4, above, for a description of Ontario college KPIs. One of the items in the survey of student satisfaction is this: "Overall, your program is giving you the knowledge and skills that will be useful in your future career." For students in the 1999–2000 year, 64.0% of the students surveyed (overall) indicated that they were very satisfied or satisfied in this respect. In the 2000–2001 year, 86.2% of the students surveyed indicated that they were very satisfied or satisfied. This percentage has been above 85% for the entire period from 2000 to 2006 (the most recent data available at the time of publication). Do you think this means that the colleges all redesigned their programs significantly between 1999–2000 and the following school year? (Source: "Key Performance Indicators 1999–00 to 2005–06," **www.acaato.on.ca/home/research/performance/survey.html**, accessed June 16, 2006).

6. A report prepared for the Association of Colleges of Applied Arts and Technology of Ontario says that "For every instructional contact hour completed, students will, on average, earn $70 more per year each year they are in the work force." (Source: "The Socioeconomic Benefits Generated by 24 Colleges of Applied Arts and Technology in Ontario," **www.acaato.on.ca/home/research/return.html**, accessed June 9, 2006) Does this mean that you should be sure to go to class when you are a student?

7. A BBC News article is titled "Short Workers Lose Small Fortune." The article goes on to say that each inch of height added USD $789 to annual pay. Professor Tim Judge from the University of Florida, who led the study, went on to suggest that the reason for this was evolution. He is quoted as saying: "When humans evolved as a species and still lived in the jungles or the plain, they ascribed leader-like qualities to tall people because they thought they would be better able to protect them." What conclusions can be justified from this kind of a study, assuming it was done in a statistically correct manner? (Source: "Short Workers Lose Small Fortune," **http://news.bbc.co.uk/go/pr/fr/-/1/hi/health/3200296.stm**, accessed June 10, 2006)

8. Your school has just approved a new policy that will make the campus entirely smoke-free. This means no smoking on the property at any time, starting at the beginning of the next semester. Because you smoke a pack a day, you are alarmed. You collect a sample of opinions about the new policy from students and staff near one of the designated smoking areas (where you spend a lot of time). You find that there are many people who share your alarm. You produce some graphs and tables, and write a report about your findings, which you take to the president of the school. She listens to your tale of woe but then tells you that your study is not representative of the views of all of the members of the school community. Where did you go wrong?

9. Lotto 6/49 is a lottery in which players select six numbers from 1 to 49. Prizes vary according to how closely players' selections match the winning set of numbers. Many players do not actually select their six numbers; they rely instead on a "quick pick," where the numbers are selected (presumably randomly) for them. Use Excel to generate a quick pick mechanism for Lotto 6/49. Select six numbers and then see if you selected winning numbers. (It is not recommended that you actually play the lottery. The probability of winning is quite low.)

10. Many companies are building customer databases through loyalty programs. One example is the Optimum program of Shoppers Drug Mart Corporation. Customers collect Optimum points when they spend money at the stores. Each purchase is recorded, and so the company collects information about customer demographics and shopping patterns. These data can be used in a variety of ways to target marketing efforts. For example, flyer distribution can be limited to neighbourhoods where the flyers are most likely to have an impact. Do some research to identify other customer loyalty programs that allow companies to collect customer information.

 Go to MyStatLab at www.mystatlab.com. You can practise many of this chapter's exercises as often as you want. The guided solutions help you find an answer step by step. You'll find a personalized study plan available to you too!

CHAPTER

Using Graphs and Tables to Describe Data

2

Learning Objectives

After mastering the material in this chapter, you will be able to:

1. Distinguish among different types of data.
2. Create frequency distributions and histograms to summarize quantitative data.
3. Create tables, bar graphs, and pie charts to summarize qualitative data.
4. Create time-series graphs.
5. Create graphs for paired quantitative data.
6. Be aware of and avoid common errors that result in misleading graphs, and understand the factors that distinguish interesting from uninteresting graphs.

INTRODUCTION

As we saw in Chapter 1, once we collect data to help us analyze a situation and make a decision, we have to organize the data so that we can make sense of it. Remember how, in Example 1.3 on page 12, the data on men's and women's purchases at a Niagara winery were difficult to assess when they were presented as two lists of numbers. When any researcher is analyzing a data set, one of the first steps taken is to create a graphical picture of the data. The type of graph depends on the type of data.

Section 2.1 begins with a description of different data types, in the context of a customer survey done by a drugstore owner. Understanding the distinctions among types of data will be crucially important as you learn more about statistical analysis, because you must be able to recognize the data type in order to choose the correct technique in descriptive or inferential statistics. In Section 2.2, you will explore a data set on vending-machine sales. You will learn how to summarize these data using frequency distributions and histograms with Microsoft®Excel. Unfortunately, the Excel output requires a series of adjustments in order to produce an acceptable histogram. Step-by-step instructions are included and, with practice, you will find this less tedious than it first appears. Section 2.3 describes how to create tables, bar graphs, and pie charts for qualitative data. The Excel tools used in this section are straightforward. Section 2.4

describes how time-series data are graphed, and raises some interesting questions about such graphs. Section 2.5 discusses graphing of paired quantitative data. Finally, Section 2.6 discusses misleading and uninteresting graphs, and describes some common graphing errors. You should pay attention to these, to avoid either making them yourself or being misled when others make them.

2.1 TYPES OF DATA

Different methods are used to analyze data and make decisions, depending on the type of data involved. Understanding data types will be crucial to your ability to correctly identify the techniques you should use. The discussion that follows is therefore not just an exercise in learning new terms: it is critical to your learning.

Suppose Max Weber surveys a random sample of the customers who shop at the drugstore he owns. The survey results contain data on the gender and age of each customer, how many times the customer has shopped at the store in the last month, and how the customer rates the store (on a scale of excellent, good, fair, and poor) in a number of areas (cleanliness, friendliness of staff, ease of locating products, speed of service, etc.). The survey results also contain data on the total amount of the customer's most recent purchase, and the customer's annual income. An excerpt (for just the first 10 customers of the sample) is shown below in Exhibit 2.1. You can view the entire set of survey results in an Excel worksheet called SEC02–1.xls in the directory called DataChap02, which you will find on the CD that accompanies this text.

SEC02-1.xls
Set

An Excerpt of Results from a Survey of Drugstore Customers

Exhibit 2.1

1 = Excellent, 2 = Good, 3 = Fair, 4 = Poor

Gender 0 = Male 1 = Female	Age	Number of Purchases Made at This Store in Past Month	Cleanliness Rating	Staff Friendliness Rating	Ease of Locating Purchases Rating	Speed of Service Rating	Purchase Amount ($)	Annual Income ($)
0	24	3	1	1	1	3	30.68	42,400
1	30	1	2	1	1	3	22.49	65,200
1	29	4	2	1	1	2	29.89	47,150
0	36	4	3	3	1	2	13.31	41,500
1	52	3	4	2	3	3	27.19	53,900
0	37	3	2	2	2	2	29.25	51,850
0	42	3	2	2	1	4	26.00	62,200
1	30	4	2	1	1	3	34.82	44,150
1	35	1	2	1	1	3	28.50	56,300
1	38	5	1	2	3	3	29.34	46,500
↓	↓	↓	↓	↓	↓	↓	↓	↓

variable a characteristic or quantity that can vary

Each of the column headings in Exhibit 2.1 could be described as a **variable**, a characteristic or quantity that can vary. When we record the actual characteristics or quantities for a particular variable, as was done for the sample of drugstore customers, we create a data set. We will use the data set illustrated in Exhibit 2.1 to distinguish among the different types of data.

Quantitative and Qualitative Data

One important distinction is whether the data are quantitative or qualitative. **Quantitative data** contain numerical information, for which arithmetical operations such as averaging are meaningful. Quantitative data are also sometimes called *numerical data*, and they may be referred to as *interval* or *ratio data* (two other data sub-types that are not important to our present work).

quantitative data data containing numerical information, for which arithmetical operations such as averaging are meaningful

Qualitative data contain descriptive information, which may be recorded in words or numbers. If qualitative data are recorded as numbers, arithmetical operations such as averaging are not meaningful. The numbers in this case represent codes for the associated words. Qualitative data are also sometimes called *nominal* or *categorical data*.

qualitative data data containing descriptive information, which may be recorded in words or numbers (the numbers represent codes for the associated words; arithmetical operations such as averaging are not meaningful in this case)

Look at the data recorded in Exhibit 2.1. Are these quantitative or qualitative data? Your first answer might be "quantitative," because the table is full of numbers. But think carefully: what do the numbers mean? If you averaged all of the numbers in column 1, on gender, and got a result of 0.58, would that be meaningful? There is no such thing as an "average" gender, and so this average of 0.58 is not really useful. In column 1, the zeroes and ones are codes to represent "male" and "female." The data on gender of the customers are not quantitative data—they are qualitative data. Notice that the numbers assigned as codes could be changed, without losing any of the information. For example, the code for male is 0 in this example, and the code for female is 1. We could just as easily have used 1 for male, and 2 for female. Or, in fact, we could have used 38 for male and 172 for female. The actual values of the numbers have no meaning in this context.

Consider the entire data set. The quantitative variables are:

- age
- number of purchases made at this store in the past month
- purchase amount
- annual income.

The qualitative variables are:

- gender
- cleanliness rating
- staff friendliness rating
- ease of locating purchases rating
- speed of service rating.

Quantitative Data: Discrete or Continuous?

continuous variable a measurement variable that can take *any* possible value on a number line (possibly within upper and lower limits)

There are some other distinctions in data types. Sometimes it is important to determine if quantitative variables are *discrete* or *continuous*. A **continuous variable** is a measurement variable that can take *any* possible value on a number line (possibly within upper and lower limits). A **discrete variable** can take on only certain identifiable values on a number line (possibly within upper and lower limits).

Which of the quantitative variables in the drugstore survey data are discrete, and which are continuous? The number of purchases made at the drugstore in the past month is an example of a discrete variable. This is a discrete variable because it can take on possible values of 0, 1, 2, 3, 4, 5, . . . n, where n is some upper limit on the number of purchases. A value of 1.52 is not possible. Exhibit 2.2 below illustrates the possible values on a number line.

One way to identify a discrete variable is to realize that there are gaps in its possible values on a number line. Counts, by definition, are discrete random variables. Age is an interesting variable, because by convention, we speak of ages in terms of the number of full years lived since birth. Although we are aging every second, we do not measure age with second-to-second accuracy. Age, as we use it, is really a counting variable (and therefore discrete), because we use it to count the number of full years lived since birth. It is useful to make a distinction here, between "actual age" and "described age." Actual age

Possible Values of the Number of Purchases Made at the Drugstore in the Past Month

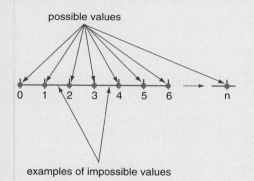

Exhibit **2.2**

is a continuous variable, and there are no gaps in the number line of possible values that actual age could take. Described age is a discrete variable because it can take on only some possible numbers, but this is really only a function of measuring conventions. We usually treat age data as if they were continuous, despite the measurement limitation. Purchase amounts and incomes, the other quantitative variables in the drugstore data set, are also normally treated as continuous data, although we do not normally measure these values beyond dollars and cents. It is not the limitations of our measuring devices but the theoretical possibilities that are important. Measurements such as height or weight are normally not measured beyond one or two decimal places, but no values on the relevant part of the number line are impossible, and so these are other examples of continuous variables.

Qualitative Data: Ranked or Unranked?

Some qualitative data are ranked. **Ranked data** are qualitative data that can be ordered according to size or quality. Ranked data are also sometimes called *ordinal* data. In the drugstore survey data, the ratings of cleanliness, staff friendliness, ease of locating products, and speed of service are examples of ranked data. We know that a rating of "excellent" is better than a rating of "good," for example, and so there is a natural order in the data.

Cross-Sectional and Time-Series Data

cross-sectional data data that are all collected in the same time period

time-series data data that are collected over successive points in time

Another distinction is between *cross-sectional* and *time-series data*. **Cross-sectional data** are all collected in the same time period. **Time-series data** are collected over successive points in time. The drugstore survey data are cross-sectional data, because they were all collected during the same time period. If the survey was repeated from year to year, then each variable could have time-series data associated with it. For example, suppose we collected the same data for 10 years. We could then calculate the average income of those surveyed each year, to create a time-series of average income data.

DEVELOP YOUR SKILLS 2.1

1. Quality control is very important in manufacturing. Several times during the week, a paint company records the number of dented cans in a random sample of 30 paint cans from the filling line. What kind of data are these?

2. An investor is interested in a particular stock, and has collected its closing price every Friday for the last three years. What type of data are these?

3. A human resources (HR) manager wants to see if she can predict job success from a college graduate's final average grade. The manager collects data for a random sample of employees hired in the last two years. The employees' grades are in the personnel files (all were college graduates). The HR manager also asks each employee's supervisor to score the employee's performance, using a detailed questionnaire to arrive at a score from 0 (meaning the worst possible performance) to 100 (an outstanding performance). What kind of data are these? Do you see any difficulty with drawing conclusions based on such a study?

4. The owner of a local franchise of a national coffee store chain hires a student to do some market research. The owner asks the student to record the selling prices of different sizes of coffee at all the coffee stores within a ten-kilometre radius. What kind of data are these?

5. Your company has an extensive database on your customers. Among the information collected is the postal code for each customer's home address. What kind of data are these?

2.2 FREQUENCY DISTRIBUTIONS AND HISTOGRAMS FOR QUANTITATIVE DATA

In this section, we will discuss two important and related ways of summarizing quantitative data: the frequency distribution (a summary table), and its accompanying graph, the histogram. Both of these are best created with a computer. However, before we describe computer-based methods for frequency distributions and histograms, we will start with a simple method of organizing quantitative data by hand, into a stem-and-leaf display. You may find this organizational method useful when you are working with small data sets. As well, a stem-and-leaf display provides an intuitive basis for summarizing quantitative data with frequency distributions and histograms.

Stem-and-Leaf Displays

A stem-and-leaf display can be used to organize a small data set quickly and easily. The display is created by breaking each number in the data set into two parts: the stem and the leaf. How many digits are in the stem and how many are in the leaf depend on the particular data set. Consider the data on the ages of the customers in the drugstore survey. The ages are as shown in Exhibit 2.3.

Survey of Drugstore Customers: Customer Ages (years)

24	30	29	36	52	37	42	30	35	38	25
54	33	40	63	33	33	26	34	38	31	31
36	42	73	35	36	33	41	85	30	32	30
32	74	39	31	30	66	28	67	29	32	32
82	58	41	39	59	54					

Exhibit 2.3

To create a stem-and-leaf display, we first identify the smallest and the largest data points. In this data set, the lowest age is 24 and the highest is 85. Since the data points have only two digits, the stem will be the first digit, and the leaf will be the second digit. We begin by setting up a column containing the stems, in order, for the entire range of the data set, as shown in Exhibit 2.4.

Stems for the Data Set of Customer Ages

```
2 |
3 |
4 |
5 |
6 |
7 |
8 |
```

Exhibit 2.4

Then, working through the data set in some logical way (across the rows or down the columns), we record the second digit in the appropriate row of the display. Exhibit 2.5 illustrates how the stem-and-leaf display will look, once the first column of the data set is recorded.

Adding the Leaves in the Stem-and-Leaf Display (first column of the data set)

```
2 | 4
3 | 6  2
4 |
5 | 4
6 |
7 |
8 | 2
```

Exhibit 2.5

Notice that the second digits are recorded as they are encountered in the data set. Do not try to order the stem-and-leaf display on the first pass. (Do a second stem-and-leaf display if ordering the data is something you want to accomplish by hand.) The completed stem-and-leaf display is shown in Exhibit 2.6.

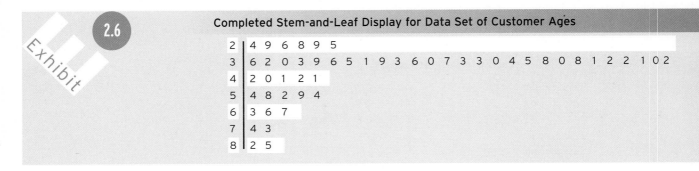

Exhibit 2.6

Completed Stem-and-Leaf Display for Data Set of Customer Ages

```
2 | 4 9 6 8 9 5
3 | 6 2 0 3 9 6 5 1 9 3 6 0 7 3 3 0 4 5 8 0 8 1 2 2 1 0 2
4 | 2 0 1 2 1
5 | 4 8 2 9 4
6 | 3 6 7
7 | 4 3
8 | 2 5
```

This stem-and-leaf display has allowed us to organize the data quickly and easily. Now we have a much better sense of the ages of customers at the drugstore. Notice that all of the original data points can be recreated from the display, so no information is lost. The display also gives us a visual picture of the data. We can easily see, for example, that there are far more customers in their 30s than in the other age ranges. The stem-and-leaf display gives us a kind of preview of two important methods for summarizing quantitative data: the frequency distribution and the histogram.

Suppose we created a table corresponding to the stem-and-leaf display to summarize the data even further, as shown in Exhibit 2.7. The new table has both lost and gained information, compared with the stem-and-leaf display. We can no longer recreate the original data from this table, but we know exactly how many customers are in their 30s (the count, or frequency, is 27). A table such as the one shown in Exhibit 2.7 is called a **frequency distribution**, a summary table that divides continuous quantitative data into ranges, and records the count (or frequency) of data points in each range.

frequency distribution a summary table that divides continuous quantitative data into ranges, and records the count (or frequency) of data points in each range

Exhibit 2.7

Survey of Drugstore Customers

Customer Age	Number of Customers
20–29	6
30–39	27
40–49	5
50–59	5
60–69	3
70–79	2
80–89	2

Because the stem-and-leaf display provides a picture of the data, it is almost a bar graph. We could take this a step further, and create a graph that corresponds to the stem-and-leaf display, replacing the leaf part of the display with bars of a corresponding length. The result would be as shown opposite in Exhibit 2.8.

A Stem-and-Leaf Display Is Similar to a Bar Graph a. Stem-and-Leaf Display b. Bar Graph

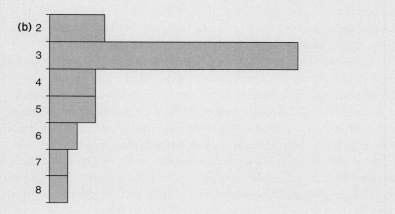

If we rotate this graph 45° counterclockwise, add information about frequencies, and provide some proper labels and a title, we get Exhibit 2.9. Such a graph is called a *histogram*. This is another standard way to represent quantitative data. Note that the histogram corresponds directly to the frequency distribution we created in Exhibit 2.7.

Histogram of Drugstore Customer: Age Data

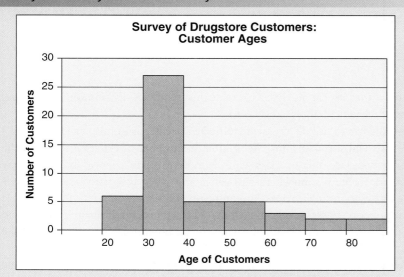

histogram a bar graph of a frequency distribution, with lower class limits shown along the *x*-axis, and class frequencies shown along the *y*-axis

A **histogram** is a bar graph of a frequency distribution, with lower class limits shown along the *x*-axis, and class frequencies shown along the *y*-axis.

Now that you have some idea of how summary tables and graphs can be used to summarize and represent data sets, we will discuss how Excel can be used to create frequency distributions and histograms.

Frequency Distributions

Anne Morgan recently graduated from a well-regarded business program at an Ontario college. Her first job is as a financial analyst for a company that installs vending machines in shopping malls. The machines provide coffee, tea, and baked goods, making them somewhat different from the norm. The company has been monitoring the vending machines at each location fairly closely, as margins are quite thin.

Anne's boss has asked her to focus on three locations: one in Newmarket, one in Barrie, and one in Orillia. Anne's instructions were vague, but her boss has told her that there is a wealth of information available on each location. Anne is facing a common situation in today's world: not *too little* information, but in a way, *too much* information.

Anne discovers that she has available to her the total weekly sales at each location for last year. Anne wants to identify similarities or differences among the three locations, and she begins by looking at the data (you can look at it too—it is available on the CD that comes with this text, in the directory called DataChap02). There are too many numbers for Anne to grasp the levels of weekly sales, and she decides to organize the sales data with a frequency distribution, something like the one shown in Exhibit 2.10.

SEC02-2.xls
Set

Exhibit 2.10

Frequency Distribution

Barrie Sales, 2006

Weekly Sales	Number of Weeks
$0–<$100	
$100–<$200	
. . .	

Anne knows that she can use Excel to create this frequency distribution, but she has to make some decisions first.

To begin, she has to decide how wide to make the categories (also called "classes") in the table. This will simultaneously determine the number of classes into which the data will be divided. Deciding on class width is more art than science. In general, any histogram should contain somewhere between 5 and 20 classes, with larger data sets having more classes than smaller ones. Sometimes experimentation is required to decide on the best number of classes (and class width). The class-width decision is important, because if Anne uses too many classes, the data will not be summarized effectively. If she uses too few, the table may hide interesting characteristics in the data.

There are a number of rules that can provide some guidance about how wide the classes should be, with the goal of summarizing the data in a representative way. Three of them are available for your use on the CD that comes with this text, in the Excel file called "Templates." This file contains a worksheet called "Class Width." Part of this worksheet is reproduced in Exhibit 2.11 below.

Template

Class Width Worksheet

$ 505.30	Copy and paste the data to be analyzed	
$ 309.90	into the first column of the spreadsheet.	
$ 609.94	Data sets of up to 500 items can be used.	
$ 776.04		
$ 735.55	**Recommendations for Class Width**	
$ 923.94	Sturges' Rule	139.23
$ 109.67	Scott's Rule	224.71
$ 524.98	Freedman & Diacomis's Rule	167.16
$ 764.66	minimum value	109.67
$ 421.32	maximum value	1,042.54
$ 337.45	n	52
↓		

Exhibit 2.11

The instructions for using this worksheet are written at the top of the worksheet. You must copy and paste[*] the data you are analyzing into the first column of the worksheet (it's a good idea to delete any existing data in the column first, as this will ensure that you are analyzing *only* the current data and not leftovers from the last data set). Data sets of up to 500 items can be analyzed with this template. The formulas for the rules for class width are built into the worksheet. These formulas take into account the number of data points being analyzed, and two of them also depend on measures of variability in the data. If you do not have a computer available, you can get some guidance about class width by doing this calculation:

$$\text{class width} = \frac{\text{maximum value} - \text{minimum value}}{\sqrt{n}}$$

where n is the number of data points in the data set.

Exhibit 2.11 shows the recommendations for the class widths for the sales data for the Barrie location (not all of Barrie's weekly sales are shown in the exhibit). Notice that there are differences in the recommended class widths. This will always be the case, although generally the rules will provide suggestions for class width that are reasonably similar. If you do not have the template available, you can use the class width formula shown above. In this case, it would be:

$$\text{width} = \frac{\text{maximum value} - \text{minimum value}}{\sqrt{n}} = \frac{1,042.54 - 109.67}{\sqrt{52}} = \frac{932.87}{7.211} = 129.4$$

Ultimately, you will have to use your judgment to set up the classes for your summary table. Sometimes you will decide on class width only after experimentation with a few different class widths (something that is fairly easy to do, with the help of a computer). Anne must keep in mind that her frequency distribution is a communication tool: she will use it to summarize the levels of Barrie's weekly sales for her boss. It would not be reasonable to use a class width of $139.23 or any of the other precise values indicated by the class width rules in the template. At the very least, the class width should be rounded to the nearest

---

[*] Use Paste Special. . . , then select Values if the data you are copying contain formulas or cell references.

dollar. Anne is considering class widths of $150 or $200, which have the same general value as those indicated by the rules but are more comfortable to work with and interpret, given that the units are dollars and cents.

Now that Anne has some idea about class widths, she must also decide where the first class starts, and where the last class ends. Obviously, the classes must encompass all of the data points in the data set, so Anne will have to know both the minimum and maximum values. You may have noticed that these values are provided in the "Class Width" worksheet for the data set, shown in Exhibit 2.11 above. The maximum weekly sales for the Barrie location are $1,042.54 and the minimum value is $109.67.

There are some other considerations for setting up classes in a frequency distribution.

1. The classes should not overlap. Each data point should belong in one and only one class. So, for example, class widths as outlined below in Exhibit 2.12 would not be acceptable, because it would not be clear where a data point of $200 would belong.

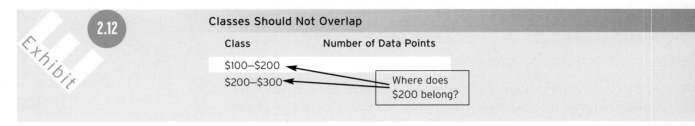

Exhibit 2.12

Classes Should Not Overlap

Class	Number of Data Points
$100–$200	
$200–$300	

Where does $200 belong?

There are a number of ways to clarify this. For example, if the classes were rewritten as shown in Exhibit 2.13 below, it would be quite clear that a data point of $200 should be counted in the second class.

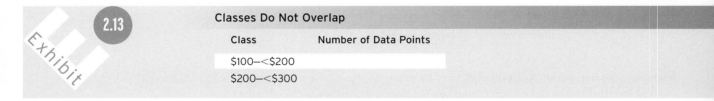

Exhibit 2.13

Classes Do Not Overlap

Class	Number of Data Points
$100–<$200	
$200–<$300	

2. The classes should all be the same width, and open-ended classes (">$300," for example) should be avoided. Readers of the frequency distribution will expect regularity in the classes, and they will be misled if classes are not the same width. It is easy to check that classes are the same width. The differences between all the neighbouring lower class limits should be the same. The same holds true for the differences in neighbouring upper class limits. This is illustrated in Exhibit 2.14 below.

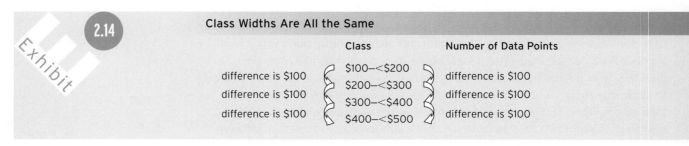

Exhibit 2.14

Class Widths Are All the Same

	Class	Number of Data Points
difference is $100	$100–<$200	difference is $100
difference is $100	$200–<$300	difference is $100
difference is $100	$300–<$400	difference is $100
	$400–<$500	

3. The lower limit of the first class should be an even multiple of the class width. So, for example, if the class width is 100, then the lower limit of the first class should be a number that is evenly divisible by 100.
4. The frequency distribution should be clearly labelled so that it is understandable to a reader, without further description.

Anne decides to visualize the frequency distributions that would arise with the two different class widths that she is considering ($150 and $200). The tables would be set up as shown in Exhibit 2.15 below.

Frequency Distributions: Different Class Widths

2.15

Exhibit

(a) Barrie Sales, 2006		**(b)** Barrie Sales, 2006	
Weekly Sales	Number of Weeks	Weekly Sales	Number of Weeks
$0–<$150		$0–<$200	
$150–<$300		$200–<$400	
$300–<$450		$400–<$600	
$450–<$750		$600–<$800	
$750–<$900		$800–<$1,000	
$900–<$1,050		$1,000–<$1,200	

Notice that although the class widths are different, in this case, the resulting frequency distributions have the same number of classes.

Anne must organize the sales data and count how many data points fall into each class. While she could do this by hand, it is much easier to use Excel (particularly when data sets are large). Anne decides to use class widths of $200, as a first pass at summarizing the data.

Click on **Data Analysis** under **Tools**. You will see the **Data Analysis** dialogue box that is shown in Exhibit 2.16 below.

Instructions

Data Analysis Dialogue Box

2.16

Exhibit

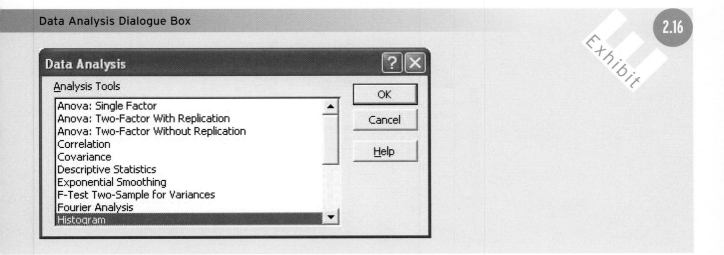

Click on **Histogram**, and **OK**.

The next dialogue box is shown in Exhibit 2.17 below.

Exhibit **2.17**

Histogram Dialogue Box

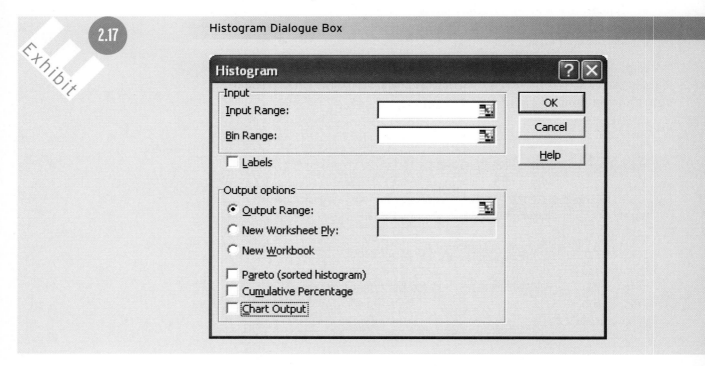

The dialogue box is filled in, as follows:

1. **Input Range** is the location of the data to be analyzed.
2. **Output Range** is the location of the output. The default location for the output is a new worksheet, but sometimes it is more convenient to have the Excel output on the same worksheet as the data. Only one cell has to be identified in the output range: it is the cell that will be the upper left-hand corner of the output range, as illustrated in Exhibit 2.18 below. If cell A1 is identified as the output range, the Excel output will be placed below and to the right of cell A1.

Exhibit **2.18**

Cell Identifying Output Range

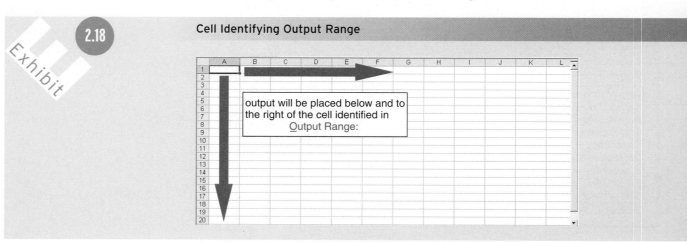

3. Bin Range must also be filled in, if you want to control how the classes are set up (and you do—what Excel does automatically is not very useful). This requires you to type bin numbers into the worksheet. An **Excel bin number** is the upper included limit of a class.

Excel bin number the upper included limit of a class

So, for example, the largest value in the first class ($0–<$200) would be $199.99. For the Barrie sales data set, the appropriate bin numbers would be as shown in Exhibit 2.19 below.

Appropriate Bin Numbers, Barrie Sales Data Set

2.19 Exhibit

Barrie Sales, 2006

Weekly Sales	Excel Bin Number
$0–<$200	199.99
$200–<$400	399.99
$400–<$600	599.99
$600–<$800	799.99
$800–<$1,000	999.99
$1,000–<$1,200	1,199.99

Exhibit 2.20 below shows the worksheet containing the Barrie sales data, and the accompanying Histogram dialogue box from Excel. Note that the bin numbers in cells G2:G7 have been typed in (of course, you can do this by using Excel's auto completion feature, by dragging the fill handle down after you have entered the first two bin numbers).

Worksheet for Barrie Sales Data, and Histogram Dialogue Box

2.20 Exhibit

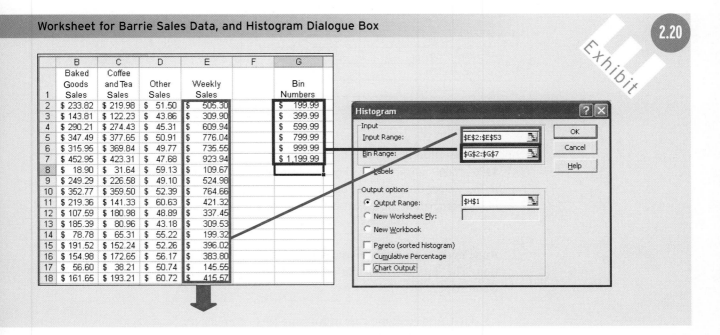

It is possible to include labels for the data being analyzed and for the bin numbers. If you tick the Labels box, Excel will treat the first row in the selections of the input range and the bin range as labels. Remember to be consistent with both inputs (both must have labels, or neither should have a label).

In the dialogue box shown in Exhibit 2.20, the output range is beside the bin numbers. The output created by Excel is reproduced in Exhibit 2.21 below.

Excel Output for Barrie Sales Data

Bin	Frequency
$ 199.99	5
$ 399.99	9
$ 599.99	19
$ 799.99	11
$ 999.99	6
$1,199.99	2
More	0

Of course, as a communication tool, this frequency distribution leaves something to be desired. Cleaned up, it becomes the more informative table shown below in Exhibit 2.22.

Frequency Distribution Table for Barrie Sales Data

Barrie Sales, 2006	
Weekly Sales	**Number of Weeks**
$0—<$200	5
$200—<$400	9
$400—<$600	19
$600—<$800	11
$800—<$1,000	6
$1,000—<$1,200	2

From this table we can see that most often, Barrie's weekly sales are in the $400–<$600 range. The weekly sales were above $1,000 in only two weeks of 2006, and in five weeks, the sales were below $200. It might be useful to investigate to see if there is any explanation for the extremely high or low weekly sales figures.

Anne must also set up a frequency distribution for the sales data for the Orillia location. The data are available on the CD that comes with the text in the directory DataChap02.

First, Anne uses the class width template to examine the data. The results are shown opposite in Exhibit 2.23.

Setting up a frequency distribution
with Excel

EXA02-2a.xls

Class Width Template for Orillia Sales Data

Recommendations for Class Width	
Sturges' Rule	135.19
Scott's Rule	171.10
Freedman & Diacomis's Rule	126.37
minimum value	544.28
maximum value	1,450.09

Anne looks at the recommendations for class width, and considers $125, $150, and $175 as possibilities. She also considers that she will probably be comparing the Barrie sales data with the Orillia sales data. This means that she should think about using the same class widths for both data sets, to make them directly comparable. She can proceed by using $200 for a class width in the Orillia data (which is wider than any of the recommended widths from the template), or redoing the Barrie frequency distribution with a class width of, for example, $150. For now, Anne decides to use $150 as the class width for the Orillia sales data. This means that her frequency distribution will have classes as shown in Exhibit 2.24 below.

Class Boundaries for Orillia Sales Data

Orillia Sales, 2006	
Weekly Sales	**Number of Weeks**
$450—<$600	
$600—<$750	
$750—<$900	
$900—<$1,050	
$1,050—<$1,200	
$1,200—<$1,350	
$1,350—<$1,500	

$450 is an even multiple of the class width of $150

The Excel bin numbers corresponding to these class boundaries are as shown in Exhibit 2.25 below. Anne types these into Excel, using the auto-fill feature.

Excel Bin Numbers for Orillia Sales Data

Orillia Sales, 2006	
Weekly Sales	**Excel Bin Number**
$450—<$600	599.99
$600—<$750	749.99
$750—<$900	899.99
$900—<$1,050	1,049.99
$1,050—<$1,200	1,199.99
$1,200—<$1,350	1,349.99
$1,350—<$1,500	1,499.99

Anne then uses the Histogram tool to produce the Excel result shown in Exhibit 2.26 below.

Exhibit 2.26

Excel Histogram Output for Orillia Sales Data

Bin	Frequency
$ 599.99	1
$ 749.99	2
$ 899.99	14
$1,049.99	17
$1,199.99	11
$1,349.99	6
$1,499.99	1
More	0

When this output is cleaned up for presentation, it looks as shown in Exhibit 2.27.

Exhibit 2.27

Frequency Distribution of Orillia Sales Data

Orillia Sales, 2006	
Weekly Sales	**Number of Weeks**
$450—<$600	1
$600—<$750	2
$750—<$900	14
$900—<$1,050	17
$1,050—<$1,200	11
$1,200—<$1,350	6
$1,350—<$1,500	1

When the data are summarized in a frequency distribution, it is easy to see some of the differences between the Orillia and Barrie sales data. For example, it is clear that the Orillia sales are generally higher than the Barrie sales.

Histograms

Frequency distributions can be a helpful means of organizing and summarizing quantitative data. It is usual to produce an accompanying graph, the histogram. So, for example, the histogram for the Barrie sales frequency distribution would look as shown in Exhibit 2.28 opposite.

Notice that there is a direct correspondence between the elements of the histogram and the frequency distribution. The titles are the same. The column headings in the frequency distribution are the axis labels on the graph.

It is easy to see from the graph that for the majority of weeks, the Barrie sales are in the $400—<$600 range. As well, we can easily see that the sales were above $1,000 in only two weeks, and were below $200 in five weeks.

Frequency Distribution and Histogram for Barrie Sales Data

Exhibit **2.28**

a. Frequency Distribution

Barrie Sales, 2006

Weekly Sales	Number of Weeks
$0–<200	5
$200–<400	9
$400–<600	19
$600–<800	11
$800–<1,000	6
$1,000–<1,200	2

b. Histogram

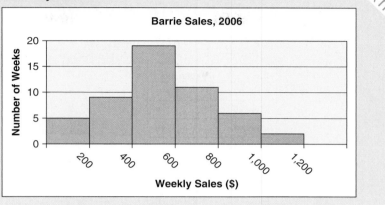

You can use Excel to create the base graph for the histogram, and this is normally done at the same time that the frequency distribution is created. Unfortunately Excel's histogram is far from acceptable in its automatic form. A number of modifications must be made to Excel's histogram to make it more useful.

Not surprisingly, the Excel histogram is produced with the Data Analysis tool called Histogram, which we have already used to produce the frequency distribution for a data set. The Excel histogram is produced by ticking the Chart Output box in the Histogram dialogue box, as illustrated in Exhibit 2.29 below.

Instructions

Creating a Chart with Histogram Dialogue Box

Exhibit **2.29**

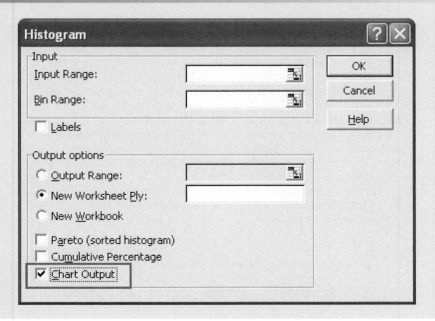

Of course, Excel's automatic histogram corresponds exactly to Excel's frequency distribution. The table and the graph produced by Excel look as shown below in Exhibit 2.30.

2.30

Raw Excel Frequency Distribution and Histogram

(a) Excel Frequency Distribution

Bin	Frequency
$ 199.99	5
$ 399.99	9
$ 599.99	19
$ 799.99	11
$ 999.99	6
$1,199.99	2
More	0

(b)

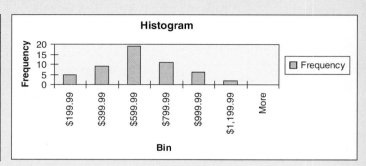

You can change elements in Excel's automatically produced histogram by clicking or right-clicking on those elements. There are a number of things to correct, as outlined in the Guide shown below.

Guide to Technique
Adjusting Excel's Histogram

1. The titles and axis labels must be informative. Click on each and type in titles and labels that allow the histogram to be interpreted without additional context.
2. The frequency legend is not required. Right-click on it and then click on Clear.
3. There should not be any spaces between the bars in a histogram (there are no spaces between the classes in the frequency distribution). Right-click on the bars, then click on Format Data Series, then click on the Options tab, then change the Gap width to 0, then click OK.
4. Convention has it that the x-axis of the histogram should show the *lower* limit of the class, but Excel's bin numbers are the *upper* included limit of each class. There is a trick to give the appearance of lower class limits: if you round the bin numbers on the worksheet, they will look like the lower limits of each class. Highlight the bin number cells on the worksheet, and then use the Format tool in Excel. Click on Cells . . . and then reduce Decimal places: to 0. Note that for this trick to work, you must always include decimal places in your bin numbers (e.g., a bin number of "199.9," not "199").[1]
5. The lower class limits should show at the left side of each associated bar, but Excel generally places the bin numbers on the chart under the middle of each bar. There is another trick to achieve approximately the right look: right-click on the x-axis labels, then click on Format Axis . . ., then click on the Alignment tab, and then set the orientation to −45 degrees.
6. Horizontal grid lines make it easier to interpret the heights of the bars on the histogram. Highlight the graph, then click on Chart on the toolbar. Click on Chart Options . . ., then tick the box beside Major gridlines under Value (Y) axis, then click OK.

---

[1] Probably because of the way Excel works, the traditional labelling convention (lower class limits on the x-axis of the histogram) is not always followed. You should communicate clearly that your histogram shows lower class limits (this will be obvious if your histogram is accompanied by a frequency distribution with clear class limits). You should also carefully examine any histogram you see, in case the standard convention is not followed.

While making all of these adjustments will seem tedious at first, you will soon become accustomed to them.[2] The result will be a histogram that is much more useful, as shown in Exhibit 2.31 below.

Adjusted Histogram of Barrie Sales Data   2.31 *Exhibit*

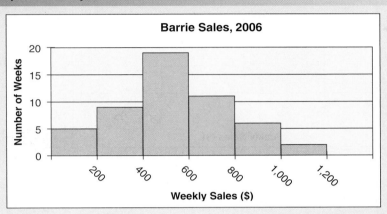

Keep in mind that it is necessary to make all of these adjustments to Excel's histogram only if you are planning to present the histogram as part of your analysis. If you are using the histogram only for your own purposes (for example, to make a decision about the distribution of a particular data set), you need not go through all the steps to make the bin numbers work correctly. For example, for the Barrie weekly sales, you might just use 200, 400, 600, etc., as your bin numbers.

The initial Excel histogram produced for the Orillia sales data (corresponding to the frequency distribution from Example 2.2a, Exhibit 2.27, page 40) looks as shown below in Exhibit 2.32.   2.2b *Example*

Modifying Excel's automatic histogram

Initial Excel Histogram for the Orillia Sales Data   2.32 *Exhibit*

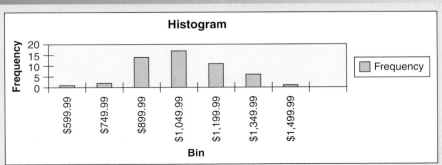

---

[2] Of course, we would all prefer that Excel did a better job in the first place!

The adjusted histogram is shown below in Exhibit 2.33.

2.33

Adjusted Excel Histogram for the Orillia Sales Data

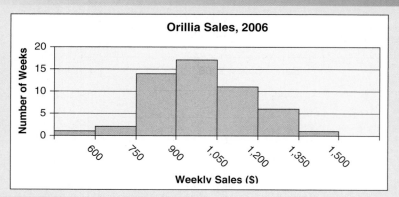

From this histogram we can see that sales are $900–<$1,050 for the greatest number of weeks. For one week, sales were above $1,350, and for one week they were below $600. There is a problem with this histogram that requires one further adjustment. By convention, the starting point for the *x*- and *y*-axes on a graph is (0, 0). However, if you look at Exhibit 2.33 above, you should see that the starting point for the *x*-axis is actually $450. This departure from convention can be misleading. The solution is to add an extra class (and an extra bin number) for the data range below the first class. Then you can indicate in the blank space created that the *x*-axis is not set up according to convention (using Excel's drawing tools, or even amending the graph by hand). See Exhibit 2.34 below.

2.34

Histogram for the Orillia Sales Data, Adjusted *x*-Axis

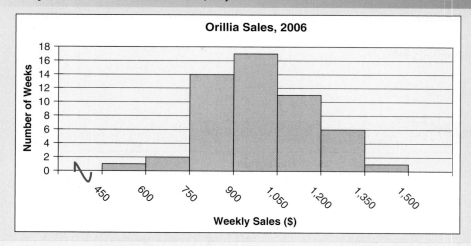

This adjustment is not often made in Excel-based histograms. It is more important when the histogram is being presented as part of a report, and less important when the histogram is an intermediary step in the analysis. In fact, the adjustment for the non-zero *x*-axis is not done for many of the histograms in this book, particularly when they are being used only to decide if a distribution has a desired shape.

Symmetry and Skewness

Histograms are very useful graphs for summarizing quantitative data, and they are widely used. Histograms can also be used to decide if a sample data set has a desired or required distribution. You will often have to make this kind of decision as you learn the techniques covered in this text.

One characteristic of a data set that is usually of interest is whether it is *symmetric* or *skewed*. In a **symmetric distribution**, the right half of the distribution is a mirror image of the left half. A symmetric distribution is illustrated in the histogram shown in Exhibit 2.35 below. If this distribution were folded over on itself at the dotted line, the left and right sides would match exactly. This kind of symmetry (and a shape like Exhibit 2.35) can be very desirable, although exact symmetry is rarely observed in real data.

symmetric distribution the right half of the distribution is a mirror image of the left half

A Symmetric Distribution

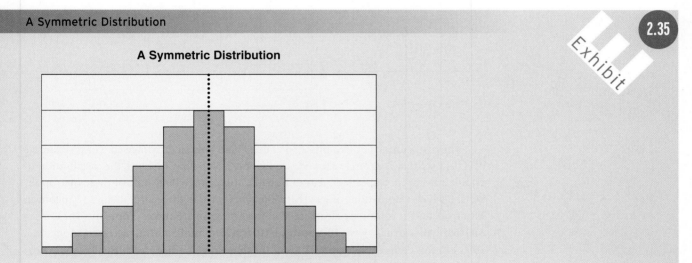

Exhibit 2.35

In contrast, a non-symmetric distribution is described as being skewed. A distribution is **skewed to the right** (or **positively skewed**), when there are some unusually high values in the data set that destroy the symmetry. An example of a positively skewed distribution is shown in Exhibit 2.36 below.

skewed to the right (or positively skewed) distribution a distribution in which some unusually high values in the data set destroy the symmetry

Positively Skewed Distribution

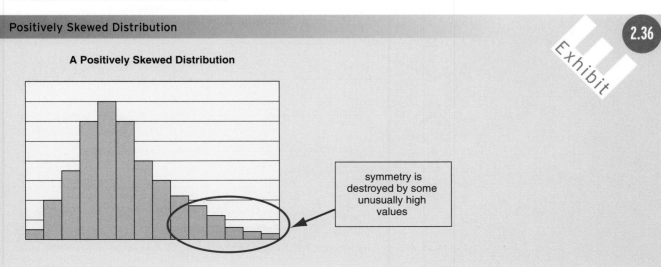

Exhibit 2.36

skewed to the left (or negatively skewed) distribution a distribution in which some unusually small values in the data set destroy the symmetry

As you might guess, a distribution is described as **negatively skewed** (or **skewed to the left**) when some unusually small values destroy the symmetry. An example of a negatively skewed distribution is shown in Exhibit 2.37 below.

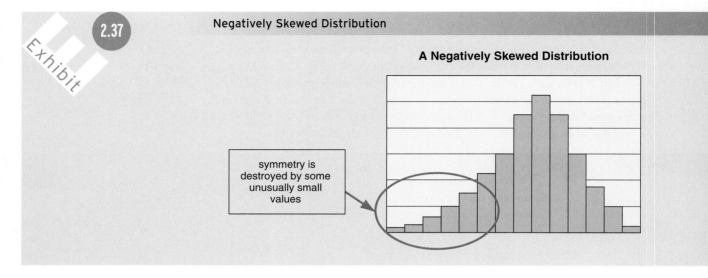

Exhibit 2.37

Negatively Skewed Distribution

The distributions in Exhibits 2.36 and 2.37 are only slightly skewed. For an example of a data set that is severely skewed, see Exhibit 2.38 below. It shows the distribution of populations of metropolitan areas in Canada. You can see that most of these metropolitan areas have populations of less than 500,000. Canada's three largest cities (Vancouver, Montreal, and Toronto) are clearly seen in the histogram. (Source: "Population of Census Metropolitan areas," **www40.stacan.ca/101/cst01/demo05a.htm**, accessed August 3, 2006.) In this data set, the populations of the three largest cities are unusually large, compared with the rest of the data. These three data points could be referred to as *outliers*. An **outlier** is a data point that is unusually far from the rest of the data.

outlier a data point that is unusually far from the rest of the data

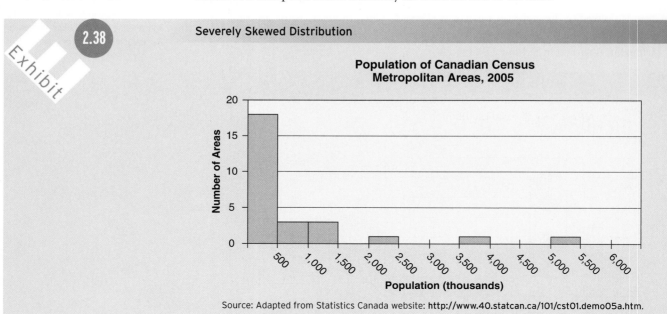

Exhibit 2.38

Severely Skewed Distribution

Source: Adapted from Statistics Canada website: http://www.40.statcan.ca/101/cst01.demo05a.htm.

The presence of outliers in a data set usually raises questions. For example, it is often a requirement that a data set have a symmetric, bell-shaped distribution, and the existence of an outlier (or outliers) can destroy that required symmetry. Outliers are usually investigated carefully. Generally, outliers can exist for one of three reasons:

1. The outlier is a correct data point, and it exists because of the variability in the population data being sampled or studied. In this case, the observation is legitimately part of the data set.
2. The outlier is an error that was made when the data was being collected or recorded. If this is the case, the error should be corrected.
3. The outlier comes from a population that is distinctly different from the one being studied or sampled. In this case, it *may* be legitimate to eliminate the outlier from the data set, but you should never do this without explaining and justifying your action.

Comparing Histograms

Anne Morgan set out to summarize the weekly sales data of the Barrie, Orillia, and Newmarket locations. When she completes the three sets of frequency distributions and histograms, she realizes that she will have to do some further work before the tables and graphs are comparable. She used a class width of 200 for the Barrie sales data, 150 for the Orillia sales data, and 100 for the Newmarket data. Taken by themselves, these would have been good decisions about class width. However, the differences in the class widths make comparison difficult. It is much easier to compare the histograms, and identify similarities and differences, if you follow the Guide shown below.

1. Use the same class width for all of the data sets being compared.
2. Use the same *x*-axis and *y*-axis scales for the data sets being compared.
3. Present the histograms one above the other on the same page, with the *x*-axis values lined up.

Guide to Technique

Comparing Histograms

Exhibit 2.39 on the next page shows the final histograms that Anne produced.

With the graphs carefully set up for comparison, it is easy to see a number of things:

• Weekly sales are lowest for the Barrie location, and highest for the Orillia location.
• There is more variability in Barrie's weekly sales than in the other two locations. Variability is least in Newmarket's weekly sales.
• The distributions of Barrie and Orillia sales are somewhat skewed to the right, meaning that there are a few exceptional weeks with higher sales in both locations.
• Weekly sales at the Newmarket location have a fairly symmetric distribution, with most weekly sales in the $600–$900 range, and a similar number of weeks above and below that range.

Exhibit 2.39

Final Histograms for the Three Locations' Sales Results

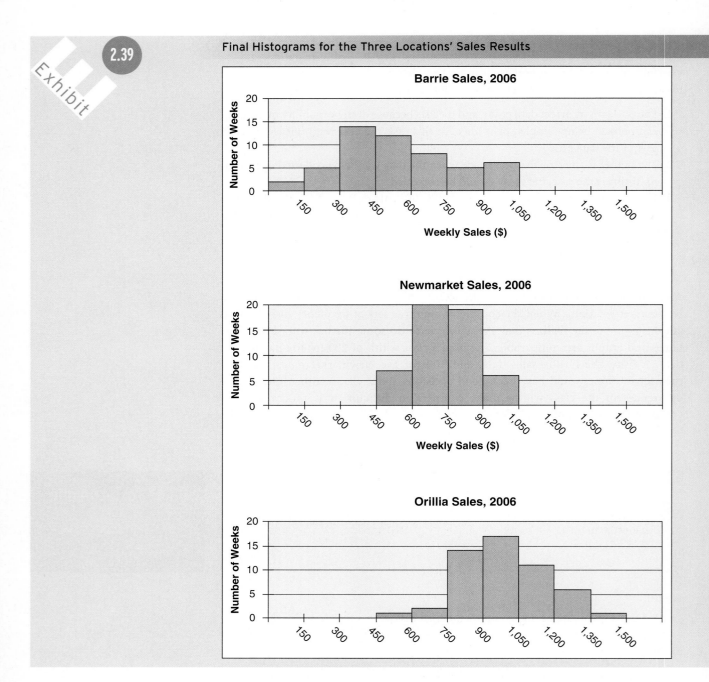

There is a further step you can take to make comparisons easy: you can convert the frequencies into relative frequencies. Relative frequencies are particularly useful when the data sets being compared have quite different frequencies. The **relative frequency** of a class is the percentage of total observations falling into that class. For example, consider the frequency distribution for the Barrie sales data, reproduced below in Exhibit 2.40.

relative frequency the percentage of total observations falling into that class

Frequency Distribution, Barrie Sales Data

Barrie Sales, 2006

Weekly Sales	Number of Weeks
$0—<$200	5
$200—<$400	9
$400—<$600	19
$600—<$800	11
$800—<$1,000	6
$1,000—<$1,200	2

There are 52 weeks of data, in total. Therefore, the relative frequency for the $0–<$200 class is $\frac{5}{52} = 0.0962$. All of the relative frequencies are shown below in Exhibit 2.41.

Relative Frequencies, Barrie Sales Data

Barrie Sales, 2006

Weekly Sales	Number of Weeks	Percentage of Weeks
$0—<$200	5	5/52 = 0.0962
$200—<$400	9	9/52 = 0.1731
$400—<$600	19	0.3654
$600—<$800	11	0.2115
$800—<$1,000	6	0.1154
$1,000—<$1,200	2	0.0385

Exhibit 2.42 on the next page shows the three relative-frequency histograms produced by Anne Morgan for the weekly sales data she is studying. Note that the shapes of the histograms are unchanged when frequencies are converted to relative frequencies: all that changes is the scale and the title on the y-axis.

DEVELOP YOUR SKILLS   2.2

1. Create a histogram for the ages of customers in the survey of drugstore customers. Do this three times, with three different class widths: 5, 10, and 15 years. Describe the histograms and comment on the differences among them. Which histogram do you think best summarizes the data? See file called DYS02-2-1.xls.

2. Create an appropriate frequency distribution and histogram for the incomes of customers in the survey of drugstore customers. Write a sentence or two to describe the data. See file called DYS02-2-2.xls.

3. Eileen McLeary runs a car repair facility in Nelson, BC. The business is always under pressure to complete repairs quickly, correctly, and at a fair price. Eileen is trying to understand how many different customers visit the shop on a daily basis, and she has collected customer counts for a random sample of days. Use a stem-and-leaf display to organize the resulting data set, shown in Exhibit 2.43 on the next page. Comment on the data.

4. Consider the histogram shown opposite in Exhibit 2.44 on p. 51. There are several problems with this histogram. Describe the problems, and how you would fix them.

Exhibit 2.42

Anne Morgan's Three Relative-Frequency Histograms

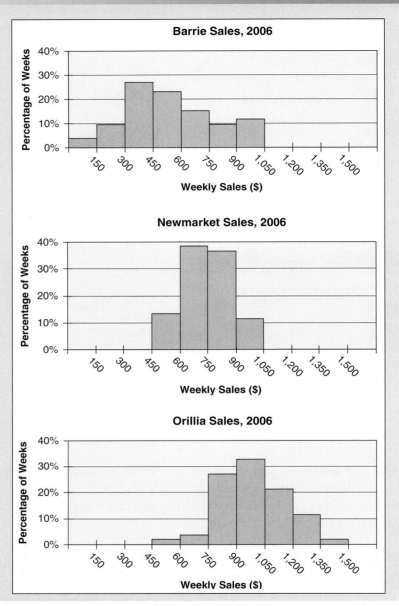

Exhibit 2.43

Data Set for McLeary Repair Shop

Daily Customer Counts, McLeary Repair Shop

24	19	27	41	17
26	34	17	25	31
23	29	26	18	24
31	24	14	29	36
31	29	40	12	26

Problematic Histogram

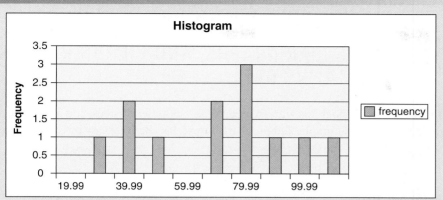

5. Patty Plainte wants to compare the final grades of the students in Mr. Mean's class with those in Ms. Nice's class. (Patty is a student in Mr. Mean's class, and thinks that her teacher's nasty personality is the reason she did so poorly in the course.) Patty has managed to collect a random sample of final grades from the students in the two classes. She has created the two histograms shown below in Exhibit 2.45 so that she can make her comparison. See file called DYS02-2-5.xls.

Histograms of Classes' Final Grades

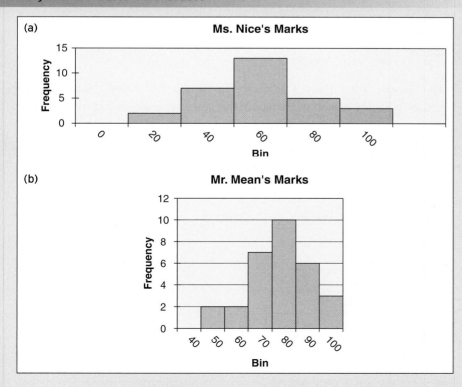

Do you think that Patty deserved her low mark in statistics, based on these graphs? What would you do to improve the graphs?

2.3 TABLES, BAR GRAPHS, AND PIE CHARTS FOR QUALITATIVE DATA

Setting up correct histograms with Excel involves a number of steps, and a number of decisions. Creating bar graphs and pie charts in Excel is relatively easy by comparison.

Bar Charts and Pie Charts for a Simple Table

Anne Morgan has been asked by her boss to analyze the types of baked goods sold at the locations she is analyzing. She begins with the data for the Barrie location. A table summarizing the total number of items sold for the year, by type, is shown in Exhibit 2.46 below. Notice that this table could be described as a frequency distribution.

Summary Table for Barrie Baked Goods Sales

Barrie Baked Goods Sales, 2006	
Type of Baked Goods	Total Number Sold
Muffins	3,231
Cookies	1,011
Doughnuts	2,988
Cupcakes	1,152

The associated bar chart is as shown in Exhibit 2.47 below. Notice the space between the bars. The heights of the bars in this graph represent counts (or frequencies)

Bar Chart for Barrie Baked Goods Sales

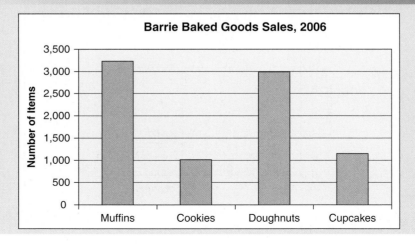

for distinct qualitative categories, so the bars must be separated by a space. This is in contrast to a histogram, where the classes have no gaps between them (and so there is no space between the bars). Also notice that the bars could have been presented in any order (again, in contrast to a histogram, where the bars correspond to quantitative data ranges on the x-axis).

This bar chart is created in Excel as follows:

1. Highlight the cells in the worksheet containing the number of items and the labels.
2. Click on the Chart Wizard on the toolbar.
3. Select Column under the Chart type: heading (this is Excel's word for a bar chart). Click Next >. See Exhibit 2.48 below.

Chart Wizard Chart Type Window

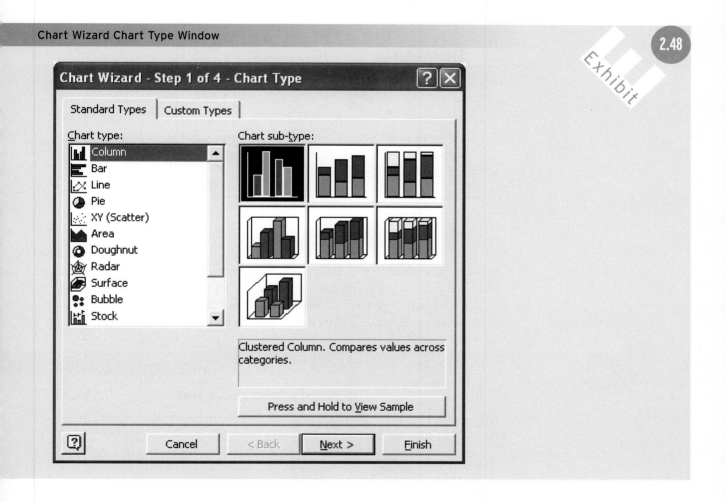

Exhibit 2.48

4. If the chart in the preview is as desired, click Next> again. If not, click on the Series tab, and make the necessary changes to the Values: and Category (X) axis labels: areas. Then click Next >. See Exhibit 2.49 on the next page.

5. Add appropriate titles under the Titles tab (and remove the legend by unticking Show legend, under the Legend tab). Click on Finish.

Exhibit

2.49

Source Data Window

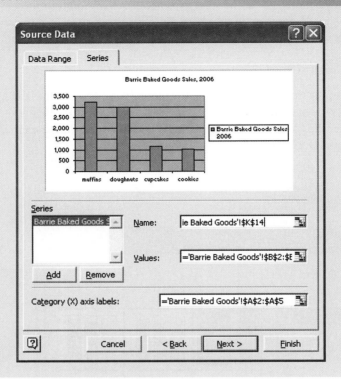

It is sometimes useful to show the bars in a particular order (from smallest to largest, or vice versa), and this is accomplished by reordering the data in the table on which the graph is based. You can use the Sort ... tool (under Data on the toolbar) to do this (you have seen this tool before, in Chapter 1). Exhibit 2.50 below shows the Barrie baked goods sales bar chart with the bars ordered from largest to smallest.

2.50

Exhibit

Ordered Bar Chart for Barrie Baked Goods Sales

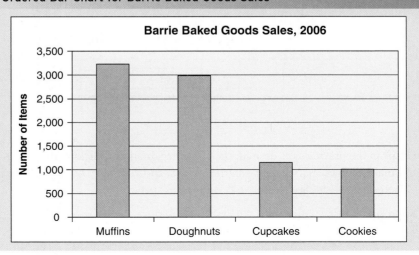

Bar charts emphasize the relative sizes of the categories in qualitative data. Pie charts can also be used to display the data. Pie charts emphasize the share of the total represented by each category. A pie chart for the Barrie baked goods sales data is shown below in Exhibit 2.51.

Pie Chart for Barrie Baked Goods Sales   2.51

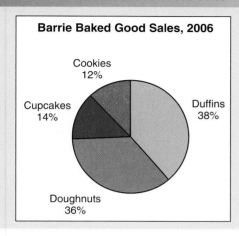

A pie chart can be created in Excel using essentially the same steps as for the bar chart, but selecting Pie under Chart Type:. In step 3 of the chart creation, you will have some choices under the Data Labels and Legend tabs. Experiment to see which option best presents the data. In the chart above, Category name and Percentage were chosen under the Data Labels tab. It is often useful to have the category names right next to the pie slices in the graph, rather than in a separate legend. This is particularly true if the graph is going to be reproduced in black and white, and you might consider using patterns rather than colours to distinguish the slices in this case. You can accomplish this by right-clicking on the slice of the pie you wish to format, selecting Format Data Point . . ., selecting Patterns, clicking on Fill Effects . . ., selecting Pattern, and then clicking on the desired pattern.

The data collected in the survey of drugstore customers should be organized. Create an appropriate graph to display the customer ratings of staff friendliness.

The first task is to arrive at counts for each category of staff friendliness. Since the ratings are recorded as numbers, it is just a matter of using Excel's Histogram tool to create a frequency distribution, using bin numbers of 1, 2, 3, and 4 (the ratings). The result produced by Excel is shown below in Exhibit 2.52.

Using Excel to create a bar graph with coded data

Excel Frequency Distribution for Staff Friendliness Ratings   2.52

Bin	Frequency
1	15
2	23
3	10
4	2
More	0

First, we can improve on this table by adding a title, and replacing the codes with their meanings. See the table shown in Exhibit 2.53 below.

2.53

Exhibit

Improved Frequency Distribution for Staff Friendliness Ratings

Survey of Drugstore Customers, Staff Friendliness Ratings	
Rating	Number of Customers
Excellent	15
Good	23
Fair	10
Poor	2

If similar changes are made on the Excel spreadsheet, creating the bar chart is fairly straightforward. The bar chart is created in Excel as follows:

1. Highlight the cells in the worksheet containing the summary table of ratings.
2. Click on the **Chart Wizard** on the toolbar.
3. Select **Column** under the **C**hart type:.
4. Click on the **Series** tab, and make the necessary changes to the **V**alues: and Ca**t**egory (X) axis labels: areas. Then click **N**ext>.
5. Add appropriate titles under the **Titles** tab (and remove the legend by unticking **S**how legend, under the **Legend** tab). Click on **F**inish.

The appropriate bar graph is shown below in Exhibit 2.54.

2.54

Exhibit

Bar Graph for Staff Friendliness Ratings

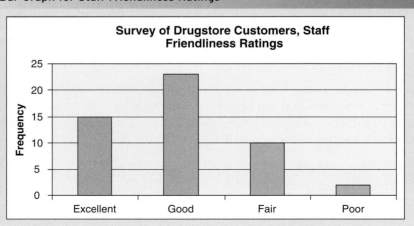

It is easy to see that most customers rate staff friendliness as either "excellent" or "good." We can also see that 10 customers rated the staff friendliness as "fair," and a few customers rated staff friendliness as "poor." If you were the owner of this drugstore, would you be happy with these results?

Bar Charts for Contingency Tables

Anne Morgan also has data on the baked goods sales at the Orillia and Newmarket locations. She can organize all of the data in one table, as shown below in Exhibit 2.55. Such a table is called a contingency table, or a cross-classification table, and it is a useful means of summarizing qualitative data.

Contingency Table, Baked Goods Sales

Exhibit 2.55

Baked Goods Sales, 2006			
Type of Baked Goods	**Barrie**	**Newmarket**	**Orillia**
Muffins	3,231	5,178	8,546
Cookies	1,011	569	2,154
Doughnuts	2,988	3,256	4,589
Cupcakes	1,152	1,013	1,736

It is also possible to summarize this data set with a bar chart, as shown below in Exhibit 2.56. A pie chart would not be useful for cross-classified data of this type.

Bar Chart, Baked Goods Sales

Exhibit 2.56

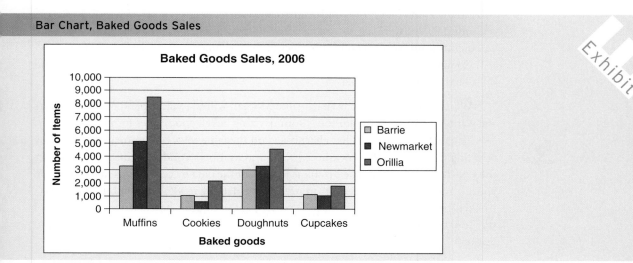

With this chart, a number of things are illustrated; for example:

1. Orillia had the highest number of items sold in all four baked goods categories in 2006.
2. Barrie sold the lowest number of muffins and doughnuts among the three locations.
3. Newmarket sold the lowest number of cookies and cupcakes among the three locations.
4. The categories of muffins and doughnuts are more important, in terms of numbers sold, than the categories of cookies and cupcakes.

It is also possible to create a bar chart that is organized according to the rows of the table, rather than the columns, as Exhibit 2.57 below illustrates.

2.57

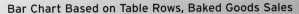
Bar Chart Based on Table Rows, Baked Goods Sales

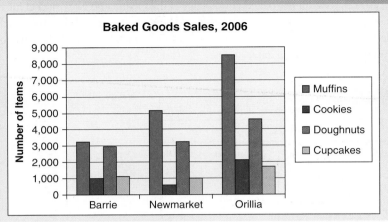

This presentation of the data makes some other observations more obvious; for example:

1. The Barrie location sold fewer items in total than the other locations.
2. All locations sold more muffins than any other category of baked goods. In Barrie, muffin sales were almost matched by doughnut sales, while doughnut sales were significantly lower than muffin sales at the Newmarket and Orillia locations.
3. Cookies represent the lowest number of items sold by category in Newmarket and Barrie, but not in Orillia.

Which version of the bar chart Anne Morgan will use will depend on what factors she wants to emphasize when she is summarizing baked goods sales for her boss.

Instructions

The more complicated bar chart based on the table rows can be created in Excel by selecting the table on the worksheet (labels and numbers), and selecting Column under the Chart type: heading. The default is to present the data by column (as in Exhibit 2.56 above). You can change the chart to present the data by row (as in Exhibit 2.57 above), by clicking on the Series tab. Start by removing the column-based series, and then add the row-based series, making the necessary selections in the Name:, Values: and Category (X) axis labels: areas.

DEVELOP YOUR SKILLS 2.3

1. Create an appropriate graph to summarize the cleanliness rating data for the survey of drugstore customers. Comment on the data. See file called DYS02-3-1.xls.

2. A candy manufacturer has definite rules about the colour mixture of its candy-coated peanuts. Currently, the manufacturing process is set up to produce candies according to the distribution shown in Exhibit 2.58 on the next page.

Candy Colour Desired Distribution

Candy Colours			
Red	Green	Blue	Yellow
40%	30%	20%	10%

The company wants to be sure it is still achieving this colour balance after a recent reorganization of the production process at one of its plants. A random sample of candies is selected. The breakdown of colours is as shown in Exhibit 2.59.

Candy Colour Sample Distribution

Candy Colours			
Red	Green	Blue	Yellow
305	265	201	96

Create an appropriate graph to assess whether the company is still achieving the desired colour balance at the plant after reorganizing the production process.

3. Exhibit 2.60 shows some data on the number of defects observed during different shifts at a manufacturing plant. Create an appropriate graph to summarize these data, and comment.

Defects Observed at a Manufacturing Plant

Shift	Items With No Apparent Defects	Items With One Minor Defect	Items With More Than One Minor Defect
8:00 A.M.–4:00 P.M.	351	34	15
4:00 P.M.–Midnight	336	51	13
Midnight–8:00 A.M.	344	40	16

4. A financial services company conducted a survey of a random sample of its customers. One of the items on the survey was as follows: "The staff at my local branch can provide me with good advice on my financial affairs." Customers were asked to respond on the following scale: (1) strongly agree; (2) agree; (3) neither agree nor disagree; (4) disagree; (5) strongly disagree. The customer responses are summarized in Exhibit 2.61 on the next page.

Exhibit

2.61

Financial Services Company Customer Survey

Financial Services Company Customer Survey

"The staff at my local branch can provide me with good advice on my financial affairs."	Number of Customers
Strongly agree	10
Agree	57
Neither agree nor disagree	32
Disagree	15
Strongly disagree	9

DYS02-3-5.xls

Set

Create an appropriate graph to summarize the results, and comment. Do the results suggest any further investigation that might be worthwhile?

5. On the CD that accompanies this text is a file containing data on favourite flavours of ice cream for a random sample of people walking around Kempenfelt Bay one summer evening. The data are coded as follows: (1) vanilla, (2) chocolate, (3) strawberry, (4) maple walnut, (5) chocolate chip, (6) pralines, (7) other. Create an appropriate graph for the data set and comment.

2.4   TIME-SERIES GRAPHS

Time-series data are a sequence of observations made over time. These observations are plotted in the order in which they occurred, with time along the *x*-axis. Anne Morgan wants to investigate the sales data to see if she can detect any seasonal patterns in sales. A time-series graph of the Barrie sales data is shown below in Exhibit 2.62.

Exhibit

2.62

Time-Series Graph of the Barrie Sales Data

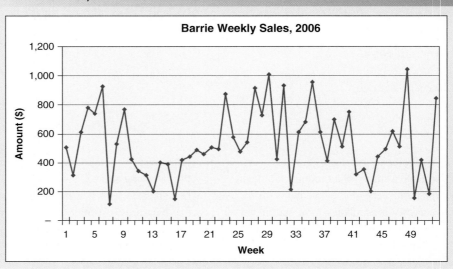

Note that the original data points are shown as points on this graph. The lines joining the points do *not* represent data: the lines are added to make it easier to see any patterns in the data. There do appear to be some time-related patterns in the sales data. A period of lower sales shows in weeks 10–22 (about mid-March to the beginning of June). Another period of lower sales occurs in weeks 41–46 (about the middle of October to the middle of November). Particularly if these patterns were evident in other years, it would make sense to investigate why they occurred. Some seasonal or cyclical factors may be affecting sales.

It is also possible to present time-series data as a bar chart, but this is only appropriate if there are only a few time periods above (if you experiment with a bar chart of the Barrie sales data, you will quickly conclude that the graph is unreadable). Bar charts can be effective for a limited number of observations, particularly if you want to clearly emphasize the differences from period to period.

One of the things Anne may do is to compare the weekly sales for all three locations, over time. She can do this by creating a line graph, with a different coloured line for each location, as shown below in Exhibit 2.63.

Line Graph Comparing Weekly Sales over Time

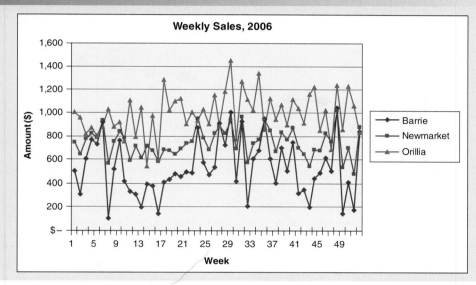

Exhibit 2.63

This graph permits several observations; for example:

1. There is some remarkable similarity in the patterns of weekly sales at the Barrie and Newmarket locations. The pattern of weekly sales in Orillia is quite different from the other locations.
2. Sales at Barrie are generally lower than at Newmarket, which in turn are generally lower than at the Orillia location.
3. Sales at the Barrie location are more variable than at the other two locations (something we also observed from the histograms of sales data).

To create a line chart in Excel, highlight the associated data table on the worksheet, click on the Chart Wizard icon on the toolbar, and then choose **Line** under the **Chart type:** heading. In step 2, click on the **Series** tab, and make the appropriate selections for the **Name:**, **Values:** and **Category (X) axis labels:** areas.

Instructions

Again, if your graph is going to be presented in black and white, you should consider formatting the lines so that they are easily distinguishable. You can accomplish this by right-clicking on a line on the graph, selecting Format Data Series ..., selecting Pattern, and then making appropriate choices for the line and the marker.

Example 2.4

Graphing time-series data

EXA02-4.xls

Set

The Collingtree Ski Shop has enjoyed a steadily growing business for about a decade. The company's owner believes that the increases in sales justify hiring another full-time sales associate. The company accountant wants to take a more cautious approach, hiring extra part-time sales staff as needed.

The owner is looking at annual sales data for the last 10 years. The accountant is looking at monthly sales data for the same period. Which data set should be the basis for analysis, and what hiring decision should be made?

Use Excel's Chart Wizard to create two time-series graphs—one for the monthly sales data, and one for the annual sales data. The Excel graphs are shown below.

Exhibit 2.64

Collingtree Annual Sales Data

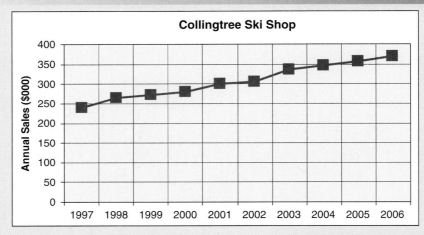

Exhibit 2.65

Collingtree Monthly Sales Data

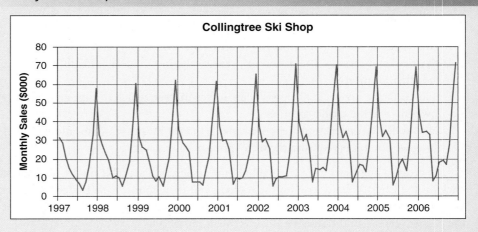

Note that it is difficult to see the increasing trend in sales in Exhibit 2.65, which shows the monthly sales. There is clearly a wide variation in sales, based on the season. It is easier to see the increasing trend in sales over the 10-year period in Exhibit 2.64, which shows annual sales.

Both graphs have their uses. For staffing purposes, the monthly sales data are more useful. While the monthly sales highs for each year have increased over the period, the monthly sales lows have not. This indicates that hiring another full-time sales associate may not be justified, because this staff member is likely not needed during the months with low sales. The accountant's recommendation to hire more part-time staff in the months with higher sales seems a more reasonable approach.

DEVELOP YOUR SKILLS   2.4

1. Suppose you are the sales manager at a car dealership. You want to examine data on past sales, with an eye to planning sales activities for the next year. Should you look at annual or monthly sales? Why?

2. Find some data on the Canada–U.S. exchange rate for the period January 2000 to December 2005 (there are many reliable sources of such data available on the web, including the Bank of Canada website). Create a line graph, and comment on the pattern apparent in the graph.

3. Exhibit 2.66 below shows the Bank of Canada Bank Rate, on a monthly basis, from January 2004 to May 2006.

Bank of Canada Bank Rate, Monthly, January 2004–May 2006

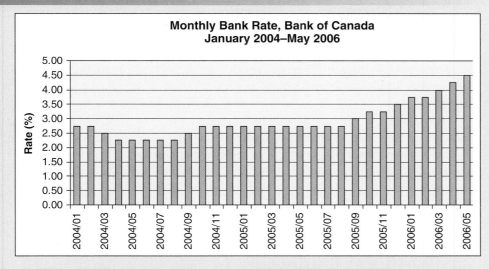

Exhibit 2.66

Source: Data from Rates and Statistics, Bank of Canada, www.bankofcanada.ca/en/rates/interest-look.html (accessed June 14, 2006). Used with permission.

a. Comment on what you observe in this graph.
b. The other option for presenting this data would be a line graph. What is the advantage of using a bar chart in this case?

4. Many companies now provide information from their annual reports on their company websites. Find a company of your choice, and collect sales data for at least 10 periods. Create a graph of the data, and comment on what the graph tells you.

5. Statistics Canada collects data and computes a monthly price index for computer prices. A separate index is calculated for computers sold to consumers (not business or government).

Set   A data set of this price index is available on the CD that comes with the text, in a directory called DataChap02. Create an appropriate graph for this data set, and comment on it. (Source: Adapted from Statistics Canada CANSIM in E-STAT, CANSIM Table 331-001:

"Computer prices indexes, by type of purchaser, monthly (index 2001=100), Jan 1990 to Apr 2006," **http://estat.statcan.ca/cgiwin/CNSMCG1.EXE?Lang= E&RootDir=ESTAT/&CANSIMFILE=EStat/English/ CII_1_E.htm**. (See file called DYS02-4-5.xls.)

2.5   GRAPHS OF PAIRED QUANTITATIVE DATA

When Anne Morgan looked at the data for types of baked good sales and locations, she was investigating the relationship between these two *qualitative* variables. It is also possible to investigate the relationship between two *quantitative* variables, such as quantity demanded or supplied, and price. Chapter 12 provides a more detailed discussion of the techniques involved, but it is possible to get a preliminary assessment of such a relationship by drawing a graph called a scatter diagram. A **scatter diagram** displays paired x–y data points of the form (x, y).

scatter diagram display of paired x–y data points of the form (x, y)

For example, Anne Morgan has records of the Barrie location's total daily sales and the number of people entering the mall at the nearest door, for 25 randomly selected days throughout the year. Anne wonders whether there is a relationship between traffic at that door and sales. The data are shown in the table in Exhibit 2.67 on the next page.

If you examine the data, you will probably see that there does seem to be a relationship between the number of people entering through the nearest door and daily sales. On the days when the number of people entering through the nearest door is higher, sales are generally higher. However, it is difficult to see the pattern from the table of numbers. It is much easier to see the relationship when the data are graphed in a scatter diagram.

It is customary to graph the explanatory variable on the x-axis, and the response variable on the y-axis, so before you create a scatter diagram, you must decide which is which. When the explanatory variable changes, it appears to (or is hypothesized to) cause a change in the response variable. The **explanatory variable** is observed (and sometimes controlled) by the researcher, and is the apparent cause of the change in the response variable. The **response variable** changes when the explanatory variable changes. Note that sometimes the explanatory variable is referred to as the "independent" variable, and the response variable is referred to as the "dependent" variable.

explanatory variable variable observed (and sometimes controlled) by the researcher, which is the apparent cause of the change in the response variable

response variable variable that changes when the explanatory variable changes

In the case of the Barrie location data, the explanatory variable is the number of people entering through the nearest door. It would be expected that changes in this number could cause changes in sales, the response variable. A reasonable hypothesis would be that greater traffic at the door would lead to higher sales.

The scatter diagram is created in Excel as follows:

1. Highlight the cells in the worksheet containing the x- and y-data.
2. Click on the Chart Wizard on the toolbar.

Data for Barrie Location Daily Sales and Traffic at Nearest Door

Exhibit 2.67

Barrie Location, 2006, 25 Randomly Selected Days

Daily Sales ($)	Number of People Entering Through Nearest Door
72.19	150
131.99	125
60.19	155
28.47	56
54.83	78
48.21	65
103.33	101
29.87	35
63.09	89
70.56	85
87.59	67
73.01	75
25.55	46
120.01	168
87.13	112
110.86	125
105.08	115
124.91	139
15.67	45
62.54	72
69.29	72
65.30	70
71.88	89
70.05	32
77.01	98

3. Select XY(Scatter) under the Chart type: heading. Click Next>.
4. If the chart in the preview is as desired, click Next> again. If not, click on the Series tab, and make the necessary changes to the X Values: and Y Values: areas. Then click Next>.
5. Add appropriate titles under the Titles tab (and remove the legend by unticking Show legend, under the Legend tab). Click on Finish.

The scatter diagram will help us to see if this hypothesized relationship is supported by the data. A scatter diagram for the Barrie data is shown below in Exhibit 2.68 on the next page.

Exhibit
2.68

Scatter Diagram for the Barrie Data

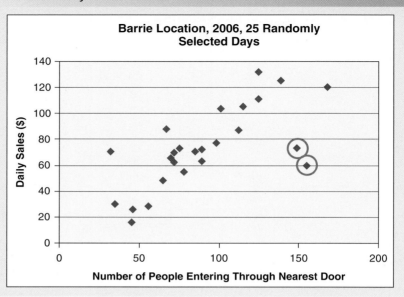

Barrie Location, 2006, 25 Randomly Selected Days

Daily Sales ($) — vertical axis: 0, 20, 40, 60, 80, 100, 120, 140

Number of People Entering Through Nearest Door — horizontal axis: 0, 50, 100, 150, 200

positive (direct) relationship
increases in the explanatory variable correspond to increases in the response variable

negative (inverse) relationship
increases in the explanatory variable correspond to decreases in the response variable

There does appear to be a positive relationship between door traffic and sales, as the general shape of the scatter diagram is an upward slope to the right. When the number of people entering through the nearest door is higher, the day's sales are generally higher as well. In a **positive (direct) relationship**, increases in the explanatory variable correspond to increases in the response variable. In a **negative (inverse) relationship**, increases in the explanatory variable correspond to decreases in the response variable.

While there does appear to be a positive relationship between door traffic and daily sales at the Barrie location, it is also clear that the sales are quite variable, and that door traffic is probably only one of the factors affecting daily sales. As well, there are (at least two) observations that do not appear to fit the general pattern, and these are circled in Exhibit 2.68 above. You will learn how to investigate and model relationships such as this one with the techniques described in Chapter 12 of this text. The first step in the more advanced techniques is always to create a scatter diagram to picture the relationship between the variables.

Example
2.5

Graphing paired quantitative data

EXA02-5.xls
Set

The marketing department at Smith & Klein Manufacturing is interested in the relationship between sales and promotion spending. Accountants have provided the annual figures in each category for the last 30 years.

The data are available on the CD that accompanies this text, in the directory called DataChap02.

The first decision is which is the explanatory (*x*-axis) variable, and which is the response (*y*-axis) variable. In this case, spending is made on promotions with the goal of increasing sales, so amount of sales is the response variable.

The Chart Wizard of Excel is used to create the scatter diagram shown in Exhibit 2.69. It appears, from the scatter diagram, that there is a positive relationship between annual promotion spending and sales.

Scatter Diagram

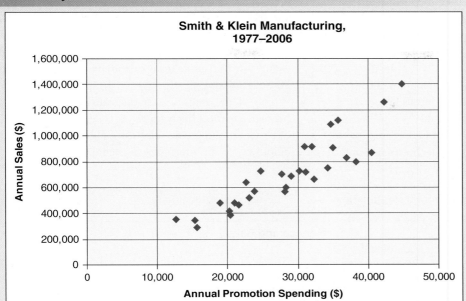

Exhibit **2.69**

DEVELOP YOUR SKILLS **2.5**

1. An economist wants to study the relationship between household income and monthly spending on restaurant meals. Data are collected from a random sample of households. Create an appropriate graph of the data, and comment. See file called DYS02-5-1.xls.

2. Jack runs a small convenience store, which sells freshly baked cookies (they are displayed near the cash register, to tempt buyers as they pay for their other purchases). Jack has been uncertain about how to price the cookies he sells (he vaguely remembers a concept called "price-elasticity of demand" from his class in economics at business school). Jack has experimented by charging a different price on a randomly selected number of days. The data he has collected are shown below in Exhibit 2.70. Create an appropriate graph for these data, and comment on the relationship. See file called DYS02-5-2.xls.

Set

Sales Data for Jack's Cookies

Exhibit **2.70**

Jack's Cookies

Price ($)	Quantity Sold
1.00	50
0.90	51
0.80	58
0.75	59
0.70	58
0.65	55
0.60	63
0.55	60
0.50	65

3. Max Weber is wondering whether the size of a customer's most recent purchase at his drugstore is related to the customer's income. Create an appropriate graph for the data from the survey, and comment. See file called DYS02-5-3.xls.

4. A college professor is very concerned that her students' academic success is affected by the number of hours the students spend working at their jobs. She selects a random sample of 45 students and asks them to keep track of their total hours of paid employment for the semester (they all do, because she has promised them a bonus mark as a reward). The professor also records each student's average mark for the semester. Create an appropriate graph for the data, and comment. See file called DYS02-5-4.xls.

5. Which of the three scatter diagrams in Exhibit 2.71 below is the most likely representation of data on years of service and annual salary for a random selection of employees in an international organization? Why?

Exhibit 2.71

Scatter Diagram Possibilities: Years of Service vs. Annual Salary

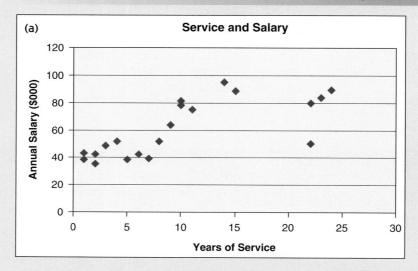

(a) Service and Salary

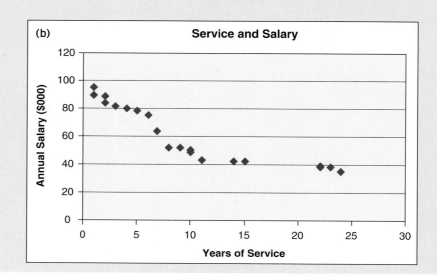

(b) Service and Salary

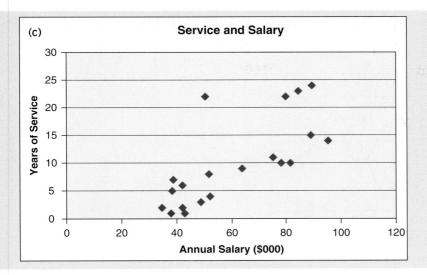

2.6 MISLEADING AND UNINTERESTING GRAPHS

Not all graphs are faithful and compelling visual representations of data sets. For various reasons, graphs can be either misleading or uninteresting, or both.

Misleading Graphs

Graphs and charts can provide useful summaries of data, but they can also mislead. As both a consumer and a producer of graphs, you should avoid misinterpreting others' graphs or misleading others with your own graphs. Some common problems with graphs are outlined below.

Non-Zero Origins   By convention, the starting point (the origin) for the *x*- and *y*-axes of any graph is the point (0, 0). Any departure from this convention must be clearly and visibly indicated on the graph.

Exhibit 2.72 on the next page shows two graphs of the same data.

Notice that a first inspection of Exhibit 2.72a might lead to the following observation: "During the 2000–06 period, the Kelowna location's sales climbed significantly, levelling off in the last three years. In contrast, the Nelson location's sales have been extremely variable, and significantly below Kelowna's sales in the last few years, with some improvement by 2006." These statements seem to be supported by the graph, until you notice that the *y*-axis starts at $100 million, *not* $0 million.

Exhibit 2.72b shows the graph with a proper scale on the *y*-axis. The fluctuations in the sales at the Nelson location do not seem so pronounced, and in fact, they are not gyrating widely, as the graph in Exhibit 2.72a seems to indicate. Objectively speaking, it could be argued that there is *more* fluctuation in the Kelowna sales over the period, something we will explore further in Chapter 3 when we discuss measures of variability. As well, as Exhibit 2.72b shows, the sales at the two locations are not so significantly different from each other.

There are cases when the (0, 0) origin cannot be reasonably used on a graph. For example, suppose you were investigating the scatter diagram shown in Exhibit 2.73.

Exhibit **2.72** Two Graphs of the Same Data, Non-Zero Origin vs. Zero Origin

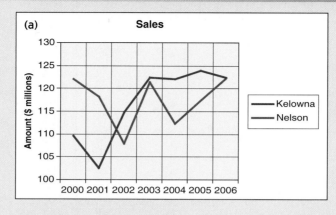

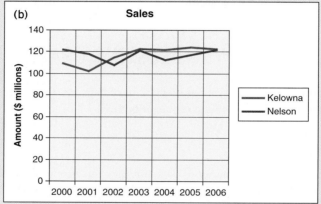

Exhibit **2.73** Scatter Diagram with Zero Origin

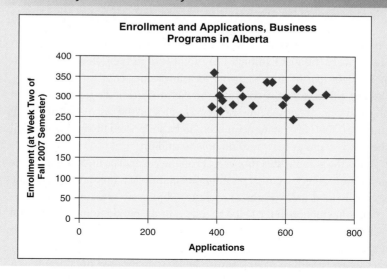

In this case, much of the area on the graph is unoccupied, and the data set is represented by a small cluster of points that cannot be seen very clearly. In a case like this, it is preferable to scale the axes of the graph (right-click on the axis in Excel, click on Format Axis . . . , then click on the Scale tab and make the necessary adjustments).

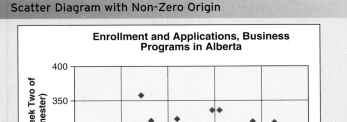

Instructions

However, when you make an adjustment like this, it is crucial that you warn the reader that you have done so. Sometimes this is done by showing breaks in the axes or the plot area, as Exhibit 2.74 below illustrates.

Scatter Diagram with Non-Zero Origin

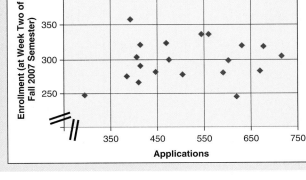

2.74

Exhibit

Misleading or Missing Titles and Axis Labels   It is not unusual, particularly in the popular press, to see titles or captions on graphs that encourage the reader to draw conclusions about the data. This can be misleading. For example, consider the graph shown in Exhibit 2.75 below.

Graph with Misleading Title, Improper Format

2.75

Exhibit

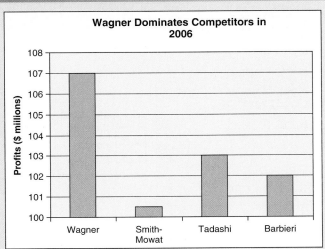

The title of the graph is not merely descriptive, because it is asking the reader to draw a conclusion. When the graph is properly formatted, as in Exhibit 2.76, it seems that the conclusion is not really justified. Notice that the title on the reformatted graph in Exhibit 2.76 is purely descriptive.

2.76
Exhibit

Graph With Descriptive Title, Proper Format

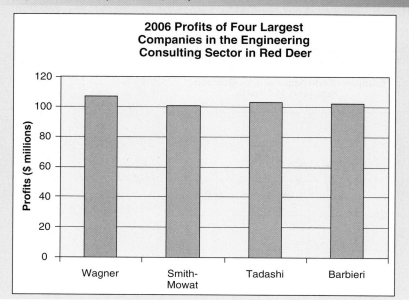

Beware of titles on graphs that ask you to draw conclusions. Avoid using such titles. Titles and labels should objectively describe the associated data.

Another misleading feature of some graphs is missing or vague labels on the axes. See, for example, Exhibit 2.77 below.

2.77
Exhibit

Graph with Missing Labels on the Axes

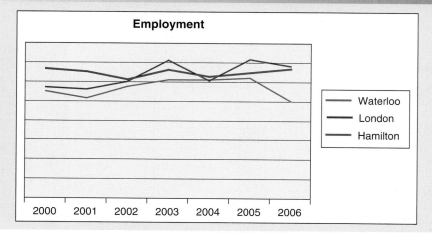

We can see that this graph is supposed to be telling us something about employment at three locations, over the 2000–06 period. But it is not at all clear what data are being illustrated here. Is it perhaps numbers of employees? Could it be index numbers illustrating how current employment relates to some base year? Is it percentage of total employment in the company? And which company is this? Because we do not know the answers to these questions, the graph is useless. Be careful not to create such graphs.

Apply this test to any graph you create: ask yourself if your graph can be read and understood without any further supporting material or explanation. You should be able to answer "yes" to this question.

Distorted Images   The wide availability of software such as Excel means that it is relatively easy to produce graphs to describe data. Unfortunately, if such software is not used judiciously, the graphs can be misleading or difficult to interpret. One of the most common errors is to add 3-D effects to a graph.

It is *never* a good idea to add 3-D effects to a graph.

To see why, consider the pie charts shown below in Exhibit 2.78 below.

Pie Charts Based on Same Data, One with 3-D Effects   **2.78**   *Exhibit*

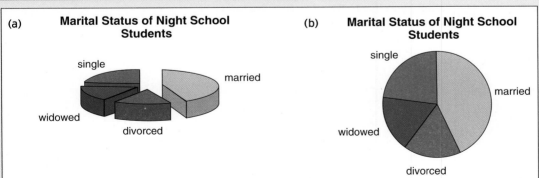

In Exhibit 2.78a, the pie chart is tilted, and has 3-D slices. Because of this, it is very difficult to judge the relative sizes of the slices of the pie. In Exhibit 2.78a, the "single" slice, at 23%, looks significantly larger than the "widowed" slice, at 17%, and it is not obvious that the "widowed" slice and the "divorced" slice are equal in size. It is far easier to judge the relative sizes of the slices in Exhibit 2.78b, where the graph is no longer tilted, and the 3-D aspect is removed. Exhibit 2.78a is not an acceptable graph, because it does not communicate clearly. Exhibit 2.78b is far better.

Sometimes graphs are cluttered with images. Often this is because the graphs themselves are not very interesting (see the section on "Uninteresting Graphs," below). Consider the graph shown in Exhibit 2.79.

Exhibit 2.79

Graph Cluttered with Images

An improved version is shown in Exhibit 2.80, below.

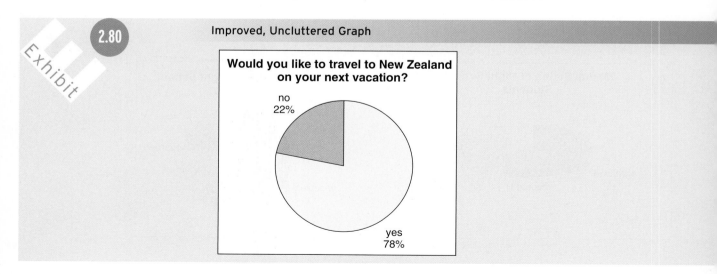

Exhibit 2.80

Improved, Uncluttered Graph

Exhibit 2.80 is easier to read, but it leaves a number of questions unanswered. Who was surveyed? When were the data collected? Even if we had answers to these questions, it is not clear that these data would be worth having. A more useful question might have been:

"Are you actively considering travelling to New Zealand for your next vacation?" This might capture data about intentions (the original question is too vague, as it refers to wishes only).

The graph shown in Exhibit 2.80 does not really contain any useful data. The graph is superficially interesting only because of its vibrant colours and images. Beware of graphs that are cluttered with extraneous images. The clutter is often an indication that the creator of the graph cared less about communicating than about how fancy the graph looked.

> The primary goal of a graph is to summarize data, in a way that communicates clearly.

Missing Data   Another trick that is sometimes used to mislead with graphs is to leave out selected data points. Consider, for example, the time-series graph shown in Exhibit 2.81a below. This graph shows the weekly sales for the Barrie vending-machine location, but for only a few weeks in 2006. When the data are put in proper context, as in Exhibit 2.81b, the conclusion that the weekly sales are on an upward trend does not seem justified.

Time-Series Graphs, One with Missing Data

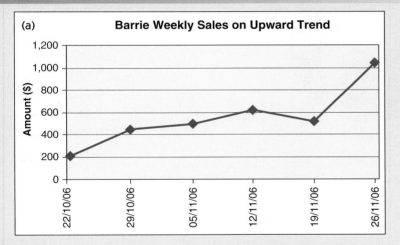

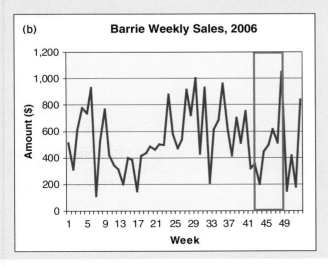

Exhibit 2.81

Always check data sources to make sure that important data has not been omitted from a graph.

Uninteresting Graphs

As mentioned above, sometimes graphs are inherently uninteresting, and this can lead to a temptation to use colours, images, or 3-D aspects to try to make them look more interesting. However, trying to add interest to a graph with visual gimmicks will not work if the underlying data are not interesting. Consider the pie chart below in Exhibit 2.82.

Exhibit 2.82

Pie Chart with Uninteresting Data

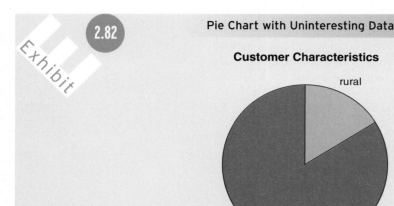

Customer Characteristics

There is too little information in this graph to make it interesting. A table summarizing the data would probably be sufficient, as shown in Exhibit 2.83 below. In this case, some additional calculations to present the relative frequencies of customer types would be helpful, but there is not enough data here to make an interesting graph.

Exhibit 2.83

Table of Data from Pie Chart in Exhibit 2.82

	Customer Characteristics	
	Number of Customers	Percentage of Customers
Rural	132	16.1
Urban	689	83.9
Total	821	100.0

Contrast the graph shown in Exhibit 2.82 with some of the graphs presented earlier in this chapter. For example, in Exhibit 2.39 (p. 48), a significant amount of data is summarized in the three histograms of weekly sales data for the Barrie, Orillia, and Newmarket vending-machine locations. Similarly, Exhibit 2.56 (p. 57) effectively summarizes a great deal of data about baked-good sales, and allows comparisons among the three different locations. These are examples of interesting graphs that are easy to understand, and that lead naturally to further avenues of investigation about the underlying data.

DEVELOP YOUR SKILLS 2.6

1. Exhibit 2.84 shows a graph of the speed-of-service ratings for the survey of drugstore customers. Comment on how you would improve the graph (if at all).

Drugstore Customers' Speed of Service Ratings

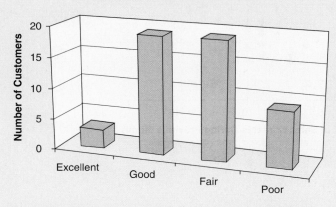

Exhibit 2.84

2. Comment on the graph shown below in Exhibit 2.85.

Drugstore Customers' Speed of Service Ratings

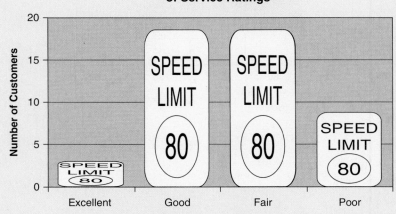

Exhibit 2.85

3. Is Exhibit 2.86 an example of a good graph? Why or why not?

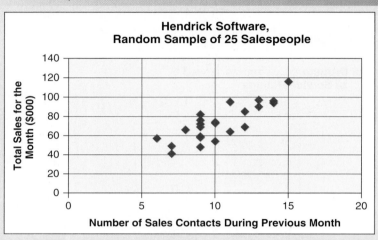

2.86 Exhibit

Scatter Graph of Sales Data

4. Is the graph shown in Exhibit 2.87 an interesting graph? Explain why or why not.

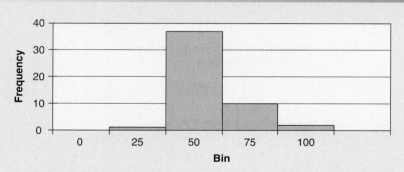

2.87 Exhibit

Histogram

5. Exhibit 2.88 on the next page is one method of displaying the data on ice cream flavour preferences, first described in Develop Your Skills 2.3, Exercise 5 on p. 60. Comment on this graph as a way of displaying the data.

Graph of Ice Cream Flavour Preferences

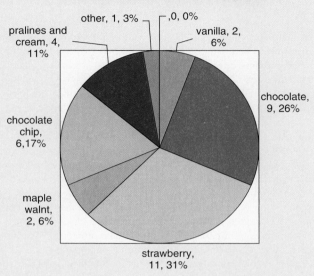

Survey of People at Kempenfelt Bay

other, 1, 3% — ,0, 0%

pralines and cream, 4, 11%

vanilla, 2, 6%

chocolate, 9, 26%

chocolate chip, 6, 17%

maple walnt, 2, 6%

strawberry, 11, 31%

2.88

Exhibit

Types of Data

The methods used to analyze data and make decisions differ according to the type of data involved. Quantitative data contain numerical information, for which arithmetical operations such as averaging are meaningful. Qualitative data contain descriptive information, which may be recorded in words or numbers.

A continuous variable can take *any* possible value on a number line (possibly within upper and lower limits). A discrete variable can take on only certain identifiable values on a number line (possibly within upper and lower limits). Ranked data are qualitative data that can be ordered according to size or quality.

Cross-sectional data are all collected in the same time period. Time-series data are collected over successive points in time.

Frequency Distributions and Histograms for Quantitative Data

A frequency distribution is a summary table that divides quantitative data into ranges (classes), and records the count (frequency) of data points in each range.

The number of classes appropriate for a particular data set depends on the number of observations, and the variability in the observations. An Excel template is available to assist with decisions about the number of classes (see p. 33). If no computer is at hand, the formula below can give some guidance about appropriate class width:

$$\text{class width} = \frac{\text{maximum value} - \text{minimum value}}{\sqrt{n}}$$

where n is the number of data points in the data set.

Chapter Summary

2

Some considerations for setting up classes:

1. The classes should not overlap.
2. The classes should all be the same width, and open-ended classes should be avoided.
3. The lower limit of the first class should be an even multiple of the class width.
4. The frequency distribution should be clearly labelled so that it is understandable to reader, without further description.

Excel can be used to count the frequencies for each class, using the Data Analysis tool called Histogram (see p. 35). Classes are controlled using Excel's bin numbers, which are the upper included limits of each class. Bin numbers must be typed into an Excel worksheet when the Histogram tool is used.

A histogram is a bar graph of a frequency distribution, with lower class limits shown along the *x*-axis, and frequencies shown along the *y*-axis. Histograms can also be created with Excel's Histogram tool (see p. 41). Unfortunately, Excel's histograms require several adjustments. See the Guide to Technique for adjusting Excel's histograms on page 42 for detailed instructions.

A distribution is symmetric if the right half of the distribution is a mirror image of the left half. A distribution is skewed to the right (or positively skewed) when there are some unusually large values in the data set that destroy the symmetry. A distribution is skewed to the left (or negatively skewed) when there are some unusually small values in the data set that destroy the symmetry.

Sometimes histograms illustrate the existence of outliers. An outlier is a data point that is unusually far from the rest of the data. Outliers are usually investigated carefully.

When you are creating histograms for comparison, you should take care to set them up so that comparison is easy. See the Guide to Technique for comparing histograms on page 47. Sometimes it is useful to create relative frequency distributions and histograms, particularly for comparison when the data sets have quite different frequencies. The relative frequency of a class is the percentage of total observations falling into that class.

Tables, Bar Graphs, and Pie Charts for Qualitative Data

Excel's Chart Wizard can be used to create bar graphs and pie charts for simple tables (see the Excel instructions on p. 53 and p. 55). Bar charts emphasize the relative sizes of the categories in qualitative data. Pie charts emphasize the share of the total represented by each category.

Bar charts can also be created to illustrate the relationship between two or more qualitative variables. Contingency tables are tables with more than one column, with data cross-classified by row and column headings. See the Excel instructions on page 58.

Time Series Graphs

Time-series graphs are usually line graphs, with observations plotted against time on the *x*-axis. See the Excel instructions on page 61.

Graphs of Paired Quantitative Data

A scatter diagram displays paired *x*–*y* data points of the form (x, y). The response variable is plotted on the *y*-axis, and the explanatory variable on the *x*-axis. The explanatory variable is observed (and sometimes controlled) by the researcher.

In a positive (direct) relationship, increases in the explanatory variable correspond to increases in the response variable. In a negative (inverse) relationship, increases in the explanatory variable correspond to decreases in the response variable.

A scatter diagram is created in Excel with the Chart Wizard, using the XY (Scatter) type of chart.

Misleading and Uninteresting Graphs

Graphs and charts can provide useful summaries of data, but they can also mislead. The primary goal of a graph is to summarize data, in a way that communicates clearly.

By convention, the starting point (the origin) for the *x*- and *y*-axes of any graph is $(0, 0)$. Any departure from this convention must be clearly and visibly indicated on the graph. Always check data sources to make sure that important data have not been omitted from a graph.

Beware of titles on graphs that ask you to draw conclusions. Avoid using such titles. Titles and labels should objectively describe the associated data.

Apply this test to any graph you create: ask yourself if the graph can be read and understood without any further supporting material or explanation. You should be able to answer "yes" to this question.

Graphs are interesting only if the underlying data are interesting. Trying to add interest with visual gimmicks will not improve a graph that is based on uninteresting data. It is never a good idea to add 3-D effects to a graph.

CHAPTER REVIEW EXERCISES

1. For the data set of student marks from Ms. Nice's class and Mr. Nasty's class (first discussed in Develop Your Skills 2.2, Exercise 5), create appropriate graphs for comparison. Comment on the differences and similarities you see in the two data sets.

 CRE02-1.xls
Set

2. Comment on the graph shown below in Exhibit 2.89.

Graph of Canadians' Expectations

Exhibit **2.89**

Everything is coming up roses

% of Canadians who do not fear job loss =

% of Canadians who expect finances to improve =

3. What type of data are these?
   a. A random sample of adult Moncton residents was chosen, and data was recorded about whether they are male or female, and whether they have fitness club memberships.
   b. The type of payment method used was recorded for a random sample of 100 customers from four different store locations.
   c. The number of pedestrians passing two prospective store locations in a given week was recorded.
   d. A restaurant owner who is trying to decide which of two chefs to promote asks a sample of diners to rate the food made by each of the chefs, on a scale of 1 to 4, where 1 corresponds to "barely edible" and 4 corresponds to "absolutely delicious."
   e. A company collects data for the past 10 years on sales and advertising.

CRE02-4.xls
Set

4. A survey of pedestrian traffic is conducted over 45 days for two locations where a manager is thinking of opening a new location. The data set is available on the CD that accompanies this text. Create appropriate frequency distributions and histograms for these data sets, and comment on similarities and differences in the data.

5. The owner of a music store is wondering if he should target female customers in particular, because he believes they tend to spend more than male customers. However, he wants to check this belief. He asks the cashiers to keep track of the spending by a random sample of female customers and a random sample of male customers, over several days. The purchases are shown in Exhibit 2.90 below. Create appropriate graphical displays to summarize and compare these data. Comment.

2.90

Exhibit

Music Store Purchases by a Random Sample of Customers

Purchases By Females ($)	Purchases By Males ($)
30.50	31.49
15.83	28.88
38.66	30.77
44.15	24.95
42.98	23.26
39.56	27.66
22.25	25.77
31.49	33.32
49.43	18.29
18.70	38.25
24.65	25.09
29.64	30.51
17.30	24.96
20.34	26.34
23.40	

6. A bank with a management training program has asked for 360° feedback for one of its trainees (that is, feedback from managers and peers). The ratings range from 1 to 6, where 1 corresponds to the best performance, and 6 to the worst. The results for one of the trainees are shown below in Exhibit 2.91. Create an appropriate graphical display and comment.

2.91

Exhibit

Results of a Trainee's 360° Feedback

Trainee Ratings
4
5
4
5
6
2
5
5
1

7. A company that produces golf balls is trying to develop a new ball that will travel farther than its current best-seller. A golf pro hits a number of balls of each type off of a tee, and the distance travelled is exactly measured. The results are shown below in Exhibit 2.92. Create appropriate graphical displays for the data sets and comment on similarities or differences. Comment on symmetry and skewness.

Golf Ball Data

Exhibit 2.92

Distances Travelled (Metres) by Current Best-Selling Golf Ball	Distances Travelled (Metres) by New Golf Ball
260	310
266	286
254	292
302	276
241	269
249	293
262	306
255	279
252	262
244	248
286	

8. A random sample of employees was asked to rate the performance of a company president. This president was fired, and a new president was hired. After six months, another random sample of employees is asked to rate the performance of the new president. A rating of 1 corresponds to the best performance, and 10 the worst possible. The ratings are shown below in Exhibit 2.93. Create an appropriate graphical display for these data. Comment on similarities or differences in the ratings of the two presidents.

Employees' Ratings of Presidents' Performance

Exhibit 2.93

Rating of the Old President's Performance	Rating of the New President's Performance
10	9
7	6
2	2
8	1
8	2
6	4
4	5
6	7
8	8
9	7

CRE02-9.xls
Set

9. The real estate listings for a random sample of three-bedroom bungalows in a Calgary suburb is available on the CD that comes with this text. Create an appropriate graphical display for these data, and comment.

10. A random sample of students was selected in Ontario, and another in British Columbia. The students were asked to rate a particular Canadian university, with a rating of 1 if they considered it excellent, down to 4 if they considered it poor. The ratings of the students are shown below in Exhibit 2.94. Create an appropriate graphical display and compare the ratings of the Ontario students and the BC students.

Exhibit 2.94

University Ratings

Ontario Student Ranking	BC Student Ranking
2	1
3	4
4	4
1	2
4	1
2	1
1	1
2	1
2	1
3	2
2	2
4	2
2	2
4	3
4	2
4	1
3	3
4	2
2	3
2	3

11. The type of payment method used was recorded for a random sample of customers from four different store locations. The data are shown below in Exhibit 2.95. Create an appropriate graphical display to summarize the data, and comment.

Exhibit 2.95

Customer Payment Method

	Store A	Store B	Store C	Store D	Total
Cash/debit card	40	65	20	25	150
Credit card	30	80	30	40	180
Cheque	30	55	50	35	170
Total	100	200	100	100	500

12. The Travel Price Index (TPI) is an aggregate index of goods and services used when travelling in Canada. Price movements are derived from detailed Consumer Price Index (CPI) series. Data on the TPI are available on the CD that accompanies this text. Create an appropriate graph for the last 10 years of data available, and comment. (Source: Adapted from Statistics Canada CANSIM in E-STAT, CANSIM Table 428-0002, "Travel price index," http://estat.statcan.ca/cgiwin/CNSMCG1.EXE?Lang=E&RootDir=ESTAT/&CANSIM-FILE=EStat/English/CII_1_E.htm.)

CRE02-12.xls
Set

13. A statistics teacher is wondering if there is a relationship between students' marks in their first-year business math course, and in their second-year statistics course. She collects data from a random sample of students, and begins her analysis by creating an appropriate graph. Which is the explanatory variable? Which is the response variable? Would it be correct to say that a high mark in business math *caused* a high mark in statistics?

CRE02-13.xls
Set

14. The marketing department of a college wanted to know if there was a difference in the proportions of students drawn from inside or outside the college catchment area by program. A random sample of 100 students from business, technology, and nursing programs revealed the results shown in Exhibit 2.96.

Origin of Students in College Programs

	Business	Technology	Nursing
From local area	65	45	58
Not from local area	35	55	42

Exhibit 2.96

Create an appropriate graphical display for these data. Does it appear that there is a relationship between the program and whether or not students come from the local catchment area?

15. Woodbon, a company that produces a limited line of high-quality wooden furniture, has enjoyed remarkable sales growth since its inception in 1980. Woodbon's owner, Kate Cameron, is looking back over the company's years of operation, and is trying to plan for the future. Kate collects the annual advertising and sales figures for the last several years. Create an appropriate graph to summarize the relationship between advertising and sales for Woodbon. The data are available on the CD that comes with this text.

CRE02-15.xls
Set

16. *USA Today* is an American newspaper that has an accompanying website, on which there is a feature called "Snapshots." These are graphical displays of data on a wide range of topics. Go to the Snapshots section of the site, at www.usatoday.com/news/snapshot.htm. View the graphical displays. What is the purpose of these graphs?

17. Jane Wedd collected data on the ages of a random sample of the people attending a local fall fair. The data are shown below in Exhibit 2.97. Use a stem-and-leaf display to organize the data. Describe the shape of the distribution.

Ages of a Random Sample of Attendees Local Fall Fair

8	12	8	20	31
9	23	40	14	32
9	22	8	20	30
50	21	31	12	9

Exhibit 2.97

18. A random sample of 78 employees at a large computer software firm was polled to determine their method of travel to work. A random sample of 80 employees of an accounting firm in the same office complex was also polled. The results are shown in Exhibit 2.98 below. Create an appropriate graphical display to summarize the data.

Method of Travel to Work

	By Transit	In Car	On Bicycle	On Foot
Software firm	51	8	16	3
Accounting firm	52	23	4	1

19. A new analyst at a soft drink company was preparing a graph to illustrate the company's net operating revenues over the last five years. He decided that the graph was boring and so he adjusted it. The resulting graph is shown in Exhibit 2.99 below. Comment on this graph.

Soft Drink Company's Net Operating Revenues

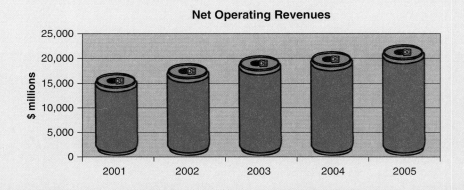

20. A human resources consultant produced the graph shown opposite in Exhibit 2.100, after selecting a random sample of employees and recording their salaries and months of experience with the company. Comment on the graph.

Employees' Salaries and Months of Experience

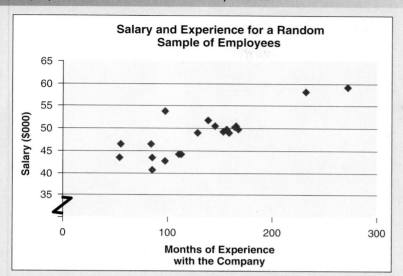

Exhibit 2.100

CHAPTER 3

Using Numbers to Describe Data

Learning Objectives

After mastering the material in this chapter, you will be able to:

1. Use conventions about the order of operations and summation notation to correctly evaluate common statistical formulas.

2. Choose and calculate the appropriate measure of central tendency for a data set.

3. Choose and calculate the appropriate measure of variability for a data set.

4. Choose, calculate, and interpret the appropriate measure of association for a paired data set.

INTRODUCTION

Anne Morgan has created some interesting graphs to describe sales data for the Barrie, Orillia, and Newmarket vending machines operated by her employer (see Chapter 2 for details). Anne has already noticed that weekly sales are different at the three locations, both in the amount of sales and in variability. Anne now wants to prepare some numerical summary measures to describe the data.

Anne has also used a graph to illustrate the relationship between the Barrie vending machine sales and the number of people entering through the nearest door in the mall. She now wants to measure how strongly the two variables are related.

In this chapter, you will be introduced to some of the numerical measures Anne could use to describe the data sets of interest to her. In particular, you will be introduced to measures of central tendency (Section 3.2), measures of variability (Section 3.3), and measures of association (Section 3.4).

Construction of these measures involves some arithmetic, which will be described by standard mathematical notation. This notation is described in Section 3.1, and if you are already familiar with it, you should proceed directly to Section 3.2.

SOME USEFUL NOTATION

Statistics involves some arithmetic, much of it repetitive. While computers permit fast and easy calculation, you will probably have to do some of the arithmetic by hand (with the use of a calculator), as you learn new techniques or write tests for your statistics course.

Doing the arithmetic by hand may help you develop an intuitive understanding of what the calculations mean, and so it is important that you master the manual techniques. A basic calculator with at least one memory will come in handy (be sure you learn how to use your calculator's memory, because without it, the arithmetic can be *very* time-consuming).

Mathematical notation will also come in handy. Sometimes the arithmetic you must do will have a number of steps, and mathematical notation can help you remember the steps, *but only if you know how to read it!*

Fortunately, the notation is not that difficult to read. In this section, you will be introduced to some standard mathematical notation, and you will be shown how to read it and use it. The examples used are bits and pieces of formulas you will encounter as you go through this text, so you will be able to use this section as a reference when you encounter a formula in some other part of the book.

Order of Operations

There are some conventions in mathematics that help keep things organized, just as the convention of driving on the right-hand side of the road in Canada helps keep vehicle traffic from becoming dangerous and chaotic. One set of conventions is that some mathematical operations are always done first, before others, when an algebraic expression is being evaluated.

The order of operations is as follows:

1. First evaluate anything in *brackets*.
2. Then evaluate anything with an *exponent*.
3. Working from left to right, do any *division or multiplication*.
4. Working from left to right, do any *addition or subtraction*.

It is important to remember that the conventions about the order of operations always apply, and if you have trouble remembering what a mathematical formula means, it may help you to go back to these conventions.

Summation Notation

Suppose we have a data set for the variable called x (this is an example of a mathematical convention—x is a commonly assigned variable name, although we could have used any other letter, such as y or z). Suppose x is the name we give to the variable that is the ages of the five students sitting in the front row of statistics class. If we collect the data from the five students, then the data set consists of

(17, 21, 20, 18, 20)

By convention, we refer to the first number in the data set (17) as x_1, that is, "x-one." This value is called x_1 simply because it is the *first* number in the list. Similarly, we would call the *fourth* number (which is 18) x_4, and so on.

Suppose we wanted to write an expression to indicate that all of the numbers in the data set should be added up, and we know that there will be five students in the front row of class, but we have not yet collected the data. We could write

$$x_1 + x_2 + x_3 + x_4 + x_5$$

as an indication of our plans. However, this is tedious to write out, and of course, writing it out could be time-consuming if there were hundreds or thousands of values.

Adding up all the numbers in a data set is one of the arithmetic tasks you will have to do repeatedly in statistics. The commonly accepted notation for this task is Σ, which is a capital Greek letter called *sigma*. Several Greek letters are commonly used in statistics notation, and you will learn several more as you work through the material in this text.

The expression $\sum_{i=1}^{5} x_i$ is mathematical notation that means: "add up the first five values in your data set called x." This notation uses the subscript i as an index number. You can expand the notation by writing out the expression nestled beside the sigma operator, moving the index number from its lower limit (1 in this example) one by one to its upper limit (5 in this example), and then adding all the values.

$$\sum_{i=1}^{5} x_i$$

Write out the expression with each successive index number

$$x_1 \; x_2 \; x_3 \; x_4 \; x_5$$

and then add the terms (this is what the Σ operator is telling you to do)

$$x_1 + x_2 + x_3 + x_4 + x_5$$

So we see that

$$\sum_{i=1}^{5} x_i = x_1 + x_2 + x_3 + x_4 + x_5$$

But what if we do not even know how many observations there are in the data set? There is a convention for this too. When we do not know, we refer to the total number of observations as n. If we wanted to indicate that all of the (unknown number of) observations in the data set should be added up, we would simply write:

$$\sum_{i=1}^{n} x_i$$

This expression is used so often that there is an even shorter version, which is

$$\Sigma x$$

By convention, whenever the sigma sign does not have upper and lower limits, it means "add them all up." This more streamlined notation is the kind that will be used throughout this text.

Some Examples

Suppose we have two data sets. One is a set of observations for a variable x, as follows:

$(1, 3, 5, 7)$

Another is a set of observations for a variable y, as follows:

$(2, 4, 6, 8)$

$$\Sigma x = x_1 + x_2 + x_3 + x_4 = 1 + 3 + 5 + 7 = 16$$

3.1a

Evaluating Σx

How would you evaluate the following expression?

Σx^2

In this case, the x-values must be squared. Since exponents must be evaluated before addition (based on the order of operations), this means that each x-value is first squared, and then the resulting terms are added.

$$\Sigma x^2 = x_1^2 + x_2^2 + x_3^2 + x_4^2 = 1^2 + 3^2 + 5^2 + 7^2 = 1 + 9 + 25 + 49 = 84$$

3.1b

Evaluating Σx^2

How would you evaluate the following expression?

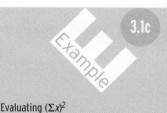

$(\Sigma x)^2$

In this case, the expression in the brackets must be evaluated *before* any squaring is done (based on the order of operations). Therefore, all of the x-values must first be added up, and then the resulting sum should be squared, as follows:

$$(\Sigma x)^2 = (x_1 + x_2 + x_3 + x_4)^2 = (1 + 3 + 5 + 7)^2 = 16^2 = 256$$

Notice that the result in Example 3.1c is quite different from the result in Example 3.1b. Be sure you understand and remember the difference between these two expressions.

3.1c

Evaluating $(\Sigma x)^2$

How would you evaluate the following expression?

Σxy

If you know that both x and y are variables, this expression would be evaluated as follows:

$$\Sigma xy = x_1 y_1 + x_2 y_2 + x_3 y_3 + x_4 y_4 = 1(2) + 3(4) + 5(6) + 7(8)$$
$$= 2 + 12 + 30 + 56 = 100$$

3.1d

Evaluating Σxy

Multiplication comes before addition in the conventions for order of operations. The first x-variable will be multiplied by the first y-variable, the second x-variable will be multiplied by the second y-variable, and so on, and the resulting terms will be added.

Example 3.1e

Evaluating $\Sigma(x - 6)$

How would you evaluate this expression?

$$\Sigma(x - 6)$$

What is in the brackets must be evaluated first for each value of x, and the resulting terms then added.

$$\Sigma(x - 6) = (x_1 - 6) + (x_2 - 6) + (x_3 - 6) + (x_4 - 6)$$
$$= (1 - 6) + (3 - 6) + (5 - 6) + (7 - 6)$$
$$= (-5) + (-3) + (-1) + 1$$
$$= -8$$

Example 3.1f

Evaluating $\Sigma(x - 6)^2$

How would you evaluate this expression?

$$\Sigma(x - 6)^2$$

In this case, each of the terms in the brackets must be evaluated first, and then these results must be squared, and the resulting squares must be added up.

$$\Sigma(x - 6)^2 = (x_1 - 6)^2 + (x_2 - 6)^2 + (x_3 - 6)^2 + (x_4 - 6)^2$$
$$= (1 - 6)^2 + (3 - 6)^2 + (5 - 6)^2 + (7 - 6)^2$$
$$= (-5)^2 + (-3)^2 + (-1)^2 + 1^2$$
$$= 25 + 9 + 1 + 1$$
$$= 36$$

Example 3.1g

Evaluating $\displaystyle\sum \frac{(x - 6)^2}{n - 1}$

How would you evaluate this expression?

$$\sum \frac{(x - 6)^2}{n - 1}$$

In this case, we can use the result from Example 3.1f to get the answer. Remember that n does not vary: it is a number. Although the number will be unknown until we determine how many observations there are in the data set, it is still just a number (not a variable). Therefore, the Σ operator has no effect on it, and this expression can be rewritten and evaluated for the data set as follows:

$$\sum \frac{(x - 6)^2}{n - 1} = \frac{1}{n - 1} \sum (x - 6)^2 = \frac{1}{4 - 1}(36) = \frac{1}{3}(36) = 12$$

How would you evaluate this expression?

$$\Sigma(x - 6)(y - 3)$$

First the terms in the brackets must be evaluated for all of the first, second, third, . . . sets of observations in the two data sets. The resulting pairs must be multiplied, and then all of those products must be added.

Evaluating $\Sigma(x - 6)(y - 3)$

$$\Sigma(x - 6)(y - 3)$$
$$= (x_1 - 6)(y_1 - 3) + (x_2 - 6)(y_2 - 3) + (x_3 - 6)(y_3 - 3) + (x_4 - 6)(y_4 - 3)$$
$$= (1 - 6)(2 - 3) + (3 - 6)(4 - 3) + (5 - 6)(6 - 3) + (7 - 6)(8 - 3)$$
$$= (-5)(-1) + (-3)(1) + (-1)(3) + (1)(5)$$
$$= 5 + (-3) + (-3) + 5$$
$$= 4$$

DEVELOP YOUR SKILLS 3.1

1. Using the y data set (2, 4, 6, 8), evaluate Σy.

2. Using the y data set (2, 4, 6, 8), evaluate Σy^2. Also evaluate $(\Sigma y)^2$. Why are the answers different?

3. Using the y data set (2, 4, 6, 8), calculate $\dfrac{\Sigma x}{n}$. Calculate $\dfrac{\Sigma x}{n}$ for the x data set (1, 3, 5, 7).

4. Calculate $\Sigma(x-4)$. Calculate $\Sigma(y-5)$.

5. Consider the data set: 34, 67, 2, 31, 89, 35. For this data set, calculate:
   a. Σx
   b. Σx^2
   c. $\dfrac{\Sigma x}{n}$
   d. $\sqrt{\dfrac{\Sigma x^2 - \dfrac{(\Sigma x)^2}{n}}{n - 1}}$

3.2 MEASURES OF CENTRAL TENDENCY

As we have already seen in Chapter 2, the weekly sales at Barrie, Orillia, and Newmarket are quite different. One of the ways to capture this difference is with a measure of central tendency. Some measure of central tendency is generally of interest when we examine a data set, and the *mean* is often used to represent a typical—or middle—value of a group of numbers. Another useful measure of central tendency is the *median*. A third, sometimes useful indication of central tendency is the *mode*.

The Mean

The mean is the most widely used measure of central tendency. You already know how to calculate a mean, although you may have referred to it as the *average*. We will capture the arithmetic in a formula, and introduce the usual notation for the mean of a data set.

mean a measure of central tendency calculated by adding up all the numbers in the data set, and then dividing by the number of numbers

Normally we are working with sample data. If this is the case, we use the notation $\bar{x}$ (x-bar) to denote the sample mean. We can then write the following formula to summarize the arithmetic involved in calculating the mean: the **mean** is calculated by adding up all the numbers in the data set, and then dividing by the number of numbers.

$$\bar{x} = \frac{\Sigma x}{n}$$

There is another symbol that we use to represent the mean (usually unknown) of a population of data. It is the Greek letter μ (called *mu* and pronounced "mew"). It is calculated the same way, that is:

$$\mu = \frac{\Sigma x}{n}$$

but the difference in notation is very important. We often say, for instance, that we are using $\bar{x}$ to estimate μ. In other words, we calculate $\bar{x}$ from the sample data, to get an estimate of the true population mean μ. (It is quite usual to use Greek letters to represent unknown population parameters, and you will encounter other Greek letters as you work through the material in this text.) The sample mean $\bar{x}$ is a sample statistic, and the population mean μ is the corresponding population parameter.

The mean is the balance point of all the numbers in the data set. This is always true, because of the way in which the mean is calculated. Consider a sample data set of the days absent for a random sample of a company's workers in 2005.

(2, 2, 4, 4, 5, 5, 5, 6, 7, 7, 8)

In this case, the mean of the sample of days absent for 2005 is

$$\bar{x} = \frac{\Sigma x}{n} = \frac{2 + 2 + 4 + 4 + 5 + 5 + 5 + 6 + 7 + 7 + 8}{11} = 5$$

The mean of 5 is the balance point of this data set, as illustrated in Exhibit 3.1 below.

Exhibit 3.1

The Mean Is the Balance Point of a Data Set

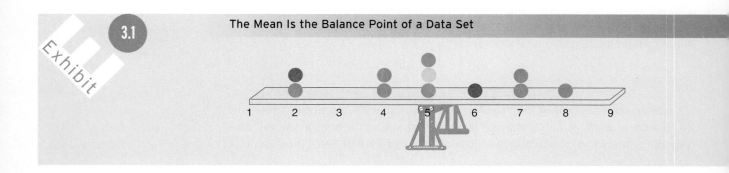

If you put a number line on a pivot at the 5 location, and added equal-sized weights at the locations corresponding to the data points, the number line would be balanced. Another related feature of the mean is as follows: the sum of all the deviations from the mean is zero. The concept of a deviation from the mean is illustrated in Exhibit 3.2.

Deviations from the Mean

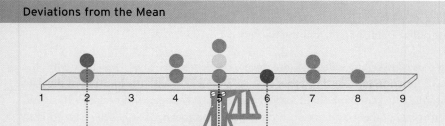

Exhibit 3.2

The **deviation from the mean** for each data point is the distance of the point from the mean value. For example, for the data point represented by the red weight (at 6) on the number line in Exhibit 3.2, the deviation from the mean would be $6 - 5 = +1$. For the data point represented by the yellow weight (at 5), the deviation from the mean would be $5 - 5 = 0$. For the data point represented by the green weight (at 2), the deviation from the mean would be $2 - 5 = -3$. Notice that a negative deviation from the mean indicates that a data point is below the mean. A positive deviation from the mean indicates that a data point is above the mean. We could use mathematical notation to indicate how we calculate this.

deviation from the mean for each data point, the distance of the point from the mean value

$$\text{deviation from the mean} = (x - \bar{x})$$

The table shown in Exhibit 3.3 summarizes the calculation of the deviation from the mean for every data point in the sample data set.

Table of Deviations from the Mean

Exhibit 3.3

Deviations from the Mean for
Employee Absences (mean is 5)

x	$x - \bar{x}$
2	$2 - 5 = -3$
2	$2 - 5 = -3$
4	$4 - 5 = -1$
4	$4 - 5 = -1$
5	$5 - 5 = 0$
5	$5 - 5 = 0$
5	$5 - 5 = 0$
6	$6 - 5 = +1$
7	$7 - 5 = +2$
7	$7 - 5 = +2$
8	$8 - 5 = +3$

sum of deviations from the mean $\sum(x - \bar{x}) = 0$

Of course, we could also use mathematical notation to summarize what we have observed, that is, that $\sum(x - \bar{x}) = 0$. We will use this mathematical relationship again, when we discuss measures of variability.

3.2a

Instructions

Using Excel to calculate the mean

Anne Morgan wants to calculate the average weekly sales for the Barrie, Newmarket, and Orillia locations. (The data are available on the CD that comes with the text, in the directory called DataChap03, and the file called EXA03–2a.xls.)

Anne uses Excel to calculate the mean weekly sales. She does this with the AVERAGE function in Excel. She types in =AVERAGE( ), with the location of the data typed into the brackets. Note that Excel will return the average, with no label. It is good practice to type a label beside the cell containing the mean, so it will be easy to read the worksheet. The average weekly sales for the three locations in 2006 are shown in Exhibit 3.4 below.

3.4

Mean Weekly Sales 2006

Location	Mean Weekly Sales, 2006
Barrie	$532.58
Newmarket	$747.26
Orillia	$993.42

As we would have suspected from the histograms we saw in Chapter 2 (see p. 47), mean weekly sales are highest for the Orillia location, and lowest for the Barrie location.

While the mean is the most widely used measure of central tendency, it has some limitations. It can be used only for quantitative data. It is also affected by extreme values (outliers), and this makes it a less satisfying indication of central tendency for skewed data sets, as Example 3.2b below illustrates.

3.2b

The mean is greatly affected by extreme values

Suppose that just one of the numbers in the sample data set of employee days absent illustrated in Exhibit 3.1 is changed. We will replace the 8 with a value of 58 (this might happen, for example, if one employee had a serious illness and missed a long period of work).

Data set 1: 2, 2, 4, 4, 5, 5, 5, 6, 7, 7, 8

Data set 2: 2, 2, 4, 4, 5, 5, 5, 6, 7, 7, 58

What is the new mean?

$$\bar{x} = \frac{\sum x}{n} = \frac{2 + 2 + 4 + 4 + 5 + 5 + 5 + 6 + 7 + 7 + 58}{11} = 9.55$$

The new mean is now greater than 10 out of 11 points in the data set, and it no longer seems to be a very good measure of central tendency. Notice that the data point of 58 would be an outlier in the new data set. Because it is so different from the other data points, it should be investigated for accuracy.

The Median

As we have seen in Example 3.2b, the mean is sometimes not the best measure of central tendency. When a data set is significantly skewed, or consists of ranked data, the median is a better measure of the middle of the data set. The **median** is the middle value (if there is a unique middle value), or the average of the two middle values (when there is not a unique middle value) in an ordered data set.

So, for example, for the original data set of days absent for 2005, the median would be 5. When the data are ordered, 5 is the unique middle value. There are five values in the data set that are higher than 5, and another five values that are lower than 5.

> Data set 1: 2, 2, 4, 4, 5, 5, 5, 6, 7, 7, 8

> Notice that 5 is still the median when the data set is altered, with the 8 replaced by 58.

> Data set 2: 2, 2, 4, 4, 5, ⑤, 5, 6, 7, 7, **58**

In this case, when the data are highly skewed, the median is a more typical value than the mean, and a better measure of central tendency.

There is (strangely enough) no generally accepted notation for the median. As well, there can be no formula for the median, but there is a formula for the *location* of the median. In a data set of n numbers, the median will be located at the $0.5(n + 1)^{th}$ place (this holds true whether we are dealing with sample or population data). So, for example, in the data set of 11 numbers, the median is located at the $0.5(n + 1) = 0.5(11 + 1) = 0.5(12) = 6^{th}$ place, as we found above.

Excel will calculate the median for a data set. The MEDIAN function is used. In a spreadsheet, type in =MEDIAN() with the location of the data typed into the brackets. Note that Excel will return the median, with no label. It is good practice to type a label beside the cell containing the median, so it will be easy to read the worksheet.

> median the middle value (if there is a unique middle value), or the average of the two middle values (when there is not a unique middle value) in an ordered data set

Instructions

Example 3.2c

The ages of a randomly selected group of applicants for the office manager's job at a small law firm are as shown in Exhibit 3.5 below.

What is the median age of the applicants? What is the mean age? Which would be the better measure of central tendency, the mean or the median—and why?

Finding the median in a data set

Exhibit 3.5

Ages of a Sample of Applicants for the Office Manager's Job at a Law Firm
43
44
48
43
22
36
41
35
36

(continued)

Exhibit 3.5   (Continued)

47
40
38
39
31
35
23
39
39
34
42

The first step in finding the median age is to order the data. Please note: one of the most common mistakes made by students in locating the median (with manual calculations) is forgetting this important step. Don't forget to order the data before you locate the median! Exhibit 3.6 below shows the ordered data set.

Exhibit 3.6

Sample of Law Firm Applicants' Ages, Ordered

Ages of a Sample of Applicants for the Office Manager's Job at a Law Firm	Ordered Ages
43	22
44	23
48	31
43	34
22	35
36	35
41	36
35	36
36	38
47	10th place: 39
40	11th place: 40
38	40
39	40
31	41
35	42
23	43
40	43
40	44
34	47
42	48

In this sample, there is no unique middle value. There are two middle values, and so we average them to get the median.

$$\text{median} = \frac{39 + 40}{2} = 39.5$$

This is straightforward, because the data set is small. We can also use the location formula to identify the median. In this sample, $n = 20$, so the median will be located at the $0.50(n + 1) = 0.50(20 + 1) = 0.50(21) = 10.5^{\text{th}}$ place. The meaning of "10.5" in this context is illustrated in Exhibit 3.7 below. The median is equal to:

10th place value $+ 0.5$(distance between 10th and 11th place value)

The 10th data point is 39, and the 11th is 40, so the median can be calculated as:

$39 + 0.5(40 - 39) = 39 + 0.5 = 39.5$

Meaning of a 10.5th Location

39	39.5	40
10th place	10.5^{th} place	11th place

Exhibit **3.7**

The median age of the job applicants is 39.5.

The average age is 37.85 (you should verify this). This data set is somewhat skewed, because there are a couple of unusually young job applicants (one is 22 and one is 23). In this case, the median is a somewhat better measure of central tendency, because it is less affected by the unusually low values.

We can check our manual calculation of the median by using Excel. The data set for this problem is available on the CD that comes with the text, in a directory called DataChap03, and a file called EXA03–2c.xls. Excel also calculates the median as 39.5.

 EXA03-2C.xls
Set

The Mode

Another measure of central tendency that is sometimes useful is the **mode**, the most frequently occurring value in the data set. In the data set of employee absences (from Exhibit 3.1), the mode is 5. It is the most frequently occurring value in the data set, and it is also a good indication of central tendency.

Original data set: $= (2, \ 2, 4, \underbrace{4, 5, 5, 5}_{\text{mode}}, 6, 7, 7, 8)$

However, if a data set contains only unique values, there will be no mode. As well, there may be more than one mode, and in such a case, the multiple modes may not be a good measure of central tendency. Consider the following slightly amended data set, which is the employee absences data, with one value removed.

Data set with one value removed: $(2, 2, 4, 4, 5, 5, 6, 7, 7, 8)$

This amended data set has four modes: 2, 4, 5, and 7. It would be hard to justify that all four are good measures of central tendency, or a good reflection of a typical value. For

mode the most frequently occurring value in the data set

this reason, the mode is most often used in reference to the shape of a histogram. For example, a histogram with the shape shown in Exhibit 3.8 would be described as *unimodal*, as there is a unique modal class.

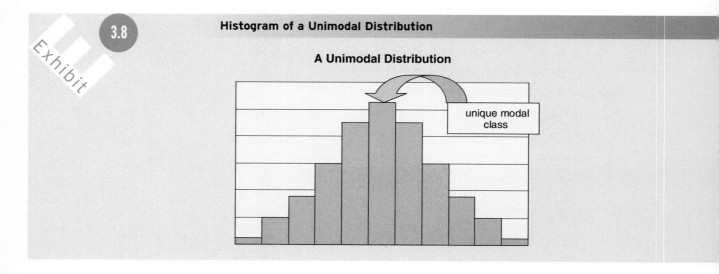

Exhibit 3.8

Histogram of a Unimodal Distribution

A Unimodal Distribution

unique modal class

In contrast, the distribution shown in Exhibit 3.9 would be described as *bimodal*, because there are two distinct modal classes.

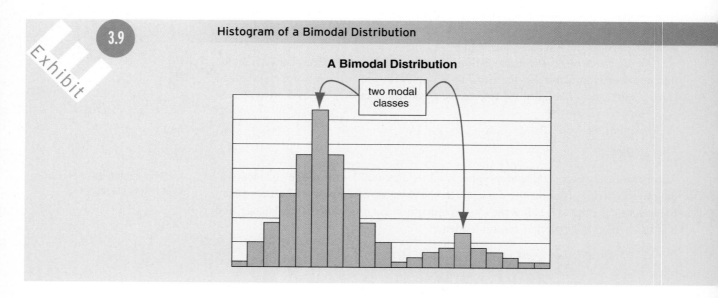

Exhibit 3.9

Histogram of a Bimodal Distribution

A Bimodal Distribution

two modal classes

Instructions

Excel will calculate the mode for a data set (if one exists), using the MODE function. In a spreadsheet, type in =MODE() with the location of the data typed into the brackets. If there is more than one mode, Excel will not identify this, and it will return only the first mode in the data set. Note that the Excel MODE function will return the mode with no label. It is good practice to type a label beside the cell containing the mode, so it will be easy to read the worksheet.

<table>
<tr><td>

1. The mean is the preferred measure of central tendency for quantitative data. However, it is significantly affected by outliers, and should not be used for significantly skewed data.
2. The median can be used as a measure of central tendency for quantitative or ranked data. It is preferred for quantitative data when the data are skewed.
3. The mode can give an indication of central tendency for quantitative or ranked data, but there may be no mode, or there may not be a unique mode.

</td><td>

Guide to Decision Making

Choosing a Measure of Central Tendency

</td></tr>
</table>

DEVELOP YOUR SKILLS 3.2

1. Calculate the mean, median, and mode for the ages of customers in the survey of drugstore customers. **Set** Which is the best measure of central tendency in this data set? Why? See file called DYS 03-2-1.xls.
2. Calculate the mean and the median for the incomes of customers in the survey of drugstore customers. **Set** Comment on the difference between the two measures of central tendency. Which one is best, and why? See file called DYS 03-2-2.xls.
3. Eileen McLeary runs a car repair facility in Nelson, BC. She has collected customer counts for a random sample of days. The data set is shown below in Exhibit 3.10. Calculate an appropriate measure of central tendency for this data set.

4. The mean amount of the most recent purchase made by customers in the survey of drugstore customers is $26.19. The median amount is $26.44. What does this tell you about the distribution of customer purchases?
5. In Develop Your Skills 2.2, Exercise 5, you looked at histograms of data collected by Patty Plainte (see p. 51). Calculate the mean marks for Ms. Nice's class and for Mr. Mean's class. Based on this calculation, which **Set** group of students performed better? Can you attribute this difference in performance to the difference in teachers? See file called DYS 03-2-5.xls.

McLeary's Repair Shop, Daily Customer Counts

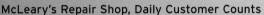

24	19	27	41	17
26	34	17	25	31
23	29	26	18	24
31	24	14	29	36
31	29	40	12	26

Exhibit 3.10

3.3 MEASURES OF VARIABILITY

We are usually also interested in the variability in a data set. When Anne Morgan created histograms for the weekly sales of the Barrie, Orillia, and Newmarket locations, she noticed that Barrie's weekly sales were more variable than the other two locations', with Newmarket's sales exhibiting the least variability. Anne is now wondering if there is some numerical measure she can use to capture the differences among the data sets.

The Range

The **range** of the data set is a number that is calculated as the difference between the maximum and minimum values in the data set.

Notice that the range is a *single* number. For the Barrie weekly sales data, the maximum value is $1,042.54, and the minimum value is $109.67.

$$\text{range} = \text{maximum} - \text{minimum} = \$1,042.54 - \$109.67 = \$932.87$$

Notice that the range is *not* "$109.67 to $1,042.54," which is how you might have described it in everyday English (this does not correspond to the precise meaning of the term in statistical language). The ranges for the weekly sales at the three locations are shown in Exhibit 3.11 below.

Exhibit 3.11

Three Locations' Ranges of Weekly Sales

Weekly Sales, 2006	Range
Barrie	$932.87
Newmarket	$539.31
Orillia	$905.81

The ranges do seem to correspond to our impressions of the differences in variability in the histograms of weekly sales (see Exhibit 2.39 on p. 48). The range is highest for Barrie, and lowest for Newmarket.

The Standard Deviation

While the range can give an indication of the variability in the data, it does not distinguish between data sets with the same maximum and minimum values but very different variability, as illustrated by the two histograms in Exhibit 3.12 below.

Exhibit 3.12

Two Data Sets, Same Maximum and Minimum Values

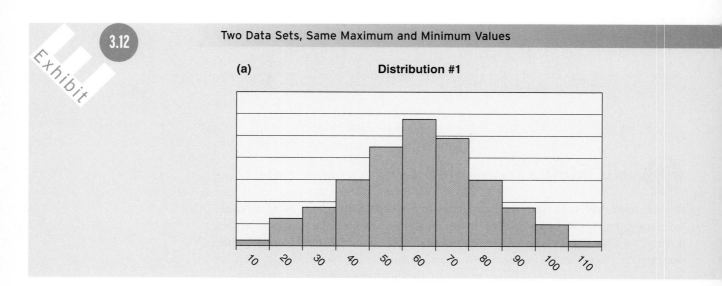

(a)   **Distribution #1**

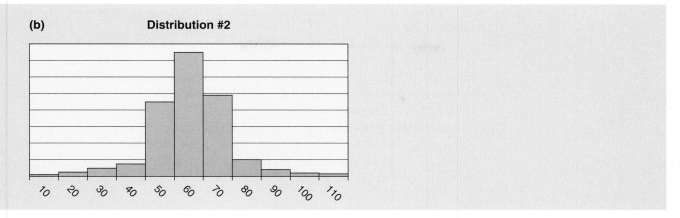

The data in distribution #2 is much less variable than in distribution #1, but the range could be exactly the same.

A better measure of variability would focus not only on the maximum and minimum values in the data set, but on every single value. The most-used measure of variability does this. It is called the **standard deviation**, and is a measure of variability in a data set that is based on deviations from the mean.

You have already been introduced to the idea of a deviation from the mean. The deviations from the mean for the data points in distribution #1 will, overall, be larger than the deviations from the mean for the data points in distribution #2. If we want a single number to represent the variability in the two data sets, we could consider calculating the average deviation from the mean for each. Unfortunately, if we did this, we would realize that the average deviation from the mean was zero for both distributions. This is because (as was pointed out earlier), for all data sets, the deviations from the mean will *total* to zero. The positive and negative deviations from the mean always exactly cancel each other out, for every data set.

In order to prevent this cancelling out, calculation of the standard deviation involves *squaring* the deviations from the mean. An average of the squared deviations is then calculated. Finally, the square root of this value is taken, to "undo" the squaring and return the measure to units like the units in the original data set.

When we refer to the standard deviation of the population, the notation is σ, which is the Greek letter *sigma* (this is the lower-case version of the upper-case Σ that is used to denote summation). The formula capturing the arithmetic for calculation of the population standard deviation is as follows.

$$\sigma = \sqrt{\frac{\Sigma(x - \mu)^2}{n}}$$

Some statistical formulas require the use of the squared version of this measure, which is called the variance, with the notation (reasonably enough) σ^2.

The notation for a sample standard deviation is different, and in this case, the formula is also slightly different. We denote the sample standard deviation with "s." The formula differs in that the divisor is $(n - 1)$, not n, as follows:

$$s = \sqrt{\frac{\Sigma(x - \bar{x})^2}{n - 1}}$$

standard deviation a measure of variability in a data set that is based on deviations from the mean

The sample mean is referred to as $\bar{x}$ in this formula for the sample standard deviation, as it should be.

We use s to estimate the (usually unknown) value of σ. The formula shown above for s (with the $n-1$ divisor) provides a reliable and unbiased estimate of σ. It can be shown that if the sample standard deviation was calculated with just n in the divisor, it would tend to underestimate the true population value, which is of course undesirable. Dividing by $n-1$ removes this bias.

Let's return to the data set from the beginning of the chapter, about employee absences for 2005, to demonstrate calculation of the standard deviation. Since we have already calculated deviations from the mean for this data set, we will build on this base, as shown below in Exhibit 3.13.

3.13

Employee Absences Data: Deviations

Employee Absences, 2005

x	$(x-\bar{x})$	$(x-\bar{x})^2$
2	$2-5 = -3$	$(-3)^2 = 9$
2	$2-5 = -3$	$(-3)^2 = 9$
4	$4-5 = -1$	$(-1)^2 = 1$
4	$4-5 = -1$	$(-1)^2 = 1$
5	$5-5 = 0$	$0^2 = 0$
5	$5-5 = 0$	$0^2 = 0$
6	$6-5 = +1$	$1^2 = 1$
7	$7-5 = +2$	$2^2 = 4$
7	$7-5 = +2$	$2^2 = 4$
8	$8-5 = +3$	$3^2 = 9$
sum	0	38 ← $\sum(x-\bar{x})^2$

There are 11 data points in this sample data set, so $n=11$. We can now use the formula, as follows.

$$s = \sqrt{\frac{\sum(x-\bar{x})^2}{n-1}} = \sqrt{\frac{38}{11-1}} = \sqrt{\frac{38}{10}} = \sqrt{3.8} = 1.949$$

The standard deviation for this sample data set is 1.949. What does this mean? Think of it, for now, simply as a measure, or a score, of variability. The larger the standard deviation is, the more variable the data are. To illustrate, let us return to the weekly sales data of the vending machines at Barrie, Newmarket, and Orillia that Anne Morgan is investigating.

3.3a

Calculating standard deviation with Excel

Anne Morgan wants to calculate the standard deviation for weekly sales at Barrie, Newmarket, and Orillia. Anne must first decide if she has sample or population data. In this case, she has weekly sales for the entire year of 2006, and she realizes that she could consider this population data, particularly if all she will ever be interested in is 2006 sales. However, Anne realizes that the vending machines have been in business since before 2006, and will be in business for some years after. With that in mind, she decides to treat the data as sample data.

Anne can use the STDEV function in Excel to find the sample standard deviation. She types in =STDEV( ), with the location of the data typed into the brackets. Note that Excel will return the standard deviation with no label. It is good practice to type a label beside the cell containing the standard deviation, so it will be easy to read the worksheet. When Anne completes this task, she produces the summary table shown in Exhibit 3.14.

Instructions

Three Locations' Standard Deviations

Weekly Sales, 2006	Standard Deviation
Barrie	239.638
Newmarket	120.758
Orillia	182.466

3.14 Exhibit

Once again, we see that the standard deviation matches what we have already observed in the variability of weekly sales at the three locations. The standard deviation is highest in the most variable data set of weekly sales (Barrie), and lowest in the least variable data set (Newmarket).

The formula for standard deviation introduced above can help you understand how deviations from the mean are used to calculate this measure of variability. However, if you want to calculate the sample standard deviation by hand with a calculator, you should use another version of the formula, as follows.

$$s = \sqrt{\frac{\Sigma x^2 - \frac{(\Sigma x)^2}{n}}{n - 1}}$$

We will refer to this as the "computational formula" for the standard deviation. This formula will result in the same value for the standard deviation, and although it looks more complicated, you will find this version of the formula quicker to use, so be sure that you master it. Example 3.3b illustrates the use of the computational formula.

We will use the computational formula to calculate the standard deviation for the employee absences data set. This will show you how to use the formula, and should reassure you that it gives the same end result. Exhibit 3.15 shows the employee absences data, and some other calculations.

3.3b Example

Calculating the standard deviation with the computational formula

$$s = \sqrt{\frac{\Sigma x^2 - \frac{(\Sigma x)^2}{n}}{n - 1}}$$

First, break the formula into pieces.

$$s = \sqrt{\frac{\Sigma x^2 - \frac{(\Sigma x)^2}{\textcircled{n}}}{n - 1}}$$

Exhibit **3.15**

Employee Absences, 2005

x	x^2
2	$2^2 = 4$
2	$2^2 = 4$
4	$4^2 = 16$
4	$4^2 = 16$
5	$5^2 = 25$
5	$5^2 = 25$
5	$5^2 = 25$
6	$6^2 = 36$
7	$7^2 = 49$
7	$7^2 = 49$
8	$8^2 = 64$
$\Sigma x = 55$	$\Sigma x^2 = 313$

As usual, n is the number of observations, and n = 11 in this case.

$$s = \sqrt{\frac{\Sigma x^2 - \frac{(\Sigma x)^2}{n}}{n-1}}$$

Σx^2 requires squaring each data point, and then adding the results (see the second column of Exhibit 3.15). In this case, $\Sigma x^2 = 2^2 + 2^2 + 4^2 + 4^2 + 5^2 + 5^2 + 5^2 + 6^2 + 7^2 + 7^2 + 8^2 = 313$

$$s = \sqrt{\frac{\Sigma x^2 - \frac{(\Sigma x)^2}{n}}{n-1}}$$

$(\Sigma x)^2$ requires adding up all the data points (see the first column of Exhibit 3.15 above), and then squaring the sum

$$(\Sigma x)^2 = (2 + 2 + 4 + 4 + 5 + 5 + 5 + 6 + 7 + 7 + 8)^2 = 55^2 = 3025$$

Now we have all the pieces necessary for the calculation, as follows.

$$s = \sqrt{\frac{\Sigma x^2 - \frac{(\Sigma x)^2}{n}}{n-1}} = \sqrt{\frac{313 - \frac{3025}{11}}{11-1}} = \sqrt{\frac{313 - 275}{10}} = \sqrt{\frac{38}{10}} = \sqrt{3.8}$$
$$= 1.949$$

which matches our earlier calculation of the standard deviation.

With some practice, you should be able to do this calculation, using the memory of your calculator, without stopping to write down any intermediate answers. Since you will probably be required to do this calculation on tests or exams, you should learn to do it efficiently.

The Empirical Rule   So far, we have used the standard deviation as a measure of variability, with a larger standard deviation indicating greater variability. However, for certain types of data sets, the standard deviation has some very useful additional properties.

We can regard the standard deviation as a typical deviation from the mean in a data set. We can also use the standard deviation as a unit of measurement, something that is very common and very useful in statistical decision-making techniques. The Empirical Rule is an introduction to this use of the standard deviation.

Consider the following data set, which represents the number of diners at a small Winnipeg restaurant, for a random sample of 30 different evenings. The sample data are shown below in Exhibit 3.16.

Number of Diners at a Winnipeg Restaurant, Random Sample of 30 Evenings

104	112	94
100	109	93
115	100	104
107	106	97
88	113	118
107	94	111
121	103	97
80	96	97
111	88	108
125	101	109

Exhibit **3.16**

For the Empirical Rule to apply, the data set must be symmetric and bell-shaped. The desired shape is shown in Exhibit 3.17 below.

Distribution Shape Required for Application of the Empirical Rule

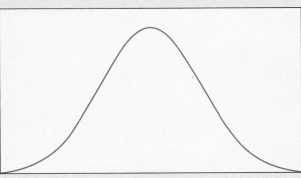

Distribution Shape Required for Application of the Empirical Rule

Exhibit **3.17**

One way to check on the symmetry and shape of the data is to create a histogram for the data set. If the histogram is approximately the correct shape, it is appropriate to apply the Empirical Rule. A histogram of the data set of diners (see the table in

Exhibit 3.16) is shown below in Exhibit 3.18. Since this histogram has the required shape, we can proceed with the Empirical Rule.

3.18 Histogram of Data on Diners at a Winnipeg Restaurant

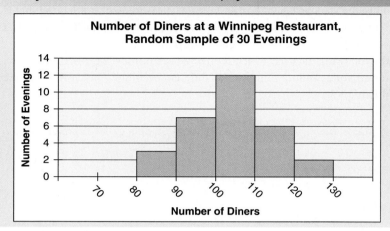

The Empirical Rule applies *only* to a symmetric bell-shaped distribution:

1. About 68% of the data points will lie within one standard deviation of the mean.
2. About 95% of the data points will lie within two standard deviations of the mean.
3. Almost all of the data points will lie within three standard deviations of the mean.

The Empirical Rule is illustrated in Exhibit 3.19 below. Strictly speaking, the Empirical Rule applies to *population* data that have a symmetric bell-shaped distribution. However, if we have a reasonably large sample data set, we can use $\bar{x}$ as an estimate of μ, and s as an estimate of σ, and apply the rule to make some inferences about the population.

3.19 The Empirical Rule for Symmetric Bell-Shaped Distributions

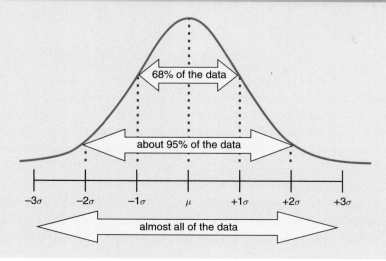

The sample data set of the number of diners at the Winnipeg restaurant has a mean of 103.6 and a standard deviation of 10.23. First, we will directly apply the Empirical Rule (we have already established that the sample data have a symmetric, bell-shaped distribution). This will illustrate the use of the standard deviation as a unit of measurement. Then we will explore the implications of the Empirical Rule.

For the Winnipeg diners data set, $s = 10.23$. This distance will be the unit of measurement in the discussion.

$$\underset{10.23}{\vdash \overset{1s}{\rule{2cm}{0.4pt}} \dashv}$$

1. About 68% of the numbers of diners visiting the Winnipeg restaurant in the evening are within one standard deviation of the mean. We will explore the data set by first locating the points that are one standard deviation away from the mean (that is, 10.23 units away from the mean of 103.6). We have to calculate

$$\overline{x} + 1s = 103.6 + 10.23 = 113.83$$

We also have to calculate

$$\overline{x} - 1s = 103.6 - 10.23 = 93.37$$

Exhibit 3.20 below illustrates this calculation.

One Standard Deviation from the Mean

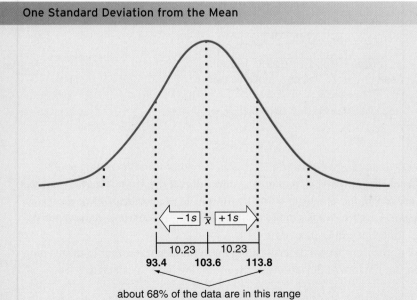

$-1s$ $\overline{x}$ $+1s$

10.23   10.23

93.4   103.6   113.8

about 68% of the data are in this range

Exhibit **3.20**

How many of the sample data points are in the interval (93.4, 113.8)? We count 22. This means that in the sample, $\frac{22}{30} = 73.3\%$ of the data points are within one standard deviation of the mean. This is a little above the 68% suggested by the Empirical Rule, but still reasonably close.

2. About 95% of the numbers of diners visiting the Winnipeg restaurant in the evening are within two standard deviations of the mean. We have to calculate

$$\bar{x} + 2s = 103.6 + (2)10.23 = 124.06$$

We also have to calculate

$$\bar{x} - 2s = 103.6 - (2)10.23 = 83.14$$

Exhibit 3.21 below illustrates this calculation.

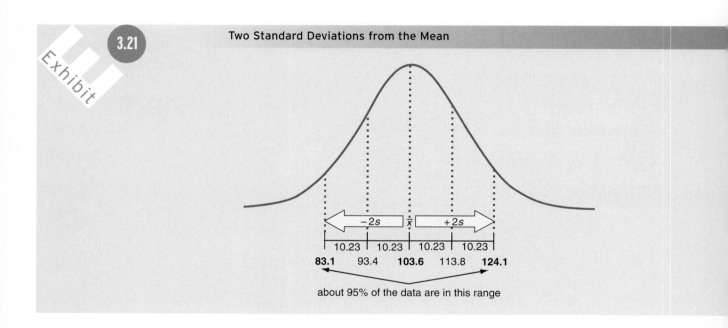

3.21 *Exhibit*

Two Standard Deviations from the Mean

about 95% of the data are in this range

How many of the sample data points are in the interval (83.1, 124.1)? We count 28. This means that in the sample, $\frac{28}{30} = 93.3\%$ of the data points are within two standard deviations of the mean. This is a little below the 95% suggested by the Empirical Rule, but still quite close.

3. Almost all of the numbers of diners visiting the Winnipeg restaurant in the evening are within three standard deviations of the mean. We have to calculate

$$\bar{x} + 3s = 103.6 + (3)10.23 = 134.29$$

We also have to calculate

$$\bar{x} - 3s = 103.6 - (3)10.23 = 72.91$$

Exhibit 3.22 below illustrates this calculation.

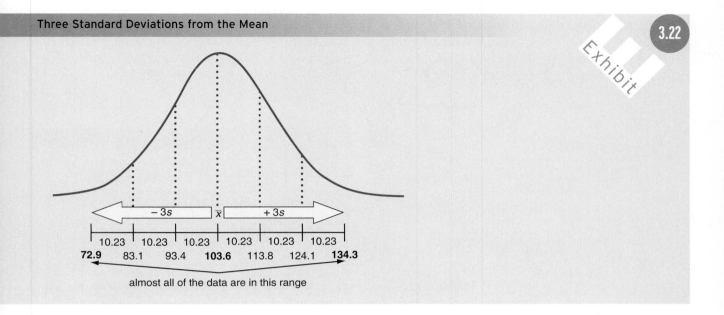

Three Standard Deviations from the Mean

3.22

Exhibit

almost all of the data are in this range

How many of the sample data points are in the interval (72.9, 134.3)? All of them are, so in the sample 100% of the data points are within three standard deviations of the mean. This is what the Empirical Rule suggests (almost all).

So what? This is a case where we can infer characteristics of the population data on the basis of the sample data, presuming that we have a representative sample. While the Empirical Rule holds (approximately) for the sample data, what is more interesting is that it also probably holds for the population data.

This means, for example (using the third part of the Empirical Rule), that this restaurant would almost never have fewer than about 73 diners in the evening, or more than about 134 diners. This could have implications for ordering supplies and setting staff schedules.

Because wasted food is expensive, the restaurant might decide to plan for a maximum of 124 diners in the evening. The second part of the Empirical Rule says that about 95% of the numbers of diners at this Winnipeg restaurant, in the evening, will be between 83.1 and 124.1. If 95% of the numbers of diners are within this range, then only 5% are outside this range, in what are referred to as the "tails" of the distribution. Since the distribution appears to be symmetric, this would indicate that about 2.5% of the time, there would be fewer than 83 diners, and about 2.5% of the time, there would be more than 124 diners. Planning for a maximum of 124 diners, then, would leave the restaurant short of supplies only about 2.5% of the time—a risk the owner might take, to save on costs. Exhibit 3.23 below illustrates this calculation.

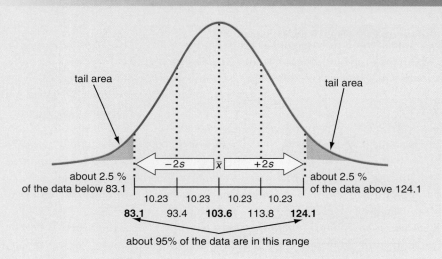

The Tails of the Distribution

tail area   tail area

about 2.5 %   about 2.5 %
of the data below 83.1   of the data above 124.1

10.23   10.23   10.23   10.23

83.1   93.4   **103.6**   113.8   **124.1**

about 95% of the data are in this range

3.23 *Exhibit*

In Chapter 8, we will explore these estimation procedures in more detail. For now, the Empirical Rule provides a way to make some educated guesses about population data, *if the sample data set is symmetric and bell-shaped.* Example 3.3c shows another application of the Empirical Rule.

3.3c *Example*

Applying the Empirical Rule

Jeff Ng has just received the mark on his first statistics test. He would like to have some idea of how his mark compares to the marks of other students on the test, but his professor will not tell him what his relative standing is. However, Jeff's professor did give Jeff a random sample of 50 of the marks of the other students who took the test. When Jeff created a histogram of the sample data set, it was fairly bell-shaped and symmetric. The sample mean mark was 58.3, and the sample standard deviation was 13.7. Jeff's mark was 75.

The sample size, at 50, is fairly large. Because a histogram of the sample data is bell-shaped and symmetric, Jeff feels comfortable applying the Empirical Rule. Jeff starts by calculating the points that are one standard deviation from the mean.

$$\bar{x} + 1s = 58.3 + 13.7 = 72$$

$$\bar{x} - 1s = 58.3 - 13.7 = 44.6$$

The Empirical Rule suggests that about 68% of the marks on the Statistics test are between 44.6 and 72. This means that about 32% of the marks are outside this range. Because the distribution is symmetric, Jeff expects that about 16% (half of 32%) of the marks are above 72, and about 16% are below 44.6. Since Jeff's mark is 75, he estimates that just fewer than 16% of his fellow students got a better mark than he did. Although Jeff was hoping to achieve a higher mark on the test, he feels better knowing that he is likely in the top 16% of the class. However, he makes a commitment to spend more time doing statistics exercises so that he can do better on the next test.

Example 3.3c illustrated the usefulness and also the limitations of the Empirical Rule. For example, Jeff's estimate of the percentage of students with a higher mark than he received is approximate, because his mark is not exactly one or two standard deviations from the mean. In fact, Jeff's mark is $75 - 58.3 = 16.7$ marks away from the mean, and this is a distance of $\frac{16.7}{13.7} = 1.22$ standard deviations. Similarly, it is difficult to estimate what percentage of students passed the test, as the mark of 50 is not exactly one or two standard deviations from the mean, but $\frac{50 - 58.3}{13.7} = -0.6$ standard deviations from the mean. In Chapter 5, you will be introduced to the normal distribution, and you will learn how to go beyond the limitations of the Empirical Rule to deal with cases like these.

The Interquartile Range

While the standard deviation is the preferred measure of variability for quantitative data, it is significantly affected by outliers (which is reasonable, since it is based on deviations from the mean, a measure also affected by outliers).

Let us return to the data sets of employee days absent we used to explore the mean.

Data set 1 (Original data): (2, 2, 4, 4, 5, 5, 5, 6, 7, 7, 8)

Data set 2 (New data): (2, 2, 4, 4, 5, 5, 5, 6, 7, 7, **58**)

Now, calculate the standard deviation for data set 1 (we will refer to this as s_1).

$$s_1 = \sqrt{\frac{\Sigma x^2 - \frac{(\Sigma x)^2}{n}}{n-1}} = \sqrt{\frac{313 - \frac{(55)^2}{11}}{10}} = 1.949$$

The standard deviation for data set 2 will be:

$$s_2 = \sqrt{\frac{\Sigma x^2 - \frac{(\Sigma x)^2}{n}}{n-1}} = \sqrt{\frac{3.613 - \frac{(105)^2}{11}}{10}} = 16.158$$

Now, there is no doubt that data set 2 is more variable than data set 1. However, the standard deviation was significantly changed by the change in only one data point. In this case, where data set 2 is significantly skewed by the outlier of 58, the standard deviation gives a somewhat misleading impression of variability. As a contrast, consider data set 3 shown below, which has a mean of 9.5 (almost the same mean as data set 2) and a standard deviation of 16.0 (very close to that of data set 2). Data set 2 is repeated, for ease of comparison.

Data set 2: 2, 2, 4, 4, 5, 5, 5, 6, 7, 7, 58

Data set 3: −12, −10, −9, 0, 2, 12, 16, 22, 27, 27, 30

Most people would agree that there is more variability in data set 3 than in data set 2. It seems that the standard deviation gives a somewhat misleading measure of variability for the skewed data set.

So, what could we use instead? The answer is: the interquartile range. But before we discuss its calculation, we must first discuss quartiles and percentiles.

P^{th} percentile x_p, the data point that is above P% of the data points

If 75% of the other marks on a test were lower than yours, then your test mark is the 75th percentile. If 38% of the other marks were lower than yours, then your test mark is the 38th percentile. In general, if P% of the data points are lower than x_p, then x_p is the **P^{th} percentile**.

Notice that the median is the 50th percentile, as 50% of the data points are below the median. To locate a particular percentile, we use a formula that is a generalization of the location formula for the median. In a data set of n numbers, the Pth percentile will be located at the $\frac{P}{100}(n + 1)^{th}$ place.

3.3d

Finding the 75th percentile

Find the 75th percentile for the following data set:

3, 6, 8, 8, 12, 34, 56, 79

In this case, there are 8 data points, so $n = 8$. The 75th percentile will be located at the $\frac{P}{100}(n + 1) = \frac{75}{100}(8 + 1) = 6.75^{th}$ place.

Since the data are already ordered, we can proceed directly to the calculation of the 75th percentile. The 6th data point is 34, and the 7th data point is 56. The value of the 6.75th location is equal to:

6th place value + 0.75(distance between 6th and 7th place values)

The 75th percentile will be:

$$34 + 0.75(56 - 34) = 34 + 0.75(22) = 34 + 16.5 = 50.5$$

Exhibit 3.24 illustrates the 6.75th location.

3.24

Meaning of a 6.75 Location

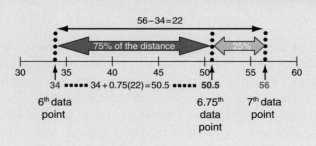

1st quartile usually denoted Q_1; is the 25th percentile

3rd quartile usually denoted Q_3; is the 75th percentile

Quartiles are particular percentiles, which divide the data set into quarters. The **1st quartile**, usually denoted Q_1, is the 25th percentile. The **3rd quartile**, usually denoted Q_3, is the 75th percentile. Of course, the median is also the 2nd quartile.

The **interquartile range (IQR)** is $Q_3 - Q_1$. It measures the range of the middle 50% of the data values. Because the IQR is calculated on the basis of the middle 50% of the data values, it is not affected by outliers, and so is a better measure of variability for skewed data sets.

Calculate the interquartile range for data set 2 and data set 3, first discussed above.

Data set 2: 2, 2, 4, 4, 5, 5, 5, 6, 7, 7, 58

Data set 3: $-12, -10, -9, 0, 2, 12, 16, 22, 27, 27, 30$

For data set 2:

Calculating the interquartile range

Q_1's location is $0.25(n + 1) = 0.25(11 + 1) = 0.25(12) = 3$

So Q_1 is the 3rd data point (the data are already ordered).

$Q_1 = 4$

Similarly, Q_3's location is $0.75(n + 1) = 0.75(11 + 1) = 0.75(12) = 9$

Q_3 is the 9th data point, so $Q_3 = 7$

$IQR_2 = Q_3 - Q_1 = 7 - 4 = 3$

Repeat for data set 3, which also has 11 data points.

Q_1 is the 3rd data point (the data are already ordered).

$Q_1 = -9$

Q_3 is the 9th data point.

$Q_3 = 27$

$IQR_3 = 27 - (-9) = 36$

Notice that IQRs are quite different for these two data sets, which share an almost equal standard deviation. In this case, the interquartile range is a better measure of variability, because it more appropriately distinguishes between these two data sets.

Notice that the interquartile range can also be used as a measure of variability for ranked data, although there are not many instances where this would be useful.

Excel does not have a built-in tool to calculate the interquartile range. However, Excel does have a function to calculate Q_1 and Q_3. Exhibit 3.25 below shows the function arguments dialogue box for the QUARTILE function, which is activated by typing =QUARTILE into a spreadsheet cell.

Instructions

3.25

Function Arguments Dialogue Box for the QUARTILE **Function**

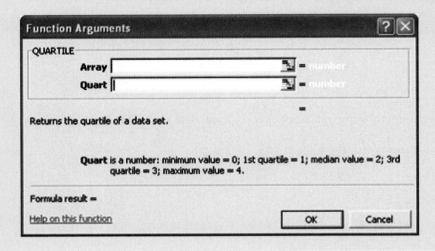

The dialogue box is filled in as follows:

1. Array is the location of the data to be analyzed.
2. Quart is where you indicate which quartile you want to calculate. As the dialogue box indicates when you activate this input area, you must enter 1 for the 1st quartile, and 3 for the 3rd quartile.

The Excel function will output the quartile value, with no label. You should type a label into an adjacent cell, so that your spreadsheet is easy to read.

Once you have calculated the 1st and 3rd quartiles, you have to enter a formula into Excel to calculate the difference. Exhibit 3.26 below shows an excerpt from an Excel spreadsheet

3.26

IQR Calculation in Spreadsheet

	A	B
1	Data Set 2	
2	2	
3	2	
4	4	
5	4	
6	5	
7	5	
8	5	
9	6	
10	7	
11	7	
12	58	
13		
14	Q1	=QUARTILE(A2:A12,1)
15	Q3	=QUARTILE(A2:A12,3)
16	IQR	=B15-B14
17		

where the IQR is calculated. The formulas are revealed for your reference. Notice that the labels in cells A14, A15, and A16 have been typed in so that the spreadsheet is easy to read.

You may be surprised to find that the values calculated by Excel for the quartiles (and thus the interquartile range) do not exactly match the manual calculations above. Exhibit 3.27 summarizes the differences.

Differences Between Manual Calculations and Spreadsheet   3.27

Exhibit

Data Set 2 Calculations		
	As Calculated by Hand	As Calculated by Excel
Q_1	4	4
Q_3	7	6.5
IQR	3	2.5

As you can see from the table above, Excel's calculations of the quartiles differ from the calculations shown in the manual method above. It is interesting that there is not widespread agreement about how to calculate percentiles and quartiles. The manual method shown above is widely accepted (and somewhat easier), and you should continue to use it with confidence. Because the methods differ somewhat in their results, you should always compare IQRs calculated using the same method so that your comparisons will be valid.

Guide to Decision Making

Choosing a Measure of Variability

1. The standard deviation is the preferred measure of variability for quantitative data. However, it is significantly affected by outliers, and should not be used for badly skewed data.
2. The interquartile range can be used as a measure of variability for quantitative or ranked data. It is preferred for quantitative data when the data are skewed. When comparing data sets, never compare an IQR calculated by hand with an IQR calculated with Excel, as the methods are not directly comparable.

DEVELOP YOUR SKILLS 3.3

1. Calculate an appropriate measure of variability for the ages of customers in the survey of drugstore customers. Would it be appropriate to use the Empirical Rule with this data set? See file called DYS 03-3-1.xls.

2. Calculate an appropriate measure of variability for the incomes of customers in the survey of drugstore customers. See file called DYS 03-3-2.xls.

3. Eileen McLeary runs a car repair facility in Nelson, BC. She has collected customer counts for a random sample of days. The data set is shown below in Exhibit 3.28. Calculate an appropriate measure of variability for this data set.

McLeary's Repair Shop, Daily Customer Counts   3.28

Exhibit

24	19	27	41	17
26	34	17	25	31
23	29	26	18	24
31	24	14	29	36
31	29	40	12	26

4. Would it be appropriate to apply the Empirical Rule to the data set of customer counts for the McLeary Repair Shop, shown above in Exhibit 3.28? Why or why not?

5. Eileen McLeary wants to have enough mechanics on hand to take care of her customer requests, but she does not want to be paying mechanics to be sitting around doing nothing. Eileen needs to know a reasonable upper limit on the number of customers, so she can plan her staff schedule. About 97.5% of the time, what is the maximum number of customers should Eileen plan for?

3.4 MEASURES OF ASSOCIATION

Correlation analysis can be used to measure the degree (and direction) of association between two variables.

The Pearson Correlation Coefficient for Quantitative Variables

In Chapter 2, Anne Morgan created a scatter diagram to investigate the relationship between daily sales at the Barrie vending machine and the number of people entering the mall at the nearest door. This scatter diagram is reproduced below, in Exhibit 3.29.

 Scatter Diagram for the Barrie Data

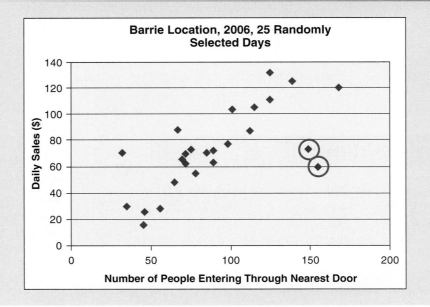

There appears to be a positive relationship between the two variables, although the relationship is less than perfect. If sales were perfectly predicted by door traffic, the relationship would appear as depicted in Exhibit 3.30.

Perfect Positive Linear Relationship

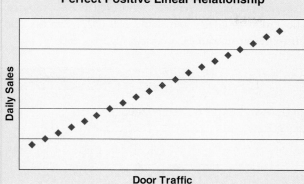

Perfect Positive Linear Relationship

Exhibit 3.30

The linear correlation between two variables is stronger, the closer the x–y data points are to lining up in a straight line.

The **Pearson correlation coefficient** is a numerical measure that indicates the strength of the linear relationship between two quantitative variables. The notation for the Pearson correlation coefficient is r (or sometimes the "Pearson r"), and the coefficient can take on values between −1 and +1. An r of −1 signifies a perfect negative linear relationship. An r of +1 signifies a perfect positive relationship. An r of 0 indicates no apparent linear relationship. The relationship is stronger, the further the r-value is from zero in either direction. Exhibit 3.31 illustrates.

Pearson correlation coefficient a numerical measure that indicates the strength of the linear relationship between two quantitative variables

Values of the Pearson Correlation Coefficient

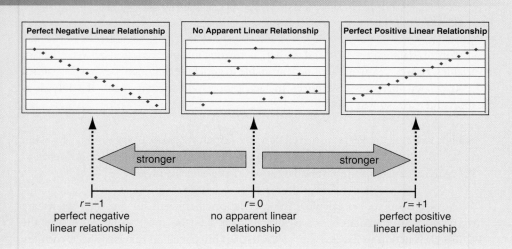

Exhibit 3.31

While interpretation of the r-value cannot follow any fixed rules, it is generally considered that an r in the range from −0.5 to +0.5 indicates that there is no strong linear relationship between the x- and y-values. Note that an r-value close to +1 or −1 does not *prove* that there is a cause-and-effect relationship between the x- and y-variables involved—all we can say is that the variables are highly correlated, and any conclusions about causality must be made on the basis of an understanding of the context of the data being analyzed.

For example, Exhibit 3.32 below shows a scatter diagram of data on Canada's Gross Domestic Product (GDP), and exports of goods and services, from 1980 to 2005. (Source: Table 380-0016, Gross Domestic Product (GDP) and Table 380-0027, Exports and Imports of Goods and Services, **http://estat.statcan.ca,** accessed August 4, 2006.)

Canadian GDP and Exports, 1980-2005

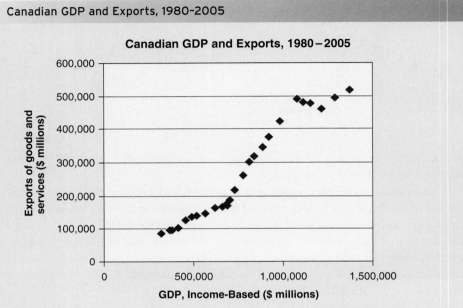

Source: Adapted from Statistics Canada CANSIM in E-STAT, CANSIM Table 380-0016, "Gross Domestic Product (GDP)" and Table 380-0027, "Exports and imports of goods and services," http://estat.statcan.ca/cgiwin/CNSMCG1.EXE?Lang=E&RootDir=ESTAT/&CANSIMFILE=EStat/English/CII_1_E.htm.

For this data set, $r = 0.95$ and so there is a strong linear correlation between the two variables. However, it would not be reasonable to conclude that increases in GDP *caused* the associated increases in exports. In fact, exports are a component of GDP, so as exports increase, so will GDP.

> A high value of the Pearson correlation coefficient, r, (close to $+1$ or close to -1) indicates a strong linear correlation between the x- and y-variables, but it does *not* prove that changes in the x-variable caused changes in the y-variable.

Instructions

We will use Excel to calculate the correlation coefficient for any data set we are investigating. To calculate r for a sample data set (the most usual case), use the **PEARSON** function in Excel. Type =**PEARSON()** into a cell on the worksheet, with the locations of the x- and y-values input into the brackets. You should create a label beside the cell where the function result is located, so that your worksheet is easy to read.

Excel calculates the correlation coefficient for the Barrie data on sales and door traffic to be $+0.71$. This is an indication of a moderately strong positive relationship between daily sales and door traffic.

Calculation of *r* Is Based on Deviations from the Mean

While the correlation coefficient is not normally calculated by hand, the formula on which it is based is of interest. This formula illustrates that r is based on deviations from the mean, for both *x*- and *y*-values.

One formula for r is as follows.

$$r = \frac{\Sigma(x - \bar{x})(y - \bar{y})}{(n - 1)s_x s_y}$$

where s_x is the standard deviation of the *x*-values in the sample, and s_y is the standard deviation of the *y*-values in the sample. The sign of r is determined by the numerator, $\Sigma(x - \bar{x})(y - \bar{y})$, because all of the terms in the denominator will always be positive.

The numerator of this formula for *r* is the sum of the products of the deviations from the mean for each pair of (x, y) variables. An example will help you understand how this formula works. Exhibit 3.33 below shows a scatter diagram of results from a study of a weight-loss program run by a fitness club that wants to advertise its success. A random sample of participants reported how many weeks they had been on the program, and the number of pounds lost.

Scatter Diagram of Weight-Loss Results

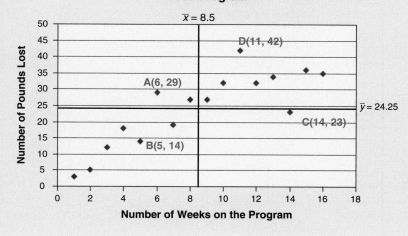

3.33 *Exhibit*

$$r = \frac{\Sigma(x - \bar{x})(y - \bar{y})}{(n - 1)s_x s_y}$$

We will focus on the numerator of this calculation, since it governs the sign of the *r*-value. While we will not evaluate every term in $\Sigma(x - \bar{x})(y - \bar{y})$ it is instructive to look at some examples. For this data set, $\bar{x} = 8.5$ and $\bar{y} = 24.25$, and these means are shown on the graph in Exhibit 3.33, dividing the graph into four areas.

Now consider the point labelled A on the graph, at (6, 29). For this point,

$$(x_A - \bar{x})(y_A - \bar{y}) = (6 - 8.5)(29 - 24.25) = (-2.5)(4.75) = -11.875$$

which is, of course, a negative number. Notice that the term for the other point in this area of the graph will also produce a negative number. This is because in this area of the graph, all of the x-values are *below* $\bar{x}$, and so $(x - \bar{x}) < 0$. However, all of the y-values are *above* $\bar{y}$, so $(y - \bar{y}) > 0$. Multiplying a negative number by a positive number yields a negative result.

With similar reasoning, we can see that all of the points in the area of the graph where B is located will contribute a *positive* term to the calculation of r. All of the x-values in this area are *below* $\bar{x}$, and so $(x - \bar{x}) < 0$. All of the y-values are *below* $\bar{y}$, so $(y - \bar{y}) < 0$. Multiplying two negative terms yields a positive result. For the point labelled B, the term is

$$(x_B - \bar{x})(y_B - \bar{y}) = (5 - 8.5)(14 - 24.25) = (-3.5)(-10.25) = +35.875$$

Following on, you should be able to see that all of the points in the area of point C on the graph will contribute a negative term to the calculation of r. All of the points in the area of point D will contribute a positive term to the calculation of r. These conclusions are summarized in Exhibit 3.34 below.

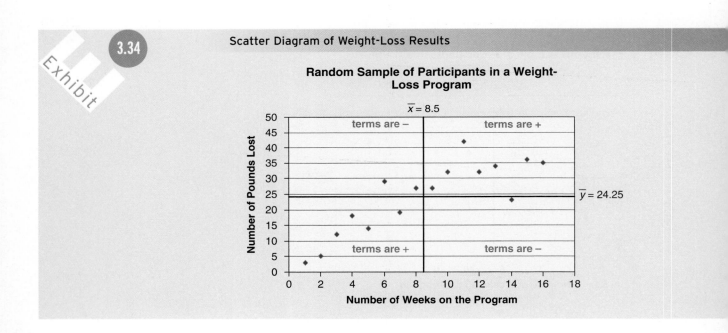

Exhibit 3.34

Scatter Diagram of Weight-Loss Results

Finally, you should be able to see that the number and the value of positive terms (there are 13 positive terms) in the calculation of r far outweigh the number of negative terms (there are only 3 negative terms) for this data set. As a result, $\sum(x - \bar{x})(y - \bar{y})$ will be a positive number, leading to a positive correlation coefficient. In fact, in this case, $r = 0.84$, indicating a strong positive correlation between the number of weeks on the program and the number of pounds lost.

Now, apply the same reasoning about positive and negative terms in the $\sum(x - \bar{x})(y - \bar{y})$ calculation for the scatter diagram shown in Exhibit 3.35 below.

r < 0 for a Negative Relationship

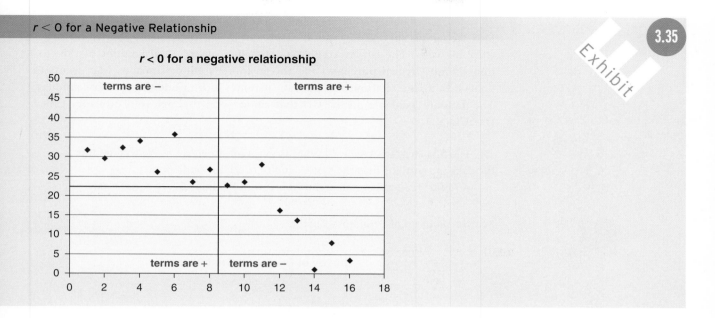

r < 0 for a negative relationship

In this case, the negative terms far outweigh the positive terms, and so the correlation coefficient will be negative. In fact, for the data set shown above, $r = -0.87$.

Now consider the case illustrated by Exhibit 3.36 below. In this case, the numbers and values of the positive and negative terms in the $\sum(x - \bar{x})(y - \bar{y})$ calculation will

r Is Close to Zero

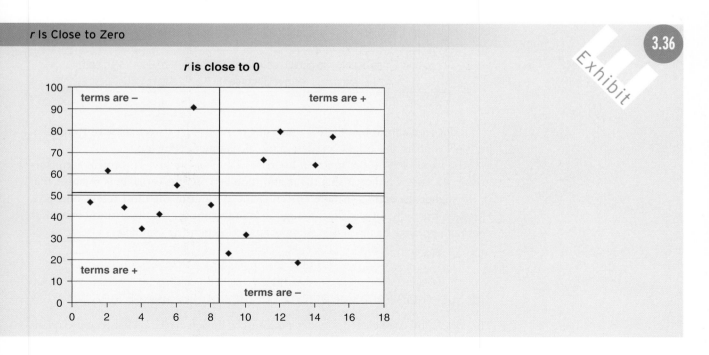

r is close to 0

approximately offset each other, leading to a correlation coefficient near zero. In fact, for this data set, $r = 0.08$.

Example 3.4a

Calculating the Pearson correlation coefficient

EXA03-4a.xls
Set

Max Weber has surveyed a random sample of the customers who shop at the drugstore he owns. The survey results contain data on the total amount of the customer's most recent purchase, and the customer's annual income. Max wants to know if there is a relationship between customer income and the purchase amount. The data are available on the CD that comes with the text, in a directory called DataChap03.

The first step is to create a scatter diagram for the data set. We will use this to see if the data appear to be linearly related, and to check for outliers.

An Excel scatter diagram is shown below in Exhibit 3.37.

Exhibit 3.37

Scatter Diagram of Drugstore Customer Survey Results

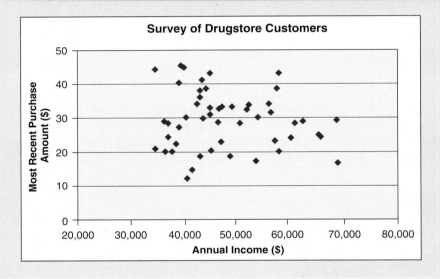

It does not appear that there is much of a relationship between these two variables, but we'll confirm the lack of correlation by calculating the Pearson r.

Use Excel's **PEARSON** function to arrive at an r of -0.119. This might seem surprising, because it indicates that the relationship between the variables is negative, that is, the higher the annual income, the *lower* the amount of the most recent purchase. However, this value of r is close enough to zero to confirm the observation that there does not appear to be much of a relationship between the two variables.

The Spearman Rank Correlation Coefficient for Ranked Variables

The correlation coefficient r provides a measure of linear correlation between two quantitative variables. However, it has some weaknesses:

1. The correlation coefficient r does not identify non-linear correlations.
2. The correlation coefficient r can be greatly affected by outliers, to the extent that it may give a misleading indication of correlation.

There is an alternative measure of correlation that identifies both linear and non-linear correlations, and is not so affected by outliers. It is called the Spearman rank correlation coefficient, and is usually denoted r_S. The Spearman rank correlation coefficient has another advantage: it can be used to calculate a measure of association between two variables when one or both of them are ranked data. The **Spearman rank correlation coefficient** is a numerical measure that indicates the strength of the relationship (linear or non-linear) for two variables, one or both of which may be ranked.

The Spearman rank correlation coefficient is calculated in the same way as the Pearson correlation coefficient, but is based on the ranks of the x- and y-variables, not the actual values of the data. The ranking process is fairly straightforward. All of the x-values are ranked from smallest to largest, with ranks from 1 to n. Similarly, all y-values are ranked from smallest to largest, with ranks from 1 to n. The only complication that arises is when a value occurs more than once. When this occurs, the ranks of the tied values are averaged. Example 3.4b below illustrates the ranking process, and calculation of the Spearman rank correlation coefficient.

Spearman rank correlation coefficient a numerical measure that indicates the strength of the relationship (linear or non-linear) for two variables, one or both of which may be ranked

Example 3.4b

A head office manager is concerned about the employee turnover rate at some of the local branches of its operation. The manager surveys employees at the branches. On the basis of the survey results, the manager ranks the branches according to how satisfied the employees are with the working conditions at the branch (the branch rated #1 is the branch where employees are most satisfied). The manager then collects some data on employee turnover. He calculates the employee turnover rate as the number of employee terminations (because of firing or someone quitting) as a percentage of the total number of employees. Since a high turnover rate may suggest retention issues, the manager wants to see if there is an association between the branch ranking by the employees and the turnover rate. The data for the 10 branches is shown in Exhibit 3.38 below.

Calculating the Spearman rank correlation coefficient

Exhibit 3.38

Employee Ranking and Turnover Rate

Branch Location	Rank of Branch by Local Employees	Employee Turnover Rate
Whitby	1	4.50
Ajax	2	4.00
Pickering	3	4.50
Oshawa	4	5.70
Scarborough	5	15.20
Oakville	6	14.70
Woodbridge	7	10.30
Mississauga	8	13.40
Hamilton	9	9.60
Waterloo	10	17.00

Since the rankings of each branch by the local employees are ranked data, the manager must use the Spearman rank correlation coefficient to measure the association between the two variables. The ranking process is illustrated in Exhibit 3.39 below.

3.39

Ranking Process

Branch Location	Rank of Branch by Local Employees	Employee Turnover Ratio	Ranks to Be Assigned	Assigned Ranks
Whitby	1	4.50	3	2.5
Ajax	2	4.00	1	1
Pickering	3	4.50	2	2.5
Oshawa	4	5.70	4	4
Scarborough	5	15.20	9	9
Oakville	6	14.70	8	8
Woodbridge	7	10.30	6	6
Mississauga	8	13.40	7	7
Hamilton	9	9.60	5	5
Waterloo	10	17.00	10	10

In this case, the ranking of the branches is already done. The employee turnover ratios must also be ranked, from smallest to largest, with ranks from 1 to 10. There are two locations with the same employee turnover ratio (Whitby and Pickering). The ranks that must be assigned to the two locations are 2 and 3. Since the employee turnover ratios are the same, the associated ranks should also be the same. This is arranged by averaging the two ranks involved, and assigning the averaged rank to each location. We assign a rank of $\frac{2 + 3}{2} = 2.5$ to each location. This is highlighted in Exhibit 3.39 above.

Now that the ranks are calculated, the Spearman rank correlation coefficient can be calculated. This can be done with Excel, as usual, using the **PEARSON** function on the ranks of the data. The result for this data set is $r_S = 0.75$ (you should check this in Excel). This indicates that the ranking of the branch by local employees is fairly strongly associated with the employee turnover ratio. The higher the turnover ratio, the lower the ranking by employees.

Notice that in Example 3.4b, the employee rating of 1 corresponds to "best," and so the lowest assigned rank corresponds to the best employee rating. If we thought that low employee turnover ratios (low assigned ranks) were associated with good ratings by employees (low assigned ranks), we would expect a positive correlation between the assigned ranks.

However, suppose the employee data was the number of employees with at least three years of service. The lowest assigned rank of 1 would then be assigned to the lowest number of employees with at least three years of experience, the worst case. In this case, if we thought that good employee ratings (low ranks) were associated with a greater number of employees with at least three years of service (high ranks), we would expect a negative correlation between the assigned ranks. Always take a minute to think about the rankings before you assign them, and you will avoid confusion about the meaning of the Spearman *r*. Otherwise, you might confuse the meaning of negative and positive correlations.

While ranking the data was straightforward in this example, it can be quite tedious for larger data sets. Unfortunately, Excel does not provide for this ranking process. There is an Excel add-in that comes with the text, which ranks the data correctly and calculates the Spearman rank correlation coefficient.

Once the add-ins are installed (see instructions on p. ii), click on Tools, then Non-parametric Tools, and then select Spearman Rank Correlation Coefficient Calculations as illustrated in Exhibit 3.40 below.

Instructions

Non-parametric Tools Dialogue Box

3.40

Exhibit

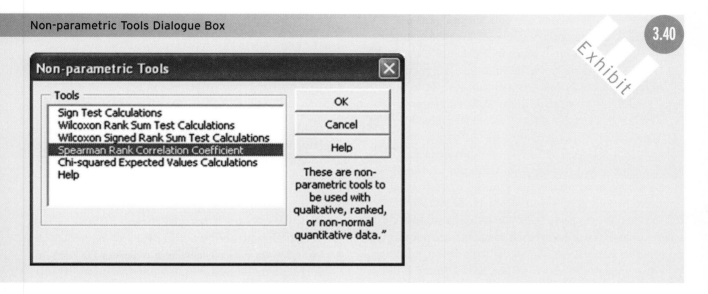

Exhibit 3.41 shows the next dialogue box, which is self-explanatory.

Spearman Rank Correlation Coefficient Calculation

3.41

Exhibit

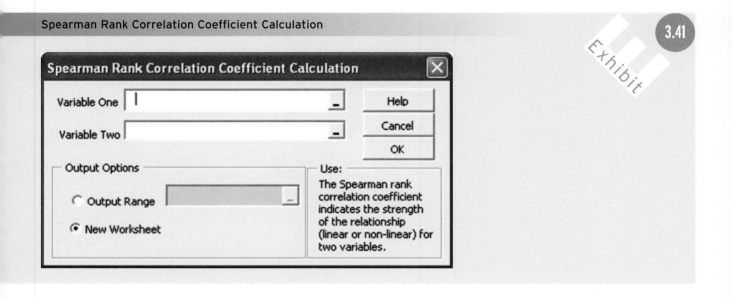

You must indicate where the sample data are located, and where you want the output to go. The output will be as shown below in Exhibit 3.42.

3.42

Spearman Rank Correlation Coefficient Calculation

Spearman Rank Correlation Coefficient Calculation	
Spearman r	0.747724

Guide to Decision Making

Choosing a Measure of Association

1. The Pearson correlation coefficient (r) is the preferred measure of association for quantitative data. However, it can be affected by outliers, and is less reliable when these are present in the data. As well, it is a measure of linear association only.
2. The Spearman rank correlation coefficient (r_S) can be used as a measure of both linear and non-linear association between two variables. It may provide a better indication of the correlation between two quantitative variables when there are outliers in the data. The Spearman rank correlation coefficient can also be used as a measure of association when one or both of the variables are ranked.

DEVELOP YOUR SKILLS 3.4

1. In Develop Your Skills 2.5, Exercise 1, you were asked to produce a scatter diagram for data on household income and monthly spending on restaurant meals. Calculate an appropriate measure of association for these two variables. See file called DYS03-4-1.xls.

2. Jack runs a small convenience store, where he sells freshly baked cookies. Jack has experimented by charging different prices for the cookies on randomly selected days, and recording the quantity sold. A scatter diagram for the data is shown below in Exhibit 3.43.

3.43

Scatter Diagram of Cookie Prices and Quantities Sold

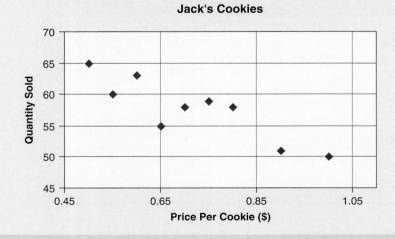

Which of the following *r*-values best matches this scatter diagram? Why?

a.   +0.75

b.   −0.88

c.   +0.22

d.   −0.11

3. The Human Resources Department is interested in seeing if there is a relationship between the rankings of new hires by the recruiter who hired them and by the employees' supervisor. A random sample of 10 employees is selected from a large group of employees hired by a single recruiter, to be assigned to a single supervisor. The recruiter is asked to rank the 10 employees at the time of hiring. The supervisor is then asked to rank them a year later. See file called DYS03-4-3.xls.

Does it appear that there is a correlation between the recruiter's rankings and the supervisor's rankings? Explain.

4. A college professor has collected data for a random sample of 45 students. She has asked them to keep track of their total hours of paid employment for the semester, and she has also recorded each student's semester average mark. Does it appear that there is a linear correlation between the hours of work and the average mark? Explain. See file called DYS03-4-4.xls.

5. Two of the data sets depicted in Exhibit 3.44 below have an *r*-value of 0.73, and one has an *r*-value of −0.90. Indicate which *r*-value belongs to each graph. How can the *r*-values be the same for the two graphs you have picked?

Three Graphs of Service and Salary

Exhibit

3.44

a)

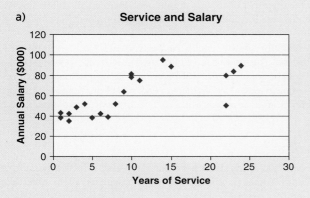

b)

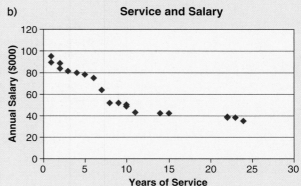

c)

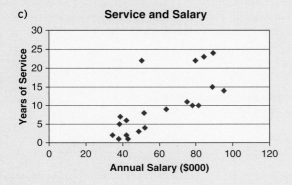

Chapter Summary

3

Some Useful Notation

Summation notation is frequently used in statistical formulas. For example:

$$\sum_{i=1}^{n} x_i = \sum x = x_1 + x_2 + x_3 + \cdots + x_n$$

Examples 3.1a–h on pages. 91–93 illustrate how to evaluate some terms you will encounter in statistical formulas.

Measures of Central Tendency

Some measure of central tendency is generally of interest when we examine a data set.

The mean is calculated by adding up all the numbers in the data set, and then dividing by the number of numbers. The sample mean is given the notation $\bar{x}$, and the population mean is given the notation $\propto$. Formulas for their calculation are:

$$\bar{x} = \frac{\sum x}{n} \text{ and } \mu = \frac{\sum x}{n}$$

The deviation from the mean for each data point is the distance of the point from the mean value. The sum of all the deviations from the mean is always zero, that is, $\sum(x - \bar{x}) = 0$.

While the mean is the most widely used measure of central location, it has some limitations. It can be used only for quantitative data. It is also affected by extreme values, and this makes it a less satisfying indication of central tendency for skewed data sets. Calculation of the mean is done with the **AVERAGE** function in Excel.

The median is the middle value (if there is a unique middle value), or the average of the two middle values (when there is not a unique middle value) in an ordered data set. There is no commonly accepted notation for the median. In a data set of n numbers, the median will be located at the $0.50(n + 1)^{\text{th}}$ place (this holds true for both sample and population data). Calculation of the median is done with the **MEDIAN** function in Excel.

The mode is another measure of central tendency that is sometimes useful. The mode is the most frequently occurring value in the data set. The mode is most often used in reference to the shape of a histogram. Calculation of the mode can be done with the **MODE** function in Excel, although this function will identify only one mode (the first in the list), and is therefore not reliable for multi-modal data.

A Guide to Decision Making for choosing a measure of central tendency is shown on page 101.

Measures of Variability

Some measure of variability is generally of interest when we examine a data set. One measure of variability is the range. The range of the data set is a number that is calculated as the difference between the maximum and minimum values in the data set.

The standard deviation is a measure of variability in a data set that is based on deviations from the mean. The sample standard deviation is given the notation s, and the population standard deviation is given the notation σ. The formulas are as follows;

$$s = \sqrt{\frac{\sum(x - \bar{x})^2}{n - 1}} \text{ and } \sigma = \sqrt{\frac{\sum(x - \mu)^2}{n}}$$

The computational formula for the sample standard deviation is:

$$s = \sqrt{\frac{\sum x^2 - \frac{(\sum x)^2}{n}}{n - 1}}$$

The standard deviation is a measure of variability, with a larger standard deviation indicating greater variability. For data sets with a symmetric bell-shaped distribution, the standard deviation has some very useful additional properties. In such cases, the Empirical Rule applies.

1. About 68% of the data points will lie within one standard deviation of the mean.
2. About 95% of the data points will lie within two standard deviations of the mean.
3. Almost all of the data points will lie within three standard deviations of the mean.

You can check to see if the distribution has the appropriate shape by creating a histogram for the data.

The sample standard deviation is calculated with the **STDEV** function in Excel. The standard deviation is affected by outliers, and so is not an appropriate measure of variability for badly skewed data. In this case, the interquartile range (IQR) should be used. IQR = $Q_3 - Q_1$, where Q_3 is the 75th percentile of the data set, and Q_1 is the 25th percentile. Q_1 is located at the $0.25(n + 1)^{th}$ place in an ordered data set. Q_3 is located at the $0.75(n + 1)^{th}$ place in an ordered data set.

Excel does not have a built-in tool to calculate the interquartile range. However, Excel does have a function to calculate Q_1 and Q_3. Once you have calculated the 1st and 3rd quartiles, you have to enter a formula into Excel to calculate the difference. Exhibit 3.25 on page 116 shows an excerpt from an Excel spreadsheet where the IQR is calculated. The formulas are revealed for your reference.

A Guide to Decision Making for choosing the best measure of variability for a data set is shown on page 117.

Measures of Association

The Pearson correlation coefficient is a numerical measure that indicates the strength of the linear relationship between two quantitative variables. The notation for the correlation coefficient is r (or sometimes the "Pearson r"). The Pearson correlation coefficient can take on values between -1 and $+1$. An r of -1 signifies a perfect negative linear relationship. An r of $+1$ signifies a perfect positive relationship. An r of 0 indicates no apparent linear relationship. The relationship is stronger the further the r-value is from zero in either direction.

A value of r that is close to $+1$ or -1 does not *prove* that there is a cause-and-effect relationship between the x- and y-variables involved. All we can say is that the variables are highly correlated, and any conclusions about causality must be made on the basis of an understanding of the context of the data being analyzed. Calculation of the Pearson r is done in Excel with the **PEARSON** function.

The correlation coefficient r provides a measure of linear correlation between two quantitative variables. However, it has some weaknesses:

1. The correlation coefficient r does not identify non-linear correlations.
2. The correlation coefficient r can be greatly affected by outliers, to the extent that it may give a misleading indication of correlation.

The Spearman rank correlation coefficient (usually denoted r_S) is an alternative measure of correlation that identifies both linear and non-linear correlations, and is not so affected by outliers. It can also be used to calculate a measure of association between two variables when one or both of them are ranked data.

The Spearman rank correlation coefficient is calculated in the same way as the Pearson correlation coefficient, but is based on the ranks of the x- and y-variables, not the actual values of the data. All of the x-values are ranked from smallest to largest, with ranks from 1 to n. Similarly, all y-values are ranked from smallest to largest, with ranks from 1 to n. When a value appears more than once in the x- or y-values, the ranks for the tied values are averaged.

An Excel add-in that comes with the text ranks the data and calculates the Spearman rank correlation coefficient. Instructions for its use are given on page 127.

A Guide to Decision Making for choosing the best measure of association is shown on page 128.

CHAPTER REVIEW EXERCISES

It is usual, when investigating a data set, to examine it both graphically and with numerical summary measures. Often, it is necessary to create a graph for the data to assess the shape of the distribution before deciding on the appropriate measures of central tendency and variability. Many of these exercises refer to data sets you have already examined graphically in Chapter 2.

CRE03-1.xls
Set

1. A survey of pedestrian traffic is conducted over 45 days for two locations where a manager is thinking of opening a new location. The data set is available on the CD that accompanies this text. Calculate appropriate measures of central tendency and variability for these data, and comment. (Refer to the graphs you created for Chapter Review Exercise 4 in Chapter 2.)

2. The owner of a music store asks the cashiers to keep track of the spending by a random sample of female customers, and a random sample of male customers, over several days. The purchases are shown in Exhibit 3.45 below.

Exhibit 3.45

Music Store Purchases by a Random Sample of Customers

Purchases by Females ($)	Purchases by Males ($)
30.50	31.49
15.83	28.88
38.66	30.77
44.15	24.95
42.98	23.26
39.56	27.66
22.25	25.77
31.49	33.32
49.43	18.29
18.70	38.25
24.65	25.09
29.64	30.51
17.30	24.96
20.34	26.34
23.40	

Calculate appropriate measures of central tendency and variability, and comment. (Refer to the graphs you created for Chapter Review Exercise 5 in Chapter 2.)

3. A company that produces golf balls is trying to develop a new ball that will travel farther than its current best-seller. A golf pro hits a number of balls of each type off of a tee, and the distance travelled is exactly measured. The results are shown below in Exhibit 3.46. Calculate

Exhibit 3.46

Golf Ball Data

Distances Travelled (Metres) by Current Best-Selling Golf Ball	Distances Travelled (Metres) by New Golf Ball
260	310
266	286
254	292
302	276
241	269
249	293
262	306
255	279
252	262
244	248
286	

appropriate measures of central tendency and variability for these data, and comment. (Refer to the graphs you created for Chapter Review Exercise 7 in Chapter 2.)

4. The real estate listings for a random sample of three-bedroom bungalows in a Calgary suburb are available on the CD that comes with this text. Calculate appropriate measures of central tendency and variability for this data set, and comment. (Refer to the graph you created for Chapter Review Exercise 9 in Chapter 2.)

CRE03-4.xls

Set

5. A random sample of Canadian students was selected and asked to rate one university in Ontario and another in British Columbia. The rating was 1 if the student considered the university excellent, down to 4 if they considered it poor. The ratings of the students are shown below in Exhibit 3.47. Calculate an appropriate measure of association for these variables, and comment.

University Ratings

Exhibit 3.47

Ontario University Rating	BC University Rating
2	1
3	4
4	4
1	2
4	1
2	1
1	1
2	1
2	1
3	2
2	2
4	2
2	2
4	3
4	2
4	1
3	3
4	2
2	3
2	3

6. A statistics teacher collects data from a random sample of students about their marks in their first-year business math course and in their second-year statistics course. Calculate an appropriate measure of association for these data, and comment. (Refer to the graph you created for Chapter Review Exercise 13 in Chapter 2.)

CRE03-6.xls

Set

7. Woodbon, a company that produces a limited line of high-quality wooden furniture, has enjoyed remarkable sales growth since its inception in 1980. Woodbon's owner, Kate Cameron, collects the annual advertising and sales figures for the last several years. The data are available on the CD that comes with this text. Calculate an appropriate measure of association for these data, and comment. (Refer to the graph you created for Chapter Review Exercise 15 in Chapter 2.)

CRE03-7.xls

Set

8. In the discussion on misleading graphs in Section 2.6 of Chapter 2, the sales of an enterprise in Kelowna and one in Nelson were depicted (see the discussion on p. 69). The point was made that despite appearances, the Kelowna sales were in fact more variable than the Nelson location's sales. The data are shown below in Exhibit 3.48. Calculate an appropriate measure of variability. Which enterprise had more variable sales over the period?

3.48 Exhibit

Annual Sales Data for the Kelowna and Nelson Locations

	Annual Sales ($000)	
	Kelowna	Nelson
2000	109.55	122.01
2001	102.52	118.14
2002	114.91	107.85
2003	122.48	121.34
2004	122.12	112.30
2005	123.96	117.29
2006	122.36	122.27

9. In Example 3.4a on page 124, no linear relationship was found between the amount of the most recent purchase and income in the survey of drugstore customers. Does this result from the survey prove that there is no relationship? Explain.

10. Joe Walsh is concerned about the high cost of cartridges for his inkjet printer. He decides to call several local suppliers of cartridges, and collect data on the prices they charge for the cartridge that fits his particular printer. The results are shown in Exhibit 3.49 below. What is the mean price? What is the median price?

3.49 Exhibit

Prices of Inkjet Printer Cartridge

$19.99 $24.97 $33.13 $26.92 $34.50 $29.99 $23.95 $21.97

CRE03-11.xls
Set

11. Calculate appropriate measures of central tendency and variability for the incomes of customers in the survey of drugstore customers, first discussed in Chapter 2, and comment. (Refer to the graph you created for Develop Your Skills 2.2, Exercise 2.)

12. A manufacturer sells plastic jars of alfalfa honey, in 500 g sizes. The actual (carefully measured) weights of 10 jars of honey are recorded in Exhibit 3.50 below (the weights are adjusted for the weight of the jar itself). What is the mean weight of honey in the jars? Do you think this result means that the company is systematically underfilling the honey jars?

3.50 Exhibit

Precise Weights (g) of 500 g Jars of Honey

510   491   489   504   490   513   502   480   488   506

13. Two financial advisors who have been working at the same company for about five years have decided to compare their customer characteristics. Wally Johnson has 167 clients with Registered Retirement Savings Plans (RRSPs). Kate Moore has 202 clients with RRSPs. The amounts in the RRSPs for both sets of customers are available on the CD that comes with this text. Use appropriate numerical measures to compare the amounts of client RRSPs for Kate and Wally.

CRE03-13.xls
Set

14. Repeat Exercise 13 above, but with the new data set for this exercise.

15. Some management trainees across several branches of an electronics store were rated by their customers and by their bosses. Comment on the correlation between the two sets of ratings. The data are shown in Exhibit 3.51 below. A rating of "1" is excellent, and a rating of "5" is poor. Do the ranking by hand, and then use Excel to calculate the Spearman rank correlation coefficient, using the **PEARSON** function on your assigned ranks. Also, use the add-in for Spearman rank correlation coefficient on the data. (You should get the same answer.)

CRE03-14.xls
Set

Management Trainees' Ratings

3.51 Exhibit

Ratings by Customers	Ratings by Bosses
2	3
2	3
3	2
4	2
3	2
3	2
2	4
2	1
1	3
2	2

16. A company is trying a new marketing approach in some of its stores. The company has selected a random sample of stores from its many locations. The average of sales at all stores was $5,000 a week, before the new marketing plan was introduced. Weekly sales at the stores trying out the new marketing approach were recorded, with the results shown in Exhibit 3.52 below.

Weekly Sales at a Random Sample of Stores Trying Out a New Marketing Approach

3.52 Exhibit

$5,117	$5,167	$5,267	$5,451	$5,430
$5,577	$4,900	$5,036	$5,601	$4,801
$5,224	$4,635	$4,592	$4,831	$4,887

Calculate appropriate measures of central tendency and variability for this data set. Would it be appropriate to apply the Empirical Rule to this data set? If so, almost all of the sales would be in what range?

17. Cans of soup are supposed to contain 540 mL. A random sample of 35 cans of soup is selected from the production line, and their contents measured carefully. The data are available on the CD that comes with this text. Assume this sample is representative of the population. The

CRE03-17.xls
Set

company wants to be sure that the soup cans contain no more than 556 mL. Based on this sample, is there any cause for concern that the cans being produced contain more than 556 mL? The company is also concerned about customer complaints. About what percentage of the soup cans being produced will have less than 530 mL?

18. An automotive parts manufacturing plant has been working hard to reduce employee absences. In the past, the average of days off work (other than vacation) per year has been 6.6. The company has introduced a wellness program to encourage workers to eat well, exercise regularly, and lead healthier lifestyles. The absences of a random sample of 25 employees were examined for the current year, and are shown in Exhibit 3.53 below.

Annual Days Off Work (Other than Vacation) for a Random Sample of Employees

4	4.5	5.5	5	5.5	9	7.5	4	7.5	6.5
6	5.5	6.5	6.5	6	5	6	4.5	7	7
8	7	4.5	5.5	7					

Calculate appropriate measures of central tendency and variability for this data set. Do you think the annual days off work have decreased because of the wellness program?

19. Walter Beamish owns a sailboat that he uses to give harbour tours out of Vancouver. The boat can take 12 paying passengers, plus the captain and one deck hand. Reservations are taken in advance. The number of passengers for a random sample of 20 days last summer is shown below in Exhibit 3.54.

Number of Passengers on Sailboat Tour

11	8	11	11
8	9	8	8
9	12	10	7
9	7	10	9
9	11	8	10

Calculate appropriate measures of central tendency and variability for these data. Walter's calculations indicate that he must have, on average, nine passengers on his tours if the return on investment is to be acceptable. Comment, on the basis of this sample.

20. A clothing manufacturer is concerned that the heights of young men aged 18–24 might be changing. Clothing patterns will have to be adjusted if this is true. A random sample of young men aged 18–24 was selected. The average height in the sample data was 177.2 cm, with a standard deviation of 7.2 cm. A histogram of the sample data was symmetric and bell-shaped. Assuming this sample is representative of the population, what proportion of young men aged 18–24 are shorter than 170 cm? What proportion of young men aged 18–24 are taller than 199 cm?

Go to MyStatLab at www.mystatlab.com. You can practise many of this chapter's exercises as often as you want. The guided solutions help you find an answer step by step. You'll find a personalized study plan available to you too!

CHAPTER

4 Calculating Probabilities

INTRODUCTION

Most business decisions must be made with incomplete information, and there is usually some uncertainty about the impacts of particular decisions. Probability analysis allows us to make the best use of the (usually limited) information that is available to us, and to measure or estimate uncertainty. More importantly, probability analysis allows us to draw generally reliable inferences from sample data. In this chapter, we will cover some basic probability concepts, and start to build the probability skills needed for statistical inference.

Probability analysis involves experiments, events, and sample spaces. An **experiment** is any activity with an uncertain outcome. An **event** is one or more outcomes of an experiment. A **sample space** is a complete list or representation of all of the possible outcomes of an experiment. **Probability** is a measure of the likelihood of an event. It indicates the percentage of times the event is likely to occur when the experiment is repeated a large number of times.

Let's put this language in a particular context. Suppose Ben Little is running a small haircutting salon, and he has an accurate database of customer information, including whether each customer has an urban or a rural address.

Here is an *experiment:* Ben randomly selects one customer from his database. Ben's database could be used to create a list of all the possible outcomes of the

experiment any activity with an uncertain outcome

event one or more outcomes of an experiment

sample space a complete list or representation of all of the possible outcomes of an experiment

probability a measure of the likelihood of an event

classical definition of probability if there are *n* equally likely possible outcomes of an experiment, and *m* of them correspond to the event you are interested in, then the probability of the event is $\frac{m}{n}$

relative frequency approach to probability probability is the relative frequency of an event over a large number of repeated trials of an experiment

experiment, *the sample space.* Here is an *event* Ben is interested in: he wants to know whether or not the customer has an urban address.

The **classical definition of probability** is based on counting. If there are *n* equally likely possible outcomes of an experiment, and *m* of them correspond to the event you are interested in, then the probability of the event is $\frac{m}{n}$. Suppose Ben has 800 customers in total, and 480 of them are urban. Then the probability of randomly selecting an urban customer is $\frac{480}{800} = 0.60$.

The standard notation for probability is P(event). The P here stands for *probability* and P followed by brackets means *the probability of*. Notice that the P and the brackets () cannot be separated (and do not, in this case, indicate multiplication). The uppercase P is a mathematical operator that is standard mathematical shorthand for *the probability of*. So, P(urban customer) = 0.60.

The **relative frequency approach to probability** is based on a large number of repeated trials of an experiment. Probability is the relative frequency of an event over this large number of trials.

Suppose Ben conducts his experiment just once, and he selects an urban customer. Based on only one trial, his estimate of the probability of selecting an urban customer would be 100%, which we know is not accurate. If Ben repeats his experiment 10 times, it is more likely that he will select some urban and some rural customers, and his estimate of the probability of selecting an urban customer will improve. If Ben repeats his experiment 10,000 times, it is quite likely that he will have randomly selected close to 6,000 urban customers, and his estimate of P(urban customer) will be very close to 0.60.

Ben may not have a customer database, or have time to conduct 10,000 experiments. It is still possible for Ben to obtain some probability information about his customers by taking a random sample of them. Suppose Ben does this, and records two types of data:

- whether they are satisfied or dissatisfied with the service at the salon
- whether they live in the town where the salon is located (urban customers), or outside the town (rural customers).

For the sake of the discussion that follows, we will assume that although Ben surveyed only 10 customers, this sample is representative of *all* of his customers. The customer data can be visually represented as shown in Exhibit 4.1, where the orange colour corresponds to urban customers, and green corresponds to rural customers.

4.1

A Random Sample of Ben Little's Salon Customers

4.1 SAMPLE SPACES AND BASIC PROBABILITIES

What is the probability that a customer in Ben's sample is satisfied with the service of his salon? By inspecting the sample, we can count 7 satisfied customers, out of 10. This yields a relative frequency of 0.70. This relative frequency gives us some information about the probability of selecting a satisfied customer in the customer base. It is, of course, only an estimate of that probability. To know the actual probability of selecting a satisfied customer, we need information about *all* customers. Generally, this information is difficult or expensive to acquire, so we use relative frequencies from samples as probability estimates. The larger the sample size is, the better the probability estimate will be.

Using probability notation, we would write:

$$P(\text{satisfied customer}) = \tfrac{7}{10} = 0.70$$

While it is appropriate to talk of probabilities in percentage form, generally we will use the decimal equivalents (0.7, instead of 70%) when we are doing probability calculations, because this makes the arithmetic easier.

We could also simplify the notation by using a letter (for example, the letter S) to correspond to the event of a satisfied customer. Then we could write:

$$P(S) = 0.70$$

This more streamlined approach is sometimes helpful for more involved probability calculations. We will often use a single letter to correspond to an event. In the following discussion, we will use letters to correspond to the following events:

- S: customer is satisfied
- N: customer is not satisfied
- R: customer is rural
- U: customer is urban

There are various ways to represent the sample data Ben collected on these two customer characteristics. We will examine four of them. The picture of the faces (Exhibit 4.1 on p. 138) is one. A similar way to represent the sample space is with a list. It is also possible (sometimes) to put the data into tables of counts or probabilities. Finally, the data can often be presented in a tree diagram. These are simply different ways to describe the sample space for these customer characteristics.

Contingency Tables   The data collected in the customer survey could be summarized in a table, as in Exhibit 4.2. This is an example of a cross-classification table, or contingency table. Such a table is a very useful way of organizing the data. When row and

Contingency Table for Ben Little's Salon Customers

	Satisfied	Not Satisfied	Total
Rural	3	1	4
Urban	4	2	6
Total	7	3	10

Exhibit 4.2

column totals are computed, the table gives us a quick and easy way to calculate probabilities. For example, we can easily see from the table that $P(S) = P(\text{satisfied customer}) = \frac{7}{10} = 0.70$. We can also easily see that $P(U) = P(\text{urban customer}) = \frac{6}{10} = 0.60$.

Joint Probability Tables   One further variation is to convert the counts in the table cells to relative frequencies, which can be interpreted as probabilities. Exhibit 4.3 illustrates this for the salon's customers. Now we can read some probabilities directly from the table. For example, $P(R) = P(\text{rural customer}) = 0.4$. We will discuss *joint* probabilities in this table more detail, later in this chapter.

4.3

Exhibit

Joint Probability Table for Ben Little's Salon Customers			
	Satisfied	Not Satisfied	Total
Rural	$\frac{3}{10} = 0.3$	0.1	0.4
Urban	$\frac{4}{10} = 0.4$	0.2	0.6
Total	$\frac{7}{10} = 0.7$	0.3	1.0

Tree Diagrams   Another way to represent the customer sample space is with a tree diagram. A tree diagram is not always an appropriate way to represent a sample space, but when it is, it can be a helpful visual aid to probability assessment. A tree diagram for Ben Little's customer data would look like Exhibit 4.4.

4.4

Exhibit

Tree Diagram for Ben Little's Salon Customers

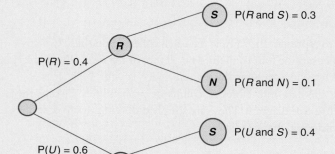

The first stage of the tree splits the data into rural and urban categories. The second stage then splits the data into satisfied and not satisfied customers. Note the probabilities along the first branches. In a tree diagram, the sum of the probabilities over the branches from one node (one of the circles in the diagram) has to equal 1 or 100% (if it does not, you have missed some part of the sample space). All of the branches have probabilities associated with them. At present, this tree diagram is incomplete. We will complete it when we have covered conditional probabilities.

Notice that at the end stage of the tree diagram are the four events that correspond to the cells of the tables we already created. The probabilities of these events also sum to 1 or 100%. The tree diagram gives us a picture of all the possible combinations of characteristics for the salon customers. Tree diagrams can be particularly helpful in keeping track of the entire sample space for an event.

A company has made a health and fitness centre available to its employees. Records show that over the last year, 210 of the 350 employees used the facilities at some time. Of the 170 males who worked for the company, 65 used the facilities.

Create a listing of the sample space for randomly selecting one employee and determining whether the person was male or female, and had or had not used the facilities. Then set up a contingency table to represent the sample space. Finally, use relative frequencies to create a joint probability table, and set up a tree diagram.

Representing a sample space with a contingency table, a joint probability table, and a tree diagram

Workers can be classified into male and female categories, and then further classified by whether or not they used the health and fitness centre in the last year. One representation of the sample space is shown below in Exhibit 4.5.

Representation of a Sample Space

4.5

Sample Space for Employee Use of a Company Health and Fitness Centre

Male and used health and fitness centre

Male and did not use health and fitness centre

Female and used health and fitness centre

Female and did not use health and fitness centre

In order to use the sample space to calculate probabilities, we will have to know the counts for each of the items in the sample space. There are 350 employees altogether, and 170 of these are male. This means there must be 350 − 170 = 180 females. We are told that 210 workers used the facilities at some time, and that 65 males used the facilities. This means that 210 − 65 = 145 females used the facilities. If 65 males out of 170 used the facilities, this means that 105 male employees did not use the facilities. If 145 out of 180 females used the facilities, then 35 female employees did not use the facilities. Exhibit 4.6 below shows the sample space with the associated counts.

Sample Space with Associated Counts

4.6

Sample Space for Employee Use of a Company Health and Fitness Centre

Male and used health and fitness centre	65
Male and did not use health and fitness centre	105
Female and used health and fitness centre	145
Female and did not use health and fitness centre	35

The contingency table to summarize the information could look as shown in Exhibit 4.7. The numbers that were given originally are shown in black. The numbers we calculated above are shown in red. Totals calculated from these are shown in blue.

4.7
Exhibit

Contingency Table

Employee Use of a Company Health and Fitness Centre

	Males	Females	Total
Used the facilities	65	145	210
Did not use the facilities	105	35	140
Total	170	180	350

It is straightforward to convert the frequencies into probabilities. The probability of a randomly selected person from the sample being a male who used the facilities is $\frac{65}{350} = 0.1857$. The probability that a randomly selected person from the sample is a female who used the facilities is $\frac{145}{350} = 0.4143$. The probability that a randomly selected person from the sample used the facilities is $\frac{210}{350} = 0.6$, and so on. A completed table of probabilities is shown below in Exhibit 4.8.

4.8
Exhibit

Joint Probability Table

Probabilities of Employee Use of a Company Health and Fitness Centre

	Males	Females	Total
Used the facilities	$\frac{65}{350} = 0.1857$	0.4143	0.6
Did not use the facilities	0.3000	0.1000	0.4
Total	0.4857	0.5143	1.0

Finally, a tree diagram to represent the sample space might look as shown in Exhibit 4.9 (notice that the tree diagram might just as well have started with the split between those who used the facilities and those who did not). We will use the letters

- M to represent the event that an employee is male
- F to represent the event that an employee is female
- U for the event that the employee used the health and fitness facilities, and
- D for the event that the employee did not use the health and fitness facilities.

4.9
Exhibit

Employee Use of a Company Health and Fitness Centre

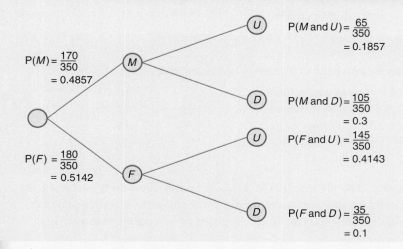

Notice that we have still not filled in the probabilities along some of the branches. We will learn how to do this in the next section, where we explore conditional probabilities.

DEVELOP YOUR SKILLS 4.1

For each of the exercises below, start by creating a representation of the sample space (your choice.) Then use it to calculate the probabilities.

1. A random sample of 350 workers at a car parts manufacturing plant are surveyed. Of the 350, all come to work by car. 246 commute more than 40 kilometres to work. 150 of the employees arrange rides with other workers. 135 of those who commute more than 40 kilometres to work drive alone.
   a. What is the probability that a randomly selected employee from the sample commutes more than 40 kilometres to work?
   b. What is the probability that a randomly selected employee from the sample arranges rides with other workers?

2. The human resources department has classified all company employees according to highest level of education attained, and job classification. Education levels are high school, up to four years of post-secondary education, graduate degree, and post-graduate studies. Job classifications are clerical, professional, and managerial. The company has 37 managers, 10 of whom have either a graduate degree or post-graduate studies. None of these has only high school education. What is the probability that a randomly selected manager has up to four years of post-secondary education?

3. Refer back to the information contained in Exercise 2 above. The company has 520 employees, of whom 372 are professionals. What is the probability that a randomly selected employee is in the professional classification? What is the probability that a randomly selected employee is in the clerical classification?

4. A random sample of 100 customers at a grocery store were asked to classify themselves as making a quick trip, doing a major stock-up, or doing a fill-in shop. 62 of the customers said they were making quick trips, and 13 were doing major stock-ups. What is the probability that a grocery store customer is doing a fill-in shop? Assume the relative frequencies from the sample are good estimates of the probabilities.

5. On the first day of class, a statistics teacher asked the class to choose one of the following items as the best description of their previous experience in math courses.

   • loved previous math courses
   • worked very hard in previous math courses, but did not enjoy them
   • thought previous math courses were far too difficult
   • equated previous math courses with sticking needles in the eyes

   Of the 225 students surveyed, 56 said they loved previous math courses. What is the probability that a randomly selected student from the survey did not love his/her previous math courses?

4.2 CONDITIONAL PROBABILITIES AND THE TEST FOR INDEPENDENCE

Conditional Probabilities

Now, while it might be interesting to Ben Little that 60% of his customers are urban, there are other, perhaps more interesting questions that he might want to ask. For example, does the level of satisfaction with his services differ between the rural customers and the urban customers? If it does, he might want to figure out why, and change his approach accordingly.

conditional probability the probability of an event *A* given that another event *B* has already occurred; the usual notation is P(*A*|*B*), read *the probability of A, given B*

In order to judge whether location (urban vs. rural) is related to customer satisfaction, you have to understand something about conditional probabilities. A **conditional probability** is the probability of an event (call it *A*), *given that* another event (call it *B*) has already occurred. The usual notation is P(*A*|*B*), read *the probability of A, given B*.

What is the probability that a randomly selected urban customer is satisfied with Ben's service? This is a conditional probability, because Ben is no longer interested in *all* of his customers. He is interested only in urban customers. A more formal way to put this would be: what is the probability that a customer is satisfied with Ben's service, *given that* the customer is urban? The standard notation for this is P(satisfied *given* urban) = P(*S*|*U*). The vertical line in the notation corresponds to the words *given that*, which will rarely appear in probability discussions. It will be up to you to recognize conditional probabilities without these words as a guide. Another word that might give you a clue that a conditional probability is required is *if* (e.g., "If the customer is urban, what is the probability that she is satisfied with Ben's service?"). Often, however, there is no explicit word clue. Remember that the probability is conditional whenever we are examining only a subset (that is, a limited part) of the entire sample space. This will be your only reliable indication that a conditional probability is required. Consider the picture of Ben's customers shown in Exhibit 4.10 below.

A Random Sample of Ben Little's Salon Customers

There are six orange faces, corresponding to the six urban customers from the sample. Of these six, four have happy faces, corresponding to being satisfied with Ben's service. Therefore, P(satisfied *given* urban) = P(*S*|*U*) = $\frac{4}{6}$ = 0.6667.

We can also use the contingency table of customer counts to calculate the probability that a customer is satisfied with Ben's service, given that he or she is urban. See Exhibit 4.11 below.

Contingency Table

Ben Little's Salon Customers

	Satisfied	Not Satisfied	Total
Rural	3	1	4
Urban	4	2	6
Total	7	3	10

We focus only on the subset of Ben's customers who are urban, which is the row that is green in the table. There are six urban customers, and of these, four are satisfied with Ben's service. We calculate that P(satisfied *given* urban) = P(*S*|*U*) = $\frac{4}{6}$ = 0.6667. We can also do a parallel calculation on the contingency table of probabilities: P(*S*|*U*) = $\frac{0.4}{0.6}$ = 0.6667.

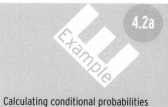

Suppose you are wondering whether your TV advertising actually affects a consumer's decision about buying your product. You conduct a random sample of 300 people in your market area, and ask them if they saw your TV ad and whether they purchased your product within the last six months. The results are summarized in Exhibit 4.12.

4.2a Example

Calculating conditional probabilities

Results of Advertising Survey

Exhibit 4.12

Random Sample of Customers In the Last Six Months	Purchased Product	Did Not Purchase Product
Saw the TV ad	152	36
Did not see the TV ad	76	36

What is the probability that one of the people in the sample purchased the product? What is the probability that one of the people who saw the TV ad purchased the product?

Out of the 300 people surveyed, 228 purchased the product (152 + 76). So P(purchased product) = $\frac{228}{300}$ = 0.76.

There were 188 people in the sample who saw the TV ad (152 + 36). Of those, 152 purchased the product. So P(purchased the product|saw the TV ad) = $\frac{152}{188}$ = 0.8085.

The Test for Independence

At the hair salon, Ben wants to figure out whether customer location is related to customer satisfaction. One way to do this is to compare the probability of satisfaction for an urban customer with the probability of satisfaction for all of his customers. We already know that in the entire sample, 7 out of the 10 customers were satisfied, so P(S) = 0.7. Above, we calculated P(S|U) = 0.6667. Comparison of these probabilities allows us to see that the customer location *is* related to customer satisfaction, as urban customers are less satisfied with Ben's service than customers overall.

There is something important that you should note at this stage: we can say only that customer location and level of satisfaction are related *in the sample*. In order to draw such a conclusion for the entire population of customers on the basis of the sample, we need some statistical tools that will be covered in Chapter 11.

This probability comparison that we have just completed is a test for independence. Two events are **independent** if the probability of one of the events is unaffected by whether the other event has occurred. If two events A and B are independent, then P(A|B) = P(A) and P(B|A) = P(B). The general approach to checking for independence is described below.

independent events two events A and B are independent if the probability of one of the events is unaffected by whether the other event has occurred; P(A|B) = P(A) and P(B|A) = P(B)

To check whether two events A and B are independent:

- compare P(A|B) with P(A), or
- compare P(B|A) with P(B).

It is necessary to do only one of these comparisons. If the compared probabilities are equal, then events A and B are independent. If the compared probabilities are not equal, then events A and B are not independent (that is, they are related).

Note that you have different options for checking for independence. In the salon example, we compared P(satisfied customer) = P(S) with P(satisfied given urban) = P(S|U) to test for independence. However, we could also have compared P(S) with P(S|R). Either of these comparisons is sufficient to establish independence (or lack of it).

Example 4.2b

Testing for independence

Suppose an industry association conducted a survey of companies in the industry to collect information about the educational background of different types of employees. The data are summarized in Exhibit 4.13.

Exhibit 4.13

Industry Association Survey of Employees

	Highest Level of Education Attained		
	High School	College/University	Graduate Studies
Hourly worker	790	265	2
Supervisor	7	145	12
Manager	1	75	23
Senior executive	0	15	10

In this sample, is the type of work done by the employee independent of educational level? If we can identify any particular case where the type of work and the educational level are not independent, we can say that type of work and educational level are related.

Suppose we compare P(hourly worker) with P(hourly worker|high school). In order to calculate these probabilities, we have to calculate the total number of workers in the data set, and the total number of employees with a high school education. The total number of employees is 1,345. The total number of employees with a high school education is 798.

P(hourly worker) = 1,057/1,345 = 0.7859

P(hourly worker|high school) = 790/798 = 0.9900

Since these two probabilities are not equal, type of work and education level are *not* independent. In other words, in this sample, education level and type of work *are* related. Employees doing hourly paid work are much more likely to have only a high school education than employees in general.

DEVELOP YOUR SKILLS 4.2

1. Out of 100 gas station customers, 80 customers pay with a credit card. Twenty-five gas station customers buy something other than gas (e.g., chips or pop) and 20 customers pay with a credit card and buy something other than gas. If a station customer buys something other than gas, what is the probability that he/she pays with a credit card? If the customer pays with a credit card, what is the probability that he/she buys something other than gas? Are paying with a credit card and buying something other than gas related?

2. A breakfast cereal comes in several versions. It can be purchased in a regular size, or a larger family size. As well, it can be purchased in regular flavour, or in a honey-nut version. Sales data are shown in Exhibit 4.14 below. If a customer buys a family size box of cereal, what is the probability that it is the honey-nut flavour? Are the size of the box and the flavour related?

Probabilities of Sales of Breakfast Cereal

	Regular Size	Family Size
Regular flavour	270	135
Honey-nut flavour	315	180

Exhibit 4.14

3. Exhibit 4.15 below shows employment in Canada in 2005, by sex and educational attainment (numbers are in thousands). (Adapted from Statistics Canada CANSIM in E-STAT, CANSIM Table 282-0004, "Labour force survey estimates (LFS), by educational attainment, sex and age group, annual (persons), 1990 to 2005," **http://estat. statcan.ca/cgiwin/CNSMCG1.EXE?Lang=E&RootDir= ESTAT/&CANSIMFILE=EStat/English/CII_1_E.htm.**)

What is the probability that an employed female in Canada in 2005 was a high school graduate? What is the probability that an employed worker with a university degree was male? What is the probability that a randomly selected employed Canadian was male? Were educational level and gender independent among Canada's employed?

4. A roofing company has analyzed its accounts receivable, and produced the cross-classification table shown

Labour Force Survey Estimates of Employment, 2005

Educational Attainment	M	F
0 to 8 years	1,258.1	690.5
Some high school	3,683.1	2,327.3
High school graduate	6,640.5	5,982.9
Some post-secondary	2,485.1	2,223.7
Post-secondary certificate or diploma	11,552.5	10,516.9
University degree	7,566.9	7,022.0

Exhibit 4.15

4.16

Accounts Receivable for a Roofing Company

Age	Amount		
	≤$5,000	$5,000–<$10,000	≥$10,000
<30 days	12	15	10
30–<60 days	7	11	2
60 days and over	3	4	1

in Exhibit 4.16. What is the probability that one of the company's accounts receivable is <30 days? What is the probability that an account of ≤$5,000 is <30 days? Are the age of the account and its amount independent?

5. A dry cleaning company has done some research into how customers rate its services, and whether or not the customer will use its services again. The data are summarized in Exhibit 4.17 below.

4.17

Customer Survey for a Dry Cleaning Company

Service Rating	Will Use Services Again	Will Not Use Services Again
Poor	174	986
Fair	232	928
Good	2,436	174
Excellent	754	116

What is the probability that a customer will use the dry cleaning company's services again? What is the probability that a customer who rates the services as "good" or "excellent" will not use the services again? What does this indicate? Are the service rating and the tendency to use the services again independent?

4.3 "AND," "OR," AND "NOT" PROBABILITIES

"And" Probabilities

There are other straightforward probabilities that we can calculate from the salon customer survey. For example, what is the probability that a randomly selected customer from Ben's sample of salon customers is urban *and* satisfied with the service? Look at Exhibit 4.18 below.

4.18

A Random Sample of Ben Little's Salon Customers

Urban customers are represented by the orange faces, four of which have smiles. We count four urban customers who are satisfied with the service. So P(urban *and* satisfied) $= \frac{4}{10} = 0.04$. We can also see this in the contingency table shown in Exhibit 4.19 below. We can see that of the 10 customers surveyed, 4 were *both* urban and satisfied, so P(urban *and* satisfied) $=$ P(U and S) $= \frac{4}{10} = 0.4$.

Ben Little's Salon Customers

	Satisfied	Not Satisfied	Total
Rural	3	1	4
Urban	④	2	6
Total	7	3	10

Exhibit 4.19

This is an example of a *joint* probability. Notice the *and* in the description. The customer had to be *both* urban *and* satisfied with the service to be counted in the probability calculation. This is illustrated with Exhibit 4.20. The probability we want is at the intersection of the first column and the second row of the table.

Ben Little's Salon Customers

	Satisfied	Not Satisfied	Total
Rural	3	1	4
Urban	4	2	6
Total	7	3	10

Exhibit 4.20

Make sure you understand the difference between a joint probability and a conditional probability. For a joint probability, we are considering the entire sample space. We want to know how many customers, out of *all* customers, are both urban and satisfied. This is different from a conditional probability, where we consider only a subset of the sample space. If we were trying to calculate the conditional probability of an urban customer being satisfied, we would be focusing on only the urban customers, a subset of the sample space.

- P(satisfied *given* urban) = P($S|U$) = $\frac{4}{6}$ = 0.6667 (a conditional probability)
- P(satisfied *and* urban) = P(S and U) = $\frac{4}{10}$ = 0.4 (a joint probability)

Now that we have introduced the idea of a joint probability, we can point out a relationship between joint and conditional probabilities.

For two events A and B, the conditional probability can be calculated as follows:

$$P(A|B) = \frac{P(A \text{ and } B)}{P(B)}$$

This formula corresponds exactly to the method we used to calculate the probability of a salon customer being satisfied, given that he or she is urban. Translating from the general statement above, we see that

$$P(\text{satisfied}|\text{urban}) = \frac{P(\text{satisifed } and \text{ urban})}{P(\text{urban})}$$

$$P(S|U) = \frac{P(S \text{ and } U)}{P(U)}$$

$$P(S|U) = \frac{0.4}{0.6}$$

$$= 0.6667$$

as we calculated before. So far we have easily calculated the joint probability for the salon customers, but we do not always have a complete listing of the sample space when we are calculating probabilities. Sometimes we need to piece together available information to calculate the probability we want, and use the general formula.

For example, suppose that we have 10 female job applicants and 12 male job applicants waiting for an interview. If the company doing the hiring randomly selects two applicants to interview, what is the probability that both of them are male? We might be interested in this, for example, if there was concern about gender bias in the interviewing process.

If you think about it, you will see that P(both applicants are male) is a joint probability. For both applicants to be male, the first one has to be male *and* the second one has to be male. But how do we figure out the probability?

Break this down into two parts. First, what is the probability that the first applicant is male? There are 22 applicants altogether (10 female + 12 male), and of these, 12 are male. P(1st applicant selected is male) $= \frac{12}{22} = 0.5455$. Now, what is the probability that the second applicant selected is male as well? There are 21 applicants left, 11 of whom are male, so P(2nd applicant selected is male|1st applicant selected was male) $= \frac{11}{12} = 0.5238$.

Now, how do we put these calculations together to arrive at the joint probability? For this, we need the rule of multiplication.

For two events A and B, the probability of A and B occurring can be calculated using the rule of multiplication (the dot is a symbol for multiplication):

$$P(A \text{ and } B) = P(A) \cdot P(B|A).$$

You should be able to see that this rule is just a rearrangement of the rule for calculating conditional probability. If $P(A|B) = \dfrac{P(A \text{ and } B)}{P(B)}$, then it follows that $P(A \text{ and } B) = P(A) \cdot P(B|A)$ (just cross-multiply to get this).

Now apply the multiplication rule directly to the job applicant problem.

P(both applicants are male)

= P(1st applicant is male *and* 2nd applicant is male)

= P(1st applicant is male) • P(2nd applicant is male|1st applicant was male)

$= \dfrac{12}{22} \cdot \dfrac{11}{21}$

$= \dfrac{132}{462}$

$= 0.2857$

For this kind of calculation, it is wise to leave the intermediate probabilities in fraction form, rather than converting them to decimals (that is, use $\frac{12}{22}$ in the calculation, rather than 0.5455, which is a rounded value). This is an easy way to preserve accuracy.

Now that we have covered conditional and joint probabilities, we can use them to complete a tree diagram corresponding to the job interview example.

Tree Diagram for Job Applicants

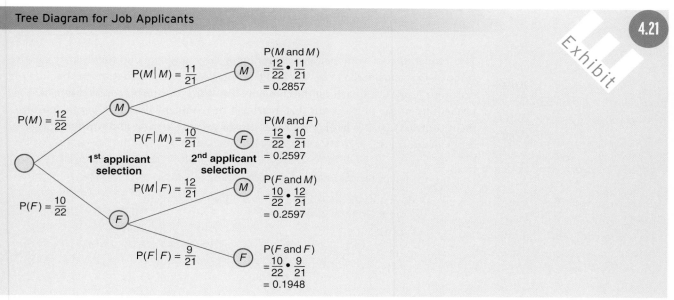

Exhibit **4.21**

Notice that after the first node (circle) in the tree diagram, the probabilities listed along the branches are conditional probabilities. This allows you to use the multiplication rule to calculate the probabilities at the end stages of the tree diagram. Notice that the sum of the probabilities along the branches from any node (circle) has to equal 100%.

The rule of multiplication has a special form when the two events involved are independent. Remember, when two events A and B are independent, the probability of one happening is unaffected by whether the other event has occurred, and $P(B) = P(B|A)$, for example. This means that for the special case of independent events, we can simplify the rule of multiplication as follows:

P(A and B)

= P(A) • P(B|A)

= P(A) • P(B)

Here is an example. Suppose an international music production company is launching new CDs for two artists. One of the artists is a country singer, and one is an opera singer. The probability that the country singer's CD will be a big hit is estimated to be 0.07. The probability that the opera singer's CD will be a hit is estimated to be 0.03. What is the probability that both CDs will be a hit for the company? Market research has indicated that country music fans generally do not listen to opera, and vice versa.

In this case, although we are not directly told that the two events are independent, we are told that customers who buy country music are different from customers who buy operatic music, so it is probably safe to conclude that the two CD launches are independent. Therefore

> P(country CD is a hit *and* opera CD is a hit)
>
> = 0.07 • 0.03
>
> = 0.0021

There is only a very small probability that both new CDs will be hits.

4.3a

The rule of multiplication: calculating "and" probability

The probability of your company winning a large government contract to supply computers is considered to be 0.3. Budget projections indicate that the probability of earning a profit this quarter if the company wins the government contract is 0.75. The probability of earning a profit this quarter if the company does not win the government contract is 0.4. What is the probability of earning a profit and winning the government contract?

> P(winning the government contract and earning a profit)
>
> = P(winning the government contract) • P(earning a profit *given* government contract won)
>
> = 0.3 • 0.75
>
> = 0.225

"Or" Probabilities

Ben Little is thinking of placing an advertisement for his salon in the local newspapers. He is not sure which newspaper(s) would be best for the ad, but the newspapers give him some information about their readership that will help him with his decision. Suppose Ben is told that 60% of local residents read the morning paper, 40% read the evening paper, and 20% read both. What percentage of residents read at least one of the two papers?

Your first reaction might be to think that almost everybody reads at least one of the papers. After all, P(morning paper read) = 0.6, and P(evening paper read) = 0.4, and the sum of those two probabilities is 100%. However, simply adding the two probabilities is not correct, because it will result in double-counting the 20% of residents who read both papers. They are counted in the probability for the morning paper, and they are counted again in the probability for the evening paper. So, we have to subtract the 20% who are double-counted to get the final probability, as follows:

P(at least one of the two papers read)

= P(morning paper read *or* evening paper read *or* both read)

= P(morning paper read) + P(evening paper read) − P(both papers read)

= 0.6 + 0.4 − 0.2

= 0.8

This is an example of an "*or*" probability. Note that there was no *or* in the original question ("at least one"). As usual, it will be up to you to recognize when an "or" probability is required. Usually this is a matter of checking to see if the event can be described correctly using the word "or." The event "*A* or *B*" means that *A* occurs, or *B* occurs, or they both occur. The rule for calculating these probabilities is the rule of addition.

For two events *A* and *B*, the probability of *A* or *B* occurring can be calculated using the rule of addition:

P(*A* or *B*) = P(*A*) + P(*B*) − P(*A* and *B*)

We can examine how this rule operates with the salon customer survey contingency table.

P(satisfied or urban)

= P(*S* or *U*)

= P(*S*) + P(*U*) − P(*S* and *U*)

= 0.7 + 0.6 − 0.4

= 0.9

Exhibit 4.22 illustrates the double-counting that must be corrected. P(urban) = 0.6, and P(satisfied) = 0.7, but this double-counts P(urban and satisfied) = 0.4.

Ben Little's Salon Customers

	Satisfied	Not Satisfied	Total
Rural	0.3	0.1	0.4
Urban	**0.4**	0.2	0.6
Total	0.7	0.3	1.0

Exhibit 4.22

The rule of addition has a special case for **mutually exclusive events**, events that cannot happen simultaneously. If two events *A* and *B* are mutually exclusive, then P(*A* and *B*) = 0.

mutually exclusive events events that cannot happen simultaneously; if two events *A* and *B* are mutually exclusive, then P(*A* and *B*) = 0

For example, suppose you have some information about your customers, according to level of income. The information is summarized in Exhibit 4.23.

Customer Income Analysis

Annual Income Level	Number of Customers
$0–<$25,000	29
$25,000–<$50,000	152
$50,000–<$75,000	353
$75,000–<$100,000	12
Total	546

What is the probability that a randomly selected customer has an income below $25,000, or $75,000–<$100,000?

$$P(\text{income} < \$25,000) = \frac{29}{546} = 0.0531$$

$$P(\text{income } \$75,000–<\$100,000) = \frac{12}{546} = 0.0220$$

$$P(\text{income} <\$25,000 \text{ or } \$75,000–<\$100,000) = \frac{29}{546} + \frac{12}{546} = \frac{41}{546} = 0.0751$$

Notice that since the income categories are mutually exclusive (a customer cannot have an income <$25,000 and at the same time have an income $75,000–<$100,000), the probabilities can simply be added.

4.3b **Your large company has suppliers all across Canada. The joint probability table shown in Exhibit 4.24 summarizes the location and size (by annual sales) of these suppliers. What is the probability that a supplier has sales <$1 million or is located in BC?**

The rule of addition: calculating "or" probabilities

Joint Probability Table for Company Suppliers

Location	Annual Sales		
	<$1 million	$1 million—<$5 million	≥$5 million
BC	0.02	0.06	0.15
AB, SK, MB	0.01	0.07	0.01
ON	0.03	0.10	0.40
QC	0.02	0.01	0.07
PE, NB, NS, and NL	0.01	0.02	0.02

First we calculate the probability of a supplier having sales of <$1 million. We get this by adding the probabilities in the second column of Exhibit 4.24 (these are all mutually exclusive outcomes, so we can just add the probabilities).

P(supplier has sales <$1 million) = 0.02 + 0.01 + 0.03 + 0.02 + 0.01 = 0.09

Similarly, we calculate the probability of a supplier being located in BC by adding the probabilities along the first row of the table.

P(supplier located in BC) = 0.02 + 0.06 + 0.15 = 0.23

For one of the company's suppliers

P(sales <$1 million *or* located in BC)

= P(sales <$1 million) + P(located in BC) − P(sales <$1 million *and* located in BC)

= 0.09 + 0.23 − 0.02 (the joint probability is simply read from the table)

= 0.30

"Not" Probabilities

If the probability that one of Ben Little's salon customers is urban is 0.6, what is the probability that a customer is *not* urban? One way to calculate this is P(not urban) = 1 − P(urban) = 1 − 0.6 = 0.4. We can do this because all of Ben's customers are either urban or not (rural). Generally, the sum of probabilities for all the non-overlapping events in a sample space has to add up to 1 or 100%. If they do not, something must be missing from the list of all possible events. *Not urban* is called the complement of *urban*. The **complement of an event A** is everything in the sample space that is not A. Various notations are used to describe complements. The complement of A might be noted as $\overline{A}$ or $\sim A$ or A^C or A'. In this text, we will use the notation A^C for the complement of A. The complement rule summarizes the relationship between P(A) and P(A^C).

complement of an event A everything in the sample space that is not A

The probability of an event **A** can be calculated using the complement rule:

P(A) = 1 − P(A^C)

The complement rule can be a very powerful tool for probability calculation. Let's look at an example. A company is submitting tenders for two road construction jobs in Calgary. The smaller of the two jobs is a contract to repair a major city street. The larger job is new street construction in an area undergoing massive development. The company's president estimates that the probability of winning the smaller job (which comes up first) is 0.70. She also believes that the probability of winning the larger job, if the company wins the smaller job, is 0.50. On the other hand, if the company does not win the smaller job, she believes the probability of winning the larger job to be only 0.20. According to the president's probability estimates, what is the probability that the company will win both jobs?

There is no probability rule for "both," but we recognize that "winning both jobs" is logically equivalent to "winning the smaller job *and* winning the larger job." We will denote "winning the smaller job" with the letter S, and winning the larger job with the letter L. We can now summarize the information we have been given:

- P(winning smaller job) = $P(S)$ = 0.70
- P(winning larger job, given that the smaller job is won) = $P(L|S)$ = 0.50
- P(winning larger job, given that the smaller job is not won) = $P(L|S^C)$ = 0.20

To calculate the probability of winning both jobs, proceed as follows.

$$P(S \text{ and } L)$$
$$= P(S) \cdot P(L|S)$$
$$= 0.70 \cdot 0.50$$
$$= 0.35$$

So, the probability of winning both jobs is 0.35.
What is the probability of losing both jobs?

$$P(\text{losing both jobs})$$
$$= P(S^C \text{ and } L^C)$$
$$= P(S^C) \cdot P(L^C|S^C)$$
$$= (1 - 0.70) \cdot (1 - 0.20)$$
$$= 0.30 \cdot 0.80$$
$$= 0.24$$

What is the probability of winning just one of the two jobs? This could be a lengthy probability calculation. We could calculate the probability of winning the smaller job and losing the larger job, and then add that to the probability of losing the smaller job and winning the larger job. However, there is an easier way, which involves the complement rule. This is a case where a tree diagram can be helpful to keep track of the sample space. Exhibit 4.25 illustrates the sample space for this example.

4.25

Exhibit

Tree Diagram for Road Construction Jobs

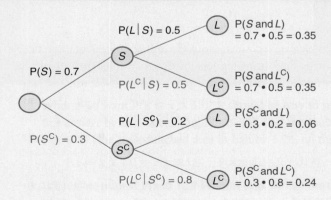

$P(S) = 0.7$

$P(L|S) = 0.5$ → L → $P(S \text{ and } L)$ = 0.7 • 0.5 = 0.35

S

$P(L^C|S) = 0.5$ → L^C → $P(S \text{ and } L^C)$ = 0.7 • 0.5 = 0.35

$P(S^C) = 0.3$

$P(L|S^C) = 0.2$ → L → $P(S^C \text{ and } L)$ = 0.3 • 0.2 = 0.06

S^C

$P(L^C|S^C) = 0.8$ → L^C → $P(S^C \text{ and } L^C)$ = 0.3 • 0.8 = 0.24

The probabilities in black in Exhibit 4.25 correspond to the probabilities given in the problem description. The probabilities in red are calculated using the complement rule. For example, if $P(L|S) = 0.5$, then $P(L^C|S) = 1 - 0.5 = 0.5$. The end-stage probabilities, in blue, are calculated using the multiplication rule. For example, $P(S \text{ and } L) = P(S) \cdot P(L|S) = 0.7 \cdot 0.5 = 0.35$.

This tree diagram now gives quite a full picture of the sample space, and a number of related probabilities. It also allows us to see clearly how to calculate the probability of winning exactly one of the contracts. Using the information in the tree diagram, we can now go through the long probability calculation for winning exactly one contract.

$P(\text{winning exactly one contract})$

$= P[(\text{winning the smaller job } and \text{ not winning the larger job})$
$\quad or \text{ (not winning the smaller job } and \text{ winning the larger job)}]$

$= P[(S \text{ and } L^C) \text{ or } (S^C \text{ and } L)]$

$= P(S \text{ and } L^C) + P(S^C \text{ and } L) \text{ (mutually exclusive events)}$

$= [P(S) \cdot P(L^C|S)] + [P(S^C) \cdot P(L|S^C)] \text{ (multiplication rule)}$

$= (0.7 \cdot 0.5) + (0.3 \cdot 0.2)$

$= 0.35 + 0.06$

$= 0.41$

However, the tree diagram also gives us a clear picture of an easier way to calculate this probability. We have already calculated P(winning both contracts) and P(losing both contracts). So, using the complement rule, we can calculate

$P(\text{winning exactly one contract})$

$= 1 - P(\text{winning both contracts } or \text{ losing both contracts})$

$= 1 - (0.35 + 0.24)$

$= 1 - 0.59$

$= 0.41$

This approach takes advantage of the calculations we have already done. The complement rule leads to a much easier calculation, in this case. A tree diagram can often be useful to determine when the complement rule would be helpful.

Return to the situation described in Example 4.3a, in which your company was bidding on a large government contract to supply computers. The information provided was:

- P(winning government contract) = 0.3
- P(earning a quarterly profit, given that government contract won) = 0.75
- P(earning a quarterly profit, given that government contract not won) = 0.4

What is the probability that the company will earn a profit in the next quarter?

Recognize that there are two (mutually exclusive) ways for the company to earn a profit in the next quarter: when it wins the government contract, and when it does

4.3c

Calculating probabilities with a tree diagram and probability rules not. It might be helpful to draw a tree diagram for this situation, to illustrate the sample space. To simplify the notation, we will use the following letters:

- W for winning the government contract
- P for earning a profit in the next quarter

The appropriate tree diagram is shown in Exhibit 4.26, below.

Tree Diagram for Company Bidding on Government Contracts

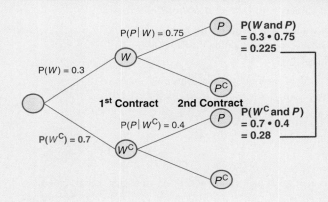

$P(P)$
$= P[(W \text{ and } P) \text{ or } (W^C \text{ and } P)]$
$= P(W \text{ and } P) + P(W^C \text{ and } P)]$ (mutually exclusive events)
$= P(W) \cdot P(P|W) + P(W^C) \cdot P(P|W^C)$
$= (0.3 \cdot 0.75) + (0.7 \cdot 0.4)$ (using the complement rule)
$= 0.225 + 0.28$
$= 0.505$

While the notation looks a little complicated, the calculations are fairly straightforward when the tree diagram is used.

Mutually Exclusive vs. Independent Events   If you are going to be successful with probability calculations, it is important that you understand the difference between mutually exclusive and independent events. These conditions are not the same. As a reminder, here are the definitions of both.

- Events A and B are *mutually exclusive* if $P(A \text{ and } B) = 0$. This means that A and B cannot both happen.
- Events A and B are *independent* if $P(A) = P(A|B)$; that is, the fact that B happened does not affect the chances of A happening (or vice versa).

DEVELOP YOUR SKILLS 4.3

1. Your company has two employees, Jane Morton and Oscar Wildman, who are experts at rescuing computers from viruses. One morning, you arrive at work to find that a virus has totally incapacitated the computers on the company network. The probability that Jane Morton will be late for work in the morning is 0.02. The probability that Oscar Wildman will be late for work in the morning is 0.04. If the employees live in different parts of the city, what is the probability that both will be late for work this morning when you really need their help?

2. Three women who have been friends since childhood have just graduated from college. The friends are very different, and have different abilities and skills. All three of them are trying to get jobs in the financial services industry. Their probabilities of succeeding are 0.4, 0.5, and 0.35. Find the probability that

   a. all of them succeed
   b. none of them succeeds
   c. at least one of them succeeds

3. A software company is about to release three new software programs, one from each of three very distinct business divisions. The first program is a new game aimed at 15–25-year-olds. Its probability of succeeding is estimated to be 0.34. The second program is an accounting application for small business. Its probability of succeeding is estimated to be 0.12. The third program is a payroll system designed for government organizations. Its probability of succeeding is 0.10. ("Success" is defined as earning enough profits to fully recover development, production, and marketing costs within one year.) What is the probability that all three software programs will succeed? What is the probability that at least two out of three of them will succeed? You may assume that the success of each product is independent of the success of the others.

4. Draw a fully labelled tree diagram for the salon problem at the beginning of the chapter (see Exhibit 4.4 on p. 140). Notice that the end-stage probabilities are the ones that show up in the cells of the related joint probability table (see Exhibit 4.3, p. 140). Use another approach to set up a different tree diagram for the salon problem.

5. Return to the situation described in Example 4.2b on page 146. An industry association conducted a survey of companies in the industry to collect information about the educational background of different types of employees. The data are repeated in Exhibit 4.27. What is the probability that a randomly selected employee in this industry is an hourly worker or someone with only a high school education?

Industry Association Survey of Employees

Exhibit 4.27

	Highest Level of Education Attained		
	High School	College/University	Graduate Studies
Hourly worker	790	265	2
Supervisor	7	145	12
Manager	1	75	23
Senior executive	0	15	10

Chapter Summary

4

Sample Spaces and Basic Probabilities

An experiment is any activity with an uncertain outcome. An event is one or more outcomes of an experiment. A sample space is a complete list or representation of all of the possible outcomes of an experiment. Sample spaces can be represented with a picture, a listing, a contingency table, a joint probability table, or a tree diagram.

In many cases, relative frequencies are used as probability estimates. Probability is a measure of the likelihood of an event. The classical definition of probability is based on counting. If there are n equally likely possible outcomes of an experiment, and m of them correspond to the event you are interested in, then the probability of the event is $\frac{m}{n}$.

The relative frequency approach to probability is based on a large number of repeated trials of an experiment. Probability is the relative frequency of an event over this large number of trials. Often relative frequencies from samples are used to estimate the probabilities of populations.

Conditional Probabilities and the Test for Independence

A conditional probability is the probability of an event (call it A), *given that* another event (call it B) has already occurred. The usual notation is $P(A|B)$, read *the probability of A, given B*. For two events A and B, the conditional probability can be calculated as follows:

$$P(A|B) = \frac{P(A \text{ and } B)}{P(B)}$$

Two events are independent if the probability of one of the events is unaffected by whether the other event has occurred. To see whether two events A and B are independent, do *one of* the following comparisons:

- compare $P(A|B)$ with $P(A)$, or
- compare $P(B|A)$ with $P(B)$.

If the compared probabilities are equal, then events A and B are independent. If the compared probabilities are not equal, then events A and B are not independent (that is, they are related).

"And," "Or," and "Not" Probabilities

For two events A and B, the probability of A and B occurring can be calculated using the rule of multiplication:

$$P(A \text{ and } B) = P(A) \cdot P(B|A)$$

For the special case of independent events, we can simplify the rule of multiplication as follows:

$$P(A \text{ and } B) = P(A) \cdot P(B)$$

For two events A and B, the probability of A or B occurring can be calculated using the rule of addition:

$$P(A \text{ or } B) = P(A) + P(B) - P(A \text{ and } B)$$

Mutually exclusive events are events that cannot happen simultaneously. If two events A and B are mutually exclusive, then

$$P(A \text{ and } B) = 0$$

For the special case of mutually exclusive events, we can simplify the rule of addition as follows:

$$P(A \text{ or } B) = P(A) + P(B)$$

The complement of an event A is everything in the sample space that is not A. The complement of event A is denoted A^C. The probability of an event A can be calculated using the complement rule:

$$P(A) = 1 - P(A^C)$$

CHAPTER REVIEW EXERCISES

1. A restaurant chain regularly surveys its customers about the quality of the food and the quality of the service. The survey responses are summarized in Exhibit 4.28 below. The relative frequencies are considered good estimates of the associated probabilities.

Survey of Restaurant Customers

	Satisfied with Service	Not Satisfied with Service
Food is excellent	0.40	0.06
Food is good	0.13	0.07
Food is fair	0.05	0.08
Food is poor	0.01	0.20

Exhibit 4.28

a. What is the probability that a randomly selected customer is satisfied with the service and rates the restaurant's food as poor?
b. What is the probability that a randomly selected customer is not satisfied with the service?
c. What is the probability that a customer who rated the food as poor was not satisfied with the service?
d. Are the service rating and the food rating related? You must use probabilities to prove your answer to this question.

2. Past experience shows that the probability that a salesperson will exceed the sales target in a given year is 14%, provided that the target was exceeded in the previous year. If the probability of a salesperson exceeding the target in any given year is 8%, what is the probability that the salesperson will exceed target two years in a row?

3. In a follow-up survey of people who purchased big-screen televisions, the buyers were asked if they were satisfied with their purchase. The answers were classified according to whether the television purchased was a high-definition television (HDTV) or not, using the probability table shown in Exhibit 4.29.

Follow-Up Survey of Customers Who Bought Big-Screen Televisions

	Satisfied	Not Satisfied
HDTV	0.30	0.05
Not HDTV	0.50	0.15

Exhibit 4.29

a. What is the probability that a customer who bought a regular big-screen TV (not HDTV) was satisfied with the purchase?
b. What is the probability that a customer who bought an HDTV was satisfied with the purchase?
c. Does the type of television purchased affect whether or not the purchaser was satisfied with the purchase? You must use probabilities to answer this question.

4. Students who wish to become chartered accountants (CAs) must pass a set of exams to qualify. Suppose that in Ontario the pass rate is 75%. Candidates who fail the exams the first time may take them again, later. Of those who fail the first time, 90% pass the second time. What is the probability that a randomly selected student will qualify to become a CA with no more than two attempts at passing the exams?

5. An insurance company has collected data on the gender and marital status of 300 customers, as shown in Exhibit 4.30 on the following page.

4.30

Customers of an Insurance Company

	Single	Married	Divorced
Male	25	125	30
Female	50	50	20

Suppose a customer is selected at random from this sample.
a. What is the probability that the customer is female or married?
b. What is the probability that the customer is married if the customer is male?
c. Are gender and marital status independent? Prove your answer.

6. At the beginning of each year, an investment newsletter predicts whether or not the stock market will rise over the year. Historical evidence reveals that there is a 75% chance of the market rising, in any given year. The newsletter predicted a rise for 80% of the years when the market actually rose, and predicted a rise for 40% of the years when the market actually fell. Find the probability that the newsletter's prediction for next year will be correct. (Use a tree diagram.)

7. A company has decided to hire some summer students. A local high school has provided the names of 10 students who have been academically successful and who have good work habits. The company decides to pick three students from this group at random, rather than taking the time to interview the students. If seven of the students are female, what is the probability that all of the students selected by the company will be female? What is the probability that all of the students selected by the company will be male?

8. Exhibit 4.31 below summarizes the community type and degree of pollution for 268 locations in Ontario.

4.31

Pollution in 268 Ontario Locations

Location	Low	Moderate	High	Total
Rural	33	23	9	65
Suburban	8	23	20	51
Urban	7	10	73	90
Commercial	3	11	48	62
Total	51	67	150	268

a. For these communities, if the location is urban, what is the probability that the air pollution is high?
b. What is the probability that one of these locations is urban or has low pollution?

9. Refer back to Example 4.2a on page 145, about a survey to determine if people saw a TV ad or purchased a product. In the sample, is purchasing behaviour related to seeing the TV ad? You must use probabilities to support your answer.

10. Refer back to Example 4.1 on page 141, about the employee health and fitness facilities. Are gender and tendency to use the health and fitness facilities related in this sample? You must use probabilities to support your answer.

11. Brandon Tamblyn has just graduated with a business diploma from a New Brunswick college. He has applied for a job in Alberta at the largest Canadian bank. The probability that he will get the job is 0.25. The probability that he will move to Alberta if he is offered this job

is 0.80. The probability that he will move to Alberta if he does not get this job is 0.35. Create a tree diagram, complete with probabilities, to describe all of the possible outcomes for Brandon. What is the probability that he will be offered the job and not move to Alberta?

12. The probability that a Canadian adult has taken some instruction in canoeing is 0.03. The probability that a Canadian adult who has taken some instruction in canoeing will go on a canoe trip this summer is 0.36. The probability that a Canadian adult who has taken no instruction in canoeing will go on a canoe trip this summer is 0.20. Create a tree diagram to represent all the possibilities for Canadian adults taking instruction in canoeing and going on a canoe trip this summer.

13. Using the tree diagram you created in Exercise 12 above, calculate the probability that a randomly selected Canadian adult is going on a canoe trip this summer, and has taken some canoeing instruction. What is the probability that a randomly selected Canadian adult is going on a canoe trip this summer, and has not taken any canoeing instruction?

14. Suppose a survey of customers from stores A, B, C, and D recorded the method of payment by customers. The data are shown below in Exhibit 4.32. Based on the survey, what is the probability that a randomly selected customer from one of these stores uses cash or a debit card, or a credit card, for payment?

Customer Payment Method

	Store A	Store B	Store C	Store D	Total
Cash or debit card	40	65	20	25	150
Credit card	30	80	30	40	180
Cheque	30	55	50	35	170
Total	100	200	100	100	500

Exhibit 4.32

15. Refer to Exhibit 4.32 in Exercise 14. Is the payment method independent of the store in this sample?

16. You are thinking about investing in a fitness facility. The current owner tells you that the probability that someone who visits the facility will buy a membership is 60%. The probability that someone who visits the facility will buy a membership and sign up for fitness classes is 20%. What is the probability that someone who visits the facility will sign up for fitness classes, if they buy a membership?

17. Refer back to Exercise 16 above. Are buying a membership and signing up for fitness classes mutually exclusive? Are buying a membership and signing up for fitness classes independent?

18. A restaurant is interested in whether there is gender difference in the tendency to drink beer, wine, and other alcoholic drinks. If there appears to be a difference, the servers will be trained to promote the most preferred types of drinks to male and female customers. A survey of a random sample of customers who bought alcoholic beverages revealed the data shown in Exhibit 4.33. Is the type of alcoholic drink ordered related to the gender of the customer in this sample?

Sample of Restaurant Customers Ordering Alcoholic Drinks

	Beer	Wine	Other Alcoholic Drinks
Male	42	36	22
Female	63	54	33

Exhibit 4.33

19. A shipment contains 500 circuit boards. Suppose that 25 of them are defective. What is the probability that if you randomly selected three circuit boards, all three of them would be defective? How does this compare to the probability you would obtain if you considered the selection of each circuit board to be independent of selection of the others, using the initial probability of selecting a defective circuit board?

20. Polls show that 35% of Canadians plan to make a contribution to their RRSPs over the next year. What is the probability that four randomly selected Canadians are all planning to make a contribution to their RRSPs over the next year?

 Go to MyStatLab at www.mystatlab.com. You can practise many of this chapter's exercises as often as you want. The guided solutions help you find an answer step by step. You'll find a personalized study plan available to you too!

5 Probability Distributions

INTRODUCTION

Chapter 4 introduced basic probability concepts and rules. Many of the problems considered in Chapter 4 involved counts of outcomes with particular characteristics. For example, how many of Ben Little's salon customers are urban? How many are satisfied? It is possible to associate a random variable with these counts. For example, we could define a random variable x as the number of rural customers Ben would find, if he randomly selected two of his customers. The value of x will be determined only when Ben randomly selects two customers and determines if they have rural addresses. A **random variable** is a variable whose value is determined by the outcome of a random experiment.

In Chapter 2, the distinction between discrete and continuous variables was made. Random variables can also be discrete or continuous. The number of rural customers out of two randomly selected customers from Ben Little's salon is a discrete random variable. The possible values that this random variable x can take are 0, 1, and 2. Because we can list all the possible values of x, it is a discrete random variable. A **discrete random variable** can take any value from a list of distinct possible values.

Learning Objectives

After mastering the material in this chapter, you will be able to:

1. Understand the concepts of discrete and continuous random variables and their associated probability distributions.

2. Recognize situations when the binomial probability distribution applies, and use a formula, Excel, or tables to calculate binomial probabilities.

3. Recognize the normal probability distribution, and use Excel or tables to calculate normal probabilities.

random variable a variable whose value is determined by the outcome of a random experiment

discrete random variable a random variable that can take on any value from a list of distinct possible values

probability distribution for a discrete random variable a list of all the possible values of the random variable, and their associated probabilities

continuous random variable a random variable that can take on any value from a continuous range

probability distribution of a continuous random variable a graph or a mathematical formula

Discrete random variables are often counts, and we looked at several examples of these kinds of experiments in Chapter 4. A probability distribution is associated with a discrete random variable. The **probability distribution for a discrete random variable** is often illustrated with a list of all the possible values of the random variable, and their associated probabilities. We will see, in Section 5.1, that these probability distributions can be constructed with the probability rules of Chapter 4. We will also see that once these distributions are known, they can be used to calculate probabilities in a wide range of situations. In Chapter 5 we will look at one particular discrete probability distribution, the binomial distribution, in Section 5.2.

A **continuous random variable** can take on any value from a continuous range. Continuous random variables are often measurements of some kind. For example, a random variable y could be defined as the height of a student in your statistics class. Because y could take on any of the values in some range[1] (from the shortest possible height to the tallest), it is a continuous random variable. In Chapter 5 we will look at one particular continuous probability distribution, the normal distribution, in Section 5.3. Of course, it is not possible to list the infinite number of possible values for a continuous random variable, so the associated probability distribution cannot take the form of a list. The **probability distribution of a continuous random variable** is described graphically, or with a mathematical formula.

Chapter 5 examines two important probability distributions (one discrete, one continuous) that have many applications for statistical inference. Later in the text, we will encounter other important probability distributions, such as the t-distribution and the Chi-squared distribution.

 ## 5.1 PROBABILITY DISTRIBUTIONS

Building a Discrete Probability Distribution

Define a random variable x as "the number of rural customers, out of two randomly selected customers from Ben Little's haircutting salon." We know that the random variable x has three possible values: 0, 1, or 2 (that is, none or one or both of the customers may be rural). There are probabilities associated with each of these possible values of x, and we can use the probability rules from Chapter 4 to calculate them.

In Chapter 4, we learned that P(rural customer) = 0.4 among Ben's salon customers. Assume for now that Ben's customer base is so large that this probability does not change when he selects two customers from his customer base (we will discuss this idea more fully later on in the chapter). Exhibit 5.1 below shows a tree diagram to illustrate the possible values for x and the associated probabilities.

---

[1] Subject to the limitations of the measuring device, as noted in Chapter 2.

Tree Diagram for Characteristics of Two Randomly Selected Customers at Ben Little's Salon

Exhibit 5.1

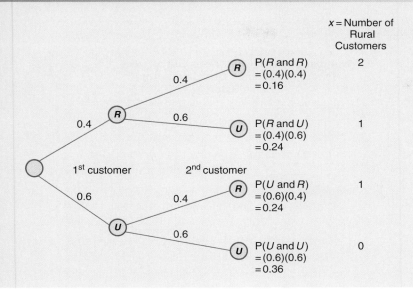

	x = Number of Rural Customers
$P(R \text{ and } R)$ $=(0.4)(0.4)$ $=0.16$	2
$P(R \text{ and } U)$ $=(0.4)(0.6)$ $=0.24$	1
$P(U \text{ and } R)$ $=(0.6)(0.4)$ $=0.24$	1
$P(U \text{ and } U)$ $=(0.6)(0.6)$ $=0.36$	0

We see that $P(x = 2) = 0.16$, and $P(x = 0) = 0.36$. We see that there are two ways for x to equal 1, and since these are mutually exclusive, we can simply add the related probabilities to get $P(x = 1) = 0.24 + 0.24 = 0.48$. This information can be summarized in a table such as the one shown in Exhibit 5.2 below.

Number of Rural Customers Out of Two Randomly Selected Customers from Ben's Salon

Exhibit 5.2

x	0	1	2
$P(x)$	0.36	0.48	0.16

Note that the possible values of the random variable x represent mutually exclusive outcomes (having exactly one rural customer is mutually exclusive with having exactly two rural customers). This means that if we want to calculate $P(x = 1 \text{ or } 2)$, we can simply add the related probabilities.

$P(x = 1 \text{ or } 2) = 0.48 + 0.16 = 0.64$

We could also have used the complement rule to get this probability.

$P(x = 1 \text{ or } 2) = 1 - P(x = 0) = 1 - 0.36 = 0.64$

The probability rules from Chapter 4 will come in handy when you are working with discrete probability distributions.

The table shown in Exhibit 5.2 is one way to represent the probability distribution of the random variable x. It is also possible to represent this information graphically, with the random variable *x* on the *x*-axis and P(*x*) on the *y*-axis, as shown below in Exhibit 5.3.

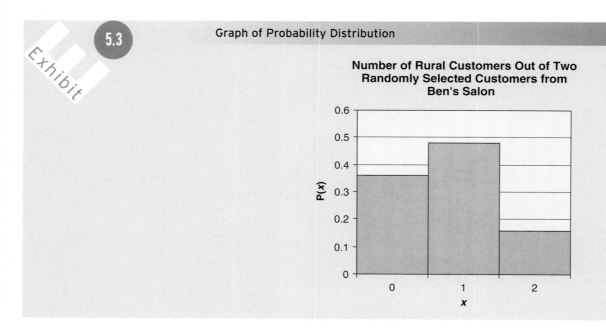

5.3

Exhibit

Graph of Probability Distribution

Number of Rural Customers Out of Two Randomly Selected Customers from Ben's Salon

Of course, the sum of the probabilities in any probability distribution has to be 100% (or 1, in decimal form), because the probability distribution lists *all* of the possible values of the random variable, and these in turn must account for all of the possible outcomes of the experiment.

Mean and Standard Deviation of a Probability Distribution

Most probability distributions can be summarized with:

- expected values (or means), which are (not surprisingly) measures of the centre of the probability distribution, and
- standard deviations, which are measures of the variability of the probability distribution.

The calculations depend on the particular probability distribution.

The mean, μ, of a discrete probability distribution can be calculated as follows.

$$\mu = \Sigma \, (x \cdot P(x))$$

That is, the mean is a weighted average of the possible values of the random variable *x*, where the weights are the associated probabilities. The mean of a probability distribution is also referred to as the *expected value* of the random variable.

The standard deviation, σ, of a probability distribution can be calculated as follows.

$$\sigma = \sqrt{\Sigma \, (x - \mu)^2 \, P(x)}$$

This formula shows that calculation of the standard deviation is based on deviations from the mean, as we would expect from our work on standard deviations in Chapter 3.

While this formula is correct, if you want to calculate the standard deviation by hand, there is another version of the formula that you will find easier to use, as follows.

$$\sigma = \sqrt{\Sigma x^2 P(x) - \mu^2}$$

We can apply these formulas to calculate the mean and standard deviation for the probability distribution for the Ben Little salon example. Exhibit 5.4 shows the probability distribution again.

Probability Distribution for Number of Rural Customers Out of Two Randomly Selected Customers from Ben's Salon

x	0	1	2
P(x)	0.36	0.48	0.16

5.4 *Exhibit*

$$\mu = \Sigma(x \cdot P(x))$$
$$= 0 \cdot 0.36 + 1 \cdot 0.48 + 2 \cdot 0.16$$
$$= 0.8$$

The expected number of rural customers, out of a random sample of two, is 0.8.

$$\sigma = \sqrt{\Sigma x^2 P(x) - \mu^2}$$
$$= \sqrt{(0^2 \cdot 0.36 + 1^2 \cdot 0.48 + 2^2 \cdot 0.16) - 0.8^2}$$
$$= \sqrt{1.12 - 0.64}$$
$$= \sqrt{0.48}$$
$$= 0.6928$$

The standard deviation of this probability distribution is 0.6928.

Suppose every year you bid for the contract to cut the lawns at a townhouse condominium in your town. The contract will pay you $5,000. Suppose also that you know that each year there is a 50% chance you will get the contract, because the condominium board makes the decision by flipping a coin to choose between you and your arch-rival, who also bids on the contract each year. Prepare a probability distribution table for the distribution of x, the amount of money you will make from this lawn-cutting contract in a particular year. Calculate the mean and standard deviation of this probability distribution.

5.1 *Example*

Calculating the mean and standard deviation of a discrete probability distribution

The associated probability distribution for this contract is illustrated in Exhibit 5.5.

Probability Distribution for Lawn-Cutting Contract

Contract value, x	$0	$5,000
Probability, P(x)	0.50	0.50

5.5 *Exhibit*

Imagine bidding on this contract year after year for many, many years. About half the time you will earn $5,000, and about half the time you will earn $0. So, your expected earnings over many years will be about $2,500, that is, $0.50(\$0) + 0.50(\$5,000) = \$2,500$. This is of course the expected value of the probability distribution.

$$\begin{aligned} \sigma &= \sqrt{\Sigma x^2 P(x) - \mu^2} \\ &= \sqrt{(0^2 \cdot 0.50 + 5,000^2 \cdot 0.50) - 2,500^2} \\ &= \sqrt{12,500,000 - 6,250,000} \\ &= \sqrt{6,250,000} \\ &= 2,500 \end{aligned}$$

The standard deviation for the contract value is $2,500.

DEVELOP YOUR SKILLS 5.1

1. Which of the following random variables are discrete, and which are continuous?
   a. The number of passengers on a flight from Toronto to Paris
   b. The time it takes you to drive to work in the morning
   c. The number of cars that arrive at the local car dealership for an express oil-change service on Wednesday
   d. The time it takes to cut a customer's lawn
   e. The number of soft drinks a student buys during one week
   f. The kilometres driven on one tank of gas

2. Revisit the situation first described in Develop Your Skills 4.3, Exercise 2 (p. 159). Three women who have been friends since childhood have just graduated from college. The friends are very different, and have different abilities and skills. All three of them are trying to get jobs in the financial services industry. Their probabilities of succeeding are 0.4, 0.5, and 0.35. Define x as the number of these three friends who get a job in the financial services industry. Build the probability distribution for x. If you did the earlier Develop Your Skills exercise, you have already calculated some of the probabilities.

3. Revisit the situation first described in Develop Your Skills 4.3, Exercise 3 (p. 159). A software company is about to release three new software programs, one from each of three very distinct business divisions. The first program is a new game aimed at 15–25-year-olds. Its probability of succeeding is estimated to be 0.34. The second program is an accounting application for small business. Its probability of succeeding is estimated to be 0.12. The third program is a payroll system designed for government organizations. Its probability of succeeding is 0.10. Define x as the number of the three new software programs that is a success for this company. Build the associated probability distribution (you should have already calculated some of the probabilities). What is the expected number of successes?

4. Revisit the situation first described in Chapter Review Exercise 19 in Chapter 4 (p. 164). A shipment contains 500 circuit boards, and 25 of them are defective. Define x as the number of defective boards in two selections from the shipment. Build the probability distribution for x. (You may find it easiest to use a computer to do these calculations.)

5. Exhibit 5.6 below shows a probability distribution for the number of customers who will order the daily special, out of the next six customers who come through the door. Fill in the missing probability, and calculate the mean and standard deviation of this probability distribution.

Exhibit 5.6

Number of Customers Who Will Order the Daily Special at a Restaurant, Out of the Next Six Customers

x	0	1	2	3	4	5	6
$P(x)$	0.03	0.05	0.28	0.45	0.12	0.04	?

5.2   THE BINOMIAL PROBABILITY DISTRIBUTION

Conditions for a Binomial Experiment

The binomial probability distribution often applies when we are interested in the number of times a particular characteristic turns up. For example, in a paint factory, we might be interested in the number of dented paint cans we find in the next 500 cans. We might want to know how many of the next 50 customers who come into the store will opt for the bonus offer. Notice that what is of interest here is a count (how many out of a particular number), which can also be expressed as a percentage or proportion (that is, 32 customers out of the next 50 corresponds to 64%).

This count that we are interested in is a random variable, because its outcome is determined by chance. A binomial random variable counts the number of times one of only two possible outcomes takes place (thus the *bi-* part of the binomial's name). Because the binomial distribution can apply in a wide range of circumstances, we use some general language to cover all of these cases. When we find what we are looking for, this is called a *success*, and the other outcome (the complement of success) is a *failure*. So, if a customer comes into the store and opts for the bonus offer, this is a success. When a customer does not opt for the bonus offer, this is a failure. Similarly, if we find a dented paint can (this is what we are looking for), this is a success. This may seem a bit odd (surely we are hoping that the paint cans will *not* be dented), but if you think of a success as *finding what you are looking for*, the language will be more comfortable.

In a binomial experiment, we are doing something repeatedly, for example, examining a paint can to see if it is dented. These repeated actions are referred to as *trials*.

> The requirements for a random variable to be binomial are as follows:
>
> 1. There are only two possible outcomes to each trial of the experiment: success and failure. The probability of success in a given trial is denoted p. The probability of failure is $1 - p$ (often denoted as q).
> 2. The binomial random variable is the number of successes in a fixed number of trials (n).
> 3. Each trial is independent of every other trial. The probability of success, p, stays constant from trial to trial, as does the probability of failure, q.

Mean and Standard Deviation of a Binomial Distribution

A binomial probability distribution has a mean (expected value) and a standard deviation, as most probability distributions do. For a binomial random variable, the general formula for the mean simplifies to $\mu = np$. For example, when there are 10 trials (so $n = 10$), and the probability of success on each trial is 0.60, the expected value (or mean) of the binomial random variable would be $10(0.6) = 6$. This seems reasonable: if we repeated this experiment many times, we could expect the average outcome to be 6.

The general formula for the standard deviation of the binomial random variable simplifies to $\sigma = \sqrt{npq}$. Following on with the example above, the standard deviation would be $\sqrt{10(0.6)(0.4)} = 1.5492$.

Checking the Conditions for a Binomial Experiment

There are many situations where the binomial distribution applies. If you can recognize these situations, then you will be able to rely on a theoretical mathematical model to calculate probabilities (which is easier than it sounds!). The key to recognizing an application of the binomial probability distribution is to check against the requirements outlined in the list above. For example, suppose we want to know the probability that a student can pass a 25-question multiple choice exam, if each question has five choices, and the student guesses. Is this a case where the binomial probability distribution applies?

First, there are 25 trials in this experiment. In each trial, the student guesses the answer to a multiple choice question. Although the student is picking from among five choices, there are in fact only two outcomes of interest: either the student guesses correctly (which has a probability of $\frac{1}{5} = 0.20$), or the student guesses incorrectly (which has a probability of $\frac{4}{5} = 0.80$). If a student is to pass the exam, then he or she must get at least 13 of the 25 questions correct. Therefore, we want to know $P(x \geq 13, n = 25, p = 0.20)$. So far, this situation seems to fit the binomial model.

The last requirement is that each trial is independent of every other trial, and that the probability of success, p, stays constant from trial to trial. If the student is truly guessing at each question, then this would be the case. We can use the binomial model to calculate the probability of passing the multiple choice test (you should do so, once you learn how to do the calculations, in case you are harbouring any misconceptions that multiple choice tests are easy to pass!).

Here is another example. What is the probability that in a sample of 20 tires in a tire factory, one will be defective, if 3% of all such tires produced at a particular plant are defective?

There are 20 trials in this experiment. Each trial consists of checking a tire to see if it is defective or not. Success in this case would be defined as finding a defective tire, and we are told that $P(\text{success}) = p = 0.03$. The only other outcome is that a tire is not defective. So, we want to know $P(x = 1, n = 20, p = 0.03)$.

The last requirement is that each trial is independent of every other trial, and that the probability of success stays constant from trial to trial. When we sample a tire to see if it is defective, we would not return the sampled tire back into the population of tires. Therefore, each time we check a tire and set it aside, we are changing the probability that the next tire we sample will be defective. In terms of the binomial distribution, this means that the probability of success is changing from trial to trial, and the trials are not independent. This would seem to indicate that the binomial distribution does *not* apply in this case. But there is more to this.

Sampling Without Replacement   In the tire example, sampling is being done *without replacement*. This means that the trials are *not* independent, and so the experiment is not truly binomial. However, the binomial distribution can still be used in *certain* situations where the trials are not truly independent.

A numerical example will help you understand why. For example, suppose a tire factory produces 100,000 tires in a production run. If 3% of the tires are defective, then there are 3,000 defective tires in the population. The first time a tire is selected, the probability of finding a defective tire will be $\frac{3,000}{100,000} = 0.03$. The probability that the second tire will be defective will depend on whether the first tire was defective:

- It will either be $\frac{2,999}{99,999} = 0.0299903$ (if the first tire was defective), or

- It will be $\frac{3,000}{99,999} = 0.0300003$ (if the first tire was not defective).

Notice that although the second-round selection probability is changing, it is not changing by much, and this is what is important here.

By the time the 20th tire is selected, the number of defective tires left in the population can be as low as 2,981 (if all of the previous 19 tires were defective) or as high as 3,000 (if none of the previous 19 tires was defective). This means that on the 20th trial, the probability of finding a defective tire can range from:

- $\frac{2,981}{99,981} = 0.0298157$ to

- $\frac{3,000}{99,981} = 0.0300057$.

While these probabilities are different from 3%, they are not much different. Because of this, we can still use the binomial distribution in this situation, because the probabilities will be close enough to the exact calculations.

This is appropriate only when the sample size is small relative to the population (otherwise, the binomial probabilities would be too far off the correct ones). How small should the sample be, relative to the population, for the binomial distribution to be used when we are sampling without replacement? Generally, if the sample is no more than 5% of the population, the binomial distribution can still be used.

> When the other conditions for a binomial experiment apply but sampling is done without replacement, the binomial distribution can be used to approximate probabilities as long as the sample is no more than 5% of the population.

In fact, most of the useful applications of the binomial distribution rely on this result, because it is rare to encounter a real-life situation where sampling is done with replacement. Opinion polls are one of the most widely known applications of the binomial distribution. Obviously, the interviews are conducted without replacement. Once a pollster has talked with a respondent, that respondent is *not* added back into the population so that he or she might be called again.

Calculating Binomial Probabilities

Now that we know how to recognize when the binomial distribution applies, the next step is to calculate binomial probabilities. We will begin by calculating a binomial probability using the probability rules from Chapter 4, and then introduce a general formula. We will also use Excel to calculate binomial probabilities, and finally, we will use tables in the back of this textbook.

Suppose a polling company has sent you to a large shopping mall to do some research into buying habits. Past polls done by the company in this mall have indicated that 60% of the shoppers are female, and there is no reason to believe that the customer base has changed significantly. You are standing by one of many entrances to the mall and approaching every customer who comes through the door to complete your survey, in the belief that this will give you a random sample of customers (suppose it does). What is the probability that two of the next three customers are female?

First we have to decide if this situation fits the binomial probability distribution. There will be three trials, as you ascertain whether each of the next three customers is female (success, in this case). The probability of a customer being female is 0.6, based on past research. Are the trials independent? No, because you are sampling without replacement. However, it is likely that your sample of three customers is much less than 5% of the population of mall customers, so we can still use the binomial distribution to figure out probabilities. Although the probability of a customer being female will change *slightly* from trial to trial, it will still be approximately 0.6, and that is the value we will use.

The tree diagram shown in Exhibit 5.7 outlines the situation. There are eight possible outcomes, of which three correspond to the desired result (two out of the next three customers are female). These are highlighted in blue on the tree diagram.

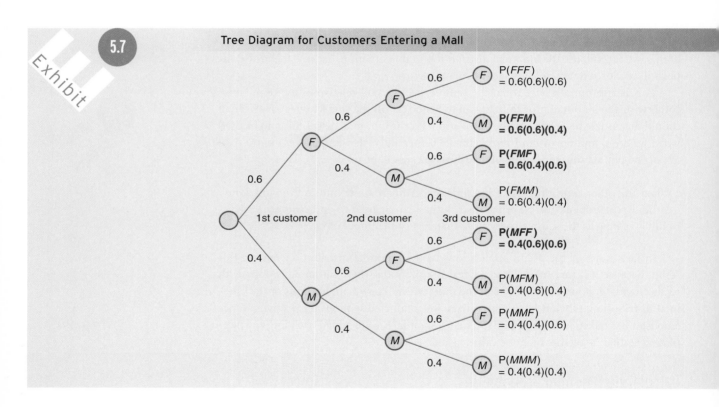

Exhibit 5.7

Tree Diagram for Customers Entering a Mall

To calculate the probability we want, we can simply add the probabilities of the three appropriate end outcomes (they are mutually exclusive). We calculate:

P(next 2 out of 3 customers female)

$$= (0.6)(0.6)(0.4) + (0.6)(0.4)(0.6) + (0.4)(0.6)(0.6)$$

$$= 0.144 + 0.144 + 0.144$$

$$= 0.432$$

Obviously, we could repeat this sort of probability calculation until we had the complete probability distribution for the random variable x, which is the number of females among the next three customers you encounter. This random variable can take four possible values (0, 1, 2, or 3). A complete probability distribution for this random variable is summarized in the table shown in Exhibit 5.8 below.

Probability Distribution for the Number of Female Customers Out of the Next Three Entering a Mall

x	0	1	2	3
P(x)	0.064	0.288	0.432	0.216

Exhibit 5.8

Particularly if you take the time to verify the other probability entries in this table, you will notice that there is a pattern to the probability calculation. This pattern applies whether we are analyzing customers at a mall or faulty tires on an assembly line. The pattern of calculations can be captured mathematically in a formula, which underlies the probability calculations in Excel and the tables in the back of the book.

Calculating Binomial Probabilities with a Formula   The formula is as follows. For a binomial experiment with n trials, probability of success p, and probability of failure $q = 1 - p$:

$$P(x \text{ successes}) = \binom{n}{x} p^x q^{n-x}$$

where $\binom{n}{x}$ is the number of combinations of x items you can choose from n items, and is evaluated as follows:

$$\binom{n}{x} = \frac{n!}{x!(n-x)!} = \frac{n(n-1)(n-2)\cdots(1)}{x(x-1)(x-2)\cdots(1)(n-x)(n-x-1)\cdots(1)}$$

This formula looks more complicated than it is. When you see the actual calculations, you will realize that they are fairly straightforward. $n!$ is read as *n factorial*. In these calculations, you will see that there is always a fair amount of cancelling out in the factorial portion of the formula. Another fact you will need to know is that $0! = 1$, by definition.

For the example above, where we wanted to know how many female customers there would be out of the next three customers entering the mall:

- $n = 3$
- $p = 0.60$ (and $q = 1 - 0.60 = 0.40$).

Suppose we want to calculate $P(x = 2)$.

$$P(x = 2) = \binom{n}{x} p^x q^{n-x}$$

$$= \binom{3}{2} 0.60^2 \, 0.40^{3-2}$$

$$= \frac{3!}{2!(3-2)!} \, 0.60^2 \, 0.40^1$$

$$= \frac{3 \cdot 2 \cdot 1}{(2 \cdot 1)(1 \cdot 1)} \, 0.36 \cdot 0.40$$

$$= 3(0.36)(0.40)$$

$$= 0.432$$

This agrees exactly with the value we calculated before (see Exhibit 5.8).

5.2a

Calculating binomial probabilities with a formula

The probability that an adult resident of Barrie is going to purchase a new vehicle in the next six months is 0.12. If six adult residents of Barrie are randomly selected and asked about whether they intend to buy a new vehicle in the next six months, what is the probability that two will indicate they plan to do so?

In this case, sampling is done without replacement, but the population of Barrie is over 100,000. The sample size of six is much less than 5% of the population, so the binomial distribution can still be used to approximate the probability.

For this experiment, $n = 6$, $p = 0.12$, and we want to calculate $P(x = 2)$.

$$P(x = 2) = \binom{n}{x} p^x q^{n-x}$$

$$= \binom{6}{2} 0.12^2 \, 0.88^{6-2}$$

$$= \frac{6!}{2!(6-2)!} \, 0.12^2 \, 0.88^4$$

$$= \frac{6 \cdot 5 \cdot 4 \cdot 3 \cdot 2 \cdot 1}{(2 \cdot 1)(4 \cdot 3 \cdot 2 \cdot 1)} \, 0.12^2 \, 0.88^4$$

$$= \frac{6 \cdot 5}{(2 \cdot 1)} \, 0.12^2 \, 0.88^4$$

$$= (3 \cdot 5)(0.0144)(0.59969536)$$

$$= 0.1295$$

You should not round the probabilities until you get to the end of the calculation.

The probability that two out of six randomly selected adult Barrie residents plan to buy a new vehicle in the next six months is 0.1295.

It is easier to use a computer (or the tables, if a computer is not at hand) to do binomial probability calculations than to do them by hand or with a calculator.

Calculating Binomial Probabilities with Excel

As with the formula, in order to use Excel or the tables, we need to identify the particular binomial distribution of interest. We need to know:

- n, the number of trials
- p, the probability of success
- x, the number of successes for which we want the probability.

In the example about the mall customers, $n = 3$, $p = 0.6$, and $x = 2$. The Excel function we need is called BINOMDIST, and has the dialogue box shown below in Exhibit 5.9.

Instructions

BINOMDIST Dialogue Box

Exhibit **5.9**

Function Arguments   ? ✕

┌─ BINOMDIST ──────────────────────────────────────┐
│   **Number_s** [   ] 🔢 = number   │
│   **Trials** [   ] 🔢 = number   │
│ **Probability_s** [   ] 🔢 = number   │
│   **Cumulative** [   ] 🔢 = logical   │
│   =   │
│ Returns the individual term binomial distribution probability. │
│   │
│   **Number_s** is the number of successes in trials. │
│   │
│ Formula result =   │
│ Help on this function   [OK] [Cancel] │
└──┘

The function arguments in Excel are:

- Number_s is x, the number of successes we are interested in
- Trials is n, the number of trials
- Probability_s is the probability of success, p
- Cumulative requires either *false* or *true* depending on whether you want a probability of a single number of successes (as in P($x = 2$), enter *false* in this case) or a cumulative probability of the form P($x \leq 2$) (enter *true* in this case).

Notice that as you place your cursor in each of the individual slots on the dialogue box, Excel provides a description of what is needed in the bottom part of the box. When you click OK, Excel returns the value into the cell in the spreadsheet where your cursor is located. You should type some text into an adjoining cell, to describe what the calculation is about.

Excel produces the same result we arrived at through calculation, P($x = 2$) = 0.432, as illustrated in Exhibit 5.10 on the following page.

Exhibit 5.10

BINOMDIST Excel Function Result

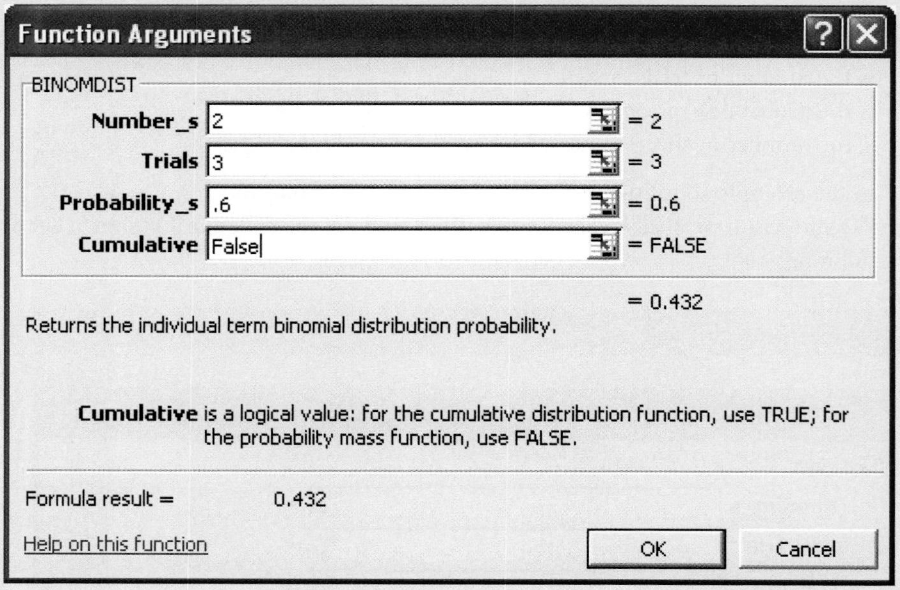

Function Arguments		? ✕
BINOMDIST		
Number_s 2	⬚	= 2
Trials 3	⬚	= 3
Probability_s .6	⬚	= 0.6
Cumulative False|	⬚	= FALSE

= 0.432

Returns the individual term binomial distribution probability.

Cumulative is a logical value: for the cumulative distribution function, use TRUE; for the probability mass function, use FALSE.

Formula result =   0.432

Help on this function   OK   Cancel

Excel's **BINOMDIST** provides not only probabilities for a single number of successes, but also *cumulative* probabilities. These are of the form $P(x \leq x^*)$, where x^* is a particular number of successes. For example, $P(x \leq 2)$, in the mall survey example, would be the answer to the question: What is the probability that two or fewer of the next three customers are female?

$P(x \leq 2) = P(x = 0 \text{ or } 1 \text{ or } 2)$. The values of x in a binomial experiment represent mutually exclusive outcomes. Cumulative probabilities are calculated by adding the associated probabilities. This is effectively what Excel does when you enter **true** in the **Cumulative** slot of the **BINOMDIST** dialogue box.

The probability function of Excel and the complement rule enable us to calculate *any* binomial probability we need.

Example 5.2b

Using Excel to calculate binomial probabilities

Use Excel to calculate the following probabilities.

1. $P(x = 13, n = 50, p = 0.12)$
2. $P(x \leq 13, n = 50, p = 0.12)$
3. $P(x > 13, n = 50, p = 0.12)$
4. $P(x < 13, n = 50, p = 0.12)$
5. $P(8 \leq x \leq 15)$
6. $P(8 < x < 15)$

Solutions

1. $P(x = 13, n = 50, p = 0.12) = 0.0034$. This is a straightforward, non-cumulative binomial probability. See the Excel result in Exhibit 5.11, on the next page.

BINOMDIST Result for P(x = 13, n = 50, p = 0.12)

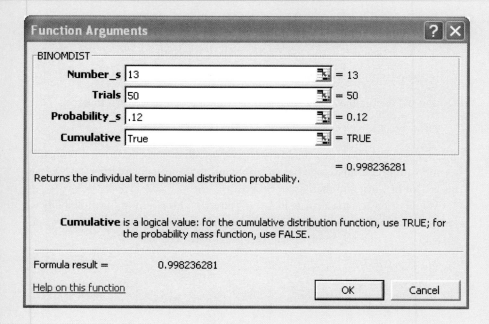

Exhibit 5.11

2. P($x \leq 13$, n = 50, p = 0.12) = 0.9982. This is a straightforward cumulative binomial probability. See the Excel result in Exhibit 5.12, below.

BINOMDIST Result for P($x \leq 13$, n = 50, p = 0.12)

Exhibit 5.12

Function Arguments		? X
BINOMDIST		
Number_s	13	= 13
Trials	50	= 50
Probability_s	.12	= 0.12
Cumulative	True	= TRUE

= 0.998236281

Returns the individual term binomial distribution probability.

Cumulative is a logical value: for the cumulative distribution function, use TRUE; for the probability mass function, use FALSE.

Formula result =   0.998236281

Help on this function   OK   Cancel

3. P($x > 13$, $n = 50$, $p = 0.12$). This poses a problem, since it does not correspond exactly to either of the two probabilities that Excel calculates. However, we can use the complement rule to calculate this answer. This allows us to work with probabilities that BINOMDIST does calculate.

P($x > 13$)

= 1 − P($x \leq 13$)

= 1 − 0.998236281 (shown above)

= 0.001763719

Be sure to use Excel to do the subtraction shown above. Exhibit 5.13 gives an example of how to set up a spreadsheet correctly. The calculations done by Excel are contained in cells B4, B6, and B9. All of the other text has been typed into Excel. This allows you (or anyone else) to be able to read the spreadsheet.

5.13 Exhibit

Correct Spreadsheet Set-up

	A	B	C
1	n	50	
2	p	0.12	
3			
4	P(x=13)	0.003351759	
5			
6	P(x <=13)	0.998236281	
7			
8	P(x>13)	=1 - P(x<=13)	
9		0.001763719	

4. P($x < 13$, $n = 50$, $p = 0.12$). This probability also does not correspond directly to one that Excel calculates. Here we have to realize that for the binomial, P($x < 13$) = P($x \leq 12$). ($x = 13$) is *not* included in this calculation, while it *is* included in P($x \leq 13$).

P($x < 13$) = P($x \leq 12$) = 0.9949

5. P($8 \leq x \leq 15$). Again, we have to do some thinking before we turn to Excel.

P($8 \leq x \leq 15$) = P($x =$ 8 or 9 or 10 or 11 or 12 or 13 or 14 or 15)

One way we could do this would be to figure out all of these individual probabilities and simply add them together (the outcomes are mutually exclusive). However, this is a lot of work and there is an easier way.

We can use Excel to calculate P($x \leq 15$) directly. This is almost the probability we want, except that it includes P($x \leq 7$), which we do not want. We can use Excel to calculate P($x \leq 7$) directly, and then subtract to get what we want.

P($8 \leq x \leq 15$)

= P($x \leq 15$) − P($x \leq 7$)

= 0.99984 − 0.75325

= 0.2466

6. P(8 < x < 15). Use similar reasoning to get this probability.

P(8 < x < 15)

= P(9 ≤ x ≤ 14)

= P(x ≤ 14) − P(x ≤ 8)

= 0.999444 − 0.860799

= 0.1386

Now that you have seen these examples, that's it! You should be able to use Excel to calculate *any* binomial probability you encounter.

Calculating Binomial Probabilities with Tables   For some situations, binomial tables are available (see Appendix 1 at the back of this textbook). As with Excel, you need to know n (the number of trials), p (the probability of success on any trial), and x (the number of successes you are interested in), to use the tables. Binomial tables are available in two forms:

- tables showing P(x = a particular value)
- tables showing P(x ≤ a particular value).

The tables in the back of this textbook are of the second form, that is, they show P(x ≤ a particular value). To get P(x = a particular value) from these tables, perform a subtraction as follows:

P(x = a particular value) = P(x ≤ the particular value) − P(x ≤ (the particular value − 1))

For example,

P(x = 4, n = 8, p = 0.3)

= P(x ≤ 4) − P(x ≤ 3) (both of these values are in the table; see the excerpt in Exhibit 5.14)

= 0.942 − 0.806

= 0.136

Cumulative Binomial Probabilities for $n = 8$

Number of Successes	P 0.01	0.05	0.1	0.2	0.25	0.3	0.4
0	0.923	0.663	0.430	0.168	0.100	0.058	0.017
1	0.997	0.943	0.813	0.503	0.367	0.255	0.106
2	1.000	0.994	0.962	0.797	0.679	0.552	0.315
3	1.000	1.000	0.995	0.944	0.886	0.806	0.594
4	1.000	1.000	1.000	0.990	0.973	0.942	0.826
5	1.000	1.000	1.000	0.999	0.996	0.989	0.950
6	1.000	1.000	1.000	1.000	1.000	0.999	0.991
7	1.000	1.000	1.000	1.000	1.000	1.000	0.999
8	1.000	1.000	1.000	1.000	1.000	1.000	1.000

Exhibit 5.14

Generally, binomial probability tables do not include the last row, $P(x \leq n)$, which is $P(x \leq 8)$ in the example above. This is because $P(x \leq 8) = 1$ when $n = 8$. The sum of the probabilities for all possible outcomes *must* add up to 100%. Of course, the tables work for only the probabilities shown across the top row. In cases where the tables do not provide the answer, you can always turn to Excel for the answer.

5.2c

Calculating binomial probabilities with tables

The probability that a paint can will be dented during the production process in a factory is 0.01. If 25 paint cans are randomly selected from production, what is the probability that three or more of them will be dented?

In this case, sampling is done without replacement, but we assume the factory produces many thousands of cans of paint. The sample size is probably much less than 5% of the population, so the binomial distribution can still be used to approximate the probabilities.

$$n = 25, p = 0.01$$

$$P(x \geq 3) = 1 - P(x \leq 2) = 1 - 0.998 = 0.002$$

The probability of getting three or more dented cans out of 25 when they are randomly selected from the paint production process is 0.002.

Graphical Representation of Binomial Probability Distributions   It is possible to present the binomial distribution graphically, by plotting probabilities on the y-axis and values of x on the x-axis. Exhibit 5.15 below shows $P(x = \text{number of successes})$, for $n = 8$ and $p = 0.3$. The probabilities were calculated using Excel.

5.15

Table of Binomial Probabilities (Non-Cumulative) for $n = 8$	
Number of Successes \\ P	0.3
0	0.05765
1	0.19765
2	0.29648
3	0.25412
4	0.13614
5	0.04668
6	0.01000
7	0.00122
8	0.00007

$P(x = 4)$, for example, is represented by the shaded area in the graph in Exhibit 5.16, opposite, where $n = 8$ and $p = 0.3$. Because this is a probability distribution, the sum of all the probabilities and the total area of the bars has to add up to 1 (or 100%).

Graph of Probability Distribution

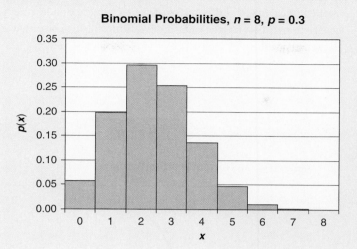

Binomial Probabilities, *n* = 8, *p* = 0.3

DEVELOP YOUR SKILLS 5.2

Do these calculations both with Excel and with tables (and with the binomial formula, if this is straightforward). You should get the same answers! Think about how you would recognize these as binomial probability calculations, if you did not have the clues here (the title of this section, for example) to let you know.

1. A campus newspaper claims that 80% of students on campus support the newspaper's position on various issues affecting the college. A random sample of 10 students is taken, and in the sample, only four students say they support the newspaper's position. What is the probability of four or fewer students agreeing with the newspaper's position, if the newspaper's claim about 80% support is correct? Do you believe the newspaper's claim?

2. What is the probability that a student can pass a 25-question multiple choice exam, if each question has five choices, and the student guesses?

3. What is the probability that in a sample of 20 tires, one will be defective, if 5% of all such tires produced at a particular plant are defective?

4. A poll on a website asked respondents what they thought was the best method of losing weight. 65% picked *exercise* as the answer. If five randomly selected visitors to the website were asked this question, what is the probability that three of them would pick *exercise*? Are you sure? Think carefully.

5. According to a recent survey conducted by a management recruiting firm, more than one-third (34.2%) of executives polled thought that business casual dress has gone too casual. Suppose you randomly selected 30 executives, and asked them if they thought that business casual dress had gone too casual. What is the probability that 10 or fewer would agree?

5.3   THE NORMAL PROBABILITY DISTRIBUTION

The normal distribution is the most important probability distribution in the world! It applies to many natural and physical situations, it is absolutely essential for many types of statistical inference, and it can also be used to approximate other distributions (even the binomial, as we will see in Chapter 6).

Even if you have never studied statistics before, you have probably seen or heard about the normal curve. It is sometimes referred to as the *bell curve*, because it is shaped like a bell. Exhibit 5.17 shows an example of a normal probability distribution centred on 100, with a standard deviation of 10. Notice that the normal distribution is symmetric.

5.17

Normal Probability Distribution with a Mean of 100, and a Standard Deviation of 10

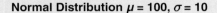

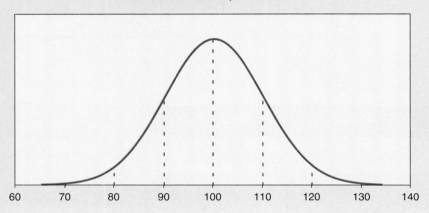

Normal Distribution $\mu = 100$, $\sigma = 10$

Many continuous random variables have normal distributions. Many normal random variables are related to a measurement of some kind. For example, if you made a histogram of the heights of all the students in your statistics class (assuming the class is fairly large), it is likely that this histogram would look fairly *normal*. As well, measurements such as the exact weight of cereal in cereal boxes tend to fit the normal distribution.

You may recall from Chapter 2 that in theory, a continuous random variable can take any value in a continuous range or interval. In practice, our measuring devices are limited (you probably cannot measure the height of your classmates more accurately than to the centimetre, unless you have some unusual measuring tools). Nevertheless, a normal random variable is theoretically continuous, and so the graph is a smooth line. As with the binomial distribution, the total area under the curve has to equal 1 (this is a probability distribution).

Because a normal random variable can take an uncountable number of possible values, it is not possible to list all values in a table with the associated probability, as we could for the binomial distribution. In this case another approach is needed, but it is very similar to the graphical approach we used for the binomial distribution.

Exhibit 5.18 shows a probability graph for a binomial distribution with $n = 10$, $p = 0.5$. $P(2 \leq x \leq 4)$ here is equivalent to the red-shaded area in the graph in Exhibit 5.18.

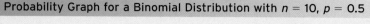

Probability Graph for a Binomial Distribution with $n = 10$, $p = 0.5$

Exhibit 5.18

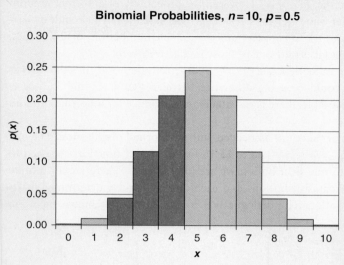

Below in Exhibit 5.19 is a normal distribution that is quite similar to the binomial distribution shown above (in Chapter 6 we will see how to create normal distributions that correspond to certain binomial distributions). The shaded area in this graph corresponds to $P(2 \leq x \leq 4)$.

Normal Distribution that Approximates the Binomial Distribution

Exhibit 5.19

Normal Distribution

Calculating Normal Probabilities with Excel But how do we figure out how much this area is? As with the binomial, this can be done with a formula (and in this case, some calculus). However, we will rely on Excel and a table to do normal probability calculations.

Before we turn to Excel, there is one more important point. For a binomial probability distribution, we can calculate the probability of the random variable taking a particular value, for example, P($x = 4$). However, the probability of a normal random variable taking a particular value is effectively 0. This is because the normal random variable is continuous. If it can take any one of an uncountable number of possible values, then the probability that it takes only one of those is effectively zero.

For a normal random variable, because P($x =$ a particular value) $= 0$, then P($x < 4$) $=$ P($x \leq 4$). While there could be a big difference between P($x \leq 4$) and P($x < 4$) for a binomial random variable, there is essentially no difference for a normal random variable.

Instructions

Excel has a number of functions associated with the normal distribution. The one we will use most often is NORMDIST. In order to use this Excel function, we need to identify the particular normal distribution we are interested in. There are an infinite number of different normal distributions, but each one is uniquely determined by its mean and standard deviation. The dialogue box for NORMDIST is shown below in Exhibit 5.20.

5.20

Exhibit

Dialogue Box for NORMDIST

Function Arguments   [?][X]

NORMDIST

X [　　　　　　　　　　　　　] = number

Mean [　　　　　　　　　　　] = number

Standard_dev [　　　　　　　] = number

Cumulative [　　　　　　　　] = logical

=

Returns the normal cumulative distribution for the specified mean and standard deviation.

X is the value for which you want the distribution.

Formula result =

Help on this function   OK   Cancel

The function arguments in Excel are:

- `x` is the upper limit of the probability you are interested in. For example if you wanted to know P($x \leq 4$), you would enter 4 here.
- `Mean` is the mean of the normal distribution you are interested in
- `Standard_dev` is the standard deviation of the normal distribution you are interested in
- `Cumulative` should *always* have "true" entered, for our purposes.

Used this way, the `NORMDIST` function will always provide

P($x \leq$ the particular value of x you provide).

Graphically, it looks like the example in Exhibit 5.21, where P($x \leq 4$) is illustrated.

P($x \leq 4$), `NORMDIST` Reports Shaded Area Under Curve

Normal Distribution

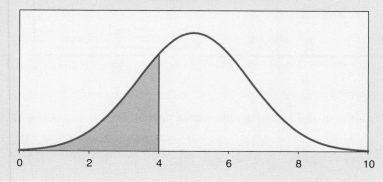

Exhibit **5.21**

For a normal distribution with a mean of 10 and a standard deviation of 2, calculate the following probabilities.

1. P($x \leq 8$)
2. P($8 \leq x \leq 13$)
3. P($x \geq 12$)

Example **5.3a**

Calculating normal probabilities with NORMDIST

Solutions

1. Probability calculations such as P($x \leq 8$) are quite straightforward with NORMDIST. Simply enter the mean, the standard deviation, and the value 8 into the appropriate areas, and the probability will be calculated for you. See Exhibit 5.22 on the next page.

Exhibit 5.22

$P(x \leq 8)$

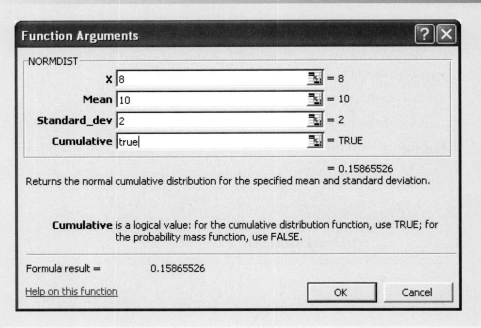

$P(x \leq 8) = 0.1587$

This probability is the shaded area under the curve shown in Exhibit 5.23 below.

Exhibit 5.23

$P(x \leq 8) = 0.1587$, Shaded Area Under Curve

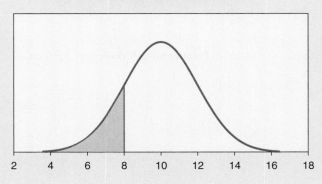

2. What if we want $P(8 \leq x \leq 13)$? It should be easy to see that we can arrive at this answer by first calculating $P(x \leq 13)$, and then subtracting off the area where $P(x \leq 8)$ (the cross-hatched area in Exhibit 5.24, on the next page).

$$P(8 \leq x \leq 13) = P(x \leq 13) - P(x \leq 8) = 0.933193 - 0.158655 = 0.774538$$

3. What if we wanted $P(x \geq 12)$? For this case, we can use the complement rule. $P(x \geq 12) = 1 - P(x \leq 12) = 1 - 0.8413455 = 0.158655$ (notice this is the same value as $P(x \leq 8)$, which we would expect, since the distribution is symmetric).

P($8 \leq x \leq 13$)

5.24
Exhibit

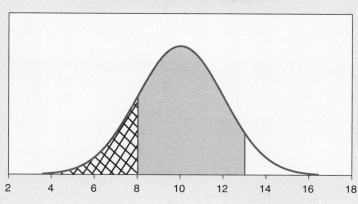

Normal Curve
Mean = 10, Standard Deviation = 2

Once you have mastered the three variations in the preceding example, you should be able to use NORMDIST to calculate any normal probability that you need. You should type some descriptive text into your spreadsheet so that you can identify the mean and standard deviation of the normal distribution you worked with, and you have a description of what the calculated probabilities refer to. Exhibit 5.25 below shows an example of how you could set up your spreadsheet.

Example of Spreadsheet Setup

5.25
Exhibit

	A	B	C
1	normal distribution		
2	mean	10	
3	standard deviation	2	
4			
5	P(x<=8)	0.158655	
6			
7	P(x<=13)	0.933193	
8	P(8<=x<=13)	0.774538	
9			
10	P(x<=12)	0.841345	
11	P(x>=12)	0.158655	

NORMDIST function results show in cells B5, B7, B8, B10, and B11. Everything else in the spreadsheet is typed in, so that the spreadsheet is easy to read and understand.

Another Excel function that we will use when calculating normal probabilities is NORMINV. We will use this function when we want the x-value that corresponds to a particular probability (this is the reverse of what we have done so far, where we started with an x-value and ended up with a probability).

Example 5.3b

Using NORMINV to calculate *x*-values
for normal probabilities

Suppose that past research has shown that the amount of paint in paint cans is normally distributed, with a mean of 3 litres and a standard deviation of 0.01 litres. The company controller is concerned that the company is giving away a lot of free paint in cans that are overfull. You want to reassure her, by telling her that 98% of the cans have no more than *x* amount of paint in them. What is *x*? Exhibit 5.26 illustrates this problem.

Exhibit 5.26

Normal Distribution of Paint Volume in Cans

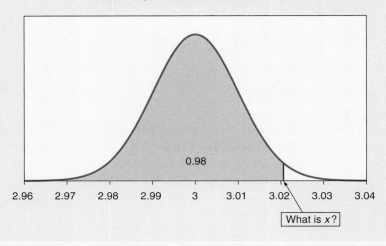

You can find the required *x* with NORMINV. The dialogue box for the function is shown below in Exhibit 5.27.

Exhibit 5.27

Dialogue Box for NORMINV

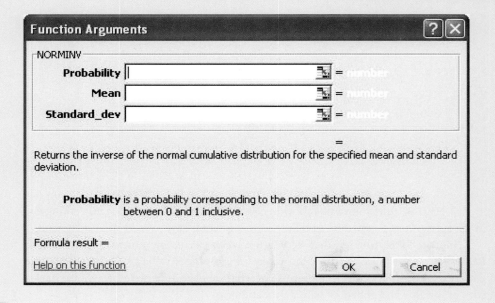

The function arguments in Excel are as follows.

- Probability is the (left-side) probability you are starting with (98%, in this case)
- Mean is the mean of the normal distribution (3, in this case)
- Standard_dev is the standard deviation of the normal distribution (0.01, in this case).

Since the probability problem is set up in a way that corresponds exactly to the Excel function, we can get the answer directly from Excel. The completed dialogue box is shown below in Exhibit 5.28.

Completed Dialogue Box for NORMINV

Exhibit 5.28

Function Arguments [?][X]

NORMINV

Probability	.98		= 0.98
Mean	3		= 3
Standard_dev	.01|		= 0.01

= 3.020537475

Returns the inverse of the normal cumulative distribution for the specified mean and standard deviation.

Standard_dev is the standard deviation of the distribution, a positive number.

Formula result =   3.020537475

Help on this function   [OK] [Cancel]

So, we can assure the controller that 98% of the paint cans have less than 3.020537 litres in them.

Calculating Normal Probabilities with a Table   What if you do not have access to Excel to calculate normal probabilities? There is a table in Appendix 2, at the back of this textbook, which can be used. It might seem surprising or mysterious that there is only *one* table, when there are an infinite number of normal distributions. The solution to the mystery lies in the fact that all normal distributions are symmetric probability distributions. The total area under each curve is equal to 1. As a result, corresponding probabilities from all of the normal distributions are equal.

This might be more obvious if we look at a couple of normal distributions. We will compare two normal distributions: one with a mean of 15 and a standard deviation of 2, and another with a mean of 16 and a standard deviation of 3. If we put both curves on the same graph (which ensures that the axis scales for the two curves are identical), the normal curves look different. This is illustrated in Exhibit 5.29.

5.29

Two Normal Distributions, Same Axis

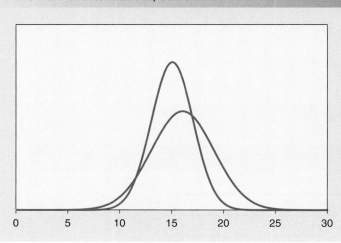

However, if we put the curves on two different graphs, and change the scales on the axes, the curves look the same, as illustrated in Exhibit 5.30 below.

5.30

Two Normal Distributions, Different Axis Scales

a)   **Normal Curve with $\mu = 15$, $\sigma = 2$**   b)   **Normal Curve with $\mu = 16$, $\sigma = 3$**

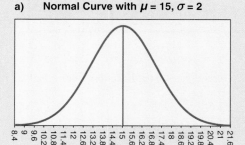 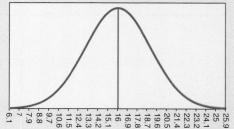

Some of the similarities are obvious. $P(x \leq 15)$ for the normal curve in Exhibit 5.30a will be equal to $P(x \leq 16)$ for the normal curve in Exhibit 5.30b. In both cases, of course, this probability will be equal to 50%, since the curves are symmetric, and half of the total 100% probability lies to the left of the mean and half to the right.

We can also see that $P(x \leq 12)$ for the normal curve centred on 15 will be equivalent to $P(x \leq 11.5)$ for the normal curve centred on 16, as illustrated in Exhibit 5.31 on the following page.

Two Normal Distributions

a)   Normal Curve With μ = 15, σ = 2   **b)   Normal Curve With μ = 16, σ = 3**

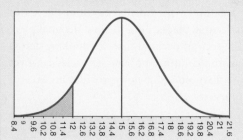
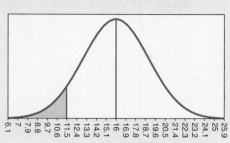

But how do we work with the normal distribution so that we can identify similar areas and probabilities? We do this by *standardizing* every normal probability calculation, that is, relating it back to a normal distribution with a mean of 0 and a standard deviation of 1 (this is the distribution that matches the table in the back of this book). We do this by calculating a *z-score*. The *z*-score translates the *x*-value of any normal distribution into a measure of how far that *x*-value is from the mean, in numbers of standard deviations. When an *x*-value is to the left of the mean (below the mean), the *z*-score will have a negative value. When an *x*-value is to the right of the mean (above the mean), the *z*-score will have a positive value.

We first used the standard deviation as a unit of measurement when we discussed the Empirical Rule, in Chapter 3. Then, we worked with *x*-values located at distances of exactly one, two, and three standard deviations from the mean. Now, with *z*-scores, we will be able to work with any *x*-value.

The *z*-score can be calculated using the following formula.

$$z = \frac{x - \mu}{\sigma}$$

As long as you follow the correct order of subtraction outlined in this formula, it will automatically assign the correct sign to the *z*-score.

We will apply the *z*-score calculation to the two examples we have been discussing. For the first distribution ($\mu = 15, \sigma = 2$), the *z*-score for an *x*-value of 12 is calculated as:

$$z = \frac{x - \mu}{\sigma} = \frac{12 - 15}{2} = -1.5$$

For the second distribution ($\mu = 15, \sigma = 3$), the *z*-score for an *x*-value of 11.5 is calculated as:

$$z = \frac{x - \mu}{\sigma} = \frac{11.5 - 16}{3} = -1.5$$

The *z*-scores are the same, so these *x*-values are an equivalent distance from the mean in their respective distributions. Therefore, the area (and probability) to the left of the *x*-values will be the same.

The table in the back of the textbook works with these z-scores, so once you have translated any x-value into a z-score, you can use the table for *any* normal distribution. You may have to rely on the complement rule to complete your calculations. The illustration at the top of the table shows what the table tells you. For a given z-score (call it z_0), the table gives $P(z \le z_0)$, that is, the area under the normal curve to the left of the z-score. The table reports z-scores to two decimal places. Find the first decimal place by looking down the first column. Locate the second decimal place by looking across the top row of the table. The intersection of the column and row you selected gives you the associated probability for the z-score. Exhibit 5.32 below provides an excerpt from the normal table, and illustrates how to use it.

5.32

Exhibit

Excerpt of Standard Normal Table

Z	0.00	0.01	0.02	0.03	0.04	0.05	0.06
0.00	0.5000	0.5040	0.5080	0.5120	0.5160	0.5199	0.5239
0.10	0.5398	0.5438	0.5478	0.5517	0.5557	0.5596	0.5636
0.20	0.5793	0.5832	0.5871	0.5910	0.5948	0.6987	0.6026
0.30	0.6179	0.6217	0.6255	0.6293	0.6331	0.6368	0.6406
0.40	0.6554	0.6591	0.6628	0.6664	0.6700	0.6736	0.6772
0.50	0.6915	0.6950	0.6985	0.7019	0.7054	0.7088	0.7123
0.60	0.7257	0.7291	0.7324	0.7357	0.7389	0.7422	0.7454
0.70	0.7580	0.7611	0.7642	0.7673	0.7704	0.7734	0.7764
0.80	0.7881	0.7910	0.7939	0.7967	0.7995	0.8023	0.8051
0.90	0.8159	0.8186	0.8212	0.8238	0.8264	0.8289	0.8315
1.00	0.8413	0.8438	0.8461	0.8485	0.8508	0.8531	0.8554

Suppose you calculated a z-score of 0.43. This table says that $P(z \le 0.43) = 0.6664$. This is illustrated in Exhibit 5.33, below.

5.33

Exhibit

$P(z \le 0.43) = 0.6664$

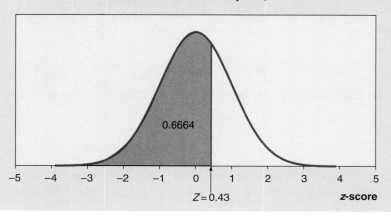

Normal Distribution with $\mu = 0$, $\sigma = 1$

0.6664

$Z = 0.43$

z-score

There is one more point about the normal tables. What if your calculations lead to a z-score that is not included in the tables? For example, what if you calculated a z-score of 4? And why do the tables go only as high as 3.99? If you look at the table, you will see that $P(z \le 3.99) = 1.0000$. This probability is equal to 100%, to four decimal places of accuracy, although a more exact value is 0.999966948158266. Although theoretically a normal random variable can be infinitely large or small, almost 100% of the probability is accounted for with a z-score of 3.99, and so the table stops there. If you have a z-score any larger than 3.99, and you are using the tables, keep in mind that there is only negligible area under the normal curve beyond a z-score of 3.99 (or -3.99).

How do we solve the problems that start with a probability and require us to find a corresponding x-value, using the normal tables? For example, how do we solve the problem from Example 5.3b (p. 190)? In this example, the amount of paint in paint cans is normally distributed, with a mean of 3 litres and a standard deviation of 0.01 litres. The company controller is concerned that the cans are overfull, and you want to reassure her that 98% of the cans have no more than x amount of paint in them. What is x?

In this case, the fact we are given is that $P(x \le$ unknown x-value$) = 0.98$. We have to scan the *body* of the normal table for an entry that is as close as possible to 0.98. The closest entry is 0.9798 (and here is one of the problems associated with using tables—often, you have to approximate the answer). This is the left-side probability for a z-score of 2.05. The z-score tells us that the correct x-value is 2.05 standard deviations above the mean. Therefore, the required x-value $= 3 + 2.05 (0.01) = 3.0205$.

Notice that this calculation is just a rearrangement of the formula for a z-score, as follows:

$$z = \frac{x - \mu}{\sigma} \text{ (cross} - \text{multiply)}$$
$$x - \mu = z \cdot \sigma \text{ (add } \mu \text{ to both sides)}$$
$$x = \mu + z \cdot \sigma$$

Because of the approximation, the x-value calculated with the table does not exactly match the value we calculated with **NORMINV** (3.020537), but it is fairly close.

It is a good idea to draw a normal curve and sketch in the area you are trying to find before you do any calculations. The use of drawings is demonstrated in this example.

Under standard conditions, an oil refinery will process an average of 150,000 barrels of oil a day. Output is normally distributed, with a standard deviation of 7,500 barrels.

1. What is the probability that more than 160,000 barrels will be processed in a day?
2. What is the probability that between 140,000 and 165,000 barrels will be processed in a day?
3. What is the probability that fewer than 130,000 barrels will be processed in a day?
4. On 75% of the days, more than _____ barrels of oil will be produced. Fill in the blank.

5.3c Example

Calculating normal probabilities with a table

Solutions

1. What is the probability that more than 160,000 barrels will be processed in a day?

5.34

Distribution of Oil Production, More than 160,000 Barrels

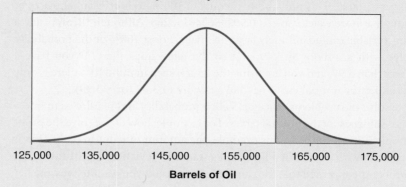

Daily Refinery Production

Barrels of Oil

$$P(x > 160,000)$$
$$= 1 - P(x < 160,000)$$
$$= 1 - P\left(z \leq \frac{160,000 - 150,000}{7,500}\right)$$
$$= 1 - P(z \leq 1.33)$$
$$= 1 - 0.9082$$
$$= 0.0918$$

2. What is the probability that between 140,000 and 165,000 barrels will be processed in a day?

5.35

Distribution of Oil Production, Between 140,000 and 160,000 Barrels

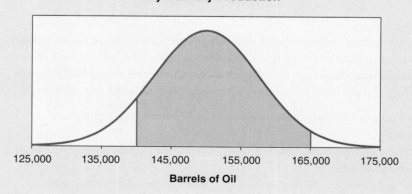

Daily Refinery Production

Barrels of Oil

$$P(140,000 \leq x \leq 165,000)$$
$$= P\left[\left(\frac{140,000 - 150,000}{7,500}\right) \leq z \leq \left(\frac{165,000 - 150,000}{7,500}\right)\right]$$
$$= P(-1.33 \leq z \leq 2)$$

$$= P(z \le 2) - P(z \le -1.33)$$
$$= 0.9772 - 0.0918$$
$$= 0.8854$$

3. What is the probability that fewer than 130,000 barrels will be processed in a day?

Distribution of Oil Production, Fewer than 130,000 Barrels

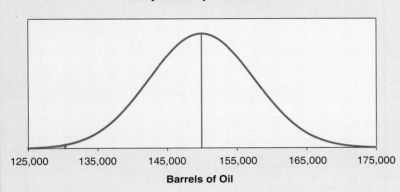

Daily Refinery Production

Barrels of Oil

5.36

Exhibit

$$P(x < 130,000)$$
$$= P\left[z < \left(\frac{130,000 - 150,000}{7,500}\right)\right]$$
$$= P(z < -2.67)$$
$$= 0.0038$$

4. On 75% of the days, more than _____ barrels of oil will be produced. Fill in the blank.

Distribution of Oil Production: Number of Barrels More Than? on 75% of Days

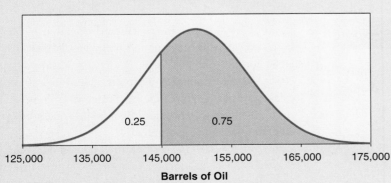

Daily Refinery Production

0.25   0.75

Barrels of Oil

5.37

Exhibit

Whatever x is, we know that 75% of the area under the normal curve lies to the right of it. This means that 25% of the area lies to the left (this corresponds to how Excel works and how the normal tables are set up). Search the body of the normal table for an entry that is as close as possible to 0.25. The closest value is 0.2514, which corresponds to a z-score of -0.67. This means that the x-value we seek is 0.67(7,500) below the mean of 150,000.

$$x = \mu + z \cdot \sigma$$
$$= 150,000 - 0.67(7,500)$$
$$= 144,975$$

Excel gives us a slightly more accurate result of 144,941.3, using NORMINV, as shown in Exhibit 5.38.

Exhibit 5.38

Excel Result: Number of Barrels More Than? on 75% of Days

Function Arguments [?][X]

NORMINV

Probability	.25	= 0.25
Mean	15,0000	= 15,0000
Standard_dev	7,500	= 7,500

= 144941.3286

Returns the inverse of the normal cumulative distribution for the specified mean and standard deviation.

Standard_dev is the standard deviation of the distribution, a positive number.

Formula result = 144,941.3286

Help on this function   [OK] [Cancel]

DEVELOP YOUR SKILLS 5.3

Do the following probability calculations with Excel first, and then with the tables in Appendix 2. You should get the same answers no matter how you do the calculations, although the tables will sometimes force you to approximate.

1. Your company manufactures light bulbs. You know from past experience that the number of hours the bulbs will last is a normally distributed random variable, with a mean of 5,000 hours and a standard deviation of 367 hours. What percentage of the bulbs will last at least 6,000 hours?

2. Using the light bulb distribution in Question 1 above, calculate what length-of-life guarantee your company should issue so that no more than 2.5% of light bulbs will fail to meet the guarantee.

3. Rocky Hill Bikes (RHB) manufactures high-end bicycles. Rocky Hill's vice-president of finance asked you to investigate the warranty expense for RHB's dual-suspension

hybrid bike. History shows that RHB has had high claims with this bike. You sampled 600 warranty claims and found that the average warranty expense per bike appeared to be normally distributed with an average of $53 (to your surprise, every bike in your sample had a warranty expense). You may assume that the standard deviation is $9. Assuming the normal distribution is an accurate probability model, answer the following questions.

a. What is the probability that a randomly selected warranty expense for these dual suspension hybrid bikes would be less than $38?

b. What is the probability that a randomly selected warranty expense for these bikes would be between $38 and $62?

c. Your boss has reminded you that RHB loses money on these bikes when the warranty expense exceeds $68. What is the probability that a randomly selected warranty expense for these bikes would be above $68?

4. Trading volume on a major stock exchange is approximately normally distributed with a mean of 646 million shares and a standard deviation of about 100 million shares.

a. What is the probability that the trading volume will be less than 450 million shares?

b. If the exchange wants to issue a press release when trading volume is in the top 2% of trading days, what trading volume would trigger a press release?

c. What percentage of the time does the trading volume exceed 800 million shares?

5. The time that it takes a worker to finish a particular assembly line task is normally distributed, with a mean of 32 seconds and a standard deviation of 10 seconds. The slowest 10% of workers (those with the slowest 10% of times) will be required to spend the weekend training, to try to improve their times. What is the minimum speed a worker must achieve to escape the weekend training?

A random variable is a variable whose value is determined by the outcome of a random experiment. A discrete random variable can take on any value from a list of distinct possible values. The probability distribution for a discrete random variable is often illustrated with a list of all the possible values of the random variable and their associated probabilities. A continuous random variable can take on any value from a continuous range. The probability distribution of a continuous random variable is described graphically, or with a mathematical formula.

Chapter Summary

Probability Distributions

It is possible to build a discrete probability distribution with probability rules. Discrete probability distributions can be represented with a table listing all possible values of the random variable and their associated probabilities. The distribution can also be represented graphically, with the possible values of the random variable along the x-axis, and the associated probabilities shown on the y-axis.

Most probability distributions can be summarized with

- expected values (or means), which are measures of the centre of the probability distribution, and
- standard deviations, which are measures of the variability of the probability distribution.

The mean of a discrete probability distribution, μ, can be calculated as follows.

$$\mu = \Sigma(x \cdot P(x))$$

The standard deviation of a probability distribution, σ, can be calculated as follows.

$$\sigma = \sqrt{\Sigma(x - \mu)^2 P(x)}$$

There is another version of the formula that you will find easier to use when doing calculations by hand, as follows.

$$\sigma = \sqrt{\Sigma x^2 \, P(x) - \mu^2}$$

The mean and standard deviation of a continuous probability distribution depend on the particular mathematical model.

The Binomial Probability Distribution

A binomial random variable counts the number of times one of only two possible outcomes takes place. In a binomial experiment, something is done repeatedly, for example, examining a paint can to see if it is dented. These repeated actions are referred to as trials.

There are a number of requirements for a random variable to be binomial, as follows:

1. There are only two possible outcomes to each trial of the experiment: success and failure. The probability of success in a given trial is denoted p. The probability of failure is $1 - p$ (often denoted as q).
2. The binomial random variable is the number of successes in a fixed number of trials (n).
3. Each trial is independent of every other trial. The probability of success, p, stays constant from trial to trial, as does the probability of failure, q.

The mean of a binomial random variable is $\mu = np$. The standard deviation of the binomial random variable is $\sigma = \sqrt{npq}$.

Most of the useful applications of the binomial distribution are not truly binomial, because sampling is done without replacement. When the other conditions for a binomial experiment apply, but sampling is done without replacement, the binomial distribution can be used to approximate probabilities, as long as the sample is no more than 5% of the population.

For a binomial experiment with n trials, probability of success p, and probability of failure $q = 1 - p$,

$$P(x \text{ successes}) = \binom{n}{x} p^x \, q^{n-x}$$

Example 5.2a on page 176 illustrates the use of the formula.

The Excel function used to calculate binomial probabilities is called BINOMDIST.

Example 5.2b on page 178 illustrates the use of Excel to calculate binomial probabilities. It is also possible to calculate a limited number of binomial probabilities using the tables in the back of the book (on pages 454–457). Example 5.2c on page 182 illustrates how to use the tables to calculate binomial probabilities.

The Normal Probability Distribution

The normal distribution applies to many natural and physical situations, it is absolutely essential for many types of statistical inference, and it can even be used to approximate other distributions. Many continuous random variables have normal distributions. Many normal random variables are related to a measurement of some kind.

For a normal random variable, $P(x = \text{a particular value}) = 0$. This means that for a normal random variable, say, 4, for example, $P(x < 4) = P(x \leq 4)$.

Excel has a number of functions associated with the normal distribution. Two that are described in this chapter are NORMDIST and NORMINV. Example 5.3a on page 187 illustrates the use of NORMDIST. Example 5.3b on page 190 illustrates the use of NORMINV.

It is also possible to use the standard normal distribution and a table (see page 458 at the back of the book) to calculate normal probabilities. It is necessary to standardize the probability calculation using a z-score, which translates the location of a particular x in a normal probability distribution into a number of standard deviations from the mean. The calculation of the z-score is as follows:

$$z = \frac{x - \mu}{\sigma}$$

See Appendix 2, pages 458–459 for instructions on how to read the normal table. Example 5.3c on page 195 illustrates the use of the normal tables to calculate probabilities.

You can also use the tables to locate an x-value that corresponds to a particular probability. Once you locate the desired probability in the body of the normal table, and the associated z-score, you can calculate the desired x-value with the following formula.

$$x = \mu + z \cdot \sigma$$

If any of your normal probability calculations lead to a z-score that is not included in the tables, remember that although theoretically a normal random variable can be infinitely large or small, almost 100% of the probability is accounted for with a z-score of 3.99, and so the table stops there. Therefore, if you have a z-score any larger than 3.99, and you are using the tables, keep in mind that there is only negligible area under the normal curve beyond a z-score of 3.99 (or −3.99).

CHAPTER REVIEW EXERCISES

1. The leading brand of toothpaste has a 10% market share.
   a. A sample of 15 customers is taken. What is the probability that three or fewer of them use the leading brand of toothpaste?
   b. A sample of four customers is selected. What is the probability that two of them use the leading brand of toothpaste?

2. Suppose that 10% of students in a business program read the financial section of the daily newspaper. Develop the probability distribution for x, the number out of three randomly selected students from the business program who read the financial section of the daily newspaper.

3. Calculate the mean and standard deviation for the probability distribution you created in Exercise 2 above. Represent the probability distribution graphically.

4. The number of pages printed before the ink cartridge has to be replaced on an inkjet printer is normally distributed, with a mean of 5000 pages and a standard deviation of 1250 pages. A new print cartridge has just been installed.
   a. What is the probability that the printer will produce more than 6000 pages before this cartridge needs to be replaced?
   b. What is the probability that the printer will produce fewer than 6000 pages before this cartridge needs to be replaced?
   c. 95% of the time, a cartridge will produce at least how many pages?

5. Warranty records show that the probability that a new computer will need warranty service in the first 90 days is 0.01.
   a. If a sample of five computers is selected, what is the probability that one of them will require service in the first 90 days?
   b. If a sample of four computers is selected, what is the probability that one of them will require service in the first 90 days?

6. Suppose the random variable x is the number of magazines subscribed to by a Canadian household. The probability distribution for x is shown in Exhibit 5.39 below.

Probability Distribution for the Number of Magazine Subscriptions in a Canadian Household

5.39

x	0	1	2	3	4	5
P(x)	0.15	0.38	0.27	0.11	0.06	0.03

   a. What is the probability that a Canadian household subscribes to three or more magazines?
   b. What is the probability that a Canadian household subscribes to two or three magazines?
   c. What is the expected number of magazine subscriptions in a Canadian household?

7. Companies that sell mutual funds charge their investors expense fees to offset the costs of research and administration. The distribution of expense fees is normal, with a mean of 2.5% and a standard deviation of 1.0%.
   a. Find the probability that a mutual fund has an expense fee of between 2.5% and 3.5%.
   b. What is the probability that a mutual fund has expense fees greater than 3%?
   c. 90% of mutual funds have expense fees below what percentage?

8. An official from the securities commission estimates that 75% of all investment bankers have profited from the use of inside information.
   a. If 15 investment bankers are selected at random, find the probability that:
      i. All 15 have profited from inside information.
      ii. At least six have profited from inside information.
   b. Suppose the experiment was repeated, and three investment bankers were selected. What is the probability that one of them profited from inside information?

9. The recent average starting salary for new college graduates in computer information systems is $47,500. Assume salaries are normally distributed with a standard deviation of $4,500.
   a. What is the probability of a new graduate receiving a salary of between $45,000 and $50,000?
   b. What is the probably of a new graduate getting a starting salary of more than $55,000?
   c. If you wanted to be earning more than 90% of new college graduates in computer information systems, what salary would you have to earn?

10. Create the probability distribution for a binomial random variable with $n = 2$ and $p = 0.4$, using basic probability rules. Verify that the expected value is equal to np using the general formula for the mean of a probability distribution.

11. A certain brand of flood lamp has a lifetime that is normally distributed with a mean of 3,750 hours and a standard deviation of 300 hours.
    a. What percentage of the flood lamps would last for more than 3,800 hours?
    b. What lifetime should the manufacturer advertise for these lamps so that only 2% will burn out before the advertised lifetime?

12. A study was made of frequent fliers, and it was found that 60% had an income of over $65,000 a year.
    a. 15 frequent fliers were selected at random, and their incomes recorded. What is the probability that at least 10 had an income of over $65,000 a year?
    b. A further group of 12 frequent fliers was selected at random. What is the probability that exactly 8 had an income over $65,000 a year?

13. The monthly credit card bills for households in the Newmarket area of Ontario are normally distributed, with a mean of $1,276.30 and a standard deviation of $345.89.
    a. What proportion of the bills are less than $1,000?
    b. What proportion of the bills are more than $1,500?
    c. 75% of the bills are more than what amount?

14. 50% of Lindsay's population is opposed to the proposed widening of Highway 35 to four lanes. If 10 Lindsay residents are selected at random, what is the probability that:
    a. all 10 of them will be opposed to the proposed highway widening?
    b. none of them will be opposed to the proposed highway widening?
    c. five or fewer of them will be opposed to the proposed highway widening?

15. In an ABC News/*Washington Post* poll conducted in June 2005, 59% of Americans described themselves as convinced that global warming was underway. However, only 33% thought that global warming would affect their own lives. Assuming these poll results still hold today, if you randomly selected 12 Americans, what is the probability that six or more of them would be convinced that global warming was underway? What is the probability that six or more of them would think that global warming would affect their own lives?

16. The probability that a college student will cheat on his or her statistics assignment by copying the work of other students is 0.043. If a professor has 175 statistics students, what is the probability that at least one of them will cheat?

17. A construction company is bidding on a contract. The company believes that it has a 25% chance of winning the contract. If the company wins, it will earn a profit of $50,000. If the company does not win the contract, it will lose the $845 it spent preparing the bid. What is the company's expected value of this contract?

18. Over time, the owner of a bicycle store has come to the conclusion that about 1% of the customers who enter her store are prepared to purchase a new bicycle. What is the probability that one out of the 25 customers who enter the store today will purchase a new bicycle? (You may assume that these 25 customers are randomly selected.)

19. The time that it takes an emergency car repair service to arrive at the broken-down car is a normally distributed random variable, with a mean of 42 minutes and a standard deviation of 12 minutes. What is the probability that the customer will have to wait more than 45 minutes for help to arrive?

20. In Chapter 6, you will see that the normal distribution can sometimes be used to approximate the binomial distribution. This exercise is designed to illustrate how good the normal approximation to the binomial can be.
    a. Consider a binomial distribution with $n = 200$, and $p = 0.5$. Calculate $P(x \leq 100)$.
    b. What is the mean and standard deviation for the distribution you used in part a?
    c. Using a normal distribution with the same mean and standard deviation you calculated in part b, calculate $P(x \leq 100)$.
    d. The probabilities that you calculated in parts a and c should be similar. Why do you think this is so?
    e. Now calculate $P(x \leq 100.5)$ for the normal distribution. The extra 0.5 is added to provide a *continuity correction factor*. It compensates for the fact that the normal distribution is continuous (so $P(x \leq 100) = P(x < 100)$, for example), and the binomial distribution is not ($P(x \leq 100) \neq P(x < 100)$). How close are the binomial and normal probabilities now?

 Go to MyStatLab at www.mystatlab.com. You can practise many of this chapter's exercises as often as you want. The guided solutions help you find an answer step by step. You'll find a personalized study plan available to you too!

CHAPTER 6

Using Sampling Distributions to Make Decisions

Learning Objectives

After mastering the material in the chapter, you will be able to:

1. Understand how probability calculations and sampling distributions can be used to draw conclusions about populations on the basis of sample results.

2. Infer whether a population mean is as claimed or desired, on the basis of a particular sample mean, using the appropriate sampling distribution and probability calculations, when σ is known.

3. Infer whether a population proportion is as claimed or desired, on the basis of a particular sample proportion, using the appropriate probability calculations.

INTRODUCTION

Eleanor Bennett is a quality control inspector in a paint factory, and she knows that machines suffer wear and tear and operators fall asleep or go for coffee breaks, so there is no guarantee that the right amount of paint is always going into the paint cans. If there is too little paint in each can, there will be customer complaints and perhaps a loss of business. If there is too much paint in each can, the company is giving away free paint, which is not good for profits.

Suppose the paint cans are designed to hold 3 litres of paint. Eleanor wants to be sure that, on average, there are 3 litres of paint in every can, with limited variability. But how will Eleanor determine if this is the case?

It is not practical to measure the amount of paint in every can. Fortunately, Eleanor can make a reliable conclusion about the average amount of paint in all the paint cans, on the basis of a random sample of paint cans, using inferential statistics. In Section 6.1, you will be introduced to the general decision-making process for statistical inference. You will see how probability calculations and sampling distributions are used to make decisions about population parameters, on the basis of sample results. You will be given all the necessary details about the sampling distribution so you can concentrate on learning how to use a sample result and a probability calculation to make a statistical inference. In Sections 6.2 and 6.3, you will learn how to determine the necessary details of two important sampling distributions yourself. In Section 6.2, you will be introduced to the sampling distribution of the sample mean, which can be used to make decisions about a population mean. In Section 6.3, you will be introduced to the sampling distribution of the sample proportion, which can be used to make decision about population proportions.

THE DECISION-MAKING PROCESS FOR STATISTICAL INFERENCE

Suppose Eleanor Bennett takes the following approach to deciding whether the paint filling line is putting the correct amount of paint in the paint cans.

1. She randomly selects 25 cans of paint from the paint filling line.
2. She carefully measures the amount of paint in each can, and computes a sample mean amount of paint ($\bar{x}$).

Eleanor will not expect to get an $\bar{x}$ of exactly 3 litres. Even when the paint-filling line is working perfectly, there will not be *exactly* 3 litres of paint in each can. Normal mechanical variability in the filling process results in some cans having a little less than 3 litres, and some having a little more. Eleanor wants to be sure to adjust the paint-filling line when there is sample evidence that it needs adjusting. But she does not want to adjust the line when it is in fact working well. So, if the calculated $\bar{x}$ is *close* to the desired 3 litres, the line will not be adjusted. If the $\bar{x}$ is *far away* from the desired 3 litres, the line will be adjusted. But how does Eleanor decide which values of $\bar{x}$ are *close* to 3 litres, and which values are *far away*? Which values should trigger adjustment of the line, and which values should not?

The decision about what values of $\bar{x}$ should trigger adjustment of the paint-filling line is straightforward if we know the sampling distribution of the sample mean. A **sampling distribution** is the probability distribution of all possible sample results for a given sample size.

Suppose Eleanor knows that when the paint-filling line is adjusted properly (with a mean of 3 litres in all cans of paint), the sampling distribution of the $\bar{x}$-values for a sample of size 25 will be normally distributed, with a mean of 3 litres and a standard deviation of 0.01 litres. Now Eleanor knows something about the $\bar{x}$-values she can expect to get from her sample of 25 paint cans. An $\bar{x}$-value of 3.01 would not be unusual, because it is only one standard deviation away from the mean. There would be no reason to adjust the paint-filling line, because this sample result is one we would not be surprised to get if the paint-filling line were properly set up. An $\bar{x}$ of 3.05 (*five* standard deviations away from the mean) would be highly unusual and improbable. We would not expect to get such a sample result if the paint-filling line were properly set up. If we did get this result, it would be a clear signal that the paint-filling line needed to be adjusted.

The sampling distribution is key to being able to distinguish unusual sample results from usual sample results. The sampling distribution is closely related to the distribution of the population from which the sample is drawn. The details of how to arrive at a

sampling distribution the probability distribution of all possible sample results for a given sample size

sampling distribution will be covered in later sections of this chapter. In this section, we will instead focus on how to use the sampling distribution to decide if a sample result is unusual. Your general understanding of this decision-making approach will allow you to use statistical inference in a variety of situations.

Depending on the situation, the sample result could be a mean, a proportion, a standard deviation, or any one of many other possible sample statistics. Whatever population parameter we are interested in, no matter what corresponding sample statistic is calculated, the decision-making process is the same. In the following discussion of the decision-making process, we will simply refer to the sample statistic as the sample result (SR). The sampling distribution used in this discussion will be normal, as many sampling distributions are (although certainly not all are).

We will examine a situation in which it is claimed or desired that the population has a mean of 3. Suppose we know that when the population has a mean of 3, the sample results for a sample of size 25 will be normally distributed, with a mean of 3 and a standard deviation of 0.01. (Note the more general language here. We are not necessarily talking about paint now.) The sample results would have the sampling distribution that is shown in Exhibit 6.1.

Exhibit 6.1   Expected Distribution of Sample Results, Mean of 3 and Standard Deviation of 0.01

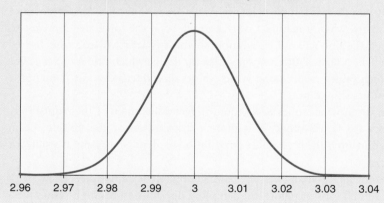

Expected Distribution of Sample Results

| 2.96 | 2.97 | 2.98 | 2.99 | 3 | 3.01 | 3.02 | 3.03 | 3.04 |

Suppose we collect a sample of 25, and calculate a sample result. Now we have to make one of two decisions:

1. The sample result *is NOT unusual*, and there is insufficient evidence that the population is not as desired.
2. The sample result *is unusual*, and there is sufficient evidence that the population is not as desired.

Which of the two possible decisions should we make if:

a. the sample result is 3?
b. the sample result is 3.04 (or 2.96)?
c. the sample result is 3.01 (or 2.99)?

d. the sample result is 3.02 (or 2.98)?

e. the sample result is 3.03 (or 2.97)?

a. If the sample result is 3 (as in Exhibit 6.2), no one would conclude that the sample result was unusual, or that there was any evidence that the population mean was not 3.

Sample Result Is 3

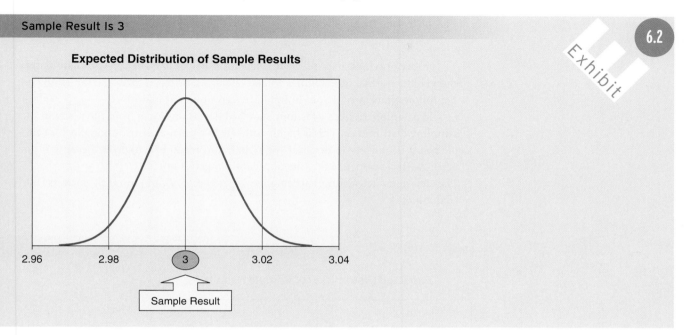

b. If the sample result is 3.04 (as in Exhibit 6.3), we would conclude that the sample result is unusual, and there is evidence that the population mean is not 3.

Sample Result is 3.04

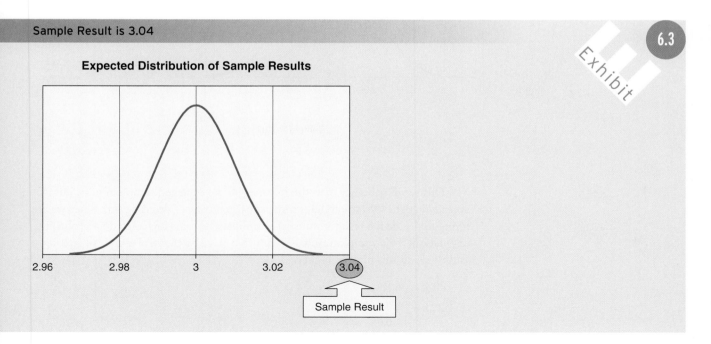

The probability of getting a sample result as high as 3.04 is:

$$P(SR \geq 3.04)$$

$$= P\left(z \geq \frac{3.04 - 3}{0.01}\right)$$

$$= P(z \geq 4)$$

$$\approx 0$$

(Excel provides a more exact calculation of 0.0000316860. Throughout this chapter, the normal probabilities will be calculated using z-scores and tables, so you can follow along even if you do not have a computer at hand.)

This sample result 3.04 is four standard deviations away from the mean of the sampling distribution. This is highly unlikely in a normal distribution. Such a sample result is unlikely to occur, if the population mean is actually 3. Because it *did* occur, we have evidence that the population mean is not 3.

c. The decisions get a little harder once we move to a sample result such as 3.01 (Exhibit 6.4).

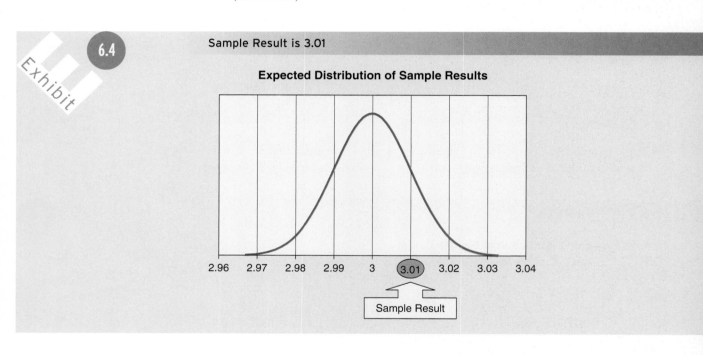

Exhibit 6.4

Sample Result is 3.01

Expected Distribution of Sample Results

2.96   2.97   2.98   2.99   3   (3.01)   3.02   3.03   3.04

Sample Result

This result is higher than the mean of all the expected sample results, but is it *unusually* high? We have to have some consistent way of deciding this. Since we are trying to decide if a result is unusual or unlikely, it seems logical to do a probability calculation. This sample result is "high;" so what is the probability of getting a sample result this high or higher?

$$P(SR \geq 3.01)$$

$$= P\left(z \geq \frac{3.01 - 3}{0.01}\right)$$

$$= P(z \geq 1)$$

$$= 1 - 0.8413$$

$$= 0.1587$$

There is an almost 16% probability of getting a sample result this high or higher. For the purposes of statistical inference, such a result would not be considered unusual. In this case, we would conclude that the sample result is *not unusual*, if the population mean is 3. The sample does not provide enough evidence to conclude that the population mean is more than 3.

We need a precise guide to our decision making, based on the probability of the sample result. In Chapter 7, we will discuss how such decision-making rules are set, and we will vary the rules. For now, we will conclude that the population is not as claimed or desired if the probability of the sample result is 5% or less.

We calculate the probability of the sample result as follows:

- if the sample result is higher than expected, calculate $P(SR \geq$ observed value)
- if the sample result is lower than expected, calculate $P(SR \leq$ observed value).

We conclude that the population is not as claimed or desired only if the probability of such an extreme sample result is 5% or less.

Notice that the decision about the population can be made only when we know the probability of the observed sample result. Without probability analysis, there is no way to know if a sample result of 3.01 is usual or unusual. Be very careful as you proceed with this type of analysis. Sometimes your intuition may suggest that a sample result is highly unusual, but you can never decide this without doing a probability calculation based on the sampling distribution.

Using the decision-making rule above as a guide, with a sample result of 3.01 or 2.99, the inspector should not adjust the paint filling line, since the sample result would occur with a probability of just under 16% if the population mean were actually 3. This is not that unusual.

d. What is the probability of getting a result like 3.02 (or 2.98)? $P(SR \geq 3.02)$ is a little more than 2% (you should check this calculation). This is an unusual sample result. Such a sample result is unlikely to occur if the population mean is actually 3. Because it *did* occur, we have evidence that the population mean is not 3.

e. Similarly, a sample result of 3.03 or 2.97 would be highly unusual if the population mean were actually 3. Because it did occur, we have evidence that the population mean is not 3.

The decisions are easy with results such as in part a or b above. In those cases, we can be fairly certain of making the right decision. With results such as in parts c to e, the decisions seem less certain. With any of the sample results, though, there is always the chance that this one sample is a fluke, and that the wrong decision is being made. Taking another sample might be tempting, but in practice, this may not be possible—the decision has to be made. We find it acceptable to live with this uncertainty (and in practice, we reduce it by using sample sizes as large as are affordable). It is worth the price of occasionally being wrong, because measuring or testing the entire population is impossible or expensive, and *most* of the time, statistical inference will lead to the correct decision.

6.1

Using a sampling distribution to decide
if a sample result is unusual

Suppose an inspector is concerned that too much cereal is going into the cereal boxes in a factory. The boxes are supposed to contain 645 grams of cereal. The inspector takes a random sample of 30 boxes of cereal, and calculates the sample mean ($\bar{x}$), which turns out to be 648 grams. Assume that if the cereal-filling line is properly adjusted, the $\bar{x}$-values will be normally distributed, with a mean of 645 grams and a standard deviation of 5 grams. Should the line be adjusted?

$$P(SR \geq 648)$$
$$= P\left(z \geq \frac{648 - 645}{5} \right)$$
$$= P(z \geq 0.6)$$
$$= 1 - 0.7257$$
$$= 0.2743$$

No, the cereal-filling line should not be adjusted, because the sample result is not unusual. If the average amount of cereal in the boxes is 645 grams, we would get a sample mean at least as high as 648 grams with a probability of 0.2742. There is not enough evidence to suggest that the cereal boxes contain more than 645 grams of cereal, on average.

DEVELOP YOUR SKILLS 6.1

1. Suppose a college claims that its graduates from the business programs earn $40,000 a year, on average, after graduation. You are making only $38,000, so you have reason to doubt the college's claim. You take a random sample of 35 graduates, and calculate an average salary of $39,368. Assume that if the college's claim is true, sample means of one-year-after-graduation salaries would be normally distributed, with a mean of $40,000 and a standard deviation of $253. Does your sample result suggest that the college's claim overstates salaries?

2. Suppose an ad for an automotive service centre claims that at least 97% of its customers would gladly recommend the centre to friends. Since you have heard nothing but complaints about this service centre, you doubt that the claim is true. You break into the centre one night, hack into its computer system, and construct a random sample of customers.[1] You conduct a survey of 300 customers, and discover that only 95% of them would recommend the centre to friends. Assume that if the centre's claim were true, sample proportions would be normally distributed, with a mean of 0.97 and a standard deviation

of 0.0098488. Does your sample result indicate that the centre's ad overstates the percentage of customers who would provide a positive recommendation?

3. A company is wondering if it should subsidize the tuition costs of employees who are furthering their education. The company feels that it could afford a subsidy program if 25% or fewer of its employees enrolled in programs that would be eligible for subsidies. The chief accountant is concerned, because he conducted a random sample of 400 employees and calculated that 26% would enroll in eligible programs if the subsidy were available. The accountant thinks this sample result is evidence that more than 25% of the employees would apply for tuition subsidies.

    Suppose that if only 25% of employees actually enrolled in eligible programs, the sample proportions would be normally distributed, with a mean of 0.25 and a standard deviation of 0.021651. Does the sample result indicate that the company cannot afford the tuition subsidy program?

4. Your statistics teacher claims that the average mark on the mid-term statistics exam for students in the business program is 72%. You survey a random sample of 30 of the business students taking statistics, and you

---

[1] This kind of illegal activity is not standard practice for statisticians, and is not recommended.

calculate an average mark of 75%. The statistics teacher tells you that if her claim is true, the sample means will be normally distributed, with a mean of 72%, and a standard deviation of 3.2%. Does your sample evidence indicate that the teacher's claim underestimates the true average mark for the mid-term stats exam?

5. According to the personnel department, the average commuting time for workers within a 50-kilometre radius of your company's head office is supposed to be 32 minutes. You suspect that, because of development in the area and increased traffic, the average commuting time has increased. Suppose you know that if the personnel department's estimate was correct, sample means would be normally distributed, with a mean of 32 minutes and a standard deviation of 5 minutes. You take a random sample of 20 employees, and calculate a sample mean of 40 minutes. Does this provide evidence that commuting times have increased?

6.2 THE SAMPLING DISTRIBUTION OF THE SAMPLE MEAN

In Section 6.1, you were always given the details about the distribution of sample results. Now the question is: how do you figure out what the sampling distribution should look like? To start with, we will cover two sampling distributions: the sampling distribution of the sample mean, $\bar{x}$, which is discussed in Section 6.2, and the sampling distribution of the sample proportion, $\hat{p}$ (pronounced "p-hat"), which is presented in Section 6.3.

The probability distribution of the sample means (the $\bar{x}$-values) is related to the distribution of the original population (the x-values). For example, the distribution of the average content for 25-can samples of paint (the $\bar{x}$-values) is related to the distribution of fill volumes for individual cans of paint (the x-values). The details are outlined below.

For a sample of size n, and a population with a claimed or desired mean of μ:

1. The standard deviation of the sample means (the $\bar{x}$-values) is equal to the population standard deviation, divided by the square root of the sample size. In other words:

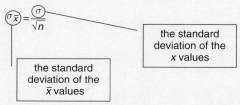

We will refer to the standard deviation of the sample means ($\sigma_{\bar{x}}$) as the *standard error*.

2. The mean of the sample means (the $\bar{x}$-values) is equal to the mean of the original population. To put this into mathematical shorthand, we would say:

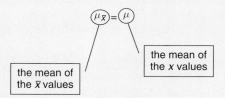

3. The sampling distribution of the sample means is normal if the original population is normally distributed, or the sample size is large enough.

Now we can apply this information about the sampling distribution and
its relationship to the population distribution, using the paint-filling line as an
example.

Suppose the average amount of paint in the population is supposed to be
3 litres. Suppose we know that the population is normally distributed, and that the
population standard deviation is 0.05 litres (of course, it is unlikely that we would
know the population standard deviation, but we will deal with this difficulty later,
in Chapter 7).

For samples of size 25, we can calculate that:

1. the standard error of the sampling distribution of the $\bar{x}$-values is

$$\sigma_{\bar{x}} = \frac{\sigma}{\sqrt{n}} = \frac{0.05}{\sqrt{25}} = \frac{0.05}{5} = 0.01$$

2. the mean of the $\bar{x}$-values is 3 litres (the same as the population mean)
3. because the population is normally distributed, the sampling distribution will be
normally distributed.

So, by using the information about the population and the sample size, we have
come up with the sampling distribution that was first discussed on page 9, as shown in
Exhibit 6.5:

6.5 Exhibit

Distribution of Sample Means, Sample Size of 25

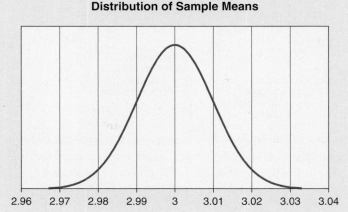

Distribution of Sample Means

2.96 2.97 2.98 2.99 3 3.01 3.02 3.03 3.04

Suppose Eleanor randomly samples 25 cans of paint, and calculates a sample mean
of 3.016 litres. Should the paint filling line be adjusted?

As we figured out above, the $\bar{x}$-values will be normally distributed, with a mean of 3 and a standard error of 0.01, as shown in Exhibit 6.6.

Distribution of Sample Means, Sample Result is 3.016 litres

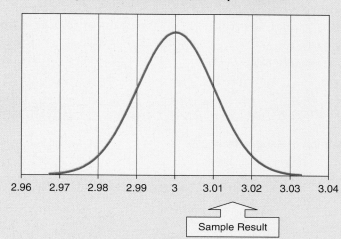

Expected Distribution of Sample Results

2.96   2.97   2.98   2.99   3   3.01   3.02   3.03   3.04

Sample Result

Exhibit **6.6**

Since 3.016 litres is more than the desired volume of 3 litres, we calculate the probability as follows:

$$= P(\bar{x} \geq 3.016)$$

$$= P\left(z \geq \frac{3.016 - 3}{0.01}\right)$$

$$= P(z \geq 1.6)$$

$$= 1 - 0.9452$$

$$= 0.0548$$

The probability of getting a sample mean as high as 3.016 is 0.0548, if the population mean is 3. Since the probability of such a sample mean is greater than 5%, the sample mean is not unusual, according to our decision rule. Therefore, although the sample mean is on the high side, no adjustment is made to the paint-filling line.

You might be slightly uncomfortable about this decision. The probability of such a high sample mean is more than 5%, but not by much! Shouldn't Eleanor adjust the paint-filling line anyway? The answer is no. While this sample mean might make us uncomfortable, the paint-filling line should not be adjusted until it truly needs adjustment.

Close decisions such as the one above may not be entirely comfortable, but over the long run, decisions made this way will generally be correct. We are willing to live with a little discomfort in decision making, since this method is far superior to guessing. The only way to be absolutely certain about the paint cans is to exactly measure the quantity of paint going into each and every can, and this is likely impossible or prohibitively expensive.

6.2a

Constructing a sampling distribution and using it to decide about a population mean

Suppose a random sample of 35 cans of paint yields a sample mean of 2.984 litres. Should the paint-filling line be adjusted? Presume, as before, that the population of individual fill volumes is normally distributed, with a desired mean of 3 litres and a standard deviation of 0.05 litres.

First, what will the sampling distribution look like? It will be normally distributed, because the population is normally distributed. It will have a mean of 3 litres (the population mean). It will have a standard error of $\sigma_{\bar{x}} = \dfrac{\sigma}{\sqrt{n}} = \dfrac{0.05}{\sqrt{35}} = 0.0084515$. The sampling distribution will look like Exhibit 6.7.

6.7

Distribution of Sample Means, Sample Size of 35

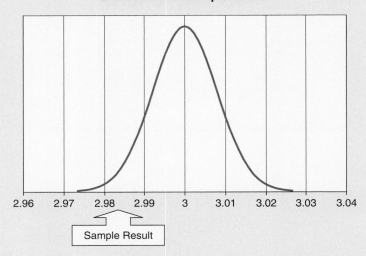

Distribution of Sample Means

Notice that this sampling distribution is different from the one we used for the previous problem, when only 25 cans of paint were sampled. With a larger sample, the standard error will be smaller, and so the distribution is narrower and taller. This sample result is exactly the same distance from the mean as the measurement in the previous example (3.016 is 0.016 above the mean, and 2.984 is 0.016 below the mean). However, because the sampling distribution has changed, this same distance from the mean represents a more extreme result.

We have to do the probability calculation to see if the paint-filling line should be adjusted.

$$= P(\bar{x} \leq 2.984)$$
$$= P\left(z \leq \frac{2.984 - 3}{0.0084515}\right)$$
$$= P(z \leq -1.89)$$
$$= 0.0294$$

When the paint-filling line is properly adjusted, the probability of getting a 35-can sample mean as low as 2.984 litres is a little less than 3%. In other words, it would be unusual to get such a sample result, were the paint-filling line properly set up. Since we actually did get such a result, this is an indication that the paint-filling line needs adjustment.

Notice that although this sample mean is the same distance from the mean as in the previous example, we made a different decision, because the sample sizes and the sampling distributions were different. We cannot simply say, "Oh, 3.016 litres isn't *that* far from 3 litres, so everything is okay." We must do a probability-based calculation to decide.

The decision-making procedure here is the same as in Section 6.1. The only difference is that now we are figuring out what the details of the sampling distribution are, rather than being told what they are. This simply means some extra work before we can do the probability calculation and make the decision.

An Empirical Exploration of the Sampling Distribution of $\bar{x}$

The relationship between the population distribution and the sampling distribution can be proven mathematically, although the mathematics is beyond the level of this text. However, you can also think of the sampling distribution as something that could be derived empirically. That is, for a given population, you could imagine taking a random sample of 25 and calculating $\bar{x}$, over and over again, a very large number of times. If you could somehow do this an infinite number of times, you could create the probability distribution of the $\bar{x}$-values for samples of size 25. You could list all the possible values of $\bar{x}$, with the relative frequencies as the probabilities. This is just the sampling distribution of $\bar{x}$.

If we do some exploration of this empirical approach, you may be able to develop some intuition about the differences between the population distribution and the sampling distributions, and how the two types of distributions are related.

We will do this by looking at Exhibit 6.8, on p. 216. This page lists (in order) the exact volumes for 500 cans of paint with a normal distribution with a mean of 3 litres and a standard deviation of 0.05 litres. You can think of this page full of numbers as a *population* of paint can volumes (*x*-values). The values have been rounded to numbers with four decimal places, which is sufficient for our purposes here.

$\sigma_{\bar{x}} = \dfrac{\sigma}{\sqrt{n}}$ —**An Exploration**   Suppose you began by taking samples of size 9 from this population. What is the largest possible $\bar{x}$ you could get, with a sample of 9? The highest possible $\bar{x}$ would come from averaging the 9 fullest paint cans. In that case would be $\dfrac{3.1090 + 3.1093 \ldots + 3.1585}{9} = 3.1211$ litres. Similarly, the smallest possible $\bar{x}$ would come from averaging the 9 least full cans, and this results in an $\bar{x}$ value of 2.8832 litres.

What if we increased the sample size to 25? With similar calculations, we find that the largest possible $\bar{x}$ from a sample of 25 cans is 3.1056 litres. The smallest possible $\bar{x}$ from a sample of 25 cans is 2.9037 litres.

Exhibit **6.8**

Population of Paint Can Volumes (Litres)

2.8679	2.9430	2.9622	2.9773	2.9906	3.0050	3.0129	3.0262	3.0426	3.0656
2.8714	2.9433	2.9626	2.9779	2.9907	3.0050	3.0134	3.0264	3.0427	3.0667
2.8718	2.9436	2.9631	2.9782	2.9908	3.0054	3.0134	3.0266	3.0442	3.0703
2.8756	2.9438	2.9635	2.9784	2.9914	3.0054	3.0134	3.0272	3.0446	3.0704
2.8817	2.9441	2.9635	2.9786	2.9918	3.0056	3.0134	3.0274	3.0446	3.0712
2.8859	2.9442	2.9636	2.9788	2.9919	3.0057	3.0136	3.0275	3.0448	3.0731
2.8936	2.9466	2.9640	2.9789	2.9920	3.0059	3.0137	3.0276	3.0457	3.0731
2.8989	2.9469	2.9640	2.9791	2.9921	3.0059	3.0143	3.0280	3.0459	3.0740
2.9022	2.9486	2.9642	2.9793	2.9923	3.0060	3.0146	3.0283	3.0474	3.0741
2.9027	2.9486	2.9645	2.9795	2.9930	3.0060	3.0147	3.0284	3.0475	3.0743
2.9058	2.9487	2.9647	2.9796	2.9934	3.0063	3.0153	3.0292	3.0476	3.0744
2.9069	2.9497	2.9651	2.9798	2.9935	3.0063	3.0161	3.0300	3.0478	3.0757
2.9099	2.9502	2.9655	2.9800	2.9935	3.0067	3.0163	3.0303	3.0479	3.0773
2.9103	2.9508	2.9657	2.9808	2.9936	3.0068	3.0171	3.0313	3.0481	3.0774
2.9121	2.9513	2.9660	2.9808	2.9937	3.0069	3.0172	3.0317	3.0492	3.0779
2.9162	2.9513	2.9666	2.9811	2.9943	3.0070	3.0174	3.0321	3.0500	3.0787
2.9163	2.9516	2.9681	2.9811	2.9945	3.0071	3.0178	3.0325	3.0503	3.0788
2.9174	2.9525	2.9681	2.9817	2.9949	3.0073	3.0179	3.0335	3.0504	3.0789
2.9184	2.9528	2.9682	2.9818	2.9951	3.0073	3.0182	3.0336	3.0508	3.0790
2.9186	2.9529	2.9686	2.9818	2.9952	3.0074	3.0187	3.0340	3.0510	3.0808
2.9196	2.9529	2.9687	2.9823	2.9955	3.0077	3.0189	3.0343	3.0513	3.0810
2.9212	2.9530	2.9691	2.9824	2.9958	3.0078	3.0195	3.0345	3.0523	3.0815
2.9221	2.9532	2.9694	2.9828	2.9962	3.0078	3.0196	3.0347	3.0525	3.0862
2.9225	2.9533	2.9696	2.9829	2.9965	3.0079	3.0200	3.0349	3.0535	3.0865
2.9236	2.9536	2.9705	2.9833	2.9965	3.0084	3.0207	3.0351	3.0543	3.0867
2.9237	2.9538	2.9708	2.9835	2.9966	3.0088	3.0208	3.0356	3.0551	3.0872
2.9243	2.9541	2.9710	2.9842	2.9967	3.0090	3.0210	3.0356	3.0556	3.0878
2.9249	2.9544	2.9716	2.9843	2.9969	3.0092	3.0215	3.0360	3.0556	3.0883
2.9254	2.9547	2.9716	2.9843	2.9969	3.0093	3.0217	3.0365	3.0557	3.0899
2.9265	2.9549	2.9724	2.9847	2.9970	3.0097	3.0218	3.0366	3.0561	3.0906
2.9266	2.9551	2.9724	2.9849	2.9975	3.0098	3.0222	3.0371	3.0564	3.0936
2.9283	2.9552	2.9725	2.9856	2.9976	3.0098	3.0223	3.0372	3.0565	3.0952
2.9283	2.9552	2.9725	2.9856	2.9981	3.0098	3.0224	3.0376	3.0570	3.0983
2.9317	2.9556	2.9726	2.9860	2.9987	3.0099	3.0227	3.0377	3.0578	3.0984
2.9324	2.9565	2.9733	2.9861	2.9988	3.0100	3.0229	3.0377	3.0583	3.0994
2.9328	2.9568	2.9739	2.9865	2.9989	3.0100	3.0229	3.0379	3.0586	3.1009
2.9333	2.9568	2.9742	2.9868	2.9990	3.0103	3.0230	3.0382	3.0605	3.1025
2.9339	2.9573	2.9742	2.9870	2.9993	3.0106	3.0232	3.0387	3.0609	3.1038
2.9345	2.9576	2.9743	2.9870	3.0000	3.0107	3.0233	3.0387	3.0609	3.1039
2.9350	2.9581	2.9747	2.9871	3.0001	3.0107	3.0235	3.0388	3.0619	3.1050
2.9351	2.9584	2.9748	2.9874	3.0003	3.0107	3.0235	3.0390	3.0626	3.1062
2.9373	2.9590	2.9748	2.9876	3.0006	3.0111	3.0236	3.0395	3.0626	3.1090
2.9386	2.9592	2.9750	2.9880	3.0010	3.0115	3.0238	3.0397	3.0629	3.1093
2.9392	2.9593	2.9752	2.9890	3.0014	3.0117	3.0247	3.0398	3.0634	3.1096
2.9410	2.9593	2.9753	2.9898	3.0019	3.0118	3.0251	3.0406	3.0637	3.1162
2.9414	2.9594	2.9758	2.9899	3.0019	3.0119	3.0254	3.0407	3.0640	3.1188
2.9414	2.9601	2.9760	2.9900	3.0031	3.0120	3.0256	3.0408	3.0642	3.1200
2.9415	2.9601	2.9761	2.9902	3.0035	3.0123	3.0258	3.0410	3.0644	3.1227
2.9418	2.9606	2.9762	2.9904	3.0036	3.0125	3.0260	3.0412	3.0652	3.1255
2.9421	2.9610	2.9766	2.9904	3.0040	3.0128	3.0262	3.0413	3.0655	3.1585

These results are summarized in the table shown in Exhibit 6.9 below. The smallest and largest $\bar{x}$-values for both sample sizes are shown, as well as the smallest and largest x-values from this population.

x-Values and x̄-Values, Paint Can Volumes

6.9 Exhibit

	Smallest Possible Value	Largest Possible Value	Standard Deviation or Standard Error
x From Population	2.8679	3.1585	$\sigma = 0.05$
$\bar{x}$ From Samples of Size 9	2.8832	3.1211	$\sigma_{\bar{x}} = \dfrac{\sigma}{\sqrt{n}} = \dfrac{0.05}{\sqrt{9}} = 0.01667$
$\bar{x}$ From Samples of Size 25	2.9037	3.1056	$\sigma_{\bar{x}} = \dfrac{\sigma}{\sqrt{n}} = \dfrac{0.05}{\sqrt{25}} = 0.01$

This information is also captured on the number line shown below in Exhibit 6.10.

Extreme x-Values and x̄-Values, Paint Can Volumes

6.10 Exhibit

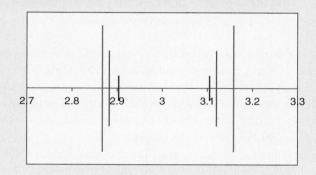

	X's Population
	$\bar{X}$'s for Sample Size 9
	$\bar{X}$'s for Sample Size 25

Clearly the $\bar{x}$-values cannot vary as much as the original x-values in the population. Additionally, the variability in the $\bar{x}$-values has to decrease when the sample size increases. Note that this is just what the formula for the standard error is telling us. For a sample size of 9, the standard error of the $\bar{x}$-values would be only $\frac{1}{3}$ of the standard deviation of the x-values. You can see this with the following arithmetic:

$$\text{If } n = 9, \; \sigma_{\bar{x}} = \frac{\sigma}{\sqrt{n}} = \frac{\sigma}{\sqrt{9}} = \frac{\sigma}{3} = \frac{1}{3}\sigma$$

Similarly, if the sample size is increased to 25, the standard error of the $\bar{x}$-values will be only $\frac{1}{5}$ of the standard deviation of the x-values.

$$\text{If } n = 25, \; \sigma_{\bar{x}} = \frac{\sigma}{\sqrt{n}} = \frac{\sigma}{\sqrt{25}} = \frac{\sigma}{5} = \frac{1}{5}\sigma$$

As the sample size (n) gets larger, the standard error gets smaller (you can see the actual values in Exhibit 6.9 above). The ends of the sampling distribution get pulled in toward the mean as the sample size increases. Exhibit 6.11 below illustrates this.

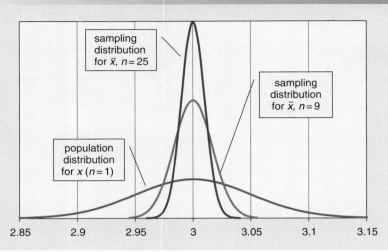

Population and Sampling Distributions

sampling distribution for $\bar{x}$, $n = 25$

sampling distribution for $\bar{x}$, $n = 9$

population distribution for x ($n = 1$)

2.85   2.9   2.95   3   3.05   3.1   3.15

$\mu_{\bar{x}} = \mu$—**An Exploration**   Something else that you will notice from Exhibit 6.11 is that the centres (the means) of the population and both sampling distributions are the same. This is what is meant by $\mu_{\bar{x}} = \mu$. The mean of the $\bar{x}$-values is the same as the mean of the x-values.

If you think about it, this should seem sensible to you. Think of selecting sample after sample after sample of size 9 from the population in Exhibit 6.8. Some of the x-values selected for the samples will be below 3 litres (about half the time), and some will be above (about half the time). Similarly, some of the $\bar{x}$-values will be below 3 litres and some will be above. Over a very large number of samples, these differences would tend to average out, and the mean of the $\bar{x}$-values would be 3 litres.

PAINT.xls

Set

You might want to experiment with this yourself. The data from Exhibit 6.8 is available on the CD that accompanies the text, in a directory called DataChap06, in a spreadsheet called PAINT.xls. You can use Excel to take a number of random samples from this data set (as described in Chapter 1), and calculate sample means. Of course, none of us has time to take an infinite number of samples. Exhibit 6.12 shows 20 sample means, based on 20 random samples from the population shown in Exhibit 6.8 (the sample size was 25).

Of course, 20 samples is nowhere near an infinite number of samples. However, even these 20 sample means show the kinds of results we would expect. Some of the sample means are below 3 litres; some are above 3 litres. The average of these sample means is 3.0029 litres, which is quite close to 3 litres.

When Is the Sampling Distribution Normal? The Central Limit Theorem

So far, all of the sampling distributions we have examined have been normal, because the original population was normal. But sampling distributions of $\bar{x}$ can also be normal— even if the original population is not normal—*if the sample size is large enough*. This somewhat surprising fact is one of the most important in statistics, and is referred to as the Central Limit Theorem. There is a practical matter first. How would we know if a

Sample Means of 20 Random Samples from the Population in Exhibit 6.8 (Litres)	
2.9874	3.0053
2.9902	3.0068
2.9917	3.0069
2.9950	3.0070
2.9956	3.0073
2.9960	3.0104
2.9961	3.0117
2.9964	3.0122
2.9997	3.0190
3.0035	3.0200

Exhibit 6.12

population was normal or not? We have to use the information we have about the population—the sample data—to make this decision.

Generally, we will create a histogram of the sample data and try to decide if it looks normal. There are formal techniques to help with this decision, but although they can be helpful, none of them works well with small sample sizes. Often, with small sample sizes, the decision about normality of the population is a judgment call.

As sample sizes get larger, the decision about normality becomes less crucial, because of the Central Limit Theorem. But how large a sample size is *large enough*? The answer is: it depends. The less normal the population is (or appears to be, based on the sample data), the larger the sample size that is necessary for the sampling distribution of $\bar{x}$ to be normal.

To assess population normality, create a histogram of sample data (unless there are too few data points). Here are some guidelines to help you decide whether a sampling distribution of $\bar{x}$ is normal.

1. If there are outliers in the sample data, you should proceed with caution, no matter what the sample size.
2. If there is more than one mode in the sample data, you should proceed thoughtfully. While large enough sample sizes could result in a normal sampling distribution of $\bar{x}$, you should investigate whether your data might be coming from more than one population.
3. With small sample sizes, less than about 15 or 20, the population data must be normal for the sampling distribution to be normal. The histogram of sample data should have a normal shape, with one central mode and no skewness.
4. With sample sizes in the range of about 15 or 20 to 40, the histogram of sample data should have a normal shape, with one central mode and not much skewness. If these conditions are met, the sampling distribution will likely be normal.
5. With sample sizes above 40 or so, the sampling distribution will probably still be normal, even if the sample histogram is somewhat skewed.

Example 6.2b

Assessing population normality, constructing a sampling distribution, and using it to decide about a population mean

It has been suggested that the average price of a three-bedroom brick bungalow in Ontario is $164,000. You collect a random sample of 30 sales of this type of house, and calculate a sample mean of $162,498. You may assume that the standard deviation for house selling prices is $7,847. A histogram of the sample data is shown below in Exhibit 6.13. Does the sample result suggest that the average price of a three-bedroom brick bungalow in Ontario is less than $164,000?

Exhibit 6.13

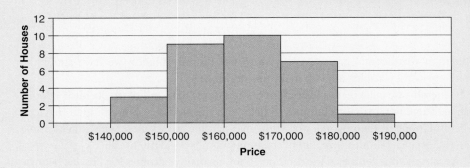

Prices of Three-Bedroom Brick Bungalows in Ontario

The histogram of the sample data looks fairly normal, and with a sample size of 30, it is reasonable to assume that the sampling distribution is normal. The mean of the sampling distribution will be $164,000, if the claim is true. The standard error of the sampling distribution will be

$$\sigma_{\bar{x}} = \frac{\sigma}{\sqrt{n}} = \frac{7847}{\sqrt{30}} = 1{,}432.6596$$

The sample mean is lower than expected. We calculate

$$P(\bar{x} \leq \$162{,}498) = P\left(z \leq \frac{\$162{,}498 - \$164{,}000}{1{,}432.6596}\right) = P(z \leq -1.05) = 0.1469$$

If the claim about the average house price being $164,000 is true, it would not be unusual to get a sample mean from 30 randomly selected houses that was as low as $162,498. In fact, we would get a sample mean that low about 15% of the time. This suggests that although our sample mean is below the claimed average house price, it is not far enough below to provide convincing evidence that the average price of a three-bedroom brick bungalow in Ontario is below $164,000.

Guide to Decision Making

Using the Sampling Distribution of $\bar{x}$ When σ Is Known

When:

- quantitative data, one sample, one population
- trying to make a decision about μ on the basis of $\bar{x}$
- σ given

Steps:
1. Identify or calculate

   - $\bar{x}$, the sample mean
   - σ, the population standard deviation
   - μ, the desired or claimed population mean
   - n, the sample size.

2. Check for normality of the sampling distribution, by assessing the normality of the population (usually with a histogram of the sample values).

3. *If* the sampling distribution is likely to be normal, proceed by identifying or calculating the mean and standard deviation of the sampling distribution, using the following formulas:

   - $\mu_{\bar{x}} = \mu$
   - $\sigma_{\bar{x}} = \dfrac{\sigma}{\sqrt{n}}$

4. Use this sampling distribution to calculate the probability of a sample result as extreme as the $\bar{x}$ from the sample

   - if $\bar{x}$ is above μ, calculate $P(\bar{x} \geq$ observed sample mean)
   - if $\bar{x}$ is below μ, calculate $P(\bar{x} \leq$ observed sample mean).

5. If the calculated probability is 5% or less, there is convincing evidence that the population is not as claimed or desired.

   Notice that this decision-making procedure depends on knowing σ. If you think about it, you will realize that if we do not know μ, it would be impossible to know σ. If σ is given, then either the people collecting the data have superhuman powers, or the data are fake. In Chapter 7, you will learn what to do when you do not know σ (which will be all the time!). The decision-making process will be very similar, but it requires a new probability distribution (the *t*-distribution, rather than the normal distribution). At this stage, the focus is on learning how the decision-making process works. Once you have mastered this, in the "pretend" world where we know σ, you should find it straightforward to transfer your knowledge to the real world, where σ is not known. It is important to remember that the decision-making process outlined above is temporary. After you cover the material in Chapter 7, you should avoid using the normal distribution to make a decision about μ.

DEVELOP YOUR SKILLS   6.2

1. Suppose the cereal boxes in a factory are supposed to contain 645 grams of cereal. Assume that when the filling line is properly adjusted, the weights of the cereal boxes are normally distributed, with a standard deviation of 5 grams. The inspector selects 10 boxes from the line, and determines that their average weight is 648 grams. What would the sampling distribution of the $\bar{x}$-values look like? What is the probability of getting an $\bar{x}$-value as high as 648 grams? Should the cereal filling line be adjusted?

2. Suppose a college claims that its graduates from the business program earn at least $40,000 a year, on average, in the first year after graduation. Assume that the year-after-graduation salaries are normally distributed, with a standard deviation of $1,500. You survey a random sample of 20 graduates of the program, and find that, one year after graduation, the average salary is $38,000. What would the sampling distribution of the $\bar{x}$-values look like? What is the probability of getting an $\bar{x}$-value as low as $38,000? Does this mean that the average salary of graduates from the business program is less than $40,000 in the first year after graduation?

3. The new tire you bought for your car is guaranteed to last an average of 25,000 kilometres. Your new tire wears prematurely, so you talk the tire store owner into surveying a random sample of 19 other tire buyers. When you survey them to see how long their tires lasted, and add your own disappointing result, you find an average of 24,000 kilometres. Assume that the tire life is a variable with a standard deviation of 500 kilometres.

Do you think you could successfully sue the company for false advertising? (Be careful!)

4. A local bank claims that it takes no more than 1.5 working days on average to approve loan requests. Examination of the bank's records for 64 randomly selected loan requests produced a sample mean of 1.8 working days. Assume that the standard deviation for the number of days to approve loan requests is 2.0 days, and that the population data are approximately normally distributed. On the basis of the sample result, does it appear that the bank's claim understates the average amount of time to approve loan requests?

5. The manager at Big Package Express knows that in the past, the packages the company handled had a mean weight of 36.7 kg. A random sample of last month's shipping records yielded a mean weight of 32.1 kg for 64 packages. Assume that the standard deviation of package weights is 14.2 kg, and that the package weights are approximately normally distributed. Does the sample result tell us that the average weight of the packages has decreased?

6.3 THE SAMPLING DISTRIBUTION OF THE SAMPLE PROPORTION

Eleanor Bennett, the quality control inspector at the paint factory, is probably interested in quality measures other than the amount of paint going into the cans. Some of these other measures may be qualitative, such as the percentage (proportion) of dented cans coming off of the paint filling line. In Section 6.3, you will see how to make decisions about the proportion of dented cans in the population of all paint cans, on the basis of a sample of paint cans.

Making Decisions About Population Proportions with the Binomial Distribution

Suppose the paint factory has decided that no more than 4% of the paint cans should be dented. Eleanor examines a random sample of 30 cans of paint. She notes that two of them are dented. If the dent rate is actually 4%, she would expect $0.04 \cdot 30 = 1.2$ dented cans, so two cans is a higher number than expected (of course, it is not actually possible to have 1.2 dented cans, but this is still the expected number). The question is whether this sample has an *unusually* high number of dented cans.

The decision-making process is the same as the one we have used before. We need to calculate the probability of getting two or more dented cans in a sample of 30, if the population proportion of dented cans is 4%. If it is unusual to get this number of dented cans, we will have evidence that something is wrong and too many cans are being dented. However, we cannot use the sampling distribution of $\bar{x}$ to calculate this probability, because the data are discrete, not continuous. What probability distribution should we use?

The appropriate probability distribution is the binomial. Although we are sampling without replacement, it is likely that the population is large enough that we can treat this as an approximately binomial problem, with $n = 30$ and $p = 0.04$ (the paint line probably produces thousands of cans). There are 30 trials; on each trial there is a success (in this case, success would be defined as getting a dented can) or a failure; the probability of getting a dented can is the same (approximately) from trial to trial; and the trials are (approximately) independent. Using Excel, for example, we discover that this probability is $P(x \geq 2, n = 30, p = 0.04) = 0.3388$. Therefore, this is not an unusual sample result. It would not be unusual to get two dented cans in a sample of 30, if the actual dent rate is 4%.

So far, there is nothing new here. We are calculating binomial probabilities, as we have before, and we are applying the decision-making criteria from Section 6.2.

A large manufacturing firm has analyzed its records and discovered that, in the past, 32% of all materials shipments were received late. The company receives many thousands of shipments, so this is a significant number of late arrivals. However, the company has recently installed a just-in-time system, which links suppliers more closely to the manufacturing process. A random sample of 400 deliveries since the new system was installed revealed 89 late deliveries. What is the probability of getting 89 or fewer late deliveries, if the percentage of late shipments is still 32%? What does this tell you about the effectiveness of the new just-in-time system in reducing late deliveries?

6.3a

Example

Using the binomial distribution to make a decision about a population proportion

Although the trials are not truly independent, we can still model this as a binomial problem, since the company receives many thousands of shipments. We can use Excel to calculate:

$$P(x \leq 89, n = 400, p = 0.32) = 0.0000104810425861441$$

This means that a sample result of only 89 late deliveries out of 400 would be *very* unlikely, if the proportion of late shipments was still 32%. We have evidence that the proportion of late shipments is lower than it was. It seems reasonable to conclude that the new just-in-time system is responsible, but we cannot draw this conclusion from the sample data alone.

The Sampling Distribution of $\hat{p}$

While it is possible to make inferences with the binomial distribution, as in the examples above, this is not the usual approach. Instead, such inferences are made by focusing not on the *number* of successes, but on the *proportion* of successes. For example, in Example 6.3a, above, there were 89 late shipments out of 400. This is equivalent to $\frac{89}{400} = 0.2225$ as a proportion of late shipments. These are two methods of representing the same information. When you are asked about a sample proportion, you can always turn it into an equivalent binomial problem, with the appropriate number of successes. As long as you have access to a computer to provide the probabilities, these problems are straightforward. However, traditionally, inferences about qualitative data have focused on the proportion of successes, and we will also cover this approach. It is possible to make such statistical inferences without the aid of a computer, in certain cases.

If we focus on the proportion of successes, rather than the count of successes, we can make decisions about a population proportion using the sampling distribution of what we will call $\hat{p}$ ("p-hat"), the sample proportion. If you are not given the sample proportion, then it should be possible to calculate it by expressing the number of successes as a percentage of the total sample, that is, $\hat{p} = \dfrac{x}{n}$. For example, if you are told that there are three dented paint cans in a sample of 30, then $\hat{p} = \dfrac{x}{n} = \dfrac{3}{30} = 0.10$.

The sampling distribution of $\hat{p}$ is normal, under the right conditions. This is because the binomial distribution can sometimes be approximated by the normal distribution. This may be somewhat surprising, since binomial random variables are discrete, while normal random variables are continuous. However, if we look at some graphs and do some calculations, you may become convinced of this fact (which is a special case of the Central Limit Theorem).

The graph of the binomial distribution looks normal whenever the probability of success (p) is close to 0.5, or whenever the number of trials is *large*. Generally, the binomial distribution can be approximated by a normal distribution whenever the following two conditions hold:

- $np \geq 10$ and
- $np \geq 10$ (where $q = 1 - p$ is the probability of failure).

Exhibits 6.14, 6.15, and 6.16 illustrate this.

6.14

Binomial Distribution, $n = 10$, $p = 0.1$

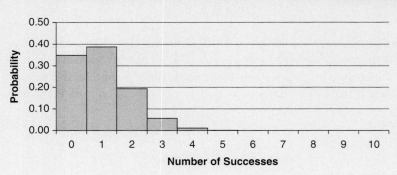

Exhibit 6.14 is a graph of a binomial distribution with $n = 10$ and $p = 0.1$. It does not look normal, because it is skewed to the right. Notice that it does not meet the required conditions ($np = 10(0.1) = 1 < 5$). In this case, we could *not* approximate the binomial distribution with the normal distribution.

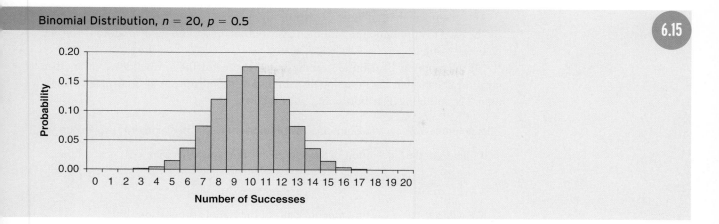

Binomial Distribution, $n = 20$, $p = 0.5$

6.15

Exhibit 6.15 is a graph of a binomial distribution with $n = 20$ and $p = 0.5$. It looks like a normal distribution. Notice that it does meet the required conditions ($np = 20(0.5) = 10$, $nq = 20(0.5) = 10$). In this case, we could use the normal distribution to approximate the binomial distribution.

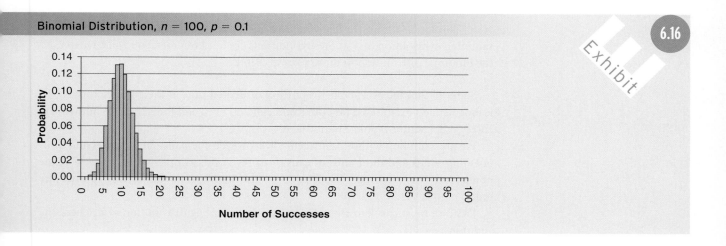

Binomial Distribution, $n = 100$, $p = 0.1$

6.16

Exhibit

Exhibit 6.16 is a graph of a binomial distribution with $n = 100$, and $p = 0.1$. In this case, the conditions for normal approximation are just met ($np = 100(0.1) = 10$, $nq = 90$). Even though the probability of success is far from 0.5, the graph still looks fairly normal, because of the high number of trials. In this case, we could use the normal distribution to approximate the binomial distribution.

Once we have established that the binomial distribution we are interested in is *normal* enough, the next question is: which normal distribution should we use to approximate it? Remember that:

- the mean of a binomial distribution is np
- the standard deviation of a binomial distribution is $\sqrt{npq}$.

So, the normal distribution with a mean of np and a standard deviation of $\sqrt{npq}$ can be used to approximate a binomial distribution, under the right conditions (np and nq both ≥ 10).

If the binomial distribution can be approximated by the normal distribution, then it can be shown that the sampling distribution of proportions is also normally distributed. The sampling distribution of $\hat{p}$ is as follows.

For a sample of size n and a binomial distribution with a claimed or desired proportion p:

1. The standard deviation of the sample proportions (the $\hat{p}$-values) is as follows:

$$\sigma_{\hat{p}} = \sqrt{\frac{npq}{n}}$$

We will refer to $\sigma_{\hat{p}}$ as the *standard error* of the sample proportion.

2. The mean of the sample proportions is equal to the population proportion. In other words:

$$\mu_{\hat{p}} = p$$

3. The sampling distribution will be approximately normal as long as both of the required conditions are met:

   - $np \geq 10$ and
   - $nq \geq 10$.

Note: This last result means that you must check these conditions before you use the sampling distribution of $\hat{p}$. If these conditions are not both met, you will have to use the binomial distribution to make your decision.

Suppose that the acceptable proportion of dented cans in the paint factory is 5%. Eleanor Bennett examines a random sample of 200 cans, and finds that 6% of them are dented. What action should Eleanor take?

We are sampling without replacement. However, the paint factory probably produces thousands and thousands of cans of paint, so this sample is less than 5% of the population. The binomial distribution is the appropriate underlying probability model.

First, we must check to see if we can use the sampling distribution of $\hat{p}$. Check the conditions:

- $np = 200(0.05) = 10 \geq 10$
- $nq = 200(0.95) = 190 \geq 10$.

The conditions are met, which means that the underlying binomial distribution can be approximated with the normal distribution, and that we can use the sampling distribution of $\hat{p}$. The sampling distribution of $\hat{p}$ will be approximately normal, with

$$\sigma_{\hat{p}} = \sqrt{\frac{pq}{n}} = \sqrt{\frac{(0.05)(0.95)}{200}} = 0.015411035$$

and

$$\mu_{\hat{p}} = p = 0.05$$

The observed sample proportion is higher than we expected, so we want to calculate $P(\hat{p} \geq 0.06)$. The tail area corresponding to the probability we need to calculate is shaded in Exhibit 6.17.

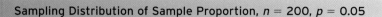

Sampling Distribution of Sample Proportion, $n = 200$, $p = 0.05$

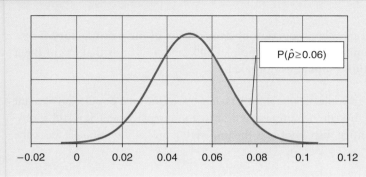

$P(\hat{p} \geq 0.06)$

Exhibit **6.17**

The probability calculation is once again a straightforward normal probability calculation.

$$P(\hat{p} \geq 0.06)$$
$$= P\left(z \geq \frac{0.06 - 0.05}{0.0154110356}\right)$$
$$= P(z \geq 0.65)$$
$$= 1 - 0.7422$$
$$= 0.2578$$

The probability of getting a sample proportion of 6% dented cans is 0.2578, if the population proportion of dented cans is 5%. This sample result would not be unusual. We do not have evidence that the true proportion of dented cans is higher than the acceptable level. So, no action is required.

For comparison's sake, we can also calculate this probability directly, using the binomial distribution and a computer. If 6% of 200 paint cans had dents, that would correspond to $(0.06 \cdot 200) = 12$ dented cans. $P(x \geq 12, n = 200, p = 0.05) = 0.3002$. You might notice that this is not that close to the approximated value of about 26% that we calculated above.

There is a reason for the discrepancy. Because we are approximating a discrete probability distribution with a continuous one, the straightforward calculation that we did using $\hat{p}$ will tend to underestimate the true probability. This bias is corrected through the use of something called the *continuity correction factor*, which is beyond the scope of this text. The good news is that the continuity correction factor is not so important for larger values of n, and that is the situation we will assume throughout the rest of the exercises. If you think about it, you will realize that it is easier to get large sample sizes when we are collecting discrete data. A quick inspection is enough to determine if a can is dented or not. This is much less time-consuming than exactly measuring the amount of paint in the can.

To demonstrate that the accuracy of the approximation is better for large sample sizes, we will redo the dented paint can example with a sample size of 500.

6.3b

Using the sampling distribution of $\hat{p}$ to make a decision about a population proportion

Suppose that the acceptable proportion of dented cans in the paint factory is 5%. Eleanor Bennett examines a random sample of 500 cans, and finds that 6% of them are dented. What action should Eleanor take?

It is likely that the sample of 500 cans is less than 5% of the total population of paint cans. Therefore, even though the sampling is done without replacement, it is still appropriate to use the binomial distribution as the underlying probability model. Check the conditions:

- $np = 500(0.05) = 25 \geq 10$
- $np = 500(0.95) = 475 \geq 10$.

A normal distribution could be used to approximate the underlying binomial distribution. It is appropriate to use the sampling distribution of $\hat{p}$, which will be approximately normal, with:

$$\sigma_{\hat{p}} = \sqrt{\frac{pq}{n}} = \sqrt{\frac{(0.05)(0.95)}{500}} = 0.009746794$$

and

$$\mu_{\hat{p}} = p = 0.05$$

The observed sample proportion is higher than the desired level, so we want to calculate $P(\hat{p} \geq 0.06)$. The area corresponding to the probability we need to calculate is shaded in Exhibit 6.18.

6.18

Sampling Distribution of Sample Proportion, $n = 500$, $p = 0.05$

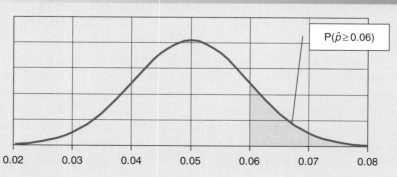

$P(\hat{p} \geq 0.06)$

0.02 0.03 0.04 0.05 0.06 0.07 0.08

$P(\hat{p} \geq 0.06)$

$= P\left(z \geq \dfrac{0.06 - 0.05}{0.009746794}\right)$

$= P(z \geq 1.03)$

$= 1 - 0.8485$

$= 0.1515$

If we do the corresponding binomial probability calculation (with the aid of a computer), we find that $P(x \geq 30, n = 500, p = 0.05) = 0.1765$. This time, the approximation (0.1515) is closer to the actual value (0.1765). Note that because the underlying binomial distribution is skewed (the probability of success is only 5%, which is quite far from 50%), the approximation will not be perfect.

Whether we calculate the probability of the sample result with the binomial distribution, or approximate it with the sampling distribution of $\hat{p}$, we will reach the same decision. Because a sample proportion as high as 6% would occur more than 15% of time, if the actual proportion of dented cans were actually 5%, the sample result is not unusual. We do not have evidence that there are more dented cans than there should be. No action should be taken.

In a recent survey about the acceptability of a new breakfast cereal, the respondents were asked to indicate whether they would use the cereal regularly after trying it. The cereal's manufacturer thought that the new cereal would be worthwhile to launch if the probability of an individual saying yes was more than 0.20.

Using the sampling distribution of $\hat{p}$ to make a decision about a population proportion

Suppose the research company actually surveyed 200 people and found 46 who said they would use the cereal regularly after trying it. What is the probability of this happening, assuming that the actual probability of using the cereal after trying it is only 0.20? Does the sample result provide evidence that the proportion of people who would use the cereal regularly after trying it is more than 20%?

First, we have to recognize that this is a situation in which the binomial distribution applies. As with most opinion surveys, sampling is done without replacement. The population of breakfast cereal eaters is probably quite large, so the sample size of 200 is probably much less than 5% of the population. The binomial distribution is an appropriate underlying model here, with $n = 200$ and $p = 0.20$.

Next, we have to see if this binomial distribution can be approximated by a normal distribution. We check np and nq.

- $np = 200(0.20) = 40$
- $nq = 200(0.80) = 160$

Both are ≥ 10, so we can use the sampling distribution of $\hat{p}$.

The sample proportion is $\frac{46}{100} = 0.23$. We now have to calculate the probability of a sample proportion as high as the observed sample result, if the population proportion is 0.20.

$$P(\hat{p} \geq 0.23) = P\left(z \geq \frac{0.23 - 0.20}{\sqrt{\frac{0.20(0.80)}{200}}}\right) = P(z \geq 1.06) = (1 - 0.8554) = 0.1446$$

The probability of getting a sample proportion as high as 23% is 0.1446, if 20% of all customers would use the cereal after trying it. This sample result is not unusual. While the sample results looked promising ($\hat{p}$ was greater than 20%), the sample result was not enough greater than 20% to be convincing. Therefore, we do not have enough evidence from the sample to conclude that more than 20% of people would use the cereal regularly after trying it. This means it would not be worthwhile to launch this breakfast cereal (if this criterion is the only one determining the launch, which is unlikely).

Guide to Decision Making

Using the Sampling Distribution of $\hat{p}$

When:

- qualitative data, one sample, one population
- trying to make a decision about p on the basis of $\hat{p}$
- sample size (n) large
- computer not available, so using a binomial probability calculation is not practical

Steps:

1. Identify or calculate

- p, the desired or claimed population proportion
- $\hat{p}$, the sample proportion
- n, the sample size.

2. If sampling is being done without replacement, check that the sample is less than 5% of the total population, so the binomial distribution is an appropriate underlying model.

3. Check that the underlying binomial distribution can be approximated by a normal distribution, which requires *both*

- $np \geq 10$ and
- $nq \geq 10$.

If these conditions are met, the sampling distribution of $\hat{p}$ will be approximately normal.

4. *If* the sampling distribution is approximately normal, proceed by identifying or calculating the mean and standard deviation of the sampling distributions, using the following formulas:

- $\mu_{\hat{p}} = p$

- $\sigma_{\hat{p}} = \sqrt{\frac{pq}{n}}$

5. Use this sampling distribution to calculate the probability of a sample result as extreme as the $\hat{p}$ from the sample.

- If $\hat{p}$ is above p, calculate P($\hat{p} \geq$ observed sample proportion).

- If $\hat{p}$ is below p, calculate P($\hat{p} \leq$ observed sample proportion).

If the calculated probability is 5% or less, there is convincing evidence that the population is not as claimed.

DEVELOP YOUR SKILLS 6.3

1. A cereal manufacturer claims that 10% of its cereal boxes contain a free ticket to the movies. Because you have eaten several boxes of cereal without finding a movie ticket, you are suspicious of this claim. You set up a website to ask people about their experience with the cereal boxes. Once you have 250 responses, you shut the website down, and do some calculations. You discover that 20 of your 250 respondents have found free movie tickets. Do you have a case against the manufacturer's claim? (Is this really a random sample? Why or why not? What do you have to think about in order to answer this question?)

2. A college claims that 97% of its graduates find jobs in their field within a year of graduation. Since you graduated from the program a year ago and have not been able to find a job, you think that the college has overestimated the job placement rate of its graduates. The alumni office contacts a random sample of 200 students from your college who graduated when you did, and discovered that 5% of the group do not have a job in their field. Does this mean that the college has overstated the proportion of graduates who find jobs in their field within a year of graduation?

3. A tire company claims that no more than 1% of its tires are defective. A national survey shows that 8 out of 500 tires purchased in the last year from this company were defective. Does the sample provide evidence that the percentage of defective tires is more than 1%? (What bias might you be concerned about, with the national survey?)

4. An advertisement for Cold-Over claims an 80% success rate in preventing a cold from developing, if the patient starts the treatment immediately upon getting a sore throat or a runny nose. A random sample of 300 patients who are just developing symptoms are given Cold-Over, and are later checked to see if the treatment was successful. It is found that 235 of them found the treatment successful. Does the sample provide evidence that fewer than 80% of patients taking Cold-Over prevent a cold from developing, if they take it as directed?

5. A survey by a research company reported that 40% of retired people eat out at least once a week. You run a restaurant, and you are wondering if you should focus more of your advertising on retired people. However, you are concerned that the research might not apply to your particular city. You decide to check on the research results. You hire a statistics student to conduct a random sample of 150 retired people in your city. The student reports that 44 of them eat out at least once a week. Do these sample results suggest that the percentage of retired people who eat out at least once a week in your city is less than in the research study? Is there anything else you should consider?

6.4 HYPOTHESIS TESTING

In Chapter 6, we have explored the use of sampling distributions and probability calculations to make decisions about population parameters, based on sample results. The formal method of doing this is called a hypothesis test, and you will be introduced to it in Chapter 7. The methods applied in this chapter, while fundamentally correct, have been somewhat informal and streamlined. The goal was to help you develop an intuitive understanding of the decision-making process, without being distracted by too many details.

We have glossed over some important issues. For example, we presumed that σ was known when we were making decisions about population means. This is clearly unrealistic, as was pointed out. However, this unrealistic approach allowed us (temporarily) to work with the familiar normal distribution. In Chapter 7, you will learn how to deal with the more realistic situation where σ is unknown, and you not need to make decisions about means with a normal sampling distribution.

In Chapter 6 we used a general rule of declaring a sample result *unusual* if the associated tail probability was 5% or less. This is a streamlined approach. In formal hypothesis tests, the probability level that is used to distinguish an unusual sample result can be different from 5%, depending on the situation (although generally it will not be more than 5%). In Chapter 7, you will learn how to deal with these different situations.

There is more to learn about the topics covered in Chapter 6, and you should realize that Chapter 6 represents an interim step in your learning. However, if you have understood what a sampling distribution is, and how it can be used to make a decision about a population distribution, this is a major accomplishment. This decision-making process is the cornerstone of inferential statistics. If you have understood it, the rest is just details. You should find that you can easily build on this understanding to conduct the formal hypothesis tests discussed in Chapter 7 and beyond.

Chapter Summary

6

The Decision-Making Process for Statistical Inference

Statistical inference is a set of techniques to allow reliable conclusions to be drawn about population data, on the basis of sample data. A random sample is drawn from the population, and a sample statistic is calculated. While the sample statistic is unlikely to be exactly equal to the claimed or desired value of the population parameter, it should be reasonably close. If it is not, the sample gives us evidence to doubt that the population is as claimed or desired.

The sampling distribution is key to the ability to distinguish whether sample results are consistent with the claimed or desired value of the population parameter. A sampling distribution is the probability distribution of all sample results for a given sample size. We use the sampling distribution to calculate the probability of getting a sample result as extreme as the one we observed from the sample, assuming the claim about the population is true. For the purposes of this chapter, we used a general rule of declaring a sample result unusual if the associated tail probability was 5% or less.

The sampling distribution is closely related to the distribution of the population from which the sample is drawn. Once we know what the population characteristics are supposed to be, we can calculate the characteristics of the sampling distribution. Two particular sampling distributions are described in this chapter.

The Sampling Distribution of the Sample Mean

Sometimes we want to make a decision about a population mean, μ, on the basis of a sample mean, $\bar{x}$. For this we need the sampling distribution of the sample mean.

For a sample of size n, and a population with a claimed or desired mean of μ:

1. The standard deviation of the sample means (the $\bar{x}$-values) is equal to the population standard deviation, divided by the square root of the sample size. In other words:

$$\sigma_{\bar{x}} = \sqrt{\frac{\sigma}{n}}$$

We refer to the standard deviation of the sample means ($\sigma_{\bar{x}}$) as the *standard error*.

2. The mean of the sample means (the $\bar{x}$-values) is equal to the mean of the original population. To put this into mathematical shorthand, we would say

$$\mu_{\bar{x}} = \mu$$

3. The sampling distribution of the sample means is normal if the original population is normally distributed, or the sample size is large enough.

The Central Limit Theorem tells us that sampling distributions of $\bar{x}$ can be normal—even if the original population is not normal—if the sample size is large enough. How large is "large enough" depends on how far from normal the population is.

To assess population normality, create a histogram of sample data (unless there are too few data points). Some guidelines to help you decide whether a sampling distribution of $\bar{x}$ is normal are outlined on p. 211. Also, there is a Guide to Decision Making using sampling distributions of $\bar{x}$ when σ is known, on p. 221. Example 6.2b on p. 220 illustrates.

The Sampling Distribution of the Sample Proportion

Sometimes we want to make decisions about a population proportion, p, on the basis of the sample proportion, $\hat{p}$. We can do this by two different methods, depending on whether we focus on the counts (the number of successes) or the proportion of successes. For example, in Example 6.3a on p. 223, the problem focused on 89 late shipments out of 400. This could also be expressed as $\frac{89}{400} = 0.2225$, a proportion of late shipments. These are just two ways of representing the same information.

No matter which method is used, if sampling is done without replacement, ensure that the sample is no more than 5% of the total population, so that the binomial distribution is the appropriate underlying probability model.

If we focus on the counts (the number of successes) rather than the proportion of successes, we can calculate the probability of a sample result as extreme as the one we observed using the binomial probability distribution. Generally this will require the use of a computer. The approach is the same as before: if the probability of getting a sample result as extreme as the one we observed is 5% or less, we consider that to be evidence that the population proportion is not as claimed. Example 6.3a on p. 223 illustrates.

If we focus on the proportion of successes, we can (in some cases) use the sampling distribution of $\hat{p}$ to assess the probability of a sample result as extreme as the one we observed.

For a sample of size n and a binomial distribution with a claimed or desired proportion p:

1. The standard deviation of the sample proportions (the $\hat{p}$-values) is as follows:

$$\sigma_{\hat{p}} = \sqrt{\frac{pq}{n}}$$

We refer to $\sigma_{\hat{p}}$ as the *standard error* of the sample proportion.

2. The mean of the sample proportions is equal to the population proportion. In other words:

$$\mu_{\hat{p}} = p$$

The sampling distribution will be approximately normal as long as both of the required conditions are met:
- $np \geq 10$ and
- $nq \geq 10$.

Note: This last result means that you must check these conditions before you use the sampling distribution of $\hat{p}$. If these conditions are not both met, you will have to use the binomial distribution to make your decision.

There is a Guide to Decision Making using the sampling distribution of $\hat{p}$ on p. 230. Example 6.3b on p. 228 illustrates.

CHAPTER REVIEW EXERCISES

When you do these exercises, you will have to decide whether to use the sampling distribution of $\bar{x}$, or the sampling distribution of $\hat{p}$ (or the binomial distribution). It should not be difficult to distinguish between the two situations, if you keep the following in mind.

- If the data are quantitative, and there is reference to averages or means, you will need to use the sampling distribution of $\bar{x}$. Remember to check for normality of the sample data set.
- If the data are qualitative, and there is reference to percentages or proportions or counts, you will need to use the sampling distribution of $\hat{p}$ (or the binomial distribution). Remember to check the conditions for normality of the sampling distribution.

There are only a few Chapter Review Exercises, but they will give you practice in handling sampling distributions. Remember that the informal, streamlined approach you are using for these questions is temporary, and that Chapter 7 will introduce you to formal hypothesis tests.

1. The manufacturer of a pill for back pain claims that 73% of those who take the pill get relief from their back pain within one hour. You work for a consumer organization, and you want to check the claim. You take a random sample of 350 people with back pain who took the pill, and find that 238 of them got relief within one hour. Is there evidence that the proportion of back pain sufferers who get relief within one hour is lower than the manufacturer claims?

2. The operations manager at the factory is interested in the lifespan of an electronic component used in one of the factory's machines. The producer of the electronic component claims that it has an average life of 6,251.35 hours, with a standard deviation of 201 hours. A random sample of 40 components is studied, and their lifespans are recorded.

    The data are available on the CD that comes with the text, in a directory called DataChap06. What is the probability of getting a sample result as low as this, if the average life of the component is actually 6,251.35 hours, as the component's producer claims? Does this sample provide evidence that the component lifespan is less than the producer claims? You may assume that the population standard deviation is equal to the sample standard deviation.

CRE06-2.xls
Set

3. The college cafeteria manager claims that 90% of cafeteria customers are satisfied with the range of food served and prices. Suppose that in a random sample of 500 cafeteria customers, 438 say that they are satisfied with the cafeteria. Does the sample result

suggest that fewer than 90% of the cafeteria's customers are satisfied with the range of food served and prices?

4. A survey of the morning beverage market shows that the primary breakfast beverage of 17% of Americans is milk. A Canadian dairy company believes the figure to be higher in Canada. The company contacts a random sample of 550 Canadians and asks what primary beverage they consumed for breakfast that day. Suppose 115 replied that milk was their primary beverage. Does this sample result provide evidence that a greater proportion of Canadians drink milk as their primary breakfast beverage, as compared to people in the United States?

5. A small college in Southern Ontario advertises that its business graduates earn an average annual income of $37,323 the first year after graduation. A researcher has been given the task of checking the claim for the 2006 year.

     A random survey of 45 of the college's business graduates produces a data set that is available on the CD that comes with the text, in a directory called DataChap06. Does this sample provide evidence that the average annual income of business graduates in the first year after graduation is less than $37,323? You may assume that the standard deviation of all graduates' salaries is equal to the sample standard deviation.

CRE06-5.xls
Set

6. A tourist attraction gets more than 50,000 visitors a year, but traffic has declined over the last few years. The manager has recently refurbished the buildings, added new activities, and generally spruced up the facility. A survey of customers done two years ago revealed that only 65% of them felt that they had had an enjoyable experience. A survey of 450 visitors, done after the upgrades, indicated that 315 of them felt that they had had an enjoyable experience. Does this provide any evidence that the upgrades improved visitor enjoyment?

7. In 1997, 60% of students attending public school in Ontario had access to a computer at school. Concerned parents, worried about budget cuts, think that the access to computers has actually decreased since then. To test their idea, they randomly sampled 400 students in a variety of Ontario public schools. They discovered that only 228 of them had access to a computer. Is there evidence that access to computers in public schools has decreased since 1997?

8. A human resources manager claims that tuition subsidies for employees are not an important benefit, as only 5% of employees would use such a program. The union president thinks that this estimate is too low. The union president conducts a survey of employees to determine how many of them would use a tuition subsidy program if it were available. The survey of 500 employees revealed that 50 of them would use the tuition subsidy program. Does the sample provide evidence that the HR manager's estimate of the percentage of employees who would use the program is too low?

9. An analyst in a government ministry is interested in the average cost of textbooks per semester for a college student. The ministry is preparing a study of the cost of a college education. The study (which is in draft form at present) uses a figure based on 1998 data, which suggests that the average cost of textbooks per semester is $500. The analyst wants to check this, and conducts a random sample of 75 college students, asking them what their textbook costs were for the last semester. The sample results show an average cost of $576, with a standard deviation of $122. Is there evidence that average textbook costs per semester have increased for college students? You may assume that the standard deviation of all textbook costs is actually $122, and that the population data are normally distributed.

10. Automated teller machines must be stocked with enough cash to satisfy customers making withdrawals over an entire weekend. At one particular branch, a random sample of the total withdrawals on 36 weekends showed a sample mean of $8,600. Suppose that

the branch manager has always claimed that the average total withdrawn over the week-end is $7,500. On the basis of the sample taken, is there evidence to suggest that the bank manager's claim about the true average total withdrawal per weekend is too low? You may assume that the population data are normally distributed, and that the standard deviation is $3,700.

 Go to MyStatLab at www.mystatlab.com. You can practise many of this chapter's exercises as often as you want. The guided solutions help you find an answer step by step. You'll find a personalized study plan available to you too!

7

Making Decisions with a Single Sample

INTRODUCTION

Chapter 6 illustrated how to use a sampling distribution and a probability calculation to make a decision about a population parameter on the basis of a sample result. In this chapter, we will use this decision-making approach in a more formal way, that is, a test of hypothesis. This chapter introduces some commonly used language for this type of decision making. Once the formal hypothesis-testing framework is set up (Section 7.1), you will see how to apply it to make decisions about proportions (Section 7.2) and means (Section 7.3), on the basis of single samples.

In Chapter 6, as an interim step, you learned how to make decisions about population means when the population standard deviation was known. This was clearly unrealistic, and so in Chapter 7, you will learn how to make decisions about a population mean when the population standard deviation is not known (which will be always).

In Chapter 6, the problems we looked at (paint in cans, cereal in boxes, etc.) started out with a goal. For example, the paint cans were supposed to hold 3 litres of paint. We recognized that not every paint can would hold *exactly* 3 litres of paint, but we wanted to recognize any case when there was a significantly different amount of paint going into the cans.

Learning Objectives

After mastering the material in this chapter, you will be able to:

1. Set up appropriate null and alternative hypotheses, and make appropriate conclusions by comparing *p*-values with significance levels.

2. Use formal hypothesis tests to make appropriate conclusions about population proportions, on the basis of a single sample.

3. Use formal hypothesis tests to make appropriate conclusions about population means, on the basis of a single sample.

If the paint-filling line is set up properly, then the population mean will be 3 litres. In this example, it is our hypothesis (that is, idea or theory or goal) that the population mean is 3 litres, because the paint-can filling line is designed to put 3 litres of paint into every can.

7.1 FORMAL HYPOTHESIS TESTING

The Null and the Alternative Hypotheses

null hypothesis what you are going to believe about the population, unless the sample gives you strongly contradictory evidence

alternative hypothesis what you are going to believe about the population when there is strong evidence against the null hypothesis

In a formal hypothesis test, there are always two hypotheses. The **null hypothesis** is what you are going to believe about the population, unless the sample gives you strongly contradictory evidence. The **alternative hypothesis** (sometimes called the *research hypothesis*) is what you are going to believe about the population when there is strong evidence against the null hypothesis.

For example, in the paint filling line example, the null hypothesis is that in the population, the mean amount of paint in the cans is 3 litres. We could use some mathematical shorthand, and say the following:

$H_0: \mu = 3$ litres

H_0, read *H-nought*, is standard notation to depict the null hypothesis.

The alternative hypothesis, denoted H_1 (or sometimes H_A), could then take one of three forms:

- $H_1: \mu > 3$ litres (if we were concerned about the cans having too much paint in them) or
- $H_1: \mu < 3$ litres (if we were concerned about the cans having too little paint in them) or
- $H_1: \mu \neq 3$ litres (if we were concerned about the cans having either too little or too much paint in them).

Notice some important things about the null and alternative hypotheses.

1. The hypotheses are statements about a population parameter (they will never be about sample statistics).
2. The hypotheses *match*, in the sense that if the null hypothesis (H_0) is that $\mu = 3$ litres the alternative hypothesis (H_1) will be some statement about μ and 3 litres.
3. The null hypothesis (H_0) always contains an equality. The alternative hypothesis never contains an equality (or $\leq$ or $\geq$).

7.1a

Example

Setting up correct null and alternative hypotheses

Which of the following are legitimate hypothesis-testing pairs? If a pair is not a legitimate hypothesis-testing pair, explain why.

a. $H_0: \mu = 15$; $H_1: \mu = 14$
b. $H_0: \sigma = 0.4$; $H_1: \sigma > 0.6$
c. $H_0: \mu = 123$; $H_1: \mu \neq 123$
d. $H_0 = 150$; $H_1 > 150$

e. H$_0$: $p = 0.15$; H$_1$: $p \geq 0.15$

f. H$_0$: $\bar{x} = 15$; H$_1$: $\bar{x} > 15$

Solutions:

a. H$_0$: $\mu = 15$; H$_1$: $\mu = 14$

No, this is not legitimate hypothesis-testing pair. Both the null and alternative hypotheses contain equalities. As well, the hypotheses refer to two different numbers.

b. H$_0$: $\sigma = 0.4$; H$_1$: $\sigma > 0.6$

No, this is not a legitimate hypothesis-testing pair. The hypotheses refer to two different numbers. The numbers must match. If there was evidence against the null hypothesis that $\sigma = 0.4$, it would not be sensible to conclude instead that $\sigma > 0.6$!

c. H$_0$: $\mu = 123$; H$_1$: $\mu \neq 123$

Yes, this is a legitimate hypothesis-testing pair.

d. H$_0$ $= 150$; H$_1$ > 150

No, this is not a legitimate hypothesis-testing pair. No population parameter is mentioned. H$_0$ and H$_1$ cannot equal anything, or be greater than anything. These are not population parameters. H$_0$ simply means *the null hypothesis* and H$_1$ means *the alternative hypothesis*. If this pair were rewritten with reference to a population parameter, the pair would be legitimate. For example:

H$_0$: $\mu = 150$; H$_1$: $\mu > 150$

e. H$_0$: $p = 0.15$; H$_1$: $p \geq 0.15$

No, this is not a legitimate hypothesis-testing pair. Both hypotheses contain an equality. If H$_1$ were rewritten to read "$p > 0.15$," the pair would be legitimate.

f. H$_0$: $\bar{x} = 15$; H$_1$: $\bar{x} > 15$

No, this is not a legitimate hypothesis-testing pair. Both hypotheses refer to $\bar{x}$, which is a sample statistic, not a population parameter. We have no doubt about what $\bar{x}$ is, because we can calculate it from the sample. The mystery is about μ, not $\bar{x}$!

Now you should have a general sense of how the null and the alternative hypotheses should look. But how do you pick them in the first place?

One-Tailed and Two-Tailed Hypothesis Tests

In general, the alternative hypothesis can take one of three forms:

1. H$_1$: population parameter $>$ some particular value
2. H$_1$: population parameter $<$ some particular value
3. H$_1$: population parameter $\neq$ some particular value

The first two forms are referred to as *one-tailed tests* because sample results in only one tail of the sampling distribution provide evidence against the null hypothesis, in favour of the alternative hypothesis.

Suppose you have been working to reduce the time it takes for loan requests to be approved (or denied) at your financial institution. You know the average time was 2 working days in the past, and this sets up the null hypothesis, H_0: μ = 2 working days. You take a random sample of loan requests, and track how long it takes until a decision is made. In this case, you are looking for evidence that the average time has been reduced. The alternative hypothesis is H_1: μ < 2 working days. This is a one-tailed (also called a left-tailed) test: only unusually low values of $\overline{x}$ from the sample (in what should be the left tail of the sampling distribution) will convince you that average time to process the loan requests has been reduced.

As another example, suppose you have developed a new marketing plan, and now you want to see if average weekly sales have increased. In the past, average weekly sales were \$5,000, so the null hypothesis will be H_0: μ = \$5,000. Since you are wondering if sales have increased, this will also be a one-tailed test (in this case, a right-tailed test), with H_1: μ > \$5,000: only unusually high values of $\overline{x}$ from the sample (in what should be the right tail of the sampling distribution) will convince you that sales have improved.

In the streamlined approach we used in Chapter 6, all of our informal tests were one-tailed. This was a simplification. Now we are also going to deal with two-tailed tests. In Chapter 6, we also looked at sample evidence about the amount of paint in paint cans. The goal was to have an average of 3 litres of paint in every can. So the null hypothesis is H_0: μ = 3 litres. The quality control procedures should identify cases in which there is either significantly too little or significantly too much paint in the cans, so the alternative hypothesis will be H_1: μ ≠ 3 litres. This is described as a *two-tailed* test of hypothesis, because both sample results that are significantly too low (from what should be the left tail of the sampling distribution) and significantly too high (from the right tail of the sampling distribution) would provide evidence against the null hypothesis. Many quality control hypothesis tests are two-tailed.

Making a Decision: Rejecting or Failing to Reject the Null Hypothesis

In a hypothesis test, we are using sample data to decide between two conflicting ideas, expressed as H_0 and H_1. If we get significant evidence from the sample data against the null hypothesis, then we are going to change our minds about something, and probably take some action. In the paint-can filling line example, if the sample data provide convincing evidence that the mean amount of paint going into the paint cans is *not* 3 litres, then some action will be taken to adjust the machines, and there will be good reason for doing so. Also notice this: if the sample does not provide convincing evidence against the null hypothesis, no action will be taken. This makes sense: the company does not want to be adjusting machines when they don't really need it. But this is a weaker result, in the sense that it does not *guarantee* that the average amount of paint going into the cans is actually 3 litres.

In the first case (convincing evidence against the null hypothesis), the usual language is to say that we *rejected* the null hypothesis, and that there is sufficient evidence to support the alternative hypothesis. This is a fairly strong conclusion. In the second case, we say that we *failed to reject* the null hypothesis, and that there is insufficient evidence to support the alternative hypothesis. This is a weaker conclusion. Above all, it does *not* imply that the null hypothesis is *true*. We can never be that definitive unless we have examined the entire population of data. Therefore, if you fail to reject the null hypothesis, you should *not* say "the null hypothesis is true," or even that you "accept" the null hypothesis. All you can say is that you do not have strong evidence against it.

Significance Level and Type I and Type II Errors

Once the null and alternative hypotheses are set up, the next step is to establish the significance level of the test. The usual notation for the significance level is α, that is, the Greek letter alpha. For example, you might see $\alpha = 0.05$, which means that the significance level is set at 5%.

But what does *significance level* mean? To understand this, you must understand that you can make two types of errors when you are doing a test of hypothesis. Both of these potential errors arise because we are using sample data to make a conclusion about a population. The best we can do is to control the possibility of these kinds of errors. We cannot eliminate them completely, as long as we are using sample data (and not population data) to make decisions.

A **Type I error** arises when we mistakenly reject the null hypothesis when it is in fact true. In the paint can filling line example, this would correspond to deciding to adjust the machines on the line when they were in fact working correctly. The **significance level** is the probability of a Type I error in a hypothesis test. It is something that you will control in the hypothesis test.

Your first instinct would probably be to set the significance level quite low, although of course, we could never set $\alpha = 0$ (whenever we use sample data, there will always be some possibility of Type I error). Suppose Eleanor Bennett, the quality control inspector at the paint factory, set the significance level at a low point, for example, $\alpha = 0.01$. Then there would be only a small chance of adjusting the machines on the paint-can filling line when they did not actually need adjusting. With α set so low, Eleanor Bennett would have to get very strong evidence from the sample data to be convinced to adjust the paint-can filling line. The only difficulty with this approach is that it has the effect of increasing the chance that machines would *not* be adjusted when they did need to be adjusted, with the result being either angry customers or lower profits because the company was giving away free paint. This is called a Type II error. A **Type II error** arises when we mistakenly fail to reject the null hypothesis when it is in fact false. Exhibit 7.1 below illustrates the trade-off.

> **Type I error** error that arises when we mistakenly reject the null hypothesis when it is in fact true
>
> **significance level** the probability of a Type I error in a hypothesis test
>
> **Type II error** error that arises when we mistakenly fail to reject the null hypothesis when it is in fact false

---

Trade-Off in Type I and Type II Error

7.1

Exhibit

a.

High Significance Level Increases the Chance of Rejecting H$_0$ (Possibly When It Is True)

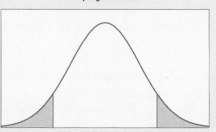

Sampling Distribution

b.

Low Significance Level Decreases the Chance of Rejecting H$_0$ (Possibly When It Is False)

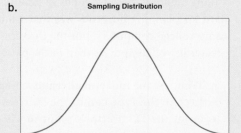

Sampling Distribution

So, how do you set α? First, realize that if you set α at 5%, this means that if you repeat the hypothesis test over and over, a large number of times, then you will end up rejecting a true null hypothesis about 5% of the time. So, over many, many quality control tests in the paint factory, the machines on the paint-can filling line would be adjusted when they did not actually need it, about 5% of the time. If you set α lower, at 2%, for example, the machines would be incorrectly adjusted only about 2% of the time, in the long run. However, lowering α would have the result that the machines would more often not be adjusted when they should be (Type II error). It is important to recognize that there is always a trade-off between Type I and Type II errors—reducing the chances of one type of error will always increase the chances of the other.

Both kinds of errors have cost and other consequences. The way to set α is to think about the costs and consequences of both types of errors, and then set α at the maximum tolerable level (which keeps the probability of Type II error as low as possible). It is possible to calculate the probability of a Type II error in a particular hypothesis test, but this is beyond the scope of this text.

In practice, the most commonly used levels of significance are 5% and 1%, and these are the levels you will most often see in problems and examples in this text. In the informal hypothesis tests in Chapter 6, we used just one significance level (5%). Now we will introduce other possibilities.

Notice that the lower the significance level is, the harder it is to reject the null hypothesis. This also means that the lower the significance level, the stronger and more persuasive your result will be if you do in fact reject the null hypothesis. If you set α fairly low, say at 1%, then you have to get a sample result that would be highly unusual (that is, it should happen only 1% of the time or less) in order to reject the null hypothesis and decide in favour of the alternative hypothesis. The sample evidence has to pass a fairly high hurdle in order for us to change our minds or take action. If we set α at 1%, and the sample evidence convinced us to adjust the machines on the paint-can filling line, we would be fairly confident that the machines did in fact need adjustment. There is one more point about the significance level of the hypothesis test. The significance level should be set *before* any data are collected, on the basis of the considerations outlined above. It can be tempting to collect some sample data and then set the significance level so that you get the result you want, but this is not the correct way to proceed.

Example 7.1b

Type I and Type II errors

The college information technology (IT) department is interested in computer usage among students, because it has to plan to provide adequate service. The former standard for planning purposes was that students spent an average of 10 hours per week using college computers, but the director of IT thinks that students are now making greater use of computers than in the past.

a. What are the null and alternative hypotheses for this situation?
b. Explain the Type I and Type II errors in the context of computer use.
c. From the IT director's point of view, which type of error would be the most important? Why?

d. From the students' point of view, which type of error would be the most important? Why?

Solutions:

a. H_0: $\mu = 10$ hours per week
H_1: $\mu > 10$ hours per week

b. A Type I error occurs when we reject the null hypothesis when it is actually true. In this context, that would mean mistakenly believing that computer use had increased, when in fact it had not.

A Type II error occurs when we fail to reject the null hypothesis when it is in fact false. In this context, that would mean concluding that computer use had not increased, when in fact it had.

c. A Type I error would mean that extra resources would be put into computing when they were not needed. This would mean incurring unnecessary extra costs.

A Type II error would mean not recognizing the case when extra resources were in fact needed. This would mean that inadequate service would be provided to students, leading to complaints and more computer down-time.

With the extreme resource limitations in the post-secondary sector in Canada, the Type I error would probably be more important to the IT director, in the short run. However, a Type II error might lead to decreased enrollment in the long run, as word got out about poor computer resources at the college.

d. A Type II error would be more important to students, as it would mean their being without crucial computing services. Ultimately, a Type I error might lead to higher educational technology fees, but those might not come into effect for a year or two after the decision was made.

Deciding on the Basis of p-Values

Although most of the problems in this text assume that data have already been collected, when you apply the hypothesis testing approach in your work, you will have to collect the sample data, as discussed in Chapter 1. Once you have the sample data, you will use it and the sampling distribution to determine whether the sample result gives you convincing evidence against the null hypothesis. This requires doing a probability calculation, based on the sampling distribution, as we did in Chapter 6.

This probability calculation results in what is called the **p-value** of a hypothesis test—the probability of getting a sample result at least as extreme as the observed sample result. The probability calculation is based on the sampling distribution that would exist if the null hypothesis were true. We have already calculated p-values, in Chapter 6. Most statistical computer software reports the p-value of any hypothesis test, so it is crucial that you understand what the p-value means. Notice that a low p-value means that the sample result would be highly unlikely (if the null hypothesis were true). Put more casually, we could say: we shouldn't be getting this sample result (not if the null hypothesis were true). But we did! This gives us evidence against the null hypothesis. On the other hand, if the p-value is high, then the sample result is not unusual, and we do not have enough evidence to reject the null

p-value in a hypothesis test, the probability of getting a sample result at least as extreme as the observed sample result; the probability calculation is based on the sampling distribution that would exist if the null hypothesis were true

hypothesis. What do *high* and *low* mean? In fact, the significance level of the hypothesis test is what decides this.

> We reject the null hypothesis whenever the *p*-value $< \alpha$. The lower the *p*-value is, the stronger is the evidence against H_0.

Comparison of the *p*-value with the significance level allows us to make the decision that is supported by the data. However, the *p*-value also gives us something more: an indication of the strength of the evidence. Suppose α is set at 5%. Both a *p*-value of 4% and a *p*-value of 1% would lead to a rejection of the null hypothesis, because both *p*-values are less than 5%. However, we would have stronger evidence against the null hypothesis when the *p*-value was 1%. A *p*-value of 1% tells us that we would get sample results like the ones we have observed only 1% of the time, if the null hypothesis were true. This is highly improbable (yet it happened), and so we can be quite confident that our decision in favour of the alternative hypothesis is true. A *p*-value of 4% gives us somewhat less confidence, even though the decision is the same.

There is one more point worth making about the *p*-value. It is unfortunate that the standard notation is so close to the notation we use for the population proportion. This can get confusing, particularly when we are doing hypothesis tests about population proportions. Keep in mind that "*p*," by itself, is the notation for a population proportion (or the probability of success in a binomial experiment). The term "*p*-value" refers to the probability calculation done for a hypothesis test.

Guide to Technique Calculating *p*-Values	The *p*-value is the probability of getting a sample result at least as extreme as the observed sample result. The probability is calculated from the appropriate sampling distribution, which is always based on the assumption that the null hypothesis is true. The *p*-value probability calculation must match the alternative hypothesis used in the test. It is: • P(sample statistic $\geq$ observed sample result) when H_1 contains ">" • P(sample statistic $\leq$ observed sample result) when H_1 contains "<" • 2 × P(tail area beyond the observed sample result) when H_1 contains "$\neq$"

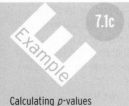

7.1c

Example

Calculating *p*-values

Suppose we have a test of hypothesis as follows:

$$H_0: \mu = 100$$
$$H_1: \mu > 100$$

A histogram of the sample data appears normal. The sample mean is 103.5 and the sample size is 40. Assume that the population standard deviation is 15.6. What is the *p*-value? If $\alpha = 0.05$, what conclusion should be made?

The histogram provides evidence that the population data are normally distributed, so the sampling distribution will also be normally distributed.

Since the alternative hypothesis contains ">," the p-value will be:

P(sample statistic ≥ observed sample result)

$= P(\bar{x} \geq 103.5)$

$= P\left[z \geq \left(\dfrac{103.5 - 100}{15.6 \Big/ \sqrt{40}} \right) \right]$

$= P(z \geq 1.42)$

$= 1 - 0.9222$

$= 0.0778$

Since the p-value is greater than the significance level of 5%, we fail to reject the null hypothesis. There is insufficient evidence to infer that $\mu > 100$.

---

1. Specify H_0, the null hypothesis.
2. Specify H_1, the alternative hypothesis.
3. Determine or identify α, the significance level.
4. Collect or identify the sample data. Calculate the p-value of the sample result.
5. If p-value $< \alpha$, reject H_0 and conclude that there is sufficient evidence to decide in favour of H_1. If p-value $> \alpha$, fail to reject H_0 and conclude that there is insufficient evidence to decide in favour of H_1.

Guide to Technique

Steps in a Formal Hypothesis Test

DEVELOP YOUR SKILLS   7.1

1. A manufacturer receives large shipments of keyboards that will be sold with its computers. It is too expensive to test every single keyboard to see if it functions properly, so the manufacturer inspects a sample of keyboards from every shipment. The computer manufacturer does not accept any shipments unless there is evidence that fewer than 5% of the keyboards are defective.
   a. What are the null and alternative hypotheses for this situation?
   b. Explain the Type I and Type II errors in the context of the keyboard shipments.
   c. From the computer manufacturer's point of view, which type of error would be the most important? Why?
   d. From the keyboard supplier's point of view, which type of error would be the most important? Why?

2. A drug company has developed a new formulation of a popular pain reliever. Initially, it appears that one of the advantages of the new formula is that it provides quicker pain relief than the old formula, which provided relief in 15 minutes, on average. The company wants to gather evidence to see if the new drug provides relief faster than the old one.
   a. What should the null and alternative hypotheses be for this situation?
   b. Explain the Type I and Type II errors in the context of the pain reliever.
   c. If the company reported that it had rejected the null hypothesis at a 10% significance level, would you be inclined to switch to the new drug? Why or why not?
   d. If the company reported that it had rejected the null hypothesis, and that the test had a p-value of 1%, would you be inclined to switch to the new drug? Why or why not?

3. The quality control manager at a plant that produces canned peaches is setting up a hypothesis test for the amount of peaches in the can. The cans are supposed to contain 142 mL of peaches.
   a. What should the null and alternative hypotheses be for this situation?

b. Explain the Type I and Type II errors in the context of the canned peaches.

c. If you were a consumer buying the peaches, which type of error would be most important to you? Why?

4. Suppose you have null and alternative hypotheses as follows.

$$H_0: p = 0.35$$
$$H_1: p > 0.35$$

The sample size is 500, sampling is done without replacement, and the sample is less than 5% of the population. The sample proportion is 0.36. What is the p-value?

5. Suppose you have null and alternative hypotheses as follows.

$$H_0: \mu = 500$$
$$H_1: \mu \neq 500$$

A histogram of the sample data appears normal. The sample mean is 556.5, and the sample size is 30. Assume that the population standard deviation is 125.6. What is the p-value?

7.2 DECIDING ABOUT A POPULATION PROPORTION

Now we can apply the formal hypothesis-testing procedure to a situation in which we are trying to make a decision about a population proportion. Remember that we can use the sampling distribution of $\hat{p}$ when np and np are both ≥ 10. Remember also that if these conditions hold, the sampling distribution of $\hat{p}$ will be approximately normal, with the mean and standard deviation as follows:

- $\mu_{\hat{p}} = p$

- $\sigma_{\hat{p}} = \sqrt{\dfrac{pq}{n}}$

We will start with a problem that we already did in Chapter 6. This will allow you to see the hypothesis-testing language being used in a situation that is already familiar to you.

7.2a

Hypothesis test about a population proportion, summary data

Let's revisit Example 6.3c on page 229. In a recent survey about the acceptability of a new breakfast cereal, the respondents were asked to indicate whether they would use the cereal regularly after trying it. The cereal's manufacturer thought that the new cereal would be worthwhile to launch only if the probability that someone would regularly use the cereal after trying it was more than 0.20. Does the sample provide evidence that this is the case?

What should the null and alternative hypotheses be in this case? The cereal will be worthwhile only if $p > 0.20$. In other words, the company needs to find convincing evidence that the proportion of people who would regularly use the cereal after trying it is more than 20%. This is the alternative hypothesis:

$$H_1: p > 0.20$$

This leads directly to a null hypothesis of $p = 0.20$. We could also say that $p \leq 0.20$, and sometimes you will see a null hypothesis specified in this way. However, we have to pick a particular value for p in order to proceed with the hypothesis test, and the value chosen must match the alternative hypothesis, so we work with $p = 0.20$. So, at this point, the null and alternative hypotheses are as follows:

H_0: $p = 0.20$
H_1: $p > 0.20$

The next step is to set the significance level for the test. To do this, we must think about the possible errors. A Type I error occurs when we reject the null hypothesis and it is actually true. This would correspond, in the current example, to deciding that more than 20% of people who tried the cereal would actually use it, when in fact they would not. The consequences of this error would be that the company would launch the new cereal, and it would not be as successful as required.

A Type II error occurs when we fail to reject the null hypothesis and it is in fact false. This would correspond, in the current example, to deciding that not enough people who tried the cereal would actually use it, when in fact they would. The consequences of this error would be that the company would not launch the new cereal, and it would have been successful.

Without more detail about the potential costs of the two kinds of errors, it is difficult to decide what the significance level of the test should be. However, it is likely that the launch of a new cereal is fairly costly, and so we would want to be fairly sure that people who tried the cereal would actually use it. In this case, we will set $\alpha = 0.01$.

The survey of 200 people found 46 who said they would use the cereal regularly after trying it. This gives us $\hat{p} = \frac{26}{200} = 0.23$, which looks promising, as $\hat{p} > 0.20$.

The next step is to calculate the appropriate p-value. This means that we must check conditions and set up the appropriate sampling distribution, as was done in Chapter 6. Since we already did this in Example 6.3c, we will not repeat the details here. We concluded that although sampling was done without replacement, the sample size was probably less than 5% of the population, so the binomial distribution was the appropriate underlying model. We calculated:

$np = 200(0.20) = 40$
$nq = 200(0.80) = 160$

Since both np and nq are ≥ 10, the sampling distribution of $\hat{p}$ will be approximately normal. Recall that the alternative hypothesis is $p > 0.20$. The p-value calculation is therefore:

$$P(\hat{p} \geq 0.20) = P\left(z \geq \frac{0.23 - 0.20}{\sqrt{\frac{0.20(0.80)}{200}}}\right) = P(z \geq .06) = 1 - 0.8554 = 0.1446$$

The p-value is more than 14%. It would not be that unusual to get $\hat{p} = 23\%$, even if only 20% of customers would actually use the cereal after trying it. The p-value, at more than 14%, is quite a lot higher than the significance level of 1%. Therefore, we fail to reject H_0, as we do not have enough evidence from the sample to conclude that more than 20% of people would use the cereal regularly after trying it. This means that on the basis of this criterion alone, it would not be worthwhile to launch this breakfast cereal.

The launch of a new breakfast cereal is a big undertaking, and it is unlikely that the decision would be made on the basis of this analysis alone. However, you should notice something important about this example. Before you learned about hypothesis testing, what would you have concluded about the proportion of people who would use the cereal after trying it? Since $\hat{p} = 0.23$ in this sample, you probably would have concluded that p was greater than 20%, and this conclusion would not be supported by the data. It would be useful to get a more comprehensive estimate of the true value of p, based on sample data, and this will be discussed in Chapter 8.

Particularly when samples are large, the data may be collected with the help of computers. Codes are often used to collect qualitative data, for example, 1 = excellent service, 2 = good service, etc. Such data have to be organized before any hypothesis test can be done. Fortunately, we have already encountered such data sets. In Chapter 2, we learned how to use Excel's Histogram tool to organize this kind of qualitative data. The next example illustrates what to do in a case such as this, and also introduces an Excel template to help with the analysis.

Example 7.2b

Hypothesis test about a population proportion with coded data

EXA07-2b.xls
Set

A mall is interested in the behaviour of its customers and, in particular, in knowing which stores are the most important in the mall. Mall management is considering not renewing the lease of a major grocery store, in favour of some electronics, photography, and outdoor stores. The grocery store manager is of course not in favour of this change. He has suggested that more than 25% of visitors to the mall come primarily to get groceries. Mall management decides to check to see if the grocery store manager's claim is true.

The data are available on the CD that comes with the text, in a directory called DataChap07. What should mall management conclude about the grocery store manager's claim? They have decided to conduct a test with a significance level of 5%.

$$H_0: p = 0.25$$
$$H_1: p > 0.25$$
$$\alpha = 5\%$$

A random sample of customers are asked to choose their most important destination in the mall, from among the following five choices:

1. Shoe store
2. Bank
3. Clothing store
4. Grocery store
5. Music store

The first step is to organize this data set so that we can determine the sample size, and what proportion of those sampled said that their most important destination was the grocery store. Using bin numbers 1–5 and Excel's Histogram tool, we find the results shown in Exhibit 7.2.

Exhibit 7.2

Excel Histogram Output for Most Important Destination in Mall

Bin	Frequency
1	38
2	68
3	66
4	82
5	46

We can use Excel formulas to calculate a sum for the frequencies, and then calculate the proportion of responses for each code. The result of these calculations is shown below in Exhibit 7.3. The "Bin" heading has been altered and the codes have been replaced with appropriate labels, to make the spreadsheet more readable (something you should always do).

Excel Calculations for Most Important Destination in Mall

Primary Destination	Frequency	Proportion
Shoe store	38	0.12667
Bank	68	0.22667
Clothing store	66	0.22000
Grocery store	82	0.27333
Music store	46	0.15333
Total	300	

Exhibit **7.3**

From the table we can see that 27.3% of those surveyed said that the grocery store was their most important destination. So, for this problem, $\hat{p} = 0.273$. We can also see that $n = 300$. Presumably, the mall has thousands of customers, so it is not unreasonable to conclude that a sample of 300 is less than 5% of the total population. Although sampling is done without replacement, we can proceed.

Using the Excel Template for Making Decisions About a Population Proportion with a Single Sample

The remaining steps are very similar to those in the previous example. Since these steps are repetitive, it is worthwhile to set up a standard worksheet approach for these problems.

A worksheet template is available on the CD that comes with the text, to help you with these calculations. Several templates are available, in a workbook called "Templates." The worksheet used here is labelled "z-Test of Proportion." The completed template for this example is shown in Exhibit 7.4

Template

Completed Excel Template

Making Decisions About the Population Proportion with a Single Sample	
sample size, n	300
hypothetical value of population proportion, p	0.25
np	75
nq	225
are both np and nq >= 10?	yes
sample proportion	0.273333333
z-score	0.933333333
one-tailed p-value	0.175323924
two-tailed p-value	0.350647848

Exhibit **7.4**

This template automates the calculations you would do by hand for a hypothesis test about a population proportion. You have to input values into the blue-shaded cells in the template, and the built-in formulas will fill in the other cells. This template has a built-in formula for checking for normality (np and $nq \geq 10$), for calculating the z-score, and for both the one-tailed and two-tailed p-values of the hypothesis test (you have to decide which you need, depending on H_1). It is most useful if you copy and paste this template onto the worksheet containing your data and initial analysis. Then you can simply link most of the values you need for the blue-shaded cells to calculated values on your spreadsheet. This reduces the possibility of a copying error.

Since this is a one-tailed test, the appropriate p-value is 0.175324. This means that the sample result would not be unusual, if the population proportion were equal to 25%. The p-value is considerably more than the 5% significance level. We fail to reject the null hypothesis, and note that there is insufficient sample evidence to conclude that more than 25% of the mall's customers come to the mall primarily to get groceries, as the grocery store manager claims.

However, does this mean that mall management should proceed to close the grocery store? Examine the data carefully. The largest proportion of the mall customers surveyed said that the grocery store was their most important destination. While it may not be as important as the grocery store manager claims it is, the grocery store is certainly an important destination in the mall.

Guide to Decision Making

Hypothesis Test About a Population Proportion

When:

- qualitative data, one sample, one population
- trying to make a decision about p, the population proportion, on the basis of $\hat{p}$, the sample proportion
- sample size (n) large

Steps:
1. Specify H_0, the null hypothesis.
2. Specify H_1, the alternative hypothesis.
3. Determine or identify α, the significance level.
4. Collect or identify the sample data. Identify or calculate:

   - $\hat{p}$, the sample proportion
   - n, the sample size.

5. If sampling is done without replacement, make sure that the sample size is less than 5% of the population, so that the binomial distribution is the appropriate underlying model.
6. Check for (approximate) normality of the sampling distribution, which requires BOTH:

   - $np \geq 10$ and
   - $nq \geq 10$.

7. *If* the sampling distribution is approximately normal, proceed by identifying or calculating the mean and standard deviation of the sampling distribution, with:

   - $\mu_{\hat{p}} = p$
   - $\sigma_{\hat{p}} = \sqrt{\dfrac{pq}{n}}$

8. Use the approximately normal sampling distribution of $\hat{p}$ to calculate the appropriate p-value for the hypothesis test. When done by hand, the calculation will involve the z-score:

$$z = \frac{\hat{p} - \mu_{\hat{p}}}{\sigma_{\hat{p}}} = \frac{\hat{p} - p}{\sqrt{\dfrac{pq}{n}}}$$

9. If p-value $< \alpha$, reject H_0 and conclude that there is sufficient evidence to decide in favour of H_1. If p-value $> \alpha$, fail to reject H_0 and conclude that there is insufficient evidence to decide in favour of H_1.

DEVELOP YOUR SKILLS 7.2

1. A poll conducted by Decima Research in September 2005 said that 27% of Canadian homeowners spent more than they planned on home renovation projects. The results were based on a random sample of 1006 homeowners. At the 5% significance level, does the survey support the notion that more than a quarter of homeowners spend more than they planned on home renovation projects? (Source: "Design Shows Blamed for High Reno Spending," *The Globe and Mail*, Friday, October 21, 2005, Section G)

2. The same poll referred to in Question 1 above said that 34% of homeowners are borrowing to renovate. At the 2% significance level, does the survey support the claim that more than a third of homeowners borrow to renovate?

3. In May 2005, SES Research conducted a random telephone survey of 500 Ontarians aged 18 and older. (Source: "Views on Ontario Government Finance," **www.sesresearch.com/library/polls/POLONT-S05-T141.pdf**, accessed July 11, 2006.) SES Research told respondents that in the past year, the provincial McGuinty Liberal government had received an extra $1 billion in tax revenue that it had not expected to have. When asked what the government's first priority for the money should be, 56% suggested that the government should increase spending on social programs like healthcare and education. Do the data support the claim that the majority of Ontarians aged 18 and older think extra government money should be devoted to social programs? Use $\alpha = 1\%$.

4. A retail electronics shop is thinking of mounting a sales push to get customers to buy the extended warranty available for their purchases. The sales manager believes that fewer than 10% of customers currently opt for the extra coverage. A random sample of 200 customers revealed that 18 opted for the extended warranty. Do the sample results confirm the sales manager's belief? Use $\alpha = 0.05$.

5. The owner of a diner wants to know if more than 25% of customers choose salad instead of fries with their main course. A random sample of 50 customers reveals that 14 chose salad instead of fries. What can you tell the diner's owner, on the basis of this sample? Use $\alpha = 4\%$.

7.3   DECIDING ABOUT THE POPULATION MEAN

In Chapter 6, we made some conclusions about population means on the basis of sample means, using the sampling distribution of $\bar{x}$. This was a useful introduction, but in Chapter 6, we assumed that we knew σ, the population standard deviation. Of course, if we do not even know μ, it is highly unlikely that we will know σ!

In this section, we will learn how to deal with the more realistic case where we do not know σ.

Remember that the sampling distribution of $\bar{x}$ will be normal if the population is normal, something that you can check by examining a histogram of the sample data. The mean and standard deviation of the $\bar{x}$-values will be:

- $\mu_{\bar{x}} = \mu$

- $\sigma_x = \dfrac{\sigma}{\sqrt{n}}$.

The difficulty is that we do not know σ, so we cannot calculate $\sigma_{\bar{x}}$.

Although we do not know σ, we can use s, the sample standard deviation, as an estimate. The bigger the sample size, the better s will be as an estimate of σ. However, s is not σ (although it may be close) and we have to take this into consideration.

The sampling distribution of $\bar{x}$ has a mean of μ, and a standard error of $\sigma_{\bar{x}} = \dfrac{\sigma}{\sqrt{n}}$.

The closest we can come to this is an approximation of the sampling distribution, with a mean of μ and an approximate standard error of $s_{\bar{x}} = \dfrac{s}{\sqrt{n}}$. While there is only one true sampling distribution, there will be a number of these approximate sampling distributions, because each one depends on the value of s taken from a particular sample. This adds some extra uncertainty into our calculations.

The *t*-Distribution

Fortunately, in 1908, a man named William S. Gosset, who worked for the Guinness brewing company in Dublin, Ireland, discovered how to handle this extra uncertainty. He developed something that is now called the *t*-distribution, which allows us to conduct reliable hypothesis tests about μ when σ is unknown.

The t-distributions are symmetric probability distributions, which look similar to the normal distribution, but with more area under the tails. There is a different *t*-distribution for each sample size, and each *t*-distribution is distinguished by its degrees of freedom. For single sample tests about μ, the degrees of freedom are calculated as $n - 1$.

Probability calculations for the *t*-distribution are based on the standardized *t*-score (even those in Excel), which is calculated for tests about μ as follows:

$$t = \frac{\bar{x} - \mu}{s / \sqrt{n}}$$

The *t*-score is calculated in a way that is parallel to the calculation of the *z*-score in the probability calculations in Chapter 6 (or in Example 7.1c on p. 244), with s replacing the unknown σ.

Exhibit 7.5 shows a *t*-distribution with three degrees of freedom (the red curve on the graph), one with six degrees of freedom (the blue curve on the graph), and a normal distribution (the green curve on the graph).

Two *t*-Distribution Curves and a Normal Curve

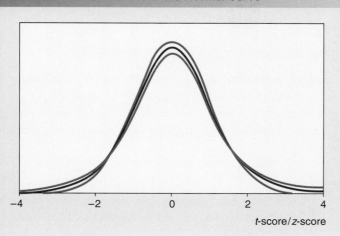

t-score/*z*-score

You can see that as the degrees of freedom (and sample size) increase, the *t*-distribution has less area under the tails. This is reasonable. As the sample size increases, *s* will be a better estimate of σ, and so there will be less variability in the *t*-score. In fact, when the degrees of freedom reach 30 or so, the *t*-distribution is very close to the normal distribution.

The *t*-distribution can be used for inferences about μ if it appears that the population data are normally distributed. We checked for normality of the population data in Chapter 6 by examining histograms of the sample data, and we must continue to do so here.

We can use Excel or *t*-tables for the probability calculations we need in order to do hypothesis tests about μ, σ unknown. Examples 7.3a, 7.3b, and 7.3c illustrate the use of Excel. Examples 7.3d and 7.3e illustrate the use of the *t*-tables.

Suppose a company is trying a new marketing approach in some of its stores. The company has selected a random sample of stores from its many locations. The average of sales at all stores was $5000 a week, before the new marketing plan was introduced. Weekly sales at the stores trying out the new marketing approach were recorded, with the results shown in Exhibit 7.6 below. Do the sample data indicate that the new marketing approach has increased weekly sales? Use a 5% significance level.

Right-tailed hypothesis test about a population mean, raw data

Weekly Sales at a Random Sample of Stores Trying Out a New Marketing Approach

Weekly Sales ($)				
5,117	5,167	5,267	5,451	5,430
5,577	4,900	5,036	5,601	4,801
5,224	4,635	4,592	4,831	4,887

In this case, we are looking for evidence that μ has increased. The null and alternative hypotheses will be as follows:

H_0: μ = $5,000 in sales per week
H_1: μ > $5,000 in sales per week

The significance level was given as 5%. Now we must determine what the sampling distribution of the $\bar{x}$-values will look like, and use it (if appropriate) to determine the p-value.

The first step is to try to assess whether weekly sales at all the locations are normally distributed. To do this, we will create a histogram of the sample data. One possible histogram is shown below in Exhibit 7.7.

7.7 Exhibit

Histogram of the Sample Data

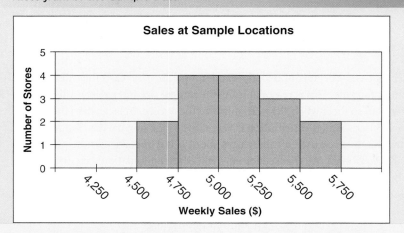

This data set looks approximately normal, so we can proceed. The next step is to calculate the appropriate t-score, so that we can assess the p-value associated with the observed sample mean.

$$t = \frac{\bar{x} - \mu}{s / \sqrt{n}}$$

Before we can calculate the t-score, we must first calculate its components. We can do this most easily with Excel, but we can also calculate the components by hand. The manual calculations are shown below. You should refer to Chapter 3 for a reminder about the use of Excel functions such as AVERAGE and STDEV.

$$\bar{x} = \frac{\Sigma x}{n} = \frac{\$76,516}{15} = \$5,101.06667$$

$$s = \sqrt{\frac{\Sigma x^2 - \frac{(\Sigma x)^2}{n}}{n-1}} = \sqrt{\frac{391,797,390.00 - \frac{(76,516)^2}{15}}{14}} = \$325.59538$$

The *t*-score can be calculated as follows.

$$t = \frac{\bar{x} - \mu}{s / \sqrt{n}} = \frac{\$5,101.06667 - \$5,000}{\$325.59538 / \sqrt{15}} = 1.20220$$

Since this is a right-tailed hypothesis test, we calculate the *p*-value as P($t \geq 1.20220$), for a *t*-distribution with 14 degrees of freedom (remember, degrees of freedom = $n - 1$).

We can use the TDIST function in Excel to calculate this probability. The dialogue box is shown below, in Exhibit 7.8

Instructions

Dialogue Box for TDIST Function in Excel

7.8
Exhibit

Function Arguments   [?][X]

┌─ TDIST ──────────────────────────────────┐
│   X [   ] = number │
│ **Deg_freedom** [   ] = number │
│   **Tails** [   ] = number │
│   =   │
│ Returns the Student's t-distribution.   │
│   │
│   **X** is the numeric value at which to evaluate the distribution. │
│   │
│ Formula result =   │
│ Help on this function   [OK] [Cancel] │
└──┘

The function arguments in Excel are as follows.

- x is the *t*-score you calculated. Note that TDIST works only with positive numbers.
- Deg_freedom is the degrees of freedom for the *t*-distribution you are working with. It is equal to $n - 1$ for single-sample tests about μ.
- Tails requires you to specify 1 or 2, depending on whether you want the probability in one or both tails of the distribution.

The completed dialogue box, with the result, is shown in Exhibit 7.9 on the next page.

Exhibit 7.9

Completed Dialogue Box for TDIST Function in Excel

Function Arguments   ? ✕

┌─ TDIST ───┐
│   │
│   **X** | 1.20220 | 📊 = 1.2022   │
│   │
│   **Deg_freedom** | 14 | 📊 = 14   │
│   │
│   **Tails** | 1 | 📊 = 1   │
│   │
│   = 0.124613207   │
│   Returns the Student's t-distribution.   │
│   │
│   **Tails** specifies the number of distribution tails to return: one-tailed distribution │
│   = 1; two-tailed distribution = 2.   │
│   │
│   Formula result =   0.124613207   │
│   │
│   Help on this function   [OK] [Cancel] │
└──┘

TDIST tells us that $P(t \geq 1.2022) = 0.124613$. Since this is a fairly high probability, the observed sample result would not be unusual, if the average weekly sales were $5,000. We do not have convincing evidence that average weekly sales have increased. The *p*-value of $0.124613 > 0.05$, the significance level of this test.

We fail to reject H_0, and can also say that there is insufficient evidence to conclude that average weekly sales have increased for the stores using the new marketing approach.

Example 7.3b

Left-tailed hypothesis test about a population mean, raw data

An automotive parts manufacturing plant has been working hard to reduce employee absences. In the past, the average of days off work (other than vacation) per year has been 6.6. The company has introduced a wellness program to encourage workers to eat well, exercise regularly, and lead healthier lifestyles. While the wellness program has had obvious positive effect on employee morale, the director of human resources is interested in whether the average of days off work has declined significantly.

The company's human resources database does not make it easy to retrieve this information, and so it was decided that the absences of a random sample of employees would be examined. The days off work for 25 employees were recorded, and are shown in Exhibit 7.10. Conduct the appropriate hypothesis test. Use a significance level of 5%.

Annual Days Off Work (Other than Vacation) for a Random Sample of Employees

7.10 Exhibit

4	4.5	5.5	5	5.5	9	7.5	4	7.5	6.5
6	5.5	6.5	6.5	6	5	6	4.5	7	7
8	7	4.5	5.5	7					

The director of human resources wants to know if the average of days off work has declined significantly. This leads to null and alternative hypotheses as follows:

$$H_0: \mu = 6.6$$
$$H_1: \mu < 6.6$$
$$\alpha = 0.05 \text{ (given)}$$

Now we have to examine the sample data to see if they appear to be normally distributed. One possible histogram of the data is presented below in Exhibit 7.11.

Histogram for the Days Off Work Data

7.11 Exhibit

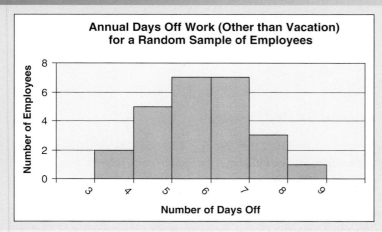

The sample data appear to be approximately normally distributed, and so we will proceed.

$$\bar{x} = \frac{\Sigma x}{n} = \frac{151}{25} = 6.04$$

$$s = \sqrt{\frac{\Sigma x^2 - \frac{(\Sigma x)^2}{n}}{n - 1}} = \sqrt{\frac{952 - \frac{(151)^2}{25}}{24}} = 1.2903488$$

The t-score can be calculated as follows.

$$t = \frac{\bar{x} - \mu}{s / \sqrt{n}} = \frac{6.04 - 6.60}{1.2903488 / \sqrt{25}} = -2.169955923$$

As always, you can use Excel functions to calculate the mean and the standard deviation, and you can create an Excel formula to calculate the *t*-score. In this case, if you try to use the calculated *t*-score in TDIST, you will get an error, because the *t*-score is a negative number and TDIST does not work with negative numbers. This is easily solved by entering the *t*-score without the minus sign. The answer will still be correct, because the *t*-distribution is symmetric. Exhibit 7.12 below illustrates.

Exhibit 7.12

| *t*-Distribution with 24 Degrees of Freedom |

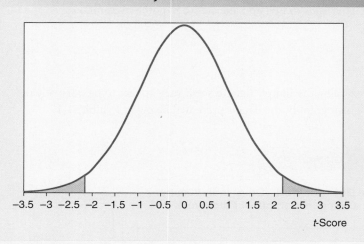

$$P(t \leq -2.169955923) = P(t \geq +2.169955923)$$

Excel calculates $P(t \geq +2.169955923) = P(t \leq -2.169955923) = 0.0200667$. This means that the sample result would be unlikely, if the null hypothesis were true. As well, the *p*-value of about 2% is less than the significance level of 5%, so we have enough evidence to reject the null hypothesis. There is sufficient evidence to suggest that the average of days off work has declined, and is now less than 6.6 per year.

It makes sense to think that the new wellness program has caused this positive change, but you should be a bit cautious here. Nothing in the data *proves* causality, and these positive results may have some other cause. For example, the average age of the workers may have declined because of a number of retirements, and younger workers may be healthier. As always, it is important that you apply common sense to your interpretation of the data.

Using the Excel Template for Making Decisions About the Population Mean with a Single Sample The calculations required to do a *t*-test of the mean are repetitive, and so it is worthwhile to set up a standard worksheet approach for these problems. An Excel template is available on the CD which comes with the text, in a workbook called "Templates." The worksheet containing this template is called "t-Test of Mean." The template is shown in Exhibit 7.13.

Excel Template for t-Test of Mean

E
Template

7.13

Exhibit

Making Decisions About the Population Mean with a Single Sample	
do the sample data appear to be normally distributed?	yes
sample standard deviation s	1.290349
sample mean	6.04
sample size n	25
hypothetical value of population mean	6.6
t-score	−2.16996
one-tailed p-value	0.020067
two-tailed p-value	0.040133

The template has a built-in formula for the *t*-score, and for both the one-tailed and two-tailed p-values of the hypothesis test (you have to decide which you need, depending on H$_1$). As usual, you will have to input values into the non-shaded cells in the template. This template will handle negative *t*-scores.

The template explicitly reminds you that the data must be normal for this test to be used. You will usually have to create a histogram for the sample data to decide this. You can use the Excel functions AVERAGE and STDEV to calculate the sample mean and sample standard deviation. An Excel function called COUNT will count the number of values in the data set to get *n*, the sample size. Of course, the p-value in the template exactly matches the p-value calculated with TDIST in Example 7.3b above.

E
Instructions

A human resources consulting firm has been hired by a company located near Toronto to do some salary research. The company is trying to find out if its junior managers' salaries are competitive, and in particular, if the average salary of such managers is more than $40,000. The consulting firm has collected a random sample of salaries of junior managers in the region.

The results are available in the directory called DataChap07 on the CD that accompanies the text. Is there evidence that the average salary of junior managers is more than $40,000? Use an α = 5%.

The first step is to specify the null and alternative hypotheses. The company wants to know if the average salary of junior managers is more than $40,000.

$$H_0: \mu = \$40{,}000$$
$$H_1: \mu > \$40{,}000$$

The level of significance is 5%. The sample mean, standard deviation, and sample size can be computed with Excel.

$$\bar{x} = 40\ 651.5972$$
$$s = 3{,}788.051692$$
$$n = 50$$

7.3c

Example

Right-tailed hypothesis test about a population mean, raw data

EXA07-3c.xls

Set

The next step is to check for normality of the sample data. One possible histogram for the data set is shown below in Exhibit 7.14.

7.14

Histogram for the Junior Managers' Salary Data

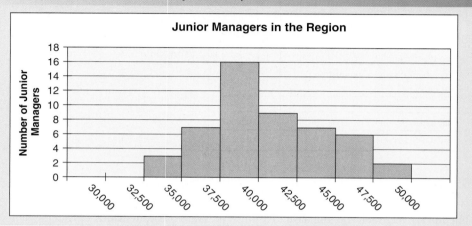

The histogram is somewhat skewed to the right, but it is unimodal and the sample size is fairly large (at 50), so using the *t*-distribution is acceptable.

An analyst at the consulting firm uses the Excel template for this problem. The result is shown below in Exhibit 7.15.

Template

7.15

Excel Template

Making Decisions About the Population Mean with a Single Sample	
do the sample data appear to be normally distributed?	yes
sample standard deviation s	3788.051692
sample mean	40651.5972
sample size n	50
hypothetical value of population mean	40000
t-score	1.216321308
one-tailed p-value	0.114844703
two-tailed p-value	0.229689406

This is a one-tailed test, so the relevant *p*-value is 0.115. Since this is > 0.05, we fail to reject the null hypothesis. The sample evidence is insufficient for us to infer that the average salary of junior managers in the region is more than $40,000.

Using the Table of Critical Values for the *t*-Distribution   It is also possible to estimate *p*-values with the help of the table of critical values for the *t*-distribution, at the back of this textbook on page 461. This table presents some limited information for a series of *t*-distributions (there are of course many of these), organized by degrees of freedom. In the current example, the sample size is $n = 50$, so the degrees of freedom value is 49. The first thing you will notice is that there is no entry in the table for 49 degrees of freedom. The closest you can come is 50, and so that is the row we will use (tables often require this kind of approximation, and that is why it is always preferable to use a computer, if possible). There are five entries in the table for 50 degrees of freedom, and they are shown in Exhibit 7.16.

Excerpt from Table of Critical Values for *t*-Distribution

Degrees of Freedom	$t_{.100}$	$t_{.050}$	$t_{.025}$	$t_{.010}$	$t_{.005}$
50	1.299	1.676	2.009	2.403	2.678

Exhibit 7.16

The notation t_x indicates that beyond this particular *t*-score, in the tail of the distribution, lies an area equal to *x*. So, for example, $P(t \geq t_{.100}) = 0.100$, and $P(t \geq t_{.005}) = 0.005$, and so on.

Exhibit 7.17 below illustrates $t_{.025}$.

Illustration of $t_{.025}$

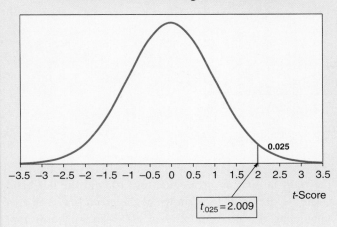

t-Distribution with 50 Degrees of Freedom

0.025

$t_{.025} = 2.009$

t-Score

Exhibit 7.17

To put this more mathematically: for a *t*-distribution with 50 degrees of freedom, $t_{.025} = 2.009$, so $P(t \geq 2.009) = 0.025$. In general:

$$P(t \geq t_x) = x$$

If we wanted to use the *t*-table to make the decision for Example 7.3c, how would we do this? The calculated *t*-score is equal to 1.216 (see Exhibit 7.14 on p. 260, and of course, we could have calculated this by hand). The *p*-value = $P(t \geq 1.216)$. There is no *t*-score of 1.216 for 50 degrees of freedom in the table, so we will not be able to get the *p*-value directly. However, if we were going to place the *t*-score of 1.216 in the row for 50 degrees of freedom, it would be located to the left of 1.299, as shown in Exhibit 7.18 below.

7.18

Exhibit

Excerpt from Table of Critical Values for *t*-Distribution

Degrees of Freedom	$t_{.100}$	$t_{.050}$	$t_{.025}$	$t_{.010}$	$t_{.005}$
50	1.299	1.676	2.009	2.403	2.678

$t = 1.216$

From the table, we see that $P(t \geq 1.299) = 0.100$. Since the *t*-score of 1.216 is less than 1.299, we know that $P(t \geq 1.216)$ must be greater than 10%. Exhibit 7.19 below illustrates this.

7.19

Exhibit

t-Distribution with 50 Degrees of Freedom

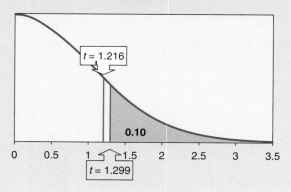

Right Side of *t*-Distribution with 50 Degrees of Freedom

$t = 1.216$

0.10

$t = 1.299$

The shaded area in the right tail has an area equal to 0.10, and the left-hand edge of this area is 1.299. The *t*-score of 1.216 is shown at the green line. The area in the tail beyond the green line is clearly more than 10%. So we know that $P(t \geq 1.216) > 0.10$.

While we cannot be precise about the *p*-value when we are using the *t*-tables, we can still make a decision. Since the *p*-value is more than 10%, we fail to reject the null hypothesis. The sample evidence is insufficient for us to infer that the average salary of junior managers in the region is more than $40,000.

The Decision Rule Approach There is another way to make the decision for this hypothesis test. In Example 7.3c, the level of significance was 5%. From the table, we see that $t_{.050}$ for 50 degrees of freedom is 1.676. Therefore, we know that if the t-value we calculate for the sample result is greater than 1.676, we should reject the null hypothesis. The area where $t > 1.676$ is called the rejection region for this test, and the t-score is called a critical value.

To recap, we could have conducted the hypothesis test for Example 7.3c as follows:

$$H_0: \mu = \$40,000$$
$$H_1: \mu > \$40,000$$

The level of significance is 5%.
Decision rule: Reject H_0 if $t > 1.676$.

$$t = \frac{\bar{x} - \mu}{s / \sqrt{n}} = \frac{\$40,651.5972 - \$40,000}{\$535.7114} = 1.216321308$$

Since $t < 1.676$, we fail to reject H_0. There is insufficient evidence to conclude that the average salary of junior managers is more than $40,000.

The decision rule approach does not require us to estimate the p-value, but of course, it provides us with less information.

7.3d

Estimating p-values from the table of critical values for the t-distribution

For the following hypothesis tests and t-scores, estimate the p-value of the sample result.

a. $H_0: \mu = 56$
$H_1: \mu > 56$
The sample size is 30, and the calculated t-score is 1.74.

b. $H_0: \mu = 100$
$H_1: \mu < 100$
The sample size is 20, and the calculated t-score is -2.96.

c. $H_0: \mu = 300$
$H_1: \mu \neq 300$
The sample size is 25, and the calculated t-score is -2.36.

Solutions:

a. $H_0: \mu = 56$
$H_1: \mu > 56$
The sample size is 30, so degrees of freedom $= 30 - 1 = 29$. The appropriate row from the t-table is shown in Exhibit 7.20 overleaf. The calculated t-score is 1.74, which is in between $t_{.050}$ and $t_{.025}$.

7.20 Exhibit

Excerpt from Table of Critical Values for *t*-Distribution

Degrees of Freedom	$t_{.100}$	$t_{.050}$	$t_{.025}$	$t_{.010}$	$t_{.005}$
29	1.311	1.699	2.045	2.462	2.756

$t = 1.74$

We see that $0.025 < P(t > 1.74) < 0.050$. This is a one-tailed test. We conclude that $0.025 < p\text{-value} < 0.050$.

b. $H_0: \mu = 100$

$H_1: \mu < 100$

The sample size is 20, so degrees of freedom $= 20 - 1 = 19$. The appropriate row from the *t*-table is shown below in Exhibit 7.21. The calculated *t*-score is -2.96. We know that $P(t < -2.96) = P(t > +2.96)$, so we locate 2.96 on the table, to the right of $t_{.005}$.

7.21 Exhibit

Excerpt from Table of Critical Values for *t*-Distribution

Degrees of Freedom	$t_{.100}$	$t_{.050}$	$t_{.025}$	$t_{.010}$	$t_{.005}$
19	1.328	1.729	2.093	2.539	2.861

$t = 2.96$

We see that $P(t > 2.96) < 0.005$. This is a one-tailed test. We conclude that $p\text{-value} < 0.005$.

c. $H_0: \mu = 300$

$H_1: \mu \neq 300$

The sample size is 25, so degrees of freedom $= 25 - 1 = 24$. The appropriate row from the *t*-table is shown below in Exhibit 7.22. The calculated *t*-score is -2.36. We know that $P(t < -2.36) = P(t > +2.36)$, so we locate 2.36 on the table between $t_{.025}$ and $t_{.010}$.

7.22 Exhibit

Excerpt from Table of Critical Values for *t*-Distribution

Degrees of Freedom	$t_{.100}$	$t_{.050}$	$t_{.025}$	$t_{.010}$	$t_{.005}$
24	1.318	1.711	2.064	2.492	2.797

$t = 2.36$

We see that $0.010 < P(t > 2.36) < 0.025$. This is a two-tailed test, so we have to double these probabilities to estimate the *p*-value.

$$0.010 \cdot 2 < p\text{-value} < 0.025 \cdot 2$$
$$0.020 < p\text{-value} < 0.050$$

For this example, we will revisit Chapter Review Exercise 10 in Chapter 6, about auto-mated teller machines (ATMs), in a more realistic context. ATMs must be stocked with enough cash to satisfy customers making withdrawals over an entire weekend. If too much cash is unnecessarily kept in the ATMs, the bank is giving up the opportunity to invest the money and earn interest. At one particular branch, a random sample of the total withdrawals on 36 weekends showed a sample mean of $8,600, and a sample stan-dard deviation of $3,700. Suppose the branch manager has always claimed that the average total withdrawal over the weekend is $7,500. On the basis of the sample, is there evidence to suggest that the true average total withdrawal per weekend is differ-ent from $7,500? You may assume that the population data are normally distributed. Use a 5% significance level.

Example **7.3e**

Two-tailed hypothesis test about a population mean, summary data

In this case, we should conduct a two-tailed hypothesis test, because we have been asked if there is evidence to suggest that the average total withdrawal per weekend is *dif-ferent from* $7,500. The question was phrased this way because either too little or too much cash in the ATM will cause problems.

H_0: μ = $7,500
H_1: $\mu \neq$ $7,500
α = 0.05

We know from the problem description that:

$\bar{x}$= $8,600
s = $3,700
n= 36

We are told to assume that the data are normally distributed. We now go on to calculate the standardized t-score.

$$t = \frac{\bar{x} - \mu}{s / \sqrt{n}} = \frac{\$8,600 - \$7,500}{\$3,700 / \sqrt{36}} = 1.784$$

With 36 observations in the sample, the appropriate t-distribution will have 35 degrees of freedom. The appropriate row from the t-table is reproduced below in Exhibit 7.23.

Excerpt from Table of Critical Values for t-Distribution

Exhibit **7.23**

Degrees of Freedom	$t_{.100}$	$t_{.050}$	$t_{.025}$	$t_{.10}$	$t_{.005}$
35	1.306	1.690	2.030	2.438	2.724

$t = 1.784$

Our calculated t-score of 1.784 is between $t_{.050}$ and $t_{.025}$, so we know:

$0.025 < P(t \geq 1.784) < 0.050$

This is a two-tailed test, so we have to double these probabilities to estimate the *p*-value.

$$0.025 \cdot 2 < p\text{-value} < 0.050 \cdot 2$$
$$0.050 < p\text{-value} < 0.100$$

We fail to reject the null hypothesis, as the *p*-value is more than the significance level of 5%. There is insufficient evidence in the sample to infer that the average cash withdrawal from the ATM over the weekend is different from $7500.

Guide to Decision Making

Hypothesis Test About a Population Mean

When:

- quantitative data, one sample, one population
- trying to make a decision about μ, the population mean, on the basis of $\bar{x}$, the sample mean

Steps:
1. Specify H_0, the null hypothesis.
2. Specify H_1, the alternative hypothesis.
3. Determine or identify α, the significance level.
4. Collect or identify the sample data. Identify or calculate:

- $\bar{x}$, the sample mean
- s, the sample standard deviation
- n, the sample size.

5. Check for normality of the sampling distribution, by assessing the normality of the population (usually with a histogram of the sample values).
6. *If* the sampling distribution is normal, proceed by calculating the appropriate *t*-score for the sample mean, using the following formula:

$$t = \frac{\bar{x} - \mu}{s / \sqrt{n}}$$

7. Use the appropriate *t*-distribution, with $n - 1$ degrees of freedom, to calculate (or approximate, if using tables) the appropriate *p*-value for the hypothesis test.
8. If *p*-value $< \alpha$, reject H_0 and conclude that there is sufficient evidence to decide in favour of H_1. If *p*-value $> \alpha$, fail to reject H_0 and conclude that there is insufficient evidence to decide in favour of H_1.

How Normal Is Normal Enough?

Step 5 above requires you to check for normality of the sampling distribution. We have done this quite informally, with an eyeball test: a histogram of the sample data is created, and if it looks normal, we proceed. This is an inexact approach, and certainly it is not always clear how normal the sample data are. We already discussed this problem in Chapter 6.

The larger the sample is, the more reliable the results of any hypothesis test about the population mean will be. There are two reasons that larger samples are better:

1. With larger sample sizes, the *s* calculated from the sample will be closer to the true value of σ, even if the population is not normal.

2. The sampling distribution of $\bar{x}$ becomes more normal as the sample size increases, no matter what the shape of the population distribution, because of the Central Limit Theorem.

The good news is that the *t*-distribution approach for deciding about μ is what statisticians call *robust*, that is, it is not strongly affected by non-normality of the data. However, this *t*-distribution–based approach should not be relied on if there are outliers in the data, or strong skewness.

Here are some general rules to guide you, until you develop enough experience and judgment to decide for yourself. You should not make important decisions about means with a sample size of less than 15 or 20, unless you have very good reason to believe that the population is normally distributed. Once sample sizes become as large as 40 or more, reliable decisions can be made even if the data are somewhat skewed. But there is no magic about these numbers, and the general rule will always be that decisions will be more reliable with larger sample sizes.

DEVELOP YOUR SKILLS 7.3

1. A marketing research organization wanted to see if the average household incomes in a particular suburb of Halifax were more than $50,000 a year.

   A random sample of 40 households revealed the household income data available in the directory called DataChap07, on the CD that comes with this text. At the 3% level of significance, what can you conclude, on the basis of the sample data? See file called DYS07-3-1.xls.

2. Research has shown that consumers are making more trips to the grocery store each week, and spending less each time. So-called quick-trip shoppers spend an average of about $25 on each trip. It is believed that such shoppers are in a hurry, and have a preference for speed of shopping over bargain shopping. You are wondering if the general research applies to your grocery store. A random sample of the bills of 100 shoppers checking out through the express lines produces an average of $31.57, with a standard deviation of $11.52. Is there sufficient evidence to conclude that the average bill of quick-trip shoppers at your grocery store is different from $25? You may assume that the population data are approximately normally distributed. Use $\alpha = 0.05$.

3. The human resources department wants to be sure that the average salary of entry-level clerks in the company (which is $37,876) is higher than the average in the surrounding area.

   A random sample of salaries of clerks in the surrounding area reveals the data available on the CD that comes with this text. At the 2% significance level, can you conclude that these salaries are lower than $37,876, on average? See file called DYS07-3-3.xls.

4. A company that produces stereo equipment for home listening is interested in the average age of the equipment in the homes of so-called baby boomers. The company has the idea that most baby boomers have not upgraded their equipment for at least 10 years, and this may present a marketing opportunity. A random sample of 60 baby boomer households was surveyed. The average age of their stereo equipment was 8.9 years, with a standard deviation of 5.5 years. The data appear to be normally distributed. Do the data contradict the company's idea that most baby boomer households have stereo equipment that is at least 10 years old? Use $\alpha = 4\%$.

5. A carpet cleaning company is doing some research to determine if its rates are lower than those of its competitors. A researcher posed as a householder to get prices for cleaning a bedroom carpet. The average of 15 such prices was $87.43, with a standard deviation of $6.23. Is this average significantly higher than the company's own price of $85 for such a job? You may assume that the population data are normally distributed. What should the company do? Use $\alpha = 0.05$.

Chapter Summary

7

Formal Hypothesis Testing

The null hypothesis (denoted H_0) is what you are going to believe about the population, unless the sample gives you strongly contradictory evidence. The alternative hypothesis (denoted H_1) is what you are going to believe about the population when there is strong evidence against the null hypothesis. In a hypothesis test, we use sample data to decide between two conflicting ideas, expressed as H_0 and H_1.

In general, the alternative hypothesis can take one of three forms:

1. H_1: population parameter > some particular value
2. H_1: population parameter < some particular value
3. H_1: population parameter ≠ some particular value

The first two forms are referred to as one-tailed tests because sample results in only one tail of the sampling distribution provide evidence against the null hypothesis, in favour of the alternative hypothesis. The third form is a two-tailed test, because sample results in either tail of the sampling distribution provide evidence against the null hypothesis, in favour of the alternative hypothesis.

If there is convincing evidence against the null hypothesis, we say that we *rejected* the null hypothesis and there is sufficient evidence to support the alternative hypothesis. This is a fairly strong conclusion. If there is not convincing evidence against the null hypothesis, we say that we *failed to reject* the null hypothesis and there is insufficient evidence to support the alternative hypothesis. This is a weaker conclusion. Above all, it does *not* imply that the null hypothesis is true. If you fail to reject the null hypothesis, you should *not* say "the null hypothesis is true," or even that you "accept" the null hypothesis. All you can say is that you do not have strong evidence against it.

There are two types of possible error in a test of hypothesis, and we cannot completely eliminate them. A Type I error arises when we mistakenly reject the null hypothesis when it is in fact true. A Type II error arises when we mistakenly fail to reject the null hypothesis when it is in fact false. Both kinds of errors have costs and consequences. The significance level of a test of hypothesis is the probability of a Type I error. It is denoted α and is set by the researcher. The p-value is the probability of getting a sample result at least as extreme as the observed sample result. The probability is calculated from the appropriate sampling distribution, which is always based on the assumption that the null hypothesis is true.

The p-value probability calculation must match the alternative hypothesis used in the test. It is:

- P(sample statistic ≥ observed sample result) when H_1 contains ">"
- P(sample statistic ≤ observed sample result) when H_1 contains "<"
- 2 × P(tail area beyond the observed sample result) when H_1 contains "≠"

A low p-value means that the sample result would be highly unlikely (if the null hypothesis were true). This gives us strong evidence against the null hypothesis. If the p-value is high, then the sample result is not unusual, and we do not have enough evidence to reject the null hypothesis. We reject the null hypothesis whenever the p-value is less than α, the significance level of the test. The lower the p-value, the stronger is the evidence against H_0.

A Guide to Technique on page 245 outlines the general steps in a formal hypothesis test.

Deciding About a Population Proportion

Hypothesis tests about p are illustrated in Examples 7.2a and 7.2b. Example 7.2a applies the formal hypothesis testing format to a Chapter Review Exercise from Chapter 6. Example 7.2b illustrates how to handle coded data with Excel, and illustrates the use of an Excel template for making decisions about the population proportion with a single sample (see p. 248).

A Guide to Decision Making for hypothesis tests about a population proportion is on page 250.

Deciding About the Population Mean

We generally do not know σ, the population standard deviation, and have to estimate it with s, the sample standard deviation. To take care of the resulting extra variability in the sampling distribution, we must use the t-distribution for hypothesis tests about the population mean. The t-distribution is actually a family of distributions, distinguished by their degrees of freedom, which are equal to $n - 1$ for tests about the mean.

Examples 7.3a (p. 253), 7.3b (p. 256) and 7.3c (p. 259) illustrate the use of Excel to conduct hypothesis tests about μ. Example 7.3b also illustrates the use of an Excel template for making decisions about the population mean with a single sample.

It is also possible to estimate p-values from a t-table of critical values. Examples 7.3d (p. 263) and 7.3e (p. 265) illustrate.

A Guide to Decision Making for hypothesis tests about a population mean is on page 266.

Use of the t-distribution is dependent on the population being normal. We check this by creating a histogram of the sample data, and checking to see if it looks normal. The t-distribution is robust, that is, it is not strongly affected by non-normality of the data. However, the t-distribution should not be relied on if there are outliers in the data, or strong skewness.

You should not make important decisions about means with sample sizes of less than 15 or 20, unless you have very good reason to believe that the population is normally distributed. Once sample sizes become as large as 40 or more, reliable decisions can be made even if the data are somewhat skewed. But there is no magic about these numbers, and the general rule will always be that decisions will be more reliable with larger sample sizes.

CHAPTER REVIEW EXERCISES

1. A toy manufacturer receives large shipments of electronic components that will be used in the dolls that it makes. It is too expensive to test every component to see if it functions properly, so the manufacturer inspects a random sample of components from every shipment. The toy manufacturer does not accept any shipment unless there is evidence that fewer than 3% of the components are defective.
   a. What are the null and alternative hypotheses for this situation?
   b. Explain the Type I and Type II errors in the context of the component shipments.
   c. From the toy manufacturer's point of view, which type of error would be the most important? Why?

2. A gasoline refinery has developed a new gasoline that theoretically reduces gas consumption per 100 kilometres driven (or, to use a non-metric phrase, provides improved gas mileage). The company wants to gather evidence to see if the new gasoline actually does provide better gas mileage. Suppose the refinery knows that for a wide range of four-passenger compact cars, the average gas consumption per 100 kilometres was 10.6 litres, for the old gasoline formulation.
   a. What are the null and alternative hypotheses for this situation?
   b. Explain the Type I and Type II errors in the context of the new gasoline.

3. The quality control manager at a plant that produces bottled water is setting up a hypothesis test for the amount of water in the bottle, which is supposed to be 750 millilitres.
   a. What should the null and alternative hypotheses be for this situation?
   b. Explain the Type I and Type II errors in the context of the bottled water.
   c. If you were a consumer buying the bottled water, which type of error would be most important to you? Why?

4. Suppose you have null and alternative hypotheses as follows.

   $H_0: \mu = 300$

   $H_1: \mu < 300$

A histogram of the sample data appears normal. The sample mean is 296.5, and the sample size is 40. The sample standard deviation is 35.6. Estimate the *p*-value for this test.

5. Suppose you have null and alternative hypotheses as follows.

$$H_0: \mu = 25$$
$$H_1: \mu \neq 25$$

Assume that the population data are normally distributed. The sample mean is 30, and the sample size is 10. The sample standard deviation is 25. Estimate the *p*-value for this test.

6. Your radio station, which has generally targeted the baby boomers, is starting to think that it must reorient its programming to a younger audience. Formats have been changed, some new on-air personalities have been hired, and generally efforts have been made to come up with a fresh approach. Now the radio station wants to see if these efforts have been successful in reaching a younger audience. In the past, the average listener's age was 48.2.
   a. What null and alternative hypotheses would be appropriate here?
   b. Explain the Type I and Type II errors in the context of the radio audience.
   c. Suppose you rejected the null hypothesis with a *p*-value of 1%. What does this tell you? Does it mean that the radio station has accomplished its goal?
   d. Suppose the situation described in part c occurs, and the sample mean is 46. Does this mean that the radio station has accomplished its goal?

7. The manufacturer of a pill for back pain claims that 73% of those who take the pill get relief from their back pain within one hour. You work for a consumer organization, and you want to check the claim. You take a random sample of 350 people with back pain who took the pill, and find that 238 of them got relief within one hour. Is there evidence that the proportion of back pain sufferers who get relief within one hour is lower than the manufacturer claims? Use $\alpha = 0.02$.

8. The operations manager at the factory is interested in the lifespan of an electronic component used in one of the factory's machines. The producer of the electronic component claims that it has an average life of 6,251.35 hours, with a standard deviation of 201 hours. A random sample of 40 components is studied, and their lifespans are recorded. You have already examined this data set, in Chapter Review Exercise 2 in Chapter 6. The data are also available in DataChap07.

   Is there evidence that the average lifespan of the electronic components is less than the manufacturer claims? Complete a formal hypothesis test, using $\alpha = 0.05$.

9. The college cafeteria manager claims that 90% of cafeteria customers are satisfied with the range of food served and prices. Suppose that in a random sample of 500 cafeteria customers, 438 say that they are satisfied with the cafeteria. Does the sample result suggest that fewer than 90% of the cafeteria's customers are satisfied with the range of food served and prices? You have already examined this problem in Chapter Review Exercise 3 in Chapter 6. Complete a formal hypothesis test. Use $\alpha = 4\%$.

10. A survey of the morning beverage market shows that the primary breakfast beverage of 17% of Americans is milk. A Canadian dairy company believes the figure to be higher in Canada. The company contacts a random sample of 550 Canadians and asks what primary beverage they consumed for breakfast that day. Suppose 115 replied that milk was their primary beverage. Does this sample result provide evidence that a greater proportion of Canadians drink milk as their primary breakfast beverage, as compared to people in the United States? You have already examined this problem in Chapter Review Exercise 4 in Chapter 6. Complete a formal hypothesis test. Use $\alpha = 0.01$.

11. A tourist attraction gets more than 50,000 visitors a year, but traffic has declined over the last few years. The manager has recently refurbished the buildings, added new activities, and generally spruced up the facility. A survey of customers done two years ago revealed that only 65% of them felt that they had had an enjoyable experience. A survey of 450 visitors, done

after the upgrades, indicated that 315 of them felt that they had had an enjoyable experience. Does this provide any evidence that the upgrades improved visitor enjoyment? You have already examined this problem in Chapter Review Exercise 6 in Chapter 6. Complete a formal hypothesis test. Use $\alpha = 0.03$.

12. In 1997, 60% of students attending public school in Ontario had access to a computer at school. Concerned parents, worried about budget cuts, think that the access to computers has actually decreased since then. To test their idea, they randomly sampled 400 students in a variety of Ontario public schools. They discovered that only 228 of them had access to a computer. Is there evidence that access to computers in public schools has decreased since 1997? You have already examined this problem, in Chapter Review Exercise 7 in Chapter 6. Complete a formal hypothesis test. Use a 5% level of significance.

13. A human resources manager claims that tuition subsidies for employees are not an important benefit, as only 5% of employees would use such a program. The union president thinks that this estimate is too low. The union president conducts a survey of employees to determine how many of them would use a tuition subsidy program if it were available. The survey of 500 employees revealed that 38 of them would use the tuition subsidy program. Does the sample provide evidence that the HR manager's estimate of the percentage of employees who would use the program is too low? Use a 2% level of significance.

14. An analyst in a government ministry is interested in the average cost of textbooks per semester for a college student. The ministry is preparing a study of the cost of a college education. The study (which is in draft form at present) uses a figure based on 1998 data, which suggests that the average cost of textbooks per semester is $500. The analyst wants to check this, and conducts a random sample of 75 college students, asking them what their textbook costs were for the last semester. The sample results show an average cost of $576, with a standard deviation of $122. Is there evidence that average textbook costs per semester have increased for college students? Complete a formal hypothesis test, with $\alpha = 5\%$. You may assume that the population data are normally distributed.

15. Automated teller machines (ATMs) must be stocked with enough cash to satisfy customers making withdrawals over an entire weekend. At one particular branch, a random sample of the total withdrawals on 36 weekends showed a sample mean of $8,600, with a sample standard deviation of $3,700. Suppose the branch manager has always claimed that the average total withdrawal over the weekend is $7,500. On the basis of the sample taken, is there evidence to suggest that the bank manager's claim about the true average total withdrawal per weekend is too low? You may assume that the population data are normally distributed. Use $\alpha = 0.04$.

16. A major company was, at one time, the sole provider of long-distance phone service in a number of areas of Canada. Currently, many other companies offer consumers long-distance service. The original company has tried to keep its rates and services competitive, and regularly checks to see if its rates are comparable with those of its competitors. Suppose the company has established that the average monthly long-distance charge of its residential customers is $23.96. An analyst selects a random sample of 70 households, and recalculates their long-distance charges, using the long-distance plan of a major competitor. The average long-distance charge in the sample is $22.24, with a standard deviation of $3.26. Does this indicate that the company's competitor has lower long-distance rates? Use a 5% level of significance. Assume that the long-distance charges are normally distributed.

17. As a student, you are suspicious that some teachers give easier tests than others. You have heard that Mr. Clarke is one such teacher. Since your current teacher, Ms. Hardy, seems very focused on covering all the material in the course outline, including the difficult sections, you are thinking of switching to Mr. Clarke's section. However, the schedule is not as convenient for you, so you want to be sure that Mr. Clarke's tests are easier. Both classes have written the first test of the semester. Ms. Hardy has told you that her class average was 58.2%. Mr. Clarke did not give out the class average, so you conduct a random sample of 20 students from his

class, and get an average mark of 65.4%, with a standard deviation of 18.6. At the 5% level of significance, does this provide evidence that the average mark was higher in Mr. Clarke's class? If so, does this mean that Mr. Clarke's test was easy? What other explanations should you consider? You may assume that the test marks are normally distributed.

18. The Student Administrative Council at your college is concerned about the number of students who are working a significant number of hours at part-time jobs while they are going to school. A random sample of 40 students were asked how many hours a week they spend at part-time jobs.

CRE07-18.xls
Set

The data are available on the CD that accompanies this text. Is there sufficient evidence to infer that students are working more than 30 hours a week, on average? Use a 5% level of significance.

CRE07-19.xls
Set

19. Max Weber has surveyed a random sample of the customers who shop at the drugstore he owns. The survey results are available on the CD that accompanies this text. Is there evidence that the average purchase amount is more than $25? Use a 5% level of significance.

CRE07-20.xls
Set

20. The survey of drugstore customers mentioned in Exercise 19 also includes data about staff friendliness. Based on the survey, can Max Weber conclude that fewer than 5% of customers rate staff friendliness as poor? Use a 4% significance level.

CRE07-21.xls
Set

21. The survey of drugstore customers also collected data on customer incomes. At the 4% level of significance, can Max Weber conclude that the average income of his drugstore customers is more than $45,000?

22. The survey of drugstore customers also collected data on customer ages. Max Weber has always claimed that the average age of his customers is 40. At the 5% level of significance, what can you conclude, based on the sample data?

23. The survey of drugstore customers also collected data on speed of service. At the 3% level of significance, is there evidence that more than 40% of customers rate the service as good or excellent?

CRE07-24.xls
Set

24. Eileen McLeary runs a car repair facility in Nelson, BC. The business is always under pressure to complete repairs quickly, correctly, and at a fair price. Eileen has collected customer counts for a random sample of days.

When she bought the facility from the previous owner, he claimed that the average number of customers per day was 25. At the 5% level of significance, can you infer that the average number of customers per day is different from 25?

25. A financial services company conducted a survey of a random sample of its customers. One of the items on the survey was as follows:

"The staff at my local branch can provide me with good advice on my financial affairs." Customers were asked to respond on the following scale: (1) strongly agree; (2) agree; (3) neither agree nor disagree; (4) disagree; and (5) strongly disagree. The customer responses are summarized in Exhibit 7.24 below.

7.24 Exhibit

Financial Services Company Customer Survey

"The staff at my local branch can provide me with good advice on my financial affairs."	Number of Customers
Strongly agree	10
Agree	57
Neither agree nor disagree	32
Disagree	15
Strongly disagree	9

Based on the sample results, can you infer that more than half of customers agreed or strongly agreed that the staff at the local branch can provide good advice on their financial affairs? Use $\alpha = 0.05$.

 Go to MyStatLab at www.mystatlab.com. You can practise many of this chapter's exercises as often as you want. The guided solutions help you find an answer step by step. You'll find a personalized study plan available to you too!

CHAPTER

Estimating Population Values

8

Learning Objectives

After mastering the material in this chapter, you will be able to:

1. Estimate a population proportion.
2. Estimate a population mean.
3. Decide on the appropriate sample size to estimate a population mean or proportion, given a desired level of accuracy for the estimate.
4. Use confidence intervals to draw appropriate hypothesis-testing conclusions.

INTRODUCTION

With the widespread use of automated teller machines (ATMs), the day-to-day operations of bank branches have changed. Many people no longer attend their bank branch in person to withdraw cash, make deposits, or pay their bills, as all of these tasks can be done at any time of the day or night at an ATM (or over the Internet, or by telephone). These changes have had implications for staffing and cash management at bank branches. Estimating the numbers and types of customers visiting the branch during peak periods helps managers decide how to schedule counter staff. Estimating the proportion of customers who visit the branch to make loan applications or to access safety deposit boxes will help managers decide what type of training their staff should have.

Estimation procedures rely on sampling (as usual), and we will continue to assume simple random sampling for the techniques described in this chapter. Estimation begins with a sample statistic that corresponds to the population parameter of interest. For example, it makes sense to estimate the population mean μ with the sample mean $\bar{x}$. The average amount of cash withdrawn from the ATM on a random sample of days might be $560. This is a starting point to estimate the average amount of cash withdrawn from the ATM on *all* days. Similarly, it makes sense to estimate the population proportion p with the sample proportion $\hat{p}$. Such sample statistics are called point estimates.

A single-number estimate of a population parameter that is based on sample data is called a **point estimate.**

We know that there is variability in sampling distributions, and so, for example, the $\bar{x}$ we calculate from the sample may or may not be close to μ. Instead of relying on a point estimate such as $\bar{x}$ or $\hat{p}$, we construct something called a confidence interval estimate. A **confidence interval estimate** of the form (a, b) is a range of numbers that is thought to enclose the parameter of interest, with a given level of probability. For example, we might estimate that the interval ($520, $600) contains the average amount of cash withdrawn from the ATM at night, with 95% confidence. It might help you to visualize this by thinking of the confidence interval as a horseshoe we are trying to throw at the (always unknown) population parameter, as depicted in Exhibit 8.1. Properly constructed, a 95% confidence interval is a horseshoe that will land on the unknown population parameter 95 times out of 100, if we repeated the sampling process and constructed the interval many, many times.

point estimate a single-number estimate of a population parameter that is based on sample data

confidence interval estimate a range of numbers of the form (a, b) that is thought to enclose the parameter of interest, with a given level of probability

A Confidence Interval Estimate Throws a Horseshoe at a Population Parameter

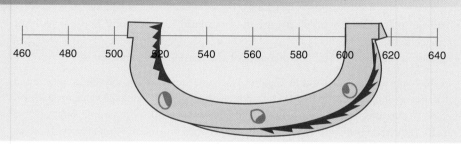

Exhibit **8.1**

Confidence interval estimates have a general form as follows:

(point estimate) $\pm$ (critical value) $\cdot$ (estimated standard error of the sample statistic)

Exhibit 8.2 illustrates the general form of a confidence interval estimate.

The General Form of a Confidence Interval Estimate

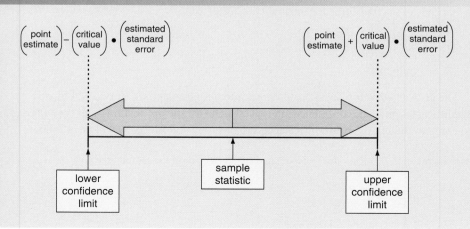

Exhibit **8.2**

In Chapter 8, we will use sampling distributions (and probability concepts) to create confidence intervals for population proportions (Section 8.1) and means (Section 8.2). As well, we will introduce some methods to help us decide how large a sample size we should take to make reliable estimates (Section 8.3). Finally, we will demonstrate the link between estimation techniques (in particular, confidence intervals) and hypothesis tests (Section 8.4).

8.1 ESTIMATING THE POPULATION PROPORTION

Suppose we wanted to estimate the proportion of bank customers who come to the branch to access their safety deposit boxes. A random sample of 200 customers revealed 43 who had come to the branch primarily to access their safety deposit boxes. We now want to estimate p, the proportion of *all* customers who come to the branch primarily to access their safety deposit boxes, with 95% confidence.

We can use the sampling distribution of $\hat{p}$ for this estimation, as long as the (probably now familiar) required conditions hold:

- The sample size must be $< 5\%$ of the population if sampling is done without replacement.
- np and nq must be ≥ 10, for normality of the sampling distribution of $\hat{p}$.

In the hypothesis tests we did in Chapter 7, we use the hypothesized values for p and q to check that np and nq were ≥ 10. In estimation, we have no hypothesized value for p (or q). Therefore, to check for normality, we use $\hat{p}$ and $\hat{q}$, calculated from the sample data.

If the required conditions are met, we construct a confidence interval estimate as follows. First, we record relevant information from the problem.

- $n = 200$
- $\hat{p} = \dfrac{43}{200} = 0.215$
- so $\hat{q} = 1 - 0.215 = 0.785$

A bank branch probably has thousands of customers, so it is reasonable to conclude that the sample of 200 is less than 5% of the population of customers.

We check the conditions for normality.

- $n\hat{p} = 200\left(\dfrac{43}{200}\right) = 43 \geq 10$
- $n\hat{q} = 200(0.785) = 157 \geq 10$

The critical value for a 95% confidence interval estimate is 1.96 (we will illustrate why a little later on). The confidence interval estimate for the proportion of all customers who come to the branch primarily to access their safety deposit boxes will be as follows.

(point estimate) $\pm$ (critical value) ● (estimated standard error of the sample statistic)

$$= \hat{p} \pm 1.96\sqrt{\dfrac{\hat{p}\hat{q}}{n}}$$

$$= 0.215 \pm 1.96\sqrt{\dfrac{0.215(0.785)}{200}}$$

$$= 0.215 \pm 1.96(0.029049527)$$
$$= 0.215 \pm 0.0569371$$

The value on the right-hand side of the confidence interval calculation above is the *half-width* of the interval. This is the amount we add to—and subtract from—the point estimate to arrive at the upper and lower confidence limits. We will use the notation HW to refer to the half-width, as Exhibit 8.3 below illustrates.

95% Confidence Interval for *p*

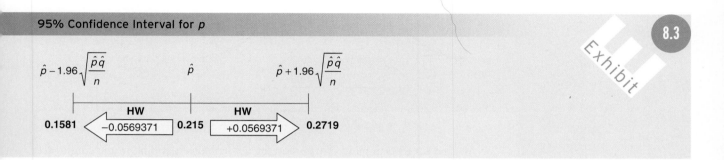

To finish the calculation:

$$0.215 \pm 0.0569371$$
$$(0.1581, 0.2719)$$

We estimate that the interval (0.1581, 0.2719) encloses the true proportion of all customers who come to the branch primarily to access their safety deposit boxes, with 95% confidence. Notice the wording that is used here. The 95% confidence is associated with the interval. Remember that we are saying we have 95% confidence that the horseshoe we constructed landed around the true population proportion. It is *not* correct to say we have 95% confidence that the population proportion is between 0.1581 and 0.2719. The population mean is *not* a random variable, and so there is no probability associated with its location, except for 100% probability that it is exactly what it is. Be careful not to make this common mistake when you are interpreting a confidence interval.

The question we have not yet answered is this: why is 1.96 the critical value in this case?

Remember that when the required conditions are met, the sampling distribution of $\hat{p}$ is approximately normal, with a mean and standard deviation as follows:

- $\mu_{\hat{p}} = p$

- $\sigma_{\hat{p}} = \sqrt{\dfrac{pq}{n}}$

The sampling distribution of $\hat{p}$ would as illustrated in Exhibit 8.4.

8.4

Sampling Distribution of the Sample Proportion

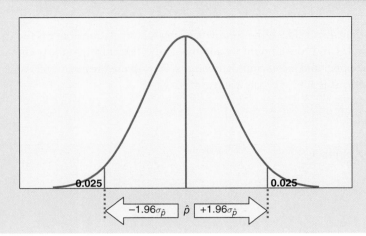

Marked on the sampling distribution are arrows corresponding to the confidence interval half-width of $1.96\sigma_{\hat{p}}$ (in the example, this distance worked out to be 0.057; in general, it will depend on the particular sampling distribution you are working with). We can use the normal table in the back of the text to confirm that a z-score of -1.96 leaves an area of 0.025 in the left-hand tail of this normal distribution. Because the distribution is symmetric, we know that there is also 0.025 in the right-hand tail of the distribution.

Now, let's simulate sampling and constructing a confidence interval, over and over. Suppose the first $\hat{p}$ we get (we'll call it $\hat{p}_1$) is somewhat to the right of the mean, as shown in Exhibit 8.5 below. When we construct the confidence interval, does it enclose the true population proportion, p? The answer is yes.

8.5

Confidence Interval for Sample 1

Sampling Distribution of Sample Proportion

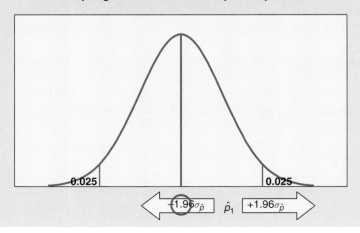

Suppose we take another sample, and this time the $\hat{p}$-value is to the left of the mean, as shown in Exhibit 8.6. Does the confidence interval enclose p? Again, the answer is yes.

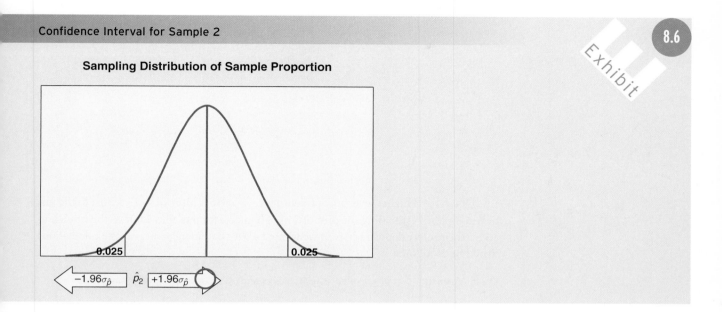

Confidence Interval for Sample 2

Sampling Distribution of Sample Proportion

0.025   0.025

$-1.96\sigma_{\hat{p}}$ $\hat{p}_2$ $+1.96\sigma_{\hat{p}}$

8.6

Exhibit

If we imagine sampling over and over again, when will the confidence intervals *not* enclose p? The answer is: Whenever the sample proportion $\hat{p}$ is in one of the tail areas of the sampling distribution. And this will happen, in the long run, just 5% of the time $(0.025 + 0.025 = 0.05)$. This means that 95% of the time, the confidence interval *will* enclose μ, and this is what gives us the 95% confidence level.

Now you should be able to figure out the critical value for a 99% confidence level. This will be the z-score that leaves 99% in the middle of the distribution, with the remaining 1% split between the two tails of the distribution, leaving 0.005 in each tail. We can use notation similar to the notation for critical t-scores here. We need to identify $z_{.005}$.

If we use the normal table in the back of the book to identify $z_{.005}$, we are faced with a problem: a z-score of -2.57 leaves 0.0051 in the tail of the distribution, and a z-score of -2.58 leaves 0.0049 in the tail. Neither of these is exactly what we want, and they are tied in terms of closeness to the desired probability. However, if we go to Excel and use NORMINV (or NORMSINV, which is the inverse for the standard normal distribution), we see that a z-score of -2.57583 will leave 0.005 in the tail of the distribution. The minus sign on the z-score is not relevant (it is already built into the formula), so the z-score we will use for a 99% confidence interval is 2.57583 (round this to 2.576 for manual calculations).

You should know how to identify the correct z-score for any confidence level, although there are just a few common ones. For a confidence level of $x\%$, the critical z-score will leave $\dfrac{(100 - x)}{2}$ % in each tail of the distribution. For example, for a confidence level of 94%, the z-score will leave $\dfrac{(100 - 94)}{2} = 3$ in each tail. The correct z-score is located by looking at the body of the normal table for an entry as close as possible to 0.03. In this case, $z_{.030}$ is 1.88.

A table showing the z-scores used for calculating some common confidence interval estimates for p is provided below in Exhibit 8.7.

Exhibit 8.7

Critical z-Scores for Calculating Confidence Interval Estimates for p

Confidence level	99%	98%	95%	90%
z-Score	2.576	2.326	1.96	1.645

Of course, a higher level of confidence means a wider interval. Let's return to the initial example, of estimating the proportion of bank customers who come to the branch to access their safety deposit boxes. If we wanted a 99% confidence interval, the calculations would be as follows:

(point estimate) $\pm$ (critical value) $\bullet$ (estimated standard error of the sample statistic)

$$= \hat{p} \pm 2.576 \sqrt{\frac{\hat{p}\,\hat{q}}{n}}$$

$$= 0.215 \pm 2.576 \sqrt{\frac{0.215(0.785)}{200}}$$

$$= 0.215 \pm 2.576(0.029049527)$$

$$= 0.215 \pm 0.0748316$$

$$= (0.1402, 0.2898)$$

Exhibit 8.8 illustrates the 99% and 95% confidence interval estimates for p. The 99% confidence interval is (0.1402, 0.2898), wider than the 95% interval we first calculated at (0.1581, 0.2719).

Exhibit 8.8

99% and 95% Confidence Interval Estimates for p

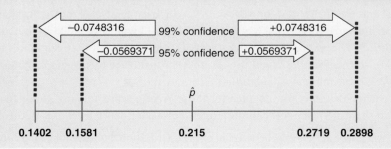

A confidence interval estimate for p is constructed as follows:

$$\hat{p} \pm (\text{critical } z\text{-score})\sqrt{\frac{\hat{p}\hat{q}}{n}}$$

Conditions required:

- If sampling is done without replacement, the sample size must be less than 5% of the population.
- $n\hat{p}$ and $n\hat{q}$ must both be ≥ 10.

A random sample of 500 Ontario respondents reveals that 230 would align themselves with the Liberal Party. Construct and interpret a 98% confidence interval for the percentage of all Ontarians who would align themselves with the Liberal Party.

8.1

Example

First, summarize the information provided.

Constructing a confidence interval estimate for p

- $n = 500$

- $\hat{p} = \dfrac{230}{500} = 0.46$

Sampling is done without replacement, but the sample of 500 is much less than 5% of all Ontario voters, so we can proceed.

Next, check conditions for normality of the sampling distribution of $\hat{p}$.

- $n\hat{p} = 500\left(\dfrac{230}{500}\right) = 230 \geq 10$

- $n\hat{q} = 500\,(0.54) = 270 \geq 10$

Conditions for normality are met.

We want a 98% confidence interval, so we need to identify $z_{.010}$. Using Exhibit 8.7 above, we identify $z_{.010}$ as 2.326.

The general form is:

$$\hat{p} \pm (z\text{-score})\sqrt{\frac{\hat{p}\hat{q}}{n}}$$

$$= \frac{230}{500} \pm (2.326)\sqrt{\frac{\left(\dfrac{230}{500}\right)\left(\dfrac{270}{500}\right)}{500}}$$

$$= 0.46 \pm (2.326)(0.022289011)$$

$$= 0.46 \pm 0.05184424$$

We have 98% confidence that the interval $(0.408, 0.512)$ contains the true proportion of Ontarians who would align themselves with the Liberal Party.

Using the Excel Template for a Confidence Interval Estimate of the Population Proportion While it is fairly straightforward to construct confidence intervals for a population proportion by hand with a calculator and a normal table, this approach will often be slightly less accurate than with a computer.

A standard worksheet template for the confidence interval for a proportion is available on the CD that comes with the text. It is in the workbook called "Templates," and the worksheet is called "CI for proportion." The template is shown below in Exhibit 8.9, with the values from Example 8.1 filled in. Note that you should always use Excel to do any calculations when you are using this template. For Example 8.1, you should enter the formula "=230/500" into the slot for $\hat{p}$, not "0.46." You should *never* use your calculator to calculate a value that you then input into an Excel spreadsheet (employers cite this behaviour as a prime indicator of lack of skill with Excel).

Template

Exhibit 8.9 Excel Template for the Confidence Interval Estimate for the Population Proportion

Confidence Interval Estimate for the Population Proportion	
confidence level (decimal form)	0.98
sample proportion	0.46
sample size n	500
np–hat	230
nq–hat	270
are np–hat and nq–hat >= 10?	yes
upper confidence limit	0.511852
lower confidence limit	0.408148

Notice that the Excel template arrived at the same answers we got when we did this by hand. As usual, some input is required for all the blue-shaded areas in the template.

DEVELOP YOUR SKILLS 8.1

Try doing these by hand, and then use the Excel template to verify your answers.

1. A company is trying to decide whether to provide an outdoor gazebo for the smokers on its staff. Before any money is spent on construction costs, the company would like to estimate the percentage of its workers who smoke. A random sample of 300 employees reveals 56 smokers. Construct a 99% confidence interval for the proportion of smokers in this company.

2. A company wants to design a daycare program for its staff. A random sample of 200 employees reveals that 142 have children of daycare age. Construct a 95% confidence interval for the proportion of all employees who have children of daycare age.

3. The manager of a research institute is thinking of subsidizing the professional membership fees for the institute's scientists. Before proceeding, the manager decides to estimate the proportion of scientists who belong to professional associations, and finds that 40% of a random sample of 75 scientists belong to professional associations. Construct a 90% confidence interval for the proportion of all the scientists who belong to professional associations.

4. You are trying to estimate the percentage of households who have high-speed Internet access in the east end of St. John's, Newfoundland. A random sample of 50 households reveals 15 with high-speed Internet access.

Estimate the percentage of all the households in the east end who have high-speed Internet access, with 98% confidence.

5. During the fall of 2005, the federal Liberal Party was leading a minority government in Ottawa. A poll conducted by The Strategic Counsel during early October found that if a federal election were held, the Liberals would get 38 percent of the vote. The survey of 1000 Canadians was described as accurate to within 3.1 percentage points, 19 times out of 20. What confidence interval can you construct from these results? (Source: "Liberals Widen Gap in Poll," **www.theglobeandmail.com**, accessed October 19, 2005.)

ESTIMATING THE POPULATION MEAN

Suppose we want to estimate the average number of customers who come into the bank branch over the noon hour, with 90% confidence. A random sample of 50 noon hours yields a sample mean of 30.98, with a sample standard deviation of 10.686. We can use the sampling distribution of $\bar{x}$ to construct the confidence interval. Because we do not know the population standard deviation σ, we will use the t-distribution, as we did for hypothesis tests about μ in Chapter 7. Of course, we cannot proceed unless we have some reason to believe that the population data are normally distributed. A histogram of the sample data is shown in Exhibit 8.10.

Histogram of Noon Hour Traffic at a Bank Branch

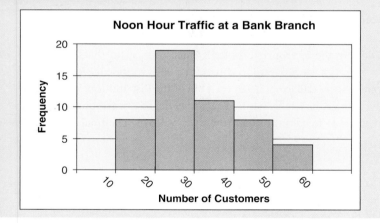

Exhibit 8.10

Although this histogram is somewhat skewed to the right, the sample size is fairly large at 50, and so we will proceed with the use of the t-distribution.

As usual, we first summarize the relevant details from the sample.

• $\bar{x} = 30.98$

• $s = 10.686$

• $n = 50$

As before, the confidence or interval will take the general form of

(point estimate) $\pm$ (critical value) • (estimated standard error of the sample statistic)

A confidence interval estimate for μ is constructed as follows:

$$\bar{x} \pm (\text{critical } t\text{-score})\left(\frac{s}{\sqrt{n}}\right)$$

Population data must be approximately normally distributed.

Exhibit 8.11 below illustrates the confidence interval estimate for μ.

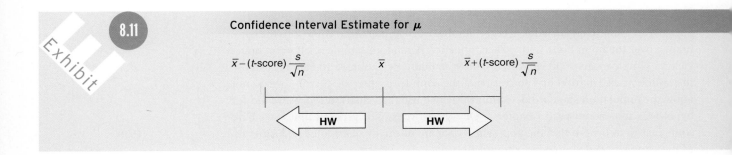

Exhibit 8.11

Confidence Interval Estimate for μ

Filling in the information from the sample, this leads to:

$$30.98 \pm (t\text{-score})\frac{10.686}{\sqrt{50}}$$

Now we must identify the appropriate t-score. Since $n = 50$ in the sample, the degrees of freedom $= n - 1 = 49$. We want to construct a 90% confidence level, meaning that the appropriate t-score will leave 5% in each tail of the distribution. This means we want to identify $t_{.050}$. Since the t-table has no row for 49 degrees of freedom, we must use the row for 50 degrees of freedom. In that row, $t_{.050} = 1.676$. The final result is as follows.

$$\bar{x} \pm (t\text{-score})\frac{s}{\sqrt{n}}$$

$$= 30.98 \pm (1.676)\frac{10.686}{\sqrt{50}}$$

$$= 30.98 \pm 2.5328192$$

$$= (28.447, 33.513)$$

Exhibit 8.12 illustrates the final result.

The 90% confidence interval for the average number of customers in the bank branch over the noon hour is (28.447, 33.513). This information will help branch management decide how many counter officers should be scheduled to work over the noon hour.

90% Confidence Interval for μ (Sample Size of 50)

Exhibit

8.12

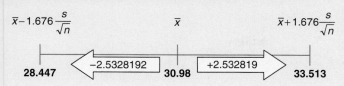

$$\bar{x}-1.676\frac{s}{\sqrt{n}} \qquad \bar{x} \qquad \bar{x}+1.676\frac{s}{\sqrt{n}}$$

28.447	−2.5328192 **30.98** +2.532819	**33.513**

A manager in the shipping and receiving area of a large company has noticed an increase in her department's number of employee absences due to work-related injuries, and she has started to wonder if the average weight of the packages handled by workers has increased. She wants to calculate a 95% confidence interval for the average package weight. A random sample of package weights (in kilograms) is shown in Exhibit 8.13 below.

Example

8.2

Constructing a confidence interval estimate for μ

Random Sample of Package Weights (in kilograms)

Exhibit

8.13

13.4	11.4	12.3	11.7	7	9.8	15.6	12.7	14.7	10.4
7.9	17.1	13.5	11.3	13.6	7.1	16.6	5.9	10.6	23

The first step is to check for normality. One possible histogram of the data, shown below in Exhibit 8.14, seems approximately normal.

Histogram of Package Weight Data

Exhibit

8.14

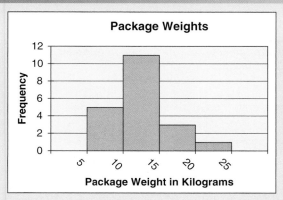

The next step is to calculate the sample mean and standard deviation.

$$\bar{x} = \frac{\Sigma x}{n} = \frac{245.6}{20} = 12.28$$

$$s = \sqrt{\frac{\Sigma x^2 - \frac{(\Sigma x)^2}{n}}{n-1}} = \sqrt{\frac{3323.5 - \frac{(245.6)^2}{20}}{19}} = 4.02317$$

There are 20 observations in the sample, yielding 19 degrees of freedom. With a 95% confidence level, there is 5% in the two tails, or 2.5% in each tail. The critical value is $t_{.025}$ with 19 degrees of freedom. The t-table tells us that this value is 2.093. The confidence interval is constructed as follows.

$$\bar{x} \pm (t\text{-score})\frac{s}{\sqrt{n}}$$
$$= 12.28 \pm (2.093)\frac{4.02317}{\sqrt{20}}$$

$$= 12.28 \pm 1.88288$$

We have 95% confidence that the interval (10.40 kg, 14.16 kg) contains the true average package weight handled in shipping and receiving.

Using the Excel Template for a Confidence Interval Estimate of the Population Mean   A standard worksheet template for the confidence interval for a mean is available on the CD that comes with the text. It is in the workbook called "Templates," and the worksheet is called "CI for mean." The template is shown below in Exhibit 8.15, with the values from Example 8.2 filled in. As usual, you will have to use this template in conjunction with the Histogram tool of Excel, so you can check for normality.

Template

Exhibit 8.15

Excel Template for the Confidence Interval Estimate for the Population Mean

Confidence Interval Estimate for the Population Mean	
do the sample data appear to be normally distributed?	yes
confidence level (decimal form)	0.95
sample mean	12.28
sample standard deviations	4.02316974
sample size n	20
upper confidence limit	14.162902
lower confidence limit	10.397098

Note that the values for the sample mean, standard deviation, and sample size can be calculated with Excel functions (AVERAGE, STDEV, and COUNT).

DEVELOP YOUR SKILLS 8.2

Do these exercises by hand, and with the Excel template.

1. A random sample of 25 families leaving a supermarket yields an average grocery bill of $112.36, with a standard deviation of $32.45. A histogram of the data is approximately normal. Construct a 95% confidence interval for the average grocery bill of all households whose members shop at this store.

2. The average spending on professional association memberships by a random sample of 75 scientists at a research institute is $125, with a standard deviation of $35. Construct a 99% confidence interval estimate for the average spending of all scientists on professional association fees. You may assume that the fees are normally distributed.

3. A random sample of monthly daycare costs for 50 households in Halifax, Nova Scotia, yields an average of $460, with a standard deviation of $65. Estimate the average monthly daycare costs for all Halifax households, with 98% confidence. You may assume that the daycare costs are normally distributed.

4. You want to know the average grade on a statistics test, but the teacher will not provide the information. You take a random sample of the marks of 20 students who wrote the test.

   The results are available on the CD that accompanies this text, in the directory DataChap08. Construct a 95% confidence interval estimate for the average grade on the statistics test. See file called DYS08-2-4.xls.

5. A human resources consulting firm wants to estimate the average salary of university graduates with a bachelor's degree in science, and 10 years of working experience, in the Toronto area. A sample of 50 such employees reveals an average of $56,387 and a standard deviation of $5,435. Assuming the salary data are approximately normally distributed, construct a 90% confidence interval for the salaries.

8.3   SELECTING THE SAMPLE SIZE

Sample Size to Estimate a Mean

Deciding on the size of the sample you plan to take is important. If you take a sample that is larger than necessary, you will be wasting money. If your sample is too small, the results may not achieve the desired level of accuracy. Deciding on the sample size is a challenge, not because it is technically difficult but because you need information you do not normally have until *after* you have taken a sample.

Suppose you wanted to take a sample to estimate the average number of customers in the bank branch over the noon hour to within 3 customers, with a 95% level of confidence. Think again of the confidence interval being a horseshoe we are trying to throw around μ. Suppose we just barely catch μ inside the horseshoe (with the true μ being at either the upper or the lower limit of the interval). Even in this worst case, the farthest $\bar{x}$ can be from μ is equal to the half-width of the interval, since $\bar{x}$ is in the centre of the confidence interval (as shown in Exhibit 8.16). For this reason, the half-width of a confidence interval is sometimes referred to as the *margin of error* or *allowable error*. Since there is actually no *error* involved, we have referred to it as the half-width (or HW).

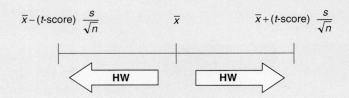

Exhibit 8.16

x̄ Will Be Within a Half-Width of μ

$$\bar{x}-(t\text{-score})\frac{s}{\sqrt{n}} \qquad \bar{x} \qquad \bar{x}+(t\text{-score})\frac{s}{\sqrt{n}}$$

HW ⟵   ⟶ HW

If we want the estimate to be within 3 units of the true value of μ, we simply set the half-width of the interval equal to 3.

$$HW = (t\text{-score})\frac{s}{\sqrt{n}} = 3$$

We cannot solve for the sample size n until we fill in the other unknowns in this equation. The first problem is that we need an estimate for s, the standard deviation. Since we have not yet done any sampling, this may pose a problem! However, there are several possible approaches.

1. Past or similar studies may provide a useful estimate of the standard deviation. For example, the bank may have done customer traffic studies in this or similar branches.

2. It may be possible to estimate the standard deviation from the range of the data. For example, counter staff may be quite sure that there are never fewer than 10 customers in the branch over the noon hour, and never more than 50. This yields a range of 40. Remember that in a normal data set, almost all of the observations will lie within three standard deviations of the mean. This means that the range of the data would occupy six standard deviations (three to the right of the mean plus three to the left of the mean). If you have reason to believe that customer traffic numbers are normally distributed (something else you are guessing about), you could estimate the standard deviation by dividing the range by 6. However, a more conservative (and the recommended) approach would be to divide the range by 4. This is less likely to give you a sample size too small for your purposes.

3. If all else fails, you may have to do a small preliminary sample to estimate the standard deviation, before you proceed with your real sample.

The other value that we have to fill into the equation is the t-score. Once again we have a difficulty: the appropriate t-score depends on the degrees of freedom, which depends on n, the sample size, which is exactly what we are trying to figure out! We solve this problem by turning to the normal distribution (which is the t-distribution with infinite degrees of freedom).

Going back to the example, we can complete the calculations as follows. For a 95% confidence interval, the z-score would be 1.96. We will use the range-based estimate of the standard deviation mentioned above; that is, we will set $s = \frac{\text{range}}{4} = \frac{40}{4} = 10$.

$$(z\text{-score})\frac{s}{\sqrt{n}} = 3$$

$$(1.96)\frac{10}{\sqrt{n}} = 3$$

$$\frac{19.6}{\sqrt{n}} = 3$$

cross-multiply to get

$$3\sqrt{n} = 19.6$$

$$\sqrt{n} = \frac{19.6}{3}$$

$$n = \left(\frac{19.6}{3}\right)^2 = 42.684$$

This calculation indicates that we need a sample size of 43 days to get an estimate with the desired level of accuracy. Notice an important point: even if the calculation had yielded a number such as 42.01, we would *still* take a sample of 43 days. We do not *round* the results of the sample size calculation. Instead we always use the whole number next-highest to the result of the calculation.

It makes sense to come up with a general formula for n to summarize the algebraic manipulations required.

The sample size for an estimate of μ is as follows:

$$n = \left(\frac{(z\text{-score})(s)}{\text{HW}}\right)^2$$

Sample size n should be set at the whole number next highest to the result of the calculation.

One of the most common mistakes students make when using this formula is for-getting to square the right-hand side—so don't forget! Of course, this formula is appro-priate only if the data turn out to be normally distributed, but we cannot assess that until a sample is taken.

Recall Example 8.2, about the average weight of packages in shipping and receiving. Suppose the manager is not satisfied with the accuracy of the estimate obtained. She wants to estimate the average weight of the packages to within half a kilogram. How large a sample must she take?

Example 8.3a

Deciding on sample size to estimate μ

From earlier calculations, we know that the data are approximately normally distributed. From earlier calculations, $s = 4.02317$. For a 95% confidence level, we use a z-score of 1.96.

$$n = \left(\frac{(z\text{-score})(s)}{HW} \right)^2$$

$$n = \left(\frac{(1.96(4.02316974)}{0.5} \right)^2$$

$$n = 248.7$$

The manager will have to take a random sample of 249 packages to get an estimate with the desired accuracy.

Sample Size to Estimate a Proportion

Similar reasoning leads us to a formula for sample size for estimating p, the population proportion. The confidence interval is set up as shown in Exhibit 8.17 below.

8.17

Confidence Interval Estimate for p

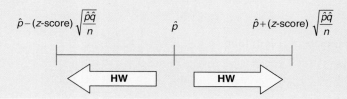

$$\hat{p} - (z\text{-score})\sqrt{\frac{\hat{p}\hat{q}}{n}} \qquad \hat{p} \qquad \hat{p} + (z\text{-score})\sqrt{\frac{\hat{p}\hat{q}}{n}}$$

HW   HW

So we can solve for the appropriate sample size by solving for n in the formula for the half-width.

$$HW = (z\text{-score})\sqrt{\frac{\hat{p}\hat{q}}{n}}$$

We are temporarily stopped by the need for $\hat{p}$ (and $\hat{q}$). As before, if some appropriate estimate of $\hat{p}$ exists from previous or similar studies, we would use that value. If no estimate of $\hat{p}$ exists, then we set $\hat{p} = 0.5$. This is because whatever $\hat{p}$ turns out to be, the sample size required will never be larger than the one required when $\hat{p} = 0.5$ (try using various levels of $\hat{p}$ in your calculations to see for yourself that this is true).

The algebraic manipulations to isolate n, the sample size, result in the formula shown opposite.

The sample size for an estimate of p is as follows:

$$n = \hat{p}\hat{q}\left(\frac{z\text{-score}}{\text{HW}}\right)^2$$

If no estimate of $\hat{p}$ is available, use $\hat{p} = 0.50$.

Sample size n should be set at the whole number next highest to the result of the calculation.

As before, we set the sample size as the whole number next highest to the results of our calculation. Again, be sure you remember to square the term on the right-hand side when you use this formula. Of course, this formula is only appropriate if the conditions for normality of the sampling distribution of $\hat{p}$ are met, but we cannot assess this until we have an estimate for p (that is, until a sample is taken).

8.3b

Recall Example 8.1, about the proportion of Ontarians who would align themselves with the Liberal Party. Suppose the party wanted to be able to estimate this proportion to within 2% of the true value, with 98% confidence. How big a sample size would be necessary?

Deciding on sample size to estimate p

From the first sample, $\hat{p} = 0.46$. As before, the appropriate z-score for a 98% confidence interval will be 2.326. Using the formula for sample size, we get the following result.

$$n = \hat{p}\hat{q}\left(\frac{z\text{-score}}{\text{HW}}\right)^2$$

$$= (0.46)(0.54)\left(\frac{2.326}{0.02}\right)^2$$

$$= 3359.8$$

For the desired level of accuracy, a random sample of 3360 Ontarians is required.

DEVELOP YOUR SKILLS 8.3

1. A company wants to estimate the proportion of smokers on staff to within 5%, with 99% confidence. A preliminary estimate of the proportion of smokers is 0.1867. How big a sample size is necessary?

2. A company wants to estimate the proportion of employees who have children of daycare age to within 5%, with 95% confidence. No estimate is available. How big a sample size is necessary? How big a sample

size would be required if the confidence level increased to 98%?

3. A researcher wants to estimate the average grocery bill of households whose members shop at a particular supermarket to within $10, with 95% confidence. How big a sample size is necessary? A preliminary sample revealed a standard deviation of $32.45.

4. A student wants to estimate the average mark on a statistics test to within 5 marks (out of 100), with 95% confidence. A preliminary sample yielded a

standard deviation of 15.54. How big a sample size is necessary?

5. The Strategic Counsel poll described in Develop Your Skills 8.1, Question 5, estimated Liberal support to within 3.1 percentage points, 19 times out of 20. How big a sample should be taken if Liberal support is to be estimated to within 2 percentage points with 95% confidence?

8.4 CONFIDENCE INTERVALS AND HYPOTHESIS TESTS

There is a direct correspondence between a two-tailed hypothesis test and the corresponding confidence interval. *If the confidence interval contains the hypothesized value of the population parameter, there is insufficient evidence to reject the null hypothesis.* And of course, the reverse is also true: *If the confidence interval does not contain the hypothesized value of the population parameter, there is sufficient evidence to reject the null hypothesis.*

Exhibit 8.18 below illustrates why this is so. The exhibit shows the sampling distribution of $\hat{p}$, based on the hypothesized value of p, and sets up the 95% confidence interval half-width. Exhibit 8.18 shows the results of four separate sample results.

8.18

Correspondence Between Confidence Intervals and Two-Tailed Hypothesis Tests

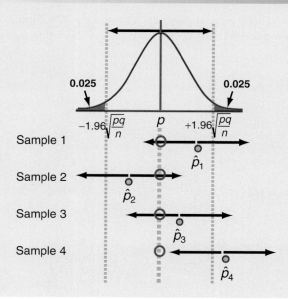

The confidence interval constructed for sample 1 contains the hypothesized value of p. As well, since the sample proportion is not extreme (not in the tail area of the distribution), we would fail to reject the null hypothesis. The same can be said for the results of samples 2 and 3. Only in sample 4 do we get a sample mean so extreme that we would reject the null hypothesis. Notice that the confidence interval constructed in this case does *not* include p.

Of course, this correspondence holds only if the tail areas from the confidence interval match the level of significance in the two-tailed hypothesis test. For example, a 95% confidence interval corresponds to a two-tailed hypothesis test with $\alpha = 0.05$. A 99% confidence interval corresponds to a two-tailed hypothesis test with $\alpha = 0.01$.

A confidence interval cannot be directly used to draw a hypothesis testing conclusion, when the hypothesis test is one-tailed. With some thought, you could work out the relationship between a particular confidence interval and a one-tailed hypothesis test. However, it is more straightforward simply to conduct the one-tailed hypothesis test, rather than to try and tie it to some confidence interval that you have constructed.

Finally, notice that while it is possible to draw a hypothesis testing conclusion from a confidence interval estimate in some situations, this approach does not provide a p-value for the hypothesis test, and so the results are somewhat limited.

Example 8.4

Refer to Example 8.2 on page 285, about the weights of packages handled at shipping and receiving. A 95% confidence interval for the average package weight was (10.40 kg, 14.15 kg). The manager thought that the average package weight was 15 kg. Based on this confidence interval, does the sample evidence support the manager's claim? What level of significance applies?

Using a confidence interval for a hypothesis test

Since the 95% confidence interval does *not* include a weight of 15 kg, there is sufficient evidence to reject the hypothesis that $\mu = 15$ kg. There is sufficient evidence from the sample to infer that $\mu \neq 15$ kg, with a 5% significance level.

DEVELOP YOUR SKILLS 8.4

Answer the following questions without doing any additional calculations beyond the confidence intervals you have already constructed.

1. Return to the confidence interval you constructed for Develop Your Skills 8.2, Question 1. The owner of the supermarket claims that the average household grocery bill is $95. Does the sample evidence support the owner's claim? What level of significance applies to your conclusion?

2. Return to the confidence interval you constructed for Develop Your Skills 8.1, Question 1. The company nurse claims that the percentage of smokers on staff is 20%.

Does the sample evidence support the nurse's claim? What level of significance applies to your conclusion?

3. Return to the confidence interval you constructed for Develop Your Skills 8.2, Question 2. The manager believes that the average fee paid by scientists for membership in professional associations is $140. Does the sample evidence support the manager's belief? What level of significance applies to your conclusion?

4. Return to the confidence interval you constructed for Develop Your Skills 8.2, Question 4. You believe that the average mark on the statistics test was 50%. Does the sample evidence support your belief? What level of significance applies to your conclusion?

Chapter Summary

8

Estimation procedures rely on sampling (as usual), and we will continue to assume simple random sampling. Estimation begins with a sample statistic that corresponds to the population parameter of interest. For example, it makes sense to estimate the population mean, μ, with the sample mean, $\bar{x}$. A single-number estimate of a population parameter that is based on sample data is called a point estimate. A confidence interval estimate of the form (a, b) is a range of numbers that is thought to enclose the parameter of interest, with a given level of probability.

Confidence intervals have a general form as follows:

$$(\text{point estimate}) \pm (\text{critical value}) \cdot (\text{estimated standard error of the sample statistic})$$

Estimating the Population Proportion

A confidence interval for a population proportion has the following general form:

$$\hat{p} \pm (\text{critical } z\text{-score})\sqrt{\frac{\hat{p}\hat{q}}{n}}$$

This is valid only if the conditions for normality of the sampling distribution of $\hat{p}$ are met ($n\hat{p}$ and $n\hat{q} \geq 10$). As well, if sampling is done without replacement, the sample size must be less than 5% of the population.

An Excel template for constructing a confidence interval for the population proportion is available on the CD that comes with the text. It is described on page 282.

Estimating the Population Mean

A confidence interval for a population mean has the following general form:

$$\bar{x} \pm (\text{critical } t\text{-score})\left(\frac{s}{\sqrt{n}}\right)$$

This is valid only if the population is approximately normally distributed. An Excel template for constructing a confidence interval for the population mean is available on the CD that comes with the text. It is described on page 286.

Selecting the Sample Size

Deciding on the sample size is a challenge because you need information that you do not normally have until *after* you have taken your sample.

The formula to select the appropriate sample size to estimate the mean is as follows:

$$n = \left(\frac{(z\text{-score})(s)}{\text{HW}}\right)^2$$

The appropriate sample size is the whole number next highest to the calculated result. HW stands for the half-width of the interval. If, for example, you wanted to estimate the mean to within 10 units, the half-width would be 10. Some estimate for s, the standard deviation, must be available. If the range of the data is known, s can be estimated as $\frac{range}{4}$. If there is no information about s, a preliminary sample may have to be taken in order to estimate s. The z-score corresponds to the desired level of confidence for the estimate.

The formula to select the appropriate sample size to estimate the proportion is as follows:

$$n = \hat{p}\hat{q}\left(\frac{z\text{-score}}{\text{HW}}\right)^2$$

HW stands for the half-width of the interval, as above. Some estimate for $\hat{p}$ must be available. If there is no estimate, use $\hat{p} = 0.50$, as this will give the most conservative estimate of sample size. The appropriate sample size is the whole number next-highest to the calculated result.

Confidence Intervals and Hypothesis Tests

There is a direct correspondence between a two-tailed test of hypothesis with a significance level of α and an interval estimate with a confidence level of $(1 - \alpha)$. If the confidence interval contains the hypothesized value of the population parameter, there is insufficient evidence to reject the null hypothesis. If the confidence interval does not contain the hypothesized value of the population parameter, there is sufficient evidence to reject the null hypothesis.

CHAPTER REVIEW EXERCISES

1. A poll taken for *Toronto Life* magazine in the fall of 2005 surveyed 316 adults in the greater Toronto area. Four in 10 said they would keep their jobs even if they won $10 million in the lottery. Provide a 95% confidence interval for the proportion of people in the greater Toronto area who would keep their jobs after winning $10 million in the lottery. (Source: "Would You Keep Job If You Won $10-Million?" **www.theglobeandmail.com**, accessed October 26, 2005.)

2. A survey of 30 employees living in a large metropolitan area yielded an average of 54.2 hours of work per week, with a standard deviation of 3.2 hours. Provide a 98% confidence interval for average hours of work per week for these employees. The data appear to be normally distributed.

3. An ice cream store wants to expand its range of flavours, and has decided to do some research to select which flavours to add. Customers were presented with a range of new flavours, and asked which one they would like to try, if any.

    The data are available in the DataChap08 directory on the CD that comes with the text. The codes are as follows: (1) pecan and fudge; (2) apple pie; (3) banana caramel ripple; (4) ginger and honey; and (5) would not try any of these flavours.

    Create a 90% confidence interval estimate for the percentage of customers who would not try any of the new flavours.

    CRE08-3.xls ◗ Set

4. How big a sample is necessary to estimate, to within 2 percentage points, the proportion of new graduates of a business program who are willing to relocate to find a job, with 90% confidence? If your college graduates only 350 students from the business program, what does this tell you?

5. A statistics professor wants to estimate the average number of hours, per week, that students in statistics classes spend (outside class) working on statistics. The professor wants to estimate the number of hours to within one hour, with 95% confidence. The professor thinks that even the least motivated students spend at least one hour, and the most highly motivated students probably spend 10 hours. How large a sample should she take? The professor knows she should be cautious about interpreting the results of any such survey. Why?

6. A random sample of 35 paint cans has an average of 2.98 litres with a standard deviation of 0.12 litres. The volumes of the paint cans appear to be normally distributed. Construct a 99% confidence interval for the average amount of paint in the paint cans.

7. Based on your calculations in answer to Exercise 6, what can you conclude about the hypothesis that the paint cans contain an average of 3 litres? What level of significance can you attach to your conclusion?

CRE08-8.xls
Set

8. A maker of toothpaste is doing quality control tests on the amount of toothpaste in the tubes. Thirty tubes of toothpaste are randomly selected, and the quantity of toothpaste in each tube is precisely measured, in millilitres. The results are available on the CD that comes with this text. Construct a 95% confidence interval for the average amount of toothpaste in the tubes.

9. A car manufacturer, worried about how increasing gasoline prices are going to affect sales, wants to estimate the percentage of the adult population in Canada who would consider buying a hybrid vehicle for their next purchase. How big a sample size should the manufacturer take, if the company wants to estimate the proportion to within 3%, and the manufacturer is fairly certain that the proportion is in the neighbourhood of 10%? The desired confidence level is 95%.

10. The City of Moose Jaw wants to estimate the percentage of households that make consistent efforts to separate recyclable materials from their garbage. How many households should be included in the random sample, if the city wants its estimate to be within 2 percentage points, with 95% confidence?

11. In a survey, 43% of the 2450 respondents said that they had phoned in sick when they were not ill. Construct a 95% confidence interval estimate for the proportion of workers who phone in sick when they are not ill. Do you think the results of such a survey would be reliable?

12. A survey conducted by Ipsos-Reid for the Royal Bank of Canada in August 2005 revealed that 42% of Canadians who plan to start a business expect that their incomes will increase within one year of starting the business. The sample size was 1,661. Construct a 95% confidence interval estimate of the proportion of all aspiring Canadian entrepreneurs who expect their incomes to increase within one year of starting the business. (Source: "Nearly One Million Canadians Want To Open Business Within The Next Year: RBC Survey," **www.rbc.com/newsroom/20051003 smallbus. html**, accessed October 5, 2005.)

13. A restaurant is trying to decide how to target its marketing. The owner thinks that diners on business expense accounts typically spend more on food and wine than other diners. The restaurant takes a random sample of 40 diners who pay with corporate credit cards. The average bill (per person) is $68.52, with a standard deviation of $14.89. Construct a 98% confidence interval estimate of the average amount spent (per person) in this restaurant by diners with business expense accounts. You may assume that the spending is normally distributed.

14. A car rental agency is trying to make staffing plans. The early morning is always a busy time for rentals. The agency keeps track of the number of customers who pick up rental cars in the 8:00 A.M.–10:00 A.M. period for a random sample of days.

CRE08-14.xls
Set

    The data are available on the CD that accompanies this text. Construct a 99% confidence interval for the average number of customers picking up rental cars in the 8:00 A.M.–10:00 A.M. period.

15. A manufacturer of cars that have had a poor quality rating in the past wants to estimate the average annual maintenance expenditure for its entry-level compact in the third year of its life. A random sample of 60 customers with such cars is selected, and annual maintenance costs are tracked.

CRE08-15.xls
Set

    The data are available on the CD that accompanies this text. Create a 98% confidence interval estimate for the annual maintenance spending on this car in the third year of its life.

16. How large a sample size should the manufacturer described in Exercise 15 take, if it wants to estimate annual maintenance costs for this entry-level compact in the third year of its life to within $10, with 98% confidence?

17. A large company is trying to manage its accounts receivable more efficiently than in the past. It selects a random sample of 100 of these accounts, and tracks how old they are. (The company's accounting system does not track account age, although there are plans for an upgrade soon.) The codes associated with the account ages are: (1) 0–30 days old; (2) 31–60 days old; and (3) more than 60 days old.

    The data are available on the CD that accompanies this text. Create a 95% confidence interval estimate for the proportion of the company's accounts that are 0–30 days old.

CRE08-17.xls
Set

18. The confidence interval created in Exercise 17 is quite wide. How large a sample would be necessary if the company wanted to estimate the percentage of its accounts receivable that were 0–30 days old to within 5%, with 95% confidence?

19. A college is concerned that the housing boom in the immediate area has made it difficult for students to find affordable accommodation. It is claimed that the average monthly rent paid by a student at the college is $500. A random sample of 40 students are surveyed, and their monthly rent costs are recorded. The sample mean was $543.21, with a sample standard deviation of $47.89. The sample data appear normally distributed. Construct a 95% confidence interval estimate for the average monthly rent paid by students at this college. What does this allow you to conclude about the claim that the average monthly rent is $500?

20. A college wants to estimate the proportion of its students who live at home with their parents. How large a sample size should be taken, if the desire is to estimate the proportion to within 3%, with 98% confidence? Past research indicated that the proportion was in the neighbourhood of 35%.

CHAPTER

9

Making Decisions with Matched-Pairs Samples, Quantitative or Ranked Data

Learning Objectives

After mastering the material in this chapter, you will be able to:

1. Choose and conduct a *t*-test to compare population differences with matched-pairs samples, for normal quantitative data.

2. Choose and conduct the Wilcoxon Signed Rank Sum Test to compare matched-pairs samples, for non-normal quantitative data.

3. Choose and conduct the Sign Test to compare matched-pairs samples, for ranked data.

INTRODUCTION

So far, we have been investigating only one population at a time. We have covered techniques to examine quantitative data (confidence intervals and hypothesis tests of the mean) and qualitative data (confidence intervals and hypothesis tests of the proportion).

In Chapters 9, 10, and 11, we will cover techniques to compare two (and sometimes more than two) populations. Chapter 9 investigates matched-pairs samples, for normal and non-normal quantitative data, and also for ranked data. Chapter 10 looks at comparisons of independent samples, again for normal and non-normal quantitative data, and ranked data. Chapter 10 also presents methods to compare populations of qualitative data.

Matched-pairs analysis is a special case of comparing two populations, but we will start here because the methods for matched pairs of normal quantitative data and ranked data are simply new applications of techniques that you have already seen. Matched-pairs experiments are also a powerful technique, because they often allow us to draw conclusions about cause and effect. For example, in Chapter 1 we discussed the difficulties in deciding whether training methods were effective in reducing the number of worker errors. We discussed comparing workers at two plants—one where the workers had not gone through the training program, and one where they had been trained. We realized that although the data could tell us if there was a difference in error rates at the two plants, we could not come to a strong conclusion that the training programs were the cause of any difference, because too many other factors could have played a part.

A better method of comparison is a matched-pairs experiment, where worker errors are recorded both before and after training. If the number of errors fell in this case, we would be able to make a stronger conclusion that the training was the cause of the improvement.

When applying the techniques covered in Chapter 9, it will be extremely important to assess the situation before proceeding. The first step will be to decide if you have matched-pairs data or independent samples. With matched-pairs samples, there is some kind of relationship between an observation in the first sample and the corresponding observation in the second sample. With independent samples, there is no such relationship.

There are two situations when sample data are matched pairs:

1. *Observational studies with matched pairs*—Suppose you wanted to compare starting salaries of graduates of the Business program with salaries of graduates of the Computer Studies program. Obviously, there are many factors that could affect salary, for example, work experience, intelligence, location of job, and so on. If you wanted to make a valid comparison by program, you would match each graduate of the Business program in your sample to a graduate of the Computer Studies program. If the graduates were matched as closely as possible according to these other factors, you could more safely suggest that any observed difference was caused by program of study. In this case, you would want to directly compare the salary of the Business graduate with the salary of the corresponding graduate of the Computer Studies program.

2. *Experimental studies with matched pairs*—Suppose a company wants to test the effects of a training program on worker errors (this situation was first discussed in Example 1.4a on page 16). A group of workers is randomly selected at a particular plant, and the number of errors made by each worker is recorded over a period of time. The workers are then put through a training program, and the numbers of errors are recorded again after the training. It makes sense to compare the errors of each worker before the training to the same worker's errors after the training.

In either situation, it is crucial that you recognize that you have matched-pairs data. If you miss this, you might draw the wrong conclusion!

If the data were produced from a matched-pairs experiment, then the techniques of Chapter 9 apply, and the other decisions you will have to make are whether the data are normal or non-normal quantitative data, or ranked data. The headings in the chapter will guide you to the appropriate techniques: Section 9.1 for matched pairs with normally distributed differences, Section 9.2 for matched pairs with non-normally distributed differences, and Section 9.3 for matched pairs of ranked data. If the samples are independent, you will need techniques from Chapter 10 or 11 to complete your analysis.

9.1 MATCHED PAIRS, QUANTITATIVE DATA, NORMAL DIFFERENCES— THE *t*-TEST

The foreman in a small assembly plant wants to see if a training program results in a reduced number of worker errors. The foreman records the weekly number of errors for a random sample of workers before the training, and again after the training. In some cases, the number of worker errors decreased, in other cases, the number of errors stayed about the same, and in still other cases, the number of errors actually increased after the training. The foreman now has to decide whether to continue the training. The foreman is in a situation that is familiar to us: he has to decide about whether the training would reduce the number of errors if it were applied to the population of *all* workers, on the basis of this data about a sample of workers.

This is a matched-pairs experiment. The foreman should compare the errors before and after the training for each particular worker. In a situation like this (a matched-pairs experiment and quantitative data), we focus on the differences in the matching observations in the samples.

If the positive and negative differences are offsetting, this results in an average difference of zero, indicating that there is no significant difference in the before and after measurements. However, even if the average difference in the population is actually zero, we would not expect the average difference in the sample to be *exactly* zero, because of sampling variability. Therefore, we have to do a test of hypothesis to determine if the average difference is significantly different from zero.

We will use the subscript D to remind us that we are dealing with the differences between corresponding observations. Generally, then, we will be comparing a null hypothesis H_0: $\mu_D = 0$ (that is, no significant difference) with one of three possible alternative hypotheses:

- $\mu_D > 0$,
- $\mu_D < 0$, or
- $\mu_D \neq 0$.

A decision about which of the three possible alternative hypotheses to use will depend on the context of the analysis, *and the order of subtraction*.

The first step in the analysis is to calculate the differences between the corresponding observations to produce the single data set that we will focus on. The order of subtraction does not matter, *as long as the subtraction is done consistently*. If you are calculating the difference as [(sample 1 observation) – (sample 2 observation)], all the differences must be calculated in the same way. The foreman might calculate the differences in the number of worker errors as [(number of errors before training) – (number of errors after training)], or the other way around. The order does not matter, as long as it is consistent. Once the data set of differences is created, you proceed with a hypothesis test of the mean, as in Chapter 7. There is really nothing new here, because we are focusing on a single data set of differences. The technique you have already learned is simply being applied to a new situation, as Example 9.1a illustrates.

Suppose you wanted to study the effect of receiving a promotion on how often people visit the gym, because you believe that promotions lead to increased work and reduced visits to the gym. You examine a random sample of people who have received a promotion, and you gather data on their monthly gym visits before and after their promotions. The data are provided in the table shown in Exhibit 9.1.

9.1a

Example

The *t*-test for matched pairs, raw data

9.1

Exhibit

Sample Data: Monthly Gym Visits Before and After a Promotion, Section 9.1

| | Monthly Gym Visits | |
Person	Before Promotion	After Promotion
Joe	10	7
Sally	13	11
Hugo	14	10
Meriel	15	15
Juanita	15	14
Tadashi	15	14
Noel	18	19
Joanne	22	21
Heather	23	25
Barb	25	20

This is certainly a matched-pairs sample. It would not make sense to compare the gym visits of Joe after promotion with the gym visits of Heather before promotion!

The first step is to calculate the differences in the number of visits. The order of subtraction does not matter, so we will simply subtract as [(visits before promotion) − (visits after promotion)]. This leads to the data set of differences shown in Exhibit 9.2.

9.2

Exhibit

Differences in Monthly Gym Visits Before and After Promotion, Section 9.1

| | Monthly Gym Visits |
Person	Monthly Gym Visits Before Promotion − Visits After Promotion
Joe	3
Sally	2
Hugo	4
Meriel	0
Juanita	1
Tadashi	1
Noel	−1
Joanne	1
Heather	−2
Barb	5

Now we will follow the steps for a hypothesis test of the mean, as outlined in Chapter 7.

First we have to specify H_0 and H_1, the null and alternative hypotheses. As noted above, the null hypothesis is that the average difference is zero, so we have $H_0: \mu_D = 0$. Now we have to determine the alternative hypothesis. In this case, it is believed that promotions lead to fewer gym visits.

This is where you have to think about the order of subtraction. If promotions reduced the number of gym visits (this is the alternative hypothesis), then the number of visits to the gym *before* the promotion should be higher than the number of gym visits *after* the promotion. We will be examining the data to see if there is evidence that the average difference is positive, given the [(before) − (after)] order of subtraction we chose. This leads to $H_1: \mu_D > 0$, for the order of subtraction used here.

What if we had used the [(after) − (before)] order of subtraction? Then the null hypothesis would be $H_1: \mu_D < 0$. This is a completely equivalent way of approaching the analysis. You should always think carefully about the order of subtraction before you specify the alternative hypothesis in a matched-pairs analysis.

Suppose we use $\alpha = 0.05$. The data have already been collected, and the differences have been calculated. We must now identify or calculate the average difference in the sample, the standard deviation of the differences in the sample, and the sample size (as in Chapter 7).

Continuing on with the subscripts to remind ourselves that we are working with differences, and using the standard formulas, we find the following values.

- There are 10 observations, so $n_D = 10$.

- $\bar{x}_D = \dfrac{\Sigma x_D}{n_D} = \dfrac{14}{10} = 1.4$

- $s_D = \sqrt{\dfrac{\Sigma x_D^2 - \dfrac{(\Sigma x_D)^2}{n_D}}{n_D - 1}} = \sqrt{\dfrac{62 - \dfrac{(14)^2}{10}}{10 - 1}} = 2.17051$

As in Chapter 7, we must check for normality of the sample data, by creating a histogram of the differences. One possible histogram is shown below in Exhibit 9.3.

Exhibit 9.3

Histogram of the Differences in Monthly Gym Visits Before and After Promotion, Section 9.1

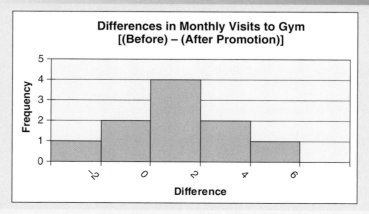

Since the histogram appears to be normal, we will assume that the population of differences is also normally distributed. We now calculate the appropriate *t*-score, again using the familiar formula.

$$t = \frac{\bar{x}_D - \mu_D}{s_D/\sqrt{n_D}} = \frac{1.4 - 0}{2.17051/\sqrt{10}} = 2.0397$$

With 10 matched pairs, there are 10 differences and $n_D - 1 = 10 - 1 = 9$ degrees of freedom. Exhibit 9.4 shows the appropriate row from the *t*-table.

---

t-Distribution Critical Values

Degrees of Freedom	$t_{.100}$	$t_{.050}$	$t_{.025}$	$t_{.010}$	$t_{.005}$
9	1.383	1.833	2.262	2.821	3.250

2.0397

Exhibit 9.4

This is a one-tailed test, so the *p*-value is somewhere between 2.5% and 5%. Since this is less than the α of 5%, we reject the null hypothesis. There is sufficient evidence to suggest that gym visits decline after a promotion.

Notice that we have put the conclusion in terms of the original question. If we had said instead that there was sufficient evidence to suggest that $\mu_D > 0$, very few people would understand the result. It is very important that you put the conclusions of hypothesis in terms that anyone can understand.

Using the Excel Template for Making Decisions About the Population Mean with a Single Sample   Of course, we could have done this analysis using an Excel formula to calculate the differences in the matched pairs of observations. Then we could have used the template introduced in Chapter 7 for hypothesis tests about the mean, with a single sample. Remember that effectively, we are dealing with only one sample here—the sample of differences. A completed template is shown below in Exhibit 9.5.

E

Template

Excel Template for Making Decisions About the Population Mean with a Single Sample

Making Decisions About the Population Mean with a Single Sample	
do the sample data appear to be normally distributed?	yes
sample standard deviation s	2.170509
sample mean	1.4
sample size n	10
hypothetical value of population mean	0
t-score	2.0397
one-tailed p-value	0.0359
two-tailed p-value	0.0718

Exhibit 9.5

As usual, the values of the standard deviation, the mean, and the sample size are calculated using the STDEV, AVERAGE, and COUNT functions of Excel. Be sure that you use Excel to calculate the differences in the before and after data values. Note that you can also use this template whenever you have only summary data from the samples.

Instructions

Using the Data Analysis *t*-Test: Paired Two Sample for Means   Excel has a built-in Data Analysis tool that allows you to do matched-pairs data comparisons, when you have normally distributed data. Exhibit 9.6 below shows the Data Analysis menu (from Tools). The correct choice is highlighted: *t*-Test: Paired Two Sample for Means.

9.6

Exhibit

Excel Data Analysis Menu

You should do some thinking about your hypothesis test before you activate the Excel tool. As well, you must check for normality of the differences. Excel does not do this; it will conduct the *t*-test whether the data are normal or not! Exhibit 9.7 below shows the *t*-test dialogue box.

9.7

Exhibit

Dialogue Box for *t*-Test: Paired Two Sample for Means

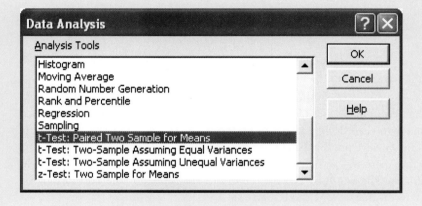

The dialogue box requires you to indicate to Excel where the sample data are stored (Variable 1 Range: and Variable 2 Range:). As indicated in Exhibit 9.7 above, the Hypothesized Mean Difference is zero (and usually will be). The Excel output for Example 9.1a is shown below in Exhibit 9.8.

Excel Output for Example 9.1a

9.8
Exhibit

t-Test: Paired Two Sample for Means		
	Before	*After*
Mean	17	15.6
Variance	23.55556	31.15556
Observations	10	10
Pearson Correlation	0.922838	
Hypothesized Mean Difference	0	
df	9	
t Stat	2.0397	
P(T<=t) one-tail	0.0359	
t Critical one-tail	1.833114	
P(T<=t) two-tail	0.0718	
t Critical two-tail	2.262159	

We can see from the output that the one-tailed *p*-value is 0.0359 (see the highlighted row in the table—note that it will *not* be highlighted in the Excel output). This of course agrees with our previous calculations. The Data Analysis tool in Excel can be used whenever you have data sets for matched-pairs data comparisons, and you have established that the data are normally distributed. *Be sure to check for normality of differences first.*

The real estate market has been very hot in the Calgary area, and it has been hard to estimate what the selling or listing price of a home should be. There is also a question about whether some real estate agents suggest higher listing prices than others.

A random sample of three-bedroom bungalows in one particular Calgary suburb was selected. In the month of July, two real estate agents were asked to look at the properties and suggest listing prices.

The data are shown in Exhibit 9.9 below (and are also available on the CD that comes with the text). At the 3% level of significance, is there evidence that Amanda Hargreave suggests listing prices that are different from those suggested by Nick O'Brien?

9.1b
Example

The *t*-test for matched pairs, raw data

EXA09-1b.xls

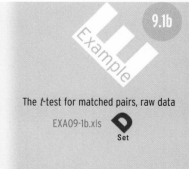

Set

Exhibit **9.9**

Two Agents' Suggested Listing Prices, Calgary Bungalows

Random Sample of Three-Bedroom Bungalows in a Calgary Suburb, July		
House	Amanda Hargreave's Suggested Listing Price	Nick O'Brien's Suggested Listing Price
1	250,900	249,600
2	242,700	242,200
3	256,600	255,200
4	263,600	263,200
5	263,600	262,800
6	264,600	264,800
7	239,050	239,900
8	251,100	250,300
9	263,900	262,300
10	244,200	243,200
11	246,000	246,000
12	239,800	240,700
13	240,500	240,400
14	245,100	243,800
15	245,700	245,300
16	241,000	240,000
17	247,300	247,000
18	249,300	248,600
19	254,600	254,100
20	249,800	248,900

Since this data set is available in an Excel worksheet, we will use Excel for the analysis. The first step is to calculate the differences in the prices recommended by the two agents, and then check to see if the differences are normally distributed. We will subtract as follows: [(Amanda Hargreave's suggested listing price) − (Nick O'Brien's suggested listing price)]. A histogram of the differences is shown in Exhibit 9.10 below.

Exhibit **9.10**

Histogram of Differences in Agents' Listing Prices

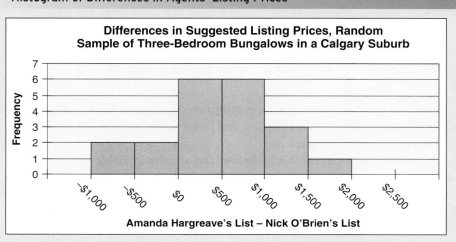

Since the differences appear to be normally distributed, we can proceed.

- $H_0: \mu_D = 0$
- $H_1: \mu_D \neq 0$
- $\alpha = 0.03$

A completed template for the differences is shown in Exhibit 9.11 below.

Completed Excel Template for Making Decisions About the Population Mean with a Single Sample

Template

Exhibit **9.11**

Making Decisions About the Population Mean with a Single Sample	
do the sample data appear to be normally distributed?	yes
sample standard deviation s	683.1573
sample mean	552.5
sample size n	20
hypothetical value of population mean	0
t-score	3.616817
one-tailed p-value	0.000918
two-tailed p-value	0.001837

This is a two-tailed test, so the appropriate *p*-value from the template is 0.0018. The *p*-value is $< \alpha$, so we reject H_0. There is sufficient evidence to suggest that the recommended listing prices of the two agents are different.

When:
- matched pairs of quantitative data with normally distributed differences
- trying to make a decision about the average difference, μ_D, on the basis of $\bar{x}_D$, the average of the sample differences

Steps:
1. Specify H_0, the null hypothesis, which will be $\mu_D = 0$.
2. Specify H_1, the alternative hypothesis.
3. Determine or identify α, the significance level.
4. Collect or identify the sample data. Identify or calculate the differences between the matching observations in the samples (keeping the order of subtraction consistent).
5. Check for normality of sample differences with a histogram. If the histogram is non-normal, particularly with small sample sizes, do not proceed with the *t*-test (use the Wilcoxon Signed Rank Sum Test instead, described on p. 311).
6. *If* the sample differences appear to be normally distributed, identify or calculate:

   - $\bar{x}_D$, the average of the differences (*including* zero differences)
   - s_D, the standard deviation of the differences
   - n_D, the number of differences (*including* zero differences)

7. Calculate the appropriate *t*-score, using the following formula:

$$t = \frac{\bar{x}_D - \mu_D}{s_D / \sqrt{n_D}}$$

Guide to Decision Making

Matched Pairs, Quantitative Data, Normal Differences–The *t*-Test

8. Use the *t*-distribution with $n_D - 1$ degrees of freedom to calculate (or approximate, if using tables) the appropriate *p*-value for the hypothesis test, keeping in mind the order of subtraction used when calculating the differences.

9. If *p*-value $< \alpha$, reject H_0 and conclude that there is sufficient evidence to decide in favour of H_1. If *p*-value $> \alpha$, fail to reject H_0 and conclude that there is insufficient evidence to decide in favour of H_1.

Confidence Interval Estimate of μ_D

Following directly from the sampling distribution and the discussion of the hypothesis test, a confidence interval estimate can be constructed for the average difference in population means, as follows:

$$\text{(point estimate)} \pm \text{(critical value)} \cdot \text{(estimated standard error of the sample statistic)}$$

$$\bar{x}_D \pm \text{critical } t\text{-score} \left(\frac{s_D}{\sqrt{n_D}} \right)$$

where the critical *t*-score corresponds to the desired level of confidence, and has $n_D - 1$ degrees of freedom. Of course, the histogram of differences must be normal for this formula to be appropriate. Example 9.1c below illustrates the construction of the confidence interval.

Confidence interval for μ_D

Financial planners collect data about their clients' circumstances, and then use a number of assumptions about the future to recommend savings plans. A researcher wanted to determine if a financial planner at a local bank branch was consistently using pessimistic assumptions about the future, resulting in recommendations for higher-than-necessary savings for clients. A random sample of 15 clients was sent to the bank's financial planner, and also to a highly respected fee-for-service financial advisor. The differences in recommended monthly savings, calculated as [(bank planner's recommended savings) − (fee-for-service advisor's recommended savings)] appeared to be normally distributed. The mean difference in monthly savings recommended was \$45.21, with a standard deviation of \$12.35. Construct a 95% confidence interval estimate for the mean difference in recommended monthly savings.

We have been told that the sample differences are normally distributed, and we will assume that the population of differences is also. We proceed by substituting the sample statistics into the confidence interval estimate formula.

$$\bar{x}_D \pm \text{critical } t\text{-score} \left(\frac{s_D}{\sqrt{n_D}} \right)$$

$$= 45.21 \pm t\text{-score} \left(\frac{12.35}{\sqrt{15}} \right)$$

The *t*-score for a 95% confidence interval with $15 - 1 = 14$ degrees of freedom is 2.145, as illustrated in the excerpt from the *t*-table shown in Exhibit 9.12.

t-Distribution Critical Values

Degrees of Freedom	$t_{.100}$	$t_{.050}$	$t_{.025}$	$t_{.010}$	$t_{.005}$
14	1.345	1.761	2.145	2.624	2.977

for 95% CI

The remaining calculations are as follows.

$$45.21 \pm 2.145\left(\frac{12.35}{\sqrt{15}}\right)$$

$$= 45.21 \pm 6.8399$$

$$= (38.37, 52.05)$$

A 95% confidence interval for the mean difference in recommended monthly savings is ($38.37, $52.05). In other words, we have 95% confidence that the interval ($38.37, $52.05) contains the average amount that the bank's financial planner is recommending in monthly savings, above the savings recommended by the fee-for-service financial planner.

Notice that since this confidence interval does not contain zero, we know that a hypothesis test would suggest that there is sufficient evidence to reject the null hypothesis of no difference in recommended monthly savings between the two financial advisors (two-tailed test, with $\alpha = 0.05$).

You can use the template for the confidence interval of a population mean (first discussed in Chapter 8 on p. 286) to construct this confidence interval. A completed template for this example is shown below in Exhibit 9.13.

Template

Completed Excel Template for the Confidence Interval Estimate for the Population Mean

Confidence Interval Estimate for the Population Mean	
do the sample data appear to be normally distributed?	yes
confidence level (decimal form)	0.95
sample mean	45.21
sample standard deviation s	12.35
sample size n	15
upper confidence limit	52.04921
lower confidence limit	38.37079

As usual, Excel yields a slightly more accurate confidence interval estimate than our manual calculations.

DEVELOP YOUR SKILLS 9.1

1. The foreman in a small assembly plant believes that playing classical music in the plant will improve worker productivity. To try to prove his point, the foreman conducts an experiment. He records the average daily production levels for a random sample of workers, over a four-week period. He then plays music in the plant, and records the average daily production levels for the same workers, over another four-week period (some time after the music was started). The results of the study are shown below in Exhibit 9.14 (they are also available in a file in the directory DataChap09). See file called DYS09-1-1.xls.

Set

Exhibit 9.14

Worker Production

Worker	Average Daily Production Before Music	Average Daily Production After Music
1	18	18
2	14	15
3	10	12
4	11	15
5	9	7
6	10	11
7	9	6
8	11	14
9	10	11
10	12	12

Is there sufficient evidence, at the 4% significance level, to suggest that playing classical music led to increased worker productivity?

2. A small company that specializes in gourmet cookies decides to redesign its packaging. The company owner is certain that the new package will lead to increased sales. Weekly sales at a random sample of stores in the Barrie area are recorded before and after the change in package design. Using the 5% level of significance, analyze the data to see if the owner's idea is correct.

The data set is available on the CD that comes with the text, and is also reproduced below in Exhibit 9.15. See file called DYS09-1-2.xls.

Set

Exhibit 9.15

Cookie Sales Data, Develop Your Skills 9.1

Weekly Sales Before and After Product Redesign

Store	Sales After	Sales Before
51 Bayfield	842.42	813.67
109 Mapleview Drive	831.54	698.71
137 Wellington	822.86	734.48
6 Collier	876.97	832.46
421 Essa Road	776.44	791.22
19 Queen	793.19	766.73
345 Cundles	730.17	668.66
D-564 Byrne Drive	576.95	631.05
24 Archer	758.87	724.39
15 Short St.	736.04	766.76

3. Telemarketers generally read from a prepared script when they make their sales calls. A firm decides to change this prepared script, making it both friendlier and shorter. Daily sales are recorded for a random sample of telemarketers, both before and after the script change. The average difference—using a [(before the change) – (after the change)] order of subtraction—is +4.2, with a sample size of 56. The differences have a standard deviation of 23.4. Do the data suggest that there is a difference in daily sales before and after the script change? Use $\alpha = 0.05$. What assumption do you have to make, in order to answer this question?

4. The Student Services Department at a Prince Edward Island college wants to see if there are differences in the study habits of male and female students. A random sample of female students are selected, and then a corresponding sample of male students is designed—same programs, ages, previous educational experience, and living arrangements (that is, all of the students are living away from their parents). The students are asked to keep track of the number of hours they study over a four-week period.

Set

   The results are available on the CD that comes with the text, in the directory called 'DataChap09.'

See file called DYS09-1-4.xls. Does it appear, based on this data, that male students study less than female students? Use a 4% significance level.

5. An automobile association has always encouraged its members to check tire pressures regularly. The association wants to demonstrate that maintaining tire pressure results in better fuel consumption. The association selected a random sample of its members, and asked them to record their fuel consumption in litres per 100 km for all of their driving for one month in the summer. It then asked the members to check and adjust tire pressures every 3–4 days, for another summer month, and record their fuel consumption again. The average difference in number of litres per 100 km was 0.4, with the standard deviation of the differences being 1.4. The order of subtraction was [(fuel consumption without checking tires) – (fuel consumption with checking tires)]. The sample size was 20. The histogram of differences appears to be normally distributed. Do these data support the association's claim that maintaining tire pressure improves fuel consumption? Use a 4% significance level. What else might explain the results in this case?

9.2   MATCHED PAIRS, QUANTITATIVE DATA, NON—NORMAL DIFFERENCES—THE WILCOXON SIGNED RANK SUM TEST

What if you have a matched-pairs sample with quantitative data, but the histogram of differences reveals significant non-normality (particularly with small sample sizes)? Fortunately, you can still proceed with the analysis, using a technique called the Wilcoxon Signed Rank Sum Test (WSRST). This is an example of a distribution-free statistical method, which does not require that the populations conform to any particular distribution (such as the normal).

The WSRST is actually a test to find out if two population distributions are the same. This means that it tests for differences in centres and also shapes and spreads. If the WSRST leads us to conclude that there is a difference in two populations, the difference might be in any of these three characteristics; Exhibit 9.16 illustrates the possibilities.

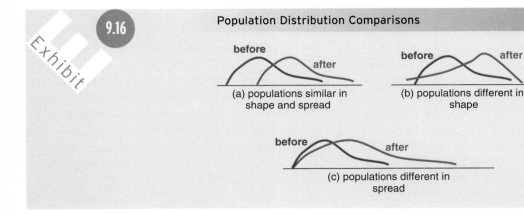

9.16

Exhibit

Population Distribution Comparisons

(a) populations similar in shape and spread

(b) populations different in shape

(c) populations different in spread

So far, we have been focusing on the average difference between two matched populations. If we are to use the WSRST to decide about the average difference in the populations, we must limit our comparisons to populations that are already similar in shape and spread, as illustrated in Exhibit 9.16a above. This can be assessed by examining histograms of the sample data, and checking if they are similar in shape and spread. Equivalently, if the histogram of differences is fairly symmetric, we can proceed with the WSRST as a test of average difference in populations. Effectively, this is a test of the locations of the populations.

If we find indications that the populations are not similar in shape and spread, such as in Exhibit 9.16b and 9.16c above, we can still use the WSRST, but we cannot make a conclusion solely about population means. In such cases, we can decide only whether there is evidence that the population distributions are different. If we conclude that they are, the differences could be in means, shapes, or spreads.

For the WSRST, the analysis begins in exactly the same way as with normal quantitative data. Differences between corresponding observations in each sample are computed. One change in the analysis with WSRST is that we will disregard any differences that are zero (these differences are included in the t-test of μ_D, but are not included in the WSRST—make sure you remember this distinction). We will refer to the number of non-zero differences as n_W.

As before, if the positive and negative differences are offsetting, we would have evidence of *no difference* in the before and after measurements. We assess the positive and negative differences by looking not at the values of the differences but at the *ranks* of the differences.[1] We begin by assigning ranks (1, 2, 3, 4, . . . , n, from smallest to largest) to the absolute values of the differences (that is, we ignore the minus signs on the negative differences). We then compare the ranks for the negative differences and the positive differences. If the positive and negative differences are approximately offsetting, then the ranks would be fairly evenly distributed between the positive and negative differences, and the sums of the ranks would be about the same. Only if the sums of the ranks are significantly different do we have evidence that there is a difference in population locations.

---

[1] You have seen the ranking process before, when the Spearman Rank Correlation Coefficient was discussed, in Chapter 3.

First we will look at a small numerical example to illustrate how to assign the ranks properly. Then we will go back to the gym visits example, with a larger data set having non-normal differences, to show the complete hypothesis testing procedure.

A small numerical example of before and after matched-pairs data is shown in Exhibit 9.17 below, with the differences calculated as [(before event) − (after event)].

Data Set for Rank Assignment Demonstration

Exhibit 9.17

	Sample Data	
Before	After	Differences
119	133	−14
105	127	−22
130	130	0
145	119	26
144	133	11
148	154	−6
101	107	−6
120	114	6
143	134	9
107	121	−14

We will go through the ranking process step by step, so that you can easily follow it. Since we ignore the signs on the differences when we assign ranks, the next step is to record the absolute value of the differences. Ultimately, though, we will want to be able to tell which ranks were assigned to positive differences, and which were assigned to negative differences. To make this easy, we will record negative differences and their assigned ranks in the colour red. This is shown below in Exhibit 9.18.

Data Set for Rank Assignment Demonstration, Absolute Value of Difference

Exhibit 9.18

	Sample Data		
Before	After	Differences	Absolute Value of Differences
119	133	−14	14
105	127	−22	22
130	130	0	0
145	119	26	26
144	133	11	11
148	154	−6	6
101	107	−6	6
120	114	6	6
143	134	9	9
107	121	−14	14

Next, we put the differences in order, from smallest to largest (in absolute value). For the WSRST, we eliminate any differences of zero. The ordered differences are shown below in Exhibit 9.19. Also shown is a column of the ranks that must be assigned to the non-zero differences.

9.19

Exhibit

Demonstration Data with Ordered Differences and Ranks to Be Assigned

Sample Data		
Absolute Value of Differences	Ordered Differences	Ranks to Be Assigned
14	0	ignore
22	6	1
0	6	2
26	6	3
11	9	4
6	11	5
6	14	6
6	14	7
9	22	8
14	26	9

We cannot assign the ranks exactly as shown here, because we have to deal with tied differences carefully. The example contains a couple of cases where the differences are of the same size, but the ranks initially assigned to them are different. For example, there are two differences of 14 (in absolute value), and in Exhibit 9.19, one has a rank of 6, and the other a rank of 7 (see the shaded area in Exhibit 9.19). Whether the negative difference gets assigned the rank of 6 or 7 depends only on whether the negative difference of 14 was recorded before or after the positive difference of 14. This hardly seems to be a reliable approach, because it means we could get a number of *different* rank sums for the same data set, depending on the order in which the numbers were recorded. So that we can be sure that there is one and only one rank assignment for each data set of differences, we average the ranks of tied differences, and assign the averaged rank to each of the tied numbers. The ranks 6 and 7 have to be allocated to the two differences of 14. We will give each a rank of $\frac{(6+7)}{2} = 6.5$.

Similarly, the first three non-zero differences in the data set are 6, 6, and 6. The three associated ranks are 1, 2, and 3. We average the ranks to get $\frac{(1+2+3)}{3} = 2$, and assign a rank of 2 to each of the first three numbers. We continue the process until we have arrived at the ranks shown in Exhibit 9.20 on the next page.

Next, we sum the ranks of the positive differences to get what we will refer to as W^+, and we sum the ranks of the negative differences to get what we will refer to as W^-. This is shown in Exhibit 9.21, on the next page.

We see that $W^+ = 26.5$ and $W^- = 18.5$. One way to check that you have assigned the ranks correctly is to total W^+ and W^-: the sum should be equal to the sum of the column of ranks to be assigned. This is a quick way to pick up any errors you might have made in averaging the tied ranks in this case, $26.5 + 18.5 = 45$.

Gym Visits, Section 9.2 With Ordering and Ranking

Monthly Gym Visits

Monthly Gym Visits Before Promotion	Monthly Gym Visits After Promotion	Differences [(Before Promotion) − (After Promotion)]	Absolute Value of Differences	Ordered Differences	Ranks to Be Assigned	Assigned Ranks	+Ranks	−Ranks
10	2	8	8	0	ignore			
13	6	7	7	1	1	4.5		4.5
14	8	6	6	1	2	4.5		4.5
15	15	0	0	1	3	4.5		4.5
15	5	10	10	1	4	4.5		4.5
15	18	−3	3	1	5	4.5	4.5	
18	25	−7	7	1	6	4.5	4.5	
22	25	−3	3	1	7	4.5	4.5	
23	25	−2	2	1	8	4.5		4.5
25	17	8	8	2	9	10		10
11	12	−1	1	2	10	10		10
14	15	−1	1	2	11	10		10
15	10	5	5	3	12	13.5		13.5
16	11	5	5	3	13	13.5		13.5
16	9	7	7	3	14	13.5	13.5	
17	12	5	5	3	15	13.5	13.5	
19	21	−2	2	4	16	16	16	
23	28	−5	5	5	17	19.5	19.5	
21	22	−1	1	5	18	19.5	19.5	
15	12	3	3	5	19	19.5	19.5	
21	17	4	4	5	20	19.5		19.5
8	9	−1	1	5	21	19.5	19.5	
5	4	1	1	5	22	19.5	19.5	
13	12	1	1	6	23	23	23	
12	7	5	5	7	24	25.5	25.5	
11	13	−2	2	7	25	25.5		25.5
23	20	3	3	7	26	25.5	25.5	
18	17	1	1	7	27	25.5	25.5	
19	20	−1	1	8	28	29	29	
19	12	7	7	8	29	29	29	
10	2	8	8	8	30	29	29	
15	10	5	5	10	31	31	31	
			sum of the ranks		496	496	$W^+ =$ 371.5	$W^- =$ 124.5

We can focus on either W^+ or W^- to make a decision. You may find one of the values more logical for your focus, in the context of the order of subtraction you chose and the alternative hypothesis.

As before, the null hypothesis is that there is no difference in the visits to the gym before promotion and after promotion. We will use a significance level of 5% for this example.

- H_0: There is no difference in monthly gym visits before and after promotion.
- H_1: Monthly gym visits decreased after promotion.

- $\alpha = 0.05$, as given above
- $W^+ = 371.5$ and $W^- = 124.5$, as calculated above
- $n_W = 31$ (there are 31 non-zero differences)

As $n_W \geq 25$, we can use the sampling distribution of W described on page 315.

We can focus on either W^+ or W^-. Because the sampling distribution of W is symmetric, P($W \geq$ largest rank sum) = P($W \leq$ smallest rank sum). This is a one-tailed test, so the p-value will be P($W^+ \geq 371.5$) = P($W^- \leq 124.5$). To see why this is so, remember that the alternative hypothesis is that monthly gym visits decreased after the person received a promotion. If this were true, then the number of before promotion monthly gym visits would generally be higher than the after promotion gym visits. Because the order of subtraction was [(before promotion) − (after promotion)], the alternative hypothesis implies more positive differences than negative ones. This also means that the sum of the ranks of the positive differences should be large, and the sum of the ranks of the negative differences should be small. A large W^+ or a small W^- would provide evidence in favour of the alternative hypothesis, contrary to the null hypothesis.

This does not mean that you can ignore the order of subtraction. In this problem, if the largest rank sum was W^-, this would seem to indicate that gym visits *increased* after promotion! So that you do not miss this situation (somewhat unlikely, given H$_1$), you should always think about the order of subtraction in these problems when you are doing a one-tailed test.

Suppose we focus on W^+.

$$\mu_W = \frac{n_W(n_W + 1)}{4} = \frac{31(31 + 1)}{4} = 248$$

$$\sigma_W = \sqrt{\frac{n_W(n_W + 1)(2n_W + 1)}{24}} = \sqrt{\frac{31(31 + 1)(2(31) + 1)}{24}} = 51.0294$$

$$z = \frac{W^+ - \mu_W}{\sigma_W} = \frac{371.5 - 248}{51.0294} = 2.42$$

The p-value = P($W^+ \geq 371.5$) = P($z \geq 2.42$) = $1 - 0.9922 = 0.0078$. The p-value is very small. If the null hypothesis were true, it would be highly unlikely that we could get a sample result like the one we got. The sample evidence gives us reason to reject the null hypothesis. There is sufficient evidence to suggest that individuals who received a promotion reduced their monthly visits to the gym.

You should notice two things about Example 9.2a. First, the conclusion is stated in language that relates to the original example, and is understandable, even by someone who did not fully understand the details of the analysis. Second, this is just a hypothesis test like any of the others we have already done. Once the initial conditions are examined and the correct sampling distribution is identified, the process is the same as usual.

As well, you should now be able to see why the Wilcoxon Signed Rank Sum Test is called a *distribution-free* technique: the decision is made based on the *ranks* of the differences; the distribution of the actual differences does not matter (although the two samples should have similar distributions). This technique is also sometimes referred to as a *non-parametric* technique, because the null and alternative hypotheses do not refer to a population parameter such as μ.

Using the Excel Add-in and Template for Sample Sizes $\geq$ 25   There is no built-in data analysis tool in Excel to allow you to conduct a Wilcoxon Signed Rank Sum Test. Some Excel add-ins are available on the CD that comes with this text, however, and once these add-ins are installed (see the instructions on p. ii), you will be able to use Excel to calculate the sums of the ranks for the Wilcoxon Signed Rank Sum Test. Click on Tools on the Excel toolbar, then click on Non-Parametric Tools. . . , then choose Wilcoxon Signed Rank Sum Test Calculations, as illustrated in Exhibit 9.24 below.

Instructions

Excel Dialogue Box for Non-Parametric Tools

9.24

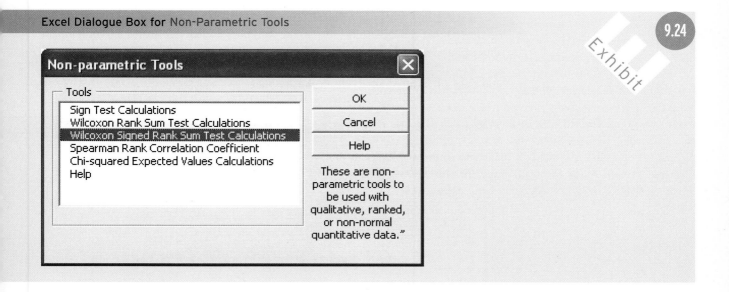

The next dialogue box is shown in Exhibit 9.25.

Excel Dialogue Box for Wilcoxon Signed Rank Sum Test Calculations

9.25

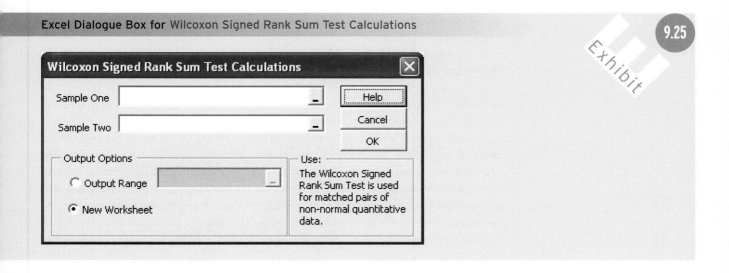

You must indicate where the sample data are located, and where you want the output to go. The output will be as shown below in Exhibit 9.26.

9.26

Wilcoxon Signed Rank Sum Test Calculations **Output**

Wilcoxon Signed Rank Sum Test Calculations	
sample size	31
W$^+$	371.5
W$^-$	124.5

You can then use the worksheet template called "WSRST matched pairs" (available on the CD that comes with the text, in the workbook called "Templates"). This template should only be used if the number of non-zero differences is at least 25.

Template

Shown below in Exhibit 9.27 is the worksheet template for Example 9.2a. As always, you must fill in the shaded cells in the template.

9.27

Worksheet Template for Wilcoxon Signed Rank Sum Test

Making Decisions About Matched Pairs, Quantitative Data, Non-Normal Differences (WSRST)	
sample size	31
is the sample size at least 25?	yes
is the histogram of differences symmetric?	yes
W$^+$	371.5
W$^-$	124.5
z-score	2.420173
one-tailed p-value	0.007757
two-tailed p-value	0.015513

Using the Wilcoxon Signed Rank Sum Test Table for Sample Sizes < 25 There is only one more variation when you are dealing with matched pairs of quantitative data with non-normal differences. The sampling distribution outlined on page 315 is approximately normal only for fairly large sample sizes, that is, $n \geq 25$. What if we have a smaller sample? The process is the same. Differences are ranked, and the sums of the ranks are computed. However, we must turn to tables to estimate p-values in these cases, because the sampling distribution is not normal.

As discussed above, when there is no difference in the populations, the sums of the ranks for the positive differences and the negative differences would be about the same. The more different the rank sums are, the more evidence there is of a difference in the populations. The Wilcoxon Signed Rank Sum Test table indicates the rank sums (for a given sample size) that are so different that they provide evidence of a difference in the populations. The tables show these selected rank sums for each sample size (n_W) from 6 to 25.

Some of the rank sums are at the lower end of possible rank sums (referred to as W_L), and some of them are at the upper end of possible rank sums (referred to as W_U).

The table lists just the rank sums with p-values that are either equal to or closest to the common p-values of 0.010, 0.025, and 0.050. An excerpt of the table is shown below in Exhibit 9.28, with $n_W = 10$.

Wilcoxon Signed Rank Sum Test, Critical Values and p-Values

Exhibit 9.28

	W_L	W_U	$P(W \le W_L)$ $= P(W \ge W_U)$
$n_W = 10$	5	50	0.010
	8	47	0.024
	9	46	0.032
	10	45	0.042
	11	44	0.053

For example, in the table above, there is no simple rank sum that has a p-value of 0.025, so the rank sums with p-values just above and below 0.025 are shown.

Suppose you calculated a rank sum of 5.5 with 10 matched pairs. No rank sum of 5.5 is shown in the table above. We can proceed as usual, by identifying where in the table the rank sum of 5.5 would belong, and estimating the p-value accordingly, as Exhibit 9.29 below illustrates.

Wilcoxon Signed Rank Sum Test, Critical Values and p-Values, Estimating p

Exhibit 9.29

	W_L	W_U	$P(W \le W_L)$ $= P(W \ge W_U)$
n_W 5.5	5	50	0.010
	8	47	0.024
	9	46	0.032
	10	45	0.042
	11	44	0.053

The rank sum of 5.5 is between 5 and 8 in the table, so its p-value is between 0.010 and 0.024.

Now that we have seen how the table is set up, we will once again return to the gym visits example, with yet another data set. In the new data set, the differences are non-normal, so we cannot use the t-test from Section 9.1. The sample size is small, so we cannot use the approximately normal sampling distribution of W, as in Example 9.2a. We will conduct a Wilcoxon Signed Rank Sum Test, but use the table to estimate the p-value. The Wilcoxon Signed Rank Sum Test table is on page 462 at the back of the text.

Wilcoxon Signed Rank Sum Test, small sample, raw data

Suppose we return to the gym visits analysis discussed in Example 9.1a, but with different data. The differences are non-normal, and the sample size is < 25. The third data set is shown in Exhibit 9.30.

Gym Visits, Example 9.2b

Exhibit 9.30

Monthly Gym Visits

Person	Before Promotion	After Promotion	Differences [(Before) − (After)]
#1	10	0	10
#2	13	6	7
#3	14	10	4
#4	15	15	0
#5	15	5	10
#6	15	6	9
#7	18	25	−7
#8	22	21	1
#9	23	25	−2
#10	25	20	5

A histogram of the differences is shown in Exhibit 9.31. It is non-normal and somewhat symmetric. With such a small sample size, it is difficult to judge normality or symmetry. We will proceed with the WSRST, but recognize that if we find evidence of a difference in the populations, it could be due to differences in means or shapes or spreads.

Histogram of Gym Visits, Example 9.2b

Exhibit 9.31

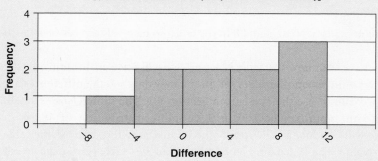

Differences in Monthly Visits to the Gym [(Before Promotion) − (After Promotion)]

The ranking process is illustrated in Exhibit 9.32 below.

Ranking Process Illustration for Gym Visits, Example 9.2b

Monthly Gym Visits

Differences in Monthly Gym Visits [(Before Promotion) − (After Promotion)]	Absolute Value of Differences (Negative Differences Recorded in Red)	Differences Reordered from Smallest to Largest (Absolute Value)	Ranks to Be Assigned	Ranks for Positive Differences	Ranks for Negative Differences
10	10	0	ignore	ignore	ignore
7	7	1	1	1	
4	4	2	2		2
0	0	4	3	3	
10	10	5	4	4	
9	9	7	5	(5 + 6)/2 = 5.5	
−7	7	7	6		(5 + 6)/2 = 5.5
1	1	9	7	7	
−2	2	10	8	(8 + 9)/2 = 8.5	
5	5	10	9	(8 + 9)/2 = 8.5	
		sum of the ranks	45	$W^+ = 37.5$	$W^- = 7.5$

A quick inspection of the table makes it clear that there are many more positive differences than negative ones in this example. As a result, $W^+ = 37.5$, which is much higher than $W^- = 7.5$. But of course, we expect some sampling variability, so we need to know if the ranks are different enough for us to suggest that there is a pattern in the differences.

First, set up the hypothesis test. Use $\alpha = 0.025$ in this case.

- H_0: The populations of monthly gym visits are the same for individuals before and after promotion.
- H_1: The population of monthly gym visits before an individual received a promotion is different from the population of monthly gym visits after the promotion.
- $\alpha = 0.025$, as given above
- $W^+ = 37.5$ and $W^- = 7.5$, as calculated above
- $n_W = 9$ (there are 9 non-zero differences)

Let's focus on W^+ (we could also have chosen to focus on W^-). The question is whether a W of 37.5 gives us sufficient evidence to reject the null hypothesis. We have to refer to the Wilcoxon Signed Rank Sum Test table on page 462 to find out. We want to know $P(W^+ \geq 37.5)$ for this sample, when $n_W = 9$. An excerpt from the table is shown below in Exhibit 9.33, for $n_W = 9$.

There is no rank sum of 37.5 in the table, so we can proceed as usual. We can identify where in the table the rank sum would belong, and estimate the *p*-value accordingly.

9.33

Wilcoxon Signed Rank Sum Test, Critical Values and p-Values

	W_L	W_U	$P(W \le W_L)$ $\ne P(W \ge W_U)$
$n_W = 9$	3	42	0.010
	5	40	0.020
	6	39	0.027
	8	37	0.049
	9	36	0.064

37.5

The rank sum calculated in Example 9.2b is 37.5. It is between 37 and 39, so the
p-value is between 0.049 and 0.027. Since this is > 0.025, we fail to reject the null
hypothesis. In this case, there is insufficient evidence to suggest that population of
monthly visits to the gym before the promotion is different from the population of
monthly visits to the gym after the promotion.

Guide to Decision Making

Matched Pairs, Quantitative Data, Non-Normal Differences—The Wilcoxon Signed Rank Sum Test

When:
- matched pairs of quantitative data, non-normally distributed differences
- trying to make a decision about the average difference in the matched observations

Steps:
1. Specify H_0, the null hypothesis, which is that the population locations are the same.
2. Specify H_1, the alternative hypothesis.
3. Determine or identify α, the significance level.
4. Collect or identify the sample data. Identify or calculate the differences between the matching observations in the samples (keeping the order of subtraction consistent).
5. Check for normality of sample differences with a histogram. If the histogram of differences appears normal, use the *t*-test (described on p. 307). If the histogram of differences is non-normal, check that it is fairly symmetric.
6. *If* the histogram of differences is non-normal and fairly symmetric, identify or calculate n_W, the number of non-zero differences between the matching observations in the samples.
7. Rank the absolute values of the non-zero differences, from 1 to n_W, averaging the ranks for tied differences.
8. Calculate
   - W^+, the sum of the ranks of the positive differences
   - W^-, the sum of the ranks of the negative differences.
9. *If* $n_W \ge 25$, the sampling distribution of W is approximately normal, with

$$\sigma_W = \sqrt{\frac{n_W(n_W + 1)(2n_W + 1)}{24}}$$

$$\mu_W = \frac{n_W(n_W + 1)}{4}$$

Using either W^+ or W^- (choose by thinking about H_1 and the order of subtrac-tion), use the normal sampling distribution to calculate the p-value of the result. When doing this by hand, the calculation will involve the z-score:

$$z = \frac{W - \mu_W}{\sigma_W}$$

10. If $n_W < 25$, use the table on page 462 to approximate the p-value of the chosen W.
11. If p-value $< \alpha$, reject H_0 and conclude that there is sufficient evidence to decide in favour of H_1. If p-value $> \alpha$, fail to reject H_0 and conclude that there is insuf-ficient evidence to decide in favour of H_1.

Quantitative Matched-Pairs Data: Which Test?

We have now looked at matched pairs of quantitative data, and we have presented deci-sion-making techniques to use both when the differences are normally distributed and when they are not.

When the differences are normally distributed, the t-test about the mean applies (you first learned about the t-test in Chapter 7). When the differences are not normally distributed, the Wilcoxon Signed Rank Sum Test can be used. This test will provide evi-dence of differences in population locations, as long as the populations have similar shape and spread.

When deciding whether to use the t-test or the WSRST, we are faced once again with the question: how normal is normal enough? The t-test is robust, but as before, it performs better with larger sample sizes. If there are outliers, do not use the t-test. If the sample size is small (less than about 15 or 20), and the differences are clearly non-normal, do not use the t-test. If the sample size is more than 15 or 20, you can use the t-test, even with some skewness in the histogram of differences. Once samples are as large as 40 or so, the t-test can be used, even if there is significant skewness in the differ-ences. The t-test is preferred to the Wilcoxon Signed Rank Sum Test, if the necessary conditions are met. The t-test is based on the actual data values, while the WSRST is based only on the ranks of the values. Using the WSRST means giving up some infor-mation, and this should be done only if necessary.

DEVELOP YOUR SKILLS 9.2

1. The foreman in a small assembly plant wants to see if a training program has reduced the number of worker errors. The foreman records the weekly number of errors for a random sample of workers before the training, and again after the training. The data set is available on the CD that comes with the text, in the directory called DataChap09. Is there sufficient evidence, at the 4% signif-icance level, to suggest that the training led to a reduced number of worker errors? See file called DYS09-2-1.xls.

2. A small company that specializes in gourmet cookies decides to redesign its packaging. The company owner is certain that the new package will lead to increased sales. Weekly sales at a random sample of stores in the Barrie area are recorded before and after the change in package design. Using the 5% level of significance, ana-lyze the data to see if the owner's idea is correct. The data set is available on the CD that comes with the text, in the directory called DataChap09. It is also shown in Exhibit 9.34. See file called DYS09-2-2.xls.

Exhibit 9.34

Cookie Sales Data, Develop Your Skills 9.2

Weekly Sales Before and After Product Redesign

Store	Sales After	Sales Before
51 Bayfield	942.00	813.67
109 Mapleview Drive	698.71	831.54
137 Wellington	646.10	734.48
6 Collier	976.97	832.46
421 Essa Road	676.44	791.22
19 Queen	793.19	766.73
345 Cundles	607.15	668.66
D-564 Byrne Drive	785.15	631.05
24 Archer	858.87	724.39
15 Short St.	636.04	766.76

3. Telemarketers generally read from a prepared script when they make their sales calls. A firm decides to change this prepared script, making it both friendlier and shorter. The numbers of daily sales are recorded for a random sample of telemarketers, both before and after the script change. The data are shown in Exhibit 9.35 below. Do the data suggest that there is a difference in the numbers of daily sales before and after the script change? Use $\alpha = 0.05$.

Exhibit 9.35

Telemarketers' Numbers of Sales

Sales Before Script Change	Sales After Script Change
52	63
35	45
47	57
69	78
54	55
63	62
47	45
36	29
51	49

4. The Student Services Department at a Prince Edward Island college wants to see if there are differences in the study habits of male and female students. A random sample of female students are selected, and then a corresponding sample of male students is designed— same programs, ages, previous educational experience, and living arrangements (that is, all of the students are living away from their parents). The students are asked to keep track of the number of hours they study over a four-week period. The results are available on the CD that comes with the text, in the directory called DataChap09. Does it appear, based on this data, that male students study less than female students? Use $\alpha = 0.04$. See file called DYS09-2-4.xls.

5. An automobile association has always encouraged its members to check tire pressures regularly. The association wants to demonstrate that maintaining tire pressure results in better fuel consumption. The association selected a random sample of its members, and asked them to record their fuel consumption in litres per 100 km for all of their driving for one month in the summer. It then selected another sample of members whose driving habits and car models were the same as the original sample, and asked these drivers to check and adjust tire pressures every 3–4 days, during the same summer month, and record their fuel consumption again. The data collected are available on the CD that comes with the text, in the directory called DataChap09. Do these data support the association's claim that maintaining tire pressure improves fuel consumption? Use $\alpha = 0.04$. See file called DYS09-2-5.xls.

9.3   MATCHED PAIRS, RANKED DATA—THE SIGN TEST

What if we want to examine matched pairs of ranked data? This section describes the appropriate decision-making technique, which is called the Sign Test.

Suppose an advertising agency wants to analyze the impact of a new advertisement about HDTVs (high definition televisions). The agency selects a random sample of potential consumers of the televisions, and asks them to rate their readiness to buy an HDTV before and after seeing the ad. The ratings are on a scale of 1–4, where 1 corresponds to *unwilling to buy*, and 4 corresponds to *ready to buy*. When the data are ranked, as they are here, we cannot calculate the difference in the corresponding sample values (how do you subtract [(ready to buy) − (unwilling to buy)], for example?). However, we can keep track of whether the difference is positive or negative (e.g., whether the ad increased or decreased the consumer's willingness to buy). We record positive differences with a plus sign, and negative differences with a minus sign, and then we examine the numbers of each in the Sign Test.

If there was no difference in the ratings in the two samples, then the number of positive differences should be about the same as the number of negative differences. About the same number of people would have increased their readiness to buy HDTVs as decreased their readiness to buy, after seeing the ad. We can use a binomial distribution with $p = 0.5$ to test whether the observed number of positive (or negative) differences is significantly different from the expected half-and-half split. If sample sizes are sufficiently large, we can also do a population proportion hypothesis test of $p = 0.5$ (generally we would do this only if the test must be done by hand). Examples 9.3a and 9.3b illustrate the two approaches to this test. In both cases, the test uses techniques you have already learned, and applies the techniques to new situations.

Suppose a polling company found a random sample of Canadian students who were considering going to university. The polling company then asked the students to rate two Canadian universities—one in Ontario and one in British Columbia—using the following rating system: (1) excellent; (2) good; (3) fair; and (4) poor.

The company wants to test the hypothesis that students rate the Ontario university less favourably than the BC university, with a 5% level of significance.

Sign Test, small sample, raw data

The results for the university ratings are shown in Exhibit 9.36 on the next page.

Exhibit

9.36

University Ratings

Ontario University Rating	BC University Rating
2	1
3	4
4	4
1	2
4	1
2	1
1	1
2	1
2	1
3	2
2	2
4	2
2	2
4	3
4	2
4	1
3	3
4	2
2	3
2	3

Once again, it is clear that we have a matched-pairs experiment. It makes sense to compare the rating of the Ontario university with the rating of the BC university by the same student. The data are ranked. Again, we will examine the data set of differences, but we cannot simply calculate the differences in the numerical ratings because the results would not be meaningful. Instead, we keep track only of whether the Ontario university's numerical rating was higher or lower than that of the BC university by the same student.

Exhibit 9.37 shows the data again, with an extra column. The column records a + whenever the numerical value of the Ontario university rating is higher than the numerical value of the BC university rating, a 0 when the student gave the university the same numerical rating, and a − when the numerical value of the Ontario university rating is lower than the numerical value of the BC university rating.

It is simplest, and most computer-friendly, simply to subtract the numerical values of the ratings to determine the pluses and minuses. This means that you will always have to think carefully about what a plus or a minus means when you are conducting this test. (As always, the order of subtraction must be consistent.)

In this example, a higher *numerical* rating means a less favourable *actual* opinion—since the highest rating is 1. This is often the case ("We're number one!" is usually a good thing), but it is not always the case. We subtracted as follows: [(Ontario university rating) − (BC university rating)]. This results in a plus sign whenever the numerical value of the Ontario university rating is higher. A plus sign occurs whenever the student rates the Ontario university less favourably than the BC university.

Positive or Negative Differences in University Ratings

Ontario University Rating	BC University Rating	Ontario Rating Versus BC Rating
2	1	+
3	4	−
4	4	0
1	2	−
4	1	+
2	1	+
1	1	0
2	1	+
2	1	+
3	2	+
2	2	0
4	2	+
2	2	0
4	3	+
4	2	+
4	1	+
3	3	0
4	2	+
2	3	−
2	3	−

In this data set, we have observed 11 plus signs, 4 minus signs, and 5 cases of no difference. The polling company wants to test the hypothesis H_1: students rate the Ontario university less favourably than the BC university. Now we have to decide whether this sample evidence supports this idea.

With the Sign Test, we ignore cases where there is no difference in the rating, so the sample size (adjusted for the Sign Test) is $n_{ST} = 15$. With 15 non-zero differences, we would expect about 7.5 (that is, 7 or 8) to be positive and 7.5 to be negative.

We can focus on either the number of pluses or the number of minuses because we are testing to see if there is about a half-and-half split in plus signs and minus signs. The binomial distribution will be symmetric, because $p = 0.5$: $P(n^+ \geq 11) = P(n^- \leq 4)$.

This does not mean that you can ignore the order of subtraction. In this problem, if the results were reversed ($n^+ = 4$, $n^- = 11$), this would seem to indicate that students rated the Ontario university more highly than the BC university! So that you do not miss this situation (somewhat unlikely, given H_1), you should always think about the order of subtraction in these problems when you are doing a one-tailed test.

In this case, we have been focusing on whether the student ratings of the Ontario university are less favourable than the BC student ratings, so we will focus on the plus signs. We observed 11 plus signs. We will use the notation n^+ to refer to the number of plus signs.

The question we have to ask is this: does the result of 11 out of 15 give us convincing evidence that the students rated the Ontario university less favourably than the BC university?

- H_0: Students rate the Ontario and BC universities about the same
- H_1: Students rate the Ontario university less favourably than the BC university
- The polling company wants to use $\alpha = 0.05$.
- The p-value will be $P(n^+ \geq 11, n_{ST} = 15, p = 0.5)$.

This is a binomial probability calculation. As we discussed in Chapter 5, we can use the binomial distribution here, even though we do not have a *true* binomial experiment (we are sampling without replacement). As long as the sample size is $< 5\%$ of the population, the binomial distribution will still give us a good estimate of the probability. It is clear that the sample size of 15 is $< 5\%$ of the total population of Canadian students considering going to university.

Of course, we can use Excel to calculate the *p*-value. In this case, we can also use the tables in the text. Locate the binomial table where $n = 9$, and find the column in which $p = 0.50$. The calculation (similar to the ones we did in Chapter 5) is as follows.

$$p\text{-value} = P(n^+ \geq 11) = 1 - P(n^+ \leq 10) = 1 - 0.941 = 0.059$$

Since *p*-value $> \alpha$, we fail to reject H_0. There is insufficient evidence to suggest that students rate the Ontario university less favourably than the BC university.

Instructions

Using the Excel Add-in and Template for Small Sample Sizes   There is an Excel add-in that will calculate the number of positive and negative differences for matched-pairs ranked data. Once the add-in is installed, click on Tools on the Excel toolbar, then click on Non-Parametric Tools . . . , then choose Sign Test Calculations. The next dialogue box is self-explanatory, as shown in Exhibit 9.38 below.

Exhibit
9.38

Excel Dialogue Box for Sign Test Calculations

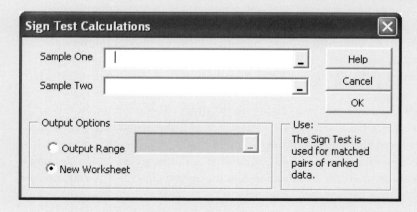

You must indicate where the sample data are located, and where you want the output to go. The output will be as shown opposite in Exhibit 9.39.

Excel Output for Sign Test Calculations

Exhibit

Sign Test Calculations	
# of non-zero differences	15
# of positive differences	11
# of negative differences	4

There is a worksheet template called "Sign Test," in the Templates workbook on the CD that comes with the text. You can use this template to complete the hypothesis test for matched pairs of ranked data. A completed template for the university rating problem is shown below in Exhibit 9.40. As usual, you must fill in the blue-shaded cells in the template.

Template

Completed Excel Template for Making Decisions About Matched Pairs, Ranked Data (Sign Test)

9.40
Exhibit

Making Decisions About Matched Pairs, Ranked Data (Sign Test)	
# of non-zero differences	15
# of positive differences	11
# of negative differences	4
one-tailed p-value	0.059235
two-tailed p-value	0.1 18469

The template is also useful if you have only summary data from the samples.

Using the Sampling Distribution of $\hat{p}$ for Large Sample Sizes   If the sample size is fairly large, it is possible to do the Sign Test as a hypothesis test of $p = 0.50$. Because $p = 0.50$, we know that the underlying binomial distribution will be symmetric. However, with smaller sample sizes, the normal approximation is not very accurate (a continuity correction factor is required, as discussed in Chapter 6), and your approach should be to use the template shown above. If the sample size is fairly large, however, and you have to do the problem by hand, you can use the approach illustrated in Example 9.3b below.

When we want to work with the sampling distribution of $\hat{p}$, we have to check for normality, which requires np and $nq \geq 10$. In every case of the Sign Test, because we are checking for *no difference in the ratings*, we use a null hypothesis of $p = 0.50$. This means that $q = 0.50$ as well. So, whenever $n \geq 20$, both np and nq will be ≥ 10.

A fine living magazine asked its subscribers to rate two local restaurants—Jane's Fish and Chips and Archie's Tea Room. Response rates were high, because the magazine was going to randomly select one respondent to receive a free meal for two at one of the two restaurants being rated. (Are the target and sampled populations actually the same here? Should this be a concern?)

There were 280 responses. Of those, 26 rated the two restaurants the same. Of the 254 remaining respondents, 145 rated Jane's Fish and Chips higher than Archie's Tea

9.3b
Example

Sign Test, large sample, summary data, using sampling distribution of $\hat{p}$

Room. From this sample, is there evidence that this magazine's subscribers rate Jane's Fish and Chips higher than Archie's Tea Room (the magazine has more than 7,000 subscribers)? Use $\alpha = 0.025$.

Since we are interested in cases where Jane's Fish and Chips gets higher ratings than Archie's Tea Room, we will calculate this proportion as $\hat{p} = \dfrac{145}{254} = 0.570866$.

Take a minute to think about the focus of the analysis. It is important to realize that if Jane's restaurant is rated higher, this is the same as Archie's restaurant being rated lower. These are just two different ways of describing the same condition.

Let's proceed with a hypothesis test like the ones we did in Chapter 7. The underlying distribution is the binomial. Although we are sampling without replacement, we are told that the magazine has more than 7,000 subscribers. A sample of 280 represents only 4% of the population, and so the binomial distribution will be a reasonable model.

- H_0: $p = 0.50$, that is, Archie's restaurant and Jane's restaurant are rated about the same
- H_1: $p > 0.50$ (with p defined as the proportion of times that Jane's restaurant is rated higher than Archie's restaurant)
- $\alpha = 0.025$

We check for normality of the sampling distribution of $\hat{p}$, and note that $n_{ST} = 254 > 20$, so the conditions are met.

We are using the normal approximation to the binomial in this case so that we can complete the test by hand (if a computer is available, there is no reason to use the approximation). We know from Chapter 7 that the standard error of the sample proportion is

$$\sigma_{\hat{p}} = \sqrt{\dfrac{pq}{n_{ST}}} = \sqrt{\dfrac{(0.5)(0.5)}{254}} = 0.03137279$$

so the z-score will be

$$z = \dfrac{\hat{p} - p}{\sigma_{\hat{p}}} = \dfrac{\hat{p} - p}{\sqrt{\dfrac{pq}{n_{ST}}}} = \dfrac{0.570866 - 0.5}{0.03137279} = 2.26$$

Using the normal tables, we find the p-value as $P(\hat{p} \geq 0.570866) \doteq P(z \geq 2.26) = (1 - 0.9881) = 0.0119$. Since this is less than 0.025, the significance level of the hypothesis test, we will reject the null hypothesis. There is sufficient evidence to suggest that the magazine's subscribers rate Jane's Fish and Chips higher than Archie's Tea Room. Remember to state the conclusion in terms of the original problem. Concluding that there is evidence that $p > 0.50$ here would be technically correct, but not helpful!

As well, in this case, the sample is self-selected, so we have to be careful about interpreting results. Respondents might have been motivated by the promise of winning a free meal, and their opinions might differ from the population of magazine subscribers.

Guide to Decision Making

Matched Pairs, Ranked Data—The Sign Test

When:
- matched pairs of ranked data
- trying to make a decision about the average difference in the matched observations

Steps:
1. Specify H_0, the null hypothesis.
2. Specify H_1, the alternative hypothesis.
3. Determine or identify α, the significance level.
4. Collect or identify the sample data. Identify or count:

   - the number of times sample 1 values are greater than sample 2 values (the + signs), n^+
   - the number of times sample 1 values are less than sample 2 values (the − signs), n^-
   - n_{ST}, the number of non-zero differences between the matching observations in the samples

5. Using the binomial distribution with n_{ST} trials, $p = 0.5$, calculate the p-value for either n^+ or n^- (depending on H_1 and the way the comparison was made). When doing the problem by hand, with a sufficiently large sample size, conduct this as

   a test of $p = 0.50$, with the p-value based on $z = \dfrac{\hat{p} - p}{s_{\hat{p}}} = \dfrac{\hat{p} - p}{\sqrt{\dfrac{pq}{n_{ST}}}}$.

6. If p-value $< \alpha$, reject H_0 and conclude that there is sufficient evidence to decide in favour of H_1. If p-value $> \alpha$, fail to reject H_0 and conclude that there is insufficient evidence to decide in favour of H_1.

DEVELOP YOUR SKILLS 9.3

1. A marketing team wanted to run a taste test between a particular brand of cola and its major competitor. A random sample of 16 cola drinkers were selected. Each was asked to taste a sample of the two colas and say which one they preferred, if any. The order in which the colas were tasted was randomly assigned. Of the 16 testers, 1 preferred the colas equally, and 9 preferred cola A. Is there evidence, at the 5% level of significance, that cola A is preferred by cola drinkers?

2. A Honda automobile dealer was interested in how well his sales staff compared with the salespeople at the Ford dealership across the road, in terms of the overall experience of buying a car. The Honda dealer hired a research organization to investigate. The research company selected a group of adults who had some car buying experience, and asked them to shop for (but not to buy) a particular make and model of car—one at the Honda dealer and one at the Ford dealer—and then rate their experiences on the following scale: (1) the best car-shopping experience I have ever had; (2) a very positive experience; (3) some positive and some negative aspects; (4) a very negative experience; and (5) the worst car-shopping experience I have ever had. The results are shown in Exhibit 9.41. At the 4% significance level, is there any evidence of a difference in the ratings for the two auto dealerships?

9.41

Car Shopping Experience

Shopper	Rating for Ford Dealer	Rating for Honda Dealer
1	5	1
2	2	3
3	3	4
4	4	2
5	2	3
6	2	2
7	5	1
8	3	2
9	3	3

3. A number of economic analysts were asked to rate their expectations for the economies of North America and Europe over the coming year, according to the following scale: (4) prospects are very promising; (3) prospects are promising in terms of growth, but with some potential for slowdown; (2) the economy is expected to slow down from the previous year; and (1) a serious downturn is expected. The analysts' ratings are shown in Exhibit 9.42 below. At the 3% level of significance, is there evidence that all economic analysts rate prospects for the North American and European economies differently?

9.42

Analysts' Ratings of Economic Prospects for North America and Europe

Analyst	Rating for North America	Rating for Europe
1	3	4
2	2	3
3	4	2
4	3	2
5	3	1
6	2	3
7	3	2
8	3	2
9	3	4
10	2	1
11	4	4

4. A random sample of 250 attendees of a wine and cheese festival were asked to rate Californian and French wines. Of the 250, 25 rated the wines about equal. Of the remainder, 150 rated Californian wines higher than French wines. At the 3% level of significance, is there evidence to suggest that all wine drinkers rate Californian wines higher than French wines?

5. An advertising agency wants to analyze the impact of a new advertisement about HDTVs (high definition televisions). The agency selects a random sample of potential consumers of the televisions, and asks them to rate their readiness to buy an HDTV before and after seeing the ad. The ratings are on a scale of 1–4, where 1 corresponds to *unwilling to buy*, and 4 corresponds to *ready to buy*.

The data set is available on the CD that comes with this text, in the directory called DataChap09. Is there evidence, at the 5% significance level, that consumers' willingness to buy would be higher after seeing the ad? Do this question with the Excel template, and compare your answer to the results you get when you do it by hand. See file called DYS09-3-5.xls.

Set

All of the techniques in this chapter apply to matched-pairs data. There are two situations when sample data are matched pairs:

1. *A matched-pairs experimental study* —There is a measurement or count, followed by an action of some kind, followed by a second measurement or count.
2. *A matched-pairs observational study* —There is a matching or pairing of observations, designed so that it is easier to decide what caused any observed change between the observations.

In all cases with matched pairs, it is essential that the order of subtraction (or comparison) be consistent. As well, you will have to think a bit about what the order of subtraction tells you about the alternative hypothesis, so that you can do the correct *p*-value calculation (or estimation).

Chapter Summary

9

Matched Pairs, Quantitative Data, Normal Differences–The *t*-Test

When the quantitative matched-pairs data have normally distributed differences, a *t*-test of the mean difference is used to make decisions. The null hypothesis is always that there is no difference, on average, between the two measurements for the matched pairs. A comparison is made of a null hypothesis $H_0: \mu_D = 0$ with one of three possible alternative hypotheses:

- $\mu_D > 0$,
- $\mu_D < 0$, or
- $\mu_D \neq 0$.

A decision about which of the three possible alternative hypotheses to use will depend on the context of the analysis, *and the order of subtraction* used to arrive at the differences.

The *t*-score is calculated as follows, with the subscript *D* reminding us that we are looking at a data set of differences:

$$t = \frac{\bar{x}_D - \mu_D}{s_D \big/ \sqrt{n_D}}, \text{ with } n_D - 1 \text{ degrees of freedom}$$

If you have raw or summary data, you can use the template illustrated on page 303 to make your calculations in Excel (as Example 9.1b on p. 305 illustrates). With raw sample data, you can also use the Excel data analysis tool "*t*-Test: Paired Two Sample for Means" (see p. 304). Its use is demonstrated on page 305, with data from Example 9.1a. A Guide to Decision Making for matched pairs, quantitative data, normal differences is shown on page 307.

Matched Pairs, Quantitative Data, Non-Normal Differences–The Wilcoxon Signed Rank Sum Test

When the histogram of differences for quantitative data is not normally distributed (particularly with small sample sizes), the Wilcoxon Signed Rank Sum Test is used to make decisions. The requirement is that the sample histograms be similar in shape and spread (or, equivalently, the histogram of differences is symmetric). The null hypothesis is that there is no difference in the population locations.

The absolute values of differences are ranked from smallest to largest. When differences are tied, the associated ranks are averaged. The sums of the ranks for the positive and negative differences are calculated. Differences of zero are ignored. The procedure for assigning ranks is described on page 313.

When n_W, the number of non-zero differences, is at least 25, an approximately normal sampling distribution can be used, with a *z*-score of

$$z = \frac{W - \mu_W}{\sigma_W} = \frac{W - \left(\dfrac{n_W(n_W + 1)}{4} \right)}{\sqrt{\dfrac{n_W(n_W + 1)(2n_W + 1)}{24}}}$$

The Excel add-ins that come with the text (Non-Parametric Tools) contain a tool called Wilcoxon Signed Rank Sum Test Calculations that will calculate the W^+ and W^- for the Wilcoxon Signed Rank Sum Test. You can then use the worksheet template titled "Making Decisions About Matched Pairs, Quantitative Data, Non-Normal Differences (WSRST)" for p-value calculations when the sample size is ≥ 25. See page 320.

When $n_W < 25$, the table on page 463 should be used to estimate p-values to make decisions, as Example 9.2b on page 322 illustrates.

A Guide to Decision Making for matched pairs, quantitative data, non-normal differences is shown on page 324.

Matched Pairs, Ranked Data–The Sign Test

When the data are ranked, the corresponding sample data points cannot be subtracted (what does [(good) – (excellent)] mean?). However, we can keep track of whether differences are positive or negative. If there is no difference in the rankings of the matched pairs, on average, then the number of positive differences should be about equal to the number of negative differences (again, for this test, differences of zero are ignored).

This binomial probability distribution, with $p = 0.50$, can be used to calculate the p-value of the sample result, as Example 9.3a on page 327 illustrates. There is no built-in data analysis function in Excel to conduct a Sign Test. The Excel add-ins that come with the text (Non-Parametric Tools) contain a tool called Sign Test Calculations that will calculate the numbers of positive and negative differences for a data set. You can then use the worksheet template titled "Making Decisions About Matched Pairs, Ranked Data (Sign Test)" for p-value calculations (see p. 331). If you have to do this test by hand, and the sample size is large, you can make a decision using a hypothesis test of $p = 0.50$, as Example 9.3b on page 331 illustrates.

A Guide to Decision Making for matched pairs, ranked data, is shown on page 333.

CHAPTER REVIEW EXERCISES

1. A new microbrewery has opened in Manitoba. Its aim is to produce an English-style ale, adapted to Canadian tastes. While developing the beer recipe, the company periodically asked a panel of beer drinkers to rate the beer, on a scale of 1 to 5, where 1 is excellent and 5 is undrinkable. The ratings for one taste test are shown below in Exhibit 9.43. At the 5% level of significance, is there evidence of a difference in ratings for the two beer recipes?

Beer Taste Test

Tester	Beer Recipe #3	Beer Recipe #4
1	1	2
2	3	2
3	2	1
4	5	3
5	3	2
6	2	1
7	4	5
8	1	3
9	2	1
10	3	2

2. A random sample of the top 1,000 Canadian companies revealed information about profits in 2004 and 2005 as shown in Exhibit 9.44. Can you conclude that profits increased between 2004 and 2005 for the top 1,000 Canadian companies? Use the 4% level of significance.

Profits for a Random Sample of Top 1000 Canadian Companies

2005 Profit ($ millions)	2004 Profit ($ millions)
89	52.7
70.4	60.2
31.8	16
31	50.8
19.9	17.5
14.3	10.1
14.7	2.6
11.2	14.5
9.7	18.7
5.7	8.8
4.8	14.5
4.8	3.4
3.8	3.7
1.4	4.8
−2.3	−1.6
−87	−58

3. Create a 95% confidence interval estimate for the average difference between Canadian company profits in 2004 and 2005, based on the data shown in Exhibit 9.44 in Exercise 2 above.

4. A large college was interested in the salaries of graduates from its business and computer studies programs. The college randomly selected a number of graduates from each program, and then matched the graduates as closely as possible in terms of age, experience, achievement at school, and location. The college collected data on the annual salaries of the graduates.

CRE09-4.xls
Set

The results are available on the CD that accompanies this text, in the directory called DataChap09. At the 2.5% significance level, is there evidence of a difference in salary between computer studies and business graduates from this college?

5. A random sample of 400 college students were asked to rate two potential designs for the new student centre on campus. Of these, 36 rated the designs equally. Of the remainder, 207 gave a higher rating to the more modern design. At the 2.5% level of significance, is there evidence to suggest that students rate the two designs differently?

6. A new tool is supposed to reduce the time it takes to assemble a component in a factory. A random sample of workers is selected, and the assembly times are measured with and without the new tool. The average difference in assembly time is 3.4 minutes, with a standard deviation of 4.7 minutes. The sample size is 15. You may assume that the differences are normally distributed. Is there evidence, at the 5% level of significance, that the new tool speeds up assembly time? The order of subtraction is [(time without tool) − (time with tool)].

CRE09-7.xls
Set

7. A company hired a consulting firm to conduct a seminar that would improve its workers' self-esteem. Employees were given a test to assess their self-esteem before the seminar, and again afterwards. The test scores are shown in Exhibit 9.45. A higher score indicates higher self-esteem. Is there sufficient evidence, at a 5% significance level, to suggest that the seminar improved employees' self-esteem?

Exhibit 9.45

Results of Employees' Self-Esteem Test

Self-Esteem Test Score Before Seminar	Self-Esteem Test Score After Seminar
70	75
84	89
74	70
61	63
82	88
55	59
43	40
56	63
84	80
67	64
63	61
76	82
62	57
83	79
56	54
44	47
52	56
85	90

8. A random sample of 10 contractors were asked to quote a price for a bathroom renovation in two different houses. The bathroom renovation was technically the same in both houses, with the same amount of labour and materials required, but one house was in a very wealthy neighbourhood and the other was in a run-down neighbourhood. At the 5% level of significance, is there evidence that contractors quote higher prices for jobs in wealthier neighbourhoods? Differences were calculated as [(price for job in wealthy neighbourhood) – (price for job in run-down neighbourhood)]. The average difference was $1,562, with a standard deviation of $578. You may assume that the differences were normally distributed.

9. Construct a 95% confidence interval for the average difference in prices quoted for the bathroom renovation, based on the data in Exercise 8 above.

10. A hardware store is trying to decide which of two new key-cutting machines to purchase. The features of both machines are about equivalent. The store owner decides to assess the speed of the machines. Exhibit 9.46 shows the times (in seconds) to cut copies of a random sample of keys. Is there evidence, at the 4% level of significance, of a difference in speed in the two machines? Which machine would you recommend to the store owner?

11. A restaurant owner wanted to gather some data on customer taste preferences about two new salads on the menu. One salad was mixed greens with a balsamic vinegar and olive oil dressing. The other salad contained greens and fruit, and had a fruit-flavoured dressing. A random sample of diners were selected. Each diner was asked to taste both of the new salads, and indicate which was preferred. There were 35 diners in the sample. Of these, 2 liked the salads equally. Of the remainder, 20 gave a higher rating to the mixed greens salad. Is there evidence, at the 3% level of significance, that diners prefer the mixed greens salad?

Cutting Time for Two Key-Cutting Machines (in seconds)

9.46
Exhibit

Machine A	Machine B
75.7	69.1
78	76.4
67.5	63.5
80.8	78.4
56.5	58.3
77.1	75
64.2	60.4
76.3	79.1
45	39.6
28.6	19.6
61.6	60.9
75.2	70.6
62.1	62.7
59.5	62.1
36.4	37.2

12. A researcher was interested in the price that people would be willing to pay for a spa week-end in the country, compared with the price that they would be willing to pay for a spa week-end in the city. The researcher collected data from a random sample of potential spa cus-tomers. When he created a histogram of the differences, he noted that it was not normal but was fairly symmetric. The researcher used the Wilcoxon Signed Rank Sum Test Calculations add-in, and produced the output shown in Exhibit 9.47 below.

    Is there evidence, at the 3% level of significance, that people are willing to pay more for a spa weekend in the country? The order of subtraction was [(price for country spa week-end) – (price for city spa weekend)].

Excel Output for Spa Research Data

9.47
Exhibit

Wilcoxon Signed Rank Sum Test Calculations	
sample size	75
W^+	1851
W^-	999

13. A large number of workers commute to work at the GM assembly plant in Oshawa, Ontario, every day. The commute can be quite long, depending on traffic conditions. The company decided to experiment with flexible hours for office workers at the plant. A ran-dom sample of these workers were asked to time (in minutes) precisely how long their drive to work took, over a random sample of days. On half of those days, the workers were to leave home to arrive for an 8:00 A.M. start, on the other half, they were to arrive for a 9:00 A.M. start. The average commuting time for each worker was recorded for each start time, and the results are shown on the next page in Exhibit 9.48 on the next page. Is there evidence, at a 4% significance level, that the earlier arrival time reduces the time it takes for workers to commute to work?

CRE09-13.xls
Set

14. An accounting firm is testing a new software program. The company selects a random sam-ple of workers and trains them on the new software until the employees are equally comfort-able with the two programs. These workers are then asked to complete a set of tasks—with

Exhibit **9.48**

Commuting Time for Workers to a GM Plant in Oshawa (in minutes)

8:00 A.M. Start	9:00 A.M. Start
23	15
74	64
116	113
76	89
94	102
56	65
74	80
76	90
72	67
91	95
85	79
93	100
101	100
105	113
91	90
62	66
80	73
57	67
56	70
91	86
67	68
71	80
58	54
89	93
70	83
50	58
76	86
82	74
99	111
52	68

the old software and then with the new software—and keep track of how long (in minutes) the work takes. A 95% confidence interval of the average difference in time is (2.9, 15.3). The order of subtraction was [(time with old software) − (time with new software)]. Without doing any further calculations, what can you conclude about whether the tasks are completed in the same amount of time with the two software programs? What level of significance applies? Which software program would you recommend? Explain your reasoning.

15. A company decides to test two package designs for canned soup by placing cans with each design at opposite ends of the soup aisle in a random sample of 25 supermarkets. Data were collected on weekly sales for each soup. Differences in sales were symmetric, but not normally distributed. The rank sum of the positive differences was 276, and the rank sum of the negative differences was 49. Is there sufficient evidence to suggest that sales of the soup in the two different packages differ? Use $\alpha = 0.05$.

16. The manager of a financial planning firm is trying to train her staff to make greater use of their working time. To see if this training is having any effect, she keeps track of monthly new business generated before and after the training, for all six staff members. The results are as shown in Exhibit 9.49. Has the manager's training resulted in increased new business? Use $\alpha = 0.025$. You may assume that the differences are normally distributed.

New Business Generated Before and After Training

9.49

Exhibit

Staff Member	Monthly New Business Before Training ($000s)	Monthly New Business After Training ($000s)
Shirley	230	240
Tom	150	165
Janice	100	90
Brian	50	100
Ed	340	330
Kim	500	505

17. Create a 95% confidence interval estimate for the average difference in monthly new business before training and after training. Based on your answer to Exercise 16, would you expect this interval to contain zero?

18. Repeat the analysis for Exercise 16 above, but this time assume that the differences are not normally distributed.

19. A dairy products company is developing a new organic yogurt. The company assembles a panel of tasters to compare two possible formulations of the new product. The panelists are asked to rate the taste of each yogurt on a scale of 1 to 5, with 1 corresponding to *absolutely delicious*, and 5 corresponding to *inedible*. The results of the taste test are shown below in Exhibit 9.50. Is there evidence, at the 2.5% level of significance, that the tasters prefer one yogurt recipe over the other?

Taste Test of Yogurt Formulations

9.50

Exhibit

Taster	Recipe #1	Recipe #2
1	1	2
2	4	1
3	2	3
4	5	4
5	3	2
6	2	1
7	3	2

20. A drill manufacturer wants to draw attention to a new design, which theoretically allows quicker changes between drill bits. The manufacturer gathers a random sample of amateurs who have some experience using drills around the home. These people are asked to complete a prescribed set of tasks with the new drill and with the old drill (which drill is used first is randomly assigned). The total time to complete the tasks (in minutes) is recorded, for each drill. The order of subtraction is [(time with the new-style drill) – (time with the old-style drill)]. The average difference is –5.2, with a standard deviation of 12.2. Is there sufficient evidence to suggest that the tasks are completed more quickly with the new-style drill? Use $\alpha = 0.05$. You may assume that the differences in completion times are normally distributed.

 **MyStatLab** Go to MyStatLab at www.mystatlab.com. You can practise many of this chapter's exercises as often as you want. The guided solutions help you find an answer step by step. You'll find a personalized study plan available to you too!

Making 10 Decisions with Two Independent Samples, Quantitative or Ranked Data

Learning Objectives

After mastering the material in this chapter, you will be able to:

1. Choose and conduct the appropriate hypothesis test to compare two populations, based on independent samples, for normal quantitative data.

2. Choose and conduct the appropriate hypothesis test to compare two populations, based on independent samples, for non-normal quantitative or ranked data.

INTRODUCTION

Suppose that a doughnut shop is considering opening a new location in the downtown area. After considering many criteria, the manager has narrowed the choices down to two. All other things being about equal, she wants to choose the location with greater pedestrian traffic. The manager hires a student to count the number of pedestrians passing by each of the two locations, on a random sample of days.

The result of the survey will be two independent samples. When samples are independent, there is no relationship between, for example, observation #1 from sample 1 and observation #1 from sample 2. Conclusions about differences in populations based on independent samples are not as strong as those based on matched pairs (as was discussed in Chapter 9).

Despite the weaker conclusions, independent samples are often used because they are less costly to obtain. In other cases, matched-pairs experiments would not be appropriate or even possible. For example, it would be impossible to design a sensible matched-pairs experiment to compare amounts of pedestrian traffic at the two potential doughnut shop locations: there are too many factors that might contribute to different traffic levels, and they cannot all be controlled.

Making a decision about which store location actually has more pedestrian traffic (if there is a difference) requires a hypothesis test of the difference between two means, which is covered in Section 10.1. As you might expect, the kind of test required depends on the normality of the populations.

In Section 10.2, we will examine comparisons of two independent samples when the populations do not appear to be normal. The hypothesis test that we'll use is another non-parametric test, the Wilcoxon Rank Sum Test (WRST). The WRST has some similarities to the Wilcoxon Signed Rank Sum Test covered in Chapter 9, and so you should find it fairly easy to understand. The WRST can also be used to compare independent samples of ranked data, and this is also discussed in Section 10.2.

INDEPENDENT SAMPLES, NORMAL QUANTITATIVE DATA–THE *t*-TEST

Let's return to the doughnut shop location decision described in the introduction. After considering many criteria for the location decision, the manager wants to focus on pedestrian traffic at the two locations. The manager believes the traffic at location 2 to be higher, but she decides to gather some data to check her belief. A survey over 45 days reveals that location 1 has an average of 108.4 pedestrians per day, and location 2 has an average of 124.4 pedestrians per day. But there is considerable variability in the daily traffic patterns, so is this really evidence that location 2 actually gets more pedestrian traffic, on average? Or is the difference in the two sample means only due to sampling variability?

The manager wants to know if μ_1 (the average daily pedestrian traffic at location 1) is smaller than μ_2 (the average daily pedestrian traffic at location 2). As in the matched-pairs analysis, the focus is the differences, this time between μ_1 and μ_2. Usually (although not always), the null hypothesis is that there is no difference between the two averages—that is, $\mu_1 - \mu_2 = 0$. This leaves three possibilities for the alternative hypothesis:

- If the population 1 mean is greater than the population 2 mean, then $\mu_1 - \mu_2 > 0$.
- If the population 1 mean is less than the population 2 mean, then $\mu_1 - \mu_2 < 0$.
- If the population 1 mean is different from the population 2 mean, then $\mu_1 - \mu_2 \neq 0$.

Of course, we will examine the difference between the two sample means (that is, $\bar{x}_1 - \bar{x}_2$) in order to decide. We need to know what the sampling distribution of $\bar{x}_1 - \bar{x}_2$ looks like in order to make a decision.

Sampling Distribution of $\bar{x}_1 - \bar{x}_2$ with Two Independent Samples

The sampling distribution of $\bar{x}_1 - \bar{x}_2$ is normally distributed if the populations are normal.

1. The standard error of the sampling distribution is

$$\sigma_{\bar{x}_1 - \bar{x}_2} = \sqrt{\frac{\sigma_1^2}{n_1} + \frac{\sigma_2^2}{n_2}}$$

2. The mean of the sampling distribution is

$$\mu_{\bar{x}_1 - \bar{x}_2} = \mu_1 - \mu_2$$

As discussed in Chapter 6, the sampling distributions of the sample means will be approximately normal as long as the populations are not extremely non-normal, or sample sizes are fairly large. The sampling distribution of the differences in the means will also be approximately normal under these conditions.

This information about the sampling distribution cannot be directly applied, as we do not know what σ_1 or σ_2 (the true population standard deviations) are. We have to approximate σ_1 and σ_2 with the sample estimates, that is, s_1 and s_2. We will proceed by using them in place of the unknown population parameters in the formula (as we have before). This means that the test statistic will become

$$t = \frac{(\bar{x}_1 - \bar{x}_2) - \mu_{\bar{x}_1 - \bar{x}_2}}{s_{\bar{x}_1 - \bar{x}_2}} = \frac{(\bar{x}_1 - \bar{x}_2) - (\mu_1 - \mu_2)}{\sqrt{\dfrac{s_1^2}{n_1} + \dfrac{s_2^2}{n_2}}}$$

When we estimate both standard deviations, the resulting sampling distribution is not actually a t-distribution, but fortunately it can be approximated with a t-distribution. Perhaps unfortunately, the approximate degrees of freedom for the relevant t-distribution are as follows:

$$df = \frac{\left(\dfrac{s_1^2}{n_1} + \dfrac{s_2^2}{n_2}\right)^2}{\dfrac{\left(\dfrac{s_1^2}{n_1}\right)^2}{(n_1 - 1)} + \dfrac{\left(\dfrac{s_2^2}{n_2}\right)^2}{(n_2 - 1)}}$$

Using Data Analysis t-Test: Two-Sample Assuming Unequal Variances   It should be obvious that such an expression is best evaluated by computer (although it is certainly possible to do it with a calculator). Excel has a built-in Data Analysis tool that supports hypothesis testing of the difference in means for normal data, with independent samples. It can be used when you have the raw data from the samples on which the analysis is based.

Instructions

Exhibit 10.1 below shows the Data Analysis menu from Tools. The correct choice is as highlighted: t-Test: Two-Sample Assuming Unequal Variances.

10.1

Exhibit

Excel Data Analysis Dialogue Box

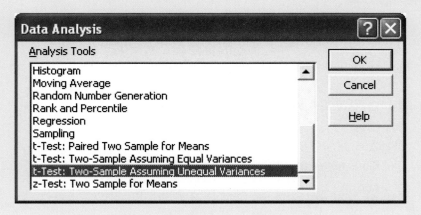

As always, you should set up the hypothesis test and do your thinking before you turn to the computer. Example 10.1a illustrates.

Set
EXA10-1a.xls

t-test for independent samples, raw data

The manager of a doughnut shop is trying to decide between two potential locations for a new shop. The manager believes the traffic at location 2 to be higher, but she decides to gather some data to check her belief. The data that were collected for the pedestrian traffic study for the doughnut shop are available on the CD that comes with the text, in the directory DataChap10.

- $H_0: \mu_1 - \mu_2 = 0$ (that is, there is no difference in the means of the two populations; this is the null hypothesis in most cases)
- $H_1: \mu_1 - \mu_2 < 0$ (this is based on our question: does location 2 actually get more pedestrian traffic?)
- Use $\alpha = 0.04$

The first thing we must assess is the normality of the populations. As usual, we do that by creating histograms of the sample data. The histograms shown below in Exhibit 10.2 are reasonably normal. Both sample sizes are fairly large, at 45, and so we can proceed.

Histograms of Daily Pedestrian Traffic at Two Potential Doughnut Shop Locations

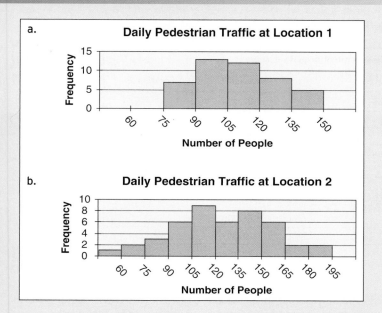

Exhibit 10.3 on the next page shows the *t*-Test dialogue box.

Instructions

t-Test **Dialogue Box**

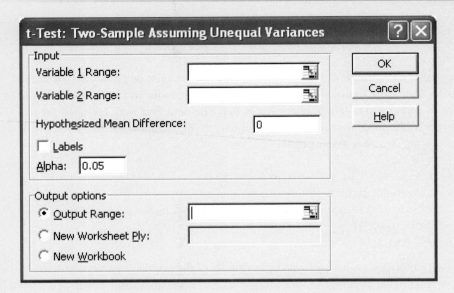

Exhibit **10.3**

The dialogue box requires you to indicate where the sample data are stored (Variable 1 Range: and Variable 2 Range:). As indicated in Exhibit 10.3 above, the Hypothesized Mean Difference is usually zero (although there are instances when it is another value). The Excel output is shown below in Exhibit 10.4.

Exhibit **10.4**

Excel Output for *t*-Test: Two-Sample Assuming Unequal Variances

t-Test: Two-Sample Assuming Unequal Variances		
	Location 1	*Location 2*
Mean	108.3778	124.4
Variance	298.6495	· 877.6545
Observations	45	45
Hypothesized Mean Difference	0	
df	71	
t Stat	−3.13379	
P(T<=t) one-tail	0.001254	
t Critical one-tail	1.666599	
P(T<=t) two-tail	0.002509	
t Critical two-tail	1.993944	

We can see from the output that the *p*-value is 0.001254 (the row is highlighted in the table, although it will not be in the Excel output). Since this is less than the α of 0.04, we reject the null hypothesis. There is sufficient evidence to conclude that average daily pedestrian traffic at location 2 is higher than at location 1. (An equivalent way to say this is that average pedestrian traffic at location 1 is lower than at location 2.)

Now, what if you want to do a comparison of means with independent samples by hand? With courage and a good calculator, you can calculate the degrees of freedom with the formula shown on page 344, and use the *t*-tables to estimate the *p*-value. However, if your courage fails, you can use a simpler approach to the degrees of freedom. Instead of the complicated formula for degrees of freedom shown on page 344, use the lesser of $(n_1 - 1)$ and $(n_2 - 1)$ as the degrees of freedom. The result will not be as accurate, but will provide a conservative answer, in that it will tend to overestimate the *p*-value (and so you will be less likely to reject the null hypothesis with the manual method).

While the computer-based approach is preferred, you can do these problems by hand with tables. Example 10.1b below illustrates the approach, and compares the results with the computer-based analysis.

A toy company is trying to decide which brand of battery to install in its battery-operated toys. The company decides to confirm battery life claims by the suppliers by testing a random sample of batteries. A random sample of 45 AA batteries from the Everlife battery company yields a mean life of 28.5 hours, with a standard deviation of 5.3 hours. A random sample of 42 AA batteries from the Durable battery company produces a mean life of 30.2 hours, with a standard deviation of 6.9 hours. At the 4% level of significance, is there evidence of a difference in mean battery life? You may assume that the battery life data is normally distributed, for both manufacturers.

t-test for independent samples, summary data

Again, recognize that these are independent samples. There is no correspondence between battery #1 in the Everlife sample and battery #1 in the Durable sample. Also, the sample size is different, which guarantees that this cannot be a matched-pairs sample.

Let's designate the Everlife sample as sample 1 from population 1, and the Durable sample as sample 2 from population 2 (you should always state your designation explicitly when you do one of these problems, so that you don't get confused about which population is which).

- H_0: $\mu_1 - \mu_2 = 0$ (mean battery life is the same for Everlife and Durable)
- H_1: $\mu_1 - \mu_2 \neq 0$ (mean battery life is different for Everlife and Durable)
- $\alpha = 0.04$
- $t = \dfrac{(\bar{x}_1 - \bar{x}_2) - (\mu_1 - \mu_2)}{\sqrt{\dfrac{s_1^2}{n_1} + \dfrac{s_2^2}{n_2}}} = \dfrac{(28.5 - 30.2) - (0)}{\sqrt{\dfrac{5.3^2}{45} + \dfrac{6.9^2}{42}}} = -1.282$

We will have to use the *t*-tables to approximate the *p*-value. We approximate the degrees of freedom as the minimum of $(n_1 - 1)$ and $(n_2 - 1)$.

$$n_1 - 1 = 45 - 1 = 44$$

$$n_2 - 1 = 42 - 1 = 41$$

The minimum is 41. We have no row in the *t*-table for 41 degrees. The closest is the row with 40 degrees of freedom, which is illustrated in Exhibit 10.5 below.

t-Distribution Critical Values

Degrees of Freedom	$t_{.100}$	$t_{.050}$	$t_{.025}$	$t_{.010}$	$t_{.005}$
40	1.303	1.684	2.021	2.423	2.705

1.282

We can see that the one-tailed *p*-value is > 10%, which means that the two-tailed *p*-value (appropriate for this test) is > 20%. We fail to reject the null hypothesis. There is insufficient evidence to conclude that there is a difference in AA battery life between the Everlife and Durable brands.

Using the Excel Template for *t*-Test of Means   Now we can turn to Excel for a more accurate result. In this example, we do not have the data on which the summary statistics are based. There is a worksheet template called "*t*-test of means, independent" in the workbook called "Templates" (available on the CD that comes with the text). You can use this template if you have only the summary statistics available (sample mean, etc.). You could also use the template if you have calculated the summary statistics from the raw data (preferably using a computer!). The completed template for Example 10.1b is shown below in Exhibit 10.6.

Completed Excel Template for *t*-Test of Means

Making Decisions About the Difference in Population Means with Two Independent Samples	
do the sample data appear to be normally distributed?	yes
sample 1 standard deviation	5.1
sample 2 standard deviation	6.9
sample 1 mean	28.5
sample 2 mean	30.2
sample 1 size	45
sample 2 size	42
hypothetical difference in population means	0
t-score	−1.29943
one-tailed p-value	0.098889
two-tailed p-value	0.197778

When we used the simplified approach for degrees of freedom and estimated the *p*-value, we concluded that it was > 20%. The *p*-value shown in the template is 20%, so our manual method was pretty close. This will not always be the case. You should always use the computer to do these tests if possible.

Equal or Unequal Variances?

In Example 10.1a, the sample variance for the location 1 data was 298.6495 (see the Excel output in Exhibit 10.4 on p. 346), and the sample variance for the location 2 data was 877.6545. In Example 10.1b, sample 1's standard deviation was 5.1 (making the variance = 5.1^2 = 26.01), and sample 2's standard deviation was 6.9 (making the variance =6.9^2 = 47.61). Since the variances were fairly far apart in both cases, it seems reasonable that we chose the *t*-test with unequal variances.

In some cases, we might suspect that population variances are equal, which would allow us to use another version of the *t*-test that is available in Excel—namely, t-Test: Two-Sample Assuming Equal Variances. There are some advantages to the equal-variances version of this hypothesis test. Since the variances are assumed to be equal, the sample data can be pooled, which should lead to a better estimate of the variance (and the standard deviation). As well, the sampling distribution is exactly a *t*-distribution when the variances are equal.

However, there is an important difficulty in using the equal-variances version of the test: how do we know if the population variances are equal? Several statistical tests are available to help with this decision, but they are sensitive to non-normality (some of them quite highly so). This makes it difficult to decide whether the variances are equal, especially when sample sizes are small. As well, any test of variances should be independent of the test of means. Testing the variances thus requires additional sampling, *before* you sample to make a decision about the means. Finally, if you mistakenly assume that the variances are equal when they are not, your results will be unreliable, particularly when sample sizes differ (and especially when the smaller sample has the larger variance).

It is recommended that you always use the unequal variances version of the *t*-test to compare population means with independent normally distributed samples, unless you have strong independent evidence that the variances are the same.

Using the unequal variances version of the *t*-test will lead to the right decision, even if the variances are in fact equal (with very few exceptions). One reason for this is that if the variances *are* equal, then s_1^2 and s_2^2 will be fairly close, so that the *pooled* version of the variance will be close to the *unpooled* version. Also, when sample sizes are close to the same, the results of the t-test assuming equal variances will be very close to the results for the *t*-test assuming unequal variances.

To illustrate, we will redo the calculations of Example 10.1b, but this time we will assume *equal* population variances. The pooled variance is a weighted average of the sample variances.

$$s_p^2 = \frac{(n_1 - 1)s_1^2 + (n_2 - 1)s_2^2}{(n_1 + n_2 - 2)} = \frac{(45 - 1)5.1^2 + (42 - 1)6.9^2}{(45 + 42 - 2)} = 36.4288$$

The *t*-score then becomes

$$t = \frac{(\bar{x}_1 - \bar{x}_2) - (\mu_1 - \mu_2)}{\sqrt{s_p^2\left(\frac{1}{n_1} + \frac{1}{n_2}\right)}} = \frac{(28.5 - 30.2) - (0)}{\sqrt{36.4288\left(\frac{1}{45} + \frac{1}{42}\right)}} = -1.313$$

Using Excel, we calculate the p-value as 0.0964. This is very close to the p-value we calculated for the unequal-variances version of the test, which was 0.0989 (see Exhibit 10.6 on p. 348). Certainly, the conclusion is not affected by the choice of the equal or unequal variances version of the t-test for Example 10.1b.

Guide to Decision Making

Independent Samples, Normal Quantitative Data–The t-Test

When:

- normal quantitative data, independent samples
- trying to make a decision about $\mu_1 - \mu_2$ (the difference in population means), on the basis of $\bar{x}_1 - \bar{x}_2$ (the difference in the sample means)
- variances are unequal (this version of the test is recommended, unless you have strong independent evidence that variances are equal)

Steps:
1. Specify H_0, the null hypothesis, which will usually be H_0: $\mu_1 - \mu_2 = 0$.
2. Specify H_1, the alternative hypothesis.
3. Determine or identify α, the significance level.
4. Collect or identify the sample data. Identify or calculate:

   - the sample means, $\bar{x}_1$ and $\bar{x}_2$
   - the sample standard deviations, s_1 and s_2
   - the sample sizes, n_1 and n_2

5. Check for normality of populations with histograms of the sample data. If even one of the histograms is non-normal, particularly with small sample sizes, do not proceed with the t-test (use the Wilcoxon Rank Sum Test instead, described on p. 354).
6. *If* the samples appear to be normally distributed, calculate the appropriate t-score, using the following formula:

$$t = \frac{(\bar{x}_1 - \bar{x}_2) - (\mu_1 - \mu_2)}{\sqrt{\dfrac{s_1^2}{n_1} + \dfrac{s_2^2}{n_2}}}$$

7. Calculate or estimate the degrees of freedom for the appropriate t-distribution. If you are using a computer, the degrees of freedom will be calculated for you. If you are doing the problem by hand, approximate the degrees of freedom by choosing the minimum of $(n_1 - 1)$ and $(n_2 - 1)$.
8. Use the t-distribution to calculate (or approximate, if using tables) the appropriate p-value for the hypothesis test, keeping in mind the order of subtraction used when calculating the differences.
9. If p-value $< \alpha$, reject H_0 and conclude that there is sufficient evidence to decide in favour of H_1. If p-value $> \alpha$, fail to reject H_0 and conclude that there is insufficient evidence to decide in favour of H_1.

Confidence-Interval for $\mu_1 - \mu_2$

Following directly from the sampling distribution and the discussion of the hypothesis test, a confidence interval estimate can be constructed for the difference in population means, as follows:

(point estimate) $\pm$ (critical value) $\cdot$ (estimated standard error of the sample statistic)

$$(\bar{x}_1 - \bar{x}_2) \pm t\text{-score}\sqrt{\frac{s_1^2}{n_1} + \frac{s_2^2}{n_2}}$$

where the *t*-score corresponds to the desired level of confidence, and has approximately

$$\frac{\left(\dfrac{s_1^2}{n_1} + \dfrac{s_2^2}{n_2}\right)^2}{\dfrac{\left(\dfrac{s_1^2}{n_1}\right)^2}{(n_1 - 1)} + \dfrac{\left(\dfrac{s_2^2}{n_2}\right)^2}{(n_2 - 1)}}$$

degrees of freedom. As above, when you are creating a confidence interval estimate by hand, you may use minimum $(n_1 - 1, n_2 - 1)$ as the degrees of freedom. Of course, normality of the populations is required for this formula to be appropriate.

Example 10.1c below illustrates construction of a confidence interval for the life of the batteries described in Example 10.1b.

Example 10.1c

Confidence interval for difference in means

The toy company wants to estimate the difference in average battery life between AA batteries from the Everlife battery company and those from the Durable battery company. A random sample of 45 AA batteries from the Everlife battery company yields a mean life of 28.5 hours, with a standard deviation of 5.3 hours. A random sample of 42 AA batteries from the Durable battery company produces a mean life of 30.2 hours, with a standard deviation of 6.9 hours. Construct a 99% confidence interval estimate for the difference in average battery life between the two kinds of batteries. You may assume that the battery life data is normally distributed.

We use the formula for the confidence interval:

$$(\bar{x}_1 - \bar{x}_2) \pm t\text{-score}\sqrt{\frac{s_1^2}{n_1} + \frac{s_2^2}{n_2}}$$

$$(28.5 - 30.2) \pm t\text{-score}\sqrt{\frac{5.3^2}{45} + \frac{6.9^2}{42}}$$

When doing this by hand, we will use the *t*-score with degrees of freedom = minimum$(n_1 - 1, n_2 - 1)$. The minimum of $(45 - 1, 42 - 1)$ is 41. We find no row in the table for 41 degrees of freedom, so we will use the row for 40. It is illustrated in Exhibit 10.7 below.

Exhibit 10.7

***t*-Distribution Critical Values**

Degrees of Freedom	$t_{.100}$	$t_{.050}$	$t_{.025}$	$t_{.01}$	$t_{.005}$
40	1.303	1.684	2.021	2.423	2.705

for 99% CI

We will now complete the calculations.

$$(28.5 - 30.2) \pm (2.705)\sqrt{\frac{5.3^2}{45} + \frac{6.9^2}{42}}$$

$$= -1.7 \pm (2.705)(1.3258)$$

$$= -1.7 \pm 3.5863$$

$$= (-5.29, 1.89)$$

With a confidence level of 99%, we believe that the interval $(-5.29, 1.89)$ contains the true difference in average battery life between the Everlife and Durable batteries. Notice that this interval contains 0, which we would expect, since the hypothesis test concluded that there was no evidence of a significant difference in battery life. (We have to be careful in establishing this correspondence between the hypothesis test and the confidence interval. They do not correspond exactly, because the significance level of 4% does not match with a confidence level of 99%.)

Template

Using the Excel Template for Confidence Interval Estimate for the Difference in Population Means
A template on the worksheet called "CI for diff in means" in the workbook called "Templates" is available on the CD that comes with this text. This template allows you to calculate confidence interval estimates more accurately. As always, you are required to fill in the blue-shaded cells in the template. A completed template for Example 10.1c is shown below in Exhibit 10.8.

10.8

Completed Excel Template for Confidence Interval Estimate for the Difference in Population Means, Example 10.1c

Confidence Interval Estimate for the Difference in Population Means	
do the sample data appear to be normally distributed?	yes
sample 1 standard deviation	5.1
sample 2 standard deviation	6.9
sample 1 mean	28.5
sample 2 mean	30.2
sample 1 size	45
sample 2 size	42
desired confidence level (decimal form)	0.99
upper confidence limit	1.757748
lower confidence limit	−5.15775

The approximation done by hand produced an interval of $(-5.29, 1.89)$. This is fairly close to the more accurate interval shown in the template of $(-5.15, 1.76)$.

DEVELOP YOUR SKILLS 10.1

1. The foreman at an assembly plant is concerned that the number of defective items produced on the night shift seems to be higher than during the day shift. A random sample of 45 night shifts had an average of 34.6 defects, with a standard deviation of 15.2. A random sample of 50 day shifts had an average of 27.9 defects, with a standard deviation of 7.9. Is there sufficient evidence, at the 5% significance level, to indicate that the number of defects is higher on the night shift than on the day shift? You may assume that the population distributions of errors are normal.

2. The owner of a drugstore is wondering if he should target female customers in particular, because he believes that they tend to spend more than male customers. However, he wants to check this belief. He asks the cashiers to keep track of the spending by a random sample of female customers, and a random sample of male customers, over several days. The purchases are shown in Exhibit 10.9 below. See file called DYS10-1-2.xls.

Drugstore Purchases by a Random Sample of Customers

Purchases by Females ($)	Purchases by Males ($)
30.50	31.49
15.83	28.88
38.66	30.77
44.15	24.95
42.98	23.26
39.56	27.66
22.25	25.77
31.49	33.32
49.43	18.29
18.70	38.25
24.65	25.09
29.64	30.51
17.30	24.96
20.34	26.34
23.40	

Exhibit 10.9

At the 2.5% level of significance, do the data provide evidence to support the drugstore owner's idea that female customers spend more than male customers?

3. Construct a 95% confidence interval estimate for the average difference in purchases made by female customers compared to male customers, based on the data in Exercise 2 above. Do you expect this confidence interval to contain zero? Why or why not?

4. A hotdog vendor who operates just outside the front door of a major hardware store wants to know if his daily sales have increased this summer, compared with last summer. The vendor sells a variety of hotdogs, sausages, cold drinks, candies, and other small items. He does not have electronic records, so he selects a random sample of days from last summer, and records the daily sales. He does the same for a random sample of days from this summer.

The data are available on the CD that accompanies this text. Is there sufficient evidence for the owner to conclude that daily sales are higher than last year, on average? Use $\alpha = 0.03$. See file called DYS10-1-4.xls.

5. A radio station is interested in whether listening habits differ by age. The station identified a random sample of 30 listeners aged 25 and younger, and asked them to keep

track of the number of minutes they listened to the station in a week. The station also identified a random sample of 35 listeners who were over 25 years of age, and asked them to record their listening times. The data from the younger listeners yielded an average of 256.8 minutes, with a standard deviation of 50.3 minutes. The data from the older listeners yielded an average of 218.3 minutes, with a standard deviation of 92.4 minutes. At the 5% significance level, is there evidence of a difference in listening times between the two age groups?

10.2 INDEPENDENT SAMPLES, NON-NORMAL QUANTITATIVE DATA OR RANKED DATA– THE WILCOXON RANK SUM TEST

There are two remaining situations when you might want to compare two independent samples. The first follows from the previous section—what if the quantitative data do not appear to be normally distributed? The second arises when the data points themselves are ranked data. In both situations, it is possible to use the Wilcoxon Rank Sum Test (WRST) to make decisions. The WRST is quite similar to the WSRST, in that it involves ordering the data, assigning ranks, and calculating rank sums. Examples 10.2a and 10.2b illustrate the use of this test.

The WRST requires you to calculate the sum of the ranks for each sample. We will call the rank sum of sample 1 W_1 and the rank sum of sample 2 W_2. It is possible to draw conclusions by examining either rank sum. For consistency, we will focus on W_1. In particular, when we are working with tables, we will designate W_1 as the rank sum of the *smaller* sample (if the samples are of different sizes).

Sampling Distribution of W_1 with Two Independent Samples

When both sample sizes are at least 10, the sampling distribution of W_1 is approximately normally distributed.

1. The standard error of the sampling distribution is calculated with the following formula, where n_1 is the size of sample 1, and n_2 is the size of sample 2.

$$\sigma_{W_1} = \sqrt{\frac{n_1 n_2 (n_1 + n_2 + 1)}{12}}$$

2. The mean of the sampling distribution of W_1 is

$$\mu_{W_1} = \frac{n_1 (n_1 + n_2 + 1)}{2}$$

If you are doing these problems by hand, you will use a z-score of the usual form, that is:

$$z = \frac{W_1 - \mu_{W_1}}{\sigma_{W_1}} = \frac{W_1 - \dfrac{n_1 (n_1 + n_2 + 1)}{2}}{\sqrt{\dfrac{n_1 (n_1 + n_2 + 1)}{12}}}$$

Independent Samples, Non-Normal Quantitative Data

The ranking process in the Wilcoxon Rank Sum Test is very similar to the ranking process for the Wilcoxon Signed Rank Sum Test, from Chapter 9, as Example 10.2a illustrates.

A company that manages a number of golf course properties is trying to decide between two types of accounting software. One of its recently acquired properties uses a program called CreditIt. Another very similar operation uses software called DoubleEntry. One of the criteria the company is using to make its decision is the number of times per day that the system locks up, requiring a supervisor override to complete an entry. The company wants to determine if there are fewer supervisor overrides with the CreditIt software. A random sample of days is chosen, and the number of supervisor overrides is recorded.

Set
EXA10-2a.xls

Example **10.2a**

Wilcoxon Rank Sum Test, sample size ≥ 10

First, notice that these are independent samples, and not matched pairs. The software users are doing a variety of tasks (not matched) on different days (also not matched).

As with the Wilcoxon Signed Rank Sum Test, it is required that the populations be similar in shape and spread, if we want to make conclusions about the locations of the two populations. With small data sets, it can be difficult to assess similarity in shape and spread. Histograms for this data set do show some similarity. The range is the same, and there is notable skewness to the right. The histograms are shown below in Exhibit 10.10.

Histograms of Overrides for Accounting Software

Exhibit **10.10**

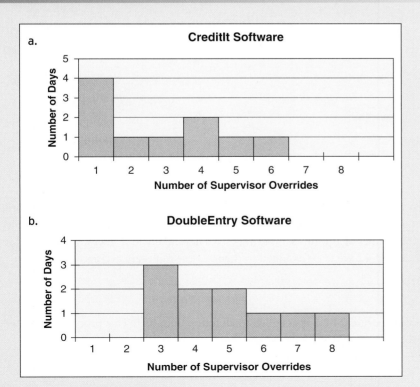

a.

CreditIt Software

b.

DoubleEntry Software

Because of the significant skewness and small sample size, it would not be appropriate to use a *t*-test to analyze this data set.

- H_0: The CreditIt and DoubleEntry software require the same number of daily supervisor overrides.
- H_1: The CreditIt software requires a lower number of daily supervisor overrides.
- Use $\alpha = 0.05$.

The Wilcoxon Rank Sum Test involves assigning ranks to the data points in the samples (all of the data are considered at once for the ranking). Ranks are averaged for tied values. Then the ranks for each sample are summed. If the samples came from populations in the same location, we would expect that the rank sums would be about equal, while allowing for different sample sizes. If the samples came from populations in different locations, we would expect the rank sums to be very different. Exhibit 10.11 below shows the assigned ranks for the two samples.

Supervisor Overrides for Accounting Software

CreditIt Supervisor Overrides	DoubleEntry Supervisor Overrides	CreditIt Supervisor Overrides (Ordered Data)	Ranks	DoubleEntry Supervisor Overrides (Ordered Data)	Ranks
6	8	1	2.5	3	7.5
1	5	1	2.5	3	7.5
4	4	1	2.5	3	7.5
5	4	1	2.5	4	11.5
3	3	2	5	4	11.5
4	3	3	7.5	5	15
1	5	4	11.5	5	15
1	6	4	11.5	6	17.5
1	7	5	15	7	19
2	3	6	17.5	8	20
			$W_1 = 78$		$W_2 = 132$

When values are tied, the associated ranks are averaged (you have seen this before, in the discussion of the Wilcoxon Signed Rank Sum Test in Chapter 9). For example, there are four values of 1 in this sample data set. They are the four lowest values, and the ranks 1, 2, 3, and 4 have to be assigned to them. These ranks are averaged.

$$\frac{1 + 2 + 3 + 4}{4} = 2.5$$

This average rank of 2.5 is assigned to all four values of 1. This process is repeated any time the values are tied.

Because the samples are the same size, we can designate either sample as sample 1. We will designate the data set for the CreditIt data as sample 1, and the sum of the ranks for this sample W_1.

The sample sizes are just large enough for the normal approximation.

$$z = \frac{W_1 - \mu_{W_1}}{\sigma_{W_1}} = \frac{78 - \dfrac{10(10 + 10 + 1)}{2}}{\sqrt{\dfrac{10(10)(10 + 10 + 1)}{12}}} = -2.04$$

In order to get the p-value, we have to think about the alternative hypothesis and what W_1 tells us. We are wondering if the supervisor overrides with the CreditIt software are lower than with the DoubleEntry software. If this were the case, then the number of overrides in sample 1 (the CreditIt sample) would be lower than in sample 2. This would lead to a lower rank sum for sample 1. Therefore, the p-value will be $P(W_1 \le 78)$.

$$P(W_1 \le 78) = P(z \le -2.04) = 0.0207$$

Since this p-value is less than the α of 5%, we reject the null hypothesis. There is sufficient evidence to infer that fewer supervisor overrides are required with the CreditIt software.

Using the Excel Add-in and Template for Sample Sizes ≥ 10   There is no built-in Data Analysis function in Excel to allow you to conduct a Wilcoxon Rank Sum Test. One of the Excel add-ins that comes with this text allows you to quickly and easily calculate W_1 and W_2 for any data set. Once the add-ins are installed, click on Tools on the Excel toolbar, then click on Non-Parametric Tools . . . , then choose Wilcoxon Rank Sum Test Calculations. As usual, you will have to fill in the dialogue box to indicate where sample 1 and sample 2 data are stored, and where you want the output placed. You should keep track of which sample you designated as sample 1, and which as sample 2, to help you understand the results. The output for the data in Example 10.2a is shown in Exhibit 10.12.

Instructions

Excel Output for Wilcoxon Rank Sum Test Calculations, **Example 10.2a**

10.12
Exhibit

Wilcoxon Rank Sum Test Calculations	
sample 1 size	10
sample 2 size	10
W 1	78
W 2	132

You can then use the worksheet template called "WRST independent" (which is available on the CD that comes with the text, in the workbook called "Templates") for *p*-value calculations. This template should only be used when sample sizes are at least 10. Exhibit 10.13 shows the worksheet template for Example 10.2a.

Exhibit 10.13

Excel Template for Making Decisions About Two Population Locations, Non-normal Quantitative Data or Ranked Data (WRST), Example 10.2a

Making Decisions About Two Population Locations, Non-normal Quantitative Data or Ranked Data (WRST)	
sample 1 size	10
sample 2 size	10
are both sample sizes at least 10?	yes
are the sample histograms similar in shape and spread?	yes
W1	78
W2	132
z-score (based on W1)	−2.041008154
one-tailed p-value	0.02062494
two-tailed p-value	0.04124988

As usual, you must fill in the blue-shaded cells in the template. The *p*-value is slightly more accurate than the one we calculated by hand.

Wilcoxon Rank Sum Test or *t*-Test?

We have now looked at two ways to draw a conclusion about two populations of quantitative data: one for normal data, and one for non-normal data. You might be tempted to choose the WRST whether the data are normal are not, since normal data fit the requirements for the WRST (that is, that the distributions be similar in shape and spread). But you should *not* succumb to this temptation.

The *t*-test is preferred to the Wilcoxon Rank Sum Test, because the *t*-test is more powerful than the WRST when the data are normal, in the sense that it is better at detecting false hypotheses. You should always use the *t*-test if you can.

How normal is normal enough? As always, this depends on sample size. The *t*-test works well, particularly when sample sizes are equal and sample histograms are similar, even if they are somewhat non-normal and skewed. The larger the sample sizes are, the more reliable the *t*-test will be. As always, you should be very cautious about using a *t*-test when there are outliers in the data.

Independent Samples, Ranked Data

As mentioned above, the WRST is also useful in comparing two populations of ranked data, as Example 10.2b below illustrates. This example also illustrates the use of the Wilcoxon Rank Sum tables for sample sizes < 10.

A restaurant owner is trying to decide which of two chefs she should promote. Both of the chefs work at a small restaurant that is known for its interesting fusion of French and Asian cooking styles. The owner is currently leaning toward Chef Lee as worthy of promotion. Her accountant has accused her of personal bias, and she is determined to refute this accusation by using data in her decision-making process. The owner decides to do a hypothesis test with a 5% level of significance.

Example 10.2b

Wilcoxon Rank Sum Test, sample size < 10

The owner selects a random sample of customers who are dining when Chef Lee is cooking, and asks them to rate the food. She does the same for a random sample of customers when Chef Girard is cooking. The ranking scale is as follows: (1) barely edible; (2) passable; (3) good; and (4) absolutely delicious.

The survey results and assigned ranks are shown in Exhibit 10.14 below. The data are similar in spread (ratings are from 1 to 4) and similar in shape, so we can use the Wilcoxon Rank Sum Test to draw a conclusion about population locations.

Restaurant Food Ratings

Exhibit 10.14

Ratings Assigned to Chef Lee's Food	Ratings Assigned to Chef Girard's Food	Ratings Assigned to Chef Lee's Food (Ordered)	Ranks	Ratings Assigned to Chef Girard's Food (Ordered)	Ranks
2	2	1	2	1	2
4	3	2	5.5	1	2
3	3	2	5.5	2	5.5
4	2	3	11	2	5.5
2	1	3	11	3	11
1	4	3	11	3	11
3	3	3	11	3	11
3	1	4	16	4	16
3		4	16		
			$W_2 = 89$		$W_1 = 64$

- H_0: the ratings for Chef Lee's food and Chef Girard's food are the same
- H_1: the ratings for Chef Lee's food are higher than for Chef Girard's food
- $\alpha = 5\%$

Since we have different sample sizes here, we designate the smallest sample (Chef Girard's ratings) as sample 1. Notice that we need calculate only W_1 to complete our analysis. We choose to calculate W_1 from the smallest sample because it's less work!

Before we calculate the p-value, we have to think about W_1 and what it tells us. In this case, higher numerical rankings correspond to higher actual rankings (the highest rank is 4, which corresponds to *absolutely delicious*). If the ratings for Chef Lee's food are higher than for Chef Girard's food, then the rank sum for the Chef Lee ratings sample should be higher, and the rank sum for Chef Girard's food should be lower. Therefore, to get the p-value, we need to figure out $P(W_1 \leq 64)$ when $n_1 = 8$ and $n_2 = 9$.

Before we go to the table, notice something very important: because sample 1 is smaller, its rank sum will be smaller, even when there is no difference in the two population locations. The Wilcoxon Rank Sum Test table is based on the calculation of W_1 from the smaller sample. It is critical that you always calculate W_1 from the smaller of the two samples when you are using the tables. Otherwise, your conclusion may be incorrect.

The table for the Wilcoxon Rank Sum Test is at the back of the book, on page 462. The table lists the rank sums (for the smaller sample) with p-values that are either equal to or close to the common levels of significance of 0.010, 0.025, and 0.05. The sampling distribution of W_1 is symmetric, so $P(W_1 \geq W_U) = P(W_1 \leq W_L)$.

When you use the table, you first have to identify n_1 (the size of the smaller sample), n_2 (the size of the larger sample), and W_1 (the rank sum for the smaller sample). In Example 10.2b, $n_1 = 8$, $n_2 = 9$, and $W_1 = 64$. An excerpt from the table is shown below in Exhibit 10.15.

10.15

Exhibit

Wilcoxon Rank Sum Test Critical Values and p-Values

n_1	n_2	W_L	W_U	$P(W_1 \leq W_L) = P(W_2 \geq W_U)$
8	9	55	89	0.057
		54	90	0.046
		52	92	0.030
		51	93	0.023
		48	96	0.010

$W_1 = 64$. This value is not on the table, but we can proceed as usual. $P(W_1 \leq 55) = 0.057$, so we know $P(W_1 \leq 64) > 0.057$. Since the p-value is greater than α, we fail to reject H_0. There is insufficient evidence to conclude that Chef Lee's ratings are higher than Chef Girard's. The data do not support promotion of Chef Lee on the basis of this criterion. The owner is going to have to find some other way to justify her promotion of Chef Lee.

Guide to Decision Making

Independent Samples, Non-Normal Quantitative Data or Ranked Data— The Wilcoxon Rank Sum Test

When:
- non-normal quantitative data or ranked data, independent samples
- trying to make a decision about the locations of the two populations

Steps:
1. Specify H_0, the null hypothesis, which is normally that there is no difference in the population locations.
2. Specify H_1, the alternative hypothesis.
3. Determine or identify α, the significance level.
4. Collect or identify the sample data.
5. Create histograms of the data, and check for normality. If the histograms appear normal and the data are quantitative, use the t-test (described on p. 343). If the histograms are non-normal, they should be similar in shape and spread for conclusions to be drawn about population locations.

6. Considering all of the data (from both samples) simultaneously, rank the data from 1 to $(n_1 + n_2)$. Average the ranks for tied data points. Calculate W_1, the sum of the ranks for sample 1, which is the *smallest* sample.

7. If both n_1 and n_2 are ≥ 10, the sampling distribution of W_1 is approximately normal, with

$$\sigma_{W_1} = \sqrt{\frac{n_1 n_2 (n_1 + n_2 + 1)}{12}}$$

$$\mu_{W_1} = \frac{n_1 (n_1 + n_2 + 1)}{2}$$

Use the normal sampling distribution to calculate the *p*-value of the result. When doing this by hand, the calculation will involve the *z*-score:

$$z = \frac{W_1 - \mu_{W_1}}{\sigma_{W_1}}$$

If either of n_1 or n_2 is < 10, use the table on page 462 to approximate the p-value. The table provides *p*-values for W_1, assuming it is calculated from the smallest sample.

8. If *p*-value $< \alpha$, reject H_0 and conclude that there is sufficient evidence to decide in favour of H_1. If *p*-value $> \alpha$, fail to reject H_0 and conclude that there is insufficient evidence to decide in favour of H_1.

DEVELOP YOUR SKILLS 10.2

1. A bank with a management training program is considering promotion of one of two trainees in the Metro West division. The bank has asked for 360° feedback for each of the trainees (that is, feedback from managers and peers). The overall ratings for each trainee are shown in Exhibit 10.16 below. The ratings range from 1 to 6, where 1 corresponds to the best performance, and 6 corresponds to the worst performance. At the 2.5% level of significance, is there evidence of a difference in the performance ratings of the two trainees? Based on these performance ratings, which trainee should be promoted?

Performance Ratings

Trainee #1	Trainee #2
1	4
5	5
3	4
2	5
3	6
4	2
4	5
5	5
4	

Exhibit 10.16

2. A company that produces golf balls is trying to develop a new ball that will travel farther than its current best-seller. A golf pro hits a number of balls of each type off of a tee, and the distance travelled is exactly measured. The results are shown below in Exhibit 10.17. Is there evidence that the new golf ball travels longer distances? Use $\alpha = 0.05$.

Exhibit 10.17 Distances Travelled by Current Best-Selling and New Golf Balls

Distances Travelled (Metres) by Current Best-Selling Golf Ball	Distances Travelled (Metres) by New Golf Ball
260	310
266	286
254	292
302	276
241	269
249	293
262	306
255	279
252	262
244	248
286	

3. A major airport has been redesigned and renovated. One of the goals of the upgrades was to decrease the amount of time that flights are delayed before takeoff. The delays (in minutes) for a random sample of flights at the airport before and after the airport upgrade are available on the CD that accompanies this text. Is there evidence, at the 5% significance level, that the upgrades reduced flight delays? See file called DYS10-2-3.xls.

4. A pharmaceutical manufacturer undertakes a study to prove the effectiveness of its diet pill. The company selects a random sample of 50 young women aged 18–25, and puts them on a weight-loss program. The women all have a meal plan and a personal trainer. Half of them (randomly selected) are given the diet pill, and half are given a placebo. Total weight loss, after 30 days, is recorded for all the participants in the study. The distributions of weight loss are non-normal, but both are skewed to the right, with some unusually high weight losses recorded. The rank sum of the weight losses with the diet pill is 700, and the rank sum of the weight losses with the placebo is 575. Do these data prove that the diet pill is effective? Use $\alpha = 4\%$.

5. John Williams, a member of the board of governors of an educational institution, is concerned about the leadership of the current president. John takes a random sample of employees, and asks them to rate the performance of the president, on a scale of 1 to 10, with 1 corresponding to the best performance, and 10 to the worst possible performance. The president is fired, and a new president is hired. After six months, John takes another random sample of employees, and asks them to rate the performance of the new president. At the 5% level of significance, is there evidence that the employees think the new president is performing better than the old president? The ratings are shown in Exhibit 10.18.

Ratings of the Old and New Presidents' Performance

Exhibit 10.18

Rating of the Old President's Performance	Rating of the New President's Performance
10	9
7	6
2	2
8	1
8	2
6	4
4	5
6	7
8	8
9	7

10.3 COMPARING MORE THAN TWO POPULATIONS

In Chapters 9 and 10, we have described techniques for making decisions when comparing two populations, with quantitative or ranked data. In Chapter 11, we will describe hypothesis tests for comparing two *or more* populations with qualitative data. This leaves a gap. What if you want to compare more than two populations with quantitative (or ranked) data? There are many situations where multiple comparisons are made. Suppose, for example, that you wanted to compare average annual vacation spending across four different age groups (e.g., 18–25, 26–40, 41–60, and over 60).

These comparisons can be made with a set of techniques called *analysis of variance*, and usually referred to as ANOVA. This name might sound surprising. The goal is to compare means, so why the focus on variance?

As you might expect, a comparison of vacation spending across a number of age groups would require calculation of mean vacation expenditure for each age group. ANOVA techniques then require calculation of a measure of the variability for those sample means. If the sample means are fairly close to each other, then this measure of variation will be small, and you would have no evidence that the population means are not equal. On the other hand, if there is a significant amount of variation in the sample means, you would have evidence that the population means are not equal. The question, as always, is: how large does the variation in sample means have to be, before it is considered significant? In order to decide this, ANOVA techniques compare the variation in the sample means with the overall variability in the data. If the sample means are significantly more variable than the underlying data, you have evidence that the population means are not the same. (This conclusion requires that the population variances be equal.)

Without actually doing any of this, you can probably anticipate that ANOVA techniques require a significant number of calculations. It really is not reasonable to do ANOVA calculations by hand. This is one of the reasons that ANOVA is not included in this introductory text, in which almost all of the techniques can be completed manually. As well, use of ANOVA requires careful experimental design, and the data collection can be quite complicated. As always, there are required conditions that must be checked carefully. Finally, even if ANOVA suggests a difference in means, further analysis is required to find out which means differ, and how. These techniques are beyond the scope of most introductory statistics courses, and are therefore beyond the scope of this text.

What you should *not* be tempted to do is to make multiple *t*-tests of two sample means as a substitute for ANOVA and related techniques. First of all, the number of *t*-tests required is large. With three populations, you must make three pair-wise comparisons. With four populations, you would have to make six pair-wise comparisons. More importantly, the probability of a Type I error (rejecting the null hypothesis when it is in fact true) increases dramatically when multiple *t*-tests are conducted.

If you ever find it necessary to make comparisons of quantitative data for more than two populations, the habits you have probably acquired while learning the techniques in this book (thinking carefully, checking required conditions) will stand you in good stead. There are many books available that provide good descriptions of techniques to compare multiple populations, and Excel has some Data Analysis tools that can help you.

Chapter Summary

10

This chapter presents hypothesis tests to make decisions when comparing two independent samples of normal or ranked data (if the data are qualitative, refer to Chapter 11). When samples are independent, there is no relationship between, for example, observation #1 from sample 1 and observation #1 from sample 2. Conclusions about differences in populations based on independent samples are not as strong as those based on matched pairs (which we covered in Chapter 9). Despite the weaker conclusions, independent samples are often used because matched-pairs data are more costly or even impossible to obtain.

Independent Samples, Normal Quantitative Data—The *t*-Test

If the data are quantitative, and the histograms of sample data appear normal, the hypothesis test is a *t*-test, assuming unequal variances, with $H_0: \mu_1 - \mu_2 = 0$. (There is an equal-variances version of this test, but since it is difficult to establish whether variances are actually equal, it is not recommended.)

The sampling distribution is approximately a *t*-distribution, with degrees of freedom as follows:

$$df = \frac{\left(\dfrac{s_1^2}{n_1} + \dfrac{s_2^2}{n_2}\right)^2}{\dfrac{\left(\dfrac{s_1^2}{n_1}\right)^2}{(n_1 - 1)} + \dfrac{\left(\dfrac{s_2^2}{n_2}\right)^2}{(n_2 - 1)}}$$

The t-score used in calculating p-values is:

$$t = \frac{(\bar{x}_1 - \bar{x}_2) - \mu_{\bar{x}_1 - \bar{x}_2}}{s_{\bar{x}_1 - \bar{x}_2}} = \frac{(\bar{x}_1 - \bar{x}_2) - (\mu_1 - \mu_2)}{\sqrt{\dfrac{s_1^2}{n_1} + \dfrac{s_2^2}{n_2}}}$$

The Excel Data Analysis tool for raw sample data, t-Test: Two-Sample Assuming Unequal Variances, is illustrated in Example 10.1a on page 345. These problems can also be done by hand, using minimum $(n_1 - 1, n_2 - 1)$ as the degrees of freedom, as illustrated in Example 10.1b on page 347. There is an Excel template for problems with summary sample data; it is illustrated on page 348.

A confidence interval estimate for the difference in means is

$$(\bar{x}_1 - \bar{x}_2) \pm t\text{-score}\sqrt{\frac{s_1^2}{n_1} + \frac{s_2^2}{n_2}}$$

where the t-score corresponds to the desired level of confidence, and has approximately

$$\frac{\left(\dfrac{s_1^2}{n_1} + \dfrac{s_2^2}{n_2}\right)^2}{\dfrac{\left(\dfrac{s_1^2}{n_1}\right)^2}{(n_1 - 1)} + \dfrac{\left(\dfrac{s_2^2}{n_2}\right)^2}{(n_2 - 1)}}$$

degrees of freedom. An Excel template is available, and is illustrated on page 352.

The Guide to Decision Making for independent samples, normal quantitative data, is on page 350.

Independent Samples, Non-Normal Quantitative Data or Ranked Data—The Wilcoxon Rank Sum Test

If the data are quantitative, sample sizes are small, and histograms are non-normal, you should use the Wilcoxon Rank Sum Test. This requires that the histograms be similar in shape and spread (if not, the test may indicate only that the population distributions are different in some way: location, shape, or spread, and this may not be all that helpful). The null hypothesis is that the population locations are the same. If the data are ranked, then the Wilcoxon Rank Sum Test is also appropriate, with the same requirements.

When sample sizes are at least 10, the sampling distribution is approximately normal, and the z-score used to calculate p-values is

$$z = \frac{W_1 - \mu W_1}{\sigma W_1} = \frac{W_1 - \dfrac{n_1(n_1 + n_2 + 1)}{2}}{\sqrt{\dfrac{n_1 n_2(n_1 + n_2 + 1)}{12}}}$$

There is an Excel add-in to allow you to calculate W_1 and W_2 from a data set, and there is an Excel template you can use to calculate p-values. These are both illustrated in Example 10.2a on page 355.

When the sample size is small, problems can be done by hand using the tables on page 462, as Example 10.2b on page 359 illustrates.

The Guide to Decision Making for independent samples, non-normal quantitative or ranked data, is on page 360.

CHAPTER REVIEW EXERCISES

1. A large accounting firm is concerned about the amount of time its managers spend dealing with email. A random sample of 25 managers taken in the past revealed that they spent, on average, 48.2 minutes per day on email. The standard deviation was 22.3 minutes. Since then, new procedures have been put in place: better spam controls have been implemented, and administrative assistants now screen managers' emails. Another random sample of 23 managers reveals that they spend, on average 38.6 minutes per day on email. The standard deviation of the second sample was 10.6 minutes. Is there evidence, at the 5% level of significance, that the new procedures have reduced the amount of time managers spend on email? You may assume that the sample data sets appear normally distributed.

2. Construct a 90% confidence interval estimate of the average amount of time that is saved for managers spending time on email, as a result of the new procedures described in Exercise 1 above.

3. A random sample of 50 Canadian men aged 25 to 54 were asked to keep a daily log of their hours spent doing unpaid work around the home. The time was averaged over the week. The survey was conducted in 1986 and 2005. In 1986, the average number of hours men spent doing unpaid work around the home was 2.1, with a standard deviation of 0.6. In 2005, the average number of hours men spent doing unpaid work around the home was 2.5, with a standard deviation of 1.2. Both sample data sets appear to be normally distributed. At the 2.5% level of significance, is there evidence that the average number of hours men spent doing unpaid work around the home increased in 2005, compared with 1986?

4. Construct a 95% confidence interval estimate of the increase in the amount of time that men spent doing unpaid work around the house in 2005, compared with 1986, based on the data in Exercise 3 above.

5. The management of a grocery store chain knows that the appearance of its stores is very important to customers. Past research has confirmed that customers prefer a clean, well-organized and well-lit store for their food shopping. As a result, regular surveys of customers are conducted, so that appearance can be rated. The results of two surveys done in a particular store are shown below in Exhibit 10.19. Is there evidence, at a 5% level of significance, of a change in the store's ratings? A rating of 5 is the best, and 1 is the worst.

Exhibit 10.19

Customers' Ratings of Store's Appearance

Random Sample of Grocery Store Customers

Appearance Ratings Six Months Ago	Current Appearance Ratings
5	1
4	3
3	4
4	5
2	4
1	4
4	5
4	3
3	5
3	4
4	3
5	

6. A financial advisor is concerned that the time she has to spend with her clients has increased, because of the increasing complexity of the investment products available. The advisor asks her assistant to keep track of exactly how many minutes she spends with a random sample of her clients every January. The results for this January and a year ago are available on the CD that accompanies this text. At the 3% level of significance, is there evidence that the amount of time the advisor spends with her clients has increased from a year ago? Can she attribute this to the increasing complexity of the investment products available?

 CRE10-6.xls
Set

7. Create a 97% confidence interval estimate of the average increase in the amount of time that the financial advisor described in Exercise 6 above is spending with each of her clients.

8. A company with a large sales force has implemented a pilot project to test new sales management software. The company hopes that the software will reduce the amount of time sales representatives spend on the computer, freeing them up to spend more time with customers. A random sample of sales reps is selected; 25 of them use the old software and 15 use the new software. They are asked to keep track of the total amount of time they spend on the computer (in hours), over a two-week period. The data are available on the CD that accompanies this text.

Is there evidence, at the 4% significance level, that the new software has reduced the amount of time sales reps spend on the computer? Are you sure that the new software is the cause of any difference you see?

 CRE10-8.xls
Set

9. Construct a 96% confidence interval estimate for the average amount of time the new software has saved sales reps, based on the data in Exercise 8 above.

10. A real estate agent wants to know if the average price of a single family home in a Winnipeg suburb has increased, compared with a year ago. A random sample of listings from last year and this year is shown below in Exhibit 10.20. At the 5% significance level, is there evidence of an increase in house prices compared with last year? What cautions should you have about your conclusion?

Real Estate Listings for Winnipeg Homes, Last Year and This Year

Single Family Homes in a Winnipeg Suburb

Last Year's Listings ($)	This Year's Listings ($)
129 900	124 000
134 900	139 900
134 900	139 900
134 900	139 900
138 900	144 900
139 900	149 900
141 500	149 900
144 900	

Exhibit **10.20**

11. Two restaurants of a fast-food chain are being compared as part of a performance assessment of the managers. Weeklys sales are collected for a random sample of eight weeks for both restaurants. The results are shown in Exhibit 10.21 on the next page. Is there evidence, at the 2.5% level of significance, of a difference in sales between the two restaurants? Think carefully before you answer.

Sales for Two Restaurants, Random Sample of Weeks

	Restaurant 1 ($)	Restaurant 2 ($)
Week 1	8,228	7,478
Week 2	3,633	8,254
Week 3	4,414	9,134
Week 4	6,856	6,061
Week 5	6,356	5,678
Week 6	2,498	4,291
Week 7	4,545	6,325
Week 8	6,923	4,658

CRE10-12.xls

12. A random sample of home computer users in Vancouver are asked to test two different types of high-speed Internet access. One type of access is provided by a cable TV company, and the other by a telephone company. The computer users are asked to rate the service after three months. The ratings are on a five-point scale, where 1 corresponds to *very satisfied* and 5 corresponds to *very dissatisfied*. At a 2.5% level of significance, is there evidence that the consumers rate the two services differently? The data are available on the CD that accompanies the text.

13. One of the criteria that statistics professors use in selecting a textbook is the number of exercises provided. One particular topic in statistics is selected: the *t*-test of the mean. A random sample of 15 professors are asked how many exercises students should do in order to master the topic. The sample average was 15.2, with a standard deviation of 5.2. A random sample of 20 students who demonstrated that they had mastered the topic by successfully completing some related questions were selected from these professors' classes. The students were asked how many exercises they had actually completed for this topic. The sample average was 8.3, with a standard deviation of 2.6. Is there evidence, at the 1% level of significance, that the professors have unrealistic expectations about the number of exercises that students need to do to master this topic? You may assume that the sample data for both professors and students appear normally distributed.

14. Construct a 99% confidence interval estimate for the difference in the numbers of exercises that professors think are necessary and that students deem necessary, for the situation described in Exercise 13 above. Do you expect the confidence interval estimate to include zero? Why or why not?

15. A lawnmower manufacturer sells partially assembled lawnmowers through large hardware stores. The manufacturer typically receives a number of calls to its toll-free line from consumers who have questions about the assembly of the lawnmowers. The manufacturer wants to reduce the number of these calls, and so it creates a new version of the written instructions that accompany the lawnmower. The manufacturer, working with retail outlets, randomly selects two groups of consumers: some who buy the lawnmower with the old assembly instructions, and some who buy the lawnmower with the new assembly instructions. The manufacturer contacts these consumers and asks them to rate the written assembly instructions, on a scale of 1 to 5, with 1 corresponding to *very easy to read and follow*, and 5 corresponding to *very difficult to read and follow*. The ratings for the two sets of instructions are shown in Exhibit 10.22. Is there evidence that consumers find the new instructions easier to read and follow? Use $\alpha = 0.05$.

Customers' Ratings of Old and New Lawnmower Assembly Instructions

Old Instructions	New Instructions
4	3
3	3
1	4
2	2
5	1
3	2
4	3
3	1
2	1

16. The lawnmower company described in Exercise 15 above also asked the consumers to report how long it took them to assemble their new lawnmowers. The results (in minutes) are shown below in Exhibit 10.23. Is there evidence that the consumers using the new instructions were able to assemble their lawnmowers more quickly than those with the old instructions? Use $\alpha = 4\%$.

Customers' Times to Assemble Lawnmower

Old Instructions	New Instructions
45	28
44	32
45	32
48	35
52	36
56	44
56	45
60	45
62	48

17. A consumer group tested two brands of laser printer cartridges for a particular printer, to see if there was a difference in the number of pages produced before the cartridge ran out of toner. The printers were tested in a random sample of offices where they were used for printing invoices. Brand A cartridges produced an average of 5,862 pages, with a standard deviation of 462, for a sample size of 30. Brand B cartridges produced an average of 6,031 pages, with a standard deviation of 623, for a sample size of 25. Is there evidence of a difference in the number of pages produced by the two brands of cartridges? Use $\alpha = 5\%$. You may assume that the sample data appear normally distributed.

18. Construct a 90% confidence interval estimate for the difference in the number of pages produced by the two different cartridges described in Exercise 17 above.

19. A large college was considering switching brands of the laptop computers it leases every three years for faculty. One of the criteria for choosing between the two brands is the

support available. As a test, IT workers made a number of calls throughout one week to the support lines for each manufacturer. The workers recorded the number of minutes that they waited on the phone before a technician became available to help them. The average wait time for the ITM brand was 13.5 minutes, with a standard deviation of 5.6 minutes, with a sample size of 32. The average wait time for the Dull brand was 17.5 minutes, with a standard deviation of 8.9 minutes, for a sample size of 35. You may assume that the wait times are normally distributed. Is there evidence of a difference in wait times between the two brands? Use $\alpha = 5\%$.

20. Construct a 95% confidence interval estimate for the difference in wait times for ITM and Dull computers, based on the data in Exercise 19 above. Do you expect this interval to contain zero? Why or why not?

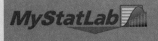 Go to MyStatLab at www.mystatlab.com. You can practise many of this chapter's exercises as often as you want. The guided solutions help you find an answer step by step. You'll find a personalized study plan available to you too!

11 Making Decisions with Two or More Samples, Qualitative Data

INTRODUCTION

There are many situations in which two or more populations of qualitative data need to be investigated. For example, market research is often aimed at finding out if there are differences or similarities in target market sub-groups. Markets might be segmented along lines of income, location, gender, and other customer characteristics. For example, a telecommunications company selling long-distance services might want to know if urban and rural customers differ in their needs for long-distance plans, so it can tailor its plans accordingly. The segmentation makes sense only if real differences among the segments can be identified. The data involved are qualitative in nature, and so researchers will be interested in counts or proportions (or percentages) in the data.

In Chapters 9 and 10, we looked at comparisons of two samples with quantitative or ranked data. In Chapter 11, we will look at comparisons of two or more samples of qualitative data, which means that we will be dealing with proportions, percentages, and counts throughout. In Section 11.1, we will compare proportions in two populations. In Section 11.2, we will compare sample data with a desired or claimed set of characteristics, by examining counts in two or more categories in one population. In Section 11.3, we will look at several samples to see how they match up according to several characteristics, comparing counts simultaneously across many populations.

11.1 COMPARING TWO PROPORTIONS

A company wanted to do some market research about fitness club memberships. A random sample of adult Moncton, New Brunswick residents was conducted. The survey results showed that out of the 153 female survey respondents, 62 had fitness club memberships. Of the 52 male survey respondents, 28 had fitness club memberships. Do the survey results suggest that males and females in Moncton have differing tendencies to have fitness club memberships?

We will refer to the sample of females as population 1, and the sample proportion as $\hat{p}_1$. We see that $\hat{p}_1 = \dfrac{62}{153} = 0.4052$. We can calculate $\hat{p}_2 = \dfrac{28}{52} = 0.5385$. The proportions of males and females who have fitness club memberships are different. As always, we must ask: are the proportions *significantly* different? As in Chapter 10, when we compared population means, we will focus on the difference in the two parameters (and the corresponding sample statistics) to decide. That is, we will examine $\hat{p}_1 - \hat{p}_2$ to draw a conclusion about $p_1 - p_2$. As usual, we must know what the sampling distribution of the difference in proportions looks like, in order to make a decision.

Of course, the underlying probability distributions here are binomial. We count how many of a certain number of trials are *successes*. In the example, we count how many of the 153 female survey respondents had fitness club memberships ($x_1 = 62$), and how many of the 52 male respondents had fitness club memberships ($x_2 = 28$). As discussed in Chapter 6, we can convert these binomial counts into proportions, and the associated sampling distributions will be approximately normal if the sample sizes are sufficiently large. The check for the normality of the sampling distribution is that np and nq are both ≥ 10 (where p is the probability of success and q is the probability of failure). As well, n has to be large enough that no continuity correction factor is needed in the approximation of the binomial distribution with the normal distribution. Similar conditions are required for the sampling distribution of $\hat{p}_1 - \hat{p}_2$.

Sampling Distribution of $\hat{p}_1 - \hat{p}_2$

For cases where the underlying binomial distributions are sufficiently normal (n_1 and n_2 sufficiently large, and $n_1 p_1$, $n_1 q_1$, $n_2 p_2$, and $n_2 q_2$ all ≥ 10), the sampling distribution of $\hat{p}_1 - \hat{p}_2$ is approximately normally distributed. Samples must be independent.

1. The standard error of $\hat{p}_1 - \hat{p}_2$ is as follows:

$$\sigma_{\hat{p}_1 - \hat{p}_2} = \sqrt{\frac{p_1 q_1}{n_1} + \frac{p_2 q_2}{n_2}}$$

2. The mean of $\hat{p}_1 - \hat{p}_2$ is:

$$\mu_{\hat{p}_1 - \hat{p}_2} = p_1 - p_2$$

This information about the sampling distribution cannot be directly applied, as we do not know what p_1 or p_2 (the true population proportions) are. We have to approximate

p_1 and p_2 with the sample estimates, that is, $\hat{p}_1$ and $\hat{p}_2$, and we will use these values in place of the unknown population parameters in the formulas for the mean and standard error. Similarly, we check the conditions for normality using $\hat{p}_1$ and $\hat{p}_2$.

In general, the test statistic will take the usual form:

$$z = \frac{(\hat{p}_1 - \hat{p}_2) - \mu_{\hat{p}_1 - \hat{p}_2}}{\sigma_{\hat{p}_1 - \hat{p}_2}} \approx \frac{(\hat{p}_1 - \hat{p}_2) - \mu_{\hat{p}_1 - \hat{p}_2}}{s_{\hat{p}_1 - \hat{p}_2}} = \frac{(\hat{p}_1 - \hat{p}_2) - (p_1 - p_2)}{\sqrt{\dfrac{\hat{p}_1 \hat{q}_1}{n_1} + \dfrac{\hat{p}_2 \hat{q}_2}{n_2}}}.$$

Special Case: H_0: $p_1 - p_2 = 0$

It is quite usual, in problems where population proportions are being compared, to work with the null hypothesis that $p_1 - p_2 = 0$ (that is, the two population proportions are equal). If the sample proportions are hypothesized to be equal, it makes sense to pool the data from the two samples to come up with a single estimate of the unknown population proportion.

When we pool the two samples in the fitness membership example, we find a total number of respondents of $n_1 + n_2 = 153 + 52 = 205$. Of the total 205 respondents, there were a total of $x_1 + x_2 = 62 + 28 = 90$ who had fitness club memberships. The *pooled* estimate of the proportion of those who have fitness club memberships (which we will call $\hat{p}$ with no subscript) will then be $\hat{p} = \dfrac{x_1 + x_2}{n_1 + n_2} = \dfrac{62 + 28}{153 + 52} = \dfrac{90}{205} = 0.439$. This means that $\hat{q} = 1 - 0.439 = 0.561$. The estimate of the standard error will become simplified. From the information on the sampling distribution above, we know that

$$\sigma_{\hat{p}_1 - \hat{p}_2} = \sqrt{\frac{p_1 q_1}{n_1} + \frac{p_2 q_2}{n_2}}$$

Since p_1 and p_2 are supposed to be equal, we will replace them in the formula with p, and similarly, we will replace q_1 and q_2 with q. We can then take out the common factor, as follows.

$$\sigma_{\hat{p}_1 - \hat{p}_2} = \sqrt{\frac{p_1 q_1}{n_1} + \frac{p_2 q_2}{n_2}}$$

$$= \sqrt{pq\left(\frac{1}{n_1} + \frac{1}{n_2}\right)}$$

The estimate of $\sigma_{\hat{p}_1 - \hat{p}_2}$, based on sample data, will then become

$$s_{\hat{p}_1 - \hat{p}_2} = \sqrt{\hat{p}\hat{q}\left(\frac{1}{n_1} + \frac{1}{n_2}\right)}$$

Here's a note about arithmetic that might be useful. In this case, we knew x_1 and x_2 (the number of successes in each sample), so we could use the formula $\hat{p} = \dfrac{x_1 + x_2}{n_1 + n_2}$ to estimate the proportion from the pooled sample data. But what if all that is given is the sample proportions and the sample sizes? The equivalent formula in this case to get the pooled sample $\hat{p}$ is as follows:

$$\hat{p} = \frac{\hat{p}_1(n_1) + \hat{p}_2(n_2)}{n_1 + n_2}$$

If you think about it, you will realize that $\hat{p}_1(n_1) = x_1$ and $\hat{p}_2(n_2) = x_2$, and so the formulas are equivalent. You should use whichever one matches the sample information you are given in the problem.

Now we can conduct the hypothesis test for the fitness memberships. The first step is to check for normality of the sampling distribution.

$$n_1\hat{p}_1 = x_1 = 62 > 10$$

$$n_1\hat{q}_1 = n_1 - x_1 = 153 - 62 = 91 > 10$$

$$n_2\hat{p}_2 = x_2 = 28 > 10$$

$$n_2\hat{q}_2 = n_2 - x_2 = 52 - 28 > 10$$

Sampling is done without replacement here. Remember, the binomial distribution is still appropriate as the underlying probability distribution as long as the sample is no more than about 5% of the population. The target population is Moncton adults, of whom there are tens of thousands, so we can be sure that the sample is less than 5% of the population.

- $H_0: p_1 - p_2 = 0$
- $H_1: p_1 - p_2 \neq 0$ (The question is whether males and females in Moncton *differ* in their tendencies to have fitness club memberships.)
- Use $\alpha = 0.05$.

We will compare $\hat{p}_1 - \hat{p}_2$ with its expected value. If we were required to do the exercise by hand using the normal table, we would calculate a z-score of the standard form.

$$z = \frac{(\hat{p}_1 - \hat{p}_2) - \mu_{\hat{p}_1 - \hat{p}_2}}{s_{\hat{p}_1 - \hat{p}_2}} = \frac{(\hat{p}_1 - \hat{p}_2) - 0}{\sqrt{\hat{p}\hat{q}\left(\frac{1}{n_1} + \frac{1}{n_2}\right)}} = \frac{(0.4052 - 0.5385) - 0}{\sqrt{(0.439)(0.561)\left(\frac{1}{153} + \frac{1}{52}\right)}}$$

$$= -1.67$$

In order to get the appropriate p-value, we first calculate $P(z \leq -1.67) = 0.0475$. Because this is a two-tailed test, the p-value $= 2(0.0475) = 0.095$. Since this is greater than the α of 0.05, we fail to reject the null hypothesis. There is insufficient evidence to infer that males and females in Moncton differ in their tendencies to have fitness club memberships.

Coded Data   The data for comparison of proportion may be in coded form (for example, *1* corresponds to *yes* and *2* corresponds to *no*). In such a case, Excel's Histogram data analysis tool can be used to sort the data before you do any hypothesis test. An Excel template is available on the CD that comes with this text to help you with your calculations. Example 11.1a illustrates.

A service organization in the public sector has recently undergone rapid growth, with the associated stresses. An employee satisfaction survey is done on an annual basis with a random sample of employees. A research officer in the organization is particularly interested in employees' perceptions of the president's competence. She wants to compare the survey data collected this year and last year in response to the question: "Do you think that the president is an effective leader?" The researcher is interested to see if significantly fewer people think that the president is an effective leader this year, compared with last year.

The data are available in the directory called DataChap11 on the CD that comes with this text. In this data set, *1* corresponds to a *yes* answer, and *0* corresponds to a *no* answer.

Comparing two proportions, special case, coded data

 EXA11-1a.xls

You will be able to use Excel to organize the coded data (as we have done before). Before you do that, you should set up the hypothesis test and think about what you need to know in order to make a good decision. Suppose we refer to last year's population of responses as population 1, and this year's as population 2. We can choose to focus on either the proportion of *yes* answers or the proportion of *no* answers. In the discussion that follows, the focus is on the proportion of *yes* answers. (Note that it is important to explicitly decide these matters before you begin, to avoid confusion.) The hypothesis test will be as follows:

- $H_0: p_1 - p_2 = 0$
- $H_1: p_1 - p_2 > 0$ (If significantly fewer people think that the president is an effective leader this year, compared to last year, then p_1 will be larger than p_2.)
- Use $\alpha = 0.025$.

Now we need to organize and summarize the data before we can proceed. One of the most straightforward ways to organize this data set is to use the Histogram tool in Excel, with bin numbers of 0 and 1 to calculate the frequencies of zeros and ones in the data for last year, and again for this year. It is then a fairly simple operation to create Excel formulas to calculate the percentages of *yes* and *no* answers for last year and this year.

For last year, Excel calculates that there were 25 *no* responses and 228 *yes* responses (and a total of 253 responses). For this year, Excel calculates 66 *no* responses and 246 *yes* responses (and a total of 312 responses).

Certainly, you could now do this problem by hand. However, since you used Excel to count the responses, and it seems reasonable to continue using Excel. A worksheet called "z-test of 2 proportions" is available in the workbook called "Templates" on the CD that comes with this text. The completed worksheet template for this example is shown below in Exhibit 11.1. As usual, you are required to fill in the blue-shaded boxes in the template. Also as usual, the template reminds you to check for normality of the sampling distribution, and that these conditions are met.

Instructions

Template

Sampling is done without replacement, and we have no information about the total number of employees in the organization. We proceed by making an assumption that the sample size is < 5% of the population, and noting that our conclusions may not be correct if this assumption does not hold.

Exhibit 11.1

Completed Excel Template, Example 11.1a

Making Decisions About Two Population Proportions, Qualitative Data	
sample 1 size	253
sample 2 size	312
sample 1 proportion	0.901185771
sample 2 proportion	0.788461538
n1p1-hat	228
n1q1-hat	25
n2p2-hat	246
n2q2-hat	66
are all np & nq at least 10?	yes
hypothesized difference in means (p1 − p2) (use decimal form)	0
z-score	3.624676071
one-tailed p-value	0.000144697
two-tailed p-value	0.000289395

This is a one-tailed test, and so the appropriate *p*-value is 0.000144697, which is quite small. There would be almost no chance of getting sample results like these if in fact there was no difference in the proportions of employees who thought that the president was an effective leader, this year compared with last year. There is very strong evidence to suggest that a lower proportion of employees think that the president is an effective leader this year, compared to last year.

General Case: H_0: $p_1 - p_2$ = Fixed Amount

It is also possible to examine qualitative data to see if the two population proportions differ by some fixed amount. The template will handle this situation. Example 11.1b below illustrates.

Example 11.1b

Comparing two proportions, general case, summary data

The dean of the business program is interested to see if student satisfaction is higher for students in classes that meet every week in a classroom, compared with students who take courses completely online. Of course, there are many factors that affect student satisfaction, and past data analysis has shown that student satisfaction can vary as much as 20% between two classes in very similar circumstances. Therefore the dean wants to check to see if there is more than a 20% difference in satisfaction levels between students with weekly classes and those enrolled online. The satisfaction level is determined by the percentage of students who answer yes to the question: "Are you generally satisfied with this class?"

A random sample of students taking face-to-face economics classes is selected, as is a random sample of students taking online economics courses. 95% of the 400 students in face-to-face classes were satisfied. 72% of the 300 students taking online courses were satisfied. Is there enough evidence to conclude that the satisfaction rate for those taking face-to-face classes is more than 20% higher than for those taking online classes?

We will refer to the satisfaction levels of those taking face-to-face classes as population 1, and of those taking online classes as population 2. The hypothesis test will be as follows:

- H_0: $p_1 - p_2 = 0.20$
- H_1: $p_1 - p_2 > 0.20$ (We want to know if the satisfaction rate for population 1 is more than 20% higher than for population 2.)
- Use $\alpha = 0.04$.

Sampling is done without replacement. We are given no data about the total number of students in face-to-face or online classes at the college. We proceed by making the assumption that the samples are < 5% of the population, and noting that our conclusions may not be valid if this is not the case.

We must also check the conditions for normality of the sampling distribution.

$$n_1 \hat{p}_1 = 380 > 10$$
$$n_1 \hat{q}_1 = 20 > 10$$
$$n_2 \hat{p}_2 = 216 > 10$$
$$n_2 \hat{q}_2 = 84 > 10$$

In this case, since we are no longer hypothesizing that the two population proportions are equal, we will not pool the sample data to get an estimate of $\hat{p}$. We will instead use $\hat{p}_1$ and $\hat{p}_2$ in our calculations, as follows:

$$z = \frac{(\hat{p}_1 - \hat{p}_2) - \mu_{\hat{p}_1 - \hat{p}_2}}{s_{\hat{p}_1 - \hat{p}_2}} = \frac{(\hat{p}_1 - \hat{p}_2) - \mu_{\hat{p}_1 - \hat{p}_2}}{\sqrt{\dfrac{\hat{p}_1 \hat{q}_1}{n_1} + \dfrac{\hat{p}_2 \hat{q}_2}{n_2}}}$$

$$= \frac{(0.95 - 0.72) - 0.20}{\sqrt{\dfrac{(0.95)(0.05)}{400} + \dfrac{(0.72)(0.28)}{300}}} = 1.067$$

$$p\text{-value} = P(z \geq 1.07) = 1 - 0.8577 = 0.1423$$

As mentioned above, it is also possible to use the Excel template in this situation. Exhibit 11.2 below shows the completed template for Example 11.1b.

Template

Note that the conditions for normality of the sampling distribution are checked in the template. Since this is a one-tailed test, the appropriate p-value is 0.143 (which differs slightly from with our manual calculations above, because of rounding of the z-score). It would not be unusual to get sample data like this if the difference in satisfaction rates in the two student groups were only 20% (or less). Based on the data, there is not enough evidence to conclude that the satisfaction rate for those taking face-to-face classes is more than 20% higher than for those taking online classes.

Completed Excel Template, Example 11.1b

Making Decisions About Two Population Proportions, Qualitative Data	
sample 1 size	400
sample 2 size	300
sample 1 proportion	0.95
sample 2 proportion	0.72
n1p1-hat	380
n1q1-hat	20
n2p2-hat	216
n2q2-hat	84
are all np & nq at least 10?	yes
hypothesized difference in means (p1 − p2) (use decimal form)	0.2
z-score	1.066845806
one-tailed p-value	0.143020765
two-tailed p-value	0.286041531

Guide to Decision Making

Comparing Two Proportions

When:
- qualitative data, independent samples
- trying to make a decision about $p_1 - p_2$ (the difference in population proportions), on the basis of $\hat{p}_1 - \hat{p}_2$ (the difference in the sample proportions)

Steps:
1. Specify H_0, the null hypothesis (usually, H_0: $p_1 - p_2 = 0$).
2. Specify H_1, the alternative hypothesis.
3. Determine or identify α, the significance level.
4. Collect or identify the sample data. Identify or calculate:
   - the sample proportions, $\hat{p}_1$ and $\hat{p}_2$
   - the sample sizes, n_1 and n_2
5. If sampling is done without replacement, make sure the sample size is less than 5% of the population, so that the binomial distribution is the appropriate underlying model.
6. Check for normality of the sampling distribution, which requires $n_1\hat{p}_1$, $n_1\hat{q}_1$, $n_2\hat{p}_2$, $n_2\hat{q}_2 \geq 10$, and n_1 and n_2 sufficiently large that no continuity correction is neccessary.
7. If the conditions are met, calculate the appropriate z-score, using the following formula:

$$z = \frac{(\hat{p}_1 - \hat{p}_2) - \mu_{\hat{p}_1 - \hat{p}_2}}{s_{\hat{p}_1 - \hat{p}_2}} = \frac{(\hat{p}_1 - \hat{p}_2) - \mu_{\hat{p}_1 - \hat{p}_2}}{\sqrt{\dfrac{\hat{p}_1 \hat{q}_1}{n_1} + \dfrac{\hat{p}_2 \hat{q}_2}{n_2}}}$$

The most usual case is of the null hypothesis that $p_1 - p_2 = 0$, and so sample data are pooled to get a single estimate of p called $\hat{p}$. The z-score then becomes

$$z = \frac{(\hat{p}_1 - \hat{p}_2) - \mu_{\hat{p}_1 - \hat{p}_2}}{s_{\hat{p}_1 - \hat{p}_2}} = \frac{(\hat{p}_1 - \hat{p}_2) - 0}{\sqrt{\hat{p}\hat{q}\left(\dfrac{1}{n_1} + \dfrac{1}{n_2}\right)}}, \text{ where } \hat{p} = \frac{x_1 + x_2}{n_1 + n_2}$$

8. Use the normal distribution to calculate the appropriate p-value for the hypothesis test.

9. If p-value $< \alpha$, reject H_0 and conclude that there is sufficient evidence to decide in favour of H_1. If p-value $> \alpha$, fail to reject H_0 and conclude that there is insufficient evidence to decide in favour of H_1.

Confidence Interval Estimate of $p_1 - p_2$

Following directly from the sampling distribution and the discussion of the hypothesis test, a confidence interval estimate can be constructed for the difference in population means, as follows:

(point estimate) $\pm$ (critical value) $\cdot$ (estimated standard error of the sample statistic)

$$(\hat{p}_1 - \hat{p}_2) \pm z\text{-score}\sqrt{\frac{\hat{p}_1\hat{q}_1}{n_1} + \frac{\hat{p}_2\hat{q}_2}{n_2}}$$

where the z-score corresponds to the desired level of confidence. Of course, the normality conditions must be met in order for this formula to be appropriate.

Example 11.1c below illustrates the construction of a confidence interval for the difference in proportions of employees who think that the president was an effective leader, last year compared with this year (these data are presented in Example 11.1a).

As described in Example 11.1a, a service organization has randomly sampled employees to understand their perceptions of the president's competence. Last year, 228 out of 253 respondents thought that the president was an effective leader. This year, 246 out of 312 respondents thought that the president was an effective leader. Construct a 95% confidence interval estimate for the difference in proportions of employees who considered the president an effective leader (last year compared with this year).

Confidence interval for difference in proportions

First, check the conditions. We have no information about how many employees there are in this organization. We proceed by assuming that the samples are $< 5\%$ of the population, and note that our estimate may not be valid if this is not the case.

We must also check the conditions for normality of the sampling distribution.

$$n_1\hat{p}_1 = x_1 = 228 > 10$$
$$n_1\hat{q}_1 = n_1 - x_1 = 253 - 228 = 25 > 10$$

$$n_2\hat{p}_2 = x_2 = 246 > 10$$
$$n_2\hat{q}_2 = n_2 - x_2 = 312 - 246 = 66 > 10$$

The formula for the confidence interval estimate is:

$$(\hat{p}_1 - \hat{p}_2) \pm z\text{-score}\sqrt{\frac{\hat{p}_1\hat{q}_1}{n_1} + \frac{\hat{p}_2\hat{q}_2}{n_2}}$$

$$= \left(\frac{228}{253} - \frac{246}{312}\right) \pm z\text{-score}\sqrt{\frac{\left(\frac{228}{253}\right)\left(\frac{253-228}{253}\right)}{253} + \frac{\left(\frac{246}{312}\right)\left(\frac{312-246}{312}\right)}{312}}$$

$$= (0.11272) \pm (1.96)(0.029775)$$

$$= (0.0544, 0.1711)$$

As before, we designated p_1 as the proportion of employees who thought that the president was an effective leader last year, and p_2 as the proportion who thought so this year. Since the interval is for $p_1 - p_2$, we can state our conclusion this way: With a confidence level of 99%, we believe that the interval (0.0544, 0.1711) contains the true decrease in proportion of employees who considered the president an effective leader this year, compared with last year.

A worksheet called "CI for diff in proportions" is available in the workbook called "Templates" on the CD that comes with this text. It allows you to calculate confidence interval estimates for the difference in proportions. As always, you are required to fill in the non-shaded cells in the template. A completed template for Example 11.1c is shown below in Exhibit 11.3.

Template

Exhibit 11.3

Completed Excel Template, Example 11.1c

Confidence Interval Estimate for the Difference in Population Proportions	
confidence level (decimal form)	0.95
sample 1 proportion	0.901186
sample 2 proportion	0.788462
sample 1 size	253
sample 2 size	312
n1 • p1hat	228
n1 • q1hat	25
n2 • p2hat	246
n2 • q2hat	66
are np and nq >=10?	yes
upper confidence limit	0.171082
lower confidence limit	0.054366

The template result agrees with the calculations we did by hand.

DEVELOP YOUR SKILLS 11.1

1. Airline mergers are sometimes followed by a decrease in performance, as operations are rationalized and staff adjusts to new operating protocols. One measure of airline efficiency is the percentage of on-time departures. Before a recent merger, Northeast Airlines took a random sample of 100 flights, and found that 85 of them had departed on time. After the merger, a sample of 100 flights showed that 78 had departed on time. At the 4% level of significance, is there evidence that the proportion of on-time flights decreased after the merger? The airline handles thousands of flights every day.

2. Many teenagers use the Internet and instant messaging services. A random sample of 500 female teenagers in Canada revealed that 430 had used instant messaging in the last week. A random sample of 500 male teenagers in Canada indicated that 410 had used instant messaging in the last week. Based on these data, can we conclude that the percentage of female teenagers using instant messaging is higher than the percentage of male teenagers using instant messaging in the past week? Use $\alpha = 0.05$. Be sure to explain your notation.

3. A major bank implemented a number of policies and procedures to try to ensure that its female employees have as much opportunity for advancement as its male employees. The bank decided to check employees' perceptions of opportunity for advancement. A random sample of 240 female employees indicated that 82.5% felt that female employees had as much opportunity for

advancement as male employees. A random sample of 350 male employees indicated that 94.3% of male employees thought that female employees had as much opportunity for advancement as male employees. Is there evidence, at a 5% significance level, that the proportion of female employees is more than 10% lower than the proportion of male employees? The total number of employees at the bank is over 65,000.

4. The marketing department is investigating methods of promoting the extended warranty for electronic equipment. In one method, customers are informed about the extended warranty by the cashier at the checkout. In another method, customers see a prominent display at the checkout. A random sample of customers who

Set

experienced each method of promotion is selected, and a 1 is recorded if the customer bought the extended warranty, and a 0 if the customer did not. See file called DYS11-24.xls

The data are available on the CD that comes with this text. At the 10% significance level, is there evidence of a difference in the proportions of customers who bought the extended warranty for the two promotion methods?

5. Create a 90% confidence interval estimate for the difference in the proportions of customers who bought the extended warranty for the two promotion methods described in Exercise 4 above. Do you expect this interval to include zero? Why or why not?

11.2   GOODNESS-OF-FIT TESTS

So far, our decision making about qualitative data has been done in a binomial context. That is, we have been interested in the proportion of the data that corresponds to a desired characteristic (the success), and all other characteristics have been characterized as failures.

We will now move from a *binomial* context to a *multinomial* context, where the data can be classified into a number of different categories, all of which are of interest to us. It is possible to test to see if sample data conform to a hypothesized distribution across a number of categories. As the examples that follow illustrate, it is possible to test to see if the candy produced at a factory has the right proportions of colours. We can also test to see if the educational attainment of managers in an accounting firm has changed over the past five years. We do these tests by focusing on the counts of data in each category.

The technique that we use in such cases is called the chi-squared (χ^2) goodness-of-fit test ("chi" is pronounced "ky" to rhyme with "sky"). The approach is quite sensible. We calculate the number of data points we would expect to see in each category, assuming the distribution is as claimed, and then compare the expected counts with the observed counts. If there is a significant difference between the observed and expected values, then we conclude that the distribution is not as we thought. Of course, we need a sampling distribution to help us make that decision. The test statistic is calculated as follows:

$$\chi^2 = \sum \frac{(o_i - e_i)^2}{e_i}$$

For each category, the difference between the observed and expected values is squared, and then divided by the expected value. The resulting terms are added up for all categories to get the χ^2 test statistic. As usual, we will use a Roman letter (X^2 in this case) to refer to the χ^2 test statistic when it is estimated from sample data.

It is always a *large* value of the test statistic that leads to rejection of the null hypothesis, because of the way the statistic is calculated. The chi-squared test offers only a conclusion about whether the observed and expected frequencies match. As a result, there is no such thing as a *right-tailed* or a *left-tailed* chi-squared test. There is only *one* test: that is, whether the distribution appears to be as desired or claimed. And it is always large values of the test statistic that lead us to conclude that the distribution is not as desired or claimed. The p-value in a chi-squared test is always $P(X^2 \geq \text{calculated value})$.

How large is large enough? That depends on the chi-squared distribution, which is another distribution that has degrees of freedom. In the case of a multinomial distribution with k categories, the degrees of freedom are $k - 1$.

Sampling Distribution of X^2

For a goodness-of-fit test, when expected values are ≥ 5, the sampling distribution of the X^2 statistic is approximately chi-squared, with $k - 1$ degrees of freedom (where k is the number of categories in the data).

The chi-squared distribution has a shape that depends on the degrees of freedom, but it is generally skewed to the right. Exhibit 11.4 below illustrates the chi-squared distribution for 8 and 16 degrees of freedom.

Chi-Squared Distribution

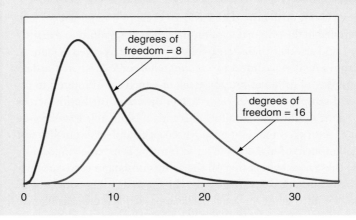

Example 11.2a below illustrates a goodness-of-fit test.

A candy manufacturer has definite rules about the colour mixture of its candy-coated peanuts. Currently, the manufacturing process is set up to produce candies according to the distribution shown in Exhibit 11.5.

Goodness-of-fit test

Candy Colours Desired Proportions

Red	Green	Blue	Yellow
40%	30%	20%	10%

The company wants to be sure it is still achieving this colour balance after a recent reorganization of the production process at one of its plants. A random sample of candies is selected. The breakdown of colours is as shown in Exhibit 11.6.

Candy Colours Count from Sample

Red	Green	Blue	Yellow
305	265	201	96

Exhibit 11.6

Is the company still achieving the desired colour balance at the plant after reorganizing the production process?

We begin by comparing the actual counts of the candies of each colour with the expected counts. There are 867 candies in the sample, in total. 40% of them should be red, so the expected number of red candies is 40% of 867 = 346.8. Now, of course we wouldn't expect the company to produce 0.8 of a red candy, so you might be tempted to round this number to the nearest whole number. Don't! For the purposes of this test, we will keep the numbers as calculated. Continuing on, we can calculate

- the expected number of green candies = 0.30 • 867 = 260.1
- the expected number of blue candies = 0.20 • 867 = 173.4
- the expected number of yellow candies = 0.10 • 867 = 86.7

Exhibit 11.7 below summarizes the calculations.

Candy Colours

	Red	Green	Blue	Yellow	Total
Observed sample values (o_i)	305	265	201	96	867
Expected percentage of values	40%	30%	20%	10%	
Expected values (e_i)	= 0.40 • 867 = 346.8	260.1	173.4	86.7	867

Exhibit 11.7

Now, we can see by looking at the table that the observed and expected values differ. But is this normal sampling variability, or is it a significant difference? In order to decide, we have to calculate the chi-squared test statistic.

The X^2 test statistic is based on the differences between the observed and expected values. Of course, if we merely added up these differences, they would sum to zero, which would not be helpful. We will deal with the problem of the cancelling out of differences as we always have, by squaring the differences. We also standardize by dividing each squared difference by its expected value.

$$X^2 = \sum \frac{(o_i - e_i)^2}{e_i}$$

Exhibit 11.8 below illustrates the calculations for the example.

11.8

Exhibit

Candy Colours Chi-Squared Test Statistic Calculations

	Red	Green	Blue	Yellow	Total
Observed sample values (o_i)	305	265	201	96	867
Expected values (e_i)	346.8	260.1	173.4	86.7	867
($o_i - e_i$)	−41.8	4.9	27.6	9.3	
($o_i - e_i$)^2	1747.24	24.01	761.76	86.49	
$\dfrac{(o_i - e_i)^2}{e_i}$	5.03818	0.09231	4.39308	0.99758	10.5211457

There are some things you should notice about these calculations.

1. A good check that you've calculated expected values correctly is to sum them. They should sum up to the sample size (867 in the case of the example).
2. The X^2 test statistic will always be a positive number, because we square the differences between the observed and expected values.
3. The further apart are the observed and expected values, the larger the X^2 test statistic will be. This gives us a clue about how we will decide if there is a significant difference between observed and expected values. If the X^2 test statistic is *large*, we will conclude that the sample evidence suggests that the data do not fit the hypothesized distribution across categories.

Remember, it is always a *large* value of the test statistic that leads to rejection of the null hypothesis, because of the way the statistic is calculated. In the example, the number of candies is larger than expected for some colours (for example, green), and for other colours, the number of candies is smaller than expected (red). The chi-squared test offers us no guidance on whether these individual category counts are too large or too small. It only offers a conclusion about whether the numbers match, that is, whether the distribution is as claimed or desired.

In the example, there are four categories, so the degrees of freedom are $4 - 1 = 3$. The p-value in this case is $P(X^2 \geq 4.53)$, with three degrees of freedom. When we are doing a problem by hand, we will use the X^2 table on page 464 to approximate this p-value. The relevant row from the table is shown below in Exhibit 11.9. This table is set up in a similar fashion to the t-distribution tables we have used before.

11.9

Exhibit

χ^2 Distribution Critical Values

Degrees of Freedom	$x^2_{.100}$	$x^2_{.050}$	$x^2_{.025}$	$x^2_{.010}$	$x^2_{.005}$
3	6.251	7.815	9.348	11.345	12.838

10.5211

From the table, we can see that $0.010 < $ p-value $ < 0.025$. This means that the observed values in the sample are significantly different from the expected values. It would be highly unusual to get sample results like ours, if the distribution of candy colours actually does match the distribution of colours desired by the manufacturer.

Let's recap all of this in standard hypothesis testing format.

- H_0: the distribution of candy colours is as desired by the manufacturer: 40% red, 30% green, 20% blue, and 10% yellow.
- H_1: the distribution of candy colours is not as desired by the manufacturer (this means that at least two of the category percentages differ)
- $\alpha = 0.05$ (given)
- $X^2 = \sum \dfrac{(o_i - e_i)^2}{e_i} = 10.5211$, degrees of freedom $= k - 1 = 4 - 1 = 3$
- p-value $= P(X^2 \geq 10.5211) < 0.025$

Reject H_0. There is sufficient evidence to infer that the distribution of candy colours differs from the distribution desired by the manufacturer.

This result tells us that the production reorganization has not been completely successful in terms of candy colours, and some adjustments must be made. The chi-squared test itself does not give us any information about how the sampled distribution differs from the desired distribution. More analysis will be required to see what is wrong. For example, we could calculate the percentages of colour in the sample, and compare them with the desired percentages. We might even draw a bar graph to illustrate. These results are shown in Exhibit 11.10 below. The bar chart allows us to see that the problems are most pronounced with the red and blue colours.

Candy Colours

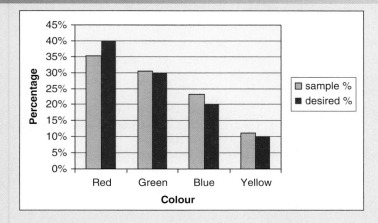

Exhibit **11.10**

The information about the sampling distribution provided above indicated that all of the expected values must be at least 5. This leads to a question: what if they are not? Usually there is some way to combine categories so that the test is still useful, and the required condition is met. Example 11.2b below illustrates such a situation.

Goodness-of-fit test, adjusting when $e_i < 5$

The human resources department at an international accounting firm claims that there has been a change in the managers' level of education during the last five years. The department presents a table of sample data showing the highest level of education achieved for managers, both five years ago and currently. Do the data support the human resources department's claim?

The data are shown in Exhibit 11.11 below.

Education Levels of Managers at Accounting Firm

Highest Level of Education	Percent of Managers Five Years Ago	Number of Managers Currently
High school diploma	15	19
College diploma	64	132
University degree	8	30
Master's degree	11	30
Higher than master's degree	2	5
Total	100	216

If there had been no change in the educational attainment of managers, the percentages of managers in each category would be about the same now as five years ago. We will proceed by calculating the expected number of managers in each category now, based on the category percentages five years ago, and then compare actual with expected numbers in each education category.

Five years ago, 15% of managers in the sample had a high school diploma as their highest level of education. The expected number of managers with a high school diploma in the sample today would be 15% of 216 = 32.4 (once again, although we obviously cannot have 0.4 of a manager (or could we?), we do not round).

Education Levels of Managers at Accounting Firm

Highest Level of Education	Percent of Managers Five Years Ago	Expected Number of Managers Currently	Number of Managers
High school diploma	15	19	32.4
College diploma	64	132	138.24
University degree	8	30	17.28
Master's degree	11	30	23.76
Higher than master's degree	2	5	4.32
Total	100	216	216

As always, we must check the conditions before proceeding any further. While all of the observed values in each category are 5 or more, notice that the expected number of managers with more than a master's degree is only 4.32, which is less than 5. Since the expected values have to be more than 5, we cannot proceed directly with our analysis.

Generally, the way to deal with this problem is to combine categories in a logical way. An obvious option for this data set is to combine the categories for the two highest levels of education, that is, the "master's degree" and "higher than master's degree" categories. The revised data table is shown below in Exhibit 11.13.

Education Levels of Managers at Accounting Firm

Highest Level of Education	Percent of Managers Five Years Ago	Number of Managers Currently	Expected Number of Managers
High school diploma	15	19	32.4
College diploma	64	132	138.24
University degree	8	30	17.28
Master's degree or higher	13	35	28.08
Total	100	216	216

Exhibit 11.13

The full hypothesis test is shown below.

- H_0: the distribution of managers by highest level of education is the same now as it was five years ago
- H_1: the distribution of managers by highest level of education is not the same now as it was five years ago
- $\alpha = 0.05$ (given)

$$X^2 = \sum \frac{(o_i - e_i)^2}{e_i} = \frac{(19 - 32.4)^2}{32.4} + \frac{(132 - 138.24)^2}{138.24}$$

$$+ \frac{(30 - 17.28)^2}{17.28} + \frac{(35 - 28.08)^2}{28.08} = 16.89233$$

The revised table has four categories, so the distribution has three degrees of freedom. The relevant row from the χ^2 table on page 464 is shown in Exhibit 11.14.

χ^2 Distribution Critical Values

Degrees of Freedom	$x^2_{.100}$	$x^2_{.050}$	$x^2_{.025}$	$x^2_{.010}$	$x^2_{.005}$
3	6.251	7.815	9.348	11.345	12.838

16.892

Exhibit 11.14

We see that p-value $= P(X^2 \geq 16.892) < 0.005$.

Reject H_0. There is sufficient evidence to infer that the distribution of managers by education level is not the same now as it was five years ago.

Once again, a bar graph might be helpful in illustrating the differences, as Exhibit 11.15 shows. We can see from the graph that there appear to be differences in all of the categories.

11.15 Managers' Highest levels of Education, Accounting Firm

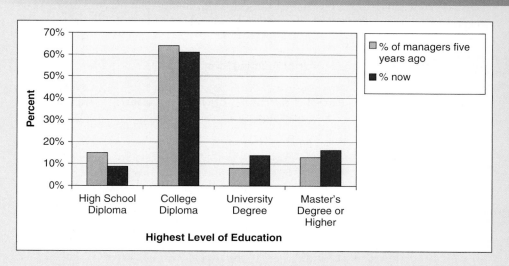

Instructions

The calculations to get the expected values for a goodness-of-fit test are quite straightforward and can be done with basic Excel formulas. However, calculation of the X^2 statistic can be quite time-consuming, and it is helpful to use a computer. Once you have the expected values in a goodness-of-fit test, you can use the Excel function called CHITEST to get the p-value.

The dialogue box for the CHITEST function is shown below in Exhibit 11.16.

11.16 CHITEST Dialogue Box

Function Arguments [?][X]

CHITEST
Actual_range [ ] = array
Expected_range [ ] = array

=

Returns the test for independence: the value from the chi-squared distribution for the statistic and the appropriate degrees of freedom.

Actual_range is the range of data that contains observations to test against expected values.

Formula result =

Help on this function   [OK] [Cancel]

The function arguments in Excel are as follows.

- Actual_range is the cells where the observed values are recorded.
- Expected_range is the cells where the expected values are recorded.

The result that is returned from the CHITEST function is the *p*-value of the X^2 statistic. As usual, you should enter some text into an adjoining cell so that the output is labelled. Excel calculates the *p*-value for Example 11.2b as 0.00199193, which is consistent with our estimation of the *p*-value from the table as being <0.005.

Guide to Decision Making

Goodness-of-Fit Tests

When:

- qualitative data, single population, with two or more categories
- trying to make a decision about the distribution across categories in the population, based on the sample distribution

Steps:

1. Specify H_0, the null hypothesis (which is that the population is distributed as claimed/desired).
2. Specify H_1, the alternative hypothesis (which is that the population is *not* as claimed/desired).
3. Determine or identify α, the significance level.
4. Collect or identify the sample data. Identify or calculate:

   - o_i, the observed frequency in each category (based on sample data)
   - e_i, the expected frequency in each category (based on the claimed/desired distribution)

5. Check that each $e_i \geq 5$, to ensure that the sampling distribution is approximately chi-squared. If any $e_i < 5$, combine categories to meet this condition.
6. If the conditions are met, calculate the appropriate test statistic, using the following formula:

$$X^2 = \Sigma \frac{(o_i - e_i)^2}{e_i}$$

7. Use the chi-squared distribution with $k - 1$ degrees of freedom to calculate (or approximate, if using tables) the appropriate *p*-value for the hypothesis test, which will be $P(X^2 \geq$ calculated value), where k is the number of categories.
8. If *p*-value $< \alpha$, reject H_0 and conclude that there is sufficient evidence to decide in favour of H_1. If *p*-value $> \alpha$, fail to reject H_0 and conclude that there is insufficient evidence to decide in favour of H_1.

DEVELOP YOUR SKILLS

1. A furniture store has a number of payment options available to customers. Some customers pay immediately. Others delay payment for six months, with no interest and no financing charges. Others delay payment for a year, but with interest and financing charges. In the past, 26% of customers paid immediately, 37% delayed payment for six months, and 37% delayed payment for a year. The store manager is wondering if current customers have changed their payment selections from the past. The manager takes a random survey of 75 store customers, and asks them to indicate which payment plan they would prefer. Of the 75, 23 would pay immediately, 32 would delay payment for six months, and the rest would delay payment for a year. At the 5% significance level, is there evidence of a change in customers' preferences for the different payment plans?

2. A new manager has been hired to run the campus student pub. The pub sells a limited selection of brands of beer. The past manager (who was fired because of incompetence) indicated that the brand preferences of the pub's customers were as shown in Exhibit 11.17 below.

The new manager wants to check on customer preferences so that he can order the correct quantities of each brand of beer. In a random sample of 85 customers, 29 preferred Labatt Blue, 6 preferred Labatt Blue Light, 21 preferred Molson Canadian, 16 preferred Kokanee, and the remainder preferred Rickard's Honey Brown. Is there evidence, at the 5% level of significance, that customers' brand preferences are different from what the previous manager thought?

11.17 Brand Preferences of Customers at Campus Pub

Labatt Blue	Labatt Blue Light	Molson Canadian	Kokanee	Rickard's Honey Brown
33%	8%	25%	19%	15%

3. John is a small businessman who gets in over his head, incurring debts he cannot pay. In desperation, he turns to the local motorcycle gang to borrow some money to keep his business afloat. He hopes to solve his money problems at the local casino. At first he does well, winning regularly, and then he makes a huge bet and loses it all. He is left alone, despondent, drinking bad Scotch and staring at one of the dice that let him down. He decides to check to see if the die is fair. He rolls it repeatedly, recording how many times each side comes up. The results are shown in Exhibit 11.18 below. Is the die fair? (Will Mary ever forgive him?) Use $\alpha = 0.025$.

11.18 Observations from Repeated Tosses of a Die

1 Spot	2 Spots	3 Spots	4 Spots	5 Spots	6 Spots
18	24	17	25	16	25

4. A travel agency collects data on the proportion of its customers who want to travel to popular destinations. Historically, the customer preferences have been as indicated in Exhibit 11.19.

11.19 Customer Preferences at a Travel Agency

Canada	U.S.	Caribbean	Europe	Asia	Australia/ New Zealand	Other
28%	32%	22%	12%	2%	3%	1%

A random sample of 54 customers revealed that:
- 22 wanted to travel in Canada
- 14 wanted to travel to the U.S.
- 8 wanted to travel to the Caribbean
- 8 wanted to travel to Europe
- 2 wanted to travel to Australia/New Zealand
- no one wanted to travel to another destination.

At the 4% level of significance, is there evidence of a change in the customer preferences at this travel agency?

5. In the past, about 40% of Ben Little's haircutting salon's customers were rural, and 60% were urban. Ben takes a random sample of 50 of his customers, and discovers that 30 are rural, and 20 are urban. Is there evidence, at the 2.5% level of significance, that the urban/rural characteristics of Ben's customers have changed?

11.3 COMPARING MANY POPULATION PROPORTIONS OR TESTING INDEPENDENCE

We first encountered contingency tables in Chapter 4. Such tables are a good means of summarizing qualitative characteristics for a number of different populations or sub-populations. For example, in Chapter 4, we used a contingency table to describe Ben Little's customers at his haircutting salon, according to whether they were urban or rural, and satisfied or not satisfied with the services of the salon.

Comparing Many Population Proportions

We are now going to test to see if contingency table data conform to our expectations. For example, Ben might have some idea about the urban/rural breakdown of his customers' characteristics, and it is possible to use the sample data to see if his idea is correct. As well, we can use the sample data to decide if there is a relationship between the location of customers and whether they are satisfied with Ben's salon.

We will start the contingency table analysis with a simple example.

Suppose a survey of customers from stores A, B, C, and D recorded the method of payment by customers. The sample results are shown in Exhibit 11.20 below.

With this data set, we could do a number of different analyses. We have sampled from four populations (the types of customer payments at the four locations). We could, for example, compare the proportions of cash/debit card sales at the four locations. Notice that this is an extension of the comparison of two proportions (discussed in Section 11.1) to comparison of four proportions in four populations. However, the

Example 11.3a

Contingency table test, comparing many populations

Exhibit 11.20

Customer Payment Method

	Store A	Store B	Store C	Store D	Total
Cash/debit card	40	65	20	25	150
Credit card	30	80	30	40	180
Cheque	30	55	50	35	170
Total	100	200	100	100	500

chi-squared analysis allows us to go beyond this. It is possible to do a comparison of the proportions of all three payment types at the four locations (that is, in all four populations simultaneously). As before, the chi-squared test focuses on counts.

The approach is still based on comparing observed and expected values. Expected values are calculated based on the null hypothesis that the proportion of sales of each type is the same for all four locations. As we did for tests of whether two proportions are equal, we will pool the sample data to get the expected proportion of each type of payment. The original table including all of the data categories is shown in Exhibit 11.21.

Exhibit 11.21

Customer Payment Method

	Store A	Store B	Store C	Store D	Total
Cash/debit card	40	65	20	25	150
Credit card	30	80	30	40	180
Cheque	30	55	50	35	170
Total	100	200	100	100	500

For example, we see from the table that out of the 500 payments included in all four samples, 150 were cash (or debit card payments, which transfer the money immediately to the store's bank account, so we'll refer to cash and debit card payments jointly as simply *cash*). This includes 40 cash payments from store A, 65 from store B, 20 from store C, and 25 from store D. Therefore:

- $\hat{p}_{cash} = \dfrac{150}{500} = 0.3$

- $\hat{p}_{credit\ card} = \dfrac{180}{500} = 0.36$, and

- $\hat{p}_{cheque} = \dfrac{170}{500} = 0.34$.

To calculate expected values, we simply apply these proportions to each of the four samples. This is quite easy to do in this example, because three of the sample sizes are 100. If the expected proportion of cash payments is 0.3, then the expected number of cash payments for store A $= \hat{p}_{cash} \cdot n_A = 0.3 \cdot 100 = 30$. Similarly, the expected number of cash payments for store B $= \hat{p}_{cash} \cdot n_B = 0.3 \cdot 200 = 60$. Exhibit 11.22 below shows the calculations of expected values. As you go through the calculations, you will see that they rely on row and column totals in the table. In fact, you can summarize the calculation of the expected value as follows:

$$\text{expected value} = \frac{\left(\begin{array}{c}\text{row}\\\text{total}\end{array}\right)\left(\begin{array}{c}\text{column}\\\text{total}\end{array}\right)}{\left(\begin{array}{c}\text{grand}\\\text{total}\end{array}\right)}$$

Exhibit 11.22

Customer Payment Method

	Store A	Store B	Store C	Store D	Total
Cash (observed)	40	65	20	25	150
Cash (expected)	$0.3 \cdot 100$ $= 30$	$0.3 \cdot 200$ $= 60$	$0.3 \cdot 100$ $= 30$	$0.3 \cdot 100$ $= 30$	$\hat{p}_{cash} = \dfrac{150}{500} = 0.3$
Credit card (observed)	30	80	30	40	180
Credit card (expected)	$0.36 \cdot 100$ $= 36$	$0.36 \cdot 200$ $= 72$	$0.36 \cdot 100$ $= 36$	$0.36 \cdot 100$ $= 36$	$\hat{p}_{credit\ card} = \dfrac{180}{500} = 0.36$
Cheque (observed)	30	55	50	35	170
Cheque (expected)	34	68	34	34	$\hat{p}_{cheque} = \dfrac{170}{500} = 0.34$
Total	100	200	100	100	500

Calculation of the X^2 statistic is the same as before, that is:

$$X^2 = \Sigma \frac{(o_i - e_i)^2}{e_i}$$

If you are doing this by hand, the calculation will be as follows:

$$
\begin{aligned}
X^2 &= \Sigma \frac{(o_i - e_i)^2}{e_i} \\[6pt]
&= \frac{(40-30)^2}{30} + \frac{(30-36)^2}{36} + \frac{(30-34)^2}{34} \\[6pt]
&\quad + \frac{(65-60)^2}{60} + \frac{(80-72)^2}{72} + \frac{(55-68)^2}{68} \\[6pt]
&\quad + \frac{(20-30)^2}{30} + \frac{(30-36)^2}{36} + \frac{(50-34)^2}{34} \\[6pt]
&\quad + \frac{(25-30)^2}{30} + \frac{(40-36)^2}{36} + \frac{(35-34)^2}{34} \\[6pt]
&= 21.7647
\end{aligned}
$$

The degrees of freedom for the chi-squared distribution for a contingency table are equal to $(r-1)(c-1)$, where r is the number of rows in the table, and c is the number of columns (not including the totals). In this case, there are three rows and four columns, so the degrees of freedom are $(3-1)(4-1) = 2(3) = 6$. Exhibit 11.23 below shows the appropriate row from the chi-squared table in the back of this text.

X^2 Distribution Critical Values

Degrees of freedom	$X^2_{.100}$	$X^2_{.050}$	$X^2_{.025}$	$X^2_{.010}$	$X^2_{.005}$
6	10.645	12.592	14.449	16.812	18.548

21.7647

Exhibit **11.23**

From the table, we can see that the p-value < 0.005. It would be highly unlikely that we would obtain a sample result such as this one, if the proportions of payment types were the same at all four store locations. Therefore we will conclude that the proportions of payment types are *not* the same at all four store locations.

To summarize, let's recap all of this in standard hypothesis testing format.

- H_0: the proportions of payment types are the same at all four store locations
- H_1: the proportions of payment types differ at the four store locations

- $X^2 = \Sigma \dfrac{(o_i - e_i)^2}{e_i} = 21.7647$, degrees of freedom $= 6$

- all $e_i \geq 5$
- p-value $= P(X^2 \geq 21.7647) < 0.005$

Reject H_0. There is sufficient evidence to infer that the proportions of payment types differ at the four store locations.

Using Excel Add-in for Chi-Squared Expected Values Calculations

Instructions

Doing the calculations for the X^2 statistic for a contingency table can be quite time-consuming, and it is helpful to use a computer. Unfortunately, there is no Data Analysis tool in Excel to allow you to calculate expected values easily. One of the Excel add-ins that comes with this text allows you to quickly and easily calculate expected values and the chi-squared statistic. Once the add-ins are installed, click on Tools on the Excel toolbar, then click on Non-Parametric Tools . . . , then choose Chi-Squared Expected Values Calculations.

The dialogue box for the Chi-Squared Expected Values Calculations is shown below in Exhibit 11.24.

Exhibit 11.24

Chi-Squared Expected Values Calculations Dialogue Box

You must indicate the range where the table of observed values is located. Note that you should include one row and one column of titles in your selection. You should *not* include totals in your selection. As well, the add-in will not work if any of the cells contain formulas. If they do, you should copy your table of observed values and Paste Special. . . , as Values. Then use the add-in with this copy of the table.

The output produced by the add-in for the data in Example 11.3a is shown below in Exhibit 11.25.

Exhibit 11.25

Chi-Squared Expected Values for Example 11.3a

Chi-Squared Expected Values Calculations					
Chi-squared test statistic	21.76471				
# of expected values ,5	0				
p-value	0.001336				
		Store A	*Store B*	*Store C*	*Store D*
Cash		30	60	30	30
Credit Card		36	72	36	36
Cheque		34	68	34	34

The output produces a table of expected values. It also provides the chi-squared test statistic, and the associated *p*-value. The output also indicates the number of expected values less than 5. Any expected values less than 5 will be highlighted in yellow in the output. Of course, you should not rely on the test statistic or *p*-value if there are any expected values less than 5. You should combine categories as necessary, and re-do the calculations.

Testing for Independence

In the sample of payment types by store discussed above, a fixed number of randomly selected payments were examined from each store. However, suppose that instead we had taken a random sample of 500 payments from the four stores, keeping track of payment type. In such a case, there is another interpretation of the result of the hypothesis test we did, as follows: there is a relationship between the types of payments and the store location. Another way to say this is that the payment types are not independent of the store locations. Such tests are tests of independence.

Tests for independence were discussed in Chapter 4. You may remember that we examined independence in samples, with contingency tables (see p. 145), but you were also warned that you would need the statistical tools presented in this chapter to draw conclusions for an entire population. Nevertheless, there is a correspondence between the calculations you did in Chapter 4 and the expected value calculations we do for the chi-squared analysis.

We learned in Chapter 4 that the test for independence is to check to see if

$$P(A \text{ and } B) = P(A) \cdot P(B)$$

Let's apply this to the example above. If, for example, "store A" and "credit card" were independent events, then P(store A and credit card) should equal P(store A) · P(credit card). From the table, we can see that:

- $P(\text{store A}) = \dfrac{100}{500} = 0.2$

- $P(\text{credit card}) = \dfrac{100}{500} = 0.36$

If the events are independent, then

$$P(\text{store A and credit card})$$

$$= P(\text{store A}) \cdot P(\text{credit card})$$

$$= 0.2(0.36)$$

$$= 0.072$$

If "store A" and "credit card" are independent, we would expect that $0.072 \cdot 500 = 36$ of the payments at store A would have been made by credit card. Notice that this exactly matches the expected value we calculated for the chi-squared analysis. All of the *expected* values are the values we would get if the factors listed in the table were independent.

The chi-squared test for independence works the same way as the test for comparing many population proportions. Example 11.3b illustrates.

11.3b

Contingency table test for independence

A manufacturing plant runs three 8-hour shifts every day. A quality control inspector is interested to see if the level of product defects varies with the shift. A random sample of 1,200 items is collected, and the defects and the shift during which the items were produced are recorded. The results are summarized in Exhibit 11.26 below.

11.26

Quality Control, Observed Values

Shift	Items with No Apparent Defects	Items with One Minor Defect	Items with More than One Minor Defect
8:00 A.M.–4:00 P.M.	351	25	10
4:00 P.M.–midnight	389	51	13
midnight–8:00 A.M.	315	37	9

Expected values are calculated as before. The output for the Chi-Squared Expected Values Calculations add-in is shown below in Exhibit 11.27.

11.27

Chi-Squared Expected Values for Example 11.3b

Chi-Squared Expected Values Calculations			
Chi-squared test statistic	6.1922304		
# of expected values < 5	0		
p-value	0.185245		
Shift	*Items with no apparent defects*	*Items with one minor defect*	*Items with more than one minor defect*
8:00 a.m.–4 p.m.	339.35833	36.34833	10.29333
4:00 p.m.–midnight	398.2625	42.6575	12.08
midnight–8:00 a.m.	317.37917	33.99417	9.626667

All of the expected values are ≥ 5, so the necessary conditions are met.

- H_0: the level of product defects is independent of the shift
- H_1: the level of product defects is related to the shift

- $X^2 = \Sigma \frac{(o_i - e_i)^2}{e_i} = 6.192230$, degrees of freedom $= (r - 1)(c - 1)$
$$= (3 - 1)(3 - 1) = 4$$

- p-value $= P(X^2 \geq 6.192230) = 0.185244968$, according to the output in Exhibit 11.27.

Fail to reject H_0. There is insufficient evidence to infer that the level of defects is related to the shift.

Notice that the conclusion of this hypothesis test is *not* "the level of defects depends on the shift." While it is clear there is a relationship, these data by themselves do not tell us anything about *why* the relationship occurs. For example, suppose the true cause of the difference in defect rates is the behaviour of the supervisors on each shift. It would not be correct to say that the level of defects depends on the shift. Instead, the level of defects depends on the supervisor. As always, you should be careful about drawing causality conclusions.

Guide to Decision Making

Contingency Table Tests

When:
- qualitative data, many populations, with two or more categories
- trying to make a decision about whether populations differ across categories
- trying to decide if category characteristics are independent

Steps:
1. Specify H_0, the null hypothesis (which is that the populations are similar, or that category characteristics are independent).
2. Specify H_1, the alternative hypothesis (which is that the populations are not similar, or that category characteristics are related).
3. Determine or identify α, the significance level.
4. Collect or identify the sample data. Identify or calculate:

   - o_i, the observed frequency in each category (based on sample data)
   - e_i, the expected frequency in each category (based on pooling the sample data across all characteristics)

   Generally, for a contingency table:

   $$\text{expected value} = \frac{\left(\begin{array}{c}\text{row}\\\text{total}\end{array}\right)\left(\begin{array}{c}\text{column}\\\text{total}\end{array}\right)}{\left(\begin{array}{c}\text{grand}\\\text{total}\end{array}\right)}$$

5. Check that each $e_i \geq 5$, to ensure that the sampling distribution is approximately chi-squared. If any $e_i < 5$, combine categories to meet this condition.
6. If the conditions are met, calculate the appropriate test statistic, using the following formula:

   $$X^2 = \Sigma\frac{(o_i - e_i)^2}{e_i}$$

7. Use the chi-squared distribution with $(r - 1)(c - 1)$ degrees of freedom to calculate (or approximate, if using tables) the appropriate p-value for the hypothesis test, which will be $P(X^2 \geq \text{calculated value})$.
8. If p-value $< \alpha$, reject H_0 and conclude that there is sufficient evidence to decide in favour of H_1. If p-value $> \alpha$, fail to reject H_0 and conclude that there is insufficient evidence to decide in favour of H_1.

Correspondence Between z-Test and X^2 Test   A two-tailed z-test of $p_1 - p_2$ with a null hypothesis that $p_1 - p_2 = 0$ and the X^2 test of a contingency table are equivalent, when we are dealing with two categories in two populations. In fact, the X^2 statistic is equal to z^2. We can demonstrate this by returning to the example of fitness club memberships discussed at the beginning of the chapter, in Section 11.1.

The survey results showed that of the 153 female survey respondents, 62 had fitness club memberships. Of the 52 male survey respondents, 28 had fitness club memberships. The question asked was: Do the survey results suggest that males and females in Moncton have differing tendencies to have fitness club memberships? We went on to test if the proportions of those belonging to fitness clubs were equal for males and females. Another way to put this would be: is there a relationship between gender and the tendency to have a fitness club membership? If the proportions of those belonging to fitness clubs are equal for both genders, there is no relationship. If the proportions are different, there is a relationship.

We can summarize the sample data in a contingency table, as shown below in Exhibit 11.28, and then test for evidence of a relationship with a χ^2 test.

11.28

Fitness Memberships Among Moncton Adults

	Yes	No	Totals
Male	28	24	52
Female	62	91	153
Totals	90	115	205

An excerpt of the output for the Excel add-in for Chi-Squared Expected Values Calculations is shown below in Exhibit 11.29.

11.29

Chi-Squared Test Results

Chi-Squared Expected Values Calculations	
Chi-squared test statistic	2.797245
# of expected values <5	0
p-value	0.094426

Template

The completed template for Making Decisions About Two Population Proportions, Qualitative Data, for this data set is also shown below in Exhibit 11.30 on the next page.

Notice that the p-value for the two-tailed test of $p_1 - p_2$ is exactly the same as the p-value for the χ^2 test. Notice also that $z^2 = 1.6724966^2 = 2.797245 = X^2$.

Of course, if you want to do a one-tailed test of $p_1 - p_2$, you will have to use the z-score approach. Remember, the χ^2 test tells us only if there is a relationship or not. It tells us nothing about the character of the relationship.

Completed Excel Template

Making Decisions About Two Population Proportions, Qualitative Data	
sample 1 size	52
sample 2 size	153
sample 1 proportion	0.538462
sample 2 proportion	0.405229
n1p1-hat	28
n1q1-hat	24
n2p2-hat	62
n2q2-hat	91
are all np & nq at least 10?	yes
hypothesized difference in means (use decimal form)	0
z-score	1.6724966
one-tailed p-value	0.047213
two-tailed p-value	0.094426

DEVELOP YOUR SKILLS 11.3

1. A random sample of the employees of a large organization were surveyed about their views of a proposed change in the company's health benefits. The results of the survey are shown in Exhibit 11.31. Is there evidence, at the 1% level of significance, that there is a relationship between the views on the proposed health benefits changes and the type of job held in the organization?

Views on Proposed Changes to Health Benefits

	In Favour	Opposed	Undecided
Management	10	18	13
Professional, salaried	56	43	15
Clerical, hourly paid	49	32	8

2. A company that sells sunscreen products wants to know if there is a relationship between people's hair colour and their tendency to apply sunscreen before going outside. For example, it may be that redheads and blondes are more sensitive to the sun, and are therefore more likely to use sunscreen. A random sample of adults were selected, and their hair colour and tendency to use sunscreen were recorded, with the results shown in Exhibit 11.32.

Do you use sunscreen when going outside?

Hair Colour	Always	Usually	Once in a While	Never
Red	26	20	10	10
Blonde	37	24	9	18
Brown	35	34	8	7
Black	23	46	20	21

At the 5% level of significance, is there evidence of a relationship between hair colour and tendency to use sunscreen?

3. A newspaper was trying to determine if there was a relationship between household income and the sections of the newspaper that were most closely read. A random survey of households revealed the results shown in Exhibit 11.33.

At the 2.5% level of significance, is there evidence that income is related to the section of the newspaper read most closely?

11.33

Which section of the newspaper do you read most closely?

Household Income	National and World News	Business	Sports	Arts	Lifestyle
Under $40,000	55	26	72	10	13
$40,000 to $70,000	56	45	43	20	25
Over $70,000	32	48	21	26	22

4. A random sample of 100 students was taken from four large schools in Montreal. The first language of the students was recorded. The results are shown in Exhibit 11.34 below. Is there evidence, at the 5% significance level, of a difference in the proportions of students whose first language is English, French, or something else for these four schools?

11.34

Survey of Montreal Schools

First Language	School #1	School #2	School #3	School #4
English	44	40	50	43
French	42	50	45	40
Other	14	10	5	17

5. The marketing department of a college wanted to know if there was a difference in the proportions of students drawn from inside and outside the college catchment area by program. A random sample of 100 students from each of the business, technology, and nursing programs revealed the results shown in Exhibit 11.35. Is there evidence, at the 2.5% level of significance, that the proportions of students drawn from inside and outside the local area are the same for all three programs?

11.35

Origin of Students in College Programs

	Business	Technology	Nursing
From local area	65	45	58
Not from local area	35	55	42

The techniques in this chapter apply when you have two or more samples of qualitative data. In some cases, the focus is on proportions, and in others, the focus is on counts.

Chapter Summary

11

Comparing Two Proportions

The hypothesis test for comparing two proportions often assumes equal proportions (that is, $H_0: p_1 - p_2 = 0$). In such a case, the sample data are pooled to get an estimate of the population proportion $\hat{p} = \dfrac{x_1 + x_2}{n_1 + n_2}$. The sample size must be large enough that no continuity correction is required, and the sampling distribution is approximately normal ($n_1\hat{p}_1$, $n_1\hat{q}_1$, $n_2\hat{p}_2$, $n_2\hat{q}_2 \geq 10$, and n_1 and n_2 are fairly large). As well, if sampling is done without replacement, the samples should be $< 5\%$ of the population.

If the conditions are met, the hypothesis test can be conducted with a z-score as follows:

$$z = \frac{(\hat{p}_1 - \hat{p}_2) - \mu_{\hat{p}_1 - \hat{p}_2}}{s_{\hat{p}_1 - \hat{p}_2}} = \frac{(\hat{p}_1 - \hat{p}_2) - 0}{\sqrt{\hat{p}\hat{q}\left(\dfrac{1}{n_1} + \dfrac{1}{n_2}\right)}}$$

Excel's Data Analysis Histogram tool can be used to organize coded data to get frequencies (as Example 11.1a on page 375 illustrates). There is an Excel template for making decisions about two population proportions (see p. 376).

It is also possible to make a decision about whether two population proportions differ by some fixed amount, as Example 11.1b on page 376 illustrates.

The Guide to Decision Making for comparing two proportions is on page 378.

A confidence interval estimate for $p_1 - p_2$ can be constructed using the following formula:

$$(\hat{p}_1 - \hat{p}_2) \pm z\text{-score}\sqrt{\frac{\hat{p}_1\hat{q}_1}{n_1} + \frac{\hat{p}_2\hat{q}_2}{n_2}}$$

where the z-score corresponds to the desired level of confidence. Again, this formula is valid only if the normality conditions are met.

An Excel template is available for confidence interval estimates for the difference in two proportions (see p. 380).

Goodness-of-Fit Tests

It is possible to test whether sample data conform to a hypothesized distribution across a number of categories. The technique is the chi-squared goodness-of-fit test, which is based on comparison of observed sample frequencies to expected frequencies. The test statistic is

$$X^2 = \sum \frac{(o_i - e_i)^2}{e_i}$$

The null hypothesis is always that the population is as claimed/desired, and the alternative hypothesis is always that the population is not as claimed or desired. The p-value is always calculated as $P(X^2 \geq$ the calculated sample test statistic), where the related chi-squared distribution has $k - 1$ degrees of freedom (k is the number of categories in the data). A requirement for using the chi-squared sampling distribution is that all expected frequencies should be at least 5. If they are not, you must combine categories in some logical way before proceeding. Example 11.2b on page 386 illustrates.

Calculation of expected values for a goodness-of-fit test is fairly straightforward in Excel, using formulas. The CHITEST function of Excel reports the p-value of the chi-squared hypothesis test, based on observed and expected frequencies. The use of the CHITEST function is described on page 388.

The Guide to Decision Making for a goodness-of-fit test is on page 389.

Comparing Many Population Proportions and Test of Independence

The chi-squared distribution can be used to compare multiple populations across multiple categories (see Example 11.3a on p. 391). It can also be used to test the independence of the categories or characteristics of the sample data (see Example 11.3b on page 396).

The test statistic is

$$X^2 = \Sigma \frac{(o_i - e_i)^2}{e_i}$$

where expected values are calculated as follows:

$$\text{expected value} = \frac{\left(\begin{array}{c}\text{row} \\ \text{total}\end{array}\right)\left(\begin{array}{c}\text{column} \\ \text{total}\end{array}\right)}{\left(\begin{array}{c}\text{grand} \\ \text{total}\end{array}\right)}$$

As with the goodness-of-fit test, the X^2 test statistic should be used only if all expected frequencies are at least 5. If they are not, categories should be combined. The degrees of freedom for the chi-squared distribution are $(r - 1)(c - 1)$, where r is the number of rows in the contingency table, and c is the number of columns (not including totals).

An Excel add-in (see p. 394) is available to do calculations of expected value, the X^2 statistic, and the p-value, as Example 11.3b on page 396 illustrates.

The Guide to Decision Making for contingency table tests is on page 397.

CHAPTER REVIEW EXERCISES

1. A quality control inspector is checking to see if the proportions of different kinds of nuts included in a mixed nuts package meets specifications. She randomly selects one of the bags of nuts off the line, and counts how many nuts of each type are included. The results are shown in Exhibit 11.36 below.

   Does this sample provide any evidence that the proportions of mixed nuts are not as they should be? Use $\alpha = 2.5\%$.

11.36 Exhibit

Company A's Mixed Nuts Package

	Almonds	Peanuts	Hazelnuts	Cashews	Pecans
Desired percentage	22%	48%	10%	10%	10%
Observed number	80	190	36	31	37

2. The company that produces the mixed nuts described in Exercise 1 claims that the percentage of peanuts in the mixed nuts package is less than 50%. Does this sample provide evidence that peanuts make up more than 50% of the mixed nuts in the packages? Use $\alpha = 2.5\%$.

3. A randomly selected package of a competing company's mixed nuts provides the information shown in Exhibit 11.37.

Company B's Mixed Nuts Package

	Almonds	Peanuts	Hazelnuts	Cashews	Pecans
Observed number	163	375	65	75	60

Is there evidence of a difference in the proportions of types of nuts for the two companies? Use $\alpha = 5\%$.

4. Based on the sample evidence in Exhibits 11.36 and 11.37 in Exercises 1 and 3 above, is there evidence of a difference in the proportions of peanuts in the two companies' mixed nuts packages? Use $\alpha = 5\%$.

5. Construct a 90% confidence interval estimate of the difference in the proportions of peanuts in the mixed nuts packages described in the previous exercises. Do you expect this confidence interval to contain zero? Why or why not?

6. A large international company often gives its managers opportunities to work in foreign countries in order to broaden their experience. The company is interested to see if the willingness to accept a foreign posting is related to the family status of the individual being offered the opportunity. A random sample of 190 individuals who had been offered foreign postings in the last year was gathered, as was information about whether they accepted the post, and what their family status was. (Information about family status was freely volunteered by employees.) The results are shown in Exhibit 11.38 below.

Random Sample of Individuals Offered Foreign Postings In the Last Year

Family Status	Accepted Foreign Postings	Declined Foreign Posting
Single, no children	50	8
Single with children	22	10
Partnered, no children	40	8
Partnered with children	38	14

Is there evidence of a relationship between an individual's family status and his/her willingness to accept a foreign posting? Use $\alpha = 5\%$.

7. A random sample of new members of a large downtown fitness club was selected, and tracked over six months. Of the 60 members who joined the club to participate in fitness classes, 38 were still working out regularly six months after joining. Of the 80 members who joined to work out with a personal trainer, 60 were still working out regularly six months after joining. At the 2.5% level of significance, is there evidence of a difference in the proportions of new members still working out regularly six months after joining the club, when comparing those who attend fitness classes and those who work out with a personal trainer?

8. Re-do Exercise 7 above as a chi-squared test. Did you get the same answer? Did you expect to?

9. A large mail order company is trying to decide between two delivery services: Canada Post and a private courier. The private firm's services are more expensive, but it claims to make quicker deliveries than Canada Post. The mail order company selects a random sample of 100 deliveries for the private courier, and another sample of 75 for Canada Post. The proportion of deliveries that were on time or early when sent via the private courier was 0.90. The proportion of deliveries that were on time or early when sent via Canada Post was 0.80. The mail order company has decided that it will pay the higher cost of the private courier if its on-time or early percentage is more than 5% higher than Canada Post's. Should the mail order company use the private courier? Use $\alpha = 2.5\%$.

10. After students apply to college, they receive offers of admission. Students can then accept one of these offers. Colleges work hard to convert offers of admission into acceptances. The sooner a prospective student indicates that he or she will be attending a particular program, the better the college can plan. One college has been experimenting with phone calls from program faculty to prospective students, to encourage students to accept offers of admission. Not all programs have faculty willing to make these phone calls. In a random sample of 275 students who were called by program faculty, 234 sent acceptances. In a random sample of 300 students who were not called, but received only a package in the mail, 232 sent acceptances. Is there evidence that the proportion of prospective students who send acceptances is higher when they get calls from program faculty? Use $\alpha = 2.5\%$.

11. Construct a 95% confidence interval estimate for the difference in proportions of students who send acceptances after receiving offers of admission, comparing those who receive phone calls from program faculty to those who receive only packages in the mail. (See Exercise 10 above.)

12. The human resources (HR) department of a large Canadian company has been sending many of its employees to conflict resolution training sessions. The HR manager is concerned that the managers of the company are resistant to the training. A random sample of 50 managers who have been on the training is selected. Of these, 36 declare the training to have been a total waste of time. A random sample of 76 non-managerial employees who have been on the training is also selected. Of these, 38 say that the training was a total waste of time. Is there evidence of a difference in the proportions of managers and non-managers who thought that the conflict resolution training was a waste of time? Use $\alpha = 2.5\%$.

13. Consider the conflict resolution training described in Exercise 12 above. If you were the manager of the HR department, would you continue the training? Why or why not? (Your answer must be supported by the data.)

14. A car parts plant is concerned that some of its employees are more likely to call in sick on Fridays or Mondays (the plant operates only five days a week). An analyst randomly selects one week, and records the number of absences each day. The data are shown below in Exhibit 11.39. Based on these sample data, is there evidence that absence levels differ over the days of the week? Use $\alpha = 5\%$.

Exhibit 11.39

Number of Absences, Randomly Selected Week at a Car Parts Plant

Monday	Tuesday	Wednesday	Thursday	Friday
15	8	12	7	16

15. A random sample of people who regularly attend movies in St. John's is selected. Each is asked which of several types of movies is his or her favourite. The answers were categorized according to the gender of the survey respondent. The results are shown in Exhibit 11.40 below. Is there evidence of a relationship between gender and preferred movie type? Use $\alpha = 0.04$.

Random Sample of St. John's Moviegoers

Favourite Movie Type	Male	Female
Action/adventure	32	32
Comedy	12	19
Drama	16	31
Fantasy	18	18
Horror	23	22
Romance	15	26
Thriller	26	15

16. A random sample of 78 employees at a large computer software firm were polled to determine their method of travel to work. A random sample of 80 employees of an accounting firm in the same office complex were also polled. The results are shown in Exhibit 11.41 below. Is there evidence that the proportions of workers who travel to work via the different methods are different between the two firms? Use $\alpha = 5\%$.

Employees' Methods of Travel to Work

	By Transit	In Car	On Bicycle	On Foot
Software firm	51	8	16	3
Accounting firm	52	23	4	1

17. A quality control inspector wants to test that the proportions of defective items in three shipments of components from different manufacturers are equal. A random sample of 125 items is selected from each shipment. The first sample has 36 defective items, the second has 30, and the third has 38. Test to see if there is evidence of a difference in the proportions of defective items, with $\alpha = 0.05$.

18. A company operates two large plants. In one plant, a random sample of 150 employees revealed that 23 had workplace accidents during the past year. In the other plant, a random sample of 125 employees revealed that 23 had workplace accidents during the past year. At the 5% level of significance, is there evidence of a difference in the proportions of employees who had accidents at the two plants?

19. Re-do Exercise 18 above as a chi-squared test. Is the p-value the same for both tests? Did you expect it to be?

20. Suppose you want to investigate the proportions of different colours in a bag of mixed hard candies. You are feeling too lazy to count the number of candies of each colour, so you hit upon the idea of weighing the candies by colour. Will you be able to use the chi-squared test to analyze the candies? Explain fully and think carefully.

CHAPTER 12

Analyzing Relationships, Two Quantitative Variables

Learning Objectives

After mastering the material in this chapter, you will be able to:

1. Create a scatter diagram and estimate the least-squares regression line for a sample of x-y quantitative data.

2. Check the conditions required for use of the regression model in hypothesis testing and prediction.

3. Conduct a hypothesis test to determine if there is evidence of a significant linear relationship between x and y.

4. Produce (with Excel) and interpret the coefficient of determination for the regression relationship.

5. Use the regression relationship (if appropriate) to make predictions about an individual y-value and an average y-value, given a particular x-value.

INTRODUCTION

Woodbon, a company that produces a limited line of high-quality wooden furniture, has enjoyed remarkable sales growth since its inception in 1980. Woodbon's owner, Kate Cameron, is looking back over the company's years of operation, and is trying to plan for the future. She would like to ensure continued growth in sales, but she's not sure just why sales have grown so steadily over the last 10 years. There are a number of factors that have probably affected sales during this time. Were the advertising campaigns effective? Were the price discounts important? Or is the company's success closely tied to housing construction in the local area? Or to the incomes of the local residents?

Answering these questions might help Kate plan for the future. With the necessary data, she will be able to build a mathematical model to estimate the relationship between sales and the various factors affecting sales. Kate will be able to use this model to assess how strongly sales seem to depend on these factors, and possibly even to make predictions for the future. Excel, and other computer software, makes this mathematical modelling easy to do.

However, Kate must be thoughtful as she analyzes the relationship between sales and various factors affecting sales. All the data in the world cannot *prove* that there is a cause-and-effect relationship between furniture sales and housing starts, for example. Even if the number of housing starts seems to be highly related to furniture sales, the true root cause may be overall economic conditions or consumer confidence. As well, if local economic conditions are changing at a rapid rate, using yesterday's data to predict the future can be unreliable.

While analyzing relationships can be very helpful to decision making, as usual, there is no substitute for careful thinking. The estimated relationships are based on a number of requirements that must be carefully checked before any predictions are made.

Chapter 12 provides an introduction to the analysis of relationships between variables. In this chapter, we will explore simple linear regression models. These mathematical models are used to understand how a variable behaves when one other related variable changes. Any analysis of this kind should start with a graph, as described in Section 12.1. A method called *least-squares regression* is used to estimate the mathematical relationship, and this is also described in Section 12.1. In Section 12.2, you will learn how to assess the sample's compliance with the required conditions for hypothesis testing and prediction. In Section 12.3, you will learn how to test to see if there is evidence of a significant linear relationship between the variables. In Section 12.4, you will see how the coefficient of determination is used to assess the strength of the regression relationship. Finally, in Section 12.4, you will learn how to use the model (and how not to use the model) to make predictions.

12.1   CREATING A GRAPH AND ESTIMATING THE RELATIONSHIP

Kate Cameron, Woodbon's owner, understands that many factors could be affecting her company's sales. Many of these factors (e.g., economic conditions, interest rates, and housing starts) are beyond her control. She decides to focus on just one factor, a factor she can control: advertising. Kate has always been uncertain about how to set her advertising budget, so she decides to examine the relationship between sales and advertising. It makes sense to start with a simple model of this nature. It may turn out that advertising alone is the biggest explanatory factor for sales. If this is the case, then Kate may be able to predict sales on the basis of advertising, without worrying very much about other related factors.

Kate collects the annual advertising and sales figures for the last several years, and realizes that she could make a number of choices about the data. She might look at quarterly or monthly figures, instead of annual ones, for instance. However, she decides that annual figures make sense, since sales are fairly steady throughout the year, and the advertising plan is set only once a year. Kate might also choose to break down her advertising spending by categories, such as spending on newspaper ads or flyers. However, the mix of advertising media used by the company has been similar in every year of operation, so Kate decides that total advertising spending is a good measure of advertising effort.

Kate's data are shown in Exhibit 12.1 on the next page.

12.1 *Exhibit*

Woodbon Sales and Advertising Data, 1984-2004

Annual Advertising Spending ($)	Woodbon Annual Sales ($)	Year
500	26,345	1980
695	31,987	1981
765	21,334	1982
890	25,584	1983
1,035	30,418	1984
1,075	38,295	1985
1,200	55,221	1986
1,300	45,732	1987
1,350	52,394	1988
1,800	53,232	1989
1,400	55,422	1990
1,570	75,385	1991
1,500	64,926	1992
1,650	58,977	1993
1,765	68,515	1994
1,900	74,817	1995
2,000	81,798	1996
2,000	86,228	1997
1,800	88,441	1998
2,000	85,954	1999
2,050	86,531	2000
2,400	87,749	2001
2,500	95,278	2002
2,150	94,600	2003
2,700	95,892	2004

Creating a Graph of the Relationship

The first thing Kate does is create a graph. As discussed in Chapter 2, the usual approach is to put the response variable on the *y*-axis. Kate is examining how sales respond to changes in advertising. As a result, Woodbon's annual sales will be plotted on the *y*-axis of the graph, with advertising spending on the *x*-axis. A scatter diagram of the data is shown in Exhibit 12.2 on the next page.

At first glance, it seems that there is a fairly strong positive relationship between sales and advertising. The relationship is described as positive because the variables increase or decrease together. In the years when advertising spending is higher, sales are higher. The points on the graph present a fairly pronounced pattern.

We notice a couple of other things about this graphical picture of the relationship.

1. First, the relationship appears to be linear. The data points line up in a relatively straight line. There is no obvious curve in the pattern of points. Because

Woodbon Sales and Advertising, First Graph

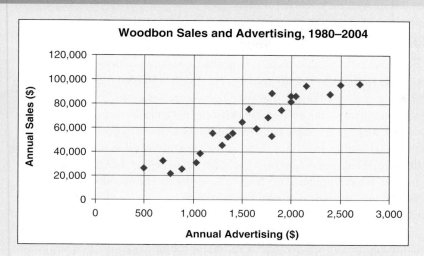

Exhibit 12.2

the relationship appears to be linear, the methods discussed in this chapter can be applied.

2. While the data points do not line up in exactly a straight-line fashion, the points are clustered fairly tightly together. This is usually a good sign, but keep in mind that how a graph looks depends very much on how it is set up (misleading graphs were discussed in Chapter 3).

This point is illustrated by Exhibit 12.3 below, which shows the Woodbon data, but with the *x*- and *y*-axes scaled differently. In this graph, the points appear to be much closer together, which seems to indicate that there is a stronger relationship between the *x*- and *y*-variables; but of course the relationship is exactly the same as shown in Exhibit 12.2. Exhibit 12.3 is provided to reinforce your understanding that the eyeball test is not necessarily reliable for assessing the strength of a relationship.

Woodbon Sales and Advertising, Second Graph

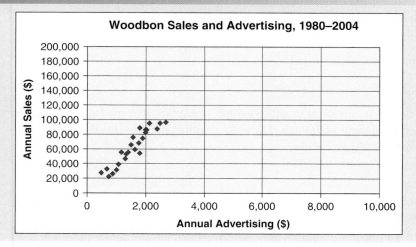

Exhibit 12.3

Misleading graphs aside, the graph of the Woodbon data (Exhibit 12.2) looks promising.

Estimating the Relationship

It appears from Exhibit 12.2 that there is a positive relationship between Woodbon's annual sales and its annual advertising spending. The question is: what is the nature of this relationship? We can examine the data that Woodbon's owner collected, and use it to arrive at a mathematical estimate of the relationship between sales and advertising for Woodbon.

The data that we have is sample data. Even if Kate Cameron has collected *all* of the data available for sales and advertising at Woodbon, we still treat it as sample data. This is because the theoretical model (discussed in more detail below) assumes that there is a range of possible sales values for every level of advertising. The Woodbon sample data is only a subset of this theoretical distribution of values.

We need to come up with the equation of a straight line that best fits the points in the scatter diagram of sample data. We want to set up a straight line because it is the simplest relationship we can specify (and it seems appropriate here, because the points line up in a fairly straight-line fashion). In order to develop the equation of the straight line, we need to estimate two things: the slope and the y-intercept. The equation for the straight line will be:

$$\text{annual sales} = y\text{-intercept} + \text{slope} \cdot \text{annual advertising}$$

In this case, the slope of the line will give us an estimate of how much annual sales increase when annual advertising increases by $1. The y-intercept is an estimate of what the annual sales will be when annual advertising is zero. However, this estimate is not likely to be reliable. As you will see in Section 12.5, it is dangerous to make predictions outside the range of the sample data. Since all the years in the sample data have an advertising budget of at least $500, we should not use these data to predict sales with $0 advertising. However, we still need the y-intercept to fully specify the mathematical relationship between sales and advertising.

We will use some general notation (and some Greek letters, as usual) to describe the theoretical relationship between annual sales and advertising in the population. (The Greek letter β is beta, pronounced "*bay*-tuh.")

$$\text{annual sales} = y\text{-intercept} + \text{slope} \cdot \text{annual advertising}$$
$$\text{annual sales} = \beta_0 + \beta_1 \cdot \text{annual advertising}$$

or, more generally

$$y = \beta_0 + \beta_1 x$$

Of course, we do not know exactly what this theoretical true model is, because we have only sample data to work with. The corresponding notation for the relationship estimated from the sample data is

$$\hat{y} = b_0 + b_1 x$$

The notation $\hat{y}$ is described as y-hat, and is used for the predicted value of y (sales), given a particular x (advertising expenditure). But how do we come up with estimates for the slope and the y-intercept (b_1 and b_0) for the equation of the straight-line relationship between annual sales and advertising?

Chances are that if five different people were asked to draw the line that *best* fits the points in the scatter diagram in Exhibit 12.1, they would draw five different lines. We need some way to decide on a single *best* line, on which everyone can agree.

We do this by focusing on what are called *residuals*. A **residual** is the difference between the observed value of y for a given x, and the predicted value of y for that x. Residuals are also sometimes referred to as the *error term*.

For example, in the Woodbon data, an observation shows actual sales of \$64,926 in a year when advertising spending was \$1,500. To put this in more general language: the observed value of y (sales) is \$64,926, for a given level of x (advertising) of \$1,500. If the best-fitting line predicts sales of \$59,273 for advertising of \$1,500, then the residual is (actual sales − predicted sales) = \$64,926 − \$59,274 = \$5,652.

Exhibit 12.4, below, illustrates the residual for a particular value of x.

residual the difference between the observed value of y for a given x, and the predicted value of y for that x

Residuals

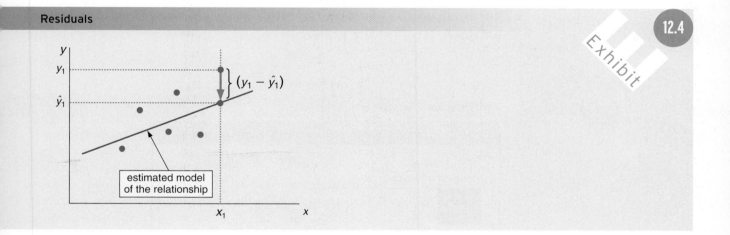

Exhibit **12.4**

In general terms, if we pick a particular value of x and call it x_1, then the corresponding observed value of y would be called y_1. The predicted value of y, given the estimated model of the relationship, is $\hat{y}_1$. The residual is the difference between the observed y-value (y_1) and the predicted y-value ($\hat{y}_1$), or $y_1 - \hat{y}_1$. This difference is represented by the red arrow in the graph above. Of course, there is a residual for every observed pair of $x-y$ data. The residual is equal to zero any time the estimated line passes through an observed sample data point.

If the line that we create fits the points well, then the residuals will be small because the line will be close to all of the points. We could get a score of how well the line fits the points by summing the residuals. However, some of the residuals are positive (observed points are *above* the line) and some are negative (observed points are *below* the line). In order to prevent cancelling out, the residuals are first squared and then added up (you should be familiar with this technique to prevent cancelling out, as we have used it before). The sum of the squared residuals $\Sigma(y_i - \hat{y}_i)^2$ will be small when the line fits the points well. The best-fitting line, called the **least-squares line** (or the *least-squares regression line*), is the one that has the smallest possible sum of the squared residuals.

least-squares line the line that has the smallest possible sum of the squared residuals

Some calculus is required to arrive at the equations for the slope and the y-intercept of the least-squares line (you may be relieved to know that the actual derivations are beyond the scope of this text). The resulting estimates for the y-intercept and the slope of the least-squares line are as follows.

$$b_1 = \frac{\Sigma(x - \bar{x})(y - \bar{y})}{\Sigma(x - \bar{x})^2} \quad \text{and} \quad b_0 = \bar{y} - b_1\bar{x}$$

where $\bar{x}$ and $\bar{y}$ are the averages of all of the x-values and all of the y-values in the sample data set.

While it is possible (particularly with variations of these formulas) to do the arithmetic involved by hand, there is no real reason to do this. Excel provides two tools that can be used to estimate the slope and the y-intercept of the least-squares line. Perhaps the easiest way to use Excel to calculate the regression line is to right-click on the points in the scatter diagram created from the data. One of the choices that comes up is Add Trendline. . . . If you click on this choice, the dialogue box shown in Exhibit 12.5 will appear.

12.5

Exhibit

Add Trendline Dialogue Box, Type Tab

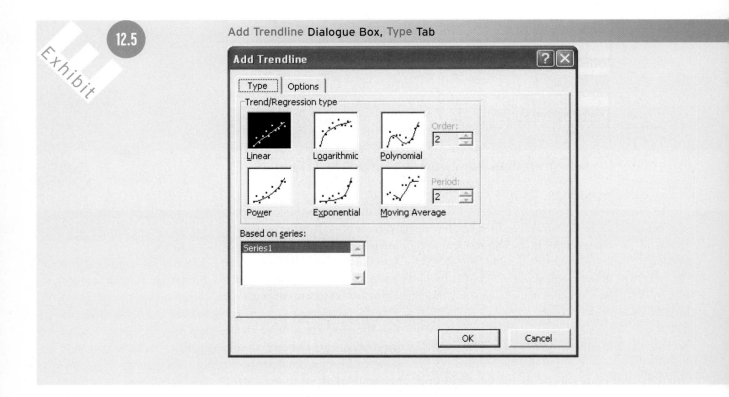

Make sure that the Linear choice is highlighted, and then click on Options. This will lead to the dialogue box shown in Exhibit 12.6.

12.6

Exhibit

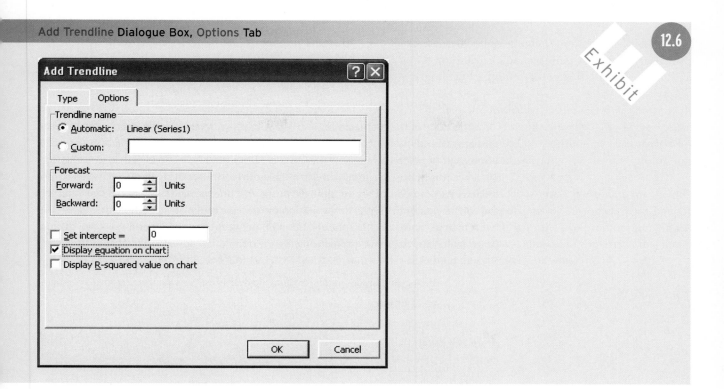

Tick the box beside Display equation on chart, as shown in Exhibit 12.6. Excel will then insert the least-squares line into the scatter diagram, and produce the equation of that line. The result for the Woodbon example is shown in Exhibit 12.7 below.

Woodbon Sales and Advertising, Least-Squares Line

12.7

Exhibit

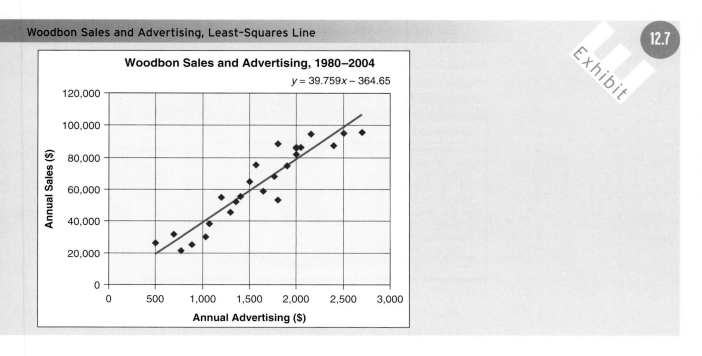

Woodbon Sales and Advertising, 1980–2004

$y = 39.759x - 364.65$

From the output, you can see that the estimated relationship is

$$\hat{y} = 39.759x - 364.65$$

or, in terms of the example

predicted annual sales $= 39.759$(annual advertising expenditure) $- \$364.65$

The slope of the estimated line is 39.759. In this case, this can be interpreted to mean that annual sales will increase by about \$39.76 for every \$1 increase in advertising. The y-intercept of $-\$364.65$ suggests that annual sales would be $-\$364.65$, if advertising were \$0. Since it is impossible to have negative sales, this estimate of the intercept is clearly not reliable. As pointed out above, though, this is not unexpected—we should not interpret the coefficients of the regression equation outside the range of the sample data set.

Once we have specified the relationship between advertising and sales, we can use it to make approximate predictions. For example, if advertising expenditure were \$1,500, predicted sales would be \$59,273.85, as follows:

predicted annual sales $= 39.759$(annual advertising expenditure) $- \$364.65$

$= 39.759(\$1500) - \$364.65$

$= \$59,638.50 - \$364.65$

$= \$59,273.85$

A word of caution is in order here. No matter how well the model fits the data, it would be wildly optimistic (and quite wrong) to think that this arithmetic suggests that spending \$1500 on advertising will lead to exactly \$59,273.85 in sales. Remember, the regression line equation is based on *sample* data. It is more useful and realistic to take an interval estimation approach to predicting sales, which we will do in Section 12.5.

Instructions

The second way to get the equation of the least-squares line is to use the Regression tool available in Data Analysis (under Tools). The choice is highlighted in Exhibit 12.8 below.

12.8

Exhibit

Data Analysis **Dialogue Box**

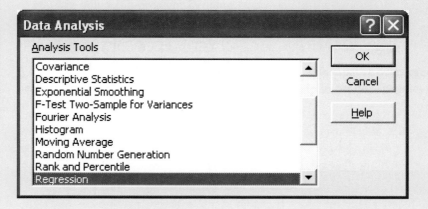

If you click OK here, the next dialogue box is as shown in Exhibit 12.9 opposite.

Regression Dialogue Box

12.9

Regression [?][X]

┌─ Input ──────────────────────────────────────┐
│ Input Y Range: [   ] [≣]   [OK   ]
│ Input X Range: [|] [≣]   [Cancel]
│ ☐ Labels   ☐ Constant is Zero   [Help]
│ ☐ Confidence Level: [95] %
└──┘
┌─ Output options ─────────────────────────────┐
│ ○ Output Range: [   ] [≣]
│ ◉ New Worksheet Ply: [   ]
│ ○ New Workbook
│ ┌─ Residuals ──────────────────────────────┐
│ │ ☐ Residuals   ☐ Residual Plots   │
│ │ ☐ Standardized Residuals ☐ Line Fit Plots│
│ └──┘
│ ┌─ Normal Probability ─────────────────────┐
│ │ ☐ Normal Probability Plots   │
│ └──┘
└──┘

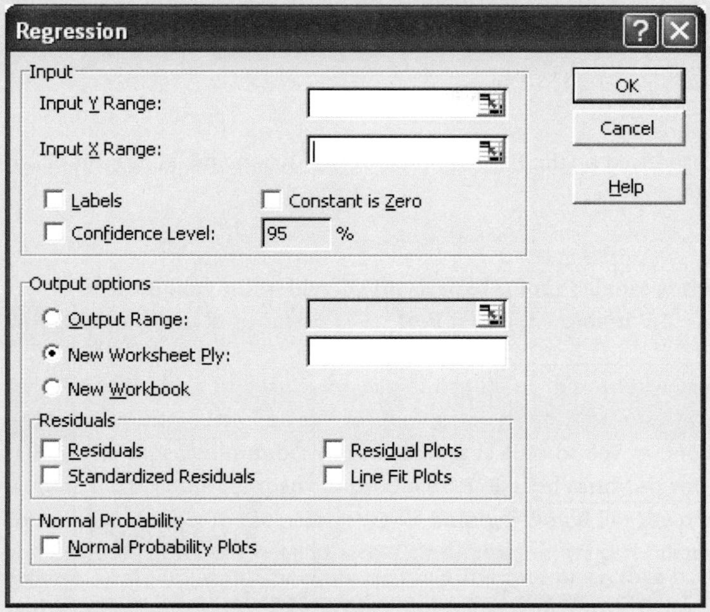

You must use this dialogue box, at a minimum, to specify where the *x*- and *y*-data are (Input Y Range: and Input X Range:), and where the output should go (Output Range:). If you tick Line Fit Plots, Excel will also produce a scatter diagram with the least-squares line shown. An excerpt of the output for the Woodbon data set is shown below in Exhibit 12.10.

Output for Regression, Woodban Data

12.10

SUMMARY OUTPUT	
Regression Statistics	
Multiple R	0.937951686
R Square	0.879753365
Adjusted R Square	0.87452525
Standard Error	8687.161393
Observations	25
ANOVA	
	df
Regression	1
Residual	23
Total	24
	Coefficients
Intercept	−364.6459102
X Variable 1	39.7592486

Excel's Regression tool produces a lot of information, and we will refer to only some of it. In particular, the coefficients of the least-squares line are highlighted in Exhibit 12.10 (but will not be, in Excel). The heading "Intercept" is the estimate of the y-intercept, b_0, and the heading "X Variable 1" is the estimate of the slope, b_1. Once again, we see that the estimated least-squares line is

$$\hat{y} = 39.759x - 364.646$$

The line fit plot produced by the Regression tool is shown below in Exhibit 12.11.

Exhibit 12.11

Excel Line Fit Plot for Woodbon Data

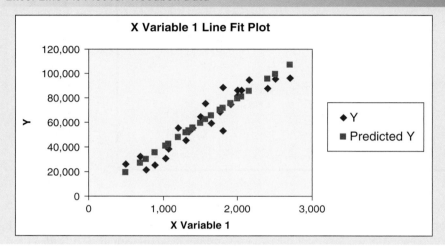

This graph is not as useful as it might be. You should change the labels and titles so that the graph communicates more information, as shown below in Exhibit 12.12.

Exhibit 12.12

Improved Line Fit Plot for Woodbon Data

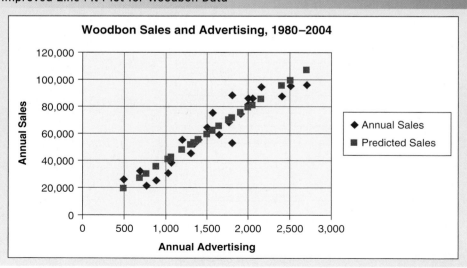

DEVELOP YOUR SKILLS 12.1

Set

1. The Hendrick Software Sales Company has collected data on the number of contacts made by its sales staff, and the software sales, for a random sample of months. Create an appropriate scatter diagram for these data. What is the least-squares regression line? Interpret it See file called DYS12-1-1. xls.

2. Data on monthly income and monthly spending on restaurant meals was collected for a random sample of households in Vancouver. An excerpt of Excel's Regression output is shown below in Exhibit 12.13. What is the equation of the least-squares regression line? Interpret it.

Excel Regression Output for Restaurant Spending

Exhibit 12.13

Regression Statistics	
Multiple R	0.420433
R Square	0.176764
Adjusted R Square	0.168364
Standard Error	34.89859
Observations	100

ANOVA	
	df
Regression	1
Residual	98
Total	99

	Coefficients
Intercept	44.90253
monthly income	0.024144

3. Smith and Klein Manufacturing have data on annual sales and the annual amount spent on promotions, for 1977–2006. Create an appropriate scatter diagram for these data. What is the least-squares regression line? Interpret it. See file called DYS12-1-3.xls.

4. A college professor has collected data for a random sample of 43 of her students. She has their final semester average marks, and the total number of hours each spent working during the semester. The professor has hired one of her students to help her analyze the data, and the student has estimated the regression equation

to be $y = 0.1535x + 90.241$. Why is the professor sure that the student has made a mistake?

5. A researcher has collected data about total revenues and total numbers of employees for a random sample of large international companies. The question that interests the researcher is this: Do companies with more employees have larger revenues? In this data set, which is the response variable and which is the explanatory variable? Create a scatter diagram, estimate the least-squares regression equation, and interpret it. See file called DYS12-1-5.xls.

12.2 ASSESSING THE MODEL

The Theoretical Model

Woodbon's owner has already speculated that many factors could be affecting company sales. Because of this, it would not be reasonable to expect a perfectly linear relationship between sales and advertising spending. For any particular value of advertising spending, there are many different possible levels of sales. These possible sales levels arise because of variations in the other factors affecting sales (economic conditions, etc.), and also because of random variability. In the theoretical model, there is a distribution of possible sales values for each level of advertising. Ideally, these distributions are normal.

Exhibit 12.14 illustrates just two of these theoretical normal distributions of possible sales values, for two particular levels of advertising, $800 and $1,700. (These two advertising levels were picked randomly, for illustration.) As you have already seen in Exhibit 12.2, the sales for an advertising expenditure of $1,700 are higher than for an advertising expenditure of only $800. This is reflected in the different locations of the two distributions shown in Exhibit 12.14 below.

12.14

The Theoretical Model, Woodbon Data

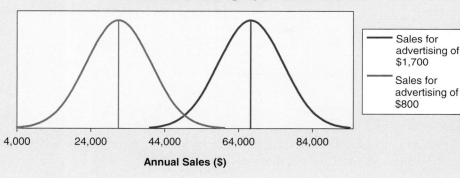

To recap: there is a distribution of sales figures for every possible level of advertising expenditure (we have shown only two of these above). The least-squares regression line focuses on the mean level of sales (μ_y) for each level of advertising expenditure.

$$\mu_y = \beta_0 + \beta_1 x$$

You have to try to see the graph opposite (Exhibit 12.15) in three dimensions to grasp this.

The Model for Predicting Sales from Advertising Expenditure

Exhibit

12.15

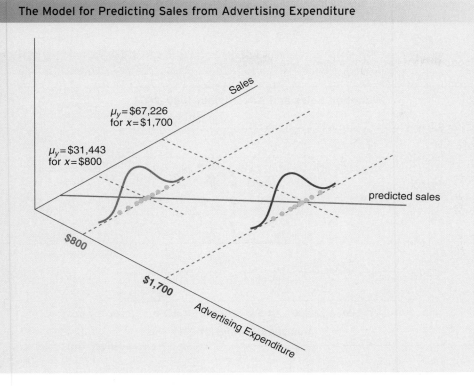

Of course, we will never know what this true straight line looks like. We can only estimate it from the sample data set. Each sample will yield a slightly different estimate of the true theoretical relationship.

Checking the Required Conditions

We have already discussed *residuals*, that is, the differences between the actual y and the predicted y for each x. The usual notation for the residuals in the theoretical model is ε, which is another Greek letter, called epsilon. As usual, we use a corresponding letter, e, to denote the residuals observed in the sample data.

Remember that $\hat{y}$ is the notation we use to denote the predicted value of y for a given x. In general, residuals can be calculated as

$$e_i = y_i - \hat{y}_i$$

for each observation in the sample data set.

For example, we previously calculated that the regression line predicts sales of $59,273.85$ ($\hat{y}$) when the advertising expenditure (x) is $1,500$. From the sample data set, we can find one observation where advertising is $1,500$. In that case, actual sales were $64,926$. For this particular observation, the residual calculation is therefore

$$e_i = y_i - \hat{y}_i$$
$$= \$64,926 - \$59,273.85$$
$$= \$5,652.15$$

We can picture this in the scatter diagram for the Woodbon data, as shown in Exhibit 12.16 below.

12.16

Woodbon Sales and Advertising, Least Squares Line

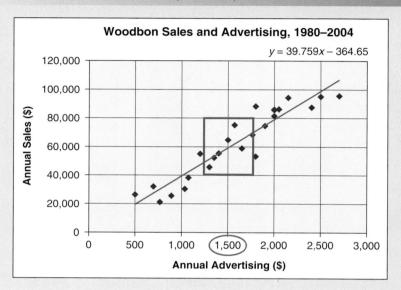

Woodbon Sales and Advertising, 1980–2004

$y = 39.759x - 364.65$

Exhibit 12.17 magnifies the area in the square shown above in Exhibit 12.16. The residual value of $5,652.15 is shown by the red arrow.

12.17

Woodbon Sales and Advertising, Calculation of a Residual

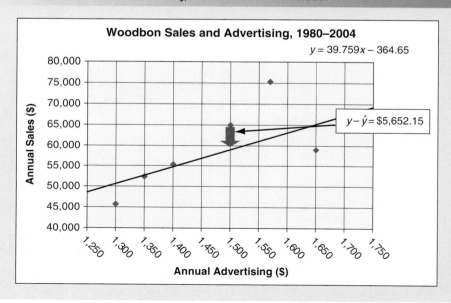

Woodbon Sales and Advertising, 1980–2004

$y = 39.759x - 364.65$

$y - \hat{y} = \$5,652.15$

Residuals can be calculated in a similar way for all of the data points in the sample. The results are summarized in Exhibit 12.18 opposite.

Residuals for Woodbon Data

Woodbon

Annual Advertising Spending, x ($)	Annual Sales, y ($)	Predicted Sales, $\hat{y}$ ($)	Residual, $e = y - \hat{y}$ ($)
500	26,345	19,514.98	6,830.02
695	31,987	27,268.03	4,718.97
765	21,334	30,051.18	−8,717.18
890	25,584	35,021.09	−9,437.09
1,035	30,418	40,786.18	−10,368.18
1,075	38,295	42,376.55	−4,081.55
1,200	55,221	47,346.45	7,874.55
1,300	45,732	51,322.38	−5,590.38
1,350	52,394	53,310.34	−916.34
1,800	53,232	71,202.00	−17,970.00
1,400	55,422	55,298.30	123.70
1,570	75,385	62,057.37	13,327.63
1,500	64,926	59,274.23	5,651.77
1,650	58,977	65,238.11	−6,261.11
1,765	68,515	69,810.43	−1,295.43
1,900	74,817	75,177.93	−360.93
2,000	81,798	79,153.85	2,644.15
2,000	86,228	79,153.85	7,074.15
1,800	88,441	71,202.00	17,239.00
2,000	85,954	79,153.85	6,800.15
2,050	86,531	81,141.81	5,389.19
2,400	87,749	95,057.55	−7,308.55
2,500	95,278	99,033.48	−3,755.48
2,150	94,600	85,117.74	9,482.26
2,700	95,892	106,985.33	−11,093.33

The residuals are important because they allow us to check whether the population data appear to conform to the requirements of the least-squares regression model. We can legitimately make predictions with the regression model—or do hypothesis tests to see whether there is a significant relationship between the x- and y-variables—only if these requirements are met.

Requirements for Predictions or Hypothesis Tests About the Linear Regression Relationship

1. For any given value of x, there are many possible values of y, and therefore, many possible values of ε (the residual, or *error* term). The distribution of the ε-values for any given x must be normal. This means that the actual y-values will be scattered in a normal fashion around the regression line, as pictured in Exhibit 12.15. (p. 419)

2. The normal distributions of ε must have a mean of 0. This means that the actual y-values will have an expected value, or mean, that is equal to the predicted y from the regression line (again, this is pictured in Exhibit 12.15).

3. The standard deviation of ε, which we will refer to as σ_ε, is the same for every value of x. This means that the actual y-values will be scattered about the same distance away from the regression line, all along the line.

4. The ε-values for different data points are not related to each other (another way to say this is that the ε-values for different data points are independent).

Instructions

Fortunately, it is easy to calculate the residuals with Excel. When you use the Data Analysis tool called Regression, the dialogue box shown in Exhibit 12.19 below is activated. You will see a heading for Residuals. Tick Residuals, Standardized Residuals, and Residual Plots to get Excel's residual analysis.

Exhibit 12.19

Regression Dialogue Box

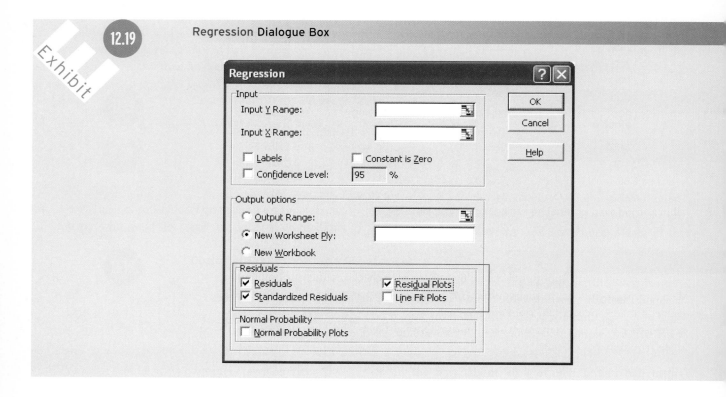

Variation in the Residuals is Constant   The graph that is created when you tick the Residual Plots option in Excel's Regression tool in Data Analysis is a plot of the residuals against x. Exhibit 12.20 shows this residual plot for the Woodbon data.

Regression **Residual plot for Woodbon Data**

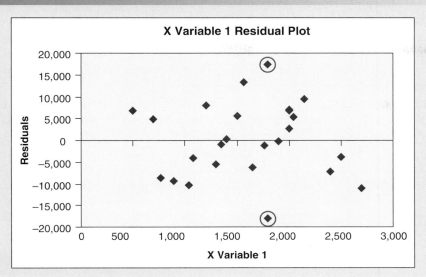

This plot should be checked to see if the residuals have the same amount of variation for all values of x (requirement #3 says that the residuals all have the same standard deviation).

The residual plot for the Woodbon data, shown in Exhibit 12.20, probably meets the requirements. This is a judgment call. You might have had a question about the extreme positive and negative residuals where x is about $1800 (these two points are circled on the diagram). We'll come back to these points later in the discussion.

Example 12.2a below illustrates a case where the requirement for constant variability in the residuals is not met.

A scatter diagram that does not meet the requirement for constant variability in the residuals is shown in Exhibit 12.21 on the next page. In this scatter diagram, the y-values are scattered more and more widely as the x-values increase.

Residuals with increasing variability

It is clear from the scatter diagram that the variability in the residuals is increasing as x increases. The dotted red lines on the graph draw attention to this pattern. The increasing variability is also clearly seen in the residual plot produced by Excel for this data set, shown in Exhibit 12.22 on the next page. Again, dotted red lines have been drawn to reinforce this point.

In this case, because the residual analysis indicates that σ_ε is probably not constant, we should not use the linear regression model to make predictions.

Exhibit 12.21

Scatter Diagram with Non-Constant Variability of Residuals

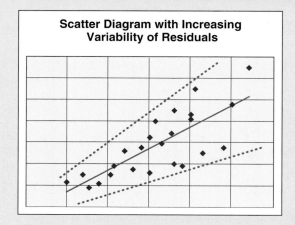

Scatter Diagram with Increasing Variability of Residuals

Exhibit 12.22

Residual Plot with Non-Constant Variablility of Residuals

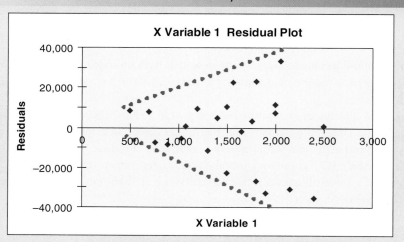

X Variable 1 Residual Plot

Independence of Error Terms One of the requirements (4) of the data is that the error terms, or residuals, are independent of one another. It can be difficult to check the independence of the error terms, since this involves imagining all of the ways in which they could be related. In the Woodbon example, it is possible that the residuals are related over time. It would not be unreasonable to speculate that there was a carryover in the effect of advertising from year to year. If the company spent a lot on advertising one year, the expenditure might still be affecting sales in the following year, even if that year's budget were smaller. This might produce a recognizable pattern in the residuals when they are plotted against time. If this turned out to be the case, we could not use the regression model without some further adjustment.

One of the most common sources of non-independence among the residuals is time. When you are working with time-series data (such as the data for Woodbon), you should plot the residuals against time to see if any pattern emerges.

Exhibit 12.23 opposite shows the Woodbon residuals plotted by year. No regular pattern is apparent in the graph, and so it is reasonable to conclude that the residuals are independent on the basis of time.

Woodbon Residuals Over Time

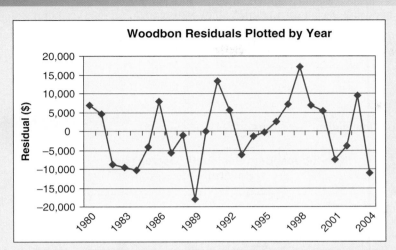

Examples 12.2b and c below show cases where the error terms (residuals) are *not* independent. In both cases, time-series data are involved, and there is a relationship between the residuals and time. If such patterns appear in the residuals when plotted against time, then the simple linear regression model is not appropriate.

Exhibit 12.24 below shows a residual plot with an alternating pattern over time. This means that the residuals are *not* independent over time, and the regression model is not reliable. When there are such regular patterns in the graph, it could be an indication that time should be added to the model as an explanatory variable. Multiple regression models (with more than one explanatory variable) are discussed briefly in Section 12.6.

Residuals not independent over time

Residuals Not Independent over Time

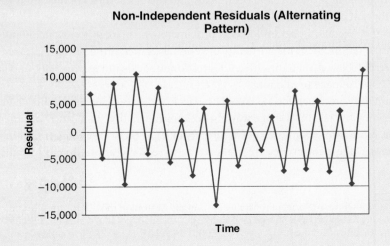

12.2c

Residuals not independent over time

Exhibit 12.25 shows a residual plot with a decreasing pattern over time. Such a residual plot would indicate that the residuals are not independent, but are related through time. Without further work, the regression relationship should not be relied upon for prediction.

12.25

Exhibit

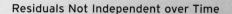
Residuals Not Independent over Time

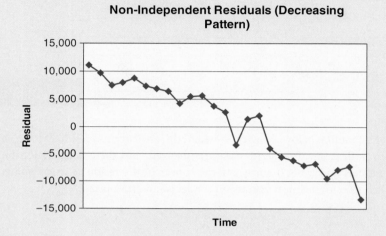

Normality of Residuals We check for normality of the residuals (requirement #1) the way we generally have—with a histogram. Since we usually do not have enough sample data to create a histogram of residuals for each individual value of *x*, we create a histogram of the residuals from all of the sample data. However, we cannot do this unless we first establish that the residuals are independent and the variations in the residuals are equal. If these checks have been made and the conditions are met, then we create one histogram of all the residuals.

As long as this overall histogram looks approximately normal, it is reasonably safe to assume that the requirement for normality of residuals is met. If the histogram of the residuals is severely skewed, then the current regression model is not appropriate, and it should not be used to make predictions.

A histogram of the residuals for the Woodbon data is shown opposite in Exhibit 12.26.

While graphing the residuals is one way to check for normality,[1] you can also sometimes see it (or, more importantly, see departures from it) in the scatter diagram. In the Woodbon data set, the data points are scattered fairly equally above and below the

---

[1] Excel contains an option for a "Normal Probability Plot" in the Regression tool. Unfortunately, it is not what is generally recognized as a normal probability plot, and does not in fact provide any guidance about the normality of residuals.

Histogram of Residuals for Woodbon Data

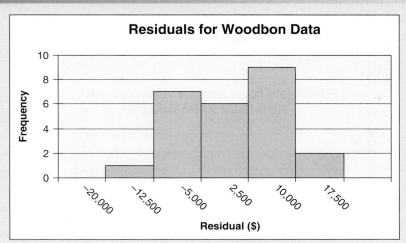

Residuals for Woodbon Data

Exhibit 12.26

regression line, with relatively more points closer to the line. This is consistent with a normal distribution of residuals.

Example 12.2d below shows a scatter diagram and histogram of residuals where the requirement for normality of the residuals is not met. In this example, you should be able to see the correspondence between the two types of graphs.

Consider the scatter diagram shown below in Exhibit 12.27. In it, the spread of data points below the regression line is much wider than above the regression line. This means that there will be several points (below the line) where the observed *y*-values are significantly below the predicted *y*-values, leading to large negative residuals. The points above the line are much closer to the line, so the positive residuals will not be as large as the negative residual.

Example 12.2d

Non-normal residuals

Scatter Diagram with Non-Normal Residuals

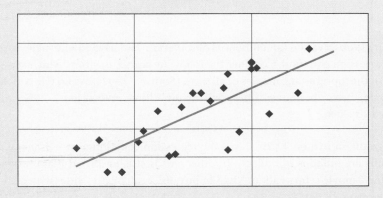

A Scatter Diagram with Non-Normal Residuals

Exhibit 12.27

The corresponding histogram of the residuals, shown in Exhibit 12.28, reveals this quite clearly. The histogram is skewed to the left because of the larger size of the negative residuals.

Histogram of Non-Normal Residuals

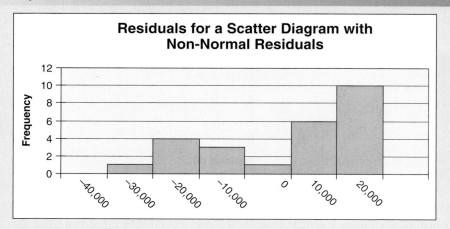

If the scatter diagram of residuals for any model was as skewed (and non-normal) as the graph shown in Exhibit 12.28, then the simple linear regression model should not be used to make predictions.

influential observation a single observation that has an extreme effect on the regression equation

Outliers and Influential Observations An **influential observation** is a single observation that has an extreme effect on the regression equation. Influential observations are usually points that have high or low values of the independent (x-) variable, and can often be seen in the scatter diagram. Removing an influential observation will radically change the regression equation, as illustrated in Example 12.2e below.

Influential observations

Sometimes a single observation (an influential observation) can have an unusually large effect on the regression equation. Consider the following scatter diagram, which shows data for some of the top-grossing movies of all time. (Source: "Top Grossing Films of All Time Worldwide," www.the-movie-times.com/thrsdir/alltime.mv?world+ByWG+All, accessed August 13, 2006.)

The first graph, in Exhibit 12.29, shows the regression equation as $y = 1.2321x + 589.48$ (the units are millions of dollars). In other words, it is estimated that every \$1 spent on making a movie returns about \$1.23 in box office sales worldwide (with a base of \$589.48 million).

Scatter Diagram for Cost and Gross of Top Movies

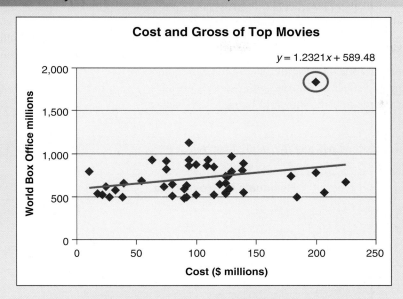

Cost and Gross of Top Movies

$y = 1.2321x + 589.48$

World Box Office millions

Cost ($ millions)

Exhibit 12.29

Notice the circled data point on the graph: it is clearly an outlier. This point corresponds to the movie called *Titanic*, which is sometimes referred to as "the biggest movie of all time." Clearly, this movie was unusual, and there is some question about whether this data point should be included in the data set. If the conditions for this movie were considerably different from the norm, then this data point might be misleading in terms of the normal relationship between cost and box office revenue.

Not only is this data point an outlier, but it is also very influential. To see this, look at the data set and the regression relationship that results when the *Titanic* data point is removed, as shown in Exhibit 12.30 below. The original regression line is shown in red, and the new regression line (without the *Titanic* data) is shown in black.

Scatter Diagram for Cost and Gross of Top Movies, Titanic Removed

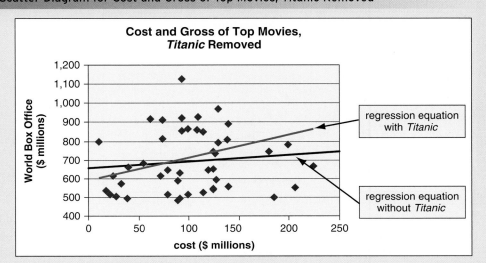

**Cost and Gross of Top Movies,
Titanic Removed**

World Box Office ($ millions)

regression equation with *Titanic*

regression equation without *Titanic*

cost ($ millions)

Exhibit 12.30

When the *Titanic* data point is removed, the regression relationship is very different. It is now $y = 0.35357x + 656.3568$ (the units are millions of dollars). In other words, the amended regression relationship suggests that every $1 spent on making a movie returns about only 35¢ in box office sales worldwide (added to a base of $656.36 million). This is significantly less than the $1.23 from the original regression equation. Removing just this one observation made a huge difference.

Note that the effect of this one point can also be clearly seen in the histogram of residuals for the movie data, shown in Exhibit 12.31 below.

Exhibit 12.31

Histogram of Residuals for Cost and Gross of Top Movies

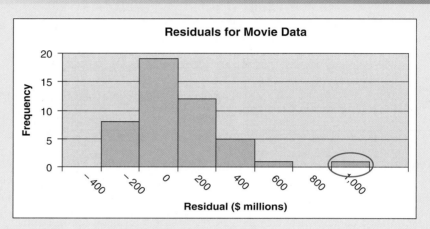

The influential observation also shows up quite clearly in the residual plot produced by Excel, as shown in Exhibit 12.32 below, although influential observations will not always reveal themselves so easily.

Exhibit 12.32

Residual Plot for Cost and Gross of Top Movies

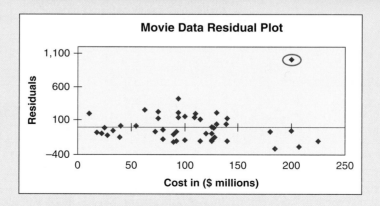

The movie data example is included to illustrate how important it is to examine the data carefully. Any influential observations should be investigated closely.

Outliers are also of interest. An outlier can be the most important data point in the sample data set. It is also possible that an outlier is the result of an error in collecting or recording the data.

Sometimes an outlier is the only indication you have that the true relationship between the variables is not linear. For example, in the scatter diagram in Exhibit 12.33, the circled observation is an outlier. It looks as if it does not belong with the rest of the data.

Sample Scatter Diagram with Outlier   12.33 *Exhibit*

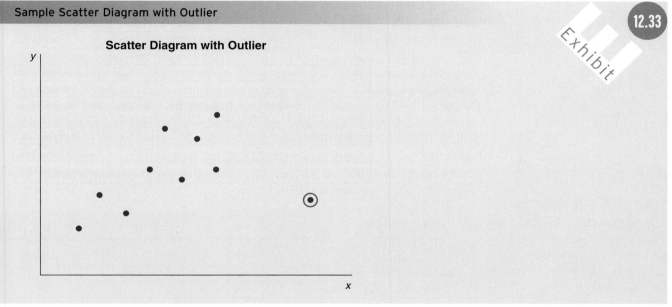

However, what if the true relationship between the variables is actually as shown in Exhibit 12.34? In this case, it is the outlier that gave us a clue that the true relationship is non-linear.

Population Scatter Diagram   12.34 *Exhibit*

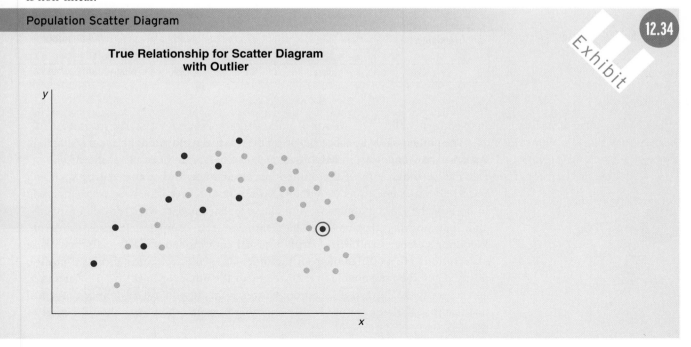

So far in our discussions, we have defined an outlier as a data point that is unusually far from the rest of the data. In the case of regression analysis, we can be a little more precise about what "unusually far" means. We will highlight any data points that have a standardized residual that is ≥ 2 or ≤ -2 (Excel produces these standardized residuals, if you tick the appropriate box in the Regression dialogue box—see p. 422). The standardized residuals are simply the residuals divided by the standard error, which results in a now-familiar measure of a particular residual's distance from the mean. In normal distributions, a distance of two or more standard deviations is fairly far from the mean, and so standardized residuals ≥ 2 or ≤ -2 (and the corresponding observations) should be checked for accuracy. Of course, these values contribute to higher variability in the residuals, making the model less precise than desired.

When we examine the standardized residuals for the Woodbon data, we see that there are two points with unusually large residuals. The two observations are shown in Exhibit 12.35a. Notice that this output describes the related data points as observations 10 and 19. If you number the observations in the original data set from 1 to n (use Excel's Autofill feature), you will be able to identify the corresponding original data points. The result is shown in Exhibit 12.35b.

Exhibit 12.35

a. Excerpt from Excel's Residual Output

Observation	Predicted Y	Residuals	Standard Residuals
10	$71,202.00	−$17,970.00	−2.1131
19	$71,202.00	$17,239.00	2.0271

b. Outliers for the Woodbon Data

annual advertising spending, (x)	annual sales, (y)	predicted sales, (ŷ)	residual, (e)	standardized residual
$ 1,800	$ 53,232	$71,202.00	−$17,970.00	−2.1131
$ 1,800	$ 88,441	$71,202.00	$17,239.00	2.0271

The outliers show up more clearly on the residual plot than on the scatter diagram. Both are shown opposite in Exhibits 12.36 and 12.37, with the outliers circled.

The fact that both of the outliers occurred when annual advertising spending was $1800 raises questions. Woodbon's owner should investigate what was happening in both of the years in question, to make sure that the data were recorded properly, and that nothing unusual was happening at the company. If Kate Cameron, Woodbon's owner, can uncover truly unusual circumstances that explain why these observations are so different from the others, and these circumstances are not the norm, it could be reasonable to remove one or the other (or both) from the data set, and respecify the regression equation. However, this should not be done without real justification. If Kate cannot identify anything unusual, the points should be left in the data set.

Woodbon Scatter Diagram with Outliers Identified

Exhibit 12.36

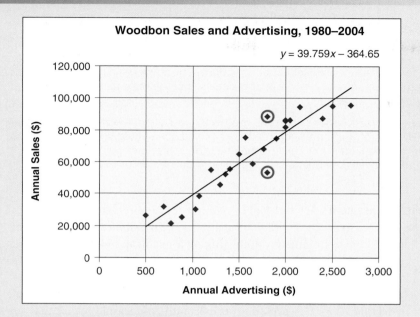

Woodbon Sales and Advertising, 1980–2004

$y = 39.759x - 364.65$

Annual Sales ($) vs Annual Advertising ($)

Woodbon Residual Plot with Outliers Identified

Exhibit 12.37

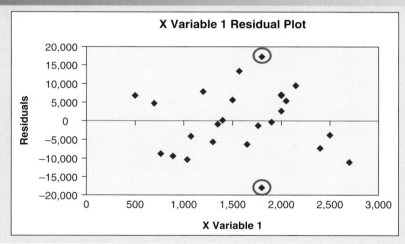

X Variable 1 Residual Plot

Residuals vs X Variable 1

When:
- before performing a hypothesis test or using the regression relationship to make predictions
- using sample data to assess if the relationship conforms to requirements

Steps:
1. Produce a scatter diagram, with a least-squares regression line. Check to see that the relationship appears linear (no pronounced curvature). Check to see that the spread of the data points on either side of the regression line is about the same, with constant spread.
2. Use Excel's Regression tool to produce the Residuals, Standardized Residuals, and Residual Plots.

Guide to Decision Making

Checking Requirements for the Linear Regression Model

3. Examine the residual plot created by Excel. The residuals should be randomly distributed around zero, with the same variability for all *x*-values.
4. Check for the independence of the error terms. With time-series data, plot the residuals against time. There should be no discernible pattern to the plot.
5. Create a histogram of the residuals. This should be approximately normal.
6. Check for outliers and influential observations. These will usually be visible on the scatter diagram, the histogram of residuals, and the residual plot. Check the standardized residuals, and investigate any with values ≥+2 or ≤−2.

Note: If these investigations indicate problems, you should not proceed with a hypothesis test of the regression relationship, and you should not create confidence or prediction intervals. These difficulties can sometimes be solved by more advanced techniques (see Section 12.6 for a brief discussion of the possibilities).

What If the Requirements Are Not Met? What if the requirements are not met? It may still be possible to proceed with your analysis. One possibility may be to transform the data, and the techniques for doing this are available in more advanced texts on model-building. Another possibility is to go back to the beginning, and perhaps choose another explanatory variable from your data. Adding another explanatory variable may also help for multiple regression (there is a brief discussion of multiple regression in Section 12.6). However, most importantly, you should realize that you should not rely on the regression model if the requirements are not met.

DEVELOP YOUR SKILLS

These exercises refer to the data sets for which you created scatter diagrams in Develop Your Skills 12.1.

1. Check that the requirements for the theoretical model are met for the data from the Hendrick Software Sales Company. Are there any outliers? Are there any influential observations? See file called DYS12-2-1.xls.

2. Check that the requirements for the theoretical model are met for the data on monthly incomes and monthly spending on restaurant meals. Are there any outliers? Are there any influential observations? See file called DYS12-2-2.xls.

3. Check that the requirements for the theoretical model are met for the data on sales and promotion spending for Smith and Klein Manufacturing. See file called DYS12-2-3.xls.

4. Check that the requirements for the theoretical model are met for the data on semester average marks and hours spent working. When the professor checked the data, she noticed that there were two unusually low marks: a 22 and a 28. When she investigated further, she realized that the students with these low marks had withdrawn from the course (all of the other students completed the course). As a result, these two data points should not be included in the data set. Reassess the data, with these two erroneous data points removed. See file called DYS12-2-4.xls.

5. Check that the requirements for the theoretical model are met for the data on the number of employees and revenues for large international companies. Are there any outliers? Are there any influential observations? See file called DYS12-2-5.xls.

 12.3 HYPOTHESIS TEST ABOUT THE REGRESSION RELATIONSHIP

So far, we have focused on estimating the regression relationship, and examining the data set to see if it conforms to required conditions for further analysis. Once we have assured ourselves that the required conditions are met, we are finally in a position to test to see if there is a statistically significant relationship between the x- and y-variables.

The least-squares regression line is the best straight line to fit the points, but there may be *no* true linear relationship between the x- and y-variables. There is always a possibility that the sample data do not realistically represent the population data. See Exhibits 12.38 and 12.39 below, which illustrate this possibility.

Sample Data Suggest a Positive Relationship

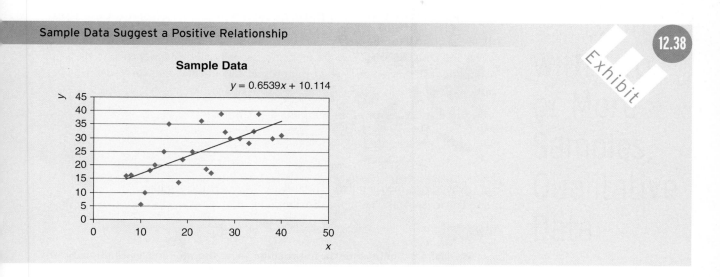

Exhibit **12.38**

Population Data Reveal No Relationship

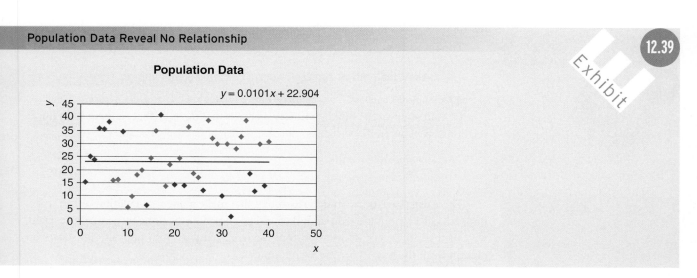

Exhibit **12.39**

Exhibit 12.39 also illustrates that when there is no relationship between the two variables, the slope of the regression line is zero. The hypothesis test for the signifiance of the relationship is a hypothesis test of the slope of the regression line. Essentially the test asks the question: given this sample data set, is there sufficient evidence to conclude that the slope of the population regression line is different from zero? The null hypothesis is always that $\beta_1 = 0$. Usually we want to find sufficient evidence to *reject* the null hypothesis, and conclude that there *is* evidence of a linear relationship between the variables.

Of course, in order to do a hypothesis test about β_1, the slope, we must have some information about the sampling distribution of b_1.

Sampling Distribution of b_1 (for Least-Squares Regression Equation)

If the required conditions of the distribution of residuals (normality, mean of zero, and constant variance) are met, and the residuals are independent, then the sampling distribution of b_1 will be approximately normal and can be described as follows.

1. The standard error of the sampling distribution is:

$$\sigma_{b_1} = \frac{\sigma_\epsilon}{\sqrt{\Sigma(x - \bar{x})^2}}$$

where σ_ϵ is the (population) standard error of ε, the residuals.
2. The mean of the sampling distribution is β_1.

As usual, we cannot apply the information about the sampling distribution directly. For example, we do not know σ_ϵ, and so we do not know σ_{b_1}. However, we can estimate σ_{b_1} from sample data (using s_ϵ to estimate σ_ϵ). Using the standard conventions about notation, we will call the standard error of the sampling distribution s_{b_1}.

The appropriate test statistic follows a t-distribution, with $n - 2$ degrees of freedom:

$$t = \frac{b_1 - \beta_1}{s_{b_1}}$$

Of course, since the null hypothesis is always that $\beta_1 = 0$ (that is, there is no linear relationship between the variables), the test statistic effectively becomes

$$t = \frac{b_1}{s_{b_1}}$$

There exist variations on these formulas that make manual calculations easier to do, but such calculations are tedious and would not normally be done by hand. Once again, we can turn to Excel's Regression tool for help. Exhibit 12.40 opposite illustrates an excerpt from the output for the Woodbon data.

Three cells are highlighted in Exhibit 12.40 to make it easy for you to see them (they will not be highlighted in Excel's output, but they will be located in the same place).

The green cell with the heading "Standard Error" in the row called "X Variable 1" is s_{b_1}, the standard error of the sampling distribution of b_1. The yellow cell with the heading "t Stat" is the t-statistic required for the hypothesis test of the slope, namely:

$$t = \frac{b_1}{s_{b_1}}$$

Instructions

Output for Regression, Woodbon Data

Exhibit 12.40

SUMMARY OUTPUT				
Regression Statistics				
Multiple R	0.939016			
R Square	0.881751			
Adjusted R Square	0.876609			
Standard Error	8446.801			
Observations	25			
ANOVA				
	df	*SS*	*MS*	*F*
Regression	1	1.22E+10	1.22E+10	171.5044
Residual	23	1.64E+09	71348446	
Total	24	1.39E+10		
	Coefficients	*Standard Error*	*t Stat*	*P-value*
Intercept	1135.147	5058.166	0.224419	0.824413
X Variable 1	39.02854	2.980195	13.09597	3.79E−12

The blue cell with the heading "P-value" shows the p-value of the *two-tailed* version of the hypothesis test. Now that we have the Excel output, we can proceed with the hypothesis test of the slope for the Woodbon data.

- $H_0: \beta_1 = 0$ (that is, there is no linear relationship between advertising and sales)
- $H_1: \beta_1 \neq 0$ (that is, there is a linear relationship between advertising and sales)
- Use $\alpha = 0.05$.
- From the Excel output, we see that $t = 13.096$.
- The p-value is 3.79×10^{-12}, or 0.00000000000379. In other words, there is almost no chance of getting sample results like the ones we got here, if in fact there is no linear relationship between advertising and sales. Therefore, we can (with confidence) reject the null hypothesis and conclude that there is evidence of a linear relationship between advertising and sales data for Woodbon.

Of course, it is also possible to test if there is a *positive* linear relationship between the variables (with the alternative hypothesis of $\beta_1 > 0$), or if there is a *negative* linear relationship (with the alternative hypothesis of $\beta_1 < 0$). In these cases, the p-value shown on the Excel output must be divided by 2. Example 12.3 below illustrates.

A professor is concerned that her students' success is being hampered by the amount of time they spend working at their part-time jobs. She randomly selects 30 of her students, and polls them about how many hours per week they worked during the semester. She also records their final mark in her statistics course. A portion of the Excel output for the regression analysis is shown below in Exhibit 12.41.

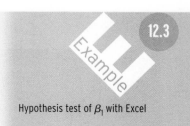

Example 12.3

Hypothesis test of β_1 with Excel

Exhibit 12.41

Output for Regression, Students Hours and Marks

SUMMARY OUTPUT				
Regression Statistics				
Multiple R	0.883933			
R Square	0.781337			
Adjusted R Square	0.773528			
Standard Error	4.924458			
Observations	30			
ANOVA				
	df	*SS*	*MS*	*F*
Regression	1	2,426.266	2,426.266	100.051
Residual	28	679.008	24.25029	
Total	29	3,105.274		
	Coefficients	*Standard Error*	*t Stat*	*P-value*
Intercept	89.24657	2.299501	38.81127	6.85E−26
Weekly Hours Spent at Work During the Semester	−1.39276	0.13924	−10.0025	9.57E−11

At the 5% level of significance, is there evidence of a negative relationship between the hours spent working and the mark in statistics? You may assume that the professor checked the necessary conditions, and has concluded that a hypothesis test will be valid.

- $H_0: \beta_1 = 0$ (that is, there is no linear relationship between hours spent working and the statistics mark)
- $H_1: \beta_1 < 0$ (that is, there is a negative linear relationship between hours spent working and the statistics mark)
- $\alpha = 0.05$
- From the Excel output, we see that $t = -10.00$.
- The p-value shown on the output is 9.57E–11, or 0.0000000000957. This is the p-value for a two-tailed test, so we have to divide by 2 to get the p-value for this hypothesis test. The p-value will be $\frac{0.0000000000957}{2} = 0.00000000004785$, which is still extremely small, and certainly less than the α of 5%.

Reject H_0. There is strong evidence of a negative relationship between hours spent working and the statistics mark.

When:

- two quantitative variables
- trying to decide if there is evidence of a linear relationship between x and y, based on b_1, the slope of the least-squares regression line

Steps:

1. Check that the required conditions are met (see the "Checking Requirements for the Linear Regression Model" Guide to Decision Making, on p. 433).
2. Specify H_0, the null hypothesis, which is always that $\beta_1 = 0$ (that is, there is no linear relationship between the variables).
3. Specify H_1, the alternative hypothesis, with three possibilities: $\beta_1 \neq 0$, $\beta_1 > 0$ (testing for a positive slope), or $\beta_1 < 0$ (testing for a negative slope).
4. Determine or identify α, the significance level.
5. Collect or identify the sample data. Identify or calculate:
   - b_1, the slope of the least-squares regression line based on the sample data
   - s_{b_1}, the standard error of b_1
   - n, the number of observations in the sample data set
6. Calculate (or locate in Excel output) the appropriate t-score, using the following formula:

$$t = \frac{b_1}{s_{b_1}}$$

7. Use the t-distribution with $n-2$ degrees of freedom to identify or calculate (or approximate, if using tables) the appropriate p-value for the hypothesis test, keeping in mind that the p-value shown in the Excel output is based on a two-tailed test.
8. If p-value $< \alpha$, reject H_0 and conclude that there is sufficient evidence to decide in favour of H_1. If p-value $> \alpha$, fail to reject H_0 and conclude that there is insufficient evidence to decide in favour of H_1.

Guide to Decision Making

Testing the Slope of the Regression Line

DEVELOP YOUR SKILLS 12.3

1. If appropriate, test to see if there is evidence of a positive relationship between the number of sales contacts and sales for the Hendrick Software Sales Company. Use $\alpha = 0.05$. See file called DYS12-3-1.xls.

2. If appropriate, test to see if there is evidence of a positive relationship between monthly income and monthly spending on restaurant meals for the data collected for households in Vancouver. Use $\alpha = 0.04$. See file callled DYS12-3-2.xls.

3. If appropriate, test to see if there is evidence of a positive relationship between sales and the amount spent on promotions for Smith and Klein Manufacturing. Use $\alpha = 0.03$. See file called DYS12-3-3.xls.

4. If appropriate, test to see if there is evidence of a negative relationship between semester average marks and hours spent working. Use $\alpha = 0.05$. See file called DYS12-3-4.xls.

5. If appropriate, test to see if there is evidence of a positive relationship between total number of employees and total sales for the random sample of large international companies. Use $\alpha = 0.02$. See file called DYS12-3-5.xls.

12.4   HOW GOOD IS THE REGRESSION?

In Chapter 3, you were introduced to the correlation coefficient (the Pearson r), which was a measure of the degree of association between x- and y-variables. (You may wish to revisit this material, on page 118, to remind yourself of this.)

Instructions

There is another (related) measure of the strength of the association between x and y, called the coefficient of determination. **The coefficient of determination, R^2,** measures the percentage of variation in the y-variable that is explained by changes in the x-variable.

R^2 is equal to the correlation coefficient squared (or, more succinctly, $R^2 = r^2$). The regression output produced by Excel also shows the coefficient of determination. It is highlighted in the excerpt from the Excel data for Woodbon, shown in Exhibit 12.42 below. Since r can take on values from -1 to $+1$, R^2 can take on values from 0 to $+1$.

Excerpt of Output for Regression for Woodbon Data

SUMMARY OUTPUT	
Regression Statistics	
Multiple R	0.937951686
R Square	0.879753365
Adjusted R Square	0.87452525
Standard Error	8687.161393
Observations	25

In order to see why the R^2-value can be interpreted this way, we must divide the difference between the observed y and the average y into two portions. This division is illustrated in Exhibit 12.43 below.

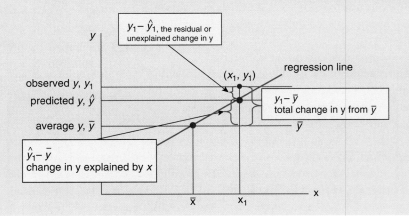

The Change in y is Explained by the Change in x

The question is, why does y vary? If there were no variation in y, then y would simply equal its average, or $\bar{y}$. But y does vary, and at the point (x_1, y_1) shown on the graph,

y has increased from $\bar{y}$ to y_1. The change in y is shown as $y_1 - \bar{y}$, the total change from the average y. This total change can be divided into two parts, also illustrated on the graph.

1. Part of the change in y is explained by the change in x (from $\bar{x}$ to x_1).
2. The unexplained part of the change in y (which we have called the residual) is the difference between the predicted $\hat{y}$ and the observed y_1.

We can write this mathematically as follows:

$$(y_1 - \bar{y}) = (\hat{y}_1 - \bar{y}) + (y_1 - \hat{y}_1)$$

In words, we could say

$$\boxed{\begin{array}{c}\text{total change}\\ \text{in } y \text{ from average } \bar{y}\end{array}} = \boxed{\begin{array}{c}\text{change in } y\\ \text{explained by}\\ \text{regression}\end{array}} + \boxed{\begin{array}{c}\text{residual}\\ \text{(or error)}\end{array}}$$

Of course, this is true for all points in the data set. A related expression, which concerns the sum of the squares of the explained and unexplained deviations, is also true.

$$\Sigma(y - \bar{y})^2 = \Sigma(\hat{y} - \bar{y})^2 + \Sigma(y - \hat{y})^2$$

$$\boxed{\begin{array}{c}\text{total sum of}\\ \text{squares for change in } y\\ \text{from average } \bar{y}\end{array}} = \boxed{\begin{array}{c}\text{sum of squares}\\ \text{for change in } y\\ \text{explained by the regression}\end{array}} + \boxed{\begin{array}{c}\text{sum of squares}\\ \text{for error (residual)}\end{array}}$$

It is usual to refer to these elements with sum of squares notation, as shown below.

$$\text{SST} = \text{SSR} + \text{SSE}$$

It can be shown that $R^2 = \dfrac{\text{SSR}}{\text{SST}}$. The R^2-value therefore tells us the percentage of the total variation in y that is explained by the regression.

If your regression relationship has an R^2 above 0.8, it is considered quite good. On the other hand, if R^2 is less than 0.50, this means that less than half of the variation in the y-values is explained by changes in the x-values, and such an R^2 is an indication that your model needs more work.

In the case of the Woodbon data, about 88% of the variation in the sales data is explained by variations in advertising. It is important to realize that "explained by" is *not* the same as "caused by." For example, in the Woodbon data, both advertising and sales increase over time. As well, several related factors—such as GDP, household incomes, and prices—have increased over time. Although the data might suggest a strong relationship between sales and household incomes, the cause of the increase in both might ultimately be attributed to a booming economy, perhaps best measured by GDP. No computer analysis is capable of proving this. There is no substitute for understanding the context of the data you are analyzing, and making well-informed judgments about causality.

12.4

Interpreting R^2

Jack runs a convenience store, and has been experimenting with the price of the freshly baked cookies he sells there. Jack has collected data for a random sample of days, with a number of different prices. Jack has used Excel to analyze his small data set, and it reports a coefficient of determination of 0.77. What does this mean?

About 77% of the variation in the number of cookies sold is explained by the price. This suggests that price is an important explanatory factor for Jack's cookie sales. This is not surprising to anyone acquainted with the law of demand.

DEVELOP YOUR SKILLS 12.4

Set

1. Interpret the coefficient of determination for the data set from the Hendrick Software Sales Company. Given this number, can you conclude that the way to increase sales is to increase the number of sales contacts made by the staff? See file called DYS12-4-1.xls.

Set

2. The coefficient of determination for the data collected on monthly income and monthly spending on restaurant meals in Vancouver is 0.18. What does this mean? See file called DYS12-4-2.xls.

Set

3. The R^2 for the data on sales and promotional spending for Smith and Klein Manufacturing is 0.82, which is a relatively high value. Does this mean that the least-squares regression line is a good model in this case? See file called DYS12-4-3.xls.

Set

4. Interpret the coefficient of determination for the data set on semester average marks. Given this number, can you conclude that the way to increase student marks is to keep students from working while they are studying? See file called DYS12-4-4.xls.

Set

5. Interpret the coefficient of determination for the data set of total revenues and total numbers of employees for a random sample of large international companies. Given this number, can you conclude that the way to increase revenues is to increase the number of employees at a company? See file called DYS12-4-5.xls.

12.5 MAKING PREDICTIONS

One of the uses of regression analysis is prediction. For example, suppose Kate Cameron wants to predict what annual sales will be if she sets her advertising budget at $1,800.

We can get a point estimate of predicted sales by plugging an advertising value of $1,800 into the estimated regression relationship, as follows.

Predicted sales

$= 39.759(\$1,800) - \$364.65$

$= \$71,566.20 - \$364.65$

$= \$71,201.55$

This point estimate is not necessarily accurate, and so an interval estimate is preferred, as it was when we estimated means and proportions.

There are two sources of error in the prediction of sales, based on a particular level of advertising.

1. The first source of error is the sampling error that results from estimating the true population relationship between sales and advertising from sample data. The regression line we create from the sample data may not match the true population

regression line. Remember, the population regression line is $\mu_y = \beta_0 + \beta_1 x$, and the estimate of $\hat{y} = b_0 + b_1\bar{x}$ is unlikely to match it exactly.

2. The second source of error is the variation of the points around the regression line. Remember, we assumed a normal distribution of possible sales values for each level of advertising (see Exhibit 12.15 on p. 419).

If the regression model fits the data fairly well, and the required conditions are met, we can use the regression model to make two kinds of predictions. A **prediction interval** predicts a particular value of y (sales) for a given value of x (advertising of $1,800 in the example above). A **confidence interval** predicts the average y (sales) for a given value of x (advertising of $1,800 in the example above). This is essentially an estimate of the location of the true regression line. As first discussed in Chapter 8, interval estimates have a general form as follows:

prediction interval interval that predicts a particular value of y for a given value of x

confidence interval interval that predicts the average y for a given value of x

(point estimate) $\pm$ (critical value) • (estimated standard error of the sample statistic)

The interval estimates based on the regression model follow this same format. The formula for a prediction interval for y, given a particular x (call it x_0) is:

$$\hat{y} \pm (t\text{-score})s_\epsilon \sqrt{1 + \frac{1}{n} + \frac{(x_0 - \bar{x})^2}{\Sigma(x - \bar{x})^2}}, \text{ where the } t\text{-distribution has } n - 2 \text{ degrees of freedom}$$

The formula for a confidence interval for μ_y, given a particular x (call it x_0) is:

$$\hat{y} \pm (t\text{-score})s_\epsilon \sqrt{\frac{1}{n} + \frac{(x_0 - \bar{x})^2}{\Sigma(x - \bar{x})^2}}, \text{ where the } t\text{-distribution has } n - 2 \text{ degrees of freedom}$$

There is no built-in Data Analysis function in Excel to calculate these interval estimates for you. Excel worksheet templates for these calculations are available on the CD that comes with the text, in the "Templates" workbook. There is a "Prediction Interval" worksheet, and a "Confidence Interval" worksheet. You must use these templates in conjunction with Excel's Regression tools so that you can get the necessary inputs to the template. As well, you must use Excel functions to calculate two of the required input values for the template. As always, the blue-shaded cells in the template require inputs.

Template

1. You must use the AVERAGE function to compute the average of all of the x-values in the sample data set. Activate the function by typing =AVERAGE and then use the mouse or pointer to select the location of the x-values from the sample data set.
2. You must use the DEVSQ function to compute $\Sigma(x - \bar{x})^2$ for the x-values. Activate the function by typing =DEVSQ and then use the mouse or pointer to select the location of the x-values from the sample data set.

The other values required for the template are either typed in, or copied from the Regression output. Exhibits 12.44a and b on the next page illustrate where the required values are found on the Regression output for the Woodbon data. An excerpt from the Excel Regression output is shown in Exhibit 12.44a. The template for the prediction interval is shown in Exhibit 12.44b.

Exhibit 12.44

Excel Regression Output and Prediction Interval Template for Woodbon Data

a.

SUMMARY OUTPUT	
Regression Statistics	
Multiple R	0.937951686
R Square	0.879753365
Adjusted R Square	0.87452525
Standard Error	8687.161393
Observations	25

ANOVA	
	df
Regression	1
Residual	23
Total	24

	Coefficients
Intercept	−364.6459102
X Variable 1	39.7592486

b.

Prediction Interval Estimate for y, Given x	
do the sample data appear to meet the required conditions?	yes
confidence level (decimal form)	0.95
AVERAGE(x)	1599.8
DEVSQ(x)	8033,324
Standard Error	8687.161
n	25
intercept	−364.646
slope	39.75925
given x	1800
upper prediction interval limit	89572.54
lower prediction interval limit	52831.47

From the template we see that the prediction interval is ($52,831.47, $89,572.54). We have 95% confidence that this interval contains the sales level that corresponds to an advertising budget of $1,800. This interval is quite wide, and probably too wide to be very useful. The width of the interval is not very surprising, because we already observed a fair amount of variability in the data.

Exhibit 12.45 shows the template for the confidence interval for the average y, given a particular level of x. It shows the confidence interval limits for the average value of sales, given advertising of $1,800.

Template

Exhibit 12.45

Excel Template for Confidence Interval for Woodbon Data

Confidence Interval Estimate for Average y, Given x	
do the sample data appear to meet the required conditions?	yes
confidence level (decimal form)	0.95
AVERAGE(x)	1599.8
DEVSQ(x)	8033 324
Standard Error	8687.161
n	25
intercept	−364.646
slope	39.75925
given x	1800
upper confidence interval limit	75013.71
lower confidence interval limit	67390.29

We have 95% confidence that the interval ($67,390.29, $75,013.71) contains the average sales when advertising is $1,800.

There are a couple of things to note about prediction intervals and confidence intervals:

1. Prediction intervals for y given a particular x are always wider (less precise) than confidence intervals for the average y given a particular x. The interval has to be wider to account for the distribution of y-values around the regression line in the population model (see Exhibit 12.15 on p. 419).
2. Both intervals are narrowest at the $(\bar{x}, \bar{y})$ point on the regression line. Both intervals get wider for x-values that are farther from $\bar{x}$. This is illustrated in Exhibit 12.46 below.

Confidence and Predictioin Intervals

Exhibit 12.46

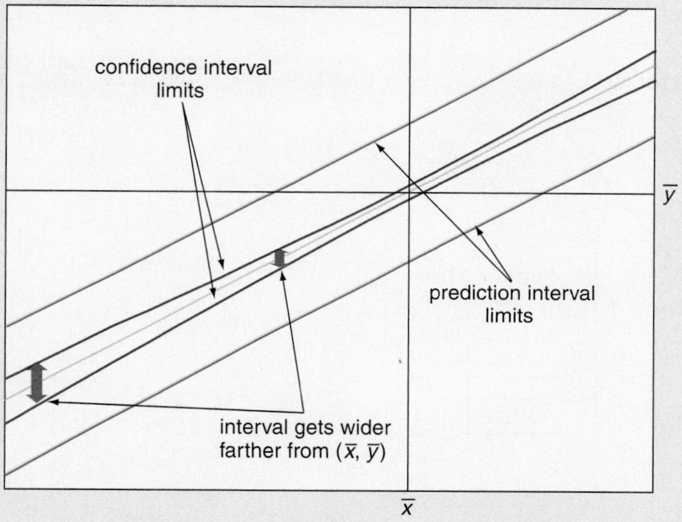

It is disappointing to have done all of the work involved in analyzing the Woodbon data, only to find that the prediction interval is so wide that it is not particularly useful. This can happen in regression analysis. The initial assessment of the data looked promising. The hypothesis test supported a conclusion that there is a linear relationship between advertising and sales. As well, the R^2-value was 0.88, which is fairly high. However, the amount of variability in the data is large, and so the predictions are not precise.

One further point should be made about prediction and confidence intervals based on regression analysis.

It is not legitimate to make predictions with a regression model for x-values outside the range of the sample data.

Even a powerful regression relationship with a high coefficient of determination and low standard error should not be relied on outside the range of the sample data. Exhibits 12.47a and b below illustrate why this is so.

Exhibit 12.47a

Sample Data and Regression Equation

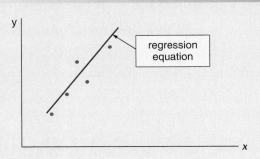

Exhibit 12.47b

Population Data and Error Arising from Incorrect Use of Regression Equation

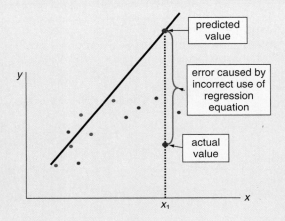

The regression equation shown in the graphs could be quite useful for the range of data from the original sample, even though the true relationship is not a straight-line relationship. The error arises when the regression relationship is used for an x-value outside this range, and as illustrated, the error can be quite large.

Example 12.5

EXA12-5.xls
Set

Calculating a confidence interval estimate for an average y, given x

Calculate a 98% confidence interval estimate for the average number of cookies Jack would sell at his convenience store, if he set the cookie price at 75¢.

Before this confidence interval estimate is calculated, we must first check that the required conditions are met.

The related data are available in a file called EXA12–5.xls. A scatter diagram of the data looks fairly linear. The residual plot produced by Excel indicates reasonably constant variability in the residuals, although there is one unusually negative residual. The observations were collected over time, but the dates are not available, so we cannot check for independence against time. There are no standardized residuals $\geq +2$ or ≤ -2, and there are no obvious influential observations. There are too few data points to create a histogram of residuals, but if we sort the residuals, we get the result shown in Exhibit 12.48 below.

Ordered Residuals for Data on Cookies at Jack's Convenience Store

−4.44961
−2.12403
−1.76357
−0.1124
−0.08915
1.53876
2.213178
2.224806
2.562016

Exhibit 12.48

It is always difficult to judge normality for a small data set. However, this one appears to be skewed to the left, with one unusually negative residual (−4.44961), and a "clump" of three residuals above but fairly close to 2.

In this case, it appears that the sample data do not meet the requirements of the theoretical model. Therefore, we will not produce a confidence interval, as it would not be reliable.

DEVELOP YOUR SKILLS 12.5

1. If appropriate, create a 98% confidence interval for the average sales at the Hendrick Software Sales Company, for 10 sales contacts. See file called DYS12-5-1.xls.

2. If appropriate, create a 95% prediction interval for the amount of monthly spending on restaurant meals, based on a monthly income of $6,000. See file called DYS12-5-2.xls.

3. If appropriate, create a 90% confidence interval for average sales when promotion spending is $10,000. See file called DYS12-5-3.xls.

4. If appropriate, create a 95% confidence interval for the average semester average mark, for students who work 200 hours during the semester. See file called DYS12-5-4.xls.

5. If appropriate, create a 99% prediction interval for the total revenue of an international company with 35,000 employees. See file called DYS12-5-5.xls.

12.6   MORE ADVANCED MODELLING

This chapter has been an introduction to an area of statistical analysis that can be both interesting and useful. Generally, when mathematical models are created, the goal is to create the simplest possible model that makes reliable predictions. Often, a simple linear regression model is sufficient.

If necessary, the techniques described in this chapter can also be extended, in several possible ways. These more advanced techniques are beyond the scope of this text, but you should be aware that they exist.

One set of techniques is called *multiple regression*. Multiple regression techniques allow the use of more than one explanatory variable. For example, Kate Cameron might attempt to predict Woodbon's sales on the basis of not only advertising, but also housing starts and/or local household incomes. Adding additional explanatory variables might improve the predictive power of the relationship.

Adding more explanatory variables also introduces the potential for a problem called multicollinearity, which arises when there is a correlation among explanatory variables. For example, there could be a high correlation between GDP and local household incomes. Introducing one of these into the model robs the other of its explanatory power, and so only one should be included. Fortunately, methods are available to identify and avoid multicollinearity problems when a multiple regression model is being constructed.

It is also possible to build models that are polynomial, to account for curvature in the relationships. It is possible to introduce qualitative explanatory variables (such as gender) using indicator variables (also called dummy variables). There are special techniques for time series trend analysis. With the appropriate training and good computer software, it is possible to build complex and sophisticated models of relationships.

However, the best models are not necessarily the most complex, and the goal should always be to create the simplest model that works well. There are many cases when a simple linear regression model can prove useful.

Chapter Summary

12

Creating a Graph and Estimating the Relationship

The first step in analyzing a relationship between two variables is to create a scatter diagram, with the dependent (response) variable plotted on the y-axis, and the independent (explanatory) variable plotted on the x-axis.

The equation of a straight line that best fits the points on the scatter diagram is of the form: $\hat{y} = b_0 + b_1x$. The coefficients b_0 and b_1 result from minimizing the sum of the squared residuals for the line. A residual is the difference between the observed value of y for a given x, and the predicted value of y for that x ($e_i = y_i - \hat{y}_i$). The coefficients of the least-squares line can be determined with Excel, either with the Add Trendline tool (see p. 412), or the Regression tool of Data Analysis (see p. 414).

Assessing the Model

Theoretically, there is a normal distribution of possible y-values for every x. The population relationship we are interested in is the average y for every x, as follows:

$$\mu_y = \beta_0 + \beta_1x$$

We cannot reliably make predictions with the regression equation, or conduct a hypothesis test to see if there is a significant relationship between the x- and y-variables, unless certain conditions are met (these are summarized in the box on p. 421). We check these conditions by focusing on the residuals in the sample data set. See the Guide to Decision Making on page 433 for checking the requirements for the regression model.

Hypothesis Test About the Regression Relationship

Once we have assured ourselves that the required conditions are met, we can test to see if there is a significant linear relationship between the x- and y-variables. This is done with a test of the slope of the line, β_1. The null hypothesis of no relationship ($\beta_1 = 0$) is tested against one of three possible alternatives:

- $\beta_1 \neq 0$ (there is some relationship between x and y)
- $\beta_1 > 0$ (there is a positive relationship between x and y)
- $\beta_1 < 0$ (there is a negative relationship between x and y).

The output of Excel's **Data Analysis** tool called **Regression** provides the t-score and p-value for the two-tailed version of this test. See page 436 for instructions on how to read the output.

The Guide to Decision Making for testing the slope of the regression line is shown on page 439.

How Good Is the Regression?

The Pearson r, the correlation coefficient, can be used to measure the degree of linear association between the x- and y-variables, as discussed in Chapter 3 (see p. 118).

Another related measure is the coefficient of determination, or R^2. The coefficient of determination measures the percentage of variation in the y-variable that is explained by changes in the x-variable. The coefficient of determination is produced in Excel's **Regression** output (see p. 440 for instructions on how to read the output). It is important to recognize that "explained by" is not the same as "caused by." Even though the R^2 may be high, the true causal relationship can only be judged on the basis of an understanding of the context of the data.

Making Predictions

Two types of predictions can be made, if the requirements are met. A prediction interval predicts a particular value of y for a given value of x. A confidence interval predicts the average y for a given value of x.

The formula for a prediction interval for y, given a particular x (call it x_0) is:

$$\hat{y} \pm (t\text{-score})s_\epsilon \sqrt{1 + \frac{1}{n} + \frac{(x_0 - \bar{x})^2}{\Sigma(x - \bar{x})^2}}$$

The formula for a confidence interval for μ_y, given a particular x (call it x_0) is:

$$\hat{y} \pm (t\text{-score})s_\epsilon \sqrt{\frac{1}{n} + \frac{(x_0 - \bar{x})^2}{\Sigma(x - \bar{x})^2}}$$

There is no built-in **Data Analysis** function in Excel to calculate these interval estimates. Excel worksheet templates for these calculations are available on the CD that comes with the text, in the "Templates" workbook. There is a "Prediction Interval" worksheet, and a "Confidence Interval" worksheet. Both are designed to be used in conjunction with Excel's **Regression** output, and both require you to copy or calculate some inputs. See the Excel instructions on page 443. Always remember that it is not legitimate to make predictions outside the range of the sample data.

CHAPTER REVIEW EXERCISES

CRE12-1.xls Set

1. What determines the price of a used car? One of the factors is the odometer reading. A data set of the number of kilometres on the odometer and the asking price for a year 2000 small car is available on the CD that accompanies this text. Create a scatter diagram for the data set, and describe the relationship between the two variables, both generally and mathematically.

2. For the data set of odometer readings and asking prices of used cars described in Exercise 1, check the requirements for regression. Would it be appropriate to use the odometer reading to predict the asking price for these used cars?

CRE12-3.xls Set

3. The Standard and Poor's Toronto Stock Exchange Composite Price Index (TSX-I) measures the performance of the broad Canadian stock market. The Dow Jones Industrials Price Index (DJIA-I) tracks the performance of U.S. stock markets. Are the values of the two indexes related? A data set of the values of the two indexes for the period from June 26 to August 4, 2006, is available on the CD that accompanies this text. Create a scatter diagram of these data, and estimate the relationship. (Source: S&P/TSX Composite Price History for Symbol TSX-1 and DJIA-I, August 4, 2006. http://investdb.theglobeandmail.com/invest. Reprinted with permission from *The Globe and Mail*)

4. What is the coefficient of determination for the data set of the TSX-I and the DJIA-I described in Exercise 3? Interpret it.

5. Check the requirements for regression for the data set of the TSX-I and the DJIA-I described in Exercise 3. Is this data set a random sample?

CRE12-6.xls Set

6. A statistics professor wants to know if a student's mark on the second statistics test is a good indicator of the student's mark on the final exam. She records the two marks for a random sample of students. The data are available on the CD that accompanies this text. Create a scatter diagram and estimate and interpret the relationship between the two variables.

7. Check the requirements for regression for the data set of student marks on the second test and the final exam in a statistics course, described in Exercise 6.

8. An excerpt from Excel's Regression output for the data set of student marks on the second test and the final exam in a statistics course, described in Exercise 6, is shown opposite in

Exhibit 12.49

Regression **Output, Students' Marks**

Regression Statistics				
Multiple R	0.960374			
R Square	0.922318			
Adjusted R Square	0.918941			
Standard Error	5.190203			
Observations	25			
ANOVA				
	df	*SS*	*MS*	*F*
Regression	1	7356.304	7356.304	273.0806
Residual	23	619.5788	26.93821	
Total	24	7975.882		
	Coefficients	*Standard Error*	*t Stat*	*P-value*
Intercept	0.446443	3.590601	0.124337	0.902129
X Variable 1	0.958644	0.058011	16.52515	2.96E−14

Exhibit 12.49. Using the output, test for evidence of a positive slope between the two variables, with $\alpha = 5\%$.

9. **a.** If appropriate, construct a 95% confidence interval estimate for the average exam mark of students who had a mark of 65% on the second test of a statistics course (using the data set described in Exercise 6).

   b. If appropriate, construct a 95% confidence interval estimate for the exam mark of a student who received 65% on the second test of a statistics course (using the data set described in Exercise 6). How does this compare with the estimate for the average exam mark of students who had a mark of 65% on the second test (your answer to Exercise 9a)? Why is there a difference?

Set
CRE12-10.xls

10. Aries Car Parts maintains an inventory of a wide array of car parts. The owner is old-fashioned and has not allowed computers to be used in the business, so records are kept manually. An auditor has calculated the actual value of inventory for a random sample of car parts, and has compared this with the recorded value. The data are available on the CD that accompanies this text. Create a scatter diagram, and estimate and interpret the relationship between the two variables. If the inventory records are generally accurate, what would you expect the slope of the line to be?

11. Check the requirements for regression for the data set of actual and recorded inventory values for Aries Car Parts from Exercise 10. When the auditor examined the relationship, he noticed two outliers, for observations 1 and 25 (why are these outliers?). Careful double-checking made the auditor realize that he had misread the written records for both data points. The recorded parts inventory for observation 1 is actually $446.23, and for observation 25 is $584.04. Amend the data set accordingly, and repeat your analysis.

12. If appropriate, test for evidence of a linear relationship between the actual and recorded inventory values for Aries Car Parts (using the amended data set from Exercise 11). Use $\alpha = 0.05$.

13. Interpret the coefficient of determination for the data on actual and recorded inventory values for Aries Car Parts (using the amended data set from Exercise 11). Does this give you confidence in the recorded inventory values?

Set
CRE12-14.xls

14. What is the relationship between revenue and profit? A random sample of the top 1000 Canadian companies was selected, and revenue and profit for 2005 were recorded. The data are available on the CD that accompanies this text. Create a scatter diagram, and comment on the relationship. What is the coefficient of determination for this data set? Does the high value mean that a linear relationship is a good model in this case? (Source: "Rankings by Profit," *Report on Business*, July/August 2006.)

Set
CRE12-15.xls

15. A large company hires many business graduates every year. The company has developed a written test to screen applicants, and the mark on this test has been a good predictor of employee suitability for the graduates that are hired. Because administering the test is time-consuming and costly, the company is wondering if it is worthwhile. One cheaper option is to rely on the overall average mark of the graduate as an indicator of suitability. An analyst has collected data on the overall average marks of a number of interviewees, and their scores (out of 70) on the company test. The data are available on the CD that accompanies this text. Create a scatter diagram for the data. Does it appear that there is a relationship between the two variables? Describe it, generally and mathematically.

16. Check the requirements for regression for the data set of overall average marks and company test scores from Exercise 15.

17. An excerpt of the Excel **Regression** output for the data set in Exercise 15 is shown below in Exhibit 12.50. If appropriate, use the output to test for evidence of a positive relationship between overall average marks and company test scores for the data set described in Exercise 15.

12.50

Regression Output, Graduates' Marks

SUMMARY OUTPUT		
Regression Statistics		
Multiple R	0.893821	
R Square	0.798917	
Adjusted R Square	0.791735	
Standard Error	3.644976	
Observations	30	
ANOVA		
	df	*SS*
Regression	1	1477.996
Residual	28	372.0038
Total	29	1850
	Coefficients	*Standard Error*
Intercept	4.977461	4.695268
X Variable 1	0.642105	0.060878

18. If appropriate, create a 98% confidence interval estimate for the average test score of a graduate with an overall average mark of 55, based on the data set described in Exercise 15.

19. If appropriate, create a 98% confidence interval estimate to predict the test score of a student with an overall average mark of 75, based on the data set describe in Exercise 15. Do you think the company should continue to administer its own test in interviewing graduates?

20. Shown opposite in Exhibit 12.51 is the residual plot for a data set on package weight in kilograms and shipping cost. Do you think it is appropriate to use package weight as a predictor of shipping cost?

CRE12-20.xls
Set

Residual Plot, Package Weight and Cost

12.51

Exhibit

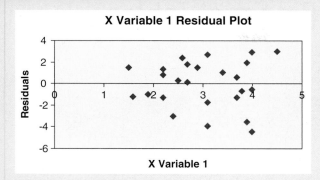

APPENDIX

Cumulative Binomial Tables

Table value = P(x ≤ number of successes)

Cumulative Binomial Probabilities for *n* = 5

no. of successes \ P	0.01	0.05	0.10	0.20	0.25	0.30	0.40	0.50	0.60	0.70	0.75	0.80	0.90	0.95	0.99
0	0.951	0.774	0.590	0.328	0.237	0.168	0.078	0.031	0.010	0.002	0.001	0.000	0.000	0.000	0.000
1	0.999	0.977	0.919	0.737	0.633	0.528	0.337	0.188	0.087	0.031	0.016	0.007	0.000	0.000	0.000
2	1.000	0.999	0.991	0.942	0.896	0.837	0.683	0.500	0.317	0.163	0.104	0.058	0.009	0.001	0.000
3	1.000	1.000	1.000	0.993	0.984	0.969	0.913	0.813	0.663	0.472	0.367	0.263	0.081	0.023	0.001
4	1.000	1.000	1.000	1.000	0.999	0.998	0.990	0.969	0.922	0.832	0.763	0.672	0.410	0.226	0.049

Table value = P(x ≤ number of successes)

Cumulative Binomial Probabilities for *n* = 6

no. of successes \ P	0.01	0.05	0.10	0.20	0.25	0.30	0.40	0.50	0.60	0.70	0.75	0.80	0.90	0.95	0.99
0	0.941	0.735	0.531	0.262	0.178	0.118	0.047	0.016	0.004	0.001	0.000	0.000	0.000	0.000	0.000
1	0.999	0.967	0.886	0.655	0.534	0.420	0.233	0.109	0.041	0.011	0.005	0.002	0.000	0.000	0.000
2	1.000	0.998	0.984	0.901	0.831	0.744	0.544	0.344	0.179	0.070	0.038	0.017	0.001	0.000	0.000
3	1.000	1.000	0.999	0.983	0.962	0.930	0.821	0.656	0.456	0.256	0.169	0.099	0.016	0.002	0.000
4	1.000	1.000	1.000	0.998	0.995	0.989	0.959	0.891	0.767	0.580	0.466	0.345	0.114	0.033	0.001
5	1.000	1.000	1.000	1.000	1.000	0.999	0.996	0.984	0.953	0.882	0.822	0.738	0.469	0.265	0.059

Table value = P(x ≤ number of successes)

Cumulative Binomial Probabilities for *n* = 7

no. of successes \ P	0.01	0.05	0.10	0.20	0.25	0.30	0.40	0.50	0.60	0.70	0.75	0.80	0.90	0.95	0.99
0	0.932	0.698	0.478	0.210	0.133	0.082	0.028	0.008	0.002	0.000	0.000	0.000	0.000	0.000	0.000
1	0.998	0.956	0.850	0.577	0.445	0.329	0.159	0.063	0.019	0.004	0.001	0.000	0.000	0.000	0.000
2	1.000	0.996	0.974	0.852	0.756	0.647	0.420	0.227	0.096	0.029	0.013	0.005	0.000	0.000	0.000
3	1.000	1.000	0.997	0.967	0.929	0.874	0.710	0.500	0.290	0.126	0.071	0.033	0.003	0.000	0.000
4	1.000	1.000	1.000	0.995	0.987	0.971	0.904	0.773	0.580	0.353	0.244	0.148	0.026	0.004	0.000
5	1.000	1.000	1.000	1.000	0.999	0.996	0.981	0.938	0.841	0.671	0.555	0.423	0.150	0.044	0.002
6	1.000	1.000	1.000	1.000	1.000	1.000	0.998	0.992	0.972	0.918	0.867	0.790	0.522	0.302	0.068

Table value = P(x ≤ number of successes)

Cumulative Binomial Probabilities for n = 8

no. of successes	0.01	0.05	0.10	0.20	0.25	0.30	0.40	0.50	0.60	0.70	0.75	0.80	0.90	0.95	0.99
0	0.923	0.663	0.430	0.168	0.100	0.058	0.017	0.004	0.001	0.000	0.000	0.000	0.000	0.000	0.000
1	0.997	0.943	0.813	0.503	0.367	0.255	0.106	0.035	0.009	0.001	0.000	0.000	0.000	0.000	0.000
2	1.000	0.994	0.962	0.797	0.679	0.552	0.315	0.145	0.050	0.011	0.004	0.001	0.000	0.000	0.000
3	1.000	1.000	0.995	0.944	0.886	0.806	0.594	0.363	0.174	0.058	0.027	0.010	0.000	0.000	0.000
4	1.000	1.000	1.000	0.990	0.973	0.942	0.826	0.637	0.406	0.194	0.114	0.056	0.005	0.000	0.000
5	1.000	1.000	1.000	0.999	0.996	0.989	0.950	0.855	0.685	0.448	0.321	0.203	0.038	0.006	0.000
6	1.000	1.000	1.000	1.000	1.000	0.999	0.991	0.965	0.894	0.745	0.633	0.497	0.187	0.057	0.003
7	1.000	1.000	1.000	1.000	1.000	1.000	0.999	0.996	0.983	0.942	0.900	0.832	0.570	0.337	0.077

Table value = P(x ≤ number of successes)

Cumulative Binomial Probabilities for n = 9

no. of successes	0.01	0.05	0.10	0.20	0.25	0.30	0.40	0.50	0.60	0.70	0.75	0.80	0.90	0.95	0.99
0	0.914	0.630	0.387	0.134	0.075	0.040	0.010	0.002	0.000	0.000	0.000	0.000	0.000	0.000	0.000
1	0.997	0.929	0.775	0.436	0.300	0.196	0.071	0.020	0.004	0.000	0.000	0.000	0.000	0.000	0.000
2	1.000	0.992	0.947	0.738	0.601	0.463	0.232	0.090	0.025	0.004	0.001	0.000	0.000	0.000	0.000
3	1.000	0.999	0.992	0.914	0.834	0.730	0.483	0.254	0.099	0.025	0.010	0.003	0.000	0.000	0.000
4	1.000	1.000	0.999	0.980	0.951	0.901	0.733	0.500	0.267	0.099	0.049	0.020	0.001	0.000	0.000
5	1.000	1.000	1.000	0.997	0.990	0.975	0.901	0.746	0.517	0.270	0.166	0.086	0.008	0.001	0.000
6	1.000	1.000	1.000	1.000	0.999	0.996	0.975	0.910	0.768	0.537	0.399	0.262	0.053	0.008	0.000
7	1.000	1.000	1.000	1.000	1.000	1.000	0.996	0.980	0.929	0.804	0.700	0.564	0.225	0.071	0.003
8	1.000	1.000	1.000	1.000	1.000	1.000	1.000	0.998	0.990	0.960	0.925	0.866	0.613	0.370	0.086

Table value = P(x ≤ number of successes)

Cumulative Binomial Probabilities for n = 10

no. of successes	0.01	0.05	0.10	0.20	0.25	0.30	0.40	0.50	0.60	0.70	0.75	0.80	0.90	0.95	0.99
0	0.904	0.599	0.349	0.107	0.056	0.028	0.006	0.001	0.000	0.000	0.000	0.000	0.000	0.000	0.000
1	0.996	0.914	0.736	0.376	0.244	0.149	0.046	0.011	0.002	0.000	0.000	0.000	0.000	0.000	0.000
2	1.000	0.988	0.930	0.678	0.526	0.383	0.167	0.055	0.012	0.002	0.000	0.000	0.000	0.000	0.000
3	1.000	0.999	0.987	0.879	0.776	0.650	0.382	0.172	0.055	0.011	0.004	0.001	0.000	0.000	0.000
4	1.000	1.000	0.998	0.967	0.922	0.850	0.633	0.377	0.166	0.047	0.020	0.006	0.000	0.000	0.000
5	1.000	1.000	1.000	0.994	0.980	0.953	0.834	0.623	0.367	0.150	0.078	0.033	0.002	0.000	0.000
6	1.000	1.000	1.000	0.999	0.996	0.989	0.945	0.828	0.618	0.350	0.224	0.121	0.013	0.001	0.000
7	1.000	1.000	1.000	1.000	1.000	0.998	0.988	0.945	0.833	0.617	0.474	0.322	0.070	0.012	0.000
8	1.000	1.000	1.000	1.000	1.000	1.000	0.998	0.989	0.954	0.851	0.756	0.624	0.264	0.086	0.004
9	1.000	1.000	1.000	1.000	1.000	1.000	1.000	0.999	0.994	0.972	0.944	0.893	0.651	0.401	0.096

Table value = P(x ≤ number of successes)

Cumulative Binomial Probabilities for n = 15

no. of successes / P	0.01	0.05	0.10	0.20	0.25	0.30	0.40	0.50	0.60	0.70	0.75	0.80	0.90	0.95	0.99
0	0.860	0.463	0.206	0.035	0.013	0.005	0.000	0.000	0.000	0.000	0.000	0.000	0.000	0.000	0.000
1	0.990	0.829	0.549	0.167	0.080	0.035	0.005	0.000	0.000	0.000	0.000	0.000	0.000	0.000	0.000
2	1.000	0.964	0.816	0.398	0.236	0.127	0.027	0.004	0.000	0.000	0.000	0.000	0.000	0.000	0.000
3	1.000	0.995	0.944	0.648	0.461	0.297	0.091	0.018	0.002	0.000	0.000	0.000	0.000	0.000	0.000
4	1.000	0.999	0.987	0.836	0.686	0.515	0.217	0.059	0.009	0.001	0.000	0.000	0.000	0.000	0.000
5	1.000	1.000	0.998	0.939	0.852	0.722	0.403	0.151	0.034	0.004	0.001	0.000	0.000	0.000	0.000
6	1.000	1.000	1.000	0.982	0.943	0.869	0.610	0.304	0.095	0.015	0.004	0.001	0.000	0.000	0.000
7	1.000	1.000	1.000	0.996	0.983	0.950	0.787	0.500	0.213	0.050	0.017	0.004	0.000	0.000	0.000
8	1.000	1.000	1.000	0.999	0.996	0.985	0.905	0.696	0.390	0.131	0.057	0.018	0.000	0.000	0.000
9	1.000	1.000	1.000	1.000	0.999	0.996	0.966	0.849	0.597	0.278	0.148	0.061	0.002	0.000	0.000
10	1.000	1.000	1.000	1.000	1.000	0.999	0.991	0.941	0.783	0.485	0.314	0.164	0.013	0.001	0.000
11	1.000	1.000	1.000	1.000	1.000	1.000	0.998	0.982	0.909	0.703	0.539	0.352	0.056	0.005	0.000
12	1.000	1.000	1.000	1.000	1.000	1.000	1.000	0.996	0.973	0.873	0.764	0.602	0.184	0.036	0.000
13	1.000	1.000	1.000	1.000	1.000	1.000	1.000	1.000	0.995	0.965	0.920	0.833	0.451	0.171	0.010
14	1.000	1.000	1.000	1.000	1.000	1.000	1.000	1.000	1.000	0.995	0.987	0.965	0.794	0.537	0.140

Table value = P(x ≤ number of successes)

Cumulative Binomial Probabilities for n = 20

no. of successes / P	0.01	0.05	0.10	0.20	0.25	0.30	0.40	0.50	0.60	0.70	0.75	0.80	0.90	0.95	0.99
0	0.818	0.358	0.122	0.012	0.003	0.001	0.000	0.000	0.000	0.000	0.000	0.000	0.000	0.000	0.000
1	0.983	0.736	0.392	0.069	0.024	0.008	0.001	0.000	0.000	0.000	0.000	0.000	0.000	0.000	0.000
2	0.999	0.925	0.677	0.206	0.091	0.035	0.004	0.000	0.000	0.000	0.000	0.000	0.000	0.000	0.000
3	1.000	0.984	0.867	0.411	0.225	0.107	0.016	0.001	0.000	0.000	0.000	0.000	0.000	0.000	0.000
4	1.000	0.997	0.957	0.630	0.415	0.238	0.051	0.006	0.000	0.000	0.000	0.000	0.000	0.000	0.000
5	1.000	1.000	0.989	0.804	0.617	0.416	0.126	0.021	0.002	0.000	0.000	0.000	0.000	0.000	0.000
6	1.000	1.000	0.998	0.913	0.786	0.608	0.250	0.058	0.006	0.000	0.000	0.000	0.000	0.000	0.000
7	1.000	1.000	1.000	0.968	0.898	0.772	0.416	0.132	0.021	0.001	0.000	0.000	0.000	0.000	0.000
8	1.000	1.000	1.000	0.990	0.959	0.887	0.596	0.252	0.057	0.005	0.001	0.000	0.000	0.000	0.000
9	1.000	1.000	1.000	0.997	0.986	0.952	0.755	0.412	0.128	0.017	0.004	0.001	0.000	0.000	0.000
10	1.000	1.000	1.000	0.999	0.996	0.983	0.872	0.588	0.245	0.048	0.014	0.003	0.000	0.000	0.000
11	1.000	1.000	1.000	1.000	0.999	0.995	0.943	0.748	0.404	0.113	0.041	0.010	0.000	0.000	0.000
12	1.000	1.000	1.000	1.000	1.000	0.999	0.979	0.868	0.584	0.228	0.102	0.032	0.000	0.000	0.000
13	1.000	1.000	1.000	1.000	1.000	1.000	0.994	0.942	0.750	0.392	0.214	0.087	0.002	0.000	0.000
14	1.000	1.000	1.000	1.000	1.000	1.000	0.998	0.979	0.874	0.584	0.383	0.196	0.011	0.000	0.000
15	1.000	1.000	1.000	1.000	1.000	1.000	1.000	0.994	0.949	0.762	0.585	0.370	0.043	0.003	0.000
16	1.000	1.000	1.000	1.000	1.000	1.000	1.000	0.999	0.984	0.893	0.775	0.589	0.133	0.016	0.000
17	1.000	1.000	1.000	1.000	1.000	1.000	1.000	1.000	0.996	0.965	0.909	0.794	0.323	0.075	0.001
18	1.000	1.000	1.000	1.000	1.000	1.000	1.000	1.000	0.999	0.992	0.976	0.931	0.608	0.264	0.017
19	1.000	1.000	1.000	1.000	1.000	1.000	1.000	1.000	1.000	0.999	0.997	0.988	0.878	0.642	0.182

Table value = P($x \leq$ number of successes)

Cumulative Binomial Probabilities for $n = 25$

no. of successes \ P	0.01	0.05	0.10	0.20	0.25	0.30	0.40	0.50	0.60	0.70	0.75	0.80	0.90	0.95	0.99
0	0.778	0.277	0.072	0.004	0.001	0.000	0.000	0.000	0.000	0.000	0.000	0.000	0.000	0.000	0.000
1	0.974	0.642	0.271	0.027	0.007	0.002	0.000	0.000	0.000	0.000	0.000	0.000	0.000	0.000	0.000
2	0.998	0.873	0.537	0.098	0.032	0.009	0.000	0.000	0.000	0.000	0.000	0.000	0.000	0.000	0.000
3	1.000	0.966	0.764	0.234	0.096	0.033	0.002	0.000	0.000	0.000	0.000	0.000	0.000	0.000	0.000
4	1.000	0.993	0.902	0.421	0.214	0.090	0.009	0.000	0.000	0.000	0.000	0.000	0.000	0.000	0.000
5	1.000	0.999	0.967	0.617	0.378	0.193	0.029	0.002	0.000	0.000	0.000	0.000	0.000	0.000	0.000
6	1.000	1.000	0.991	0.780	0.561	0.341	0.074	0.007	0.000	0.000	0.000	0.000	0.000	0.000	0.000
7	1.000	1.000	0.998	0.891	0.727	0.512	0.154	0.022	0.001	0.000	0.000	0.000	0.000	0.000	0.000
8	1.000	1.000	1.000	0.953	0.851	0.677	0.274	0.054	0.004	0.000	0.000	0.000	0.000	0.000	0.000
9	1.000	1.000	1.000	0.983	0.929	0.811	0.425	0.115	0.013	0.000	0.000	0.000	0.000	0.000	0.000
10	1.000	1.000	1.000	0.994	0.970	0.902	0.586	0.212	0.034	0.002	0.000	0.000	0.000	0.000	0.000
11	1.000	1.000	1.000	0.998	0.989	0.956	0.732	0.345	0.078	0.006	0.001	0.000	0.000	0.000	0.000
12	1.000	1.000	1.000	1.000	0.997	0.983	0.846	0.500	0.154	0.017	0.003	0.000	0.000	0.000	0.000
13	1.000	1.000	1.000	1.000	0.999	0.994	0.922	0.655	0.268	0.044	0.011	0.002	0.000	0.000	0.000
14	1.000	1.000	1.000	1.000	1.000	0.998	0.966	0.788	0.414	0.098	0.030	0.006	0.000	0.000	0.000
15	1.000	1.000	1.000	1.000	1.000	1.000	0.987	0.885	0.575	0.189	0.071	0.017	0.000	0.000	0.000
16	1.000	1.000	1.000	1.000	1.000	1.000	0.996	0.946	0.726	0.323	0.149	0.047	0.000	0.000	0.000
17	1.000	1.000	1.000	1.000	1.000	1.000	0.999	0.978	0.846	0.488	0.273	0.109	0.002	0.000	0.000
18	1.000	1.000	1.000	1.000	1.000	1.000	1.000	0.993	0.926	0.659	0.439	0.220	0.009	0.000	0.000
19	1.000	1.000	1.000	1.000	1.000	1.000	1.000	0.998	0.971	0.807	0.622	0.383	0.033	0.001	0.000
20	1.000	1.000	1.000	1.000	1.000	1.000	1.000	1.000	0.991	0.910	0.786	0.579	0.098	0.007	0.000
21	1.000	1.000	1.000	1.000	1.000	1.000	1.000	1.000	0.998	0.967	0.904	0.766	0.236	0.034	0.000
22	1.000	1.000	1.000	1.000	1.000	1.000	1.000	1.000	1.000	0.991	0.968	0.902	0.463	0.127	0.002
23	1.000	1.000	1.000	1.000	1.000	1.000	1.000	1.000	1.000	0.998	0.993	0.973	0.729	0.358	0.026
24	1.000	1.000	1.000	1.000	1.000	1.000	1.000	1.000	1.000	1.000	0.999	0.996	0.928	0.723	0.222

Standard Normal Table

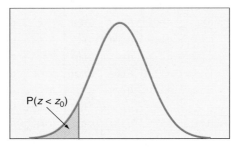

$P(z < z_0)$

z	0.00	0.01	0.02	0.03	0.04	0.05	0.06	0.07	0.08	0.09
−3.9	0.0000	0.0000	0.0000	0.0000	0.0000	0.0000	0.0000	0.0000	0.0000	0.0000
−3.8	0.0001	0.0001	0.0001	0.0001	0.0001	0.0001	0.0001	0.0001	0.0001	0.0001
−3.7	0.0001	0.0001	0.0001	0.0001	0.0001	0.0001	0.0001	0.0001	0.0001	0.0001
−3.6	0.0002	0.0002	0.0001	0.0001	0.0001	0.0001	0.0001	0.0001	0.0001	0.0001
−3.5	0.0002	0.0002	0.0002	0.0002	0.0002	0.0002	0.0002	0.0002	0.0002	0.0002
−3.4	0.0003	0.0003	0.0003	0.0003	0.0003	0.0003	0.0003	0.0003	0.0003	0.0002
−3.3	0.0005	0.0005	0.0005	0.0004	0.0004	0.0004	0.0004	0.0004	0.0004	0.0003
−3.2	0.0007	0.0007	0.0006	0.0006	0.0006	0.0006	0.0006	0.0005	0.0005	0.0005
−3.1	0.0010	0.0009	0.0009	0.0009	0.0008	0.0008	0.0008	0.0008	0.0007	0.0007
−3.0	0.0013	0.0013	0.0013	0.0012	0.0012	0.0011	0.0011	0.0011	0.0010	0.0010
−2.9	0.0019	0.0018	0.0018	0.0017	0.0016	0.0016	0.0015	0.0015	0.0014	0.0014
−2.8	0.0026	0.0025	0.0024	0.0023	0.0023	0.0022	0.0021	0.0021	0.0020	0.0019
−2.7	0.0035	0.0034	0.0033	0.0032	0.0031	0.0030	0.0029	0.0028	0.0027	0.0026
−2.6	0.0047	0.0045	0.0044	0.0043	0.0041	0.0040	0.0039	0.0038	0.0037	0.0036
−2.5	0.0062	0.0060	0.0059	0.0057	0.0055	0.0054	0.0052	0.0051	0.0049	0.0048
−2.4	0.0082	0.0080	0.0078	0.0075	0.0073	0.0071	0.0069	0.0068	0.0066	0.0064
−2.3	0.0107	0.0104	0.0102	0.0099	0.0096	0.0094	0.0091	0.0089	0.0087	0.0084
−2.2	0.0139	0.0136	0.0132	0.0129	0.0125	0.0122	0.0119	0.0116	0.0113	0.0110
−2.1	0.0179	0.0174	0.0170	0.0166	0.0162	0.0158	0.0154	0.0150	0.0146	0.0143
−2.0	0.0228	0.0222	0.0217	0.0212	0.0207	0.0202	0.0197	0.0192	0.0188	0.0183
−1.9	0.0287	0.0281	0.0274	0.0268	0.0262	0.0256	0.0250	0.0244	0.0239	0.0233
−1.8	0.0359	0.0351	0.0344	0.0336	0.0329	0.0322	0.0314	0.0307	0.0301	0.0294
−1.7	0.0446	0.0436	0.0427	0.0418	0.0409	0.0401	0.0392	0.0384	0.0375	0.0367
−1.6	0.0548	0.0537	0.0526	0.0516	0.0505	0.0495	0.0485	0.0475	0.0465	0.0455
−1.5	0.0668	0.0655	0.0643	0.0630	0.0618	0.0606	0.0594	0.0582	0.0571	0.0559
−1.4	0.0808	0.0793	0.0778	0.0764	0.0749	0.0735	0.0721	0.0708	0.0694	0.0681
−1.3	0.0968	0.0951	0.0934	0.0918	0.0901	0.0885	0.0869	0.0853	0.0838	0.0823
−1.2	0.1151	0.1131	0.1112	0.1093	0.1075	0.1056	0.1038	0.1020	0.1003	0.0985
−1.1	0.1357	0.1335	0.1314	0.1292	0.1271	0.1251	0.1230	0.1210	0.1190	0.1170
−1.0	0.1587	0.1562	0.1539	0.1515	0.1492	0.1469	0.1446	0.1423	0.1401	0.1379
−0.9	0.1841	0.1814	0.1788	0.1762	0.1736	0.1711	0.1685	0.1660	0.1635	0.1611
−0.8	0.2119	0.2090	0.2061	0.2033	0.2005	0.1977	0.1949	0.1922	0.1894	0.1867
−0.7	0.2420	0.2389	0.2358	0.2327	0.2296	0.2266	0.2236	0.2206	0.2177	0.2148
−0.6	0.2743	0.2709	0.2676	0.2643	0.2611	0.2578	0.2546	0.2514	0.2483	0.2451
−0.5	0.3085	0.3050	0.3015	0.2981	0.2946	0.2912	0.2877	0.2843	0.2810	0.2776
−0.4	0.3446	0.3409	0.3372	0.3336	0.3300	0.3264	0.3228	0.3192	0.3156	0.3121
−0.3	0.3821	0.3783	0.3745	0.3707	0.3669	0.3632	0.3594	0.3557	0.3520	0.3483
−0.2	0.4207	0.4168	0.4129	0.4090	0.4052	0.4013	0.3974	0.3936	0.3897	0.3859

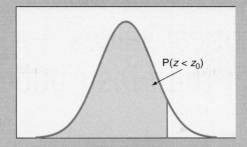

$P(z < z_0)$

z	0.00	0.01	0.02	0.03	0.04	0.05	0.06	0.07	0.08	0.09
−0.1	0.4602	0.4562	0.4522	0.4483	0.4443	0.4404	0.4364	0.4325	0.4286	0.4247
−0.0	0.5000	0.4960	0.4920	0.4880	0.4840	0.4801	0.4761	0.4721	0.4681	0.4641
0.0	0.5000	0.5040	0.5080	0.5120	0.5160	0.5199	0.5239	0.5279	0.5319	0.5359
0.1	0.5398	0.5438	0.5478	0.5517	0.5557	0.5596	0.5636	0.5675	0.5714	0.5753
0.2	0.5793	0.5832	0.5871	0.5910	0.5948	0.5987	0.6026	0.6064	0.6103	0.6141
0.3	0.6179	0.6217	0.6255	0.6293	0.6331	0.6368	0.6406	0.6443	0.6480	0.6517
0.4	0.6554	0.6591	0.6628	0.6664	0.6700	0.6736	0.6772	0.6808	0.6844	0.6879
0.5	0.6915	0.6950	0.6985	0.7019	0.7054	0.7088	0.7123	0.7157	0.7190	0.7224
0.6	0.7257	0.7291	0.7324	0.7357	0.7389	0.7422	0.7454	0.7486	0.7517	0.7549
0.7	0.7580	0.7611	0.7642	0.7673	0.7704	0.7734	0.7764	0.7794	0.7823	0.7852
0.8	0.7881	0.7910	0.7939	0.7967	0.7995	0.8023	0.8051	0.8078	0.8106	0.8133
0.9	0.8159	0.8186	0.8212	0.8238	0.8264	0.8289	0.8315	0.8340	0.8365	0.8389
1.0	0.8413	0.8438	0.8461	0.8485	0.8508	0.8531	0.8554	0.8577	0.8599	0.8621
1.1	0.8643	0.8665	0.8686	0.8708	0.8729	0.8749	0.8770	0.8790	0.8810	0.8830
1.2	0.8849	0.8869	0.8888	0.8907	0.8925	0.8944	0.8962	0.8980	0.8997	0.9015
1.3	0.9032	0.9049	0.9066	0.9082	0.9099	0.9115	0.9131	0.9147	0.9162	0.9177
1.4	0.9192	0.9207	0.9222	0.9236	0.9251	0.9265	0.9279	0.9292	0.9306	0.9319
1.5	0.9332	0.9345	0.9357	0.9370	0.9382	0.9394	0.9406	0.9418	0.9429	0.9441
1.6	0.9452	0.9463	0.9474	0.9484	0.9495	0.9505	0.9515	0.9525	0.9535	0.9545
1.7	0.9554	0.9564	0.9573	0.9582	0.9591	0.9599	0.9608	0.9616	0.9625	0.9633
1.8	0.9641	0.9649	0.9656	0.9664	0.9671	0.9678	0.9686	0.9693	0.9699	0.9706
1.9	0.9713	0.9719	0.9726	0.9732	0.9738	0.9744	0.9750	0.9756	0.9761	0.9767
2.0	0.9772	0.9778	0.9783	0.9788	0.9793	0.9798	0.9803	0.9808	0.9812	0.9817
2.1	0.9821	0.9826	0.9830	0.9834	0.9838	0.9842	0.9846	0.9850	0.9854	0.9857
2.2	0.9861	0.9864	0.9868	0.9871	0.9875	0.9878	0.9881	0.9884	0.9887	0.9890
2.3	0.9893	0.9896	0.9898	0.9901	0.9904	0.9906	0.9909	0.9911	0.9913	0.9916
2.4	0.9918	0.9920	0.9922	0.9925	0.9927	0.9929	0.9931	0.9932	0.9934	0.9936
2.5	0.9938	0.9940	0.9941	0.9943	0.9945	0.9946	0.9948	0.9949	0.9951	0.9952
2.6	0.9953	0.9955	0.9956	0.9957	0.9959	0.9960	0.9961	0.9962	0.9963	0.9964
2.7	0.9965	0.9966	0.9967	0.9968	0.9969	0.9970	0.9971	0.9972	0.9973	0.9974
2.8	0.9974	0.9975	0.9976	0.9977	0.9977	0.9978	0.9979	0.9979	0.9980	0.9981
2.9	0.9981	0.9982	0.9982	0.9983	0.9984	0.9984	0.9985	0.9985	0.9986	0.9986
3.0	0.9987	0.9987	0.9987	0.9988	0.9988	0.9989	0.9989	0.9989	0.9990	0.9990
3.1	0.9990	0.9991	0.9991	0.9991	0.9992	0.9992	0.9992	0.9992	0.9993	0.9993
3.2	0.9993	0.9993	0.9994	0.9994	0.9994	0.9994	0.9994	0.9995	0.9995	0.9995
3.3	0.9995	0.9995	0.9995	0.9996	0.9996	0.9996	0.9996	0.9996	0.9996	0.9997
3.4	0.9997	0.9997	0.9997	0.9997	0.9997	0.9997	0.9997	0.9997	0.9997	0.9998
3.5	0.9998	0.9998	0.9998	0.9998	0.9998	0.9998	0.9998	0.9998	0.9998	0.9998
3.6	0.9998	0.9998	0.9999	0.9999	0.9999	0.9999	0.9999	0.9999	0.9999	0.9999
3.7	0.9999	0.9999	0.9999	0.9999	0.9999	0.9999	0.9999	0.9999	0.9999	0.9999
3.8	0.9999	0.9999	0.9999	0.9999	0.9999	0.9999	0.9999	0.9999	0.9999	0.9999
3.9	1.0000	1.0000	1.0000	1.0000	1.0000	1.0000	1.0000	1.0000	1.0000	1.0000

Critical Values
for the *t*-Distribution

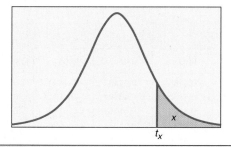

Degrees of Freedom	$t_{.100}$	$t_{.050}$	$t_{.025}$	$t_{.010}$	$t_{.005}$
1	3.078	6.314	12.706	31.821	63.656
2	1.886	2.920	4.303	6.965	9.925
3	1.638	2.353	3.182	4.541	5.841
4	1.533	2.132	2.776	3.747	4.604
5	1.476	2.015	2.571	3.365	4.032
6	1.440	1.943	2.447	3.143	3.707
7	1.415	1.895	2.365	2.998	3.499
8	1.397	1.860	2.306	2.896	3.355
9	1.383	1.833	2.262	2.821	3.250
10	1.372	1.812	2.228	2.764	3.169
11	1.363	1.796	2.201	2.718	3.106
12	1.356	1.782	2.179	2.681	3.055
13	1.350	1.771	2.160	2.650	3.012
14	1.345	1.761	2.145	2.624	2.977
15	1.341	1.753	2.131	2.602	2.947
16	1.337	1.746	2.120	2.583	2.921
17	1.333	1.740	2.110	2.567	2.898
18	1.330	1.734	2.101	2.552	2.878
19	1.328	1.729	2.093	2.539	2.861
20	1.325	1.725	2.086	2.528	2.845
21	1.323	1.721	2.080	2.518	2.831
22	1.321	1.717	2.074	2.508	2.819
23	1.319	1.714	2.069	2.500	2.807
24	1.318	1.711	2.064	2.492	2.797
25	1.316	1.708	2.060	2.485	2.787
26	1.315	1.706	2.056	2.479	2.779
27	1.314	1.703	2.052	2.473	2.771
28	1.313	1.701	2.048	2.467	2.763
29	1.311	1.699	2.045	2.462	2.756
30	1.310	1.697	2.042	2.457	2.750
35	1.306	1.690	2.030	2.438	2.724
40	1.303	1.684	2.021	2.423	2.704
45	1.301	1.679	2.014	2.412	2.690
50	1.299	1.676	2.009	2.403	2.678
60	1.296	1.671	2.000	2.390	2.660
70	1.294	1.667	1.994	2.381	2.648
80	1.292	1.664	1.990	2.374	2.639
90	1.291	1.662	1.987	2.368	2.632
100	1.290	1.660	1.984	2.364	2.626
150	1.287	1.655	1.976	2.351	2.609
200	1.286	1.653	1.972	2.345	2.601
∞	1.282	1.645	1.960	2.326	2.576

Wilcoxon Signed Rank Sum Test Table, Critical Values and *p*-values

n	W_L	W_U	$P(W \leq W_L) = P(W \geq W_U)$
4	0	10	0.062
	1	9	0.125
5	0	15	0.031
	1	14	0.062
6	0	21	0.016
	1	20	0.031
	2	19	0.047
	3	18	0.078
7	0	28	0.008
	1	27	0.016
	2	26	0.023
	3	25	0.039
	4	24	0.055
8	1	35	0.008
	2	34	0.012
	3	33	0.020
	4	32	0.027
	5	31	0.039
	6	30	0.055
9	3	42	0.010
	5	40	0.020
	6	39	0.027
	8	37	0.049
	9	36	0.064
10	5	50	0.010
	8	47	0.024
	9	46	0.032
	10	45	0.042
	11	44	0.053
11	7	59	0.010
	10	56	0.021
	11	55	0.027
	13	53	0.042
	14	52	0.051
12	9	69	0.008
	10	68	0.011
	13	65	0.021
	14	64	0.026
	17	61	0.046
	18	60	0.055
13	12	79	0.009
	13	78	0.011
	17	74	0.024
	18	73	0.029
	21	70	0.047
	22	69	0.055
14	16	89	0.010
	21	84	0.025
	25	80	0.045
	26	79	0.052

n	W_L	W_U	$P(W \leq W_L) = P(W \geq W_U)$
15	19	101	0.009
	20	100	0.011
	25	95	0.024
	26	94	0.028
	30	90	0.047
	31	89	0.054
16	23	113	0.009
	24	112	0.011
	30	106	0.025
	35	101	0.047
	36	100	0.052
17	28	125	0.010
	35	118	0.025
	41	112	0.049
	42	111	0.054
18	33	138	0.010
	40	131	0.024
	41	130	0.027
	47	124	0.049
	48	123	0.054
19	38	152	0.010
	46	144	0.025
	53	137	0.048
	54	136	0.052
20	43	167	0.010
	52	158	0.024
	53	157	0.027
	60	150	0.049
	61	149	0.053
21	49	182	0.010
	59	172	0.025
	67	164	0.048
	68	163	0.052
22	56	197	0.010
	66	187	0.025
	75	178	0.049
	76	177	0.053
23	62	214	0.010
	73	203	0.024
	74	202	0.026
	83	193	0.049
	84	192	0.052
24	69	231	0.010
	81	219	0.025
	91	209	0.048
	92	208	0.051
25	77	248	0.010
	89	236	0.024
	90	235	0.026
	100	225	0.048
	101	224	0.051

Source: Data extracted from C.H. Kraft and C. van Eeden, *A Nonparametric Introduction to Statistics* (New York: Macmillan, 1968). Used with permission.

Wilcoxon Rank Sum Test Table, Critical Values

n_1	n_2	W_L	W_U	$P(W_1 \le W_L) = P(W_1 \ge W_U)$
4	4	12	24	0.057
		11	29	0.029
		1	26	0.014
4	5	13	27	0.056
		12	28	0.032
		11	29	0.016
		10	30	0.008
4	6	14	30	0.057
		13	31	0.033
		12	32	0.019
		11	33	0.010
4	7	15	33	0.055
		14	34	0.036
		13	35	0.021
		12	36	0.012
		11	37	0.006
4	8	16	36	0.055
		14	38	0.024
		13	39	0.014
		12	40	0.008
4	9	17	39	0.053
		15	41	0.025
		13	43	0.010
4	10	18	42	0.053
		16	44	0.027
		15	45	0.018
		14	46	0.012
		13	47	0.007
5	5	19	36	0.048
		18	37	0.028
		17	38	0.016
		16	39	0.008
5	6	21	39	0.063
		20	40	0.041
		19	41	0.026
		18	42	0.015
		17	43	0.009
5	7	22	43	0.053
		21	44	0.037
		20	45	0.024
		19	46	0.015
		18	47	0.009
5	8	23	47	0.047
		22	48	0.033
		21	49	0.023
		20	50	0.015
		19	51	0.009
5	9	25	50	0.056
		23	52	0.030
		22	53	0.021
		21	54	0.014
		20	55	0.009

n_1	n_2	W_L	W_U	$P(W_1 \le W_L) = P(W_1 \ge W_U)$
5	10	26	54	0.050
		24	56	0.028
		23	57	0.020
		22	58	0.014
		21	59	0.010
6	6	28	50	0.047
		27	51	0.032
		26	52	0.021
		25	53	0.013
		24	54	0.008
6	7	30	54	0.051
		28	56	0.026
		26	58	0.011
		25	59	0.007
6	8	32	54	0.054
		30	60	0.030
		29	61	0.021
		27	63	0.010
6	9	34	62	0.057
		31	65	0.025
		29	67	0.013
		28	68	0.009
6	10	36	66	0.059
		35	67	0.047
		33	69	0.028
		32	70	0.021
		30	72	0.011
		29	73	0.008
7	7	39	66	0.049
		37	68	0.027
		36	69	0.019
		35	70	0.013
		34	71	0.009
7	8	41	71	0.047
		39	73	0.027
		38	74	0.020
		36	76	0.010
7	9	44	75	0.057
		41	78	0.027
		40	79	0.021
		38	81	0.011
		37	82	0.008
7	10	46	80	0.054
		45	81	0.044
		43	83	0.028
		42	84	0.022
		40	86	0.011
		39	87	0.009
8	8	52	84	0.052
		49	87	0.025
		46	90	0.010

(continued)

n_1	n_2	W_L	W_U	$P(W_1 \leq W_L) = P(W_1 \geq W_U)$
8	9	55	89	0.057
		54	90	0.046
		52	92	0.030
		51	93	0.023
		48	96	0.010
8	10	57	95	0.051
		54	98	0.027
		53	99	0.022
		50	102	0.010
9	9	67	104	0.057
		66	105	0.047
		63	108	0.025
		60	111	0.012
		59	112	0.009

n_1	n_2	W_L	W_U	$P(W_1 \leq W_L) = P(W_1 \geq W_U)$
9	10	70	110	0.056
		69	111	0.047
		66	114	0.027
		65	115	0.022
		62	118	0.011
		61	119	0.009
10	10	83	127	0.053
		82	128	0.045
		79	131	0.026
		78	132	0.022
		78	135	0.012
		74	136	0.009

Source: Data taken from the Wilcoxon Signed Rank Sum Test Table as prepared by Dr. Richard Darlington at **http://comp9.psych.cornell.edu/Darlington/wilcoxon/wilcox.5.htm.** Used with the permission of Dr. Richard Darlington.

APPENDIX

Critical Values for the χ^2-Distribution

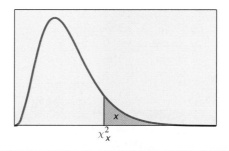

degrees of freedom	$\chi^2_{.100}$	$\chi^2_{.050}$	$\chi^2_{.025}$	$\chi^2_{.010}$	$\chi^2_{.005}$
1	2.706	3.841	5.024	6.635	7.879
2	4.605	5.991	7.378	9.210	10.597
3	6.251	7.815	9.348	11.345	12.838
4	7.779	9.488	11.143	13.277	14.860
5	9.236	11.070	12.832	15.086	16.750
6	10.645	12.592	14.449	16.812	18.548
7	12.017	14.067	16.013	18.475	20.278
8	13.362	15.507	17.535	20.090	21.955
9	14.684	16.919	19.023	21.666	23.589
10	15.987	18.307	20.483	23.209	25.188
11	17.275	19.675	21.920	24.725	26.757
12	18.549	21.026	23.337	26.217	28.300
13	19.812	22.362	24.736	27.688	29.819
14	21.064	23.685	26.119	29.141	31.319
15	22.307	24.996	27.488	30.578	32.801
16	23.542	26.296	28.845	32.000	34.267
17	24.769	27.587	30.191	33.409	35.718
18	25.989	28.869	31.526	34.805	37.156
19	27.204	30.144	32.852	36.191	38.582
20	28.412	31.410	34.170	37.566	39.997
21	29.615	32.671	35.479	38.932	41.401
22	30.813	33.924	36.781	40.289	42.796
23	32.007	35.172	38.076	41.638	44.181
24	33.196	36.415	39.364	42.980	45.558
25	34.382	37.652	40.646	44.314	46.928
26	35.563	38.885	41.923	45.642	48.290
27	36.741	40.113	43.195	46.963	49.645
28	37.916	41.337	44.461	48.278	50.994
29	39.087	42.557	45.722	49.588	52.335
30	40.256	43.773	46.979	50.892	53.672
35	46.059	49.802	53.203	57.342	60.275
40	51.805	55.758	59.342	63.691	66.766
45	57.505	61.656	65.410	69.957	73.166
50	63.167	67.505	71.420	76.154	79.490
60	74.397	79.082	83.298	88.379	91.952
70	85.527	90.531	95.023	100.425	104.215
80	96.578	101.879	106.629	112.329	116.321
90	107.565	113.145	118.136	124.116	128.299
100	118.498	124.342	129.561	135.807	140.170

Glossary

A

alternative hypothesis – what you are going to believe about the population when there is strong evidence against the null hypothesis

C

classical definition of probability – if there are n equally likely possible outcomes of an experiment, and m of them correspond to the event you are interested in, then the probability of the event is m/n

coefficient of determination, R^2 – a value that measures the percentage of variation in the y-variable that is explained by changes in the x-variable

complement of an event A – everything in the sample space that is not A

conditional probability – the probability of an event A given that another event B has already occurred; the usual notation is $P(A|B)$, read the probability of A, given B

confidence interval estimate – a range of numbers of the form (a, b) that isthought to enclose the parameter of interest, with a given level of probability

confidence interval – interval that predicts the average y for a given value of x

continuous random variable – a random variable that can take on any value from a continuous range

continuous variable – a measurement variable that can take any possible value on a number line (possibly within upper and lower limits)

coverage errors – errors that arise because of inaccuracy or duplication in the survey frame

cross-sectional data – data that are all collected in the same time period

D

descriptive statistics – a set of techniques to organize and summarize raw data

deviation from the mean – for each data point, the distance of the point from the mean value

discrete random variable – a random variable that can take on any value from a list of distinct possible values

discrete variable – a variable that can take on only certain identifiable values on a number line (possibly within upper and lower limits)

E

estimation errors – errors that arise because of incorrect use of techniques, or calculation errors

event – one or more outcomes of an experiment

Excel bin number – the upper included limit of a class

experiment – any activity with an uncertain outcome

experimental study – the researcher actively intervenes, designing the study so that conclusions about causation can be drawn

explanatory variable – variable observed (and sometimes controlled) by the researcher, which is the apparent cause of the change in the response variable

F

1st quartile – usually denoted Q_1; is the 25th percentile

frame – a list of the elements in a population

frequency distribution – a summary table that divides continuous quantitative data into ranges, and records the count (or frequency) of data points in each range

H

histogram – a bar graph of a frequency distribution, with lower class limits shown along the x-axis, and class frequencies shown along the y-axis

I

independent events – two events A and B are independent if the probability of one of the events is unaffected by whether the other event has occurred; $P(A|B)$ 5 $P(A)$ and $P(B|A)$ 5 $P(B)$

inferential statistics – a set of techniques that allow reliable conclusions to be drawn about population data, on the basis of sample data

influential observation – a single observation that has an extreme effect on the regression equation

I

interquartile range (IQR) – $Q_3 - Q_1$; it measures the range of the middle 50% of the data values

L

least-squares line – the line that has the smallest possible sum of the squared residuals

M

mean – a measure of central tendency calculated by adding up all the numbers in the data set, and then dividing by the number of numbers

median – the middle value (if there is a unique middle value), or the average of the two middle values (when there is not a unique middle value) in an ordered data set

mode – the most frequently occurring value in the data set

mutually exclusive events – events that cannot happen simultaneously; if two events A and B are mutually exclusive, then $P(A$ and $B) = 0$

N

negative (inverse) relationship – increases in the explanatory variable correspond to decreases in the response variable

nonresponse error – error that arises when data cannot be collected for some elements of the sample

nonsampling errors – other kinds of errors that can arise in the process of sampling a population

nonstatistical sampling – the elements of the population are chosen for the sample by convenience, or according to the researcher's judgment; there is no way to estimate the probability that any particular element from the population will be chosen for the sample

null hypothesis – what you are going to believe about the population, unless the sample gives you strongly contradictory evidence

O

observational study – the researcher observes what is already taking place, and does not attempt to affect outcomes

outlier – a data point that is unusually far from the rest of the data

P

p-value – in a hypothesis test, the probability of getting a sample result at least as extreme as the observed sample result; the probability calculation is based on the sampling distribution that would exist if the null hypothesis were true

parameter – a summary measure of the population data

Pearson correlation coefficient – a numerical measure that indicates the strength of the linear relationship between two quantitative variables

point estimate – a single-number estimate of a population parameter that is based on sample data

population data – the complete collection of *all* of the data of interest

positive (direct) relationship – increases in the explanatory variable correspond to increases in the response variable

prediction interval – interval that predicts a particular value of y for a given value of x

primary data – data that you collect yourself, for a specific purpose

probability distribution for a discrete random variable – a list of all the possible values of the random variable, and their associated probabilities

probability distribution of a continuous random variable – a graph or a mathematical formula

probability – a measure of the likelihood of an event

processing errors – errors that occur when the data are being prepared for analysis

Pth percentile – x_p, the data point that is above $P\%$ of the data points

Q

qualitative data – data containing descriptive information, which may be recorded in words or numbers (the numbers represent codes for the associated words; arithmetical operations such as averaging are not meaningful in this case)

quantitative data – data containing numerical information, for which arithmetical operations such as averaging are meaningful

R

random variable – a variable whose value is determined by the outcome of a random experiment

range – a number that is calculated as the difference between the maximum and minimum values in the data set

ranked data – qualitative data that can be ordered according to size or quality

relative frequency – the percentage of total observations falling into that class

relative frequency approach to probability probability is the relative frequency of an event over a large number of repeated trials of an experiment

residual – the difference between the observed value of y for a given x, and the predicted value of y for that x

response errors – errors that arise because of problems with the survey collection instrument (e.g., the questionnaire), the interviewer (e.g., bias), the respondent (e.g., faulty memory), or the survey process (e.g., not ensuring that the respondent fits into the target group)

response variable – variable that changes when the explanatory variable changes

S

sample data – a subset of population data

sample space – a complete list or representation of all of the possible outcomes of an experiment

sampling distribution – the probability distribution of all possible sample results for a given sample size

sampling error – the difference between the true value of the population parameter and the value of the corresponding sample statistic; arises because we are examining only a subset of the population

scatter diagram – display of paired x–y data points of the form (x, y)

secondary data – data that were previously collected by someone else

significance level – the probability of a Type I error in a hypothesis test

simple random sampling – a sampling process that ensures that each element of the population is equally likely to be selected

skewed to the left (or negatively skewed) distribution – a distribution in which some unusually small values in the data set destroy the symmetry

skewed to the right (or positively skewed) distribution – a distribution in which some unusually high values in the data set destroy the symmetry

Spearman rank correlation coefficient – a numerical measure that indicates the strength of the relationship (linear or non-linear) for two variables, one or both of which may be ranked

standard deviation – a measure of variability in a data set that is based on deviations from the mean

statistic – a summary measure of the sample data

statistical sampling – the elements of the population are chosen for the sample in a random fashion, with a known probability of inclusion

symmetric distribution – the right half of the distribution is a mirror image of the left half

T

3rd quartile – usually denoted Q_3; is the 75th percentile

time-series data – data that are collected over successive points in time

Type I error – error that arises when we mistakenly reject the null hypothesis when it is in fact true

Type II error – error that arises when we mistakenly fail to reject the null hypothesis when it is in fact false

V

variable – a characteristic or quantity that can vary

Index

A

ABI/INFORM, 4
addition rule, 153–155
alternative hypothesis, 238–239
analysis of variance (ANOVA), 363–364
"and" probabilities, 148–152
ANOVA, 363–364
arithmetic by hand, 89
association. *See* measures of association
axis labels, misleading or missing, 72–73, 72f

B

bar charts
    for contingency tables, 57–60, 57f, 58f
    creation in Excel, 53–54, 53f, 56
    ordered bars, 54, 54f
    relative sizes of categories, 55
    for simple table, 52–57, 52f, 54f
bar graph, 30–31, 31f, 385, 385f
BC Pharmacies and Personal Care
    Stores, 3f
bell curve, 183
    see also normal distribution
bimodal distribution, 100, 100f
bin numbers, 37f
Bin Range, 37
binomial experiment, 170–171, 173
binomial probability
    calculation of, 173–182
    cumulative, for n=8 trials, 181f
    Excel, calculation with, 176–181
    formula, calculation with, 175–176
    noncumulative, for n=8 trials, 182f
    tables, calculation with, 181–182
binomial probability distribution
    checking conditions for binomial
        experiment, 171–173
    conditions for binomial experiment,
        170–171
    graph, n=10, p-0.1, 224f
    graph, n=20, p-0.5, 224f–225f
    graph, n=100, p-0.1, 225f
    graphical representation, 182
    mean, 171
    population proportions, decisions
        about, 222–230
    probability graph, n=10, p=0.5, 184f
    sampling without replacement,
        172–173
    standard deviation, 171
binomial random variable, 171
binomial tables, 181–182, 454–457
business publications, 4
Business Source Premier (BSP), 4

C

Canadian Business & Current Affairs
    (CBCA), 4
Canadian Business magazine, 4
categorical data, 26
    see also qualitative data
cause and effect, 16
central limit theorem, 218–220
central tendency, measures of. *See*
        measures of central tendency
charts
    bar charts. *See* bar charts
    pie charts. *See* pie charts
chi-squared expected values calculations,
        394–395, 394f
chi-squared goodness-of-fit tests,
        381–389
chi-squared test for independence,
        395–398
class
    relative frequency, 48
    setup considerations, 34–35, 34f, 35f
class width, 32–34, 32f–33f, 35f
class width template, 38f–39f
classical definition of probability, 138
clutter, image, 74, 74f
coded data, 374–376
coefficient of determination (R2), 440–442
communication, 18
comparison of histograms, 47–52
complement of an event A, 155
complement rule, 155–158
computational formula (standard
        deviation), 105–106
conditional probability, 143–145
confidence interval, 443
confidence interval estimate
    average difference in population
        mean, 308–309
    for average *y*, given *x*, 446–447
    critical *z*-scores, 280f
    defined, 275
    for difference in population means,
        350–354
    for difference in proportions, 379–380
    Excel template, 282, 286–287
    general form of, 275f
    harsh around population parameter,
        275f
    and hypothesis tests, 292–293
    population mean, 284f, 285–287, 285f,
        308–309
    population proportion, 277f, 280f,
        281–282, 290f
    and two-tailed hypothesis tests, 292f

contingency table test for independence,
        395–398
contingency tables, 57–60, 139,
        141f, 144f
continuous random variable, 166, 184
convenience sample, 6
correlation analysis, 118
correlation coefficient
    formula for, 120–124
    Pearson correlation coefficient,
        118–124, 119f
    Spearman rank correlation coefficient,
        124–127
counting, 138
counts, 27
coverage errors, 11
cross-sectional data, 28
cumulative binomial tables, 454–457

D

data
    coded data, 374–376
    cross-sectional data, 28
    missing data, 75, 75f
    ordinal data, 27
    population data, 5, 5f, 108
    primary data, 3
    qualitative data, 26, 27
    quantitative data, 26–28
    ranked data. *See* ranked data
    sample data, 5, 5f
    secondary data, 3–4
    symmetry and shape, 107
    time-series data, 28
    types of, 2–28
    unranked data, 27
data analysis. *See* statistical analysis
data-based decision making framework,
        19–20
data sets
    class width worksheet, 33
    distribution, determination of, 45
    outlier, 46–47
    skewed distribution, 45–46, 45f, 46f
    symmetric distribution, 45, 45f

decision making
cause and effect, 16
data-based decision making framework, 19–20
estimation. *See* estimation
experimental study, 16–17
with hypothesis testing, 240
independent samples. *See* independent samples
matched-pair analysis. *See* matched-pair analysis
null hypothesis, rejecting or failing to reject, 240
observational study, 15
p-values, 243–245
population mean, 251–266
population proportions, 222, 230, 231, 246–251
sampling distribution, 221
single sample. *See* single sample
for statistical inference, 205–211
store location, 342
two or more samples. *See* two or more samples
decision rule approach, 262–266
descriptive statistics
correlation analysis, 118
defined, 13
deviation from the mean, 95, 103
interquartile range (IQR), 113–117, 116*f*
mean, 93–96, 94*f*
measures of association, 118–128
measures of central tendency, 93–101
measures of variability, 101–117
median, 96–99
mode, 99–100
Pearson correlation coefficient, 118–124, 119*f*
probability. *See* probability
range, 101–102, 102*f*
Spearman rank correlation coefficient, 124–127, 127*f*
standard deviation. *See* standard deviation
deviation from the mean, 95, 103
dialogue box. *See* Excel
differing error rates, 16
direct relationship, 66
discrete random variable, 165
discrete variable, 26, 27
distorted images, 73–75
distribution
bimodal distribution, 100, 100*f*
determination of, 45

frequency distribution. *See* frequency distribution
negatively skewed distribution, 46, 46*f*
population distribution, 215–217
positively skewed distribution, 45, 45*f*
probability distributions. *See* probability distribution
sampling distribution. *See* sampling distribution
severely skewed distribution, 46*f*
skewed distribution, 45–46, 45*f*, 46*f*
symmetric bell-shaped distribution, 107–108
symmetric distribution, 45, 45*f*
t-distribution, 252–258, 252*f*
tails of the distribution, 111, 111*f*
unimodal distribution, 99, 100*f*
distribution-free technique, 318
double-counting, 153

E

empirical approach, 215–218
Empirical Rule, 106–113, 107*f*, 108*f*
error term, 421, 424–426
see also residuals
errors
see also standard error
coverage errors, 11
differing error rates, 16
estimation errors, 11
nonresponse error, 11
nonsampling errors, 11
in predictions, 442
processing errors, 11
response errors, 11
sampling error, 11
Type I error, 241–243, 241*f*, 247
Type II error, 241–243, 241*f*, 247
estimation
confidence interval estimate. *See* confidence interval estimate
point estimate, 274–275
population mean, 283–287, 290
population proportion, 276–282, 290–291
relationship, 410–416
sample size for estimation of mean, 287–290
sample size for estimation of proportion, 290–291
sampling, reliance on, 274
estimation errors, 11
event, 137

Excel
bar charts, 53–54, 53*f*, 56
bin numbers, 37
BINOMDIST function dialogue, 177, 177*f*
binomial probability, 176–181
chi-squared expected values calculations, 394–395, 394*f*
chi-squared goodness-of-fit test, 388–389
coefficient of determination (R2), 440
confidence interval estimate for average *y*, given *x*, 446–447
confidence interval estimate for difference in population means, 352
confidence interval estimate for population mean, 286–287
confidence interval estimate for population proportion, 282, 282*f*
correlation coefficient, 120
data analysis dialogue box, 35*f*, 36
Data Analysis *t*-test, 304–305, 344–347
frequency distribution, 42*f*
goodness-of-fit test, 388–389
histogram dialogue box, 36*f*, 41*f*
histograms, 42–44, 42*f*, 43*f*, 44*f*
interquartile range, 115, 116*f*
interval estimates, 443–445
least-squares line, slope and *y*-intercept, 412–416, 412*f*, 413*f*, 414*f*, 415*f*, 416*f*
matched-pairs ranked data, 330–331
mean, calculation of, 96
median, calculation of, 99
mode, calculation of, 100
Non-parametric Tools, 127, 127*f*
normal probability, 185–191
Normal Probability Plot, 426
NORMDIST function, 187, 187*f*
NORMINV dialogue box, 190*f*, 191*f*
Pearson correlation coefficient, 124
pie charts, 55
population mean, 255–256, 255*f*, 257–258, 260, 303–304, 307, 309
population proportion, 248–250, 248*f*, 249*f*
quantitative data, *t*-test, 304–305
quantitative data, WSRST, 319–320
QUARTILE function, 115–116, 115*f*
random number generation, 8–10, 8*f*, 9*f*, 10*f*
Regression tool, 422, 436–438
residual output, 432, 432*f*

residuals, calculation of, 422
sample means, 218
scatter diagram, 65–66
Sign Test, 330–331
Spearman rank correlation coefficient,
    126–128
standard deviation, calculation of, 104
t-test, 304–305
t-test of mean, 258–259, 258*f*, 348
TDIST function, 255*f*
two-proportion comparison, 376,
    375*f*–376*f*, 377, 377*f*
two-sample, assuming unequal
    variances, 344–347
and Wilcoxon Rank Sum Test
    (WRST), 357–358
and Wilcoxon Signed Rank Sum Test
    (WSRST), 319–320
Excel bin number, 37
experiment
    binomial experiment, 170–171, 173
    defined, 137
    event, 137
    matched-pair experiments,
        298–299
    repeated trials, 138
    sample space, 137
experimental study, 16–17
explanatory variable, 64

F

failing to reject the null hypothesis, 240
1st quartile, 114
formal hypothesis testing, 238–246
frame, 7–8
frequency distribution
    class setup considerations, 34–35,
        34*f*, 35*f*
    class width, 32–34, 32*f*–33*f*, 35*f*
    class width template, 38*f*–39*f*
    correspondence with histogram, 40
    data analysis dialogue box, 35*f*, 36
    defined, 30
    described, 32–40
    raw Excel frequency distribution, 42*f*
    sample, 32*f*, 38*f*, 40*f*, 41*f*

G

The Globe and Mail Report on
    Business, 4
goodness-of-fit tests, 381–389
Gosset, William S., 252
graphs
    bar graph, 30–31, 31*f*, 385, 385*f*
    binomial probability distribution, 182

histogram. *See* histogram
misleading graphs, 69–75
of paired quantitative data, 65–68
of relationship, 408–410
scatter diagram, 65–68, 65*f*–66*f*, 68*f*
time-series graphs, 60–65, 60*f*
uninteresting graphs, 76–78

H

histogram
    adjusting Excel's histogram, 42–44,
        43*f*, 44*f*
    bimodal distribution, 100*f*
    class width, 32–34, 32*f*–33*f*
    comparison of histograms, 47–52
    correspondence with frequency
        distribution, 40
    defined, 32
    described, 40–107
    dialogue box, 36*f*, 41*f*
    problematic sample, 51*f*
    raw Excel histogram, 42*f*
    relative frequency, 48–49, 49*f*
    sample, 32*f*, 31*f*, 40*f*, 41*f*
    skewed distribution, 45–46,
        45*f*, 46*f*
    symmetric distribution, 45, 45*f*
    symmetry and shape, checking, 107
    unimodal distribution, 100*f*
    use of, 45
    x-axis, 42
hypothesis testing
    alternative hypothesis, 238–239
    and confidence intervals, 292–293
    decision making, 240
    decision rule approach, 262–266
    described, 231–232
    formal hypothesis testing, 238–246
    left-tailed hypothesis test, 256–258
    null hypothesis, 238–239, 240
    one-tailed hypothesis test, 239–240
    p-values, 243–245
    population mean, 251–266
    population proportions, 246–251
    regression relationship, 434–439
    rejecting or failing to reject null
        hypothesis, 240
    research hypothesis, 238–239
    right-tailed hypothesis test, 253–256,
        259–260
    significance level, 241–243
    two-tailed hypothesis test, 239–240,
        265–266, 292*f*
    Type I error, 241–243, 241*f*, 247
    Type II error, 241–243, 241*f*, 247

I

independence of error terms, 424–426
independence testing, 395–398
independent events, 145–147, 159
independent samples
    analysis of variance (ANOVA),
        363–364
    comparison of more than two popula-
        tions, 363–364
    non-normal quantitative data, 354–362
    normal quantitative data, 343–350
    ranked data, 358–360
    sampling distribution, 354
    t-test, 343–350
    two-sample, assuming unequal
        variances, 344–347
    Wilcoxon Rank Sum Test (WRST),
        354–362
Industry Canada, 4
inferential statistics
    decision-making process, 205–211
    defined, 7
    probability distribution. *See* probability
        distribution
    sampling distribution. *See* sampling
        distribution
influential observations, 428–432
interquartile range (IQR), 113–117, 115, 116*f*
inverse relationship, 66

J

joint probability, 149–150
joint probability tables, 140
judgment, 17

L

least-squares line, 411, 412–416
least-squares regression equation, 436
least-squares regression line, 411,
    412–416
left-tailed chi-squared test, 381
left-tailed hypothesis test, 256–258
linear regression model
    see also regression relationship
    checking requirements, 433–434
    constant variation in residuals,
        422–423
    decision making guide, 433–434
    error term, independence of, 424–426
    least-squares line, 411, 412–416
    more advanced modelling, 447–448
    normality of residuals, 426–428
    outliers and influential observations,
        428–432
    required conditions, 419–432

linear regression model (*Continued*)
  requirements not met, 434
  residuals, 419–422
  theoretical model, 418–419
linear relationship, positive, 118, 118f

M

Maclean's magazine, 4
matched-pair analysis
  described, 298\299
  matched-pair experiments,
      298–299
  matched-pairs experimental study, 299
  matched-pairs observational
      study, 299
  quantitative data, and choice
      of test, 325
  quantitative data, non-normal
      differences, 311–325
  quantitative data, normal differences,
      299–311
  ranked data, 327–333
  Sign Test, 327–333
  t-test, 300–311
  Wilcoxon Signed Rank Sum Test
      (WSRST), 311–325
matched-pair experiments, 298–299
matched-pairs experimental study, 299
matched-pairs observational study, 299
mathematical notation. *See* notation
mean
  binomial probability distribution, 171
  generally, 93–96, 94f
  population mean. *See* population mean
  probability distribution, 168–170
  of the sample means, 211
  sample size for estimation, 287–290
  of sampling distribution, 343
measures of association
  choosing, 128–129
  correlation analysis, 118
  Pearson correlation coefficient,
      118–124, 119f
  Spearman rank correlation coefficient,
      124–127, 127f
measures of central tendency
  choosing, 101
  deviation from the mean, 103
  mean, 93–96, 94f
  median, 96–99
  mode, 99–100
measures of variability
  choosing, 117
  interquartile range (IQR),
      113–117, 116f

range, 101–102, 102f
  standard deviation. *See* standard
      deviation
median, 96–99
misleading graphs
  distorted images, 73–75
  misleading or missing titles and axis
      labels, 72–73, 72f
  missing data, 75, 75f
  non-zero origins, 70–71
misleading titles and axis labels, 72–73, 72f
missing data, 75, 75f
missing titles and axis labels, 72–73, 72f
mode, 99–100
multicollinearity, 448
multiple-proportion comparison, 391–395
multiple regression, 448
multiple samples. *See* two or more samples
multiplication rule, 151–152
mutually exclusive events, 154, 159

N

negative (inverse) relationship, 66
negatively skewed distribution, 46, 46f
nominal data, 26
  see also qualitative data
non-parametric technique, 319
non-zero origins, 70–71
nonresponse error, 11
nonsampling errors
  coverage errors, 11
  defined, 11
  estimation errors, 11
  nonresponse error, 11
  processing errors, 11
  response errors, 11
nonstatistical sampling, 6
normal distribution
  see also normal probability
  centred on 100, with standard devia-
      tion of 10, 183f
  comparison of two normal distribu-
      tions, 191, 191f, 192f
  continuous random variables, 184
  importance of, 183
  sample, 185f
  symmetry of, 183
normal probability
  see also normal distribution
  Excel, calculation with, 185–191
  standardizing, 193
  tables, calculation with, 191–197
normal probability distribution. *See*
      normal distribution
normal random variable, 184

normal sampling distribution, 218–220,
      266–267
normal table, 193f, 194–195, 458–459
normality of residuals, 426–428
"not" probabilities, 155–158
notation
  estimated relationship, 410
  examples, 91–93
  mean, 95
  order of operations, 89
  probability, 138
  sample standard deviation, 103
  summation notation, 89–90
  use of, 89
null hypothesis, 238–239, 240
numerical data, 26
  see also quantitative data

O

observational study, 15
one-tailed hypothesis test, 239–240
online databases, 4
online polls, 6
"or" probabilities, 152–155
order of operations, 89
ordinal data, 27
  see also quantitative data
outlier
  defined, 46
  and influential observation,
      428–432
  presence in data set, 47
  scatter diagram, 431f
  standard deviation, effect on, 113
output range, 36f

P

p-values, 243–244, 263–264
paired quantitative data, 65–68
parameter, 7
Pearson correlation coefficient,
      118–124, 119f
perfect positive linear relationship,
      118, 118f
pie charts
  creation in Excel, 55
  share of total, emphasis on, 55
  for simple table, 52f, 55f
point estimate, 274–275
polling companies, 10
polls, 6
polynomial models, 448
population data, 5, 5f, 108
population distribution, 215–217, 218f,
      312, 311f–312f

population mean
average difference in, and confidence interval estimate, 308–309
comparison of, with *t*-test, 349
confidence interval estimate, 284*f*, 285–287, 308–309, 350–354
decision making, 251–266
decision rule approach, 262–266
difference in, 350–354
estimation, 283–287
Excel template, single sample, 258–260, 303–304
left-tailed hypothesis test, 256–258
p-values, 263–264
right-tailed hypothesis test, 253–256, 259–260
sample size for estimation, 287–290
sampling distribution, 214–215
t-distribution, 252–258, 252*f*, 260–262, 261*f*, 262*f*, 263*f*, 264*f*
t-test of mean, 258–259, 258*f*
two-tailed hypothesis test, 265–266
population normality, 219, 220
population proportions
binomial distribution, 222–230
comparison of many proportions, 391–395
comparison of two proportions. *See* two-proportion comparison
confidence interval estimate, 277*f*, 278*f*, 279*f*, 280*f*, 281–282, 290*f*
decisions about, 222–230
estimation, 276–283
hypothesis testing, 246–251
sample size for estimation, 290–291
sampling distribution, 229–230, 231
single sample, 246–251
positive (direct) relationship, 66
positive linear relationship, 118, 118*f*
positively skewed distribution, 45, 45*f*
prediction interval, 443
predictions, 442–447
primary data, 3
probability
addition rule, 153–155
"and" probabilities, 148–152
binomial probability. *See* binomial probability
calculations, 139
classical definition of probability, 138
complement rule, 155–158
completed table of probabilities, 142*f*
conditional probability, 143–145
contingency tables, 139, 141*f*, 144*f*

defined, 137
independent events, 159
joint probability, 149–150
joint probability tables, 140
multiplication rule, 151–152
mutually exclusive events, 159
normal probability. *See* normal probability
"not" probabilities, 155–158
"or" probabilities, 152–155
relative frequency approach to probability, 138
sample space. *See* sample space
standard notation for, 138
test for independence, 145–147
tree diagrams, 140–141, 142
probability distribution
binomial probability distribution, 170–182
building a discrete probability distribution, 166–168
of continuous random variable, 166
for discrete random variable, 166
graph of, for random variable *x*, 167*f*–168*f*
mean of, 167–170
normal probability distribution. *See* normal distribution
standard deviation of, 168–170
probability distribution for a discrete random variable, 166
probability distribution of a continuous random variable, 166
processing errors, 11
provincial government websites, 4
*P*th percentile, 114

Q
qualitative data, 26, 27
bar charts for contingency tables, 57–60, 57*f*, 58*f*
bar charts for simple table, 52–57, 52*f*, 54*f*
comparison of many population proportions, 391–395
comparison of two proportions, 372–379
goodness-of-fit tests, 381–389
independence testing, 395–398
pie charts for simple table, 52*f*, 55*f*
quantitative data
choice of matched-pairs tests, 325
continuous variable, 26
defined, 26
described, 26–27

discrete variable, 26–27
frequency distribution. *See* frequency distribution
graphs of paired quantitative data, 65–68
histogram. *See* histogram
matched pairs, non-normal differences, 311–325
matched pairs, normal differences, 299–311
non-normal, and independent samples, 354–362
normal, and independent samples, 343–350
organization of, 28–29
scatter diagram, 65–68, 65*f*–66*f*
stem and leaf displays, 29–32, 29*f*, 30*f*, 31*f*
t-test, 300–311, 343–350
Wilcoxon Signed Rank Sum Test (WSRST), 311–325
quantitative variables, 26, 65

R
random number generation, 8–10, 8*f*, 9*f*, 10*f*
random variable, 165
range, 101–102, 102*f*
ranked data
defined, 27
independent samples, 358–360
matched-pair analysis, 327–333
Wilcoxon Rank Sum Test (WRST), 358–360
ratio data, 26
see also quantitative data
regression relationship
assessment of linear regression model, 418–434
coefficient of determination (R2), 440–442
estimating the relationship, 410–416
graph of relationship, 408–410
hypothesis test, 434–439
incorrect use of regression equation, 446, 446*f*
more advanced modelling, 447–448
multiple regression, 448
polynomial models, 448
predictions, 442–447
sample data and regression equation, 446*f*
strength of regression, 439–442
testing slope of regression line, 439
rejecting the null hypothesis, 240

relationship analysis. *See* regression relationship
relative frequency, 48–49, 49*f*
relative frequency approach to probability, 138
research
experimental study, 16–17
observational study, 15
research hypothesis, 238–239
residual term, 421
residuals
see also linear regression model
analysis of, 419–422
constant variation in residuals, 422–423
defined, 411
graph of, 411*f*
independence of error terms, 424–426
normality of, 426–428
use of, 411
response errors, 11
response variable, 64
right-tailed chi-squared test, 381
right-tailed hypothesis test, 253–256, 259–260
robust, 267
rule of addition, 153–155
rule of multiplication, 151–152

S
sample data, 5, 5*f*
sample means
difference between two sample means, 343–344
in formula for sample standard deviation, 103
sampling distribution, 343–344
sampling distribution of, 211–222, 212*f*, 213*f*, 214*f*, 218*f*–219*f*
sample proportion, 222–231, 227*f*, 228*f*
sample results, 206–210, 206*f*, 207*f*, 208*f*
sample size
estimation of mean, 287–290
estimation of proportion, 290–291
smaller sample sizes, 320–324
Wilcoxon Signed Rank Sum Test (WSRST), 320–324
sample space
with associated counts, 141*f*
contingency tables, 139
defined, 137
joint probability tables, 140
probability, calculation of, 141–143

representation of, 141*f*
tree diagrams, 140–141, 142
sampling
convenience sample, 6
coverage errors, 11
estimation errors, 11
frame, 7–8
necessity of, 5
nonresponse error, 11
nonsampling errors, 11
nonstatistical sampling, 6
population data, 5, 5*f*
processing errors, 11
response errors, 11
sample data, 5, 5*f*
sampling error, 11
simple random sampling, 7
statistical sampling, 7–10
true random sample, 10
without replacement, 172–173
sampling distribution
of *b*1, 436
central limit theorem, 218–220
comparison of two proportions, 372–373
construction of, 214–215
decision making guide, 221
defined, 205
described, 205–206
empirical approach, 215–218
mean of, 343
normal sampling distribution, 218–220, 266–267
and population distribution, 215–217, 218*f*
population mean, 214–215
population proportion, 229–230, 231
of the sample means, 211–222, 212*f*, 213*f*, 214*f*, 218*f*–219*f*, 343–344
of the sample proportion, 222–231, 227*f*, 228*f*, 277*f*–278*f*
sample results, 206–210, 206*f*, 207*f*, 208*f*
standard error, 343
with two independent samples, 343, 354
unusualness of sample result, 210
Wilcoxon Signed Rank Sum Test (WSRST), 315–316
sampling error, 11
S&P/TSX Composite Index, 14*f*
scaled axes, 71*f*
scatter diagram, 65–68, 65*f*–66*f*, 68*f*

secondary data
defined, 3
sources of, 4
severely skewed distribution, 46*f*
sigma, 103
Sign Test, 327–333
significance level, 241–243
simple random sampling, 7
simple tables, 52–57
single sample
formal hypothesis testing, 238–246
population mean, 251–266
population proportion, 246–251
Six Sigma approach, 3
skewed distribution, 45–46, 45*f*, 46*f*
skewed to the left, 46, 46*f*
skewed to the right, 45, 45*f*
slope of regression line, 439
Spearman rank correlation coefficient, 124–127, 127*f*
spreadsheets. *See* Excel
squared deviations, 103
standard deviation
binomial probability distribution, 171
calculation of, 102–106
computational formula, 105–106
defined, 103
Empirical Rule, 106–113, 107*f*, 108*f*
Excel, calculation with, 104
one standard deviation from the mean, 109*f*
outliers, effect of, 113
probability distributions, 168–170
sample, 104*f*
of the sample means, 211
of the sample proportions, 226
three standard deviations from the mean, 111*f*
two standard deviations from the mean, 110*f*
standard error
of the sample means, 211
of the sample proportion, 226
of sampling distribution, 343
standard normal table, 193*f*, 194–195, 458–459
statistic, 7
statistical analysis
described, 12–13
descriptive statistics, 13
inferential statistics, 7
and judgment, 17
statistical inference. *See* inferential statistics
statistical sampling, 7–10
Statistics Canada, 4

stem and leaf displays, 29–32, 29*f*, 30*f*, 31*f*
Strategis Canada, 4
subjective language, 19
summation notation, 89–90
symmetric bell-shaped distribution, 107–108
symmetric distribution, 45, 45*f*

T

t-distribution, 252–258, 252*f*, 303*f*, 308*f*–309*f*
t-distribution critical values table, 260–262, 261*f*, 262*f*, 263*f*, 264*f*, 348*f*, 351*f*, 460
t-test
  comparison of population means, 349
  Data Analysis *t*-test, 304–305, 344–347
  equal-variances version, 349–350
  independent samples, 343–350
  matched pair analysis, 299–311
  of mean, 258–259, 258*f*, 348
  population mean, 258–259, 258*f*
  unequal variances version, 344–347
  vs. Wilcoxon Rank Sum Test (WRST), 358
tables
  binomial probability, calculation of, 181–182
  binomial tables, 181–182, 454–457
  contingency tables, 57–60, 139, 141*f*, 144*f*
  cumulative binomial tables, 454–457
  joint probability tables, 140
  normal probability, calculation of, 191–197
  normal table, 193*f*, 194–195, 458–459
  simple tables, 52–57
  standard normal table, 193*f*, 194–195, 458–459
  t-distribution, critical values, 260–262, 261*f*, 262*f*, 263*f*, 264*f*, 348*f*, 351*f*, 460
  Wilcoxon Rank Sum Test, critical values, 462–463
  Wilcoxon Signed Rank Sum Test, critical values and *p*-values, 461
  x^2-distribution, critical values, 464
tails of the distribution, 111, 111*f*
test for independence, 145–147

3rd quartile, 114
time-series data, 28
time-series graphs, 60–65, 60*f*
titles
  descriptive title, proper format, 72*f*
  misleading or missing, 72–73, 72*f*
tree diagrams, 140–141, 142
true random sample, 10
two or more samples
  comparison of many population proportions, 391–395
  comparison of two proportions, 372–379
  goodness-of-fit tests, 381–389
  independence testing, 395–398
two-proportion comparison
  coded data, 374–376
  confidence interval estimate, 379–380
  decision-making guide, 378–379
  described, 372–379
  Excel, 376, 375*f*–376*f*, 377, 377*f*
  general case, 376–377
  null hypothesis that p1 - p2 = 0, 373–374
  sampling distribution, 372–373
two-tailed hypothesis test, 239–240, 265–266, 292*f*
Type I error, 241–243, 241*f*, 247
Type II error, 241–243, 241*f*, 247

U

unimodal distribution, 99, 100*f*
uninteresting graphs, 76–78
unranked data, 27

V

variability, measures of. *See* measures of variability
variable
  binomial random variable, 171
  continuous random variable, 166, 184
  continuous variable, 26
  defined, 26
  discrete random variable, 165
  discrete variable, 26, 27
  explanatory variable, 64
  normal random variable, 184
  qualitative variables, 65
  quantitative variables, 26, 65

random variable, 165
response variable, 64
variance
  analysis of variance (ANOVA), 363–364
  described, 103
  equal variances, 349–350
  unequal variances, 344–347

W

Wilcoxon Rank Sum Test (WRST)
  decision-making guide, 360–361
  independent samples, comparison of, 354
  non-normal quantitative data, 355–358
  population locations, 358–360
  ranked data, 358–360
Wilcoxon Rank Sum Test (WRST) table, 462
Wilcoxon Signed Rank Sum Test (WSRST)
  before and after matched-pairs data, 313, 313*f*
  analysis using, 312
  critical values and *p*-values, 321*f*, 324*f*
  critical values and *p*-values, estimating *p*, 321*f*
  decision making guide, 324–325
  described, 311–312
  distribution-free technique, 318
  example, 316–318
  and Excel, 319–320
  non-parametric technique, 319
  population distribution comparisons, 312, 312*f*
  ranking process, 313–315, 313*f*, 314*f*
  sampling distribution, 315–316
  smaller sample sizes, 320–324
  table, critical values and *p*-values, 461

X

x^2-distribution critical values table, 464

Z

z-score, 193–280*f*
z-test, 397–398